Teacher's Manual

ELEMENTS OF LITERATURE

SIXTH COURSE

Teacher's Manual

ELEMENTS OF LITERATURE

SIXTH COURSE

Richard D. Parrish
Michigan State University
East Lansing, Michigan

June Gaede
North High School
Bakersfield, California

HOLT, RINEHART AND WINSTON, INC.

AUSTIN   NEW YORK   SAN DIEGO   CHICAGO   TORONTO   MONTREAL

A teacher's manual is not automatically included with each shipment of a classroom set of textbooks. However, a manual will be forwarded when requested by a teacher, an administrator, or a representative of Holt, Rinehart and Winston, Inc. A teacher's manual is available for every level of *Elements of Literature*. For information, please contact your sales representative.

Acknowledgments

For permission to reprint copyrighted material, grateful acknowledgment is made to the following sources:

Jonathan Cape, Ltd., on behalf of Henry Reed: From "Naming of Parts" from *A Map of Verona* by Henry Reed. Copyright 1947, 1975 by the Estate of Henry Reed.

Harper & Row, Publishers, Inc.: From "Hawk Roosting" from *New Selected Poems* by Ted Hughes. Copyright © 1959 by Ted Hughes.

Henry Holt and Company, Inc.: From "The Night Is Freezing Fast" from *The Collected Poems of A. E. Housman.* Copyright 1922 by Holt, Rinehart and Winston, Inc.; copyright renewed 1950 by Barclays Bank, Ltd. From "With Rue My Heart Is Laden" from *The Collected Poems of A. E. Housman,* authorized edition. Copyright 1939, 1940, © 1965 by Holt, Rinehart & Winston, Inc. Copyright © 1967, 1968 by Robert E. Symons.

Little, Brown, Inc.: Excerpt from *Pentimento* by Lillian Hellman. Copyright © 1973 by Lillian Hellman.

New American Library: From *The Tragedy of Macbeth,* edited by Sylvan Barnet. Copyright © 1963 by Sylvan Barnet.

New Directions Publishing Corporation: From "Fern Hill" from *Poems of Dylan Thomas.* Copyright 1943 by New Directions Publishing Corporation; 1945 by The Trustees for the copyright of Dylan Thomas.

Oxford University Press, Inc.: From "The Wanderer" from *An Anthology of Old English Poetry,* translated by Charles W. Kennedy. Copyright © 1960 by Oxford University Press, Inc.

Random House, Inc.: From "The Express" from *Collected Poems 1928–1953* by Stephen Spender. Copyright 1934 and renewed 1962 by Stephen Spender.

Deborah Rogers, Ltd., Literary Agency: From "The Wanderer" from *The Battle of Maldon and Other Old English Poems,* translated by Kevin Crossley-Holland. Copyright © 1966 by Kevin Crossley-Holland.

Charles Scribner's Sons, Inc.: Excerpt from *A History of English Literature* by William Vaughn Moody and Robert Moriss. Copyright © 1964 by Charles Scribner's Sons, Inc.

University of Nebraska Press: From "The Seafarer" from *Poems from the Old English,* translated by Burton Raffel. Copyright © 1960, 1964 by University of Nebraska Press.

Contents

Using the Teacher's Manual

This manual contains student objectives and teaching strategies for each unit and selection in the anthology. It provides complete coverage of the text's instructional features, as well as sample student essays, extension activities, and supplementary reading suggestions. Following the teaching guides you will find special sections on assessment, reading development, critical thinking, reading rates, vocabulary growth, and classroom techniques.

For each selection, the manual's introductory material includes, as appropriate, an **outline of major elements,** suggestions for **introducing the selection,** helpful **background information,** and a **plot summary.** The teaching strategies focus on discussions of **cultural differences** pertinent to the selection; teaching approaches for students of **different ability levels; vocabulary study,** including Glossary words and teaching suggestions; considerations in **reading the selection,** including prereading activities, oral reading, method of assignment, and audio-visual presentation; and **reteaching alternatives.** Additionally, the manual offers suggestions for teaching the essays that appear throughout the student text under the headings **Elements of Literature** (or **Style**), **Primary Sources,** and **The English Language.**

The manual also reprints the analysis questions from the anthology and suggests answers, which are to be considered guidelines. Answers are provided as well for each of the language and vocabulary exercises in the text, as are ideas for presenting the writing assignments. A notable feature is **evaluation criteria** for the writing assignments in each unit. These criteria suggest major points you may look for in assessing students' writing.

The Scope and Sequence Chart beginning on the next page shows the literary elements, writing assignments, exercises, and "Focusing on Background" features in each unit of the student text.

The *Elements of Literature* program also includes a *Teacher's Resource Organizer* for each grade level. Its major components are a test booklet with answer key; audio cassettes of many of the text selections, with program notes (a symbol appears in the manual, under the title of the selection, for those selections with accompanying cassettes); *Connections Between Reading and Writing,* supplementary student worksheets for twenty of the text selections; instructional transparencies and blackline masters; and posters.

SCOPE AND SEQUENCE OF THE PROGRAM IN *ELEMENTS OF LITERATURE*: Sixth Course

Grade 12: Unit 1 The Anglo-Saxon Period (450–1066)	Elements Taught in Question or Introduction or Exercise	Writing	Analyzing Language and Style	Critical Comment	Primary Sources	The Elements of Literature
Introduction	The Celts and Their Religion Animism The Romans: The Great Administrators The Anglo-Saxons: From King Arthur to King Alfred The Reemergence of Christianity Life in Anglo-Saxon England: Loyal Dependency The Anglo-Saxon Religion Bards and Poets in Anglo-Saxon England Monasteries and Anglo-Saxon Literature Old English Poetics Iamb Iambic Tetrameter Alliteration Caesura Kennings					
from Beowulf, translated by Burton Raffel	Motivation Imagery Symbolism Characterization Central Conflict Elegy Theme	*Creative* Changing the Point of View From John Gardner's *Grendel* *Critical* Analyzing a Character Analyzing the Epic	Kennings and Alliteration	from *The Guest-Hall of Eden,* Alvin A. Lee	The Mark of Cain The Treasure at Sutton Hoo, Robert P. Creed	

Grade 12: Unit 1 The Anglo-Saxon Period (450–1066)	Elements Taught in Question or Introduction or Exercise	Writing	Analyzing Language and Style	Critical Comment	Primary Sources	The Elements of Literature
The Wanderer, translated by Charles W. Kennedy	Elegiac Mood, Imagery, Tone, Symbolism	*Creative* Imitating a Verse Style *Critical* Analyzing the Poem, Comparing and Contrasting Translations		The Original Language		
The Seafarer, translated by Burton Raffel	Metaphors, Setting, Characterization, Atmosphere	*Critical* Supporting an Opinion, Comparing and Contrasting Poems				
Anglo-Saxon Riddles, translated by Burton Raffel	Personification, Paradox	*Creative* Writing a Riddle				
from Ecclesiastical History of the English People	Extended Simile, Symbolism, Simile, Metaphor	*Creative* Imitating the Writer's Technique				
The English Language, Old English: Where English Came From	Out of the East: The Ancestor of English, Wanderlust: The Migrations, Meeting the Neighbors, What Tongue Is This?, Our Anglo-Saxon Heritage		Locating countries where Indo-European Languages are spoken, Guessing the etymologies of Latin words, Looking up names of a writing system			

Grade 12: Unit 1 The Anglo-Saxon Period (450–1066)	Elements Taught in Question or Introduction or Exercise	Writing	Analyzing Language and Style	Critical Comment	Primary Sources	The Elements of Literature
Exercises in Critical Thinking and Writing Analyzing a Passage	Plot Setting Analysis Evaluation Synthesis Generalization Hypothesis Intellectual Response Affective Response Thesis Statement					

SCOPE AND SEQUENCE OF THE PROGRAM IN ELEMENTS OF LITERATURE: Sixth Course

Grade 12: Unit 2 The Middle Ages 1066–1485	Elements Taught in Question or Introduction or Exercise	Writing	Analyzing Language and Style	Critical Comment	Primary Sources	The Elements of Literature
Introduction The Norman Conquest						
Feudalism and Knighthood	The Woman's Place in Medieval Society Chivalry and Courtly Love					
The New City Classes						
The Great Happenings	The Crusades The Martyrdom of Thomas Becket The Magna Carta The Hundred Years' War The Black Death					
Ballads The Three Ravens	Mood Tone Refrain					
Lord Randall	Beats Rhyme Incremental Repetition Refrain					
Get up and Bar the Door	Repetition Plot Ironic Humor	*Creative* Retelling a Ballad as a News Report Writing a Folk Ballad *Critical* Comparing Ballads				Ballad Meter

Grade 12: Unit 2 The Middle Ages 1066–1485	Elements Taught in Question or Introduction or Exercise	Writing	Analyzing Language and Style	Critical Comment	Primary Sources	The Elements of Literature
The Canterbury Tales, Geoffrey Chaucer The Prologue	Characterization Satire	*Creative* Writing a Frame Story *Critical* Responding to a Critic Comparing and Contrasting Two Characters	Rhymes Couplet Half Rhymes			
from The Nun's Priest's Tale	Characterization Conflict Allusions Irony Moral	*Creative* Continuing the Frame Story				
from The Pardoner's Tale	Personification Irony Symbolism Satire Moral	*Creative* Finishing Up the Frame Story *Critical* Comparing Storytellers Evaluating the Tales as Short Stories Analyzing Character	Imagery	A Comment on *The Canterbury Tales*		
Sir Gawain and the Green Knight	Romance Quest Conflict Characterization Symbolism Imagery Theme	*Creative* Using a Different Point of View Displacing the Story *Critical* Analyzing a Romance	The Bob and Wheel Alliteration			The Romance

Grade 12: Unit 2 The Middle Ages 1066–1485	Elements Taught in Question or Introduction or Exercise	Writing	Analyzing Language and Style	Critical Comment	Primary Sources	The Elements of Literature
from Le Morte Darthur, Sir Thomas Malory	Mood Setting Symbolism Allusions Supernatural	*Creative* Using Another Point of View *Critical* Writing a Research Report	Archaic constructions and context clues	John Steinbeck on the Arthurian Legend		
The English Language, Middle English: The Language in Transition	What Happened to the Endings? Pronunciation Changes That Produced Middle English Endings and Order: Grammatical Changes That Produced Middle English Effects on Gender Effects on Mood Effects on the Plural Form Effects on Case Endings		Comparing two versions Finding dates when words entered English Guessing word origins			
Uninvited Guests: The Norman Conquest and French in England	The Battle of the Languages and the Triumph of English					
Both a Borrower and a Lender Be	Loan Words from French					
Exercises in Critical Thinking and Writing Evaluating Literature in Group Discussion	Characterization Motivation Point of view Theme					

Grade 12: Unit 3 The Renaissance 1485–1660	Elements Taught in Question or Introduction or Exercise	Writing	Analyzing Language and Style	Critical Comment	Primary Sources	The Elements of Literature
Introduction The Renaissance	The Italian Renaissance Humanism Printing Erasmus and More					
The English Renaissance	Establishment of the English Church The Tudor Monarchs					
Renaissance Poetry	Epithalamia Epigrams Epitaphs Songs Madrigal Epic					
Renaissance Drama	The Forerunners Miracle/Mystery Plays Moralities Interludes Renaissance Dramatists					
Renaissance Prose						
Decline of the Renaissance						
Whoso List to Hunt, Sir Thomas Wyatt		*Creative* Responding to the Poem				
They Flee from Me, Sir Thomas Wyatt	Pun Tone	*Creative* Responding to the Poem *Critical* Analyzing Diction				Petrarchan Sonnets

Grade 12: Unit 3 The Renaissance 1485–1660	Elements Taught in Question or Introduction or Exercise	Writing	Analyzing Language and Style	Critical Comment	Primary Sources	The Elements of Literature
Love That Doth Reign, Henry Howard and The Long Love, Sir Thomas Wyatt	Metaphor Conceit	*Creative* Creating a Petrarchan Conceit *Critical* Comparing and Contrasting Translations				Poetic Meter Iamb Trochee Anapest Dactyl Scansion Dimeter Tetrameter Pentameter Hexameter Iambic Pentameter Spondee Caesura
Nature, That Washed Her Hands in Milk, Sir Walter Raleigh	Personification	*Creative* Creating Personification *Critical* Analyzing Variations in a Poem's Ending				
What Is Our Life? Sir Walter Raleigh	Metaphor Pun	*Critical* Expressing an Opinion				
from The Faerie Queene, Edmund Spenser	Allegory Conflict Symbolism Epic Simile	*Creative* Creating Allegorical Characters *Critical* Translating Spenser	Spenser's Language			
from Amoretti: Sonnet 30 and Sonnet 75, Edmund Spenser	Paradox	*Critical* Comparing Poems				

Grade 12: Unit 3 The Renaissance 1485–1660	Elements Taught in Question or Introduction or Exercise	Writing	Analyzing Language and Style	Critical Comment	Primary Sources	The Elements of Literature
The Nightingale, Sir Philip Sidney	Setting	*Critical* Responding to a Critical Remark				
from Astrophel and Stella, Sir Philip Sidney	Octave Hexameter Pentameter	*Creative* Describing a Process *Critical* Analyzing Petrarchan Conventions				
Of Studies, Sir Francis Bacon	Parallel Structure Balanced Sentence Paradox	*Creative* Imitating Style *Critical* Interpreting an Author's Bias				
from The Essays: Axioms, Sir Francis Bacon						
from Doctor Faustus, Christopher Marlowe	Foreshadowing Soliloquy Iambic Pentameter Meter	*Creative* Showing Internal Conflict *Critical* Applying a Theme				
The Passionate Shepherd to His Love, Christopher Marlowe and The Nymph's Reply to the Shepherd, Sir Walter Raleigh	Pastoral Writing Tone	*Creative* Responding to the Poem *Critical* Analyzing Argument				

Grade 12: Unit 3 The Renaissance 1485–1660	Elements Taught in Question or Introduction or Exercise	Writing	Analyzing Language and Style	Critical Comment	Primary Sources	The Elements of Literature
The English Language, The Birth of Modern English	The Language Changes That Made Modern English Shifting Vowels Lagging Spelling O Brave New World: The Spread of English and Foreign Influence The New Learning: Classical Influences The Rise of Standard English		Studying Renaissance English			
The Renaissance Theater						
The Globe	The Structure of the Globe Scenery Act and Scene Divisions Props and Effects Private Halls and Indoor Theaters					
William Shakespeare	Shakespeare's Early Plays Shakespeare's "Tragic Period" The Last Years Shakespeare's Genius					
Macbeth	The Sources of the Play					

Grade 12: Unit 3 The Renaissance 1485–1660	Elements Taught in Question or Introduction or Exercise	Writing	Analyzing Language and Style	Critical Comment	Primary Sources	The Elements of Literature
The Tragedy of Macbeth, William Shakespeare Act I	Conflict Irony		Blank Verse			
Act II				Macbeth's Porter		
Act III	Characterization Setting Turning Point					
Act IV	Characterization Dumb Show			The King's Evil Hecate		
Act V	Foreshadowing Internal Conflict External Conflict Resolution Theme Climax	*Creative* Extending a Character Updating a Scene Changing the Outcome *Critical* Interpreting Characterization Analyzing a Character Evaluating Dramatic Effect Analyzing the Playwright's Intent Analyzing Irony Applying Logic Responding to a Critic	Imagery and Figurative Language Figures of Speech Climax Metaphors Similes Personification	The Characters Macbeth and Lady Macbeth		

Grade 12: Unit 3 The Renaissance 1485–1660	Elements Taught in Question or Introduction or Exercise	Writing	Analyzing Language and Style	Critical Comment	Primary Sources	The Elements of Literature
On the Knocking at the Gate in *Macbeth* Sonnets	The Sonnet's Form Iambic Pentameter Quatrains Couplet Turn					
Sonnet 29, William Shakespeare	Turn Tone Simile					
Sonnet 30, William Shakespeare	Turn Metaphors Tone					
Sonnet 71, William Shakespeare	Alliteration Mood Turn					
Sonnet 73, William Shakespeare	Metaphors Paraphrasing Turn Imagery Tone					
Sonnet 116, William Shakespeare	Metaphors Personification Turn Mood Couplet					

Grade 12: Unit 3 The Renaissance 1485–1660	Elements Taught in Question or Introduction or Exercise	Writing	Analyzing Language and Style	Critical Comment	Primary Sources	The Elements of Literature
Sonnet 130, William Shakespeare	Couplet	*Creative* Writing a Parody *Critical* Comparing Poems				
Songs from Shakespeare's Plays						
Winter, William Shakespeare	Imagery Attitude	*Creative* Imitating the Writer's Technique				
Under the Greenwood Tree, William Shakespeare	Imagery					
Blow, Blow, Thou Winter Wind, William Shakespeare	Personification Paraphrasing					
O Mistress Mine, William Shakespeare		*Creative* Answering the Speaker				
Fear No More the Heat o' the Sun, William Shakespeare	Theme Simile					
Full Fathom Five, William Shakespeare	Imagery Alliteration					
The English Language, Shakespeare's Language	Speaking the Speech: Shakespeare's Pronunciation Shakespeare's Grammar Shakespeare's Words		Studying Shakespeare's Language			

Grade 12: Unit 3 The Renaissance 1485–1660	Elements Taught in Question or Introduction or Exercise	Writing	Analyzing Language and Style	Critical Comment	Primary Sources	The Elements of Literature
The Bait, John Donne	Syntax Rhyme Meter	*Creative* Constructing a Conceit *Critical* Comparing Two Poems				Metaphysical Poetry
Song, John Donne	Hyperbole Tone	*Creative* Using Hyperbole				
A Valediction: Forbidding Mourning, John Donne	Simile Rhythm	*Creative* Writing a Farewell *Critical* Analyzing Conceits				
Meditation 17, John Donne	Metaphor Main Idea Tone	*Critical* Analyzing Metaphors	Context Clues			
Donne's Sonnets						
At the Round Earth's Imagined Corners, John Donne	Octave Sestet					
Death Be Not Proud, John Donne	Paradox	*Critical* Comparing Two Sonnets				
Batter My Heart, John Donne	Simile Imagery Alliteration Paradox	*Critical* Analyzing Rhythm and Sound Effects				
To Fool or Knave, Ben Jonson						

Grade 12: Unit 3 The Renaissance 1485–1660	Elements Taught in Question or Intro-duction or Exercise	Writing	Analyzing Language and Style	Critical Comment	Primary Sources	The Elements of Literature
To the Ghost of Martial, Ben Jonson						
On My First Son, Ben Jonson	Epitaph	*Creative* Responding to a Theme				
Song to Celia, Ben Jonson						
Song: Still to Be Neat, Ben Jonson		*Creative* Responding to the Main Idea				
Delight in Disorder, Robert Herrick	Oxymoron Message	*Creative* Writing a Parody *Critical* Comparing Poems				
To the Virgins, to Make Much of Time, Robert Herrick	Imagery	*Creative* Extending the Poem Answering the Poet				
Virtue, George Herbert	Title Paraphrase		Figures of Speech			
The Altar, George Herbert	Metaphor	*Creative* Writing a "Picture Poem"				
The Pulley, George Herbert		*Critical* Supporting the Main Idea				

Grade 12: Unit 3 The Renaissance 1485–1660	Elements Taught in Question or Introduction or Exercise	Writing	Analyzing Language and Style	Critical Comment	Primary Sources	The Elements of Literature
John Milton	Milton's Political Activity Milton's Epics					
On His Blindness, John Milton	Octave Sestet	*Critical* Paraphrasing the Poem				
On Shakespeare, John Milton		*Critical* Comparing Poems				
Paradise Lost	Reading *Paradise Lost* Blank verse					
The Temptation of Eve, John Milton	Metaphor Characterization	*Creative* Extending the Narrative *Critical* Paraphrasing a Speech Researching Sources	Milton's Poetic Style Epic Simile Syntax Blank Verse Unrhymed Iambic Pentameter Iamb			
To His Coy Mistress, Andrew Marvell	Exaggeration Understatement	*Creative* Writing a Response *Critical* Comparing and Contrasting Poems				

Grade 12: Unit 3 The Renaissance 1485–1660	Elements Taught in Question or Intro-duction or Exercise	Writing	Analyzing Language and Style	Critical Comment	Primary Sources	The Elements of Literature
The English Language, The Growth of Modern English	The First Grammars and Dictionaries The Battle of Styles: Ornate Vs. Plain Euphuism Metaphysical Conceit What Is Style? Types and Elements of Style		Studying the development of Modern English Studying the Influence of the Language of the Bible Comparing Two Styles			
Exercises in Critical Thinking and Writing Analyzing a Poet's Work	Primary Sources Secondary Sources Documentation					

SCOPE AND SEQUENCE OF THE PROGRAM IN *ELEMENTS OF LITERATURE*: Sixth Course

Grade 12: Unit 4 The Restoration and the Eighteenth Century 1660–1800	Elements Taught in Question or Introduction or Exercise	Writing	Analyzing Language and Style	Critical Comment	Primary Sources	The Elements of Literature
Introduction	Augustan and Neoclassical Reason and Enlightenment Changes in Religion Religion and Politics The Bloodless Revolution Writers and Religion					
The Age of Dryden	Dramatic Unities					
The Age of Pope and Swift						
Augustan Poetry	Ode Pastoral Poetry Meter Rhyme					
The Age of Johnson	Novel					
Shakespeare, John Dryden	Argumentation Opposing Viewpoints Generalizations	*Critical* Applying a Generalization				
from Baucis and Philemon, John Dryden	Moral Symbolism Comic Relief Theme Tone	*Creative* Changing the Setting *Critical* Analyzing Characterization				

Grade 12: Unit 4 The Restoration and the Eighteenth Century 1660–1800	Elements Taught in Question or Introduction or Exercise	Writing	Analyzing Language and Style	Critical Comment	Primary Sources	The Elements of Literature
from The Diary of Samuel Pepys, Samuel Pepys	Primary Source	*Creative* Planning a Diary *Critical* Using a Primary Source	Eighteenth-Century Usage			
from Robinson Crusoe, Daniel Defoe	First-Person Point of View Characterization	*Creative* Narrating a Different Outcome *Critical* Explaining a Literary Appeal Analyzing a Character's Response Comparing and Contrasting Two Treatments of Solitude				
from A Journal of the Plague Year, Daniel Defoe	Tone	*Creative* Narrating from Primary Sources *Critical* Comparing and Contrasting Literary Works Supporting an Opinion				
from Gulliver's Travels, Jonathan Swift from Part I	Parody Satire Symbolism	*Creative* Using First-Person Point of View		A Comment on the Story		
from Part II	Characterization Verbal Irony	*Creative* Varying a Plot				Satire Exaggeration Irony

Grade 12: Unit 4 The Restoration and the Eighteenth Century 1660–1800	Elements Taught in Question or Introduction or Exercise	Writing	Analyzing Language and Style	Critical Comment	Primary Sources	The Elements of Literature
A Modest Proposal, Jonathan Swift	Characterization Satire Purpose	*Creative* Writing a Newspaper Editorial Responding to the Essay *Critical* Relating the Essay to Current Events	Diction and Connotations Diction			
Heroic Couplets, Alexander Pope			Pope's Poetics Antitheses			
from An Essay on Criticism, Alexander Pope		*Creative* Writing Couplets				
from An Essay on Man, Alexander Pope		*Creative* Writing an Illustration				
from The Rape of the Lock, Alexander Pope	Satire Tone Irony Theme	*Creative* Using the Mock-Heroic Style *Critical* Analyzing a Satire Comparing and Contrasting Epics				Wit
Articles in Tragedy, Joseph Addison		*Critical* Describing Comic Devices	Satirical Techniques and Tone			
Alexander Selkirk, Sir Richard Steele Joseph Addison	Characterization Theme	*Critical* Examining a Conclusion	Precise Meanings			

Grade 12: Unit 4 The Restoration and the Eighteenth Century 1660–1800	Elements Taught in Question or Introduction or Exercise	Writing	Analyzing Language and Style	Critical Comment	Primary Sources	The Elements of Literature
from A Dictionary of the English Language, Samuel Johnson		*Creative* Writing Dictionary Definitions *Critical* Drawing Inferences				
Letter to Lord Chesterfield, Samuel Johnson	Purpose Irony Tone	*Creative* Replying to a Letter Paraphrasing a Letter *Critical* Identifying Satirical Elements				
from The Preface to Shakespeare		*Critical* Analyzing a Character				Style
Elegy Written in a Country Churchyard, Thomas Gray	Imagery Personification Stereotyping Message	*Creative* Writing an Epitaph Imitating the Writer's Technique *Critical* Comparing and Contrasting Poems	A Poetic Style			The Elegy Pastoral Elegy Gothic Element Generalizations
from The Life of Samuel Johnson, James Boswell		*Creative* Writing a Biographical Sketch *Critical* Writing an Explanation				
from Pilgrim's Progress, John Bunyan	Allegory	*Creative* Changing a Character Outlining an Allegory Recasting the Story				Allegory

Grade 12: Unit 4 The Restoration and the Eighteenth Century 1660–1800	Elements Taught in Question or Introduction or Exercise	Writing	Analyzing Language and Style	Critical Comment	Primary Sources	The Elements of Literature
The English Language, Decorum and Order	Change, Degeneration, and Growth Refining, Ascertaining, and Fixing English The Dictionary Change All Around Us What Is Good English?		Using Dictionaries to Study English			
Exercises in Critical Thinking and Writing: Using Logical Reasoning to Write a Persuasive Essay	Hasty Generalizations Circular Reasoning Inductive Reasoning Deductive Reasoning					

SCOPE AND SEQUENCE OF THE PROGRAM IN *ELEMENTS OF LITERATURE*: Sixth Course

Grade 12: Unit 5 The Romantic Period 1798–1832	Elements Taught in Question or Introduction or Exercise	Writing	Analyzing Language and Style	Critical Comment	Primary Sources	The Elements of Literature
Introduction	Political and Economic Changes The Term "Romantic" The Interrelationship of Nature, the Mind, and the Imagination The Idea of the Poet Romanticism The Forms of Literature in the Romantic Period					
To a Mouse, Robert Burns	Tone Alliteration	*Creative* Imitating the Writer's Technique *Critical* Responding to the Poem				
John Anderson, My Jo, Robert Burns	Symbolism	*Creative* Changing the Point of View *Critical* Rewriting Dialect				
Blake's Poems The Tyger, William Blake	Imagery	*Critical* Analyzing the Poem Comparing and Contrasting Two Versions of a Poem				
The Lamb, William Blake	Speaker	*Critical* Comparing and Contrasting Poems				
The Chimney Sweeper (Songs of Innocence), William Blake	Irony Tone					

Grade 12: Unit 5 The Romantic Period 1798–1832	Elements Taught in Question or Introduction or Exercise	Writing	Analyzing Language and Style	Critical Comment	Primary Sources	The Elements of Literature
The Chimney Sweeper (Songs of Experience), William Blake	Irony Purpose	*Creative* Writing a Narrative *Critical* Writing an Analysis				
London, William Blake	Imagery	*Creative* Writing a Description *Critical* Comparing Two Poets	Puns			
Jerusalem, William Blake	Tone Symbolism	*Critical* Comparing Visions	Parallelism		"Blake is a real name . . .," Charles Lamb	
Lines Composed a Few Miles Above Tintern Abbey, William Wordsworth	Meter Run-On Lines Theme	*Creative* Describing a Scene *Critical* Analyzing the Structure of a Poem	Verse Paragraphs Run-On Lines			
Strange Fits of Passion Have I Known, She Dwelt Among the Untrodden Ways, A Slumber Did My Spirit Steal, William Wordsworth	Audience Metaphor Theme Imagery	*Creative* Using Another Point of View *Critical* Analyzing Romantic Themes				
London, 1802, William Wordsworth	Poem Metaphor Symbolism	*Creative* Writing an Apostrophe				

Grade 12: Unit 5 The Romantic Period 1798–1832	Elements Taught in Question or Introduction or Exercise	Writing	Analyzing Language and Style	Critical Comment	Primary Sources	The Elements of Literature
I Wandered Lonely as a Cloud, William Wordsworth	Mood Personification	*Creative* Creating a Simile *Critical* Comparing Poems Evaluating a Metaphor				
Composed Upon Westminster Bridge, William Wordsworth	Personification Mood Paradox	*Creative* Imitating the Writer's Technique				
The Solitary Reaper, William Wordsworth	Rhythm	*Critical* Comparing Poems				Romantic Lyrics Sonnet Italian or Petrarchan Sonnet Ode Apostrophy Meditative Poem Blank Verse
Kubla Khan, Samuel Taylor Coleridge	Imagery Rhyme Scheme Meter Alliteration Symbolism	*Creative* Completing the Poem *Critical* Analyzing the Poem				
The Lime-Tree Bower My Prison, Samuel Taylor Coleridge	Paradox Tone	*Creative* Writing a Description *Critical* Comparing Two Meditative Lyrics Supporting a Topic Statement				

Grade 12: Unit 5 The Romantic Period 1798–1832	Elements Taught in Question or Intro- duction or Exercise	Writing	Analyzing Language and Style	Critical Comment	Primary Sources	The Elements of Literature
The Rime of the Ancient Mariner, Samuel Taylor Coleridge	Narrator Moral Imagery Sound Effects Simile Metaphor Personification Alliteration Assonance Internal Rhyme Ballad Stanza	*Creative* Extending the Poem *Critical* Analyzing Plot Identifying Allegory	Archaic Words		A Letter from Coleridge	
She Walks in Beauty, George Gordon, Lord Byron	Simile					
So We'll Go No More A-Roving, George Gordon, Lord Byron		*Critical* Analyzing Techniques				
The Destruction of Sennacherib, George Gordon, Lord Byron	Simile Meter	*Critical* Analyzing Similes				
from Don Juan, Canto II, George Gordon, Lord Byron	Setting Figures of Speech Simile Rhyme Scheme Alliteration Tone Satire	*Creative* Continuing the Story *Critical* Comparing Epics				

Grade 12: Unit 5 The Romantic Period 1798–1832	Elements Taught in Question or Introduction or Exercise	Writing	Analyzing Language and Style	Critical Comment	Primary Sources	The Elements of Literature
from Childe Harold's Pilgrimage, Canto IV, George Gordon, Lord Byron	Figure of Speech / Rhyme Scheme / Rhythm	*Creative* Writing an Apostrophe *Critical* Analyzing a Stanza Form			Byron Writes to Shelley	
Ode to the West Wind, Percy Bysshe Shelley	Paradox	*Critical* Analyzing Sound Effects	Terza Rima and the Sonnet	A Comment on the Poem		Apostrophe Extended Apostrophe
To a Skylark, Percy Bysshe Shelley	Simile	*Critical* Comparing Poems				
England in 1819, Percy Bysshe Shelley	Figures of Speech / Paradox		Connotations			
Ozymandias, Percy Bysshe Shelley	Narrative Frame / Irony	*Critical* Comparing and Contrasting Poems				
On First Looking into Chapman's Homer, John Keats	Rhyme Scheme / Simile	*Creative* Writing Similes *Critical* Analyzing the Poem's Structure				
Bright Star, Would I Were Steadfast as Thou Art, John Keats	Personification	*Critical* Analyzing Figures of Speech				
When I Have Fears, John Keats	Simile / Tone	*Creative* Answering the Speaker *Critical* Analyzing the Poem's Structure				

Grade 12: Unit 5 The Romantic Period 1798–1832	Elements Taught in Question or Introduction or Exercise	Writing	Analyzing Language and Style	Critical Comment	Primary Sources	The Elements of Literature
La Belle Dame Sans Merci, John Keats	Imagery Meter	*Creative* Setting a Ballad to Music Writing a Short Story				
Ode to a Nightingale, John Keats	Setting Mood	*Critical* Analyzing Symbolism Comparing and Contrasting Odes Comparing and Contrasting Poems	Imagery Synaesthesia	A Comment on the Poem		
Ode on a Grecian Urn, John Keats		*Creative* Imitating the Writer's Technique *Critical* Analyzing a Main Idea		A Comment on the Poem		
To Autumn, John Keats	Personification	*Creative* Writing a Description *Critical* Analyzing Poetic Technique				
The Eve of St. Agnes, John Keats	Setting Symbolism	*Creative* Creating and Staging a Dramatic Version *Critical* Comparing Stories Supporting a Statement	Imagery	A Comment on the Poem	Keats's Last Letter	
Dream Children: A Reverie, Charles Lamb	Tone	*Creative* Writing a Reverie	The Familiar Essay		Lamb's Letter to Coleridge	

Grade 12: Unit 5 The Romantic Period 1798–1832	Elements Taught in Question or Intro-duction or Exercise	Writing	Analyzing Language and Style	Critical Comment	Primary Sources	The Elements of Literature
from Frankenstein, Mary Wollstonecraft Shelley		*Creative* Extending the Story *Critical* Identifying a Theme				
from The Journals, Dorothy Wordsworth	Figures of Speech	*Critical* Comparing the Journal to the Poem			Dorothy Wordsworth Describes Coleridge	
The English Language, Variety in Language	What Are Dialects? How Odd You Should Say That American Regional Dialects American Ethnic Dialects	Recognizing Familiar Terms				
Exercises in Critical Thinking and Writing Interpreting Poetry	Speaker Situation in Poem Literal Meaning Tone Meter Rhyme Scheme Sound Effects Imagery					

SCOPE AND SEQUENCE OF THE PROGRAM IN *ELEMENTS OF LITERATURE*: Sixth Course

Grade 12: Unit 6 The Victorian Period 1832–1901	Elements Taught in Question or Intro-duction or Exercise	Writing	Analyzing Language and Style	Critical Comment	Primary Sources	The Elements of Literature
Introduction	Peace and Economic Growth The Idea of Progress Problems of Victoria's Reign The Movement for Reform Decorum and Authority Intellectual Progress: The March of Mind					
Victorian and Romantic Literature	Questions and Doubts					
Victorian Literature and Victorian Life						
London Streets, Thomas Babington Macaulay		*Creative* Conducting an Interview *Critical* Presenting an Oral Report				
Tears, Idle Tears, Alfred, Lord Tennyson	Imagery					
Now Sleeps the Crimson Petal, Alfred, Lord Tennyson	Repetition Parallel Syntax Imagery	*Creative* Setting the Lyric to Music				

Grade 12: Unit 6 The Victorian Period 1832–1901	Elements Taught in Question or Introduction or exercise	Writing	Analyzing Language and Style	Critical Comment	Primary Sources	The Elements of Literature
Break, Break, Break, Alfred, Lord Tennyson	Atmosphere Tone Imagery	*Critical* Analyzing Words and Images *Critical* Analyzing the Poem's Structure				
Crossing the Bar, Alfred, Lord Tennyson	Metaphor	*Creative* Writing a Letter *Critical* Comparing and Contrasting Imagery				
The Lady of Shalott, Alfred, Lord Tennyson	Setting Rhythm Rhyme Scheme Foreshadowing Imagery	*Creative* Filming the Poem *Critical* Analyzing the Ending		A Comment on the Poem		
The Eagle: A Fragment, Alfred, Lord Tennyson	Setting	*Creative* Extending the Poem Imitating the Writer's Technique *Critical* Interpreting the Poem				
Ulysses, Alfred, Lord Tennyson	Characterization	*Creative* Extending the Poem *Critical* Analyzing the Epic Hero				
from In Memoriam, Alfred, Lord Tennyson	Setting Rhyme Scheme	*Critical* Writing an Essay				

Grade 12: Unit 6 The Victorian Period 1832–1901	Elements Taught in Question or Introduction or Exercise	Writing	Analyzing Language and Style	Critical Comment	Primary Sources	The Elements of Literature
My Last Duchess, Robert Browning	Rhyme Rhythm Character Monologue	*Creative* Writing a Dramatic Monologue *Critical* Analyzing the Theme				
Porphyria's Lover, Robert Browning	Setting	*Creative* Extending the Poem *Critical* Comparing and Contrasting Two Dramatic Monologues				
Meeting at Night, Parting at Morning, Robert Browning	Rhythms	*Creative* Extending the Poems Using Another Point of View				
Prospice, Robert Browning	Imagery Attitude	*Critical* Comparing and Contrasting Two Poets' Views				
from Sonnets from the Portuguese, Elizabeth Barrett Browning		*Creative* Extending the Poem *Critical* Analyzing Concrete and Abstract Words				
Dover Beach, Matthew Arnold	Setting Mood Allusion Metaphor Simile Rhyme Scheme Rhythm	*Creative* Analyzing a Problem		A Comment on the Poem		

Grade 12: Unit 6 The Victorian Period 1832–1901	Elements Taught in Question or Introduction or Exercise	Writing	Analyzing Language and Style	Critical Comment	Primary Sources	The Elements of Literature
Requiescat, Matthew Arnold	Metaphor Repetition Tone	*Creative* Writing a Character Sketch *Critical* Analyzing the Poem				
To Marguerite—Continued, Matthew Arnold	Extended Metaphor Mood Connotation	*Creative* Writing an Extended Metaphor *Critical* Comparing and Contrasting Two Poems				
The Blessed Damozel, Dante Gabriel Rossetti	Mood Atmosphere	*Creative* Illustrating the Poem *Critical* Analyzing the Poem		A Comment on the Poem		
A Birthday, Christina Rossetti	Simile Imagery					
Spring and Fall, To a Young Child, Gerard Manley Hopkins	Alliteration Assonance	*Critical* Writing a Paraphrase				
Felix Randal, Gerard Manley Hopkins	Sonnet					
Pied Beauty, Gerard Manley Hopkins	Imagery Theme Alliteration Antithesis Rhythm	*Creative* Extending the Poem *Critical* Analyzing Diction				

Grade 12: Unit 6 The Victorian Period 1832–1901	Elements Taught in Question or Intro-duction or Exercise	Writing	Analyzing Language and Style	Critical Comment	Primary Sources	The Elements of Literature
The Darkling Thrush, Thomas Hardy	Setting	*Creative* Writing a Prediction *Critical* Comparing and Contrasting Two Poems				
Channel Firing, Thomas Hardy	Irony	*Creative* Writing an Editorial *Critical* Analyzing Point of View				
The Convergence of the Twain, Thomas Hardy	Title Main Idea	*Creative* Writing a Commentary *Critical* Writing an Essay			The Sinking of the *Titanic*	
Ah, Are You Digging on My Grave? Thomas Hardy	Anticlimax Tone	*Creative* Writing a Character Sketch *Critical* Analyzing Irony				
Drummer Hodge, Thomas Hardy		*Critical* Comparing and Contrasting Themes				
from The Return of the Native, Thomas Hardy	Mood Imagery	*Critical* Analyzing the Writer's Style				
When I was One-and-Twenty, A. E. Housman	Repetition Theme					

Grade 12: Unit 6 The Victorian Period 1832–1901	Elements Taught in Question or Intro-duction or Exercise	Writing	Analyzing Language and Style	Critical Comment	Primary Sources	The Elements of Literature
The Night Is Freezing Fast, A. E. Housman	Connotations Rhyme Scheme Extended Metaphor Theme					
With Rue My Heart Is Laden, A. E. Housman	Rhythm Rhyme	*Creative* Imitating the Writer's Technique *Critical* Comparing and Contrasting Poems				
On Moonlit Heath and Lonesome Bank, A. E. Housman		*Critical* Writing a Paraphrase Analyzing the Effects of Setting				
from David Copperfield, Charles Dickens	Imagery Characterization Point of View	*Creative* Predicting Outcomes *Critical* Analyzing Character Analyzing Cause and Effect				
from Through the Looking Glass, Lewis Carroll	Setting Events Characters Structure Satire	*Creative* Imitating the Author's Technique *Critical* Supporting an Opinion	Portmanteau Words			
The Miracle of Purun Bhagat, Rudyard Kipling		*Creative* Writing a Story or a Personal Narrative *Critical* Supporting an Opinion				

Grade 12: Unit 6 The Victorian Period 1832–1901	Elements Taught in Question or Intro-duction or Exercise	Writing	Analyzing Language and Style	Critical Comment	Primary Sources	The Elements of Literature
Victorian Drama						
The Importance of Being Earnest, Oscar Wilde	Farce					
Act One	Foreshadowing Tone Characterizations Epigrams					
Act Two	Satire Motif Repetitions					
Act Three	Irony Farce Deus Ex Machina Tone			A Comment on the Play, Donald H. Ericksen		
The Play as a Whole	Plot	Creative Writing Epigrams Writing a Sequence Critical Writing an Analysis	Puns and Paradoxes Epigrams			
The English Language, One Nation—Many Languages	English as an International Language Dialects of English					
Two Close Cousins: British and American English	Pronunciation, Spelling, and Grammar		Comparing British and American Words			

Grade 12: Unit 6 The Victorian Period 1832–1901	Elements Taught in Question or Intro- duction or Exercise	Writing	Analyzing Language and Style	Critical Comment	Primary Sources	The Elements of Literature
Exercises in Critical Thinking and Writing, Developing and Supporting Valid Generalizations	Generalization Validity Response					

SCOPE AND SEQUENCE OF THE PROGRAM IN *ELEMENTS OF LITERATURE*: Sixth Course

Grade 12: Unit 7 The Twentieth Century	Elements Taught in Question or Introduction or Exercise	Writing	Analyzing Language and Style	Critical Comment	Primary Sources	The Elements of Literature
Introduction Prose	Darwin, Marx, and The Great War Experimentation in the Arts The Rise of Dictatorships Contemporary British Writing					
The Secret Sharer, Joseph Conrad	Motivation Double Symbolism Allusion Theme Point of View Atmosphere Mood	*Creative* Extending the Story Writing About a Secret Sharer *Critical* Analyzing a Theme Analyzing a Character Analyzing Imagery Interpreting the Ending		A Comment on the Novel	Letter from Joseph Conrad	
Sredni Vashtar, Hector Hugh Monro (Saki)	Direct Characterization Indirect Characterization Theme Situational Irony Dramatic Irony	*Creative* Recasting the Story *Critical* Responding to a Critical Comment			Munro's Sister Writes About Their Aunts	
Araby, James Joyce	Setting Atmosphere Connotations Theme Irony Tone Plot Characters	*Creative* Changing the Setting *Critical* Analyzing the Story Analyzing a Character Analyzing a Theme Comparing Characters			Ezra Pound Reviews *Dubliners*	Irony Verbal Irony Sarcasm Irony of Situation Dramatic Irony
from A Portrait of the Artist as a Young Man, James Joyce	Point of View Free Association Tone	*Creative* Using the Stream-of-Consciousness Technique *Critical* Comparing and Contrasting Characters				The Stream-of-Consciousness Puns

Grade 12: Unit 7 The Twentieth Century	Elements Taught in Question or Introduction or Exercise	Writing	Analyzing Language and Style	Critical Comment	Primary Sources	The Elements of Literature
The Rocking-Horse Winner, D. H. Lawrence	Character Symbolism Theme Tone Satire	*Creative* Writing a New Resolution *Critical* Analyzing a Character Applying a Quotation to a Story Comparing and Contrasting Characters			D. H. Lawrence on Money	
Miss Brill, Katherine Mansfield	Basic Situation Irony Symbolism Theme Ambiguity	*Creative* Narrating What Happens Next *Critical* Analyzing Point of View		A Comment on the Story, Eudora Welty	from Katherine Mansfield's Letters and Journals	
The Demon Lover, Elizabeth Bowen	Setting Mood Imagery Foreshadowing Omniscient Narrator Theme Dramatic Irony Flashback	*Creative* Describing a Character Mixing Media *Critical* Comparing Literature				
My Oedipus Complex, Frank O'Connor	Narrator Conflict Irony Character Theme	*Creative* Using a Different Point of View *Critical* Comparing and Contrasting Characters Responding to the Story				
The Destructors, Graham Greene	Motivation Irony Connotations Theme	*Creative* Using Another Point of View *Critical* Explaining Imagery	Slang			

Grade 12: Unit 7 The Twentieth Century	Elements Taught in Question or Introduction or Exercise	Writing	Analyzing Language and Style	Critical Comment	Primary Sources	The Elements of Literature
No Witchcraft for Sale, Doris Lessing	Plot Irony Theme	*Creative* Extending a Character *Critical* Analyzing Conflict Analyzing Another Point of View				
The Soft Voice of the Serpent, Nadine Gordimer	Protagonist Simile Title Theme	*Creative* Using Similes in a Description *Critical* Analyzing a Character				
The Death of the Moth, Virginia Woolf		*Creative* Imagining a Different Environment *Critical* Analyzing the Writer's Discovery				
A Child's Christmas in Wales, Dylan Thomas		*Creative* Writing a Sensory Description *Critical* Analyzing the Writer's Style				
from The Road to Wigan Pier, George Orwell		*Creative* Writing About a Social Problem *Critical* Analyzing a Writer's Technique				
from In Patagonia, Bruce Chatwin		*Creative* Describing a Childhood Event *Critical* Comparing Two Works				

Grade 12: Unit 7 The Twentieth Century	Elements Taught in Question or Introduction or Exercise	Writing	Analyzing Language and Style	Critical Comment	Primary Sources	The Elements of Literature
Introduction Twentieth Century Poetry	World War I and the Trench Poets The American Influence: Eliot and Pound The English Group of the 1930's Dylan Thomas and the New Apocalypse The Contemporary Scene					
Anthem for Doomed Youth, Wilfred Owen	Metaphor Alliteration Assonance Consonance Extended Metaphor	*Creative* Writing a Paraphrase Writing an Extended Metaphor *Critical* Analyzing Imagery				
Dulce et Decorum Est, Wilfred Owen	Rhyme Scheme Half Rhymes Figure of Speech Metaphor Theme Tone	*Critical* Writing an Essay Comparing and Contrasting Poems				
Strange Meeting, Wilfred Owen	Setting Half Rhymes Theme	*Creative* Extending the Poem *Critical* Comparing Poems				
The Rear-Guard, Siegfried Sassoon	Onomatopoeia Irony	*Critical* Comparing Two Poems				
The Lake Isle of Innisfree, William Butler Yeats	Tone	*Creative* Imitating the Writer's Technique *Critical* Comparing Poems	Assonance and Alliteration			

Grade 12: Unit 7 The Twentieth Century	Elements Taught in Question or Introduction or Exercise	Writing	Analyzing Language and Style	Critical Comment	Primary Sources	The Elements of Literature
The Wild Swans at Coole, William Butler Yeats	Symbolism Theme	*Critical* Comparing Poems Analyzing a Poem				
The Second Coming, William Butler Yeats	Imagery Irony	*Creative* Evaluating the Effect of a Poem *Critical* Comparing and Contrasting Two Works Commenting on Famous Lines				
Sailing to Byzantium, William Butler Yeats	Imagery Theme	*Creative* Describing a Symbolic Setting *Critical* Comparing and Contrasting Two Poems Exploring a Symbol		A Comment on the Poem		
Still Falls the Rain, Edith Sitwell	Rhyme Scheme Refrain Meter	*Creative* Preparing a Choral Reading *Critical* Relating Technique to Theme				
Snake, D. H. Lawrence	Internal Conflict Imagery Symbolism Allusions	*Critical* Explaining an Allusion Comparing and Contrasting Two Poems Comparing Settings	Free Verse Onomatopoeia Alliteration Repetition			
Warning to Children, Robert Graves	Repetitions Theme Rhythm	*Creative* Writing a Reply Imitating the Writer's Technique				

Grade 12: Unit 7 The Twentieth Century	Elements Taught in Question or Intro- duction or Exercise	Writing	Analyzing Language and Style	Critical Comment	Primary Sources	The Elements of Literature
Death in Leamington, John Betjeman	Attitude	*Creative* Shifting the Point of View *Critical* Analyzing a Theme Comparing the Poem to a Story				
Musée des Beaux Arts, W. H. Auden	Theme	*Creative* Describing a Painting *Critical* Researching a Myth				
Song: As I Walked Out One Evening, W. H. Auden	Metaphor Imagery Figures of Speech Reversals Irony Tone Sounds Metrics	*Creative* Responding to the Poem				
The Unknown Citizen, W. H. Auden	Tone Theme	*Creative* Shifting the Point of View Imitating the Writer's Technique *Critical* Analyzing Satire				
Prayer Before Birth, Louis MacNeice	Point of View Simile Metaphor Epigraph Tone	*Creative* Using a Different Point of View *Critical* Connecting Two Poems	Free Verse Rhyme Alliteration Onomato- poeia			

Grade 12: Unit 7 The Twentieth Century	Elements Taught in Question or Intro-duction or Exercise	Writing	Analyzing Language and Style	Critical Comment	Primary Sources	The Elements of Literature
Departure in the Dark, C. Day Lewis	Allusion Rhyme Half Rhyme	*Creative* Imitating the Writer's Technique *Critical* Evaluating a Poem	Connotations			
The Express, Stephen Spender	Simile Metaphors Alliteration Onomatopoeia	*Creative* Imitating the Writer's Technique *Critical* Comparing and Contrasting Poems				
Naming of Parts, Henry Reed	Setting Tone	*Creative* Writing a Dialogue	Diction			
Fern Hill, Dylan Thomas	Personification Paradox Rhythm Alliteration Onomatopoeia	*Creative* Imitating the Writer's Technique *Critical* Analyzing a Theme	Word Play Cliché Puns			
A Refusal to Mourn the Death, by Fire, of a Child in London, Dylan Thomas	Tone	*Creative* Relating the Poem to Contemporary Experience *Critical* Paraphrasing the Poem				
Do Not Go Gentle into That Good Night, Dylan Thomas	Pun Metaphors	*Creative* Responding to the Speaker Writing a Villanelle	The Villanelle			
Church Going, Philip Larkin	Rhyme Scheme Title Tone	*Critical* Writing a Character Sketch Comparing Two Poems				

Grade 12: Unit 7 The Twentieth Century	Elements Taught in Question or Intro- duction or Exercise	Writing	Analyzing Language and Style	Critical Comment	Primary Sources	The Elements of Literature
Hawk Roosting, Ted Hughes	Paraphrasing	*Creative* Writing a Poem *Critical* Analyzing Theme				
Digging, Seamus Heaney	Imagery Figures of Speech	*Creative* Extending the Poem				
Pygmalion, Bernard Shaw Act One	Exposition Foreshadowing Character		Cockney Dialect			
Act Two	Paradoxes Satire Character Conflict Resolution					
Act Three	Character Appearance Speech Incongruity					
Act Four	Reversals Crisis					
Act Five						

Grade 12: Unit 7 The Twentieth Century	Elements Taught in Question or Introduction or Exercise	Writing	Analyzing Language and Style	Critical Comment	Primary Sources	The Elements of Literature
The Play as a Whole	Protagonist Character Types Theme Satire	*Creative* Extending the Play Updating the Story Adapting Another Myth to the Stage *Critical* Analyzing Dialogue Analyzing Themes Analyzing an Adaptation Responding to Shaw's Women Characters Responding to a Critic Responding to Shaw's Epilogue				
Modern British Drama	Departures from Conventions: New Subjects and Forms Irish Dramatists: Yeats, Synge, and O'Casey English Comedy and Noel Coward The Angry Young Men Theater of the Absurd: Samuel Beckett The Plays of Harold Pinter British Theater Today					

Grade 12: Unit 7 The Twentieth Century	Elements Taught in Question or Intro- duction or Exercise	Writing	Analyzing Language and Style	Critical Comment	Primary Sources	The Elements of Literature
The English Language, English Today and Tomorrow	Tracking New Words: Where They Come From Loanword: Sacking Other Languages Compounds: Stacking Words Together Affixes: Tacking Parts On Shortenings and Back-Formations: Hacking Parts Off Blends: Packing Words Together Shifted Words: Racking Up New Meanings Tomorrow's English		Discovering Word Origins			
Exercises in Critical Thinking and Writing Analyzing a Writer's Style	Thesis Statement					

Unit One: *The Anglo-Saxons The Emergent Period 450–1066*

Teaching Anglo-Saxon Literature

Perhaps more than any other age in British literature, the Anglo-Saxon Period is often viewed by students and some teachers with fear or at least apprehension. Part of this response is triggered by the prospect of dealing with the language of the period, Old English. Still, Anglo-Saxon literature offers students unique perspectives on life in Britain during early times.

The history of these times is vitally important to a consideration of representative works, for these works squarely are products of the age in which they were written. It should thus be stressed to students that the Anglo-Saxon Period is characterized by the contributions of the four groups that invaded England. These groups—the Angles, Saxons, Jutes, and Danes—brought with them not only the desire to conquer but the inevitable merging of their several cultures.

During the Anglo-Saxon Period, literature reflected the juxtaposition of the church and the pagan world. In the most important work of the period, *Beowulf*, readers may easily discern these two divergent worlds. Much criticism regarding *Beowulf*, in fact, deals with Christian and pagan references in the epic. A preoccupation with ecclesiastical matters is evident in another seminal work of the period, Bede's *Ecclesiastical History*.

Inasmuch as poetry is the dominant genre of this early period, direct students' attention, before assigning any single poem, to the following three key characteristics of Anglo-Saxon poetry: its tendency toward didacticism, its unique verse form, and its exploration of "epic" topics. Begin by pointing out that the poetry of the era was usually instructive in nature and that characteristic works, hence, often addressed moral, religious, or ethical concerns. Next, have students note the reliance of Anglo-Saxon poets on the division of lines into two *hemistichs*, or half-lines, an effect generally achieved by use of a *caesura*, or pause. Have them observe, in addition, the strong dependence on *alliteration*, or repetition of initial consonant sounds, as a means of enhancing the structure inherent in the poetry's four-beat rhythm. Finally, stress the preoccupation among Anglo-Saxon poets with the deeds of heroes and with acts of strength, courage, and derring-do. You might emphasize that the most famous of the heroes celebrated in epic verse is Beowulf.

The excerpt from *Beowulf*, which contains six sections of the epic, is the only selection that will require more than a single class period for coverage. As with all poetry this, and the balance of poetic selections in the unit, will be enhanced immeasurably by oral interpretation. Reserve space in your class schedule as well for the incidental source-and-analogue material presented under the "Primary Sources" heading at various points in the unit.

Objectives of the Anglo-Saxon Unit

1. To improve reading proficiency and expand vocabulary
2. To gain exposure to notable Anglo-Saxon poetry
3. To define and identify elements of poetry: figures of speech (metaphor, simile, personification), conflict, epic, imagery, paradox, sound effects (alliteration, kenning), point of view, setting, symbol, tone, and atmosphere
4. To respond to poetry orally and in writing
5. To practice the following critical thinking and writing skills:
   a. Recognizing a character's motive
   b. Identifying images and symbols
   c. Analyzing theme
   d. Comparing points of view
   e. Analyzing character

from Beowulf

Text page 12

Objectives

1. To recognize a character's motive
2. To identify images and symbols
3. To evaluate a writer's use of characterization
4. To identify the central conflict in a work
5. To identify and analyze theme
6. To write a portion of a narrative from a different point of view
7. To write a character analysis

8. To write an analysis of an epic

9. To identify examples of kennings and alliteration

Introducing the Epic

In outline form, for your reference, here are the major elements of the epic:

- **Protagonists:** Beowulf, Hrothgar
- **Antagonists:** Grendel, Grendel's mother
- **Conflict:** person vs. self (self-doubt); good vs. evil
- **Point of view:** third-person limited (omniscient)
- **Significant techniques:** characterization, imagery, symbolism, conflict, theme, point of view, kenning, alliteration
- **Setting:** Northern Europe, eighth century or earlier

Background on the Epic. As Kevin Crossley-Holland states in *The Anglo-Saxon World* (Suffolk, England: Boydell, 1982), few works of literature "represent the temper of a particular time" as does *Beowulf*. In fact, the epic not only represents the Anglo-Saxon Period, but showcases all of the important stylistic devices of that period: the use of the four-beat rhythm, the prominence of songs, or lays, and the representation of the struggle between the pagan and the Christian worlds. In *Beowulf*, students will find tales of heroism and valor and other studies in human psychology.

The Plot. Herot, the great hall of the Danish king Hrothgar, is abandoned for twelve years following a series of murderous assaults by the monster Grendel. Beowulf, a noble warrior, learns of the king's plight and arrives in Denmark with fourteen of his ablest men. After Beowulf slays Grendel, the monster's mother attacks Herot and carries off Hrothgar's closest friend. Armed with the legendary sword Hrunting, Beowulf confronts the witch in her underwater lair and kills her. In his final adventure, fifty years later, Beowulf is sent to battle a dragon and, after being betrayed by his men, is mortally wounded.

Teaching Strategies

Providing for Cultural Differences. Students may be slightly confused by Hrothgar's sponsoring a feast for Beowulf upon his arrival. Explain that the notion of breaking bread in Anglo-Saxon society was both an expression of brotherhood between men and a ritual preparation for battle. The concept is slightly analogous to a team handshake or to a battle cry in war.

Providing for Different Levels of Ability. Better students may wish to study the characteristics of other epic heroes, evaluating the similarities and differences apparent in them. Slower students will need careful and sometimes painstaking guidance in their study of *Beowulf*. Even with the epic translated into modern English, descriptions and sentence structure may impose difficulties. At times you may want to read aloud sections, asking students to see in their minds the action occurring between Beowulf and the others.

Introducing Vocabulary Study. Students, by this point in their education, should be familiar with the concept of alliteration. It will thus suffice simply to elicit from them an operational definition of the device and to remind them of its importance in Anglo-Saxon poetry. The notion of kenning, on the other hand, will be new to them. Point out that this type of specialized metaphor continues to surface in present-day English in such terms as *love-child* and *plumber's helper*.

Reading the Epic. When first considering *Beowulf*, many students and some teachers may think the poem far removed from today. Some may ask what a poem written during the eighth century could possibly have to do with contemporary life in the United States. Those persons should consider the importance historically placed on Western heroes. They remain larger than life, with attributes ranging from courage, strength, and determination, to the ability to lead others. They will possess a clear view of right and wrong, good and evil. For such heroes, the ultimate end is success.

You will want to divide your teaching of the epic over two class periods, the first ending with the review questions on page 30. Use the discussion questions as a barometer to any problems, and take remedial action against these before resuming the reading.

Reteaching Alternatives. You may want to have students act out particularly important passages. For instance, two students in a reader's theater might act out the dialogue between Beowulf and Unferth. Alternatively, you might direct students to write a persuasive essay about the dual nature of Beowulf. They may consider how their own perceptions of Beowulf have changed during their reading of the excerpt. Ask them to contemplate, moreover, whether the depiction of Beowulf's dual nature was most likely a flaw on the poet's part, or whether it serves a good purpose.

Responding to the Epic   Text page 30

Analyzing the Epic

Identifying Details

1. What does the poet tell us about Grendel's origins? The poet says that Grendel was conceived by a pair of demons who were offspring of Cain.

2. Why does Herot remain empty for twelve years? Herot remains empty for twelve years because of Grendel's murderous raids. The warriors of King Hrothgar are afraid to gather in their hall.

3. Explain why Grendel does not touch King Hrothgar's throne. The poet says that Hrothgar's throne is protected by God.

What means does Hrothgar resort to in his desperate effort to save his guest-hall? Hrothgar resorts to pagan sacrifice, which the poet condemns as impious.

4. What is Beowulf's *motive* for traveling to Hrothgar's country? Beowulf travels to Hrothgar's country to help the king.

What do he and his men do with their weapons when they arrive at Herot? When they arrive at Herot, the hero and his men set their shields and spears aside as Beowulf addresses Hrothgar.

5. How is Beowulf taunted by the jealous Unferth? Unferth, who resents Beowulf's courage and his superior fame, taunts the hero by calling him a boaster and by charging that he was bested in the swimming match with Brecca.

How does Beowulf reply to these taunts? Beowulf says that he and Brecca were separated by a storm and that, afterwards, Beowulf slew nine sea-monsters. The hero says that neither Brecca nor Unferth is strong enough to challenge him. Then he condemns Unferth for murdering his own brothers.

6. Describe what happens to Grendel when he raids Herot and finds Beowulf in charge. After destroying one Geat, Grendel tries to grasp Beowulf. The hero grips the monster and traps him. The hall trembles from the noise of the battle. Beowulf's followers attempt to protect their prince with swords, but Grendel is impervious to their swords. Beowulf mortally wounds the monster by tearing off his arm at the shoulder, and Grendel flees from the hall.

Interpreting Meanings

7. In what specific ways does Herot contrast with the place where Grendel lives? Herot is a bright hall, a place of drinking, singing, and feasting. Grendel lives in a cold, dark lake. According to Hrothgar, this place is so forbidding that even hunted deer prefer to lie down on its shores and die, rather than plunge into the waters to save their lives.

What reasons can you propose for Grendel's hatred of Herot? Student answers will vary. Many students will suggest that Herot represents order and light—and, perhaps by extension, divine creation. Grendel, the enemy of the Almighty and offspring of monsters whom God exiled, is portrayed as an outcast. He thus hates the hall as the symbol of ordered, human society.

8. In lines 3–13, the poet describes the songs of the bard in Hrothgar's hall. How does the content of the songs contrast with Grendel and his world? (Could you say that the songs are about creation and that Grendel is associated with destruction?) Most students will agree with this suggestion. In fact, the text of the poem specifi-

cally indicates that the bard's songs are about God's creation of the world (see lines 7–13).

9. What significance can you see in the fact that Grendel attacks at night? What *images* describing Grendel might associate him with death, destruction, and darkness? Grendel, who is evil and destructive, is consistently associated with death, destruction, and darkness: see especially lines 2, 18–19, 30, 49–50, 82, 112, 392–396, 547–548, and 562. Most students will agree that this association is symbolically appropriate.

10. Considering Grendel's origin and lair, what *symbolic* meaning might underlie the confrontation between Grendel and Hrothgar? Students may suggest that the confrontation has a broader, symbolic meaning—a meaning that hints at the universal struggle between light and dark, good and evil, life and death.

What symbolism do you see in the uselessness of human weapons against Grendel? Student answers will vary. Some students may suggest that this motif (relatively common in folk tales) symbolically indicates that the struggle is really on a spiritual level, rather than on a literal, physical level. In other words, the battle against Grendel is really a battle against the forces of evil.

11. Analyze the narrative function of the tale-within-a-tale about Beowulf's swimming match with Brecca. How does this story contribute to the *characterization* of Beowulf? The tale-within-a-tale provides a concrete foreshadowing of Beowulf's great strength and courage. Although Beowulf does not boast about his victories, he is appropriately proud of them. In general, the story reveals Beowulf to be a strong, confident leader, justly proud of his great achievements. The tale also serves to contrast Beowulf with the jealous Unferth: the former is truly heroic, courageous, and truthful, whereas the latter is pretentious, envious, and—by implication—cowardly.

How does it establish Beowulf's superiority to sea beasts and to the sea itself? Beowulf's astonishing feats clearly reveal his superiority to the sea and to the sea monsters, nine of whom he slew. This superiority, in turn, foreshadows Beowulf's victory over Grendel, whose habitat is said to be the dark waters of the marshy lake.

12. Does this account of Grendel and Beowulf have anything in common with fantasy or adventure movies today? Explain. Student answers will vary. Many students may suggest parallels with contemporary fantasy or adventure movies. Encourage the students to elaborate on their suggestions in class.

Primary Sources Text page 30
The Mark of Cain

Have student volunteers read the brief passage from Genesis aloud. Point out that this story has been used allegorically in literature throughout the ages. An important twentieth-century application of the story of Cain and Abel is to be found in John Steinbeck's *East of Eden*.

Responding to the Epic Text page 38

Analyzing the Epic

Identifying Details

1. Describe how Beowulf manages to kill Grendel's mother. Beowulf finds that his own sword, Hrunting, is useless against the monster, so he grapples with her with his bare hands. At one point, she pins him to the ground and tries to stab him with a dagger, but Beowulf is protected, both by his mail shirt and by supernatural aid. The hero then spies a heavy sword hanging on the wall. Even though the sword is massive, the hero manages to grasp and draw it, and with one stroke he mortally wounds Grendel's mother in the neck.

2. Who comes to the aid of Beowulf in his final battle with the dragon? Why does he help Beowulf? The only warrior to come to Beowulf's aid is Wiglaf, who pities Beowulf's suffering and honors his oaths of loyalty.

3. What sad scene concludes the epic? The funeral of Beowulf and the raising of his burial mound conclude the epic.

Interpreting Meanings

4. What *images* suggest that the lair in which Grendel and his mother live is like Hell? Among the images students may mention are the fiery lake, the claws of Grendel's mother, the invulnerability of the evil monster's skin, and the sudden shining of light when Grendel's mother is slain.

5. A hoarded treasure in Old English literature usually *symbolizes* spiritual death or damnation. How might this fact add significance to the hero's last fight with the dragon? What happens to the dragon's hoard? This fact might suggest that the dragon, who guards the treasure, is symbolic of death and evil, perhaps even of the devil. It is significant that, even though Beowulf wants to give the captured treasure to the Geats, the treasure is finally buried, along with Beowulf's body.

6. Find details that describe the dragon in terms of a serpent. (Remember that a dragon *is* a kind of serpent.) Details describing the dragon as a serpent occur in lines 711 ("coiled and uncoiled") and 726 ("scaly hide").

What might the dragon symbolize as Beowulf's final foe? As suggested above, the dragon may symbolize death or the devil.

7. Beowulf battles Grendel, Grendel's mother, and the dragon. But none of these battles could be called the *central conflict* of the epic, though each certainly relates to it. How would you state the central conflict in *Beowulf*? How is it resolved? The central conflict might be described as the struggle of good against evil. The conflict is resolved in favor of good, but at the price of the death of the hero.

8. Given what you know about the structure of Anglo-Saxon society, explain what is especially ominous about the behavior of Beowulf's men during the final scene. What might this suggest about the future of the kingdom? Given that the structure of Anglo-Saxon society was built on loyalty to a king or protector, the men's failure to help Beowulf loyally is especially ominous. This failure perhaps foreshadows the disintegration of the kingdom after Beowulf's death.

9. The epic closes on a somber, *elegiac* note—a note of mourning. What words and *images* contribute to this tone? Among the words and images students may mention are the following: "telling their sorrow" (line 851), "mourning their beloved leader" (line 839), and "crying that no better king had ever lived" (lines 840–841). Students may also mention the somber implications of lines 834–837: Beowulf, who had been "their shield and protector," is now dead.

10. Great epic poetry generally embodies the attitudes and ideals of an entire culture. In what ways do you think *Beowulf* reveals the values of the Anglo-Saxon society? What universal themes does it also reveal? Student answers will vary. In general, students should mention instances from the epic that reveal the values of courage, loyalty, and strength (both physical and spiritual). The poem also clearly contains universal themes: loyalty and self-sacrifice are admirable traits, good will triumph over evil (but at a painful cost), different members of society have obligations toward one another, and fame can be achieved through great deeds.

11. How are these Anglo-Saxon values and heroic ideals both similar to, and different from, our own? Student answers will vary. Ask the students to support and defend their opinions about the similarities and differences.

Primary Sources Text page 41

The Treasures at Sutton Hoo

Ask students to comment on the discovery mentioned in this addendum to the lesson. What, in particular, is suggested by the fact that bards used harps? What kinds of music might have accompanied the telling of a tale like *Beowulf*? What modern composer do students think might be able to provide music for heroics of the sort detailed in the epic?

Extending the Epic

Ask students to invent and describe an adventure in Beowulf's career somewhere between his killing of Grendel's mother and his last battle with the dragon. Encourage them to imagine Beowulf in this in-between time, lacking some of the vigor of a young warrior but not quite as old as the slightly frail man who succumbed to the wounds of a routine battle. Students should be imaginative in their selection of enemies for Beowulf.

Further Reading

Students interested in learning how historians reconstruct events may want to read Kenneth Harrison's *The Framework of Anglo-Saxon History* (Cambridge, 1976).

The Wanderer

Text page 42

Objectives

1. To identify images

2. To analyze tone

3. To evaluate symbolic meanings

4. To write an imitation of a verse style, using alliteration and kennings

5. To write an analysis of a poem

6. To write an essay comparing and contrasting transitions

Introducing the Poem

In outline form, for your reference, here are the major elements in the poem:

- **Protagonist:** an unnamed warrior
- **Antagonist:** a cold, indifferent world
- **Conflict:** person vs. self; person vs. society
- **Point of view:** first- and third-person (omniscient)
- **Significant techniques:** imagery, tone, symbolism, alliteration, kenning
- **Setting:** barren, unidentified lands and seas

Background on the Poem. By now students are familiar with *The Odyssey*, which, you might remind them, is also a work that treats in part the notion of wandering. Discuss with them briefly the point behind Odysseus's wandering in Homer's epic, and have them assess what probable effects perpetual wandering has on the human spirit.

The Plot. The poem consists of two main parts, preceded by a prologue. The introduction of five lines explains that the Christian sometimes lives in exile as a means of penance. Following this introduction is the first part of the poem, lines 6–62, in which the poet speaks through the exiled man. The narrator-character expresses his sorrow at losing his lord and companions. He then explains his search for a new lord and the hardships he has had to endure in the search. The poet moves into a homily, explaining that the world is coming to an end and telling readers to beware the transitory nature of this life. The poem ends with a rhetorical question: ''Where are the glories of the past?'' The epilogue of five lines then explains that God provides grace and comfort and that security may be found in Him.

Teaching Strategies

Providing for Cultural Differences. Students who lack a firm foundation in the feudal tradition may be confused by the references to the warrior's liege-lord in the poem. Explain that the relationship here is similar to that between King Arthur and his knights in Arthurian legend. Mention also that service of a feudal lord was both an honor and a lifetime mission.

Providing for Different Levels of Ability. Slower students may fail to grasp the essential rhythm of the poem. To reinforce their appreciation of the four-beat line, read—or have one of the better readers among students read—a stanza or two of the poem aloud prior to assigning the poem for homework. Make sure all students have a sense of the lilting rhythm imposed by the verse style.

Reading the Poem. Before students read, have them consider the plight of the homeless in contemporary society. Probe, in particular, the probable feelings of those isolated from society, and ask students to identify emotions involved. If they have difficulty getting started, suggest the idea that those so isolated are angry, leaving it to students to identify in discussion the cause of that anger. Tell them the ancient poem they are about to read tells the story of an individual who shares some of those emotions.

Reteaching Alternatives. Ask students to write a short one-man or one-woman monologue, in which the speaker describes in modern English an attempt to find friendship and understanding. Ask students to maintain the general purpose found in "The Wanderer," but they may use modern language and real-world referents to describe the circumstances.

Responding to the Poem   Text page 46

Analyzing the Poem

Identifying Details

1. What has the Wanderer learned about sorrow and misfortune? The Wanderer has learned that human beings who desire honor should veil their sorrow, for misfortune is inevitable in this life.

2. Why did the Wanderer leave his home and embark on this sea voyage? After the death of his liege-lord, the Wanderer left home and embarked on a voyage to find another king who would be willing to serve as his protector.

3. What happier memories does the Wanderer recall? In lines 30–32, the Wanderer recalls memories of his youth, when he was happy in the hall with his lord and his companions.

4. What mournful events does the Wanderer describe? The Wanderer describes the death of his lord, his own endless voyaging, the loss of his kin and friends as a result of his exile, the decay of battlements and wine-halls, and the death of a proud host.

5. How does the Wanderer describe a wise man? At lines 59–63, the Wanderer says that a wise man is patient, even-tempered, not hasty of speech, not greedy, and not eager to make vows that he may not be able to keep.

Interpreting Meanings

6. List all the wintry *images* created by the writer of "The Wanderer." How are these wintry images in the poem suited to the speaker's mood? Would you say that the speaker is a "wintry person"? Explain. Students may mention wintry images in lines 3, 4, 23, 29, 40, 42, 51, 58, 69, 94, and 97. The wintry images correspond to and reinforce the speaker's bleak mood. Most students will agree that the Wanderer is a "wintry" person in the sense that he is melancholy and pessimistic; the speaker himself reminds us that "No man may know wisdom till many a winter/Has been his portion" (lines 58–59).

7. When the Wanderer says that no man may know wisdom "till many a winter has been his portion" (line 58), what do you think he means? He means that no man is truly wise until he has endured suffering.

Who do you think is "the warden of men" (line 77)? The "warden of men" is probably God, who will bring the end of the world on the Last Day. This is the "doom" that is described in lines 66–79.

8. Would you describe the Wanderer's *tone* as resigned, ironic, bitter, or self-pitying? Explain. Student answers will vary. Most students will agree that the tone is not bitter, or harshly ironic. Perhaps the word "melancholy" would be the best description of the speaker's tone.

9. Summarize the comments that frame the Wanderer's speech. Do you think they offer hope to the speaker? Explain. In lines 1–7, the poet refers to "God's pity," which comes often to the Wanderer, even in his most melancholy moments. In the concluding comment at lines 103–108, the speaker says that men who guard their faith and trust in God's mercy are good. Both comments seem to offer hope to the speaker.

10. What *symbolic* meaning do you think this wandering exile might have? Some critics have noted a connection between the Wanderer and Adam's exile from the Garden of Eden. Can you see this relationship? Student answers will vary. Encourage the students to support their opinions.

11. In the modern world, is there any experience equivalent to the loss of an overlord's protection that might drive someone to an emotional state like the Wanderer's? Explain. Again, student answers will vary. Some students may suggest that the loss of a parent, a relative, a spouse, or even a job might produce a similarly anguished emotional state.

Primary Sources   Text page 47

The Original Language

Students might enjoy hearing a passage of the poem read in the original Old English. If you are able to obtain a recording of a reading of either "The Wanderer" or *Beowulf*, play several passages for the class. Allow students the opportunity to air their reactions to the sound of their own language at a much earlier point in time.

Extending the Poem

Have students imagine a conversation between the warrior and his lord. The dialogue should reflect the warrior's loyalty, along with his assertion that he would feel lost without his mentor's guidance.

Objectives

1. To identify and explain metaphors
2. To evaluate the contribution of poetic devices to setting, characterization, and atmosphere
3. Writing a supporting opinion
4. Writing a comparison of two poems

Introducing the Poem

In outline form, for your reference, here are the major elements in the poem:

- **Protagonist:** an old sailor
- **Antagonist:** an indifferent culture
- **Conflict:** person vs. self; person vs. nature
- **Point of view:** first-person, with narrator as character
- **Significant techniques:** metaphor, setting, characterization, atmosphere
- **Setting:** somewhere in northern Europe, sometime before 950

Background on the Poem. Like "The Wanderer," "The Seafarer" is an elegiac lyric poem, or a poem that creates a single, important impression concerning the narrator's view of death. It was found in the *Exeter Book*, one of the four oldest remaining works of early British literature. While not as seminal as *Beowulf*, "The Seafarer" allows us to build on what we learned from the great epic.

The Plot. "The Seafarer" describes the sea voyage of its narrator, an old sailor. Readers are introduced to the narrator's love of the sea, his exile, and the fear and pain he experiences. In lines 64–102, he explains that he believes life on the sea is more exciting and fulfilling than life on dry land. This section also concerns the transitory nature of earthly pleasures and glories, and of life itself. The last twenty-one lines contain the narrator's belief that all people should look to the Supreme Being who created the world for an answer to the question of life's meaning.

Teaching Strategies

Providing for Cultural Differences. Students should be encouraged to view this poem as they did "The Wanderer," a work that trades both literally and symbolically on Anglo-Saxon love of the sea. Remind students that the sea was viewed by Anglo-Saxons as both a transportation route and a giver and taker of life. You may want students to discuss what sort of parallels, if any, can be found in contemporary life.

Providing for Different Levels of Ability. Slower students might benefit from a review of class discussion and follow-up questions that attended the reading of both *Beowulf* and "The Wanderer." Have these students review as well pedagogical matter on the four-beat line, but stress to them that this poem dispenses with the caesura.

Reading the Poem. Owing to its brevity, the poem might best be handled in class, with the post-reading writing assignments serving as homework. You may wish to have several students read, in which case you will want to observe the natural line and/or thematic breaks occurring at lines 27, 39, 64, 81, and 103.

Reteaching Alternatives. To help students focus on the elegiac nature of "The Seafarer," have them write a short original poem that laments some social or cultural woe of modern society. They might write, for instance, on the problem of homelessness, already mentioned with respect to "The Wanderer," or on some politically charged conflict abroad toward which they have strong personal convictions.

Responding to the Poem Text page 51
Analyzing the Poem
Identifying Details

1. In lines 5–26, what scene does the speaker describe? In these lines, the speaker describes himself on watch on the bow of a ship in a stormy, wintry sea.

2. What passages explain why the seafarer seeks the rigors of the sea rather than the delight of the land? Lines 27–29 imply that the speaker dislikes "the passion of cities, swelled proud with wine." Lines 33–38 and 58–64 suggest the speaker's love of journeys and adventures.

3. According to the speaker, what are the three "threats" of fate? At lines 69–71, the speaker describes the three threats of fate as illness, age, and death from an enemy's sword.

4. How does the speaker contrast the present state of the world with the past (lines 80–102)? The speaker says that the present is a pale reflection of the past. Men have grown old and weak, and "all glory is tarnished."

5. What prayer concludes the poem? The speaker praises the eternal God, creator of the earth.

Interpreting Meanings

6. What meaning do you give to *home* in line 117? "Home" here probably means heaven.

7. What do you think the seafarer is searching for? Student answers will vary. Direct the students to explain and support their opinions.

8. This short lyric is full of striking metaphors. Select three of these metaphors and explain what each contributes to the *setting, characterization,* and/or *atmosphere* in the poem. Student answers will vary. Among the metaphors students may select are the following: "frozen chains" (line 10), "whirled in sorrow" (line 15), "drowning in desolation" (line 26), "the coldest seeds" (line 33), "summer's sentinel" (line 53), "ravenous with desire" (line 61), "The praise the living pour on the dead/Flowers from reputation" (lines 72–73). "All glory is tarnished" (line 88), "a soul overflowing with sin" (line 101), "Death leaps at the fools who forget their God" (line 106). Make sure that students relate each metaphor they select to setting, characterization, and atmosphere in context.

9. What role does fate play in this poem? Fate is an inevitable force that seems bound up with human restlessness, anxiety, and the general decline of the world.

How was fate regarded by the Wanderer (page 43)? Fate was similarly regarded by the Wanderer as a force against which men are powerless to struggle.

10. Do you hear the sentiments in lines 87–90 still expresses by people today? Explain. Most students will agree that these sentiments—praise of the past, unhappiness at the decline of the present—may still be heard today.

Extending the Poem

Have students use their imagination and, working as a team, gather materials from newspapers and magazines that may be used in a visual representation of the problem delineated in "The Seafarer." The resultant artwork may be as abstract as students' tastes dictate, though students should be prepared to defend their reasons for including each element. Display the finished work in your classroom.

Further Reading

Students eager to know more about the elegiac form in Anglo-Saxon poetry, along with some interesting facts about laws of the period, should be advised to read *Poetry and Prose of the Anglo-Saxons* by Martin Lehnert (Berlin, 1955).

Riddles

Text page 52

Objectives

1. To identify personification
2. To identify a paradox
3. To write a riddle

The Poems at a Glance

- **Rhyme:** none
- **Rhythm:** varying between four and five metric feet
- **Figures of speech:** personification

Background on the Riddle. Tell students that these early riddles, which (like "The Wanderer" and "The Seafarer") are taken from the *Exeter Book*, are anonymous. Riddle tradition can be traced to as early as the seventh century, when Aldhelm composed riddles in Latin. Emphasize the vernacular, or popular, nature of the form.

Teaching Strategies

Providing for Cultural Differences. Students may need to make a mental leap backward in time if they are to solve the riddles, which is certainly one of the key pleasures of reading them. Remind students to think in terms of the life styles and range of experiences of the Anglo-Saxon people as these are suggested in the works.

Providing for Different Levels of Ability. Have slower students peruse the riddles several times, prior to in-class consideration of the poems. If time permits, "walk through" the poems with these students, noting possible referents in Anglo-Saxon time to the images presented.

Reading the Riddles. The riddles are short enough to be read in class. Have one student read each riddle, and allow time for students to attempt to solve them. Have students check their answers by looking at the footnote at the end of the riddle section.

Reteaching Alternatives. Students who find the riddles impossible to solve may require a refresher course in solving riddles of a more contemporary hue. Create lists of characteristics of simple objects about the classroom, and have students attempt to name the objects based on your clues. As they become more adept at positing solutions, choose more and more abstract or arcane clues until you feel students are prepared to tackle the trio of riddles in the text.

Responding to the Riddles   Text page 53
Analyzing the Riddles
Identifying Details

1. List all the clues given to describe the object in Riddle 32. What does each clue actually refer to? Students should mention the following clues: "sliding against the sand" (line 4, actually referring to the ship's being beached), "traveled in an open country" (line 7, actually referring to the ship sailing on the sea), "loads its belly with food (lines 10–11, actually referring to the ship's cargoes).

2. What words *personify* the speaker in Riddle 33? Among the words that personify the speaker in this riddle are: "calling to shore" (line 2), "its voice loud and deep" (lines 2–3), "its laughter froze men's blood" (lines 3–4), "its sides were like sword-blades" (line 4), "It swam contemptuously" (lines 4–5), "A bitter warrior and a thief" (line 6), "plundering" (line 7), "it wove spells" (line 8), "shouting" (line 8). Students may also mention the quotation in lines 9–13, referring to the speaker's mother.

3. What does the speaker think is strange in Riddle 47? The speaker thinks that it is strange that a worm could eat words.

Interpreting Meanings

4. Riddles usually open with a deliberate deception. Do you think these examples follow this pattern? Explain. Student answers will vary. Most students will probably agree that these riddles do not open with a deliberate deception.

5. Can you explain the significance of the last five lines of Riddle 33? Student answers will vary. Urge the students to support their interpretations of this paradoxical passage.

6. What lines in Riddle 47 present a *paradox*—a seeming contradiction? Paradoxes occur in lines 1, 3, and 6.

7. What clues are most significant in each riddle? Students will have their own opinions about which clues are most significant. Possibilities might include lines 4 and 9 in Riddle 32, lines 3 and 6–7 in Riddle 33, and lines 1 and 3 in Riddle 47.

   Are any details too misleading? Explain. Student answers will vary.

8. Can you think of any forms of entertainment popular today that are similar to the Anglo-Saxon riddles? Again, student answers will vary. Possibilities might include parlor games, crossword puzzles, games like "20 Questions," acrostics, anagrams, and solving rebuses.

Extending the Riddles

Based on their readings in the unit thus far, have students imagine other possible topics for Anglo-Saxon riddles. The ideas they come up with might be based on phenomena described in some of the poems—for example, the mead-hall. Have students make sure that the clues they drop are consistent with the item as it is conveyed in the work.

The Venerable Bede   Text Page 54

from Ecclesiastical History of the English People   Text Page 55

Objectives

1. To analyze an extended simile
2. To analyze a symbol
3. To explain a metaphor
4. To write an imitation of a writer's technique

Introducing the History

Background on the History. A key reason for studying Bede's *Ecclesiastical History* is its uniqueness as the sole nonfiction work of the period. Bede explained that he wrote his major work at the request of Albinus, the abbot of a monastery located in Canterbury. The two men never actually met, but through repeated appeals in the abbot's letters, Bede was inspired to construct what strikes scholars today as an accurate depiction of life in Anglo-Saxon Europe and of the early spread of Christianity. Point out to students that the passages appearing in their text represent a tiny part of Bede's voluminous work.

Summary. The first of the two passages recounts the conversion of the Northumbrian king Edwin from pagan worship to Christianity. In his efforts to persuade the king to renounce idol worship, the priest Paulinus recommended the desecration of the pagan temples. The second passage is a panegyric to the poet Caedmon, whose accomplishments included the reshaping of secular poetic forms into prayers.

Teaching Strategies

Providing for Cultural Differences. Most of your students, as members of established religious denominations, may need some grounding in the rites associated with pagan worship. Explain that in many pagan cults, nature itself was often the target of religious devotion and meditation—that no specific single deity was usually served.

Providing for Different Levels of Ability. Slower students may find some of the concepts introduced in the reading slightly difficult to fathom. It might be suggested to such students that they review the portion of the unit introduction on page 9 titled "Monasteries and Anglo-Saxon Literature." This will provide them with added background.

Reading the History. The excerpts can be handled in a single evening's reading, although you may want to guide students through the prefatory matter on page 54 before they undertake the assignment. Ask students, as they read, to consider two important aspects of the work: what they reveal about the early church and about the nature of early prose.

Reteaching Alternatives. Have students review other selections they have read in this unit and to consider what those selections suggest about religious values and practices in northern Europe during the first millennium. Students might develop, based on those works, a profile of Anglo-Saxon religion that can be evaluated in light of information they glean through a reading of Bede.

Responding to the History   Text page 58

Analyzing the History

Identifying Details

1. At the opening of the first extract, Bede reports a famous *extended simile* made by one of King Edwin's counselors. State the simile in your own words: What are the terms of the comparison? The terms of the comparison are, on the one hand, the brief life of human beings, and, on the other, the swift flight of a sparrow in and out of a warm banqueting hall in winter time. The simile might be paraphrased this way: A person's life is as fleeting as the flight of a single sparrow through a banqueting hall.

2. Why does Coifi recommend that Paulinus's teachings be accepted? He recommends the acceptance of Paulinus's teachings because the practice of the pagan religion has failed to provide its followers with sure and certain truth.

How does Coifi himself profane the Saxon temple? He rides up to the temple, thrusts a spear into it, and then orders the people to burn the shrine.

3. Who is Caedmon, and what is his special gift? Caedmon is a brother in the monastery at Streanaeshalch. His special gift is the composition of religious and devotional songs.

Where, according to Bede, did this gift come from? The gift came from God.

4. What were some of the subjects of Caedmon's songs? Caedmon's songs were on Biblical and devotional themes. Among his subjects were the creation, the origin of the human race, the story of Genesis, the Exodus from Egypt and the entry into the Promised Land, the Lord's Incarnation, Passion, Resurrection, and Ascension, the coming of the Holy Spirit, the teaching of the Apostles, the terrors of the Last Judgment, the pains of Hell, and the joys of the Kingdom of Heaven.

Interpreting Meanings

5. In the *extended simile* about the sparrow, what could the sparrow *symbolize*? The sparrow might be said to symbolize the vulnerability and fragility of human life.

What does the guest-hall symbolize, and the storms outside the hall? The guest-hall may symbolize life on earth; the storms outside the hall may symbolize the dangers of the unknown, perhaps the unknown nature of existence after death in particular.

6. How does this sparrow simile connect with the attitudes of the Wanderer (page 43) and the Seafarer (page 48)? All three speakers view life as brief, dangerous, uncertain, and fraught with misfortunes.

7. Does the *simile* about the sparrow seem valid for us today? That is, do many people agree that a human life span is a brief flash of warmth in an eternity of cold and darkness? Explain. Student answers will vary. Urge the students to support their opinions.

How might such a belief affect a society's values? Again, student answers will vary. Encourage the students to supply illustrations from foreign cultures with which they are familiar.

8. Explain the *metaphors* Caedmon uses in his song to describe God and the act of creation. Caedmon implicitly compares God the creator to a fashioner of fabric. He also compares heaven to a "roof-tree" and Middle Earth, where humans live, to a mansion.

9. What *simile*, drawn from ordinary rural life, describes Caedmon's creative process? Bede compares Caedmon to "one of the clean animals chewing the cud."

10. How does Caedmon's story illustrate the idea that lowly people can be exalted? Students should point out that Caedmon, apparently a humble, uneducated man, was able to master the creative art of poetry.

Is this motif ever pointed out in histories today? Explain. Student answers will vary. Most students will agree that the motif is often pointed out in American history: the lives of Presidents Abraham Lincoln and Harry Truman, among others, furnish examples.

Extending the History

Based on Bede's clear reverence for Caedmon, have each student prepare a five-minute oration by Bede on the virtues of some twentieth-century personage the student admires. The language and tone should be consistent with those appearing in the translation of Bede.

Further Reading

Some students may find the life and times of Bede worthy of further investigation. Direct them to Peter Hunter Blair's *The World of Bede* (New York, 1970).

The English Language
Text page 59

This special essay on the origins and development of the English language is intended to answer questions that may have arisen in students' minds as they worked through the poems and prose selection included in this unit. For many readers, the main conundrum to be resolved is one related to the translator's credit that, seemingly paradoxically, follows selection titles. How, after all, one might reasonably ask, can a literary work in our own language need to be translated?

The answer to that question and others is implicit in this essay, which opens with a discussion of the source of all human languages (the putative proto-languages), proceeds to the influences of settlers of the area now known as England (including some mention of scribal practices and alphabets), and concludes with a brief descriptive glimpse of English as it exists today.

Assign the essay for homework. Then have students work collaboratively on the Analyzing Language assignment that follows the essay.

Exercises in Critical Thinking and Writing
Text page 65

The assignment calls upon students to write an essay of at least five paragraphs that analyzes the plot and setting in one of the selections of *Beowulf*. A background section tells students how to go about analyzing and synthesizing data. Prewriting and writing sections advise students to answer preset incisive questions about the passage they choose and to organize their notes prior to writing.

Read through the assignment with students, discussing with them the difference between analysis and synthesis. Ask them to demonstrate their mastery of these concepts by providing examples of the analysis and synthesis of some facet of their education to date.

Criteria for Evaluating the Assignment. Effective paragraphs will open with a strong topic sentence and follow a clear organizational pattern.

Suggestions for Teaching and Evaluating the Writing Assignments

A Creative Response

For assignments that require students to create an original poem, story, or incident, have them consider seriously their objective before they set out to write. In the assignment that asks them to write a riddle, as a case in point, you might suggest that they look for an item that is singularly defined by a particular trait—such as a donut, which is uniquely identifiable by the hole at its center. Advise them also always to plan out their response in a formal blueprint or outline, even when such strategies are not immediately evident.

Criteria for Evaluating the Assignments. Effective creative responses will show a high degree of originality and preparatory thought. Where literary techniques lend themselves to the implementation of an assignment, such as the use of figurative language in the creation of an original poem, better efforts will be rich in the use of such devices.

A Critical Response

Students are asked variously to analyze characters from a selection, to analyze the work itself, to compare and contrast literary elements, and to apply elements and techniques introduced in the lesson. The most sensible approach to most of these assignments is to invite students to participate in a forum or brainstorming session. To facilitate the free exchange of ideas, you might in cases need to start the ball rolling by presenting students with a hypothesis. Where the assignment calls, for example, for the retelling of a story or poem from an alternate point of view, you might have the students ask themselves, "What if I were _____," filling in the name of the character in question. Suggest that students attempt to become the character—to investigate the character's motivations, his or her more salient personality traits, his or her probable responses to given stimuli, and so on.

Criteria for Evaluating the Assignments. Successful paragraphs and essays will open with a strong thesis statement and flow smoothly and logically from that point forward. Where it is incumbent on the student to provide supporting details or quotations from the selection, the best efforts will rise to the challenge. Finally, expect students to follow rules of punctuation, capitalization, and style, and look for evidence that the student has taken time to proofread.

Answers to Analyzing Language

Analyzing Language and Style

Text page 40

Kennings

1. Kennings as hyphenated compounds include: *sea-paths*, *swift-moving*, *razor-sharp*, *sea-road*, *wind-swept*, *swift-flowing*, *gray-haired*, *ring-giver*, *gold-ringed*, *bracelet-wearing*, *bright-tongued*, *mead-halls*, and *treasure-holds*. Kennings as prepositional phrases include *fiercest of demons*, *hot with ale*, *firmness of spirit*, and *best of all mead-halls*. Kennings as possessives include *ocean's face*, *God's bright beacon*, *monster's hot jaws*, *hell's fires*, *Grendel's fierce grip*, and *Geat's brave prince*.

2. Students should have no difficulty gleaning meanings from the context.

3. Answers will vary. Help students develop a sensitivity to those kennings that operate on a purely poetic level and to appreciate the difference between literal and nonliteral meanings.

Alliteration

1. Examples include: *Wiglaf went*, *Treasure they'd*, *breast broke*, and *What . . . Wiglaf*.

2. Vowel repetition is discernable in *Wiglaf . . . back*, *too soon*, *lord . . . words*, and *this . . . His*.

3. Student responses will vary. Words that might seem old-fashioned or stilted to students include *thus*, *chieftains*, (for *warriors*), and *foe* (for *enemies*).

1. Possible answers include: Dutch (South Africa), Portuguese (Brazil), and French (Canada).
2. Words of Latin origin are: *belt*, *non*, *pillow*, and *pipe*. Words of Old English origin are: *brother*, *horse*, *house*, and *night*. Words of Norse origin are: *filly*, *rug*, *skin*, and *until*.

3. The terms are neologisms formed from the first six letters of the alphabet. You might mention to students that the word *alphabet* is itself such a neologism, this one formed from the first two letters of the Greek writing system, *alpha* and *beta*.

Unit Two: *The Middle Ages 1066–1485*

Teaching Medieval Literature

In order for students to have a clear understanding of the literature of the Middle Ages, begin by reviewing with them the introductory material on pages 68–75 of their text. Students should gain an understanding of why 1066 has been chosen to reflect the end of the Anglo-Saxon Period and the beginning of the Medieval Period. The material in their text will address this issue. You may also wish to have more able students consult history texts in order to gain a more thorough understanding of the sociopolitical climate of the age. Also, filmstrips that discuss the historical perspectives of the period will be helpful to slower classes.

Whatever you choose as an approach, point out that this age was a time of great turbulence in England. From 1066, changes in the English language reflected this turbulence. The language was infiltrated and, hence, altered to a considerable degree by both Latin, the language of scholars and of the Church, and French, brought to England by the Norman Conquest.

With the Medieval Age also came a revival of learning, as exemplified by the Latin chronicles written by monks during the twelfth and thirteenth centuries. The legacy of these monks also includes tracts on the Crusades and the institution of chivalry, the mystical and philosophical aspects of the Church, and the wonders of the East. To help students appreciate these contributions to our understanding of the age, you may wish to review material found in George Sampson's insightful *Concise Cambridge History of English Literature* (Cambridge, 1970). Consider mentioning, finally, that the literature of the period reflects the revival of alliterative verse, with its reliance on the repetition of initial consonant sounds. Point out that Chaucer's poetry dominated the age, with imitators thriving after his death.

Whether you assign all or only some of the selections in the unit, you will want to preserve the chronological order of the works chosen to provide the students with a sense of continuity. Consider, too, devoting some time to the useful pedagogy contained in the two sections appearing under the heading The Elements of Literature, one of which addresses ballad meter, the other the medieval romance.

Objectives of the Medieval Unit

1. To improve reading proficiency and expand vocabulary
2. To gain exposure to notable authors and works of the period
3. To define and identify significant literary techniques: mood, tone, refrain, rhythm, rhyme, repetition, plot, irony, meter, character, satire, conflict, moral, personification, symbolism, imagery, theme, point of view, alliteration, mood, setting, allusion, and context clues
4. To interpret and respond to fiction and poetry, orally and in writing, through analysis of its elements
5. To practice the following critical thinking and writing skills:
   a. Comparing ballads
   b. Responding to criticism
   c. Comparing and contrasting characters
   d. Comparing storytelling techniques
   e. Evaluating a short story
   f. Analyzing a character
   g. Analyzing a romance
   h. Writing a research report

Ballads

Text page 76

You may choose to review fully the discussion of ballads in *An Outline-History of English Literature* (Barnes, 1952), but the explanation and introduction that follow may provide an adequate and interesting point of departure in teaching this section.

An *Outline-History* offers two theories concerning the beginning of ballads. The first, called the Communal or Cooperative Folk-Intelligence Theory, holds that ballads were composed by entire communities, in which individual members contributed various aspects toward the overall whole. The other theory, called the Literary, Artistic, or Individual Theory, explains that the ballads are the byproducts of "more 'literary' work" such as metrical romances. The latter theory holds that individual writers contributed their respective works.

Also, you may mention the fact that many ballads have come to us in a variety of forms. In *The New Century Handbook of English Literature* (Appleton, 1956), mention is made of some three hundred ballads in existence today in well over a thousand versions. Some, in fact, have been shortened from original works not initially in the ballad form.

Finally, before students begin reading ballads, you should review the introductory material preceding the works, paying particular attention to the derivation of the term *ballad* and the verse forms used for them.

The Three Ravens

Text page 77

Objectives

1. To identify mood
2. To identify tone
3. To evaluate a refrain

The Ballad at a Glance

- **Rhyme:** (from line 8) *aabbcc* . . .
- **Rhythm:** mixed tetrameter
- **Figures of speech:** none

Teaching Strategies

Providing for Cultural Differences. Point out that many of the nursery rhymes and other simple poems students learned as children are distant cousins to the medieval ballads. Ask students to recite some of these verses as a means of calling to their attention the fact that they are familiar with such elements as the use of nonsense words.

Providing for Different Levels of Ability. Slow students might benefit from perusing the footnotes at the end of the poem prior to reading. Doing so should mitigate the seemingly foreign nature of the lyric.

Reading the Ballad. Before students read this ballad, discuss *mood* and *tone* with them. *A Handbook to Literature* (Bobbs-Merrill, 1972) provides clear, concise discussions to which you may wish to refer. In any case, discuss the use of the supernatural and its influence on this ballad. Ask how this phenomenon is developed in the ballad. Direct students to find specific references to it.

Also, discuss the interweaving of narration and dialogue. For what possible reasons and under what conditions does the narrator introduce dialogue? Is this use of dialogue at the expense of the narration or action?

Finally, discuss with students whether they consider this ballad tragic or comic. Answers will vary, of course, but require that students provide reasons for their responses. In either case, ask them to determine the location of tragic or comic elements in the ballad.

Reteaching Alternatives. Obtain, if possible, a recording of "The Three Ravens," or another medieval ballad, performed by a balladeer. Permit students to hear the poem as it was intended to be heard, and then solicit their reactions. Determine whether hearing the ballad in a musical setting enhances their appreciation of it.

Responding to the Ballad Text page 77
Analyzing the Ballad
Identifying Details

1. What do the ravens discuss in the poem? The ravens ask each other where they will take their breakfast. One of the birds reports that a knight lies slain in a green field. The raven says that a doe comes to grieve over the knight's dead body and to bury it, before she herself dies.

2. According to the ballad, why is the fate of the dead knight enviable? The dead knight was attended in life by faithful hawks and hounds and by a loyal mistress.

Interpreting Meanings

3. What elements of the supernatural are found in this ballad? Supernatural elements include the speaking ravens, the mistress in the form of a doe, and the mysterious death of the mistress.

Are such elements common in popular music today? Student answers will vary. Many students will agree that such elements are common in popular music today. Have the students suggest specific examples.

What do you think the presence, or absence, of the supernatural indicates about the culture in which a song flourishes? Student answers will vary. Many students will suggest that the presence of the supernatural might obliquely indicate certain religious patterns in a culture.

4. Who might the red deer be? The red deer might be the knight's mistress.

What might be the significance of the fact that she is "great with young"? This fact may signify that the mistress is pregnant with the knight's child.

5. Describe what you feel is the mood of this ballad. How would you say this mood is created? Most students will agree that the mood of the ballad is somber and melancholy. The poet has created this mood in a variety of ways: for example, the melancholy refrain (with its repetition of

the word "down"), the inclusion of supernatural elements, the connotations of the ravens (often symbols of death), and the overt references to the deaths of the knight and the deer.

6. What seems to be the tone of the ballad—the singer's attitude toward love and death? Student answers will vary. On the whole, the speaker seems to value the love of the knight and the mistress, and to mourn their deaths.

Is it an attitude common in popular music today? Most students will agree that this is a common attitude in contemporary popular music.

7. The song's refrain is a series of nonsensical words. In music today, do you ever hear this type of nonsense "patter"? Student answers will vary. Have the students support their opinions with specific suggestions.

Lord Randall Text page 78

Objectives

1. To identify meter

2. To identify rhyme

3. To analyze the effect of incremental repetition

4. To evaluate a refrain

The Ballad at a Glance

• **Rhyme:** half rhyme
• **Rhythm:** mixed tetrameter
• **Figures of speech:** none

Teaching Strategies

Providing for Cultural Differences. Students unfamiliar with the English feudal system may be puzzled by a mother's addressing her son as "Lord." Explain that a title handed down through generations of a family or conferred by a king virtually became a part of an individual's name. Note that the phenomenon exists to this day in the case of peers of the realm, such as actor Laurence Olivier, who is correctly addressed as "Lord Olivier."

Providing for Different Levels of Ability. Better students might be encouraged to conduct a search for variants of the ballad, which they may present to the class. Several standard variants are alluded to in the introduction to "Lord Randall" on page 78. Invite these students to read their discoveries aloud, perhaps accompanying them with appropriate music.

Reading the Ballad. This is an example of a ballad coming to us in three forms, the English, the German, and the Italian. Explain that this ballad, like others, relies on language that reflects the dialects in evidence during early times.

In teaching this ballad, read the selection aloud, or ask a particularly capable student to do so. In either case, you will help students understand the rhythmic pattern of the work. Students may then discuss whether they believe the language on the page is appropriate for oral interpretation. Ask students to consider the function of repetition and plot in the ballad. At what point, if any, did they determine what was going to happen to Lord Randall?

Reteaching Alternatives. Present the class with printed copies of a Robert Burns poem as a means of helping them become better acquainted with the Scottish dialect. You may, if you wish, direct them to one of the poems in this book that will be presented later in the course.

Responding to the Ballad Text page 78
Analyzing the Ballad
Identifying Details

1. Who are the speakers in this ballad? The speakers in the ballad are Lord Randall and his mother.

2. What has happened to Lord Randall? He has been hunting and has dined with his true love. His hounds have swelled and died, and now he is deathly ill, having been poisoned.

3. How many strong beats do you hear in each line? There are four strong beats in each line.

What observation can you make about the rhyme? The same end rhymes are used in each stanza. The rhyme scheme is generally *aabb*. The rhymes "son" and "man" and "soon" and "down" display slant, or half, rhyme.

Interpreting Meanings

4. This ballad provides a good example of incremental repetition—the repetition of lines with a new element introduced each time to advance the story until the climax is reached. At what point in this ballad did you discover what is wrong with Lord Randall? How would the incremental repetition increase the listeners' suspense? Line 17 makes Lord Randall's poisoning explicit. The incremental repetition leads up to this climax suspensefully by mentioning Lord Randall's dinner and the death of his bloodhounds in stanzas 2–4.

5. What line is repeated in the first four stanzas? The last line of each stanza is repeated: "For I'm weary wi'

hunting, and fain wald lie down."

How is this refrain echoed in the fifth stanza, and what is the emotional effect of this variation? The last line of the fifth stanza varies this line in its first half: instead of "For I'm weary wi' hunting," Lord Randall says "For I'm sick at the heart." The emotional effect is to foreshadow the speaker's death, and also to convey his emotional anguish ("sick at the heart") at his betrayal by his "true love."

6. Typical of ballads, "Lord Randall" ends with only half the story told. Why do you suppose the young man's lover has poisoned him? Student answers will vary. Ask the students to support their suggestions.

What other questions regarding the plot are left unanswered? Again, student answers will vary. Possibilities include the identity of the "true love," the means that were used to poison Lord Randall, and the relationship of the mother to the plot as a whole.

7. Do any contemporary songs remind you of "Lord Randall," in subject matter, tone, or technique? Student answers will vary.

Get Up and Bar the Door

Text page 80

Objectives

1. To identify examples of repetition

2. To analyze plot

3. To identify ironic humor

The Ballad at a Glance

- **Rhyme:** *abcb*, *defe*, . . .
- **Rhythm:** iambic, alternating tetrameter and trimeter
- **Figures of speech:** none

Teaching Strategies

Providing for Cultural Differences. Some students may find the notion of black pudding repulsive. Explain that this peasant dish is still popular among inhabitants of the British Isles and is regarded in other cultures as a delicacy. Point out also that "tasty" is in the eye of the beholder and that some American culinary customs—such as adding ketchup to French-fried potatoes—would appall some outsiders.

Providing for Different Levels of Ability. Slower students may need more assistance than is provided in the foot-

notes. Explain to them that a "paction" (line 13) is a pact. Tell them, in addition, that in the fifth stanza, the man and his wife have presumably retired for the night, which explains why the two gentlemen see no lights in the house.

Reading the Ballad. A study of this ballad will allow students to contrast the tragic natures of the previous ballads with the lighter, more comic tone of this one. Students should analyze the message of the narrator concerning the husband-wife relationship depicted here. Which character seems more in control as the ballad begins, and which seems so by the end? In general, what philosophy concerning domestic life and marriage does the writer seem to be conveying through his narrators and characters?

Have students determine exactly how the comic nature of this work is achieved. Ask them to locate particular instances of humor, determining the purpose of each such use. To do so, you may wish students to analyze the development of characters.

Reteaching Alternatives. Ask students to act out the poem, substituting modern English for the antiquated locutions in the poem. The playacted version will require five students—one to serve as the narrator, one to play the husband, one the wife, and one for each of the gentlemen.

Responding to the Ballad Text page 82

Analyzing the Ballad

Identifying Details

1. What do the husband and wife argue about? The husband and the wife argue about who will get up and bar the door.

What pact do they make? They say that they will keep silent, come what may; the first one to utter a word will have to get up and bar the door.

2. What causes the husband to speak first? The husband is enraged at the disrespectful attitude the visitors display toward him and his wife.

3. This ballad does not have a repeated refrain, yet it does contain repetition. What phrase is repeated? The phrase ''bar the door'' is repeated.

Interpreting Meanings

4. What prominent parts do puddings or sausages play in the plot of this story? In the first stanza, the wife is boiling puddings for the Martinmas feast. In the seventh stanza, the two gentlemen who come uninvited to the house eat the puddings. In the ninth stanza, one gentleman humorously advises the other to use the pudding broth to shave off the husband's beard.

5. Explain how the poet combines hints of violence with ironic humor in this ballad. The argument of the husband and wife and the final injunction to ''get up and bar the door'' are humorously ironic. The gentlemen's threats to kiss the wife and humiliate the husband by shaving off his beard are menacing and violent.

6. As you read the ballad, did you find yourself siding with the husband or the wife? With neither? Student answers will vary. Encourage the students to support their opinions with reasons.

Further Reading

Students who desire to know more about ballads may read the section on the poetic form found in *Outlines of English Literature* (Heath, 1930). It discusses the origin of ballads, as well as their structure, metrical form, subject matter, and general characteristics.

The Elements of Literature Text page 83

Ballad Meter

This parting glimpse at ballad structure contains a passage from McEdward Loach's *Ballad Book* detailing several fine points of the verse form's meter. Students are to read the passage, select one of the three ballads, and answer six questions in light of the points raised by each.

As an alternative to the assignment as presented—and to ensure a fuller coverage—you may wish to have students scrutinize and respond to all three ballads in a round-table discussion. In answering the questions, which for the most part probe reader taste and sensibility, students should be advised to approach the comments and views of classmates with an open mind.

Geoffrey Chaucer Text page 84

In introducing students to the most important poet of the Middle Ages, explain that critics classify Chaucer's works into three periods: the French (from early years to 1372), the Italian (from 1372–85), and the English (from 1385–1400). These divisions may be made because of the various influences on Chaucer during each time span. In the French period, Chaucer's works evince the French love of skill, in the Italian the influence from Dante, Petrarch, and Boccaccio. During the English period, Chaucer worked on a few short poems and on *The Canterbury Tales*, which he worked on from 1387 to 1400. Of the 120 tales he had planned, he completed only 22 before his death; however, students should know that *The Canterbury Tales* is Chaucer's most-read work.

Before beginning a study of each of the tales included in the text, students should review the introduction that prefaces the tales. Discuss with them the differences between the language of Chaucer's time and our own, making sure that students appreciate, in general terms, how Old English evolved into Middle English-how, that is, the heroic characteristics of the Old English period were supplanted in the Middle English period by Latinate characteristics.

Objectives

1. To analyze character

2. To identify instances of satire

3. To write a story framed by an observer

4. To write a response to a critic

5. To write a comparison of two characters

6. To identify uses of half rhyme

Introducing the Prologue

In outline form, for your reference, here are the major elements in the Prologue:

- **Point of view:** third-person limited
- **Significant techniques:** characterization, satire
- **Setting:** England in the Middle Ages, a pilgrimage to the shrine at Canterbury

Background on the Prologue.   Discuss the oral tradition of telling tales. Explain that critics and historians believe that our first recorded literature actually came from monks telling one another lays, or songs, they had learned. Also, discuss twentieth-century society before the advent of television. Ask students to imagine family life without a television or even a radio. What would families do to keep themselves occupied?

The Plot.   The narrator, after explaining that he is part of a group on a religious pilgrimage to the shrine of St. Thomas à Becket, describes each of the pilgrims. The key identifying characteristics of each are as follows:

The Knight—courteous to others and sincere

The Squire—reliant on his case studies; representative of changing attitudes or ideas

The Clerk or Scholar—an intellectual, training to take holy orders

The Physician—a believer in astrology as a means of treating illness; a man who loves money

The Reeve—superintendent of an estate; not to be trusted; not pleasant

The Summoner—sent by the Church to summon persons suspected of breaking Church law; enjoys excessive food and drink and manipulating others

The Monk—does not take his vows seriously

The Yeoman—often unwilling to talk about himself; enjoys life but is unprincipled

The Prioress—affected in manners; obsessed with keeping dogs in the court and feeding them delicacies instead of taking care of the poor; sentimental

The Friar—a man whose job is to preach and take care of the poor but who better enjoys drinking and sex

The Pardoner—a man whose job is to listen to confessions and determine the sincerity with which others express their sins; this Pardoner accepts payment for his absolution, which is immoral

The Parson—contrasts with the Pardoner; a sincere, honest man

The Merchant—enjoys making profit; very rich

The Miller—described in physical terms; loud and unrefined

The Wife of Bath—enjoys male companionship; rids herself of husbands by wearing them out sexually or by nagging them to death; coarse woman who enjoys a good, dirty joke

The Manciple—clever man whose job is to purchase goods for a college or law school

The Cook—enjoys preparing epicurean delights; suffers from an ulcer on the knee

The Host—in the Cook's Prologue, called Harry Bailly; in Chaucer's time, a man by this name did operate a tavern in Southwark

The Franklin—county landowner; enjoys extravagant living, especially indulgent eating

Five Guildsmen

The Sergeant-at-the-Law—member of legal profession; servant to the king

Teaching Strategies

Providing for Cultural Differences.   Explain that the notion of pilgrimage, which on its face may strike students as an odd ritual, still exists to this day. Note, moreover, that not all pilgrimages are strictly religious. Suggest that a journey, say, to a hall of fame is a type of pilgrimage.

Providing for Different Levels of Ability.   If you plan to assign the reading for a single evening's homework, you may wish to give slower students a head start. Make sure, before they proceed, that they have read and understood the introduction to *The Canterbury Tales* on page 86. Suggest that, as they read, they keep a running log of questions relating to points that confuse them.

Introducing Vocabulary Study.   Direct students to "listen" for the rhyme as they silently read. If you are able to read the portion of the Prologue in Middle English or obtain a recording, as suggested below under Reading the Prologue, have students note that the words, though foreign to speakers today, nonetheless rhyme.

Reading the Prologue. You may wish to read for students the section of the Prologue in Middle English found in their text on page 88. Students, in listening, should gain a feeling for the similarities in oral language found between Middle English and Modern English. You may choose, instead, to secure a recording of *The Canterbury Tales*, read in Middle English. For example, J. B. Bessinger, Jr., reads the entire Prologue on a recording titled *Canterbury Tales General Prologue, in Middle English* (Caedmon TC 1151). Also, you may find helpful Nevill Coghill and Norman Davis's reading of the Prologue on *Geoffrey Chaucer* (Spoken Arts 919).

The Prologue, though in principle no longer than some short stories students have read in a single sitting, will make for a challenging evening's reading. Nevertheless, the full impact of Chaucer's dazzling collection of character portraits comes home only when the entire Prologue is read at a single clip. To ease the burden, attempt to arrange to give the student's a weekend's time to complete the reading, and/or permit them to begin work on the selection in class.

Reteaching Alternatives. Avail students of the opportunity to learn from pictorial guides of Chaucer's time. Ian Serraillier has provided a fine reference work in his *Chaucer and His World* (Walck, 1968). The time spent in reviewing such a text will aid students in understanding an age about which they have heretofore known precious little.

Responding to the Prologue Text page 108
Analyzing the Prologue
Identifying Details

1. When, where, and for what purpose do the pilgrims gather? The pilgrims gather at the Tabard Inn in Southwark, a district of London. The time is April, at the beginning of spring. The purpose of the gathering is to prepare for a pilgrimage to the shrine of St. Thomas a Becket, in Canterbury.

2. What plan does the Host propose to the pilgrims? The Host proposes that each pilgrim should tell two tales on the journey from London to Canterbury, and an additional two tales on the return journey. The pilgrim who tells the best tale, as judged by the Host, will be rewarded with a free dinner at the Tabard Inn when the group returns to London.

3. Chaucer's pilgrims come from a cross section of medieval society, and they include three important groups. Categorize the pilgrims into those from the feudal system (related to the land); those from the Church; and those from the city (merchants and professionals). Pilgrims from the feudal system include the yeoman, the franklin, the knight, the squire, the reeve, the plowman, and the manciple. Pilgrims from the Church include the parson, the prioress, the friar, the monk, the Oxford cleric, the summoner, and the pardoner. Pilgrims from the city include the merchant, the sergeant-at-the-law, the cook, the skipper, and the doctor.

4. What plea does Chaucer make to his readers concerning his own report about the pilgrimage? Chaucer tells his readers that he will faithfully report what everyone said on the pilgrimage because he is obliged to tell the truth. On the other hand, his readers should not hold it against him if they find some of his account ribald or offensive.

Interpreting Meanings

5. Chaucer is a master at using physical details—eyes, hair, complexion, body type, clothing—to reveal character. Find at least three pilgrims whose inner natures are revealed by outer appearances. Students will have various choices. Possibilities include the pardoner, the squire, the monk, the wife of Bath, and the miller.

6. Clearly, Chaucer satirizes the Church of his time in the Prologue. Show how this is true by analyzing two characters connected with the Church. Analyses will differ, depending on the pilgrims that students select. Possibilities for analysis include the monk, the friar, the summoner, and the pardoner.

Where does Chaucer balance his satire by presenting a "good" churchman or woman? Chaucer presents a favorable picture of the Church in the descriptions of the Oxford cleric, the prioress, and the parson.

7. Where does Chaucer satirize other aspects of his own society? Students will have various answers. For example, in the portrait of the merchant, Chaucer seems to satirize "know-it-all" experts in business. In the portrait of the franklin, Chaucer seems to be poking fun at the pleasure-loving habits of the lesser nobility. The portrait of the doctor satirizes medical obscurantism and the greed of the profession for gold. Finally, the miller is portrayed as a petty thief.

8. Which characters do you think Chaucer idealizes? Again, student answers will vary. The portraits of the knight and the prioress might be included in this group.

9. In describing his pilgrims, what has Chaucer revealed about his own personality, biases, and values? Student answers will vary. In general, Chaucer reveals himself as worldly, keenly observant of the appearances and motives of others, even-tempered and good-natured, and intensely curious.

10. Which of the pilgrims' professions or trades have survived in society today? Possibilities would include the skipper, the merchant, the monk, the sergeant-at-the-law, the cook, and the doctor.

Which of the character "types" presented here have contemporary equivalents? Student answers will vary.

Ask the students to support their suggestions with specific details.

11. What events in contemporary life could be compared to the pilgrimage to Canterbury? That is, when would people from all walks of life today travel together in large groups for a common purpose, whether that purpose is religious or not? How are these "journeys" similar to, and different from, the journey that Chaucer's pilgrims undertake? Possibilities include: protest marches for political or social change and religious pilgrimages (such as the Moslem pilgrimage to Mecca). Ask stu-

age to Mecca), and so on. Ask the students to explain their suggestions with specific details.

Extending the Prologue

Have the students create a character of their own. Suggest that they begin by using the "checklist" given in the third writing assignment. Encourage the students to be imaginative, precise, and logical, and to try to give their characters not only a physical presence, but psychological and emotional depth as well. Have volunteers read their profiles aloud.

---

from **The Nun's Priest's Tale**   Text page 110

Objectives

1. To describe character

2. To identify conflict

3. To analyze ironic allusions

4. To identify a moral

5. To continue a story framed by an observer

Introducing the Tale

In outline form, for your reference, here are the major elements in the tale:

- **Protagonists:** a rooster and a hen
- **Antagonist:** a fox
- **Conflicts:** person vs. self, person vs. nature
- **Point of view:** third-person limited
- **Significant techniques:** characterization, conflict, irony, moral
- **Setting:** a farmyard

*B*ackground on the Prologue. The Nun's Priest is not mentioned in the Prologue, so here you must focus on the tale itself. It is a "beast fable," also called an "exemplum" or "mock-heroic poem." Chaucer's source is the *Roman de Renart*, coming from the French and German *Reinecke Fuchs*. According to *An Outline-History of English Literature* (Barnes, 1952), it is the first important mock-heroic poem in English.

*T*he Plot. Chanticleer, a rooster, dreams that something is trying to catch him. Pertelote, the hen to whom he is married, insists that it is silly—and even cowardly—to put stock in dreams. Some days later, Chanticleer sees the

"something" from his dream, in the form of a fox named Sir Russel. Using flattery, the fox puts Chanticleer off his guard and captures the rooster in his jaws. Just as Sir Russel is about to drag the rooster off, Chanticleer persuades him to hurl insults at the band of hens pursuing them. Sir Russel opens his mouth to speak, and Chanticleer gains his freedom.

Teaching Strategies

*P*roviding for Cultural Differences. Students may initially respond to a tale about anthropomorphized animals as both silly and childish. Point out to them that they have encountered this form of substitution before, in the fables of Aesop, and that the purpose of it is to provide a new slant on a legitimate object lesson or moral. Mention, moreover, that the characters in this extended fable are so like human beings that, after a while, the reader is barely cognizant of the fact that Chanticleer and Pertelote are fowl.

*P*roviding for Different Levels of Ability. Slower students may encounter difficulty with some of the vocabulary in the selection. Remind them that the meanings of unfamiliar words can often be guessed from context—that is, from surrounding phrases and sentences. Direct these students to record any difficult words on a separate sheet of paper and to place a check mark next to those whose definitions they divined through context clues.

*R*eading the Tale. The tale should be manageable for most students in a single reading. Before students proceed with the reading, mention that in this poem, the characterization is more important than the action. You may thus wish to review with students the differences between *plot* and *story line*. In the first, emphasis is placed on the action, while emphasis in the second is on characterization.

*R*eteaching Alternatives. Make available to students copies of selections from James Thurber's *Fables for Our Times*. The humorist's updated versions of the fables of Aesop, especially with their novel moral twists, will enable students to appreciate the different-and far from childish-tack writers can take with the same material.

Responding to the Tale   Text page 121

Analyzing the Tale

Identifying Details

1. Describe the three main *characters* in the tale. The three main characters are Chanticleer (the cock), Pertelote (the hen) and Sir Russel Fox.

What is their problem, or *conflict*? The conflict is that, despite the warnings of Chanticleer's dream, Sir Russel Fox nearly succeeds in luring the cock to his doom.

2. Describe Chanticleer's dream. In Chanticleer's dream, a red, beastlike hound appears in the yard and frightens the cock.

How does the practical Pertelote respond to it? Pertelote tells Chanticleer that he is a coward; she adds that dreams are often deceptive and should be disregarded. Then she tells him that she will treat his condition with various medicines, including worms!

3. What examples does Chanticleer give to support his view of dreams? Chanticleer is humorously made to give examples from classical mythology and from the Bible. He also tells a lengthy tale of two comrades on a pilgrimage, one of whom had a premonition of his friend's murder.

4. What trick does Chanticleer use to escape his captor? Chanticleer tricks Sir Russel Fox by persuading him to open his mouth to taunt his pursuers. When the fox does so, he lets Chanticleer drop, and the cock flies away.

Interpreting Meanings

5. What human characteristics are reflected in the portrait of Chanticleer? Among the human characteristics revealed in Chanticleer are superstitiousness, timidity, susceptibility to flattery, and pride.

In the portrait of Lady Pertelote? The portrait of the hen displays the characteristics of practicality and level-headedness.

How did you respond to these characterizations? Student answers will vary. Have them support their views with examples.

6. The Nun's Priest fills his tale with *allusions* to classical literature. Given the characters in his story, why are these classical allusions *ironic*? The allusions are ironic because they juxtapose the noble characters and themes of classical mythology with lowly, personified animal characters.

7. How do the Host's comments reflect ironically on the teller of this tale? The Host amusingly describes the Nun's Priest as strong and good-looking enough to take care of far more than seven wives, if he were a "secular."

What do you think the tale reveals about the character of the Nun's Priest? Student answers will vary. In general, the priest is described in the General Prologue as merry, festive, and rather unprincipled (see lines 212ff.). The merry tale of Chanticleer, who keeps seven wives, seems consistent with this characterization.

8. How would you state the *moral* in the tale of Chanticleer? Is the story serious, or is it told to poke fun at "the battle of the sexes"? Explain. One statement of the moral might be that pride and susceptibility to flattery can lead to disaster. In general, the students will probably agree that the story is not that serious, but is told primarily for entertainment.

Extending the Tale

Have students imagine the next "battle" in the war between Chanticleer and Sir Russel. This new incident should build on the personalities of the two characters as they were developed in the story-both of them, that is, are devious, susceptible to flattery, capable of being outwitted, and so on.

---

from The Pardoner's Tale   Text page 122

Objectives

1. To identify ironic examples of personification

2. To analyze symbols

3. To identify targets of satire

4. To identify a moral

5. To complete a story framed by an observer

6. To write a comparison of storytellers

7. To write an evaluation of *The Canterbury Tales* as short stories

8. To write a character analysis

9. To identify and evaluate examples of imagery

Introducing the Tale

In outline form, for your reference, here are the major elements in the tale:

- **Protagonists:** three young revelers
- **Antagonists:** greed and gluttony
- **Conflict:** people vs. selves
- **Point of view:** third-person limited
- **Significant techniques:** personification, irony, symbolism, moral
- **Setting:** Flanders, Middle Ages

Background on the Tale. *The Pardoner's Tale* is an exemplum or medieval sermon. The source is unknown, but the earliest versions are found in the Hindu collection *Vedabbha Jataka*. In *An Outline-History*, Otis points out that a recent example of such a tale is Kipling's *Second Jungle Book* (''The King's Ankus'').

The Plot. Three young revelers are seated at a table in a tavern, when a coffin passes bearing the body of a man who, they learn, has been murdered by a thief called ''Death.'' The three resolve to kill Death. Shortly after they set out on their mission, they encounter an old man who informs them that Death awaits them under a nearby tree. Upon reaching the tree they discover a pile of gold coins, which, they agree, they will divide after dark. When the youngest of the trio heads down to fetch food and drink, the remaining two conspire to kill him and split his share of the wealth between themselves. The youngest man, for his turn, poisons the wine he knows his cohorts will drink. When he returns to the tree, the other two carry out their plan and, after imbibing, die.

Teaching Strategies

Providing for Cultural Differences. Explain to students that a pardoner in the Middle Ages was not a priest but an agent of the Church who traveled from locale to locale hearing confessions. He was something of a trouble-shooter insofar as one of his functions was to assess the sincerity of a confession to determine whether the penitent was deserving of absolution. While pardoners were forbidden from accepting payment from penitents for their services, Chaucer implies here that not all of these clerics were above accepting ''bribes.''

Providing for Different Levels of Abililty. The ingeniously constructed story within a story should be self-motivating. You may need to go through the prologue to the tale with slower students and make sure they understand its relevance to the larger context of the tale.

Introducing Vocabulary Study. Have students keep a running log, as they read, of examples of especially vivid imagery in the tale. Direct them to keep uppermost in their minds what Chaucer's use of vivid language adds to the tale. Suggest that they be prepared to discuss these examples in class.

Reading the Tale. The notion of irony, which is addressed in the review questions following the selection, is a vital component of the tale. Before students read, discuss the concept with them, noting that there are two types of irony-dramatic and situational. Point out that, in this tale, they will encounter a disparity between word and deed and that this disparity is an important element in the Pardoner's character.

You may wish to read the prologue to the tale with students in class, and assign the tale itself for homework. After you have read the prologue, ask students what adjectives they might use to describe a man like the Pardoner. Where in today's world might students encounter individuals who share these personality traits?

Reteaching Alternatives. Have students discuss experiences in which other people made lasting impressions on them. Ask what these people were like and what qualities about their manner and their views made these people so memorable. Discuss with them the concept of persuasion. Then direct students to write a brief sermon that might be delivered by a persuasive person, either real or imagined.

Responding to the Tale   Text page 130
Analyzing the Tale
Identifying Details

1. How does the Pardoner describe his own character and morals in his Prologue? The Pardoner frankly admits that he is venal and avaricious.

2. According to the Pardoner's Tale, why are the three rioters looking for Death? They want to kill him.

3. What does the old man tell the three rioters? He tells the three rioters that they may find Death under a nearby tree.

How do they treat him? They treat him roughly and scornfully.

4. What plan do the rioters form together? After they discover the pile of gold coins, the rioters decide that one of their number should go to town for provisions; the other two will stay with the treasure until nightfall. Then the three of them will carry the gold away.

Explain how this plan proves fatal to all three men. The two rioters left behind to guard the gold decide that they will attack the youngest man when he returns and murder him; this way, they will be able to split the gold between themselves in only two shares. However, the youngest rioter forms a plan to kill the other two with poisoned wine; he thinks he will thus be able to have all the gold for himself. When the youngest man returns, the other two swiftly dispatch him. Then they sit down to eat and drink. When they drink the poisoned wine, they die.

5. After the Pardoner finishes his tale, why does a quarrel arise between him and the Host? The Host refuses to kiss the Pardoner's holy relics.

Who patches up the quarrel? The Knight patches up the quarrel.

Interpreting Meanings

6. How do the little tavern knave and the publican use personification to describe Death? At line 67, the tavern knave describes Death as a "privy thief." Later, at line 82, the publican says that Death has killed many people in the village; he imagines that Death "lives round there" (line 82).

Explain how the rioters' response to the personification is _ironic_. The idea of "killing" Death is overtly ironic.

7. What do you think the poor old man _symbolizes_? The poor old man may himself symbolize Death.

8. How many layers of _irony_ can you identify in this story? (Did the rioters, for one thing, really find Death under the tree?) The rioters did literally find Death under the tree, through their greed for the gold. It is also ironic that their plots backfire on them and lead to their own destruction.

9. Describe the contrast between the ethics of the Pardoner as described in the Prologue and the moral of the sermon he preaches. The moral of the Pardoner's sermon is that it does not pay to be greedy; the moral ironically contrasts with the ethics of the tale's teller, who frankly admits that he is avaricious.

How would you account for the psychology of the Pardoner: Is he truly evil? Is he just drunk? Or is he so used to cheating that he does it automatically? Student answers will vary. Encourage the students to support their opinions.

10. What is Chaucer _satirizing_ in the Pardoner's Tale? Chaucer seems to be satirizing greed, pride, and violence—all of these qualities are embodied in the young men, and greed is one of the Pardoner's leading traits.

11. What moral does the Pardoner want us to draw from his tale? He wants us to draw the moral that greed may lead to death and destruction.

What moral do you think Chaucer wants you to draw from the story of the Pardoner? Student answers will vary. In general, Chaucer probably intends for us to draw both the explicit moral of the Pardoner (that avarice leads to even greater evil) and the ironic moral of the tale as a whole (that those who preach against avarice may themselves be greedy).

12. Do people with the Pardoner's ethics and tricks still exist today-in any field of life? Explain. Student answers will vary. Ask the students to explain and support their opinions.

Further Reading

Chaucer's World: A Pictorial Companion (Cambridge, 1968), which provides photographs and maps of fifteenth-century England, will assist students in better understanding Chaucer and his age. Background comments and illustrations are provided, as well as criticism.

Sir Gawain and the Green Knight Text page 132

Objectives

1. To identify conflict

2. To evaluate character

3. To analyze a symbol

4. To evaluate the use of imagery

5. To identify the theme of a romance

6. To write an episode from a different point of view

7. To write a paragraph placing medieval romance in modern times

8. To write an analysis of a medieval romance

9. To analyze the bob and wheel in medieval poetry

Introducing the Tale

In outline form, for your reference, here are the major elements in the romance:

- **Protagonist:** Sir Gawain
- **Antagonist:** a Green Knight
- **Conflicts:** person vs. person, person vs. self
- **Point of view:** third-person omniscient
- **Significant techniques:** personification, conflict, character, symbolism, theme, point of view
- **Setting:** King Arthur's court, Middle Ages

Background on the Romance. It may be helpful to differentiate between the several kinds of *romance*. The word, itself, is derived from the Old French *romanz*, or "verse narrative." It refers to any medieval story or poem concentrating on the heroic exploits of a person or persons. Such romances were first translated from Latin.

Explain to students that romances are classified according to their subject matter. Such divisions include "the Matter of England," based upon Germanic traditions; "the Matter of France," based on stories drawn from the Chansons; "the Matter of Antiquity," based on legends having to do with Alexander the Great and the legends of Troy; and "the Matter of Britain," based on the Arthurian legends. This last "matter" includes the metrical romances, of which *Sir Gawain* is one.

The Plot. A huge green stranger appears at King Arthur's court and proposes a "game." A knight is to cut off the stranger's head and then receive the same treatment from the stranger a year and a day later. Sir Gawain accepts the challenge, and the decapitated stranger rides away carrying his severed head. We next find Gawain a year later, visiting a lord and his lady. While the lord is away at the hunt, his wife kisses Gawain and presents the knight with a girdle that is supposed to make him invincible. When the lord reveals himself to be the green stranger in disguise, Gawain prepares to make good on his agreement but, thanks to his knightly virtues, is barely wounded when the stranger strikes.

Teaching Strategies

Providing for Cultural Differences. Students who associate the term *romance* with the popular fiction work available on paperback display racks in this day and age should be instructed to peruse carefully the introductory material on page 132 and the essay on page 147. You might mention that the contemporary romance novel is descended, in fact, from the medieval form insofar as both usually involve some test of passion.

Providing for Different Levels of Ability. More advanced students might want to supplement their reading of *Sir Gawain* with relevant passages from *Kings, Beasts, and Heroes* (Oxford, 1972). This book draws connections between *Beowulf* and other early works dealing with heroes and their antagonists. You might want to make the offer of extra course credit to students agreeable to reporting to the class on their findings.

Introducing Vocabulary Study. You may wish students to review all vocabulary words and definitions provided in footnotes found with the text. Alternatively, you may choose to ask students to keep a written list of words and definitions as they progress through the narrative. In addition to the vocabulary in the student text, review students on the following words and definitions:

- **metrical romance:** a romantic story in verse form
- **allegory:** a story in which the characters and settings and events stand for certain other people or events or concepts
- **symbolism:** substitution of a person, a place, a thing, or an event that stands for itself and for something beyond itself as well
- **theme:** the central idea of a work of literature
- **the bob and wheel:** the construction of a poetic line in which two elements are unified by a tight formal structure

Reading the Romance. Before beginning the actual reading, students may find it interesting to know that Gawain, as a character, appears in other romances. For example, he is a main character in an early medieval romance titled *The Marriage of Sir Gawain*. He also may be found in *The Wife of Bath's Tale*. Tell students that, though the character of Sir Gawain is generally good and noble, in Malory's *Morte Darthur*, he is the "destroyer of good knights."

Reteaching Alternatives. Have students create their own romance, including a protagonist who sets out to accomplish some important feat. In their creation, students must include an antagonist, or evil character, out to threaten or even destroy the hero.

Responding to the Story
Text page 146
Analyzing the Story
Identifying Details

1. What exactly is the Green Knight's challenge to King Arthur's court? The Green Knight challenges the knights at King Arthur's court to exchange one blow with another with the two-bladed ax. The Green Knight will suffer the first blow; in return, the challenger who strikes him must agree to withstand a blow from the Green Knight a year hence, on New Year's Day.

2. What is his agreement with Sir Gawain? Sir Gawain agrees to meet the Green Knight at the Green Chapel, on the next New Year's Day.

3. Describe the *conflict* Gawain faces in the castle. Sir Gawain's conflict pits his loyalty to his host against the blandishments of the host's wife, who seems eager to seduce Gawain.

4. How does Gawain break his promise to the lord? Sir Gawain fails to keep his promise because he is silent about the magic sash that the lady has given him.

5. Describe what happens when Gawain meets the Green Knight on New Year's Day. At the first stroke of the ax, Sir Gawain flinches slightly, and the lord of the castle upbraids him. At the second stroke, Sir Gawain stands boldly, the ax nicks the nape of his neck and wounds him slightly. When Sir Gawain prepares to attack the lord, the latter reveals that he is really the Green Knight, that the lady of the castle is his own wife, and that he knows all that has passed between the lady and Sir Gawain. Magnanimously, the Green Knight forgives Sir Gawain's lapses from the code of chivalry, and gives him a gold-embroidered girdle as a memento of their encounter.

Interpreting Meanings

6. Who would you say finally wins the conflict between Gawain and the Green Knight? Student answers will vary. Most students will agree that the Green Knight finally wins the conflict.

7. Discuss the *character* of Sir Gawain. How is he a superhuman romance hero? How is he flawed, just as any real person may be flawed? On the one hand, Sir Gawain is a superhuman romance hero in that he is superbly handsome and courageous. On the other hand, he displays human qualities: susceptibility to passion and desire in his encounters with the lady of the castle, an understandable fear of he Green Knight's ax, and a less than truthful (though strategic) willingness to sacrifice absolute truthfulness to the goal of protecting his own life.

8. The figure of the Green Knight remains a puzzle to many critics. In what ways is he a "shape-changer," like so many characters in romances? Is he totally evil, or totally good, or somewhere in between? What might he *symbolize* in the narrative? The Green Knight is a "shape-changer" in the sense that he is able to ride away carrying his own head at the beginning of the poem; later, he is able to disguise himself successfully as the lord of the castle, and then to reappear at the end in his own guise as the Green Knight. Student opinions will differ on what the Green Knight may symbolize and on whether he is totally evil or totally good: encourage the students to support and defend their opinions.

9. Explore the possible *symbolic* use of the color green in this work. (Green usually symbolizes hope, it is associated with the appearance of new life in the plant world.) Why do you think the meeting with the Green Knight takes place on New Year's Day? The color green may symbolize hope and renewal: in this connection, it is significant that the encounter with the Green Knight takes place on New Year's Day, since the result of this encounter is a more perfect renewal of Sir Gawain in the knightly code. Note that the girdle given by the Green Knight to Sir Gawain as a token of the latter's trial and temptation is also green in color.

10. What *images* make the setting of the confrontation seem demonic? Students should refer to the details in the two stanzas at the beginning of Part Two (lines 164–213). Gawain himself says that he fears that "the Fiend himself" has brought him to this place to slay him.

Do you think there is any *symbolism* suggested by this setting? Explain. Student responses will differ. Some students may suggest that there is something of a parallel in this passage with the episode in the New Testament in which Satan leads Christ up to a high mountain to tempt him three times.

11. Why might the lord's wife have had such power over Gawain? The narrative obliquely suggests that, despite his distinction in so many other respects, Gawain's "besetting sin" may have been sensuality. The knight is obviously susceptible to the lady's blandishments, and he struggles within himself to control his passion.

12. How would you state the *theme* of this romance? Student summaries of the theme will differ. One statement might run as follows: To achieve nobility, human beings must rely on and constantly practice a number of virtues, especially courage, honesty, and self-denial.

13. In romance literature, women are often represented as (a) maidens, (b) mothers, (c) temptresses, or (d) crones. How is the lady in this story characterized? The lady in the story is characterized principally as a temptress.

Do these character roles for women still exist in fiction and movies today? Explain. Most students will agree that these roles still exist in contemporary fiction and movies. Ask the students to give specific examples.

14. Compare the romantic triangle in this story—the two men and a woman—with romantic triangles in contemporary fiction or movies. Is Gawain's response credible? Student answers will vary. Ask the students to supply specific parallels to Gawain's behavior if they can.

Extending the Story

Students might enjoy extending their modern versions of the Gawain story. You might suggest a group brainstorming session in which the class develops a modern version into a movie romance. Have the students create settings, characters, situations, events, and new plot twists.

The Elements of Literature

The Romance

Text page 147

This essay by Robert Foulke and Paul Smith offers students yet another critical view of the romance. The authors delve into the origins of the romance and offer external justification for the exalted position in the world of letters ascribed to it by some scholars. Have students read the essay following completion of *Sir Gawain*, and permit time to discuss the points raised in it.

Sir Thomas Malory

Text page 148

from Le Morte Darthur

Text page 149

Objectives

1. To analyze mood and its reliance on setting
2. To identify symbolism and allusions
3. To identify supernatural elements
4. To write an episode from a different point of view
5. To write a research report
6. To analyze archaic constructions through context clues

Introducing the Tale

In outline form, for your reference, here are the major elements in the tale:

- **Protagonist:** King Arthur
- **Antagonists:** human frailty, Sir Mordred
- **Conflict:** person vs. self, person vs. person
- **Point of view:** third-person omniscient
- **Significant techniques:** mood, setting, symbolism, allusion, point of view
- **Setting:** King Arthur's court, Middle Ages

*B*ackground on the Tale.   Review with students the introductory material on the life of Malory on page 148. Amplify the information furnished there by telling students that little was known about Malory's life until the 1920's, when a cache of relevant documents was unearthed at the Public Record Office in London. You might mention also that these documents—mostly arrest reports for middling crimes—revealed, more than anything else, Malory's penchant for getting into trouble.

*T*he Plot.   King Arthur, returning from France, discovers that his illegitimate son, Sir Mordred, has usurped his throne. Arthur mounts a retaliatory attack on Mordred, in the course of which Sir Gawain is killed and Mordred is subdued. Arthur, himself mortally wounded, instructs Sir Bedivere to throw his sword, Excalibur, into the lake. At first Bedivere attempts to deceive Arthur by concealing the sword behind a tree, but ultimately the knight does the king's bidding. At the end of the tale, Arthur is placed on a barge, and Bedivere goes into the forest to grieve for his dying friend.

Teaching Strategies

*P*roviding for Cultural Differences.   Students may have difficulty with the inverted sentence structure Malory sometimes uses. Select a few sentences that deviate from the standard modern English subject-verb-object pattern, and discuss the inversions with students. Then ask students to ''translate'' these sentences.

*P*roviding for Different Levels of Ability.   In addition to the difficulty cited immediately above under Providing for Cultural Differences, slower students may find the sentence length challenging at times. Advise them to look for the dividing point between clauses (i.e., the conjunction) in these unwieldy sentences and to attempt to extract from them the propositions contained within them.

*I*ntroducing Vocabulary Study.   In addition to the words treated in the footnotes, the passage contains several archaic words and constructions that you might want to caution students about. As a case in point you might note the verb *ween*, which occurs several times. Advise students to attempt to use surrounding words and phrases to gather the meaning of these words, and suggest that they maintain a running log of the words for later discussion.

Reading the Tale. Set the stage by explaining that the section in the text concerns Arthur's death and the complete dissolution of the Round Table and its notions of chivalry. By this point in the work, Malory has turned to the final tragedy: Arthur's death. You may wish to discuss the meaning of the title now.

Reteaching Alternatives. Ask students to write a narrative in which Arthur does not die. He may face extreme danger or may show himself a hero like Beowulf, but he does not face defeat. Then discuss the effect that the changed ending has on your students' perception of the romance. You may wish to compare Arthur with Beowulf, asking students how they would have responded had Beowulf lived at the end of the epic.

Responding to the Story   Text page 155
Analyzing the Story
Identifying Facts

1. What does King Arthur learn in his dream on Trinity Sunday? In his dream on Trinity Sunday, King Arthur learns from Sir Gawain that if he fights with Sir Mordred they must both be slain.

What is Sir Lucan's advice to Arthur? Lucan advises the King to remember his dream and not attack Sir Mordred.

2. Explain what causes the battle to start. An adder stings one of the knights in the foot. When the host on both sides see the knight draw his sword to kill the adder, they blow their trumpets, draw their weapons, and clash in general battle.

3. As he is about to die, what does Arthur request of Sir Bedivere? Arthur requests that Sir Bedivere throw the sword Excalibur into the lake.

How does Bedivere comply with this request? Bedivere hesitates to comply twice with this request; finally, at the King's insistence, he casts the royal sword into the lake.

4. What mysterious possibility is contained in the final paragraph? The final paragraph suggests that King Arthur may one day return.

Interpreting Meanings

5. In a word or phrase, sum up the atmosphere, or *mood*, of this story. How does Malory use details of *setting* to achieve that mood? Student summaries of the mood may differ. In general the mood is somber, elegiac, and

mysterious. The concluding description of the mysterious ladies in the barge, waiting to bear King Arthur to Avilion, especially reinforces this mood.

6. What Christian symbolism or allusions do you find in this excerpt? Consider the way the battle starts, Sir Bedivere's responses to Arthur's dying request, and any other details. What might these Christian overtones signify about Arthur's role in British mythology? Student comments may include the following observations: The battle starts as a result of a serpent's bite or sting, perhaps an echo of the temptation of Adam and Eve in the Garden of Eden by the Devil, disguised as a serpent; Sir Bedivere's denials of King Arthur's dying request echo St. Peter's denials of Christ in the New Testament; and the conclusion of the tale includes the possibility of a resurrection of King Arthur. From these references, one may possibly conclude that King Arthur had a heroic, perhaps semidivine, place in British mythology.

7. In what ways do you think *Le Morte Darthur* reflects the dreams and values of the time during which it was written? Student responses will vary. They should certainly mention that *Le Morte Darthur* reflects the wish for a universal culture hero. Ask the students to support and defend their opinions.

8. Near the end of the romance, Malory says of Arthur, "Here in this world he changed his life." Is such an accomplishment important in literature (and life) today? Student answers will vary. Encourage the students to support and defend their opinions.

9. What aspects of this story might appeal especially to people living in the last years of the twentieth-century? Or do you think the story has little appeal to people today? Explain. Student answers will vary. Many students may observe that, in the last years of the twentieth century, we are especially eager to find hero-figures. Ask students to support and defend their opinions.

10. List all the supernatural elements in this story. Among the supernatural elements are the following: King Arthur's prophetic dream, the appearance of the arm above the water that clasps the sword Excalibur, and the final scene of the three ladies in the barge.

Do you recognize any of these elements as similar to those used in other romances (including contemporary movies, television stories, and science fiction novels)? Student answers will vary. Ask the students to explain and comment on the parallels that they suggest.

Extending the Story

Have students envision a follow-up scene in which King Arthur comes back, as is presaged at the end of the tale. They might describe what he looks like upon his return from Avilion and what information he has to report about the world of the dead.

The English Language

The essay traces the evolution of English through the Middle period, describing the grammatical and phonological changes that took place in it. The most important development in the first of these areas was in the loss of complex word endings and the metamorphosis toward the periphrastic language English is today. The essay also discusses the effects of the Norman conquest and mentions our linguistic borrowings from the French.

Have students read the essay at home, or, if time permits, read it with them in class. Permit time for them to pose questions about developments not covered in the essay. You might then ask volunteers who are willing to undertake a research project for extra credit to explore some of these issues and report back to the class. A good source that might be consulted in Thomas Pyles's *The Origins and Development of the English Language* (Harcourt, Brace, Jovanovich, 1980).

After completing the essay and allowing for research commentaries, review the Analyzing Language section in class.

Exercises in Critical Thinking and Speaking

You may want to start by discussing this assignment, section by section, with the class. Make sure that the students are comfortable with all the guidelines for evaluating a story. After they have reread "The Pardoner's Tale," taken notes, and prepared their note cards, begin the discussions by breaking the class up into groups. After the individual group discussions, conduct a class discussion. Encourage the students to tell what they gained from the group evaluations.

Criteria for Evaluating the Assignment. As you conduct the general class discussion, check to see that the students have (1) understood the story, (2) learned how to evaluate a story effectively, and (3) benefited from their group evaluations.

Suggestions for Teaching and Evaluating the Writing Assignments

A Creative Response

In this unit the students will be asked to work creatively with folk ballads, to create an original frame story, to write from different points of view, and to modernize a story. For the assignments dealing with ballads, be sure the students know the plots and understand the other main elements of the ballad form. For their frame stories, remind the students to make their characters distinct, and to render their tales and accompanying dialogue so as to reflect the individual characters. For the assignments involving alternate points of view, make sure the students fully understand the characters from whose point of view they are writing. Finally, for the assignment calling on the students to "displace" a story, have them keep the main plot points in mind and update the settings, circumstances, and certain elements of character behavior. In general, the students should begin by thinking the assignment through and then creating an outline to work from. Encourage the students to be imaginative and fanciful in their writing.

Criteria for Evaluating the Assignments. The student responses to these creative writing assignments should demonstrate thoughtfulness, imaginativeness, and originality. Check to see that the students have thoroughly understood the main idea of each assignment, and that they are comfortable with the particular literary elements that the assignments focus upon.

A Critical Response

In this unit the students are asked to compare and contrast the ballad form and the characters in a narrative; to respond to a critical comment; to analyze story structure, characters, and the romance as a literary genre; and to write a research report. For all of these assignments, advise the students to begin by thinking the assignment through, taking some detailed notes, and writing at least a rough outline to work from. You might also encourage the students to participate in a class brainstorming session. For instance, where the assignment calls for the student to respond to a critic, first read, or have a volunteer read, the comment aloud; then ask the students to try to explicate the main points of the comment. This kind of preliminary ''thinking aloud'' will help the students to start on their individual responses.

Criteria for Evaluating the Assignments. Check to see that all essays begin with a clear topic sentence, and that they are logically organized throughout. In the better responses, all general statements and arguments will be supported by details, quotations, and other specific references to appropriate texts. Where research is required, the students should be thorough and precise, and should be careful to cite their sources.

Answers to Analyzing Language

Analyzing Language and Style

Text page 109

Rhymes

1. Possibilities include ''coy/loy!'' in lines 123–124, ''seemly/extremely'' in lines 127–128, and ''greased/priest'' in lines 203–204.

2. An example is ''breath/heath'' in lines 5–6. In general the translation avoids use of half rhymes.

3. Have students say these words aloud, and check their pronunciation. The rhyming words are as follows:
   a. liquor
   b. heath
   c. melody
   d. pilgrimage
   e. resound

4. Have students share their efforts with the class.

Analyzing Language and Style

Text page 131

Imagery

1. Some possibilities include Chaucer's reference to the Knight's ''fustian tunic/stained and dark/With smudges where his armor had left mark'' (lines 77–78), to the Prioress's wiping ''her upper lip so clean/That not a trace of grease was to be seen'' (lines 137–138), and to the Franklin's beard being ''white as a daisy petal'' (line 342).

2. Colors include red, coral, black, jet, azure, lily white, and burnished gold.

3. a. They seem to signify that she is widely traveled.
   b. He is compared to a ram, a sow, and a fox. These creatures, known respectively for their strength, their uncleanliness, and their slyness, all are apt.
   c. They are described as being as ''black as they are wide.''
   d. Thin, fastidious types seem to be associated with that affliction.
   e. These vices, according to the description, would seem to cover one with pus-filled sores.

4. a. These traits are suggested by his choice of songs and his flaxen hair.
   b. He is described as having a goat's voice.
   c. The man's eyes are bulging, like a hare's.
   d. His hair, as previously mentioned, is described as ''yellow as wax.'' Students might reply that the Pardoner's physical attributes create a singular impression. He certainly seems like a person about whom one would, at best, have to suspend judgment until more information were available.

The Bob and Wheel

The ideas emphasized by the device are: Sir Gawain's preparation to accept his fate (lines 209–213), the Green Knight's response to Gawain's arrival (lines 235–239), Gawain's fear (lines 234–238), the Green Knight's chiding (lines 278–282), the lifting of the ax (lines 302–306), the Green Knight's advice (lines 323–327), Gawain's admission of treachery (lines 379–383), and the Knight's assurance that no further harm will befall Gawain (lines 396–400).

Analyzing Language and Style   Text page 156

Archaic Constructions and Context Clues

1. . . . in his dream it seemed to him that he saw. . . .

2. . . . he did not awaken until it was nearly day. . . .

3. It actually seemed to the king as thought Sir Gawain had come to him. . . .

4. "I thought that you had all died."

5. "And now I see that you are still alive."

6. ". . . Who are these ladies who come here with you?"

Additional possibilities include *everich*, *foin*, *tay*, *yede*, and *bees*.

Analyzing Language   Text page 162

1. In terms of spelling, students will notice especially the use of /d/ for /t/ and the use of /u/ for /v/. In terms of syntax, they will observe that there is some inversion ("be thi wille don," for example). As for its resemblance to the language at another stage, they might better appreciate how much closer Middle English is to contemporary English than to Old English if you read the passages from *Beowulf* in the original; that is, the language in its earliest stage was for all intents and purposes a "foreign" tongue.

2. army—fourteenth century
castle—before twelfth century
chief—thirteenth century
gentleman—thirteenth century
guide—fourteenth century
herb—thirteenth century
justice—twelfth century
master—before twelfth century
roast—thirteenth century
royal—fourteenth century
servant—thirteenth century
soldier—fifteenth century

3. The old English words are *barrow*, *kin*, *stool*, *store*, and *town*. The Middle English loan words are *chair*, *car*, *city*, *gender*, *table*, and *tablet*. The modern loan words are *chaise lounge*, *automobile*, *boutique*, *genre*, *habitue*, and *tableau*.

Unit Three: *The Renaissance 1485–1660*

Teaching Renaissance Literature

A chief difficulty in teaching this unit is that many students will have brought to the experience an inherent dislike or distrust of a period that contains such "hard reads" as Shakespeare. Initially, many will balk at the seeming disparity between characters and actions featured in the literature and the realities of today's world. Others will find the study of poets like Milton an exercise in futility, offering nothing meaningful in return for their efforts. Still others will respond to the reading of metaphysical poetry as unnecessary and even boring. To forestall these negative responses, you will want to instill in students, before they turn to the literature, an appreciation for the dynamism and rich intelligence that are both the hallmarks and the enduring legacy of this period.

Begin by writing the word *renaissance* on the chalkboard, and ask students to attempt to derive its meaning from its parts—the prefix *re-* should be easy for them, and you might volunteer words that share the meaning of the root such as *nativity* and *postnatal*. Ask what sorts of events students might associate with a rebirth. Then point out that this particular rebirth saw advances in the arts (with Michelangelo, Raphael, Leonardo da Vinci), in science (with Galileo and Leonardo da Vinci), in philosophy (with Erasmus), and, of course, in literature.

Have students read the unit overview beginning on page 166 of their text. Direct them to note, in particular, the breakdown of the literature into poetry, drama, and prose. Tell them that in the weeks to come they will be reading a number of ground-breaking literary works, including a full-length play by a man who is arguably the greatest playwright the world has ever known.

As with the two earlier units of this book, the history of the period is the element that unites the various subunits. Make sure, therefore, as you proceed from selection to selection, that you spend some time on the relevant background data included in the student text. You may also wish to draw from some of the outside sources referred to under the heading Further Reading at the end of selected lessons.

Objectives of the Renaissance Unit

1. To improve reading proficiency and expand vocabulary
2. To gain exposure to notable authors and works of the period
3. To define and identify significant literary techniques: pun, tone, sonnet, meter, personification, metaphor, allegory, internal and external conflict, symbol, alliteration, epic simile, paradox, imagery, setting, pentameter, parallel structure, foreshadowing, dialogue, theme, blank verse, suspense, resolution, mood, couplet, syntax, rhyme, hyperbole, conceit, irony, octave, sestet, exaggeration, understatement, and figure of speech
4. To interpret and respond to fiction and poetry, orally and in writing, through analysis of its elements
5. To practice the following critical thinking and writing skills:
   a. Comparing and contrasting poems, prose works, and authors
   b. Responding to criticism
   c. Analyzing effects of literary techniques
   d. Evaluating a poem, play, or prose work
   e. Analyzing a character
   f. Writing a research report

Sir Thomas Wyatt & Henry Howard, Earl of Surrey

Text page 187

Whoso List to Hunt

Text page 188

Objectives

1. To understand the symbolic meaning of the poem
2. To interpret the poem in terms of historical background
3. To relate the poem to everyday experience
4. To write a paragraph responding to the situation in the poem

The Poem at a Glance

- **Rhyme:** *abbaabba*, *cdcdee*
- **Rhythm:** iambic pentameter
- **Significant techniques:** extended metaphor, allusion

Teaching Strategies

Providing for Cultural Differences. The headnote on page 188 should help make the poem more accessible to the students, who, though unfamiliar with courtly behavior, certainly know about being attracted to someone who is unavailable because of involvement with another.

Providing for Different Levels of Ability. With slower or less mature students, point out the glosses and go over the meanings in advance. These students will also benefit from your reading the poem aloud.

Introducing Vocabulary Study. Students will benefit from knowing the meanings of the following words before they read the poem.

    graven   travail

Reading the Poem. Have students read the introduction to Wyatt and Surrey on page 187, and then the headnote to the poem. Suggest the parallel contemporary situations of people being attracted to someone who is involved with someone else. Entertain the possibility with students that Surrey's attraction to Anne Boleyn may indeed have been a fatal one, since it doubtless stoked the jealousy of the man who was to order his death when Surrey was only thirty. Once the situation has been established, read the poem aloud to the class.

Reteaching Alternatives. To be sure that all students have understood at least the basic meaning of the poem, have them turn it into a Modern English prose reflection. Students may work in pairs if this seems desirable.

Responding to the Poem   Text page 188
Analyzing the Poem
Identifying Details

1. According to the speaker, why is he ending his hunt of the hind? He is ending his pursuit of the hind because he is weary and because he thinks that the hind is unattainable.

2. What advice does he give to potential hunters of this hind? He tells them that they will spend their time in vain if they hunt the hind.

3. What does he say is written about the hind's neck? Around the hind's neck is written the Latin phrase *Noli me tangere*, or "Don't touch me."

Interpreting Meanings

4. Given the information in the headnote, tell who the hind is and who Caesar is. The hind is Anne Boleyn, and Caesar is King Henry VIII.

5. When you try "in a net . . . to hold the wind" (line 8), what are you doing? What does this imply about the hunter's chances? When you try to hold the wind in a net, you are engaging in a futile endeavor. The phase implies that the hunter's chances for success are very poor.

6. Whether the poem is autobiographical or not, it does describe an experience that is fairly common in life. What is that experience? Students will generally agree that the experience has to do with a yearning or desire that is unattainable.

They Flee from Me   Text page 190

Objectives

1. To identify contrasts in the poem
2. To understand a pun in the poem
3. To describe the tone of the poem
4. To respond in writing to questions posed in the poem
5. To analyze the diction of the poem

The Poem at a Glance

- **Rhyme:** *ababbcc* in each stanza
- **Rhythm:** predominantly iambic pentameter with some irregularities

Teaching Strategies

Providing for Cultural Differences. As with the previous poem, the form and language may be remote to students' experience. However, the headnote on page 190 explicates the situation—a situation to which young people can readily relate.

Providing for Different Levels of Ability. An oral reading will greatly assist slower or less mature readers. Remind students to refer to the glosses when they come across words or expressions with which they are not familiar.

Introducing Vocabulary Study. Students will benefit from knowing the meanings of the following words before they read the story.

array   forsaking
fain   meek

Reading the Poem. Allow some time for a brief discussion of the difficulties involved in relationships with the opposite sex. Why is it that it is sometimes hard to "read other people's signals"? What misunderstandings can occur? What may sometimes cause people to change their attitudes toward someone they were once attracted to? How "real" do such situations seem after some time has passed? Depending on your assessment of students' abilities, assign the poem for independent reading or have one of them read it aloud.

Reteaching Alternatives. Have students compose a letter to someone—real or imagined—with whom they were earlier involved. What feelings might they want to express? What image might they want to project? What would they want to know about another person's present life?

Responding to the Poem Text page 191

Analyzing the Poem

Identifying Details

1. What contrast between the past and the present is emphasized in stanza 1? The contrast has to do with the women's behavior: in the past they were gentle and meek, whereas in the present they are wild and unpredictable.

2. In the encounter described in stanza 2, which lover takes the initiative? In this encounter the woman takes the initiative.

3. In stanza 3, whom does the speaker blame for the breakup of the passionate affair with one special woman? He blames himself, saying that "all is turned through my gentleness."

4. What does the speaker ask at the poem's end? He wonders what the woman "has deserved," namely, what has happened to her and whom she has met after her desertion of him.

Interpreting Meanings

5. The word *kindly* (line 20) is probably a pun because it has two meanings: (a) "naturally, typically" and (b) "graciously, sweetly." Why might the word seem sarcastic as it is used here? The word might seem sarcastic because the speaker is obviously displeased with the way the special woman has treated him.

6. How would you describe the tone of the whole poem? Student answers will vary. Most students will agree that the tone mingles nostalgia with bitterness.

7. This poem was largely ignored before the twentieth century, but it is now highly regarded by people who like poetry. How would you account for its popularity? Student answers will vary. Ask the students to support their opinions in class.

The Elements of Literature Text page 191

Petrarchan Sonnets

Have students read this brief essay, noting especially the divisions of the Petrarchan sonnet (which will be contrasted later with the Shakespearean sonnet). Stress also that the Petrarchan sonnet is sometimes called the "Italian" sonnet (just as the Shakespearean sonnet is also known as the "En-glish" sonnet). Tell students that the demands of the rhyme scheme are much more easily accomplished in Italian, which is rich in mellifluous vowel endings, than it is in English. Students may differ in their opinions of the specific location of the turn in "Whoso List to Hunt," and of whether, for that matter, such an emotional shift exists at all.

Objectives

1. To compare and contrast metaphors in poems

2. To identify conceits in poems

3. To write a Petrarchan conceit

4. To support a preference for one of the translations

The Poems at a Glance

- **Rhyme   (Surrey):** *ababcdcd, efefgg*
  (Wyatt): *abbaabba, cdeedd*
- **Rhythm:** iambic pentameter
- **Significant techniques:** conceits

Teaching Strategies

Providing for Cultural Differences. The specific conceits of the poems will be unfamiliar to students, but the heartbreak of unspoken love is something that most will be able to relate to easily.

Providing for Different Levels of Ability. These poems may prove difficult even for capable readers. Plan to have two good readers prepare to read the poems aloud. If time permits, work with these students in advance on phrasing and inflection.

Introducing Vocabulary Study. Students will benefit from knowing the meanings of the following words before they read the poem.

   ire   wherewithal
   reverence

Reading the Poems. Ask students to mention incidents in literature or the media in which someone dies of unrequited love. How do people feel who are prevented, through fear, shyness, or otherwise, from declaring their love for someone? After brief exploration of these questions, have the poems read aloud.

Reteaching Alternatives. Have the students write a journal entry from the woman's point of view about an incident in which the lover has let down his guard and let his feelings show. What are her reactions? What are the reasons behind them?

Responding to the Poems   Text page 193

Analyzing the Poems

Identifying Details

1. According to each translation, what happens to the lover's face (lines 1–4)? According to each translation, the lover's face blushes.

2. According to lines 5–8 in each poem, how does the woman respond to the lover's feelings? She urges him to be more moderate and to conceal his hope and desire.

3. According to lines 9–12 in each poem, how does love respond to the woman's reactions? Love responds by retreating to the lover's heart and hiding there.

4. According to the last two lines, what are the compensations of dying for love? The compensations are sweetness and faithfulness.

Interpreting Meanings

5. What metaphor does each translator use to characterize love? Each translator implicitly compares love to a master, or lord, in a military context.

What specific details extend the metaphor in each poem? In Surrey's poem, such details include the notion of love ''reigning'' (line 1), the mentions of ''arms'' and ''banner'' in lines 3 and 4, and the idea that the lover will stand by his lord (line 13). In Wyatt's poem, such details include the words ''campeth'' and ''banner'' (line 4), the mentions of an ''enterprise'' and a ''master'' in lines 10 and 12, and the reference to a ''field'' (battlefield) in line 14.

6. If, according to the familiar conceit, love is warfare, who is more likely to be victor—the lover or the woman? What do you think of this notion? Student answers will vary. Encourage the students to support their opinions.

Poetic Meter

Review the essay with the students in class. You may want to write key terms on the chalkboard to reinforce their importance and to make sure students fully grasp them. For practice, you may also want to scan with students a relatively simple poem whose meter is unusually pure, such as

"Twinkle, Twinkle, Little Star." The irregular lines in "They Flee from Me" are: lines 2, 4, 5, 7, 9, 11, 13, 15, 17, and 18. Inform students that in Wyatt's day, the past participle ending -ed was often pronounced as a separate unstressed syllable—hence the failure to include lines 16, 20, and 21 (all of which contain past participle verb forms) among the irregularities.

Sir Walter Raleigh

Text page 194

Nature, That Washed Her Hands in Milk

Text page 195

Objectives

1. To identify examples of personification

2. To write a personification of an emotion

3. To write an analysis of the effect of a variant ending

The Poem at a Glance

- **Rhyme:** *ababcc* in each stanza
- **Rhythm:** predominantly iambic tetrameter, with variations
- **Significant technique:** personification

Teaching Strategies

Providing for Cultural Differences. Although students will likely have encountered the use of personification in poetry prior to now, they may have difficulty adjusting to the ascription of human traits to abstract ideas such as love and nature. Reading through the poem with them aloud and placing emphasis on these words should assist students in making the necessary mental leap.

Providing for Different Levels of Ability. Except for the potential stumbling block alluded to above in Providing for Cultural Differences, the poem presents no significant reading problem. Less mature students may not grasp the personifications even through a focused reading, but this should be resolvable by focusing on the questions after the poem.

Reading the Poem. Prior to reading the poem, direct students to the introductory material on Raleigh's life on page 194. Supplement the facts by noting that the Tower shared some of the properties of today's minimum-security facilities in that prisoners were permitted to write and conduct affairs of business.

Reteaching Alternatives. Have the students compare the images and ideas here with Raleigh's "The Nymph's Reply to the Shepherd" (page 195). Ask them to state the theme of both poems.

Responding to the Poem

Text page 196

Analyzing the Poem

Identifying Details

1. What exactly does Love request Nature to do? What are his explicit requests? Love asks Nature to make a beautiful woman for him. He requests that she have eyes of light, a violet breath, and lips of jelly; he also requests that her hair be neither black nor overbright, and that her belly be of soft down; finally, he wants her inside to consist of "wantonness and wit."

2. What defect does Love's mistress have? She has a heart of stone.

3. What becomes of Love as a result? Love dies, because his mistress will not save him.

4. What changes does Time make in the young woman? Time causes the young woman to turn to dust; he dims her eyes, belly, lips, and breath; and he dulls her wit and wantonness.

Interpreting Meanings

5. What specific human attributes and actions personify Nature, Time, and Love? Nature is a motherly, benign creator; Time is a cruel destroyer; and Love is an entreating, passionate lover.

Do you think the personifications are appropriate? Most students will agree that the personifications are appropriate.

6. Why is it significant that Nature composes the woman from snow and silk, rather than from the earth? Both snow and silk are fragile and can easily be destroyed by time: snow can melt, and silk can fall apart with age.

7. Does the story of Love's mistress remind you of any other stories, ancient or modern, that you have heard? Student answers will vary. Ask them to explain the analogues that they suggest for the story.

What Is Our Life?

Text page 197

Objectives

1. To identify metaphors
2. To identify a pun
3. To write a paragraph expressing an opinion about the basic comparison in the poem

The Poem at a Glance

• **Rhyme:** couplets
• **Rhythm:** iambic pentameter
• **Significant techniques:** conceit, metaphor

Teaching Strategies

Providing for Cultural Differences. This short poem should provide no impediment to students once they have become acclimated to the poetic sensibilities of the era.

Providing for Different Levels of Ability. This poem presents fewer problems than the earlier ones in this unit. After a preview of the glosses for less able students, all should be able to handle the poem independently.

Introducing Vocabulary Study. Students will benefit from knowing the meanings of the following words before they read the poem.

  amiss   mirth
  judicious

Reading the Poem. After having students read the headnote, have them suggest any contemporary songs or poems they know of that compare life with a play. Then assign the poem.

Reteaching Alternatives. Have the students compare this poem with Jaques's speech "All the world's a stage . . ." from *As You Like It* (Act II, Scene ii, lines 139-166).

Responding to the Poem   Text page 197
Analyzing the Poem
Identifying Details

1. Identify all the metaphors used to describe life in terms of a drama. The metaphors are as follows: life as a "play of passion" (line 1), joy or "mirth" as the "music of division" (line 2), mothers' wombs as the dressing rooms or "tiring houses" (line 3), heaven as the spectator (line 5), graves as drawn curtains (lines 7-8), and progress through life as a march in a play (line 9).

2. Which aspect of life is *not* a comedy? Death is said to be "in earnest" (line 10).

Interpreting Meanings

3. Where in the poem does Raleigh make a pun by using two common but different meanings of the word *play*? This pun occurs in line 9, where "playing" can mean "trifling" and also "acting."

4. Why do you think Raleigh calls life a "short comedy," and not a tragedy? Student answers will vary. Some students will suggest that life is a comedy because the speaker seems to view our human actions as trivial or insignificant—as "play"—in the grand scheme of things.

5. Do you think that people can bear their ups and downs better if they regard life as a performance or as an act? Is there any harm in regarding life as a play? Explain. Student answers will vary. Ask the students to explain and defend their opinions.

Edmund Spenser

Introduce this luminary of the Renaissance by discussing his role as a bridge between the early Middle English poets and the later Elizabethans. The introduction beginning on page 198 of the student text provides a fairly comprehensive first glimpse of the poet—certainly it includes as much back-ground information as your students will need to work through the reading. Since many of your students will per-haps never have heard of Spenser, point our that the author of *The Faerie Queene* is generally ranked alongside Shake-speare and Milton by scholars.

from The Faerie Queene

Objectives

1. To interpret allegorical characters
2. To evaluate conflict
3. To explain symbolic elements
4. To identify epic similes
5. To create allegorical characters
6. To rewrite an excerpt of the poem in contemporary English
7. To analyze the use of alliteration

The Epic at a Glance

- **Rhyme:** *ababbcbcc*
- **Rhythm:** eight lines of iambic pentameter, ninth line (al-exandrine) is iambic hexameter

Together these features make up what is known as the Spen-serian stanza.

- **Significant techniques:** allegory, epic simile

Background on the Epic. Review with students the intro-duction to *The Faerie Queene* beginning on page 200 of their text. Give particular attention to the fourth paragraph, which introduces the notion of the Spenserian stanza. Note that the last line, the alexandrine, often provides a closing comment. Later, when you study the English sonnet with students, you may cite the alexandrine as a possible prece-dent of—or at least a correlate to—the closing couplet.

The Plot. The Redcrosse Knight, having been separated from his guiding light Una, is imprisoned by Duessa, an evil sorceress. Una has enlisted the aid of Prince Arthur and his Squire to rescue the knight. The knight, availing himself of this assistance, gains his freedom after doing battle with two of Duessa's agents—a great dragon and a giant.

Teaching Strategies

Providing for Cultural Differences. Reinforce the point made in the introduction to the poem that the term *fairy* is more akin to the modern superhero than to, say, the tooth fairy. Make sure, as well, that the students have a clear understanding of the ingredients of an epic. Jog their mem-ories, if necessary, by briefly considering the elements of *Beowulf*.

Providing for Different Levels of Ability. Slower read-ers, who may find some of the archaic spellings burden-some, will benefit from hearing the selection read aloud by a capable reader. For average students, you may want to read the first eleven stanzas aloud and then have students contin-ue on their own. Probably only your most advanced students should be expected to handle the entire selection independ-ently.

Introducing Vocabulary Study. Ask students to attempt to be sensitive to Spenser's use of alliteration as they read. Review the term with them before proceeding to the read-ing.

Reading the Epic. You may wish to conduct the reading in class so that you are available for consultation with stu-dents who encounter difficulty with the allegorical under-pinnings of the selection. Pause briefly after students have read through stanzas 11 and 29 to be certain students have understood the action to that point.

Reteaching Alternatives. Although Spenser was born af-ter the deaths of Wyatt and Surrey, his language here seems much more archaic than theirs. Have students discuss why this may be so and give specific examples of how the lan-guage fits the seriousness and solemnness of the subject. More advanced students may enjoy comparing Spenser's language with Chaucer's.

Responding to the Epic

Text page 211

Analyzing the Epic
Identifying Details

1. What are the magical properties of the horn described in stanza 4? The horn inspires terrible fear; it can be heard for three miles around; its sounds are echoed three times; it defeats magical enchantments and magically opens gates and locks.

2. In stanza 6, what is the "manyheaded beast"? The manyheaded beast is evidently a dragon.

3. In your own words, describe the action in stanzas 7 and 8. What happens to Prince Arthur? The giant tries to crush Prince Arthur with a blow from his massive club. But Arthur leaps nimbly aside and the stroke misses. The force of the blow creates a furrow three yards deep in the earth.

4. What is the action is stanza 18? Describe it in your own words. The giant lifts his club with his left hand and strikes the Knight's shield. The force of the blow is so great that the Knight falls to the ground.

5. What powers does Arthur's shield have? Arthur's shield emits a light that is so radiant that is causes the giant to drop his weapon and to become blind and paralyzed.

6. What moral does Arthur deliver in stanza 44? Arthur delivers the moral that mortal bliss is fleeting.

Interpreting Meanings

7. The characters Una, Duessa, Arthur, Orgoglio, the squire, and Redcrosse play roles in this canto. How is each one used as an allegorical figure to embody some abstract concept? How does each one also seem human? Student answers will vary. In general, it might be said that Una allegorically represents truth, Duessa represents falsehood, Arthur represents courage, Orgoglio represents pride, the squire represents loyalty, and Redcrosse represents holiness. Students may point to numerous physical descriptions and other details that make each figure seem human.

In what ways could people today identify with each of them? Student answers will vary. Ask the students to explain their opinions.

8. In the conflict between the Giant and Duessa and Arthur and his squire, the contestants on both sides have supernatural, even magical, powers. What makes Arthur's magic more effective than the Giant's? Arthur's magic seems divinely sanctioned.

9. What do Arthur's shield and its magical properties symbolize? It might be said that Arthur's shield and its magical properties symbolize the power of goodness to overwhelm evil.

10. The description of Duessa with her clothes off is full of grotesque details. What defense can you think of for this offensive language? Student answers will vary. In general, Spenser's objective seems to be to "expose" Duessa both literally and figuratively; as an allegorical representation of "falsehood," she is shown to be the direct opposite of what she seems to be—namely, ugly rather than beautiful.

11. Stanza 9, which is devoted entirely to comparing the Giant's club with Jove's thunderbolt, is an example of an epic simile, in which the narrative stands still for a moment while the poet develops an elaborate comparison between something in the narrative and something entirely outside it (frequently an animal or other living creature). Find other examples of epic similes in the poem. What effect are they apparently supposed to have on the reader? Other examples of epic similes occur at lines 95–99 in stanza 11, at lines 140–144 in stanza 22, and in all of stanza 23. The similes are evidently supposed to have a pleasing, vivid effect on the reader. Perhaps they are vehicles as well for the poet's elegant display of his knowledge of the classical tradition in epic.

---

from Amoretti

Text page 212

Objectives

1. To identify a paradox
2. To recognize multiple meanings of words
3. To write a comparison of two poems

The Poems at a Glance

- **Rhyme:** *abab*, *bcbc*, *cdcd*, *ee*
- **Rhythm:** iambic pentameter
- **Significant technique:** paradox

Teaching Strategies

Providing for Cultural Differences. The notion of "sonnet sequence" (also known as "sonnet cycle") alluded to in the headnote will be unfamiliar to most of your students. You might point out that there are some (albeit not many!) parallels between the sonnet sequence and the love song today. That is, in the England of Spenser's time it was both fashionable and popular for a young man to write a series of poems pledging his undying love for a particular woman.

Providing for Different Levels of Ability. All students should be able to handle these sonnets independently. Remind less capable students to refer to the glosses as necessary. Explain that *strand* in the first line of the second poem means "beach."

Introducing Vocabulary Study. Students will benefit from knowing the meanings of the following words before they read the poem.

allayed   entreat
augmented   manifold
congealed

Reading the Poems. Cover Sonnet 30 in class, calling to students' attention the rhyme scheme. Review with them the particulars of the Petrarchan sonnet, and discuss how this one deviates from it. Then assign Sonnet 75 for reading at home.

Reteaching Alternatives. Have students write a brief essay telling which sonnet they prefer and why. Then allow students to share their work and compare their reactions.

Responding to the Poems   Text page 213

Analyzing the Poems

Identifying Details

1. What puzzles the speaker about ice and fire in Sonnet 30? The speaker is puzzled because, if his love is like ice and he is like fire, how is it that the ice does not melt, but only grows harder? And how is it that his fire and heat are not allayed by the ice of the love, but made warmer?

2. What kindles the man's fire? Love for the mistress kindles the man's fire.

3. What paradoxes, or seeming contradictions, can you find in Sonnet 30? The poem might be said to depend on two central paradoxes: ice "kindles" fire, and the fire makes ice colder and harder.

4. Summarize the conversation that takes place between the man and the woman in Sonnet 75. The woman tells the man that it was futile to write her name in the sand where it would be washed away by the tide; she says that she herself will decay and die, just as the letters of her name disappeared. The man responds that, on the contrary, the woman will live eternally in his verses.

Interpreting Meanings

5. Many fire and ice poems are clever, but in Sonnet 30 Spenser also says something serious about love, as Shakespeare does in Sonnet 116. Explain how Spenser turns the conventional frustrations of the lover into a positive statement about the power of love. The serious dimension of the poem is revealed in the last line, where Spenser pays tribute to the power of love as capable of altering the course of nature.

6. What different meanings can the word *vain* have in Sonnet 75? The word could mean "futile," or it could mean "self-centered."

7. In what sense does the love of the two people in Sonnet 75 still live? This love still lives in the sense that Spenser's poem, which commemorated it, is still read and admired.

8. Some attitudes toward love and toward men and women have changed since these sonnets were written. Do you find them dated, or still pertinent? Student answers will vary. Ask the students to support their opinions.

Sir Philip Sidney   Text page 214

The Nightingale   Text page 216

Objectives

1. To relate setting to meaning
2. To write a response to a critical remark

The Poem at a Glance

- **Rhyme:** *ababcddceeff* in each stanza
- **Rhythm:** mixed iambic
- **Significant technique:** refrain

Teaching Strategies

Providing for Cultural Differences. Students with little grounding in the Greek tradition may need some background on the role of the gods, since reference is made to them in the headnote to the poem on page 216. Explain that the gods were omniscient overseers of earthly activity who occasionally felt impelled to intervene in the affairs of mortals, meting out punishments and awards. This system of justice was often used by the poets to explain various real-world phenomena.

Providing for Different Levels of Ability. The poem is sufficiently brief and direct to be handled independently by most students.

Introducing Vocabulary Study. Students will benefit from knowing the meanings of the following words before they read the poem.

    bewailing   prevailing
    languish

Reading the Poem. Begin by covering the biographical and introductory matter on Sidney beginning on page 214. Give students an opportunity to read, and reserve time for questions. Note with them the mention of the fact that Sidney enjoyed no fame or following as a writer during his lifetime. Ask if students know of any other artists whose works were celebrated posthumously.

Introduce the poem by asking whether anyone in the class is conversant in the defining traits of particular birds. Perhaps there are students whose hobby is bird watching or who live in a more or less rural environment. Permit volunteers to describe some of the peculiarities of certain birds, then note the title of this first selection by Sidney. Have students read the headnote on page 216, which provides important background on the poem, and mention other notable poems—Keats's famous ode, chief among them-that draw on the properties of the nightingale.

Reteaching Alternatives. Have students select another bird or an animal with a distinctive cry and write a brief comparison of that cry with a human emotion. The students may choose to present their original thoughts in the form of either a poem or prose piece.

Responding to the Poem   Text page 217
Analyzing the Poem
Identifying Details

1. Locate three or more places in the poem where the time of year is mentioned. The time of year—spring—is mentioned or alluded to in lines 1, 3, 11, and 23.

2. The speaker explains in the first stanza what is making the nightingale sad. What is it? The nightingale is sad because of Tereus's violence.

3. According to the second stanza, who is worse off—the speaker or the nightingale? Why? The speaker is worse off because of his frustrated love.

Interpreting Meanings

4. How might the setting increase the poignancy of the speaker's complaint? The setting, springtime, increases the poignancy of the complaint because spring is usually associated with joy, love, and renewal.

5. Explain whether the first thorn in lines 12 and 24 has the same meaning as the second thorn in these two lines. The first ''thorn'' refers to Tereus, the cause of anguish for the nightingale; the second thorn refers to the speaker's unhappiness, or possibly to the beloved, who does not requite his love.

6. Do you agree that ''wanting is more woe than too much having'' (line 20)? Student answers will vary. Encourage the students to discuss their opinions.

from Astrophel and Stella   Text page 218

Objectives

1. To identify the subject of an octave

2. To distinguish between lines of differing metric length

3. To write a description of a process

4. To write an analysis of poetic conventions

The Poem at a Glance

• **Rhyme:** *ababababcdcdee*
• **Rhythm:** iambic hexameter
• **Significant technique:** personification

Teaching Strategies

Providing for Cultural Differences. Students may experience some difficulty with the personification of an abstraction. You may review your discussion of Raleigh's ''Nature, That Washed Her Hands in Milk,'' on page 194, which utilizes the poetic device in a similar fashion.

Providing for Different Levels of Ability. The longer lines and the more complex sentence structure of the octave make this somewhat more difficult than some of the other sonnets students have read. All but the very best students will benefit from hearing the poem read aloud.

Reading the Poem. Ask students what approaches work best for them when they are having trouble with their writing. Ask specifically if they ever read other writers for inspiration. How helpful do they find this strategy? Read the sonnet aloud, or have students read it independently.

Reteaching Alternatives. Have students compare this sonnet with one of Spenser's on pages 212–213. Direct students to write a paragraph or two telling which sonnet they prefer and why. Urge them to consider form as well as language and content.

Responding to the Poem   Text page 219

Analyzing the Poem

Identifying Details

1. The octave—the eight-line part of the sonnet—is a single sentence. What is its subject? The subject of the sentence is ''I'' (line 5).

2. By what steps does Astrophel hope Stella will come to love him? The steps are pleasure, reading, knowledge, pity, and grace.

3. What does Astrophel decide to do when ''studying'' fails him? Astrophel hears his muse bidding him to look into his heart and write.

Interpreting Meanings

4. In line 11, Astrophel complains that other poets' feet are always getting in the way of his own. In what sense of the word *feet* do poets have a great many feet? What is the term for a world like *feet* in this poem? Poets have a great many ''feet'' because they have written metrical verses. We might use the term ''meter.''

5. This sonnet is unusual in form because its lines have twelve syllables instead of the usual ten; that is, it is written in hexameter instead of pentameter. Do you think that having an even number of feet in each line makes the poem sound more balanced that a sonnet written in pentameter (Thomas Wyatt's ''They Flew from Me,'' for example)? What other effects does the longer line create? Student answers will vary. Ask the students to discuss their opinions in class.

6. The last line of the poem is famous. A poet has said that it ''continues to echo through the history of literature and through every classroom where students are asked to write compositions.'' What do you think of this advice as a solution to the well-known problem of writers' block? Student answers will vary. Ask the students to support their opinions.

Sir Francis Bacon   Text page 220

Of Studies   Text page 221

Objectives

1. To identify examples of parallelism and balanced sentences

2. To explain a paradox

3. To write an imitation stylistic device

4. To write and support an interpretation of the author's bias

Introducing the Essay

- **Tone:** serious
- **Point of view:** third person
- **Significant techniques:** parallelism, balanced sentences

Background on the Essay. Augment the introductory information beginning on page 220 of the student text by acquainting students with the once hotly debated allegation that Bacon was responsible for some or all of the plays of Shakespeare. Explain that this charge, now roundly dismissed by serious scholars as pure myth, was perpetrated by Delia Bacon, a descendant of the philosopher, perhaps in an effort to call attention to herself.

Teaching Strategies

Providing for Cultural Differences. Students should appreciate that the term "studies" in the title of Bacon's essay might properly be replaced nowadays by "school." Point out that long ago, before the advent of publicly supervised education, the responsibility of acquiring an education fell to the individual. Ask students, prior to reading, to imagine what sort of course of studies they would set for themselves if this were the only route to learning available to them.

Providing for Different Levels of Ability. Although specific words may pose problems for some students, the essay is short and direct enough for most students to be able to handle on their own.

Introducing Vocabulary Study. Students will benefit from knowing the meanings of the following words before they read the poem.

affectation	disposition
contemn	impediment
discourse	subtile

Reading the Selections. Have students discuss briefly what each of the subjects they take in school contributes to their overall growth and development. Which do they think are directly useful? Which develop thinking and reasoning skill but have no immediate application in their lives? Then assign the selections for in-class independent reading. Be alert to the needs of less able students, who may need assistance.

Reteaching Alternatives. Have each student select an axiomatic sentence from "Of Studies" and explain its meaning and the reason for choosing it. Have students compare and defend their choices.

Responding to the Essay · Text page 222

Analyzing the Essay

Identifying Facts

1. What are some of the ways in which studies improve people's abilities? Studies help people to form good coun-

sel, to weigh and consider matters, and to improve their exactness.

2. What are some specific problems that studies can remedy? Some specific problems that studies can remedy include a wandering wit, an inability to distinguish differences, and an inability to discuss matters thoroughly.

Which studies can remedy each problem? The study of mathematics can improve a wandering wit; the study of the schoolmen can help us to make distinctions; and the study of lawyers' cases can improve our ability to discuss, prove, and illustrate matters.

3. Bacon's fondness for parallel structure and balanced sentences is apparent in "Of Studies." For example: "Some books are to be tasted, others to be swallowed, and some few to be chewed and digested." Reread the essay, looking for other examples of parallel structure and balance. Examples students may mention include the sentences beginning: "To spend too much time in studies is sloth . . . "; "Crafty men contemn studies . . . "; "Reading maketh a full man. . . ."

Interpreting Meanings

4. Bacon says that too much studying is laziness. Explain how this paradox can be true. Bacon means that excessive studying, to the expense of the conduct of practical affairs in the world, exhibits a lazy nature—that someone who studies too much is unwilling or unable to engage in the practical affairs of life.

5. Bacon has the reputation of being a hard, ambitious man, and his essays are frequently said to be cynical and lacking in warmth. Find remarks in "Of Studies" that seem to support this view. Student answers will vary.

Extending the Essay

Have students imagine what advice on education might be appropriate for people living in the year 2500. Remind them of the current state of technology, and ask them to project what advances may lie in store. Would people, for example, use books in their studies? What subjects would they learn about? Invite students to present the ideas in a brief oral report.

Read the axioms aloud, or have student volunteers take turns reading them. After each one, stop and evaluate the wisdom contained in it. Possible student assessments of the man behind the axioms might include the views that Bacon was wise, forthright, moral, religious, and witty.

Christopher Marlowe

Text page 224

from Dr. Faustus

Text page 226

Objectives

1. To interpret foreshadowing
2. To identify metric irregularities and explain their effect
3. To write a dialogue illustrating a character's conflict
4. To write an essay stating the theme of the play

Introducing the Play

- **Protagonist:** Faustus
- **Antagonist:** his own base nature
- **Conflict:** person vs. self
- **Significant technique:** soliloquy

Background on the Play. After students have read the introductory matter on pages 224–225 of the student text, discuss with them Marlowe's early demise and the promising career it cut short. Consider with them other geniuses throughout history who never achieved their full potential— the name of Mozart might suggest itself in this discussion. Have students note also that the introduction identifies Marlowe as yet another possible ghostwriter of the works of Shakespeare.

Teaching Strategies

Providing for Cultural Differences. The introduction draws attention to a system of religious belief that underlies the play—a system quite remote from the experience of most modern students. It is important for students to understand this background to be able to appreciate the work.

Providing for Different Levels of Ability. Less mature readers may need guided reading in several stages for this selection. After each section, discuss briefly the action or situation in what they have just read. Read all headnotes and discuss any problems before continuing.

Introducing Vocabulary Study. Students will benefit from knowing the meanings of the following words before they read the poem.

abjure	hapless
contrition	incessant
dross	perpetual
engendered	servile
execrable	

Reading the Play. Although average and better students can certainly manage an independent reading, all students will gain an appreciation of dramatic effect by hearing it. Assign a good reader with a strong, dramatic voice to read Faustus and choose two other students to read the Good and Bad Angels. If you wish, a fourth reader may serve as a kind of narrator by reading the headnotes and the section titles.

Reteaching Alternatives. Have the students write a scene that includes the angels and that might come between "The Conflict with Faustus" and "Helen of Troy". The situation should focus on one of Faustus's plans that has gone awry, leaving him frustrated and torn between continuing with his bargain and turning back.

Responding to the Play   Text page 230

Analyzing the Play

Identifying Facts

1. **What does Dr. Faustus plan to do with his new powers?** Dr. Faustus plans to order the spirits to do the follow-

ing: search India for gold and ransack the ocean floor for pearls; search the world for fruits and other delicacies; read his philosophy and tell him the secrets of foreign kings; wall Germany with brass and make the Rhine circle Wittenberg; fill the preparatory schools with silk; raise an army to chase the Prince of Parma from the land; and make him king.

2. When the good angel and the bad angel vie for Faustus's soul, how does each attempt to persuade Faustus? The good angel tells Faustus to think of heaven and heavenly things and to repent. The bad angel bids Faustus think of honor and wealth.

To whom does Faustus finally pledge allegiance? Faustus pledges allegiance to Mephistophilis, the devil.

3. What happens when Faustus kisses Helen of Troy? He feels his soul being sucked out of his body.

4. As Faustus waits for the devil to come fetch his soul, how does he try to escape his damnation? First, he bids time stand still. Then he calls upon Christ. Finally, he tries to bargain with God, pleading that he be punished in hell for only a thousand years and not for eternity.

Whom does he blame for his predicament? He curses himself and Lucifer.

Interpreting Meanings

5. Does Faustus seek power and knowledge for admirable purposes? Student answers will vary. In general, students will agree that, while Faustus's projects described in ''Faustus Gloats'' may benefit others as well as himself, the purposes described are all materialistic and worldly.

What evidence in the drama lets the audience infer Faustus's purposes? Students may point to the projects that are described in the first passage, ''Faustus Gloats,'' as well as to the bad angel's mention of ''honor and wealth'' in the

second passage. Finally, they may point to Faustus's request to see and kiss Helen of Troy.

6. Faustus says to Helen of Troy, ''I will be Paris.'' Considering the result of Paris's actions and of his relationship with Helen, what might that statement foreshadow? Paris's rape of Helen was the traditional cause of the Trojan War in ancient Greek legend. In light of this, the statement foreshadows doom for Faustus.

7. Examine Faustus's final soliloquy for metrical irregularities—places where Marlowe has taken liberties with the iambic pentameter line. For example, the first line of the soliloquy consists only of the words ''Ah / Faustus''—one iamb, and a long silence where listeners would expect four more metrical feet. The silence communicates more effectively than words the gravity of Faustus's predicament. Find other examples in the soliloquy of striking irregularities in meter, and explain what you think their effects are. Among the lines with metrical irregularities that students may point to are the following: 6, 10, 14, 15, 19, 20, 22, 24, 33, 42, 45, 56, 57, and 58. Student opinions on the effects of these irregularities will differ. Encourage the students to relate the metrical oddities to the content and context of each line, as well as to the speaker's emotions as the lines are said.

8. Do you sympathize with Faustus at any point in the play? Explain why or why not. Student answers will vary. Ask the students to explain their opinions.

Extending the Play

Have students imagine a scenario in which the devil has failed to tempt Faustus to enter into a bargain. Ask students to write a soliloquy that may be modeled on the verse style of Marlowe in which the devil describes his frustration over his failure.

The Passionate Shepherd to His Love

Text page 232

The Nymph's Reply to the Shepherd
(by Sir Walter Raleigh)

Text page 234

Objectives

1. To identify pastoral elements

2. To identify the tone of a poem

3. To write a response to a poem

4. To write an analysis of an argument

The Poems at a Glance

- **Rhyme:** *aabb* in each stanza of both poems
- **Rhythm:** iambic tetrameter
- **Significant techniques:** pastoral imagery, argumentation

Teaching Strategies

Providing for Cultural Differences. Students may respond to the language of the poems as too formal and atypical of courting practices as they know them. Remind them that customs and values tend to change radically in the space of four hundred years.

Providing for Different Levels of Ability. The poems present no special problems in form, language, or content. Less mature students may need some help in recognizing the tone in "The Nymph's Reply." Remind less able students to refer to the glosses as needed.

Introducing Vocabulary Study. Students will benefit from knowing the meaning of the following word before they read the poem.

wanton

Reading the Poems. After students have read the first headnote, ask them to suggest settings, life styles, and so on that enter into the contemporary mating rituals between males and females. After brief discussion, direct students to read both poems on their own, either in class or as homework. Alternatively, choose a good male reader to read the Marlowe poem aloud stanza by stanza, alternating with a good female reader who responds to each appeal with a stanza from the Raleigh poem.

Reteaching Alternatives. Have each student write a contemporary argument entitled "The Passionate Student to His Love." The students should then exchange papers with neighbors and write a response.

Analyzing the Poems
Identifying Details

1. Describe the life that the shepherd envisions with his love. How will they be dressed? How will they spend their time? The speaker envisions a life of carefree pleasure. The speaker will make the following clothes for his love: a cap of flowers, a kirtle (gown) embroidered with myrtle leaves, a gown of the finest wool, slippers with gold buckles, and a belt of straw and ivy buds, decorated with coral clasps and amber studs. The couple will sit upon the rocks, watching the shepherds, who will dance and sing for their delight.

2. In the nymph's reply, what flaws does she find with the shepherd's idyllic vision? The nymph points out that fleeting time flaws the idyllic vision: the rivers rage in the winter, and the flowers fade and wither. She also implies that not every shepherd speaks the truth, although he may have a "honey tongue."

Under what conditions would she agree to be his love? She would agree to be his love if youth could last forever.

Interpreting Meanings

3. In pastoral writing, the harsher realities of country life do not exist; there is no dirt, pain, or struggle, and there is certainly no ugliness or violence. Which details make Marlowe's poem seem distinctly pastoral? Among the details that seem distinctly pastoral are the references to "melodious birds," to the flowers and lambs, and to the dancing and singing shepherds.

4. What is the tone of the nymph's reply? The nymph speaks of harsher realities: raging rivers, cold rocks, the silent nightingale, the flocks in their folds, and fading flowers.

5. What modern kinds of writing about love are as idyllic as Marlowe's poem? Do you think the idea of an idyllic escape with a loved one still has strong appeal? Student answers will vary. Most students will agree that the idea of an idyllic escape with a loved one still has strong appeal.

The essay traces the evolution of our language into the "Modern" period, noting that the most salient single indicator of that change was the Great Vowel Shift (also known by linguists as "gradation"). Comments are made as well on the peculiarities woven into the system of orthography by the retention of old spelling conventions and on the spread of English to the far reaches of the globe.

Assign the essay for home reading, along with the Analyzing Language assignment that follows it. Plan to spend part of the following class period answering questions that may have occurred to students in the course of reading and to consider their responses to the language exercises. Many of them will take particular delight in the fourth question, which calls upon them to use Shaw's alphabet. Encourage students so inclined to create riddles of their own using this alphabet.

William Shakespeare

Text page 247

The miniunit on Shakespeare, which opens technically with the introduction to the Renaissance theater beginning on page 241, almost constitutes a course in Renaissance literature unto itself. The section, which includes *Macbeth* in its entirety, a sampling of the Bard's sonnets, and assorted songs from the plays, will require at least several weeks of class time. Lead the students through the introductory material patiently, pausing to entertain questions that arise. Proceed with great care, for it is out of a positive early exposure to such monumental works as *Macbeth* that lifelong loves of Shakespeare have been known to develop.

Begin by dispelling any myths and misconceptions that might exist about the life and times of Shakespeare. Perhaps because of the glamor and heroism sometimes attached to the image of the "starving artist" slaving away in a frozen garret, students sometimes draw connections between greatness and self-sacrifice, assuming that any artist worth his or her salt must, of necessity, have been poor. Clarify that Shakespeare, far from being an obscure poet, was, on the contrary, well-known, well-loved, and successful in his lifetime. Point out that he was one of the guiding forces behind the theater that was called the Globe. Because he had good instincts regarding business, he was able to live out his years comfortably.

Students might also enjoy learning more about the methods scholars have used through the ages to reconstruct, among other things, the chronology of the plays. Those who are interested might be directed to the readings that follow *Macbeth* in the present book. Some of these reference works consider such phenomena as the Stationer's Register (the Elizabethan counterpart of the Copyright Office), Henslow's diary, and the like.

A Preface to Macbeth

Text page 253

In teaching *Macbeth*, you must be guided by the time you have to spend on the play and by the ability levels of your students. Still, if at all possible, two important instructional strategies should be implemented. First, students should hear *Macbeth* read by an actor or performed on stage or on film. Several good aural recordings are available as are cassette tape recordings. Students who hear *Macbeth* read aloud will be aided by actors' speech intonations, so that understanding of the plot likely will increase.

Second, refer to Aristotle's definition of tragedy and the seven characteristics of tragedy. Students should understand the play better if they consider whether it fits Aristotle's definition and follows the guidelines for tragedy. Also, discuss the nature of the tragic hero and the tragic flaw, for in the characterization lie the cause and effect of the action.

Before students begin reading *Macbeth*, place Aristotle's definition of tragedy, provided below, on the chalkboard and discuss thoroughly. Aristotle said: "Tragedy is an imitation of some action that is important, entire, and of a proper magnitude, by language embellished and rendered pleasurable, but by different means in different parts, in the way not of narration, but of action, effecting through pity and terror the refinement of such passions." Perhaps the most important parts of this definition should be considered here. First, tragedy is an imitation of an action important enough to cause a series of related actions to occur. The playwright, through his actors, will use language to convey the action. The playwright will emphasize the action, itself, and not a simple telling of the action. Finally, he will provide pity and terror in his characterization and in the cause-and-effect relationship in which the tragic hero finds himself. This last aspect is very important because, with it, the playwright can bring about a catharsis, or a purging.

Objectives

1. To analyze Shakespeare's use of blank verse

2. To understand Shakespeare's use of foreshadowing to build suspense

3. To identify methods of characterization

4. To analyze mood

5. To recognize instances of foreshadowing

6. To identify conflict and resolution

7. To identify themes

8. To identify climax

9. To write an extension of a character, an updating of a scene, paragraphs reflecting a change in outcome, an interpretation of character, a character analysis, an evaluation of a dramatic effect, an analysis of the play-wright's intentions, an analysis of irony, an essay reflecting an application of logic, a response to a critic

10. To analyze imagery and figurative language

Introducing the Play

In outline form, for your reference, here are the major elements in *Macbeth*:

- **Protagonist:** Macbeth
- **Antagonists:** Lady Macbeth, ambition
- **Conflict:** person vs. self
- **Point of view:** third-person omniscient
- **Significant techniques:** foreshadowing, characterization, mood, conflict, resolution, theme, climax, imagery, figurative language
- **Setting:** Scotland, England

Providing for Different Levels of Ability. Slower students may require assistance both with elements of plot and with the allusions appearing among the glosses. Encourage them to keep a running log of any questions that occur to them in the course of the at-home phase of the reading. You may, in instances, wish to meet with them separately for several minutes of each class during your coverage of the play to assess their grasp of the story line. Where necessary, add relevant details that will clear up misunderstandings so that these students may achieve as full and unimpeded a reading of the play as possible.

Introducing Vocabulary Study. Students will benefit from knowing the meanings of the following words before they read the play.

abhor	missive
appease	multitudinous
assailable	nonpareil
avaricious	oracle
blaspheming	patricide
benediction	pernicious
censure	perturbation
chastise	pristine
cistern	prowess
clamorous	purgative
cloistered	recoil
compunctious	recompense
credulous	redress
diminutive	requite
ere	sacrilegious
exasperate	sanctity
furbished	sundry
harbinger	surfeit
implore	surmise
incense	trammel
indissoluble	undaunted
interim	unsanctified
jocund	usurper
largesse	verity
laudable	voluptuousness
malevolent	withal

Teaching Strategies

Help students establish a purpose in reading *Macbeth* by referring them to the objectives listed at the beginning of this section. You can also help students to monitor their own reading by asking able readers to take turns reading parts. As students read aloud, ask others to determine the possible motivations of the characters being depicted.

It is important to focus students toward understanding *Macbeth* in terms of tragedy. As they read the play, refer students to both Aristotle's definition and what he said we expect of tragedy. In doing so, you will be aiding students in understanding the characterizations of Macbeth and Lady Macbeth. You may even wish students to determine whether they think either or both main characters are tragic, in Aristotle's sense.

In addition, you may wish students to write their own summaries of each scene in *Macbeth*; if they do so, make sure to ask them to include their own comments expressing their views of the tragedy. For example, they might write about how they perceive the importance of fate and free personal choice, as implied in a particular scene. They might discuss the changes in the characters of Macbeth and Lady Macbeth. The might consider the cause-and-effect relationship depicted in the tragedy.

Another important strategy is the placing of Shakespeare's work on a time chart or line. As students do so, they will come to understand Shakespeare's place in British history and literature in terms of other important writers. From a time chart, students will better understand that the language of Shakespeare is not the same as that of Chaucer; nor is it the same as that of Milton. After students have read selections from *The Canterbury Tales*, and have looked at the Prologue in Middle English, they will understand that the language of the Renaissance was much more similar to modern English than was Chaucer's language. Nor is Shakespeare's language as difficult to understand as Milton's, with its often inverted sentence structure.

Have students take note, as they read, of Shakespeare's imagery and his reliance on figures of speech. Remind students that, while Shakespearean drama is precisely that—drama—Shakespeare was a poet at heart and that, as a consequence, much of the language of his plays is highly poetic. Before they embark on the first act, review with them the meaning of the terms *metaphor*, *simile*, and *personification*, asking them to provide examples of each.

Reading the Play. The play's division into five acts makes it neatly teachable in five consecutive class periods. As was mentioned earlier, if it is possible to obtain a professional recording, you might wish to provide the students with an oral interpretation of selected scenes. Otherwise, you are advised to read aloud portions yourself. Devote a part of each class period to the oral coverage of several scenes, assigning the balance for homework. Use the beginning of the following period to cover the post-act questions and to address any issues or problems raised by students. The final series of questions and the writing assignments, which are voluminous, will require another class period. You might also plan on setting aside additional time for the essays that appear at strategic points throughout the student text, if it is your intention to use them.

For your convenience, scene-by-scene plot summaries have been provided before the answers to review questions for each of the five acts.

Act I
Text page 255

The Plot

Scene 1. Three witches plan to meet Macbeth later in the day. The scene typifies Shakespeare's reliance on the supernatural, an interest of many persons living in England during the Renaissance. In addition, notice that we are introduced

to Macbeth by other characters in the play, not directly as Macbeth comes on the stage.

Scene 2. Shakespeare reveals Macbeth and Banquo's prominence as soldiers. Also, we learn that the Thane of Cawdor must give up his title and that Duncan will give it to Macbeth. Shakespeare continues his dramatic buildup by keeping the audience from seeing Macbeth.

Scene 3. Macbeth and Banquo meet the three witches, who make three predictions. Banquo dismisses the predictions, but Macbeth does not. The scene presents the initial depiction of Macbeth's interest in and reliance on the supernatural. It also contrasts the differences between Banquo and Macbeth.

Scene 4. Duncan proclaims his son, Malcolm, heir to the throne. This fact may drive Macbeth even more to desire the throne for himself. Dramatic irony occurs as Duncan claims that no one can judge a man's true character just by appearance.

Scene 5. Lady Macbeth is introduced here. We learn that Macbeth confides in her and reveals his most private thoughts to her. Shakespeare depicts her as a very strong woman, juxtaposing her qualities with Macbeth's. The plot to murder Duncan advances as the two plan their attack.

Scene 6. Duncan arrives at Macbeth's castle. Dramatic irony occurs as Duncan assumes he is safe in Macbeth's home. Lady Macbeth appears gracious, even as she plots Duncan's murder.

Scene 7. Macbeth provides his first important soliloquy, explaining that he possesses vaulting ambition that leads him to murder Duncan. Lady Macbeth encourages her husband to commit the murder. Again, we discern Macbeth's inability to act and his wife's strength of will.

Reteaching Alternatives. Have students locate news accounts, current or in the past, of individuals who ''struck deals'' to get ahead against the advice of top aides. Tell them that an updated version of the *Macbeth* story was made some years ago in a grade-B movie titled *Joe Macbeth*. In this rendition, the setting was gangland Chicago during Prohibition.

Responding to the Play
Text page 270

Analyzing Act I

Identifying Facts

1. In Scene 1, where do the witches plan to meet again, and why? The witches plan to gather on the heath to meet Macbeth.

2. What news about Macbeth does the bloodstained Captain bring to the king in Scene 2? The Captain reports that Macbeth has distinguished himself by his fearlessness in battle and has turned the tide of the conflict by slaying Macdonwald. Macbeth and Banquo have also bravely repelled a second assault by the king's enemies.

3. What news does Ross bring about the Thane of Cawdor? Ross says that the Thane of Cawdor has traitorously assisted the Norwegian king.

4. What does the king determine to do for Macbeth? The king orders that the Thane of Cawdor be executed and that his title be conferred on Macbeth.

5. What do the witches tell Macbeth and Banquo in Scene 3? The witches tell Macbeth that he shall be Thane of Cawdor and then king hereafter. They tell Banquo that, although he will not be king, he will be the father of a line of kings.

6. In Scene 5, what is Lady Macbeth's response to her husband's letter with the news about his title and the witch's prophecy? Lady Macbeth ambitiously looks forward to her husband's becoming king, but she fears that he may not be strong enough to acquire the crown through dishonest means.

7. What speech tells you what Lady Macbeth plans to do to Duncan when he visits the castle? The speech that reveals that Lady Macbeth plans to murder King Duncan begins with the words, ''The raven himself is hoarse. . . .'' Note that Lady Macbeth refers to her ''keen knife.''

8. What are Macbeth's misgivings in Scene 7? Macbeth hesitates to murder the king because Duncan is a kinsman and a guest and because the king's goodness will cause the people to pity his murder. Macbeth is also reluctant to risk his own good reputation.

9. What is his wife's response? His wife tells him that he is a coward. She then describes specific plans for the murder and a plot to throw the blame on Duncan's guards.

Interpreting Meanings

10. In the very first scene of a play, a dramatist must tell the audience what kind of play they are about to see. What does the brief opening scene of *Macbeth* reveal about the play that will follow? How does the weather reflect the human passion revealed in the rest of the act? The opening scene suggests that this play will be stormy and violent and that supernatural elements will play a leading role.

11. The witches apparently recognize Macbeth as a man marked for success. Explain why their prophecy of Macbeth's coming greatness is actually a temptation to him. The fulfillment of part of the prophecy (that Macbeth will be the Thane of Cawdor) occurs with such swiftness that Macbeth is tempted to think that, if he took matters into his own hands, the rest of the prophecy might also be fulfilled (see I.iii.130-142).

12. Explain the seeming contradiction in the witches' greeting to Banquo in Scene 3: "Lesser than Macbeth, and greater." How is this true? The statement is true because, although Banquo will be Macbeth's subject when the latter becomes king, he will be ''greater'' than Macbeth in the sense that a long line of his descendants will rule Scotland.

13. How do Banquo's reactions to the witches differ from Macbeth's? Whereas Macbeth is tempted to believe the witches' prophecies, Banquo shows himself suspicious of the ''instruments of darkness.'' He compares the witches to bubbles of the earth, and he questions whether or not he and Macbeth have eaten of the ''insane root/That takes the reason prisoner.'' Altogether, Banquo seems far more skeptical than Macbeth of the witches' prophecies.

What does Macbeth's reaction suggest at once about his character? Macbeth's reaction may suggest that he is credulous and also ambitious.

14. One critic has said that the witches are ''in some sense representative of potentialities within'' Macbeth. Explain that statement. Is there any evidence that Macbeth has wanted to be king before? Student answers will vary. Ask the students to discuss their opinions in class.

15. The most interesting part of any serious play is what goes on inside the characters' minds. What conflict rages in Macbeth after he hears the witches' prophecy? The conflict in his mind is between his ambition and his horror of any violence that he might commit against the king.

What effect do the events of Scene 4 have on the conflict? The events of Scene 4, in which Duncan apparently blocks Macbeth's path to royalty by naming his eldest son the Prince of Cumberland (and thus the official heir to the throne), tip the balance in Macbeth's mind in favor of violence. Notice that he refers to his ''black and deep desires'' as I.iv.51.

16. We see Lady Macbeth alone for most of Scene 5, then with Duncan and his party in Scene 6. What impressions do you have of her by the end of Scene 6? Among the impressions students may mention are: violence, ruthlessness, ambition, and skill at dissembling.

17. Describe the temperamental differences between Macbeth and his wife. Who is more single-minded and logical? Who is more imaginative and sensitive? Which one wins the argument? Lady Macbeth is, without doubt, more single-minded and logical, while Macbeth is more imaginative and sensitive. Lady Macbeth wins the argument.

18. What irony would the audience feel as they watch Duncan enter the castle and hear him praise its peacefulness? The audience would feel irony because they know that the castle's outward calm conceals a violent plot to murder Duncan.

Act II

Text page 272

The Plot

Scene 1. The weather is important here, foreshadowing the darkness and evil of Macbeth and Lady Macbeth's plan of murder. Banquo is described as being troubled because of the witches' predictions. Dialogue between Banquo and Macbeth reveals that the latter is unconcerned with the predictions. However, after Banquo leaves, Macbeth shows that he does think of them. In his soliloquy, he sees a dagger before him, covered in blood. Here the audience may see the first evidence that Macbeth's mind is affected. The bell sounds, and Macbeth leaves to commit the murder.

Scene 2. After murdering Duncan, Macbeth greets his wife in a state of confusion. Lady Macbeth has been unable to commit the murder because Duncan reminds her of her own father. While Lady Macbeth is calm and yet thrilled with the murder, partially from alcohol, Macbeth is deeply troubled. Lady Macbeth must take the daggers from Macbeth and place them beside the sleeping grooms.

Scene 3. Here Shakespeare introduces comic relief, in the form of a drunken porter. The ''knocking at the gate,'' however, is ironic, because the porter assumes with each knock he is admitting a criminal to hell. Macbeth now appears calm. Macduff discovers Duncan's murder, while Lennox describes the strange occurrences in the weather and the horses. The speech intensifies the importance of the supernatural in the play and parallels the horror of the time. Malcolm and Donalbain enter, learn what has happened, and flee the country. Macbeth exclaims that he has murdered the grooms because of their guilt in killing Duncan. Lady Macbeth faints, leaving the audience to question whether her action is genuine or planned. It should be emphasized here that, in killing Duncan, Macbeth had serious reservations; in killing the grooms, he no longer has such reservations. The effects of his decision have already begun.

Scene 4. The horror of nature parallels that of the murders. Ross and the old man talk about the wild and frightening happenings about them. Macduff reveals the fact that he will not be present for Macbeth's coronation at Scone and that he fears conditions under the new crown.

Reteaching Alternatives. Have students think of other literary or artistic works in which the weather can be seen in some sense to go hand in hand with the action. Ask them to discuss why the weather is such a useful symbol for indicating the mood of a passage in a work of fiction.

Responding to the Play

Text page 284

Analyzing Act II

Identifying Facts

1. In Scene 1, Macbeth asks Banquo to meet him later for ''some words.'' What incentive does he offer Banquo? Macbeth tells Banquo that if he supports him when the time comes, he will receive honors.

How does Banquo reply? Banquo says that he will agree, provided that Macbeth does not ask him to do anything that will compromise a clear conscience.

2. Describe the vision that Macbeth has at the end of Scene 1. What details foreshadow the action to come? Macbeth has a vision of a dagger in the air that gradually grows red with blood. Details that foreshadow the action to come include the gouts of blood, the figurative description of ''withered murder,'' and Macbeth's comments on the bell that summons Duncan ''to heaven, or to hell.''

3. In Scene 2, as Macbeth kills Duncan, what does Lady Macbeth hear? Lady Macbeth hears the shriek of an owl and the cry of crickets.

What does Macbeth hear? Macbeth hears the laughter of one of the guards in his sleep and the cries of ''Murder'' and ''God bless us.'' Then he thinks that he hears repeated cries that say, ''Macbeth shall sleep no more.''

4. Why, according to Lady Macbeth, was she unable to kill Duncan herself? She says that Duncan resembled her father as he slept.

Which task related to the murder does she perform? Lady Macbeth plants the daggers near the grooms and tells Macbeth to wash the blood from his hands and put on his nightgown.

5. In Scene 2, Lady Macbeth sensibly suggests that Macbeth go wash the ''filthy witness'' from his hands after the murder. How does Macbeth respond? He says that not even ''great Neptune's ocean'' can make his hands clean; rather, the blood on his hands will make the sea turn from green to red.

6. In Scene 3, what is the porter pretending as he goes to open the gate? The porter is pretending that he is knocking on the gate of hell.

7. Why has Macduff come? Macduff has come because the king had commanded him to meet him at the castle early in the morning.

8. What reason does Macbeth give for killing Duncan's two guards? He says that he killed them out of fury at their ''murder'' of the king.

9. Where do Duncan's sons decide to go? Malcolm decides to go to England, and Donalbain makes for Ireland.

10. In Scene 4, whom does Macduff suspect of Duncan's murder? Macduff, ironically, suspects the king's sons because they have fled.

Interpreting Meanings

11. Though Macbeth encounters no actual opposition until long after Duncan is murdered, Shakespeare must foreshadow some trouble for him and, to build up suspense, must start one character edging toward suspicion of Macbeth. Who is this character, and what inkling does he give of his dissatisfaction with Macbeth? The character is Malcolm, who implies that Macbeth is both murderous and merciless. He also implies that Macbeth's sorrow at Duncan's murder is feigned.

12. In Act I, Scene 7, Lady Macbeth seems to be planning to murder Duncan herself. But at the last moment, in Act II, Scene 2, she is unable to wield her dagger. Consider the reason she gives, and decide what her actions and explanation reveal about her character. Lady Macbeth's reason is that the king resembles her father as he sleeps. Student responses will vary. Ask the students to explain their opinions in class.

13. Many people are killed onstage in Shakespeare's plays. Why, then, do you suppose he decided to have the murder of Duncan and his guards take place offstage? Student answers will vary. Some students may argue that the murders become even more horrible if the audience is allowed to imagine them.

14. In Scene 3, when Duncan's corpse is discovered, Macbeth utters a hypocritical lament beginning, ''Had I but died . . . .'' But is it really hypocritical? The critic A. C. Bradley argued that, although the speech is meant to be a lie, it actually contains ''Macbeth's profoundest feelings.'' Explain this apparent contradiction. How does Macbeth feel about having murdered Duncan? What clues tell you how he feels? The speech can be interpreted in two ways. On the level of a hypocritical lament, it is intended to convey sorrow at the king's violent death and to avert suspicion from Macbeth. But Macbeth's words are ambiguous: they may be taken to mean that, with the murder, he knows he has lost his true peace of mind, renown, and grace. Interpreted in this way, the speech reveals Macbeth's regret and guilt.

15. Lady Macbeth's fainting spell, like everything else she has done so far, has a purpose. What message do you think she wants her fainting spell to convey? She probably wants her fainting spell to distract attention from Macbeth's elaborate explanation of why he killed the guards. She may also be sending him the message not to reveal too much information.

16. Malcolm and Donalbain are little more than boys, yet they already know enough about life to keep their mouths shut. What is in their minds, but left unsaid? How do they hint about it to each other? In their minds is the possibility that Macbeth, despite his professions of sorrow, has actually murdered the king. They hint about this possibility by indirectly referring to an ''unfelt sorrow'' and ''daggers in men's smiles.''

17. Macduff is an important character in the three remaining acts. Describe how Shakespeare characterizes Macduff in Scenes 3 and 4. Shakespeare characterizes Macduff as direct, loyal, and perhaps a bit naive.

18. What would you say is the mood of Act II? What images and actions help to create this mood? The mood of Act II is sinister and violent. Among the images that help to create this mood are Banquo's opening description of the starless night, the repeated references to blood, the dagger, Lennox's description of the storm, the shriek of the owl, and the porter's references to the gate of hell.

Act III   Text page 285
The Plot

Scene 1. Banquo reveals that he suspects Macbeth of having murdered Duncan and the grooms. He realizes that the predictions of the witches are coming true for Macbeth and wonders if they will also come true for him. Banquo is now a threat to Macbeth, who realizes that the witches have predicted he would become king but his descendants would not.

The scene also depicts Macbeth and Lady Macbeth as king and queen. Macbeth invites Banquo to the banquet that night but learns that Banquo is leaving the castle and does not plan on arriving back in time. Macbeth attempts to change Banquo's mind. Banquo finally agrees to attend the banquet but explains that he and Fleance must first leave the castle for awhile. Realizing that Banquo suspects him, Macbeth plots his death. Dismissing the group until seven that night, he summons the two murderers. Playing on the failures they have experienced in life and on their blame of Banquo for those failures, Macbeth entreats them to commit the murder of Banquo and Fleance. Here we discern that Macbeth has lost all sense of ethics in his quest to rid himself of all those who would suspect him.

Scene 2. Lady Macbeth states that she has nothing as queen if she does not have peace of mind. She expresses her remorse at Duncan's death. Macbeth enters, and she works to encourage him to be strong and fearless. Macbeth explains that he envies Duncan, who, in death, no longer has to worry about poisoned food. Macbeth states that he fears Banquo and his children but that a ''deed of dreadful note'' will soon be accomplished. Lady Macbeth questions her husband regarding his statement, but he will tell her nothing of his plans.

Scene 3. Banquo is murdered, but Fleance escapes. The witches' prediction—that Banquo's descendants will become king—has a chance of becoming reality.

Scene 4. The banquet scene. Macbeth's mental disintegration is apparent. The first murderer beckons Macbeth to him. Macbeth's joy at Banquo's death is overcome by his depression at Fleance's escape. After Lady Macbeth warns her husband of being away from the guests too long, he comes back to sit with the others. Now he sees Banquo's ghost and is horrified. Lady Macbeth tries to explain that her husband is ill, but then she admonishes him for being weak. Macbeth comes back to himself, pledging a toast to everyone, especially Banquo. At this point, he is in danger of exposing the crimes he has committed, speaking as he does directly to Banquo's ghost. Lady Macbeth realizes his near confession and overtakes him, dismissing the guests. However, it is too late now, as Lennox explains upon his leaving. The scene ends with Lady Macbeth's severe depression. She laments what is happening, as Macbeth explains that they are still new to violence. Once they become more experienced, they will overcome their weaknesses. He leaves to find the witches and speak with them further about their predictions.

Scene 5. This scene may have been written by someone other than Shakespeare. The plot is not advanced at all.

Scene 6. The scene is the palace. Lennox explains to another lord what he suspects Macbeth of having done. He asks where Macduff is now, and the lord answers that he is in England, planning with Edward the Confessor to overtake Scotland. Macbeth hears of these plans and begins preparations of his own. Students should note that Macbeth has summoned Macduff, who has refused to see him. Thus, Macbeth is sure that Macduff does suspect the truth.

Reteaching Alternatives. Review with the students the notion of "climax" in the development of a plot. Provide a visual aid by drawing a makeshift line graph on the chalkboard, on which the plot is represented as a line that gradually ascends and then suddenly plummets. Point out to students that in such a representation, the high point signifies the climax.

Responding to the Play   Text page 300
Analyzing Act III
Identifying Facts

1. In the short soliloquy that opens Scene 1, what does Banquo reveal that he knows about Macbeth? He reveals that he knows that Macbeth "played most foully" to gain the crown.

What does he decide to do? He decides to wait for the fulfillment of the witches' hopeful prophecies about his descendants.

2. How and why does Macbeth arrange Banquo's murder? How is Lady Macbeth involved in the murder? Macbeth fears Banquo's noble nature; he also cannot endure the thought of Banquo's descendants succeeding him on the throne. He therefore arranges to have Banquo and his son Fleance murdered by professional assassins. Lady Macbeth is a participant insofar as she persistently goads her husband into taking aggressive action.

3. In Scene 3, who escapes the murderers? Fleance escapes the murderers.

4. Describe what happens in Scene 4 when Ross, Lennox, and the other lords invite Macbeth to share their table. What does Macbeth do? What does Lady Macbeth do? Macbeth is terrified by the appearances of the bloody ghost of Banquo. Lady Macbeth tries in vain to reassure the guests, saying that her husband has suffered from strange, momentary fits ever since his youth. Privately, Lady Macbeth reproaches her husband for his weakness.

5. By Scene 6, what opinion do Lennox and the other lord hold of Macbeth? They think he is a murderous tyrant.

6. Macduff does not appear at all in Act III. Where is he, and why? Macduff has joined Malcolm in England. They are gathering allies to challenge Macbeth's power.

Interpreting Meanings

7. Why do you suppose Shakespeare did not have Macbeth kill Banquo with his own hands, as he killed Duncan and his two guards? What can you infer about Macbeth's changing character from seeing how readily he engages in this complex plan involving professional murderers? Perhaps Shakespeare meant to suggest how rapidly Macbeth's moral nature has deteriorated. He now commands others to perform his bloody work for him.

8. The relationship between Macbeth and his wife has changed in several ways since they became rulers of Scotland. Describe some of these changes. What reasons can you suggest for these changes? Macbeth and his wife have grown somewhat estranged and more formal with each other. In addition, Macbeth now takes the initiative in the violent plot to murder Banquo; Lady Macbeth seems more passive. Guilt and fear are the probable reasons for these changes.

9. In Scene 2, Shakespeare helps the audience imagine the setting by having Macbeth say, "Light thickens, and the crow makes wing to the rooky wood." How can these remarks also be seen as a metaphorical commentary on the events of the play? The words suggest that the distinction between good and evil has at first been blurred and then completely erased in the hero's mind, just as we find it difficult to distinguish one concrete object from another at twilight. The crow might be regarded as a symbol of evil or murder.

Find other remarks of this sort that Shakespeare has Macbeth make, and explain how they function. At I.iii.141, Macbeth soliloquizes that "nothing is but what is not," implying the blurring of reality and illusion. His remarks in his soliloquy in II.i about the "fatal vision" of the bloody dagger touch on the same motif. Finally, his anguish at the sight of the ghost compels him again to question the distinction between illusion and reality. Notice Lady Macbeth's reference at the end of the banquet scene to the time of night: "Almost at odds with morning, which is which."

10. How is Fleance's escape a turning point in the play? Fleance's escape is a turning point because it signifies that the witches' prophecies concerning Banquo's descendants may indeed come true.

11. Nobody except Macbeth sees Banquo's ghost. In some productions of the play the ghost does not appear onstage; in others, it does. What is gained by having Banquo appear at the banquet, made up as a ghost? What is gained by having nobody actually appear to motivate Macbeth's terrified behavior? Student answers will vary. In general, students may suggest that the appearance of Banquo might contribute to realism, while having nobody actually appear would emphasize Macbeth's inner conflicts and guilt.

12. How does the banquet scene blur the clear-cut and common-sense distinction that most of us make between the real and the imaginary? The failure of anyone else to see Banquo's ghost causes Macbeth to wonder if the dead can come out of their graves and if he is going mad.

In what other scenes has this distinction also been blurred? Students may point to a number of scenes (see the comments under question 9, above). They may add that the witches' remarks—"Fair is foul, and foul is fair./Hover through the fog and filthy air"—suggest the blurring of this distinction in the very first scene of the play.

Act IV   Text page 301
The Plot

Scene 1. Macbeth goes back to the witches, demanding that they show him the future. By now, he relies on their assistance, believing them to be in favor of him. The witches decline his request, but he persists. The apparitions begin—an armed head, a bloody child, a child with a crown on its head. As Macbeth demands to learn more, the witches discourage him against knowing too much. At his insistence, they show him another apparition, a display of eight kings. Finally, the ghost of Banquo appears and points to the kings as his descendants. The mirror indicates the continuation of the royal line, something that infuriates Macbeth. The symbol of the two balls means that James, the king of England, had called himself the king of France and Scotland. The three scepters represent his reign over England, Ireland, and Scotland.

After the display of apparitions, the witches vanish. Lennox appears, telling Macbeth that Macduff has fled to England. Here, Macbeth realizes that Macduff is going to conspire with those already abroad. The scene ends with Macbeth's plan to murder Lady Macduff and the children.

Scene 2. A messenger has warned the victims just before the assassins enter, but with no success. It is possible that Lady Macbeth, with remorse at what has occurred so far, has sent the messenger to warn the victims. Still, Shakespeare never explains the mystery. Macduff's family are killed, and the audience discerns clearly Macbeth's moral disintegration.

Scene 3. The forces gather to oppose Macbeth. Macduff attempts to secure Malcolm's aid in fighting Macbeth. Malcolm begins testing Macduff, asking why he has left his family at this difficult time for Scotland. Malcolm explains that he believes himself incapable of ruling Scotland. Finally, he is convinced of Macduff's integrity and agrees to assist him.

Ross enters with news of Lady Macduff's death and that of her children. With anger and grief, Macduff prays that he will be allowed to meet Macbeth in battle. The scene ends as Malcolm states that his plans are complete toward overtaking Macbeth.

Reteaching Alternatives. Students who have difficulty accepting the supernatural elements in the first scene might be reminded that these very elements—apparitions of the future and a visit from the ghost of a former associate—are acceptable to most audiences in Dickens's *A Christmas Carol*. The difficulty in adjustment here, then, is related to time, not to culture.

Responding to the Play   Text page 316
Analyzing Act IV
Identifying Facts

1. What kinds of ingredients go into the witches' stew? What is the purpose of this vile concoction? Among the ingredients are a toad, a slice of snake, the eye of a newt, the toe of a frog, the wool of a bat, a dog's tongue, a lizard's leg, the wing of an owl, the scale of a dragon, the tooth of a wolf, the mummified flesh of a witch, the stomach and gullet of a shark, the root of hemlock, the liver of a blaspheming Jew, the gall of a goat, slips of yew, the nose of a Turk, the lips of a Tartar, the finger of a strangled baby, the entrails of a tiger, and the blood of a baboon. The purpose is to summon Hecate and the other witches to cast an evil spell, or enchantment.

2. Describe the three apparitions Macbeth sees when he visits the witches. What does each apparition tell him? The first apparition, an armed head, tells Macbeth to beware of Macduff. The second apparition, a bloody child, tells Macbeth that he cannot be harmed by any man born of woman. The third apparition, a crowned child, tells Macbeth that he will never be vanquished until Birnam Wood shall come to Dunsinane Hill against him.

3. What question has Macbeth come to ask the witches, and how do they answer? Macbeth has come to learn if

Banquo's descendants will ever gain the throne. The witches show him a procession of eight kings who are obviously Banquo's descendants.

4. Which nobleman does Macbeth plan to murder after talking with the witches? He plans to murder Macduff.

How is his plan foiled? His plan is foiled because of Macduff's flight to England.

5. At the end of Scene 1, what does Macbeth vow? He vows he will murder Macduff's wife, young children, and relatives.

Describe the way his vow is carried out in Scene 2. Murderers burst in on Lady Macduff and her young son and kill them.

6. According to the conversation between Malcolm and Macduff in Scene 3, what has happened to Scotland during Macbeth's reign? Under Macbeth's reign, the countryside has become desolate.

7. What does Malcolm "confess" about his own faults? Malcolm pretends to confess that he is intemperate and corrupt.

8. How does Macduff respond to Malcolm's "confessions"? Macduff responds by declaring that Malcolm is unfit to live, much less to govern, and he weeps for Scotland.

Interpreting Meanings

9. In this act Macbeth seeks out the witches, just as they took the initiative in approaching him in Act I. How has his situation changed since he last talked with them? How has his character changed? His situation has changed because he is unnerved by opposition and by the escape of Fleance. His character has changed in that he has become more corrupt and bloodthirsty.

10. Do you think the witches have caused any of these changes, directly or indirectly? Explain your reasons for thinking as you do. Student answers will vary. Encourage the students to discuss and defend their opinions.

11. In Scene 1, the eight kings appear in what was called in Shakespeare's day a dumb show—an interpolated brief scene in which nothing is said. What is the point of this particular dumb show? The point is to stress to Macbeth the validity of the witches' prophecy that Banquo's descendants will rule Scotland.

12. In Scene 2, the lines spoken by Macduff's wife and son illustrate Shakespeare's great skill at characterization. Using only a few words, he brings the woman and the child to life, showing both faults and virtues in each. How would you describe Lady Macduff? How would you describe the boy? Lady Macduff is portrayed as tender, weak, and a bit hysterical; she has drawn the wrong conclu-

sion about her husband. Macduff's son is portrayed as overcurious, witty, and courageous.

13. The murder of Macduff's wife and small son is one of the most pitiful and shocking scenes in Shakespeare. Why do you suppose he decided to show it onstage, rather than just having it reported after it happens? Student answers will vary. Ask the students to explain their opinions. Perhaps the graphic violence here is intended to show how ruthless Macbeth has become.

14. Both the murderer and Lady Macduff herself call Macduff a traitor. In what sense does each mean it? Lady Macduff means it in the sense that she thinks her husband has abandoned his family. The murderer means Macduff is a traitor to the king, Macbeth.

Do you think Macduff is a traitor, in either sense? Most students will probably concur in *not* thinking Macduff is a traitor in either sense.

15. In Scene 3, Malcolm deliberately lies to Macduff. What does this behavior, and the reason for it, reveal about Malcolm? This behavior and its motivation reveal that Malcolm is cautious, skeptical, and prudent in testing Macduff's moral character before he allies himself with him.

16. Describe how you felt as you read Scene 4. How does Shakespeare build suspense and emotions in the scene? Some of the methods students may suggest for the building of suspense and emotion include Malcolm's false "confession" and Ross's announcement that Macduff's wife and children have been murdered.

Act V   Text page 317
The Plot

Scene 1. Lady Macbeth's mental and physical conditions have deteriorated. As she sleepwalks, she reveals the truth about the conspiracy against Duncan. The lady in waiting and the physician have watched Lady Macbeth for two nights by now, and once again watch her. She enters, holding a candle and rubbing her hands, attempting to rid herself of the blood she believes is still on her hands. The doctor explains that nothing can be done to help her.

Scene 2. The scene is Birnam Wood, where Malcolm, Macduff, and others have gathered in their plan to overtake Macbeth. In his castle, Macbeth believes for a time that he is invincible. Some critics believe him to be insane by this time, but others state that he suffers instead from a false sense of security.

Scene 3. Macbeth gives a moving soliloquy in which he bemoans the fact that old age cannot be accompanied by friendship and love.

Scene 4. The Scottish troops have joined the British in preparation for overtaking Macbeth. In a move that fulfills the witches' prophecy, Malcolm instructs all of the troops to cut branches from trees in Birnam Wood and carry them as camouflage of their numbers.

Scene 5. Offstage, a cry is heard, and Macbeth states that he is not disturbed by it as he once would have been. He mentions his increasing insensitivity to such circumstances and explains that it is caused by the evil he has committed.

Seyton enters with news that Lady Macbeth is dead. Macbeth delivers his most famous soliloquy, beginning "Tomorrow, and tomorrow, and tomorrow. . . ." The speech further reflects his helplessness and despair. He sees life as being "full of sound and fury, signifying nothing."

Scene 6. Malcolm gives orders to his troops. The trumpets sound, signifying the beginning of the battle.

Scene 7. Macbeth kills Siward and gains hope that he may, in fact, win the battle against Malcolm.

Scene 8. At first, Macbeth refuses to fight Macduff, sure now that the other prophecies may come true. However, Macduff tempts him into battle by explaining that if he does not fight, he will be placed in a cage where everyone can view him as a fearful captured animal. The final fight begins.

Offstage, Macduff kills Macbeth and beheads him. Onstage, Ross explains that Siward was killed. Macduff returns with the head of Macbeth on the tip of his sword. Malcolm agrees to accept the position of king, and the play ends with an invitation to all to see him crowned at Scone, the ancient location of such events.

Reteaching Alternatives. Have students read either or both of the brief essays that conclude the reading—"Soliloquies and Asides" on page 329 and the commentary on the characters of Macbeth and Lady Macbeth beginning on page 330. The second of these two pieces, which probes the complex psychology behind the two main characters, will prove to be a particularly invaluable aid to the student reader.

Responding to the Play Text page 332
Analyzing Act V
Identifying Facts

1. Why, according to the doctor, is Lady Macbeth walking in her sleep? According to the doctor, she has more need of the divine than the physician—in other words, she has a guilty conscience.

2. In Scene 2, what opinion of Macbeth do the Scottish lords now hold? The Scottish lords think Macbeth is either mad or cruelly violent because of guilt at his "secret murders."

3. Describe how and when Lady Macbeth dies. Lady Macbeth dies by suicide during the final battle.

4. Describe Macbeth's plan for dealing with the attacking troops. He says he would prefer to deal with the troops in a different way; why has he been forced to choose this plan instead? Macbeth plans to allow his castle to be besieged by the enemy troops. He says he would have preferred to meet the opposition face to face, but he has been forced to choose this plan because the enemy has forcibly enlisted the aid of troops that should have been his.

5. In Scene 5, Macbeth describes changes in his own personality. What are those changes? He says that he has forgotten how to be afraid because of all the horrors he has experienced.

6. In the speech in Scene 5 that begins, "Tomorrow, and tomorrow, and tomorrow . . . " (lines 19-28), how does Macbeth describe life? What metaphors does he use? He describes life with the metaphors of a brief candle, a poor player strutting for a brief time upon the stage, and a tale told by an idiot. His description of life characterizes it as brief, dreary, and insignificant.

7. In Act IV, Scene 1, the three apparitions shown Macbeth by the witches all referred, in reverse chronological order, to events in Act V. Find the things in Act V that correspond with the three apparitions in Act IV. The fact that Malcolm's troops rip down trees from Birnam Wood to protect themselves as they mount their assault against the castle corresponds with the third apparition's warning, that Macbeth should be fearless until Birnam Wood comes to Dunsinane. The fact that Macduff reveals that he was "untimely ripped" from his mother's womb corresponds with the second apparition, that Macbeth would never be vanquished by any man born of woman. Finally, the fact that Macduff slays Macbeth corresponds with the warning of the first apparition, the armed head, that Macbeth should beware Macduff.

8. At the end of the play, what has become of Macbeth? He is stripped of all illusions, hated by his people, and finally slain in battle.

Interpreting Meanings

9. Theatrically, the spectacle of Lady Macbeth walking in her sleep is one of the most striking scenes in the play. It is entirely Shakespeare's invention, not found or suggested in his source. Why do you suppose Shakespeare has her walk in her sleep? How is this scene related to the remarks Macbeth makes about sleep in Act II, Scene 2, just after he kills Duncan? Shakespeare probably has Lady Macbeth walk in her sleep to emphasize the torment and pathos of her guilt. The scene is related to Macbeth's comments after the murder that he heard a voice crying, "Macbeth shall sleep no more." Also note the relationship with the couple's sleeplessness in Act III, when Lady Macbeth remarks to her husband, after the terrifying banquet scene, ''You lack the season of all natures, sleep'' (III.iv.141).

10. In the sleepwalking scene, Lady Macbeth refers to many of her waking experiences. For example, the words ''one; two'' may refer to Act II, Scene 1, when she struck the bell signaling Macbeth to go kill Duncan. Find traces of other experiences in what she says in her sleep. Among the traces of other experiences that students may mention are the following: the washing of the hands and the command to put on the nightgown (referring to her actions on the night of the murder of Duncan); the reference to the wife of the Thane of Fife (referring to the murder of Lady Macduff); the reference to the burial of Banquo (alluding to Macbeth's horror at seeing Banquo's ghost in the banquet scene of III.iv); and the reference to the knocking at the gate (alluding to the porter's actions directly after the murder of Duncan).

11. Malcolm, at the very end of Act IV, says, ''The night is long that never finds a day.'' In what metaphorical sense did he use the terms ''night'' and ''day''? How does his remark foreshadow the outcome of the play? He uses the terms ''night'' and ''day'' in a metaphorical sense to indicate tyranny and freedom, or enslavement and liberation. The remark foreshadows the outcome of the play because it hints that Macbeth will, in the end, be defeated.

12. Shakespeare gave most of his tragic heroes an impressive dying speech in which they say something significant about their life and death. He did not write such a speech for Macbeth. Which speech of Macbeth's do you think serves in the play as his dying speech? Why do you select this speech rather than some other one? Many students will suggest that Macbeth's ''dying speech'' is, in effect, the brief soliloquy at V.v.19, beginnings with ''Tomorrow, and tomorrow, and tomorrow . . . .'' Ask students to explain their selection of a particular speech as the dying speech.

13. ''Nothing in his life became him like the leaving of it.'' Malcolm says this in Act I, Scene 4, about the execution of the traitorous Thane of Cawdor. Malcolm also says that this Thane of Cawdor threw away the dearest thing he owned. Might these two statements also apply to Macbeth? Explain. Student answers will vary. Ask students to explain and defend their opinions in class.

The Play as a Whole
Interpreting Meanings

1. Internal conflicts rage within Macbeth, and he has external conflicts with other characters. Explain some of the play's main conflicts, and trace their resolution. The internal conflicts within Macbeth include ambition vs. loyalty, honor vs. shame, rationality vs. delusion, hope vs. despair, and strength vs. weakness. The external conflicts include his conflicts with Banquo, the witches, Macduff, Malcolm, and—for a time—with his wife.

2. One of the themes of *Macbeth* centers on evil, which Shakespeare saw as a force beyond human understanding. Do you think Shakespeare also saw evil as stronger than the forces of good? To answer, consider the events and outcome of *Macbeth*. Explain your reasons for thinking as you do. Student answers will vary. Ask the students to explain and defend their opinions in class.

3. The last act of *Macbeth* contains the play's climax—the most emotional and suspenseful part of the action—the moment when the characters' conflict in finally resolved. Which part of Act V do you consider the climax? Explain. Student answers will vary. Many students will suggest that the actual death of Macbeth in battle is the climax. Some students may propose that the climax occurs when Macduff announces that he was prematurely ripped from his mother's womb; this fulfills the third waring of the apparitions, and from this moment on Macbeth suspects that his doom is sealed.

4. One critic has observed that a part of Macbeth's tragedy is the fact that many of his strengths are also his weaknesses. Explain this apparent contradiction. What are Macbeth's strengths? Which ones also work against him? Students may suggest that Macbeth's strengths include military courage, loyalty, ambition, imagination, and persuasive ability. The last three of these strengths could be said also to work against him.

5. Think of a modern figure, real or fictional, whose downfall, like Macbeth's, came after an attempt to gain great power. How is this modern figure like Macbeth, and how different? Do you think the modern figure would make a good tragic hero or heroine? Student answers will vary. Ask the students to compare the figures they choose with Macbeth as specifically as they can.

On the Knocking at the Gate in *Macbeth*

Text page 335

This essay by the early nineteenth-century essayist Thomas De Quincey, alluded to in the commentary at the close of Act II on text page 283, addresses Shakespeare's reasons for including the porter scene and the effects this inclusion may have been intended to have on the reader. Preface the reading of the essay by pointing out to students that Shakespeare scholarship, since the century following the Bard's death, has explored numerous questions along these lines. After students have read the essay, ask them to respond to the following questions, perhaps in brief essays: Is De Quincey's digression in the second paragraph necessary—that is, does it help the reader to understand the point he makes later about the central subject of the essay? How is De Quincey's distinction between the ''two worlds'' in *Macbeth* central to his argument?

Extending the Play

Have students work as a team to write a scene that details developments in King Malcolm's first year on the throne. Encourage them to set the scene up as a portion of a play, using dialogue, stage directions, and, if possible, blank verse. The character portrayal of Malcolm should be consistent with Shakespeare's. Remind students, however, that power leads to changes in people, as *Macbeth* so eloquently attests.

Further Reading

Students interested in learning more about Shakespeare and his dramatic craft might be directed to the following titles.

Barber, C. L. and Richard P. Wheeler. *The Whole Journey: Shakespeare's Power of Development*. Berkeley: U of California P, 1986. Discusses Lady Macbeth and Macbeth's relationship in terms of her maternal power over him. Considers the sonnets the result of "a self at deep levels of need." Includes several good essays on *Hamlet* as well.

Brennan, Anthony. *Shakespeare's Dramatic Structures*. Boston: Routledge and Kegan Paul, 1986. Considers the variety of ways Shakespeare altered the basic techniques of structure and the order he assigns events. Discusses the separation of Lady Macbeth and Macbeth from each other as well as from others, and the effect of this isolation.

Brown, John Russel. *Discovering Shakespeare: A New Guide to the Plays*. New York: Columbia UP, 1981. Explains thesis that readers should imagine live performances of plays. Discusses notion that character and theme are secondary to the excitement and strength readers must first experience.

Chute, Marchette. *An Introduction to Shakespeare*. New York: Dutton, 1951. Discusses Shakespeare's early life, marriage, children, investments; considers Shakespeare as actor and member of companies. Offers clear explanation of the sources of *Macbeth*.

Cunningham, J. V. *Woe or Wonder: The Emotional Effect of Shakespearean Tragedy*. Denver: U of Denver P, 1951. Considers what emotional effects Shakespeare wanted evoked by the catastrophes of his tragedies. Differentiates between effects spoken by characters and those expressing the playwright's intentions concerning a play as a whole.

Dillon, Janette. *Shakespeare and the Solitary Man*. Totowa, NJ: Rowman and Littlefield, 1981. Discusses transition, during Renaissance, from solitude as fashionable and attractive state to immoral and antisocial one. Considers Macbeth as a solitary man who was also "villain-hero."

Eastman, Arthur M. *A Short History of Shakespearean Criticism*. New York: Random House, 1968. Evaluates Shakespearean criticism of the eighteenth, nineteenth, and twentieth centuries, reviewing first British and then American scholarship. Discusses the work of Bradley, Knights, Spurgeon, Granville-Barker, Frye, Tillyard, Coleridge, and others.

Hawkes, Terence, ed. *Twentieth Century Interpretations of* Macbeth: *A Collection of Critical Essays*. Englewood Cliffs, NJ: Prentice-Hall, 1977. Includes essays by Caroline Spurgeon ("Shakespeare's Imagery in *Macbeth*"), Francis Fergusson ("*Macbeth* as the Imitation of an Action"), and L. C. Knights (*Macbeth*). Very useful to instructors and more able students desiring critical commentaries concerning various aspects of *Macbeth*.

Knight, G. Wilson. *The Wheel of Fire: Interpretations of Shakespearean Tragedy*. London: Methuen, 1972. Discusses major hindrances in understanding Shakespeare. Considers similarities between Macbeth and Brutus, the nature of evil in *Macbeth*, Lear's universe, Shakespeare's use of personification, and music in Shakespearean tragedy.

Van Doren, Mark. *Shakespeare*. New York: Holt, 1939. Analyzes all of Shakespeare's plays. Explains *Macbeth* as a play whose "central horror" is enclosed within a "universe of good." Discusses the brevity of *Macbeth* and the changes and inconsistencies found in the play.

Sonnets

Text page 338

Supposedly, Shakespeare wrote his sonnet cycle between 1593 and 1603, although its publication was not until 1609. He wrote 154 sonnets in all, dedicated to "Mr. W. H.," whose identity still is not known.

Although the sonnets differ in content, a general theme may be discerned in them: love and the transitory aspects of mortal life. Many sonnets are concerned with the differences between the past and the present or future. In several sonnets, for example, Shakespeare writes of the effects of time and the belief that all that remains are memories of people and circumstances of the past.

In *An Interpretation of Shakespeare*, Hardin Craig refers to comments made by Tucker Brooke, who writes that Shakespeare's sonnets contain language that is "perhaps the simplest by which any English poet has achieved comparable effects. . . .'' He further states that the sonnets contain an ''almost unequalled range of subjects and breadth of treatment. They present human situations and relations of the most universal occurrence'' (113, New York: Dryden, 1948). Ask students to consider Brooke's comments, determining whether they believe them correct. Students may wish to consider their own experiences with the transitory nature of life and love. In particular, what effect does memory have for each student?

This selection of sonnets includes several of the most famous of Shakespeare's compositions, lyric or dramatic. Taken as a group, they make a good introduction to this important body of English poetry, as they amply illustrate Shakespeare's unsurpassed technical artistry, the richness of his imagination, and the extraordinary range of his variations on the theme of love.

Objectives

1. To analyze tone

2. To analyze simile

3. To identify turn

4. To evaluate mood

5. To write a parody of a sonnet

6. To compare sonnets

The Poems at a Glance

- **Rhyme:** *ababcdcdefefgg* in all sonnets
- **Rhythm:** iambic pentameter
- **Significant techniques:** simile, tone, mood

Teaching Strategies

Providing for Cultural Differences. Students should have little difficulty relating to the speaker's feelings and thoughts in these sonnets. Remind the students that the common theme is love, and that, in general, the speaker views life and the world around him in terms of his love.

Providing for Different Levels of Ability. Slower readers may yet have difficulty with the language of these poems and with some of the more elaborate metaphors, such as those in lines 2-10 of Sonnet 116. These difficulties can be gotten over to a large degree by rereading and by reading aloud. Again, remind the students that the poet's constant theme is love.

Introducing Vocabulary Study. Students will benefit from knowing the meanings of the following words before they read the poems.

temperate   sullen

Reading the Sonnets. As with any poem whose language is unfamiliar, or whose imagery or thought is complex, it is important to read these sonnets slowly and more than once. Suggest to the students that they begin by studying the headnote to each sonnet and the marginal glosses that define and explain difficult words and passages. Help the students read the poems ''conversationally''—that is, as if the speaker were talking directly to them. Thus, instead of reading line by line, they might try reading thought by thought, or according to the poem's punctuation. This way of reading will make the language seem easier and will convey the movement of thought more naturally.

Consider assigning the last two of the poems for homework once the first three have been considered in class.

Reteaching Alternatives. Have the students select one of the sonnets they especially like. Have them write a prose paraphrase of the sonnet, recasting into Modern English the main ideas, images, and comparisons in the original.

Sonnet 29

Responding to the Poem

Analyzing the Poem

Identifying Details

1. Name the traits of others that the speaker is envious of. Among these traits are: material prospects and optimism, physical appearance, friends, literary ability, and wide-ranging talents.

2. Which line carries the turn of the sonnet? The turn occurs in line 10.

3. What remembrance changes the speaker's state of mind? The remembrance of the beloved changes the speaker's state of mind.

Interpreting Meanings

4. Show how the turn signals a change in the speaker's tone. What tone does the lark simile add to the poem? After the turn in line 10, the tone changes from a depressed mood to a happy mood. The lark simile, which mentions the songs of the bird "arising" to heaven, reinforces the happy mood of the second part of the sonnet.

5. What is the effect of devoting so many lines in the sonnet to the speaker's mental problems and so few to their cure? Student answers will vary. Some students may suggest that the effect is to indicate that many things may be the cause of depression but that these numerous problems may all be solved by one happy or bracing thought. Other students may suggest that the structure of the sonnet reflects an undertone: that the speaker's happiness, described in so few lines, may be fleeting, especially in the face of so many causes of unhappiness.

Sonnet 30

Responding to the Poem

Analyzing the Poem

Identifying Details

1. What are the various grievances the speaker remembers when he starts thinking? Among these grievances are the following: frustration of the speaker's hopes, the speaker's waste of his "dear time," the deaths of friends, and the woe of love that is "canceled."

What is he describing in line 5? In line 5, he is describing his weeping.

2. What thoughts cheer him up? Thoughts of his friend cheer him up.

3. Where does the turn take place? The turn of the sonnet takes place in line 13.

Interpreting Meanings

4. There are a number of related metaphors in lines 7–14. Identify them, and explain how they are related and how they reinforce what the speaker is saying. The related metaphors appear with the references to "canceled" (line 7), "expense" (line 8), "tell" (line 10), "account" (line 11), "pay" and "paid" (line 12), and "losses" (line 14). These words all refer to financial terms. The metaphors reinforce what the speaker is saying because they constitute, in effect, a single suppressed metaphor: the speaker's thought of the friend brings him a benefit that compensates for all his prior losses.

5. Describe the tone of most of the sonnet. Most of the sonnet has a pessimistic, sober tone.

6. Sonnet 30 is a companion to Sonnet 29, but differs from it in one important respect. What is that difference? The two sonnets are alike in that they both refer to the compensation that the thought of the speaker's beloved brings him. They are different in that in Sonnet 30 the motif of envy or jealousy is absent: the speaker is depressed, not because he envies other people, but because he is conscious of the passage of time.

Sonnet 71

Responding to the Poem

Analyzing the Poem

Identifying Details

1. The speaker gives two reasons for wanting his beloved to forget about him. What are they? The first reason is that the speaker does not wish the memory of himself to cause grief to the beloved. The second reason is that the speaker does not want himself, and the beloved, mocked by the world after his death.

2. Where does the poet use alliteration to create sound effects? Examples of alliteration occur in line 2 ("the surly sullen bell"), line 3 ("warning to the world"), line 4 ("this vile world, with vilest worms"), line 10 ("compounded am with clay"), line 12 ("let your love even with my life"), and line 13 ("the wise world").

William Shakespeare   59

Interpreting Meanings

3. List the descriptive words and phrases that you think make this poem powerful. Student answers will vary. Ask the students to defend their opinions in class.

4. The shift in mood is more subtle than in the preceding sonnets. Where does the turn occur? The turn occurs in line 12.

What mood does the speaker shift into? The speaker shifts into a mood of protectiveness for the beloved.

5. Support of refute this statement: *The speaker of the sonnet is somewhat morbid*. Give evidence from the sonnet. Student answers will vary. Ask the students to give evidence for their opinions.

6. Discuss this statement: *The speaker is using irony when he calls the world "wise" in line 14*. Student answers will vary. Many students will agree that the use of the word is ironic, given the speaker's evidently sincere emotion for the beloved. Ask the students to define how the use of this word may be ironic and to justify their opinions.

Sonnet 73 Text page 344

Responding to the Poem Text page 344
Analyzing the Poem
Identifying Details

1. What three metaphors describe the speaker? The three metaphors compare the speaker to a bare tree in autumn, the twilight after sunset, and the glowing embers of a fire.

2. What should make love even stronger? The beloved's love should become even stronger with the realization that the speaker must die soon.

Interpreting Meanings

3. In what sense can "night" (line 7) be called "Death's second self" (line 8)? "Night" can be called "Death's second self" because of the metaphorical conception of death as an endless void, or night.

4. The idea of line 12 is somewhat compressed. Paraphrase it in your own words, after you have thought about what originally fed ("nourished") the speaker's fires-fires that are now choked ("consumed"). One paraphrase of this line might run as follows: My youth was nourished by love for you, but love for you has extinguished my youth and made me grow old.

5. Where is the turn in this sonnet? What is the logical relationship between the statements coming after the turn and those coming before it? The turn of the sonnet occurs in line 13. The logical relationship is: I am growing old; you are conscious of the fact that I must die soon; and, therefore, you love me even more, because you will soon be without me.

6. How do the seasonal and daily imagery contribute to the tone of this poem? The references to autumn and twilight reinforce the sober, melancholy tone of the sonnet.

Sonnet 116 Text page 345

Responding to the Poem Text page 345
Analyzing the Poem
Identifying Details

1. What metaphors does the speaker use to describe the steadiness of love? In line 5, love is said to be a sea-mark that is not shaken by any tempest; in line 7, love is said to be the star that serves as a steady navigational aid to ships; in line 9, love is said not to be "Time's fool."

2. Where does the speaker define love by what it is *not*, and by what it does *not* do? He defines love this way in lines 2–4 and in lines 9–11.

3. How is time personified in the poem? Time is personified as a reaper with a sickle.

Interpreting Meanings

4. Between which lines does the turn—the change in moods—occur? Describe how the speaker's voice might change. The turn, or change in moods, occurs between lines 12 and 13. Student suggestions as to the change in the speaker's voice will vary.

5. What is the function of the final couplet? The final couplet serves to sum up the theme and to "personalize" the sonnet as a whole, implying that the speaker himself is both a writer and a lover.

6. What single quality of true love does the sonnet emphasize? The sonnet emphasizes the constancy and steadfastness of love.

7. How does the sonnet solve the problem of a disparity in the ages of two lovers, or the death of one of them? Student answers will vary. In general, the emphasis on the steadfastness of love, and of love's immunity to time, helps to solve both of these problems.

8. Do you agree with this definition of love? Explain.
Student answers will vary. Ask the students to support their opinions.

Sonnet 130   Text page 346

Responding to the Poem   Text page 346
Analyzing the Poem
Identifying Details

1. Shakespeare uses the classic objects of comparison in describing his mistress. What are they? The objects of comparison are the sun (for the eyes), coral (for the lips), snow (for the breasts), roses (for the cheeks), perfume (for the breath), and music (for the voice).

Interpreting Meanings

2. Describe what the speaker's mistress might look like. Student descriptions will vary. Ask the students to cite details in the poem to support their descriptions.

3. Some of the ways the speaker chooses to praise his mistress are humorous. Which descriptions did you find comical? How is the sonnet as a whole humorous? Among the comical descriptions are the references to the mistress's hair as ''wires,'' the description of the mistress's breath, and the ironic understatement referring to the mistress treading ''on the ground'' in line 12. The sonnet is humorous on the whole because it reverses conventional romantic conceits.

4. Why is the couplet absolutely necessary, to keep the sonnet from being misunderstood? The couplet shows that the speaker is passionately devoted to his mistress, despite her flaws and imperfections.

Songs   Text page 348

These songs present a lighter, less complex, and somewhat more playful side of Shakespeare, and so make a nice complement to the sonnets. Whereas the sonnets develop the theme of love, this group of songs involves different themes, including the different aspects of winter, the importance of seizing the moment, and nature's miraculous power to transform. Whereas the sonnets all adhere to the same strict poetic form, these songs employ a variety of techniques and forms and rely heavily on *onomatopoeia*, language that sounds like what it means.

Winter   Text page 349

Under the Greenwood Tree   Text page 351

Blow, Blow, Thou Winter Wind   Text page 352

O Mistress Mine   Text page 353

Fear No More the Heat o' the Sun   Text page 354

Full Fathom Five   Text page 356

Objectives

1. To identify and analyze imagery
2. To analyze personification
3. To identify theme
4. To write a song imitating the poet's technique
5. To write a reply to the speaker

The Poems at a Glance

- **Rhyme:** (''Winter'') *ababccdee*
  (''Under the Greenwood Tree'') *aabbcaac*
  (''Blow, Blow, Thou Winter Wind'') *aabccbeeee*
  (''O Mistress Mine'') *aabccb*
  (''Fear No More the Heat o' the Sun'') *ababcc*
  (''Full Fathom Five'') *ababccded*
- **Rhythm:** mixed trochaic
- **Significant techniques:** imagery, personification, theme

Teaching Strategies

Providing for Cultural Differences. These relatively simple lyrics, which express familiar, youthful, and even childlike ideas and feelings, should present few difficulties for the students.

Providing for Different Levels of Ability. Shakespeare's language and diction should be less a problem here than with the sonnets; likewise his imagery, which here is quite direct and simple—winter scenes, birds singing, wind blowing, and so on. Again, with slower readers, much can be gained by reading, or having them read, the problematic passages aloud.

Introducing Vocabulary Study. Students will benefit from knowing the meanings of the following words before they read the poems.
  feign   consummation

Reading the Songs. Tell the students that, unlike the sonnets, these songs on the whole are not about terribly serious ideas or themes but are instead rather playful expressions of ordinary feelings about such things as winter, the joy of being in love, and nature's seemingly magical power to change things. Nevertheless, as with the sonnets and any good poetry, the students will gain the most from their reading by reading slowly, carefully, and more than once.

Arrange, again, to read several of the songs in class, reserving the balance for homework.

Reteaching Alternatives. Have the students reread ''Fear No More the Heat o' the Sun,'' which is the one somewhat complex song in this group. After they have reread the poem, conduct a discussion in which the students analyze its theme and paraphrase the speaker's sentiments.

Winter   Text page 349

Responding to the Poem   Text page 349
Analyzing the Poem
Identifying Details

1. What images does Shakespeare use to help us see and hear this winter scene? What images help us feel the cold? Among the images are the following: the mention of icicles (line 1), the reference to Dick blowing on his nail (line 2), the mentions of logs and frozen milk (lines 3–4), the reference to freezing of the blood and the foul ways (line 5), the blowing wind (line 9), the parson coughing (line 10), the snow (line 11), Marian's red nose (line 12), and the roasted crabs hissing in the bowl (line 13).

Interpreting Meanings

2. The owl's note is said to be merry, although the sound of an owl hooting at night is usually regarded as mournful and melancholy. Perhaps the owl's call seems merry only in contrast to the other wintry images in the poem. What is the general effect of these images? The general effect of the images is to suggest a bleak, unhappy time of year.

3. What is the poet's attitude toward winter? Student answers will vary. In general, the song suggests that the poet regards winter as a time of suffering and difficulty.

4. What does this song tell you about sixteenth-century life? What do you suppose Joan is stirring in that pot? Why do you think she is greasy? Student answers will vary. Ask them to support their suggestions.

Under the Greenwood Tree Text page 351

Responding to the Poem   Text page 351
Analyzing the Poem
Identifying Details

1. Who is the only ''enemy'' in this song? The only ''enemy'' is winter and rough weather.

2. Which images suggest harmony with nature? Among the images that suggest harmony with nature are the sweet bird's song, the mention of the sun, and the specific setting—under the greenwood tree.

Interpreting Meanings

3. Which words or phrases in this song give it a light and upbeat feeling? Students may suggest that the following phrases produce a light and upbeat feeling: ''Come hither, come hither, come hither'' (lines 5 and 13), ''And loves to live i' the sun'' (line 10), and ''pleased with what he gets'' (line 12).

4. What comment does the song make on the life led by the exiles in the forest? The song suggests that life in the forest may be idyllic.

5. Relate this song to Christopher Marlowe's ''The Passionate Shepherd to His Love.'' What do the two works have in common? Student answers will vary. Students should observe that both poems idealize the pastoral setting.

presses opinions on hedonism, ingratitude, pretense, and folly. Ask the students to support their suggestions in class.

5. Samuel Johnson paraphrased lines 4–5 of this song as follows: ''Thy rudeness gives the less pain as thou are not seen, as thou art an enemy that dost not brave us with thy presence, and whose unkindness is therefore not aggravated by insult.'' Explain whether this paraphrase helps you understand lines 4–5. Most students will agree that the paraphrase is more complex than the original.

6. How does the merry-sounding chorus with its nonsense words modify the impression made by the preceding verse? The chorus contrasts with the serious sentiments about human attributes in the preceding verses. Students will differ in their descriptions of the effect created, but most students will agree that Shakespeare is deliberately creating some sort of clash, or paradoxical effect.

Blow, Blow, Thou Winter Wind
Text page 352

Responding to the Poem   Text page 352
Analyzing the Poem
Identifying Details

1. Which aspects of human nature does the singer criticize? The speaker criticizes ingratitude, hypocrisy, and folly.

2. How does the singer compare man's bite with winter's? The speaker says that man's bite is more keen than winter's cold.

3. What details personify the wind and the sky? The wind is personified by being addressed in line 1 and with the mention of the ''tooth'' (line 3) and the ''breath'' (line 6). The sky is personified with the references to its ''bite'' (line 12) and ''sting'' (line 15).

Interpreting Meanings

4. ''Under the Greenwood Tree'' and ''Blow, Blow, Thou Winter Wind'' are probably the first dramatic songs used to characterize the singer, a practice that since Shakespeare's day has been common and expected in musical comedy and opera. What can you deduce from the songs about Amiens's character? Student answers will vary. Some students will suggest that Amiens is something of a philosopher, inclined to see suggestions of human attributes in his natural surroundings. Amiens ex-

---

O Mistress Mine   Text page 353

Responding to the Poem   Text page 353
Analyzing the Poem
Identifying Details

1. To whom is the singer speaking? The speaker is singing to his mistress.

How old is this person? The mistress is twenty years old.

2. In the beginning of the second stanza, the speaker asks ''What is love?'' How is the question answered? The answer describes love as a phenomenon of the present; whatever else it may be, it does not exist in delay or in the uncertain ''hereafter.''

Interpreting Meanings

3. Though the song is not in the form of an argument, as so many invitations to love are, it does include some reasons for loving now rather than later. What are they? The reasons are that the future is unsure and that there is no fulfillment in delay.

4. Explain how Feste's song is not a ''song of good life.'' Use lines from the song to back up your answer. Student answers will vary. The students should point out that a ''song of good life'' would be composed to point up a moral, whereas this song is an invitation to the fulfillment of pleasure in the present.

Fear No More the Heat o' the Sun

Text page 354

Responding to the Poem
Text page 354

Analyzing the Poem

Identifying Details

1. What are the things the dead person can no longer fear? The dead person can no longer fear the summer's heat, the rages of the winter, the displeasure of great tyrants, the lightning and thunder, and slander and disapproval (''censure rash'').

2. According to this dirge, what are the advantages of being dead? What are the dangers? The advantages are that the dead person need not fear all the threats that make human life unpleasant; the dangers are that the dead person might be disturbed by exorcism, witchcraft, and ghosts.

Interpreting Meanings

3. Identify the lines that carry the theme of death as a leveler. Lines 5–6, 11–12, and 17–18 carry this theme.

4. In the famous simile in lines 5–6, what are the connotations of ''golden lads and girls'' and of ''chimney sweepers''? How are they different? The first phrase, ''golden lads and girls,'' carries connotations of wealth, handsomeness, and good luck. The second phrase, ''chimney sweepers,'' carries connotations of humble social status, dirt, poverty, and bad luck.

5. Who are the ''scepter,'' ''learning,'' and ''physic''? The ''scepter'' is a symbol for royalty; ''learning'' suggests those who are learned (perhaps professors); and ''physic'' suggests doctors.

6. The events in *Cymbeline* supposedly take place long before Christianity was introduced into Britain. How does the dirge reflect the time of the play? The dirge reflects the time of the play by mentioning exorcism and witchcraft in lines 19–20, both of which would have been regarded in a different light by Christianity.

Full Fathom Five
Text page 356

Responding to the Poem
Text page 356

Analyzing the Poem

Identifying Details

1. Where does Ariel say Ferdinand's father is? Ariel says that Ferdinand's father lies at the bottom of the sea.

2. What images of sight and sound do you find in the poem? Images of sight and sound include coral (line 2) and pearls (line 3). Images of sound include the ringing of the knell (line 7) and the phrase ''ding-dong'' in lines 8 and 9.

Interpreting Meanings

3. Which lines of this dirge suggest Ariel's playful and cheerful character? Student answers will vary. Some students may mention lines 8–9 as indicative of Ariel's playful character.

4. What examples of alliteration make the first line so interesting? The first line contains alliteration of the *f* sound (''full,'' ''fathom,'' ''five,'' and ''father'') and of the *th* sound (''fathom,'' ''thy,'' and ''father''), as well as of *l* (''full'' and ''lies'').

5. The subject of this dirge, King Alonso, is a thoroughly bad man who, during the course of the play, turns into a good man. What other ''sea change'' takes place in this dirge? The body of Alonso turns from a decaying corpse into a gem-studded, ''rich and strange'' marvel.

The English Language
Text page 357

This special essay focuses on Shakespeare's language and on the differences in pronunciation, grammar, and vocabulary between his English and Modern English. The essay is systematic and thorough, and refers frequently to the text of *Macbeth*. By reading this essay, the students will be better able to return to *Macbeth* with considerably less puzzlement over the language. They will also gain an appreciation of the richness of Shakespeare's language.

Assign the essay as homework. Encourage the students to go back to the text of *Macbeth* and find other examples of the points of Shakespeare's language that are discussed. Then have the students work together on the Analyzing Language assignment that follows the essay.

The biography beginning on page 362 provides a well-rounded summary of Donne's life and achievements. You may wish to reiterate that very little of his poetry was published during his lifetime, though many of his love poems and satires did circulate in manuscript form among the intellectuals of Elizabethan and Jacobean London. After some two hundred years of comparative neglect, Donne's work enjoyed a great resurgence of interest in the twentieth century, sparked by the impact that his style had on the two dominant forces in modern English poetry, W. B. Yeats and T. S. Eliot. Through their work, John Donne has had an inestimable influence on modern writing.

The Elements of Literature
Text page 363

Metaphysical Poetry

Have the students read this brief essay, which makes a good introduction to Donne's poems. The students may find the poetry difficult and even a little strange at first. (You may also want to have the students review other examples of "sweet-sounding" poetry; this would make the contrast with Donne that much sharper.) It is especially important that the students understand the ways in which Donne departed from prevailing styles in poetry. His harshness (even cynicism), colloquialisms, "hard" tone, intellectuality, and often outlandish images and comparisons—all these elements made Donne unusual as a poet and have helped make his poetry timeless.

The Bait
Text page 364

Objectives

1. To understand shifts in syntax
2. To analyze rhyme and meter
3. To write a poem or paragraph centering on an extended conceit
4. To write a comparison of two poems

The Poem at a Glance

- **Rhyme:** couplets
- **Rhythm:** iambic tetrameter
- **Significant techniques:** rhyme, rhythm

Teaching Strategies

Providing for Cultural Differences. Explain that the poem they are about to read is as filled with conscious exaggeration as a tall tale. The speaker's intent is to amuse and charm his love with one extravagant piece of flattery after another.

Providing for Different Levels of Ability. This poem is more accessible than the previous ones by Donne, and most students should be able to handle it on their own.

Reading the Poem. Have students refresh their memories of Marlowe's "The Passionate Shepherd to His Love," and ask them to recall the details of the idyllic life the lover proposes. Explain that they are about to read quite a different poem that begins with the same line. Assign the poem for independent reading either in class or at home.

Reteaching Alternatives. Have students write a response to "The Bait" similar to Raleigh's "The Nymph's Reply to the Shepherd."

Responding to the Poem
Text page 364
Analyzing the Poem
Identifying Details

1. According to the second stanza, how will the river be warmed? The river will be warmed by the woman's eyes.

2. Explain why the lady does not need "deceit." She

does not need deceit because her captivating beauty is sufficient to function as "bait" for the fish.

3. Where in the poem is the syntax or word order of a sentence shifted about to accommodate the rhyme and meter? In line 8, the direct object "themselves" occupies an unusual place in the syntax of the sentence for the sake of the rhyme and meter.

Interpreting Meanings

4. What tone do the adjectives "golden," "crystal," "silken," and "silver" establish for the poem as a whole? These adjectives establish an alluring, almost magical tone for the poem.

5. Why would the woman in the poem be a very desirable companion on a fishing trip? She can catch the fish simply by bathing in the river.

6. Which line of this poem could Shakespeare have been thinking of when he wrote Sonnet 130? Perhaps line 6, "Warmed by thy eyes more than the sun," might have served as the paradigm for Shakespeare's ironic inversion in the first line of Sonnet 130, "My mistress' eyes are nothing like the sun."

7. Explain why the compliment paid to the lady in the last stanza is a rather dubious one. The lady is being complimented on her appearance, but the compliment is negated by its wholesale indictment of all women.

8. Some people regard this poem as cold, clammy, unattractive. Do you agree? Students will have different answers. Ask them to support their assertions.

Song

Text page 365

Objectives

1. To identify hyperbole in the poem

2. To identify the tone of the poem

3. To write a paragraph imitating the hyperbole in the poem

The Poem at a Glance

- **Rhyme:** *ababccddd* in each stanza
- **Rhythm:** mixed iambic
- **Significant technique:** hyperbole

Teaching Strategies

Providing for Cultural Differences. Explain that this cynical poem on the inconstancy of women does not represent a completely different attitude from the idealization of women common in Renaissance poetry. We must assume that the speaker in "Song" has been bitterly disappointed in love; and in lashing out at his love, he includes all women in his indictment. His condemnation of women is just as exaggerated as his earlier idealization.

Providing for Different Levels of Ability. This poem will probably be difficult for all but your best readers to handle independently. You will want to plan to read it aloud and discuss it carefully with most students.

Reading the Poem. Ask students how they have responded to the idealized pictures of women in most of the poems they have read so far in the unit. Point out that the poem they are about to hear takes a very different point of view toward women. Be sure students have read the introduction and the headnote before you read the poem to them.

Reteaching Alternatives. Have students write a paragraph agreeing or disagreeing with Donne's assertion that fidelity and physical beauty cannot coexist in the same women.

Responding to the Poem   Text page 365
Analyzing the Poem
Identifying Details

1. What commands does the speaker make in the first stanza? What do the commands have in common? The commands are: go and catch a falling star (line 1), get with child a mandrake root (line 2), tell me where past years are (line 3), tell me who cleft the devil's foot (line 4), teach me to hear mermaids singing (line 5), teach me how to avoid the sting of envy (line 6), and tell me how to find how an honest mind may advance in the world (lines 7–9). The commands are all linked because the speaker evidently regards them as impossible requests.

2. What does the speaker say about the ideal of a woman both "true" and "fair" in the second stanza? The speaker implies that this ideal can never be fulfilled in reality.

3. What does the speaker say he will not do in the last stanza? Why? He says that even if a woman who is both true and fair is discovered, he will not go on a pilgrimage to see her, because in the interim she will have doubtless been false.

Interpreting Meanings

4. What examples of *hyperbole*, or exaggeration for rhetorical effect, can you find in the poem? Students may mention the following examples: the commands in the first stanza, the reference to ten thousand days and nights (line

12), the mention of "snow white hairs" (line 13), and the implication that the woman will have been false to "two or three" in the last stanza.

5. What song-like qualities does the poem possess, in your view? Student answers will vary. Ask them to defend their opinions in class.

6. How would you describe the speaker's *tone*? Most students will agree that the speaker's tone is rather cynical.

What keeps the song from being offensive in the way it characterizes women? Student answers will vary (some of the students may actually find the song offensive). Ask the students to defend their opinions in class.

A Valediction: Forbidding Mourning

Objectives

1. To paraphrase a simile
2. To analyze rhythm
3. To write a letter of valediction
4. To write an analysis of metaphysical conceits

The Poem at a Glance

- **Rhyme:** *abab* in each stanza
- **Rhythm:** iambic tetrameter
- **Significant techniques:** simile, metaphysical conceits

Teaching Strategies

Providing for Cultural Differences. The comparison in this poem of the poet's soul and that of his wife being like the two legs of a compass, forever joined though parted, may strike your students as strange appearing in a love poem. Explain that this image was also startling to many of Donne's readers in his own day, who were accustomed to bland, unsurprising metaphors.

Providing for Different Levels of Ability. Average and above students should be able to handle the poem alone after a careful reading of the headnote. You will probably want to provide guided reading for less capable students.

Introducing Vocabulary Study. Students will benefit from knowing the meaning of the following word before they read the poem.

profanation

Reading the Poem. Explain that *valediction* means "farewell" and have students discuss the usual tone of songs and poems of farewell that they are familiar with. Instruct all students to read the headnote carefully and then proceed to the reading of the poem. (See Providing for Different Levels of Ability above.)

Reteaching Alternatives. Before assigning "A Critical Response," have students recall the introductory discussion about the general nature of farewells and discuss briefly what keeps the poem from being either excessively grim or overly sentimental. Elicit the notion that the intellectual nature of the imagery (conceits) controls the emotional content. You may wish to direct students to provide an introductory paragraph to A Critical Response (page 367) addressing this question.

Responding to the Poem
Analyzing the Poem
Identifying Details

1. Who is the speaker in this poem? Whom is he addressing, and on what occasion? The speaker is a man who is about to leave his wife because he must go on a journey.

2. Paraphrase the simile in the first two stanzas. One paraphrase might run as follows: Just as virtuous men die in peaceful silence, so now let us say goodbye to each other in silence and tranquility, relying on our secret knowledge that we are a loving couple.

3. How does the speaker distinguish himself and his lover from other couples in the fourth and fifth stanzas? He says that, whereas other couples fear separation, he and his wife are bound by a love that is so strong that it is not affected by physical separation.

4. What are compasses used for? Compasses are used to draw perfect circles.

Explain the conceit Donne uses in the final stanzas, and show how it applies to the couple's situation. Donne compares himself and his wife to the two legs on a pair of compasses; the wife leans toward the husband if he wanders or journeys, but her fixity makes him come home in a "circle just."

Interpreting Meanings

5. What is the point of the references to irregular events on earth and irregular events in the spheres (or outer space) in lines 9–12? What kind of event is like the separation of the lovers? These references—to earthquakes and to irregular movements of the celestial spheres—underscore the trauma that "dull sublunary lovers" feel in the event of separation.

6. Why does the speaker insist that the lovers—obviously two people—are actually one? He insists that they are actually one in order to emphasize the sense of union, harmony, and trust that he feels with his beloved.

7. Comment on the way these words are used in the poem: "melt" (line 5); "inter-assured" (line 19, a coinage of Donne's); "airy thinness" (line 24). Student answers will vary. Ask the students to support their comments in class. In general, these expressions reinforce the concept of love as a refined, trusting, interdependent union of two lovers.

8. How does Donne enliven the stanzas on the compasses, so that they do not become mechanical? Again, student answers will vary. Students may point to the techniques of enjambment and syncopated rhythm as enlivening aspects of these stanzas.

9. Comment on rhythm of the poem. The rhythm is predominantly iambic tetrameter. However, Donne introduces unexpected rhythmic irregularities at numerous points in the poem.

10. How does the attitude toward the lover here contrast with the attitude in "Song"? In "Song," the speaker's attitude is cynical about ever finding a lady who is fair and true. In "A Valediction," the speaker evidently loves and trusts his beloved.

11. How would you describe the personality of the speaker of this poem? Does the poem give you any hints? Student answers will vary. Ask the students to support their portraits of the speaker with specific references to the poem.

Meditation 17

Text page 368

Objectives

1. To recognize and analyze significant metaphors

2. To identify main ideas

3. To identify and explain tone

4. To write an analysis of metaphors

5. To use context clues to determine the meanings of unfamiliar words

Introducing the Meditation   Text page 368

***B**ackground on the Meditation.*   The headnote that preceeds this selection informs the students that the meditations

were a series of compositions that Donne wrote on the occasion of a near-fatal illness. You may wish to tell the students that the meditations are part of a larger work called *Devotions Upon Emergent Occasions* (published in 1624). This work is organized in twenty-three sections, each consisting of a "meditation," an "expostulation," and a "prayer." Overall, the work traces the progress of the disease and its eventual cure, draws extraordinary analogies between the poet's own illness and the general spiritual illness of all humankind, and powerfully delineates the theme of universal brotherhood.

Teaching Strategies

***P**roviding for Cultural Differences.*   The meditation as a literary form is little used today and will be unfamiliar to most students. To make it less intimidating to students, you might compare it to a reflective journal entry or a personal essay.

Providing for Different Levels of Ability. Mature students and good readers will have no difficulty reading the selection independently. Others, however, will need guided reading and some additional help with vocabulary.

Introducing Vocabulary Study. Remind students that context—surrounding phrases and sentences—often provides useful clues to an unfamiliar word's meaning. Instruct students, as they read ''Meditation 17,'' to be on the lookout for such clues.

Reading the Selection. Have students discuss types of situations that might cause great concern. What thoughts and fears arise at such times? Explain that the selection that they are about to read was written by Donne during a serious illness. Assign the meditation as independent or guided reading as suggested in Providing for Different Levels of Ability above.

Reteaching Alternatives. Have students discuss what positive meanings tend to be associated with the sound of bells. If possible, read them Poe's poem, ''The Bells,'' and have them note the particular images and sound devices the poet uses to achieve his effects.

Responding to the Meditation
Text page 369
Analyzing the Meditation
Identifying Facts

1. What sound prompts the speaker to begin his meditation? The sound that prompts him to begin is the tolling of a bell for a funeral.

2. List the metaphors used to show that the speaker is part of all humanity and not an isolated individual. Among the metaphors that show the speaker is part of all humanity are the following: the comparison of the speaker to a part of the body of which Christ is the Head; the metaphor comparing the speaker to a page in a book that God has translated; the comparison of every man to a piece of the continent; and the comparison of another man's affliction to gold, which is then transferred to the speaker.

3. Why does the speaker feel that affliction is a treasure? In what ways is tribulation like money? Affliction is a treasure because it helps us to get nearer to our ultimate home, heaven.

Interpreting Meanings

4. How would you explain what Donne means by saying ''the bell . . . tolls for thee''? He intends to remind us that we must all die, and that the death of another person should serve as a visible reminder to us of that fact.

5. What are Donne's main ideas in this meditation? Do you agree with all of them? Donne's main ideas include the following: We are all interconnected; we all must die; we must not resent affliction; tribulation helps us to get to heaven. Student opinions of these ideas will vary.

6. Do you think any lines from this meditation should have particular relevance to life in the late twentieth century? Explain. Student answers will vary. Ask the students to support and defend their opinions.

7. How would you describe the speaker's tone? Is it depressed, angry, resigned, or something else? The speaker's tone might be described as dignified and optimistic.

What beliefs and values account for this tone? The speaker evidently holds profoundly religious values, including a belief in the afterlife and in divine protection and mercy.

Extending the Meditation

Have students devise their own analogies to express the place of the individual in society, or the fundamental relationship between each individual and the rest of humankind. Suggest to the students they they first define clearly for themselves what that relationship is, and then go on to imagine a comparison that encompasses the relationship.

At the Round Earth's Imagined Corners
Text page 371

Objectives

1. To analyze the function of the octave

2. To analyze function of the sestet

3. To identify shifts in sound

4. To contrast the speaker with that in other poems by the author

John Donne 69

The Poem at a Glance

- **Rhyme:** *abbaabbacdcdee*
- **Rhythm:** iambic pentameter
- **Significant technique:** Petrarchan sonnet

Teaching Strategies

Providing for Cultural Differences. Explain that in the Bible (Revelation 7:1), it is said that Judgment Day will begin with four angels standing at the four corners of the earth and holding back the winds. Donne describes the earth's corners as "Imagined" out of deference to the knowledge that the earth is a sphere.

Providing for Different Levels of Ability. Slower readers and less mature students will certainly need help with this sonnet. However, because of the enjambment (See Reteaching Alternatives below), all students will benefit from hearing the poem read by a competent reader.

Reading the Poem. Have students read the headnote to Donne's sonnets on page 370. Ask them to skim the sonnet on the opposite page, noting the rhyme scheme. Then ask them to determine if the sonnet is a Petrarchan sonnet or a Shakespearean sonnet. Ask also what criteria they used to arrive at this answer. Once they have determined that this is a Petrarchan sonnet, ask what expectations they have about the poet's arrangement of ideas within the fourteen lines.

Have the students discuss briefly what they know about Christian beliefs concerning the end of the world and Judgment Day. Have students read the introductory material and the headnote privately and then follow along as you or an outstanding student reader reads the poem aloud.

Reteaching Alternatives. Unlike sonnets students have read earlier, Donne does not always end a thought at the end of a line or even after a pair of lines. Rather, he often carries a thought from one line to the next, using a device called *enjambment*. Have students analyze how the use of this device affects the sound and meaning of the poem.

Responding to the Poem   Text page 371
Analyzing the Poem
Identifying Details

1. Whom does the speaker address in the octave of the sonnet? In the octave of the sonnet, the speaker addresses the angels; he bids them blow their trumpets to signal the day of the Last Judgment.

Whom does he address in the sestet? In the sestet, he addresses Christ.

2. Where does the speaker change his mind in the sonnet? How does Donne use the sonnet form to signal this change of mind? The speaker changes his mind in line 9. He uses the structure of the octave and sestet to signal this change of mind.

3. To what event does the speaker refer in the last line? He refers to Christ's redemption of humanity through the crucifixion.

Whom is he addressing here? He is addressing Christ.

Interpreting Meanings

4. Essentially, the poem is a plea for more time. Time for what? The speaker pleads for more time so that he can repent of his sins.

5. Explain how the sound of the poem changes as it moves from its beginning to its end. The sound in the first eight lines is bright and syncopated, as the speaker conjures up the sound of the angels' trumpet and the list of those who are dead. In the last six lines, the sound becomes more fluid and somber.

6. How would you contrast the sensibility of the speaker here to the sensibility of the speaker in "Song" or "The Sun Rising"? Is it difficult for you to imagine that these poems are all the work of the same author? Explain why or why not. Student answers will vary. Ask the students to defend their opinions in class.

Death Be Not Proud   Text page 372

Objectives

1. To explain a metaphor
2. To explain the central paradox of the poem
3. To compare two sonnets on the same subject

The Poem at a Glance

- **Rhyme:** *abbaabbacddcee*
- **Rhythm:** iambic pentameter
- **Significant technique:** paradox

Teaching Strategies

Providing for Cultural Differences. Point out that personifying death, as Donne does in this poem, has a long history. Paul wrote in I Corinthians, ''O death where is thy sting?'' In the art of the Middle Ages, death was often represented by a skeleton. Explain that personification is a kind of metaphor in which an idea is talked about as though it were a person.

Providing for Different Levels of Ability. After students' experience with the previous sonnet, most should be able to read this one on their own. Be sure students have read the headnote, and remind them to refer to the glosses as needed.

Reading the Poem. Discuss contemporary attitudes toward death and an afterlife. Have students speculate as to why death may seem less fearful to one who holds a belief in some form of life after death. Then assign the poem for private reading.

Reteaching Alternatives. Provide students with copies of the Dylan Thomas poem mentioned in the headnote. Have them compare the two poems.

Responding to the Poem   Text page 372

Analyzing the Poem

Identifying Details

1. According to the poem, why should death not be proud? Death should not be proud because those whom death overthrows do not really die.

Whom must death serve as a slave? Death must serve fate, chance, kings, and desperate men.

2. Show how, as the sonnet develops, the speaker shifts the grounds of his attack on death. In the first part of the sonnet, the speaker says that death may actually be a source of relief to mankind, since it offers rest, sleep, and release from the cares of the world. However, in the last two lines, the grounds of the attack change: here, the speaker positively affirms that death is the gateway to eternal life.

Interpreting Meanings

3. Explain how rest and sleep are the ''pictures'' of death (line 5). By ''pictures,'' Donne means ''imitations'' here; rest and sleep resemble death because a sleeping person might be said to resemble a dead person.

4. The sonnet seems to involve a paradox or contradiction: Those who die do not die, but *Death* itself will die. Explain how the paradox can be resolved. Student answers may vary. One explanation of the paradox might be as follows: Death does not really conquer us, since death is a prelude to eternal life. Therefore, death itself is really a false concept.

5. What book uses this poem's opening lines as its title? How is the title appropriate to that book? The book is John Gunther's account of his son's heroic battle against cancer. The title is appropriate insofar as John Gunther Jr. had his whole life ahead of him, and his untimely early demise was, in a sense, a loss for the entire race.

Batter My Heart   Text page 373

Objectives

1. To explain a simile
2. To analyze imagery
3. To discuss use of imagery
4. To identify a paradox
5. To write an analysis of rhythm and other sound effects

The Poem at a Glance

- **Rhyme:** *abbaabbacdcdee*
- **Rhythm:** iambic pentameter
- **Significant technique:** alliteration

Teaching Strategies

Providing for Cultural Differences. Some students may not be familiar with the concept of the Trinity, referred to in line 1 as ''three-personed God.'' According to orthodox Christian doctrine, three divine persons-Father, Son, and Holy Spirit-are united in one God.

Providing for Different Levels of Ability. All students should be able to read this sonnet on their own. However, less mature students will need considerable help in unraveling the poem's true meaning. In addition to careful discussion of the questions in Analyzing the Poem, some groups may require a line-by-line analysis.

Introducing Vocabulary Study. Students will benefit from knowing the meanings of the following words before they read the poem.

    enthral   ravish

Reading the Poem. Discuss situations the students may be familiar with in which someone feels overcome by the inability to change a behavior alone. Consider whether extreme measures are sometimes needed for change to come about. Average students and above can then read the poem independently while you work with slower or less mature students.

Reteaching Alternatives. Have students develop another metaphor for change and reformation (a potter with clay, a weaver, a glassblower or silversmith, etc.). Have them begin with an imperative sentence of direct address to the transforming agent and then work out the details of the metaphor and how the change is to be accomplished. (The final product need not be a poem.)

Responding to the Poem   Text page 373

Analyzing the Poem

Identifying Details

1. What does the speaker ask God to do to him? The speaker asks God to batter his heart, to imprison him, and to ravish him.

2. Explain the simile in line 5. This simile compares the speaker to a town that has been besieged and captured by an usurper.

Where else in the poem does the image of the siege of a town seem appropriate? This image could appropriately be applied to the reference to "captivated" reason in lines 7 and 8.

Interpreting Meanings

3. Comment on the poem's use of alliteration. Student comments will vary. They should note the following examples of alliteration: "break, blow, burn" (line 4), "dearly I love you, and would be loved fain" (line 9), and "nor ever chaste, except you ravish me" (line 14).

4. How does Donne use paradox throughout the sonnet? Paradoxes abound in the sonnet. In line 3, for example, the speaker asks God to overthrow him so that he can rise and stand; in line 4, he asks God to break, blow, and burn him to make him new. In lines 9 and 10, the speaker says he dearly loves God but that he is betrothed to God's "enemy" (Satan). In the final two lines there are two paradoxes: God must imprison the speaker to make him free and must ravish him to make him chaste.

5. Why is God "three-personed" in line 1? This epithet refers to the Christian belief in the Holy Trinity: God is three persons (Father, Son, and Holy Spirit) in one God.

Who is the "enemy" in line 10? The enemy is Satan.

6. Does this seem like the prayer of a weak person or of a strong person, in your view? Explain your answer. Student answers will vary. Most students will agree that the vigor of the imagery makes the poem seem like that of a strong person. Other students may add that only a strong person would have the courage to admit his moral weaknesses the way the speaker does in the poem.

Ben Jonson   Text page 374

On My First Son   Text page 377

Objectives

1. To recognize and analyze irony
2. To evaluate an assertion in the poem
3. To write a response to the poem's theme

The Poem at a Glance

- **Rhyme:** couplets
- **Rhythm:** iambic pentameter
- **Significant technique:** irony

Teaching Strategies

Providing for Cultural Differences. Because in Jonson's time large loans were often made for seven years, Jonson was able to use the idea of a loan as the metaphor for his son's seven years of life.

Providing for Different Levels of Ability. Jonson's poetry will seem quite straightforward, particularly immediately after Donne. Given the background information in the headnotes, all students should be able to read the poem independently.

Reading the Poem. This entire short section on Ben Jonson makes an ideal homework assignment. The introduction beginning on page 374 and the headnotes on page 376 provide all necessary background information, and the poems themselves are quite direct. Use the Responding to the Poem sections to check students' understanding.

Reteaching Alternatives. In other poems that they have read earlier in the unit, students have encountered the notion of achieving immortality for another through poetry. Have students write a paragraph agreeing or disagreeing with this concept.

Responding to the Poem   Text page 377

Analyzing the Poem
Identifying Details

1. What comfort does Jonson provide himself in lines 7-8? Is this comfort sufficient to make him "lose all father"? Jonson gives himself the comfort that at least his son has avoided the ills of old age. Students will differ on the question of whether this consolation is a sufficient compensation for the speaker's losing all sense of fatherhood.

Interpreting Meanings

2. Why can the early death of a boy named *Benjamin* be regarded as ironic? Because the name "Benjamin" means "lucky," the early death of a boy with this name might be regarded as unexpected and therefore ironic.

3. Jonson borrowed some of the poem's features from Latin works: the direct address to the boy in line 9 and the first three words of the epitaph or inscription, "Here doth lie. . . ." But the idea that the son is his best poem is original with Jonson. What do you think of this statement? Student answers will vary. Ask the students to support their opinions in class.

Song: To Celia   Text page 378

Song: Still to Be Neat   Text page 379

Objectives

1. To understand the basic metaphors in the poem
2. To identify a pronoun referent
3. To write a response to a main idea

The Poems at a Glance

- **Rhyme:** ("To Celia") *abcbabcb* in each stanza ("Still to Be Neat") couplets in two six-line stanzas
- **Rhythm:** iambic tetrameter in both poems

Teaching Strategies

Providing for Cultural Differences. Point out that *wreath* and *wreathe* in "To Celia" and *drest* and *feast* in "Still to Be Neat" were good rhymes for Johson's day; changes in pronunciation have given them different sounds today.

Providing for Different Levels of Ability. Students should have no difficulty reading these poems independently.

Reading the Poems. If you have not assigned the entire section as a single assignment, have students read at least the two songs together, either in class or as homework.

Reteaching Alternatives. Have the students consider both the idealized goddess-like woman in "To Celia," whose mere breath can turn a wreath into a growing thing, and the simplicity and naturalness expected of women in "Still to Be Neat." Have them write a paragraph giving a composite of what Jonson's ideal woman might be like.

Analyzing the Poem

Interpreting Meanings

1. Explain how a woman might drink to a man with her eyes and how a man could "pledge" himself to her with his eyes in return. The expression relies on a common figure of speech: the meeting of lovers' eyes conveys their desire and pledge of faithfulness to each other.

2. What does "thine" refer to in line 8? "Thine" refers to the lady's "nectar," or, by extension, to her love.

3. Why did the speaker send the wreath? The speaker sent the wreath in the hope that it would not be withered if it were in the presence of his beloved.

What powers does he attribute to Celia? He attributes to Celia the magical powers of keeping the wreath forever fresh.

4. How did Celia transform the wreath? Celia breathed on the wreath and sent it back to the lover; now it smells of her.

Analyzing the Poem

Identifying Details

1. What does the speaker presume about a woman who is always neat and dressed up? He presumes that such a woman is unchaste.

2. What kind of "look" does the speaker prefer? He prefers a more natural, free, and simple "look."

Interpreting Meanings

3. What is the "art" in line 11? The "art" probably refers to cosmetics.

4. What does "they" refer to in line 12? "They" probably refers to the "adulteries" (or "cheats") of "art": namely, makeup and elaborate clothes and hair styles.

5. Where does Jonson show he may have known the old proverb, "He who always smells good doesn't smell good"? Lines 5 and 6 perhaps imply that Jonson was familiar with the proverb.

6. What connotations of the word *adulteries* do you think Jonson might have expected his readers to recognize? Student answers will vary. Jonson might have expected his readers to recognize at least two connotations: a) marital infidelities, and b) the "mixtures" in which cosmetics were prepared at the time.

Robert Herrick   Text page 380

Delight in Disorder   Text page 382

Objectives

1. To identify and explain oxymoron
2. To analyze a poem's message
3. To write a parody
4. To write a comparison of two poems

The Poem at a Glance

- **Rhyme:** couplets
- **Rhythm:** iambic tetrameter
- **Significant technique:** oxymoron

Teaching Strategies

Providing for Cultural Differences. Though students may be unfamiliar with the details of dress in the Renaissance, they certainly are aware that different kinds of clothing can produce different "looks" and suggest different attitudes and lifestyles. A picture of a seventeenth-century lady in full formal dress may be a useful introduction to the poem.

Providing for Different Levels of Ability. Given the material provided in the headnote and the glosses, students should have no problems reading this poem on their own.

Introducing Vocabulary Study. Students will benefit from knowing the meaning of the following word before they read the poem.

tempestuous

Reading the Poem. Discuss with the students various patterns of dress from formal through casual to sloppy, from preppy to punk. Point out how fashions change and elicit the idea that even the most casual results can sometimes involve a calculated attempt to create the desired look. After a brief discussion, have the students read the poem on their own.

Reteaching Alternatives. Have students take the Puritan attitude and write a refutation of the poem beginning "A careful order in the dress."

Responding to the Poem　　Text page 382
Analyzing the Poem
Identifying Details

1. What is the effect of a slightly disordered dress? The effect is to kindle sexiness, or "wantonness" (line 2).

Interpreting Meanings

2. This poem makes use of a figure of speech called oxymoron. This is a group—usually a pair—of words that seem contradictory; *cruel kindness* is often given as an example. Find the oxymoron in: "Delight in Disorder." How does it sum up the poem's message? The oxymoron occurs in line 12 in the phrase "wild civility." The phrase sums up the poem's message by compressing the opposites of which the poet speaks: disorder and delight, carelessness and precision, naturalness and art.

To the Virgins, to Make Much of Time　　Text page 385

Objectives

1. To identify an image
2. To write a paragraph describing a situation that may have occasioned the poem
3. To write a response to the poem

The Poem at a Glance

- **Rhyme:** *abab* in each stanza
- **Rhythm:** iambic tetrameter alternating with iambic trimeter
- **Significant technique:** image

Teaching Strategies

Providing for Cultural Differences. Your students' attitudes toward their future and their expectations and goals will greatly color their attitude toward this poem. Girls' responses will be affected by whether they plan careers or early marriage; boys' by the qualities they value and admire in women. The question of what constitutes a woman's "prime" and the place of marriage in a woman's life may provoke some lively discussion.

Providing for Different Levels of Ability. Less mature students and less capable readers may benefit from hearing the poem read aloud and from discussing the content after each stanza. Average and better students can proceed on their own.

Reading the Poem. Have students respond to the saying "Time flies" and what it means to them. Then proceed according to the suggestions in Providing for Different Levels of Ability above.

Reteaching Alternatives. Have the students contemplate other reasons individuals might be prompted to take advantage of their youth. Have students present some of these ideas to the class in a brief address.

Responding to the Poem　　Text page 385
Analyzing the Poem
Identifying Details

1. What warning does the speaker give the virgins in the first stanza? The speaker warns the virgins that the same flower that blooms today will be dying tomorrow.

2. What solar image does he use to enforce his point in the second stanza? He says that the higher the sun mounts in the sky, the nearer it is to its setting.

3. How does the speaker feel about age in the third stanza? He says that the best age is the first, when youth and blood are warm.

4. What warning does he sign off with? He tells the virgins not to be coy but to go and get married; having lost their prime, the girls may be out of luck-in other words, they may never get married.

Interpreting Meanings

5. Which line of the poem seems to reflect Herrick's profession as a priest? Perhaps line 14, ''go marry,'' might reflect the poet's profession as a priest.

6. How would you respond to Herrick's urgent advice? Student answers will vary. Encourage them to discuss the theme of *carpe diem* (''seize the day''), of which this poem is one of the most notable Renaissance examples.

George Herbert

Virtue

Text page 387

Objectives

1. To recognize the relationship of the title to the poem

2. To paraphrase the last stanza

3. To identify figures of speech

The Poem at a Glance

· **Rhyme:** *abab* in each stanza
· **Rhythm:** mixed iambic
· **Significant technique:** repetition of key words

Teaching Strategies

Providing for Cultural Differences. Although mortality and the ravages of time do not ordinarily concern most high-school students, by now students should have developed some acceptance of these themes in Renaissance poetry. This poem reiterates the belief that all earthly things must die and that only spiritual qualities last forever.

Providing for Different Levels of Ability. The poem should not pose any reading problems, but an oral reading by a good reader will make students more aware of its lyrical elements. Be sure all students have read the introductory material on Herbert on page 386.

Introducing Vocabulary Study. Instruct students to remain alert, as they read, for instances of figurative language. Direct them, in particular, to pay attention to the poet's use of simile and metaphor.

Reading the Poem. Have students recall the notion of immortality as treated in Donne's sonnets. Explain that the poem they are about to hear is a variation on that theme. Then read the poem aloud so students can appreciate its musical qualities.

Reteaching Alternatives. Have students analyze, either in writing or through discussion, the language of the poem—the sounds, repetition, and refrain that contribute to its songlike quality.

Responding to the Poem   Text page 387
Analyzing the Poem
Identifying Details

1. What examples does the speaker give to prove his statement that ''all must die''? The speaker mentions the day, which must die at night; the rose; and the spring. In the last stanza, he alludes to the world turning ''to coal''—namely, being consumed by fire on the day of the Last Judgment.

2. According to the last stanza, what kind of soul will live forever? The sweet and virtuous soul will live forever.

Interpreting Meanings

3. What does the title add to the message of the poem? The title reinforces the theme—that virtue is a spiritual, rather than a physical or worldly, matter.

76   Unit Three: The Renaissance

4. How would you paraphrase the last stanza? One paraphrase might run as follows: A virtuous soul, like seasoned wood, endures for eternity, even after the day of reckoning and the destruction of the world at the Last Judgment.

5. What is the effect of the twist in the last line of the last stanza? How is it different from the final lines of the other stanzas? The twist derives from the fact that this line stresses life, rather than death. The effect is to reinforce the poet's optimistic prediction about the rewards of virtue in this life: the virtuous soul will survive the destruction of this earth and will live forever.

6. Many poems on the passage of time end with the advice, "Let us eat, drink, and be merry, for tomorrow we die"—or words to that effect. How does Herbert's poem differ from these others? Herbert's poem differs in that it commends exactly the opposite course: the speaker counsels that true rewards are to be gained through virtue, rather than through the indulgence of ephemeral pleasures.

The Altar

Text page 388

Objectives

1. To interpret the central metaphor of the poem

2. To understand the metaphysical conceit

3. To write a picture poem

The Poem at a Glance

- **Rhyme:** couplets
- **Rhythm:** mixed iambic
- **Significant techniques:** metaphor, picture poem

Teaching Strategies

Providing for Cultural Differences. Although this poem is somewhat more formal—including having meter and rhyme—than other picture poems students may be familiar with, they should be able to see clearly the relationship of the shape to the title. You might use some contemporary picture poems to introduce the concept before students read this poem.

Providing for Different Levels of Ability. Average students and above should be able to manage the poem on their own. However, you will need to work closely with less capable students.

Reading the Poem. Have students discuss experiences they may have had with poems whose shape suggests an object or idea. Point out that while most people think such poems are quite modern, their antecedents go back to the seventeenth century. Then proceed to the reading of the poem.

Reteaching Alternatives. Before assigning Writing About the Poem, assemble a collection of books of picture poetry for students to examine. Include, if you can, other examples of Herbert's picture poems, such as his "Easter Wings." Have each student choose one picture poem to compare and contrast with "The Altar."

Responding to the Poem   Text page 388
Analyzing the Poem
Identifying Details

1. What is the speaker's altar made of? The altar is made of a heart, cemented by tears.

2. According to the speaker, what alone can "cut" a stony heart? The only thing that can cut a stony heart is the power of the Lord.

3. What is the purpose of the altar the speaker is building? The speaker is building the altar in order to praise the Lord's name.

Interpreting Meanings

4. When does it become apparent to you that the altar is the poem? Student answers will differ. Many students will suggest that the peculiar shape of the poem plants this possibility in the reader's mind at the very beginning.

What does the speaker mean, metaphorically, by the stones in line 14? He may mean the parts of his heart (referred to in lines 9–10); or perhaps he means his poems.

5. Why might an altar of "hewn stone" be less acceptable than one made of natural stones that are not chipped away at? On the metaphorical level, an altar of natural stones might represent a pure and natural love of God, unsullied by any sin; an altar of "hewn stones" would represent the love of God that comes about as a result of human repentance for sin and of the Lord's power.

6. Of someone lacking in compassion, we say that he or she has "a heart of stone." What are the ways in which Herbert plays with that idea? Student answers will vary.

The students should mentions Herbert's theme of the refractory human heart—at least where the love of God is concerned.

The Pulley

Text page 389

Objectives

1. To analyze multiple meanings of a word
2. To interpret the relationship of the title to the poem
3. To write a paragraph supporting the poem's main idea

The Poem at a Glance

- **Rhyme:** *ababba* in each stanza
- **Rhythm:** mixed iambic

Teaching Strategies

Providing for Cultural Differences. The poem rests on the belief that all people have is a gift from God. Although this belief may not be personally shared by all students, by now most will recognize it as consistent with the beliefs of Renaissance society.

Providing for Different Levels of Ability. It is unlikely that any but your very best students will be able to handle this poem on their own. It is best to plan on a careful guided reading in class.

Introducing Vocabulary Study. Students will benefit from knowing the meaning of the following word before they read the poem.

   repining

Reading the Poem. Plan to read the poem aloud to the class. With less mature students, it will be best to pause after each stanza to get responses to the questions in Analyzing the Poem. Then plan to reread the poem aloud in its entirety to give students a sense of the complexity of the whole.

Reteaching the Poem. Have students select another gift that God might have withheld instead. What might have been His reason for doing so? How would it have affected people? Have students work out the details in a brief paragraph or poem.

Responding to the Poem   Text page 389
Analyzing the Poem
Identifying Details

1. According to stanza 1, what did God do for man? God poured a glass of blessings on him and gave him the world's riches.

2. According to stanza 2, what specific riches did he pour into man? He gave man strength, beauty, wisdom, honor, and pleasure.

3. Why didn't God bestow His "jewel" on man? He did not bestow His "jewel"—rest—on man because He believed that man might adore His gifts instead of Him.

4. Why, according to the last stanza, did God make man "rich and weary" with "repining restlessness"? God did this in order to insist that weariness—if not goodness—would cause man to turn back to Him.

Interpreting Meanings

5. The word *rest*, as it is used in this poem, has two possible meanings: the simple one, "remainder," and a more complex one containing the ideas of peace, repose, satisfaction, absence of restlessness, and the like. Locate all the places in the poem where *rest* is used. Where in the poem does *rest* have the simple meaning? Where the more complex one? In line 16, the word has the simple meaning. In lines 10 and 14, the word has the complex meaning.

6. Why, according to the poem, does God not give human beings "rest" in the complex sense? God does not give human beings "rest" in the complex sense because He suspects that human beings may become complacent and idolatrous.

7. Explain the connnection between the poem and the title. Student answers will vary. In general, the title suggests a reciprocal, or oscillating, movement—mirrored in turn by God's vision of human beings as "repining" and "restless," and as ultimately turning back to Him, their Creator.

Sir John Suckling
Richard Lovelace

Objectives

1. To identify tone

2. To support a personal response to a poem

The Poems at a Glance

- **Rhyme:** ("Out Upon It!") *abab*
  ("Why So Pale and Wan, Fond Lover?") *ababb*
- **Rhythm:** mixed trochaic in both poems
- **Significant technique:** tone

Teaching Strategies

Providing for Cultural Differences. To prepare students for the conversational tone of the poems, have them suggest songs they are familiar with in which the lyrics are addressed to another person, rather than simply spoken about the subject of the song.

Providing for Different Levels of Ability. Given the material in the introduction and the headnotes, students should have no difficulty with these poems.

Reading the Poems. The Suckling material makes an ideal homework assignment. You may also include Lovelace if think your students can handle both poems. Using the Responding to the Poem material for in-class discussion will ensure that students have understood the poems.

Reteaching Alternatives. Have the students look up cavalier in a standard collegiate dictionary. Then have them

write a paragraph explaining in how many different senses this word (capitalized and otherwise) is applicable to Suckling.

Responding to the Poems Text page 391
Analyzing the Poems
Interpreting Meanings

1. It has been said of "Out Upon It!" that in the very act of claiming his devotion and constancy, the speaker gives us good reasons to doubt that he is temperamentally capable of either. Where, in the poem, are these "good reasons" to be found? Students may cite the first stanza, in which the speaker seems amazed that he has been faithful for three whole days! He also says that he will love for three more, if there is fair weather. In the last stanza, the speaker alludes to the dozen ladies he might have loved instead of his mistress.

2. What advice does the speaker give the pale lover? What is his tone? He tells the lover to quit his suit, since nothing but herself will make the mistress love. His tone is practical and down-to-earth.

3. This poems lacks interesting metaphors and similes, and it is barren of other poetic devices and decorations. What, then, makes it a likeable poem? (How did you respond to it?) Students may cite the effects of rhythm, rhyme, repetition, parallelism, and the surprise ending. Student responses to the poem will differ. Ask the students to support and defend their opinions in class.

Objectives

1. To explain paradoxes

2. To identify a message

3. To write a reply from Lucasta

4. To write an essay relating a poem to current events

The Poems at a Glance

- **Rhyme:** ("To Lucasta . . .") *abab* in each stanza ("To Althea . . .") *ababcdcd* in each stanza
- **Rhythm:** mixed iambic in both poems
- **Significant technique:** paradox

Teaching Strategies

Providing for Cultural Differences. Both poems are about separation, one anticipated and the other enforced. To get the students into the right frame of mind, you might have them recall poems or songs about separation that they may be familiar with.

Providing for Different Levels of Ability. Once students have read the headnotes as background, they should have no difficulty reading both poems on their own at a single setting.

Introducing Vocabulary Study. Students will benefit from knowing the meaning of the following word before they read the poem.

   inconstancy

Reading the Poems. If you did not assign these poems along with Suckling, you may wish to make them a separate homework assignment, since they require little, if any, explication.

Reteaching Alternatives. Have students compare Suckling and Lovelace in their attitudes toward women, love, fidelity, and honor. All statements should be supported with evidence from the poems.

Responding to the Poem   Text page 392
Analyzing the Poem
Identifying Details

1. What new mistress is the speaker about to chase? He goes to chase the first foe he meets on the battlefield.

2. Instead of Lucasta, what is he about to embrace? He is going to embrace a sword, a horse, and a shield.

3. Why will Lucasta adore his inconstancy, or unfaithfulness? She will adore his unfaithfulness because it is a sign of his honor.

Interpreting Meanings

4. The poem implies the paradox that inconstancy (line 9) is really constancy, that loyalty to a woman is dependent on loyalty to something else. Explain these paradoxes. The paradoxes are all resolved in the last stanza, where the speaker says that he could not love the mistress so much if he did not love honor more. His departure for the battlefield (or "inconstancy") results from his sense of honor and loyalty to duty.

5. Can you find in the poem evidence for believing that Lucasta has the same values as the speaker and will therefore not whine or scold him for leaving her? Most students will point to the speaker's confident assurance that Lucasta still loves him as evidence that she, too, has the same values.

Responding to the Poem   Text page 393
Analyzing the Poem
Identifying Details

1. In stanzas 1–3, the last two lines make a comparison. What two things are being compared in each stanza? In the first stanza, the lovers are compared to birds that play in the air. In the second stanza, they are compared to fishes in the deep. In the third stanza, the speaker is compared to winds.

Interpreting Meanings

2. What message is the speaker sending Althea from prison? He sends the message that, despite his literal imprisonment, he is really free in his heart and mind.

3. How would you explain line 6? The phrase "fettered to her eye" means that the speaker has eyes for Althea alone and is, figuratively speaking, "chained" to her glance.

4. The poem's most famous lines, lines 25-26, state a paradox. What is it? Explain why the prisoner does not feel imprisoned. The paradox is the apparent contradiction between freedom and imprisonment. Although the speaker is literally imprisoned, he feels free because he may still love Althea and praise his king.

5. According to the implication made in the poem, what *does* make a prison? How do you feel about this idea? The poem implies that infidelity and disloyalty make a prisoner of the person who commits them. Student opinions will vary.

The King James Bible

In teaching these excerpts from the Bible, you may find it helpful to read, or have volunteers read, passages aloud (after the students have read the passages silently at least once). This practice will help the students hear the distinctive rhythms of the prose. Hearing these rhythms will, in turn, help the students better understand the ideas conveyed in the Bible.

Objectives

1. To recall and interpret details from the narrative
2. To understand foreshadowing
3. To infer aspects of human nature from the narrative

Introducing the Narrative

- **Point of view:** third person
- **Significant technique:** foreshadowing

Teaching Strategies

Providing for Cultural Differences. It is important to make clear to the students that they are being asked to read these excerpts from the Bible as examples of the high literary quality of the King James Bible, not as doctrines proposed for their belief. Regardless of students' individual religious backgrounds and beliefs, most will be familiar with the account of Creation given in Genesis.

Providing for Different Levels of Ability. Familiarity with the basic outlines of the narrative make it readily accessible to all students. Therefore, it is ideal as a homework assignment or for other independent reading.

Introducing Vocabulary Study. Students will benefit from knowing the meanings of the following words before they read the poem.

dominion   replenish
enmity

Reading the Narrative. Have students recall the bare outlines of the biblical account of creation—the story of Adam and Eve in the Garden of Eden. Then assign the introductory material and the portion of Genesis as independent reading, either at home or in class.

Reteaching Alternatives. Obtain and distribute to the class copies of James Weldon Johnson's poem, "The Creation." Read it aloud as students follow along. Then discuss with them their reactions to this variant telling of the story in Genesis. Have them state which they prefer, along with the reasons for their preference.

from Genesis

Responding to the Narrative Text page 399
Analyzing the Narrative
Identifying Details

1. How is the Creation an example of divine fiat or decree? The Creation is an example of divine fiat or decree because God repeatedly utters a command starting with "Let."

2. Contrast the two accounts of the creation of man. In the first account, God creates man and woman from nothing, in His own image and likeness. In the second account, God first creates Adam from the dust of the ground and breathes a soul into him; He then creates Eve from Adam's rib.

3. Of all animals, why is the serpent able to tempt Eve? The writer says that the serpent is the subtlest animal of all the beasts in the field.

The King James Bible   81

4. What punishment does God mete out to Adam, Eve, and the serpent? God punishes Adam by telling him he will have to toil for his living and that he will die; He tells Eve that He will greatly multiply her labor in conception, and He punishes the serpent by ordering that it move on its belly.

Interpreting Meanings

5. What characteristics or qualities of God does the narrative reveal? (In your answer consider the phrases "and it was so" and "it was good.") Student answers will vary. In general, the students may suggest the following qualities: omnipotence, majesty, benevolence, and justice.

6. How does Adam's creation from dust foreshadow his ultimate fate? Adam's creation from dust foreshadows the return of his body to dust after he dies.

7. Why do you think the serpent tempts Eve instead of Adam? Student answers will vary. Perhaps the serpent thinks that Eve may be more susceptible to flattery.

8. What aspects of the human condition does the story of Adam and Eve account for? The story accounts for the following aspects of the human condition: suffering, pain, death, and the ability to choose between good and evil.

Extending the Narrative

Have the students write a concise summary of the main events of the Creation, as related in Genesis. You also might suggest that the students imagine a Creation myth of their own: For instance, how did a certain group of animals come into being? Or, how did the climate of a particular region come to be as it is? Or, why is the grass green and the sky blue and the sunset red?

Psalms

Psalm 8

Text page 401

Psalm 23

Text page 402

Psalm 24

Text page 403

Psalm 137

Text page 404

Objectives

1. To identify images
2. To describe the relationship of figurative language to tone
3. To note parallel structures
4. To write a comparison of two translations of a psalm

The Psalms at a Glance

- **Rhyme:** none
- **Rhythm:** free verse
- **Significant techniques:** imagery, figurative language, tone

Teaching Strategies

Providing for Cultural Differences. Many students will be familiar with some of the psalms from religious services. Even those outside the Judeo-Christian tradition may be familiar with the Psalm 23, which is commonly included in funeral or burial services they may have witnessed. Explain that one of the reasons why the psalms remain in common use today and continue to be popular is their expression of such universal human emotions as hope, joy, despair, sorrow, and wonder.

Providing for Different Levels of Ability. Slower readers and less mature students will need some guided reading in class; other students will be able to read the material on their own.

Introducing Vocabulary Study. Students will benefit from knowing the meanings of the following words before they read the psalm.

anoint   noisome

Reading the Psalms. To reinforce the idea of psalms as songs, play recordings of selected psalms for the students. There are many tapes and records available with settings ranging from classical to plainchant to contemporary. You might also point out that psalms are often still sung as part of many religious services. Remind students to read the introductory material and then to read the headnotes before reading the psalms.

Reteaching Alternatives. Provide collections of psalms for the students to look through. Ask each student to chose a favorite and write a paragraph analyzing it and explaining why it appeals to him or her.

Responding to the Psalms   Text page 404
Analyzing the Psalms
Identifying Details

1. In Psalm 8 which images suggest the enormous power of God? Among these images are the references to the moon and the stars, the reference to God's name in all the earth, the juxtaposition of babes and conquered enemies, and the catalogue of gifts that God has ordained for man.

2. In Psalm 23 which images show that God will protect the psalmist? Among the images are the lying down of the psalmist in green pastures, leading beside still waters, the rod and the staff that comfort the psalmist in the valley of the shadow of death, the preparing of the table, the anointing of the head with oil, and the overflowing cup.

3. In Psalm 24 which images describe God in military terms? Among these images are ''the Lord mighty in battle'' and the ''Lord of hosts.''

4. In Psalm 137 which lines refer to the speaker's loss of talent as a harpist and singer? Lines 3–4 and 8–9 refer to the speaker's loss.

Interpreting Meanings

5. In what ways does Psalm 8 resemble the Creation narratives in Genesis? The psalm and the narratives are alike in that they emphasize God's omnipotence. Lines 7–8 of the psalm refer to part of the creation of the heavens, and lines 12–18 refer to aspects of earthly creation.

6. How does the figurative language used to describe God in Psalms 23 and 24 affect the psalms' tone? Student answers will vary. The figurative language in Psalm 23, describing the Lord as a shepherd, contributes to the consolatory tone of the poem. In Psalm 24, God is figuratively described as a triumphant military commander, reinforcing the tone of joy and praise.

7. The speaker in Psalm 137 is both homesick and revengeful. Which lines convey these emotions most vividly to you? How did you react to the final line? Homesickness is conveyed by lines 1–2 and 10–14, while revenge is conveyed by lines 15–21. Student reactions to the final lines will vary. Ask the students to discuss their opinions in class.

Jonah   Text page 406

Objectives

1. To interpret a character's reaction
2. To identify the intended audience and lesson
3. To write an essay stating the theme of the narrative

Introducing the Narrative

- **Point of view:** third person
- **Significant technique:** audience

Teaching Strategies

Providing for Cultural Differences. The main action of this narrative is straightforward. That is, the events and their sequence, fantastic as they are, are clear. However, it is unquestionable that the story's theme is controversial and that its language is archaic and will sound strange to the students initially. The first difficulty can be alleviated by class discussion and debate; the second by reading—and having volunteers read—passages aloud.

Providing for Different Levels of Ability. The selection should not pose any significant problem for any students.

Introducing Vocabulary Study. Students will benefit from knowing the meanings of the following words before they read the selection.

discern   vehement

Reading the Narrative. Have students mention stories and characters from the Bible with which they may be familiar. If Jonah is mentioned, ask what students remember about the story; if not, ask how many know anything about the story. Then assign the introductory material, headnote, and story as independent reading.

Reteaching Alternatives. Have students write an additional paragraph or two rounding out the Jonah story with Jonah's response to the Lord—either verbal or in actions.

Responding to the Narrative Text page 408

Analyzing the Narrative

Identifying Details

1. How does God persuade Jonah to go to Nineveh? At first, Jonah disobeys God's command and sets out for Tarshish rather than Nineveh. But then God causes a great storm on the sea that endangers the ship carrying Jonah. The mariners throw Jonah into the sea, where he is swallowed by a great fish. Jonah cries out to the Lord, who then causes the fish to vomit him up on the shore. When God orders Jonah to go to Nineveh a second time, Jonah agrees.

2. What miraculous events occur as a result of Jonah's warning the people of Nineveh? As a result of Jonah's warning, the people repent. A gourd miraculously appears, to console Jonah in his grief, and then just as miraculously withers and dies.

Interpreting Meanings

3. Jonah claims to believe that God is "gracious and merciful"; why, then, does he become infuriated when God spares Nineveh? He probably becomes infuritated because he feels that God has used him unnecessarily.

4. Who do you think is the audience for the story of Jonah? Student answers will vary. Ask them to support their opinions in class.

What lesson do you think the story is teaching? Again, student answers will vary. Many students may suggest that the story is emphasizing the values of repentance and mercy. The story also suggests that it is wrong to second-guess God's purposes and to harbor a yearning for violent revenge against others.

Extending the Narrative

Have the students discuss how the general outlines of this story—the kinds of things that happen to Jonah—might be applied to modern life. What sorts of events and situations in life have parallels to the events in the narrative?

The Parable of the Good Samaritan

Text page 410

Objectives

1. To explain ironies in the parable
2. To provide a personal interpretation of the parable

Introducing the Parable

· **Point of view:** third-person limited
· **Significant technique:** parable

Teaching Strategies

Providing for Cultural Differences. Given the brevity of the tale, the simplicity of its moral lesson, and the information related in the headnote, the students should have little difficulty reading and responding to this selection.

Providing for Different Levels of Ability. All students will be able to read this selection on their own.

Introducing Vocabulary Study. Students will benefit from knowing the meaning of the following word before they read the selection.

raiment

Reading the Parable. You may wish to go over the introduction with the class to be sure all understand the parable form. Students who are familiar with the parables mentioned may want to give a brief summary and explanation (though some are quite unfathomable). The parable represented here is quite straightforward and one of the most familiar, so you may simply wish to assign it without any additional introduction at all. Do, however, be sure students read the headnote in order to understand the irony.

Reteaching Alternatives. Explain to the students that many states now have "Good Samaritan laws," laws protecting from liability a passer-by who stops to give CPR, first aid, or other kinds of emergency assistance to accident victims. Such protection is often limited to certain types of individuals, such as those who have taken a certified CPR course, for example. Have students research more about such laws in your own or a neighboring state and write an essay supporting or opposing the law. Remind them to consider possible benefits and risks to both helper and victim, as well as the ethical and humanitarian factors.

Responding to the Parable   Text page 410
Analyzing the Parable
Identifying Details

1. What question is the parable answering? The parable is answering the question, "Who is my neighbor?"

2. What are the hearers of the parable asked to do? The hearers of the parable are asked to show mercy to others in distress, no matter who they may be.

Interpreting Meanings

3. Why is it ironic that the priest and the Levite ignore the wounded man, but the Samaritan helps him? It is ironic because the audience might have expected both the priest and the Levite to help; the despised Samaritan, an outsider, would have been the last person expected to have compassion for the wounded man.

4. After reading the parable, how do you answer the question: Who is my neighbor? Student answers will vary. In general, many students will suggest "everyone in trouble."

Extending the Narrative

Discuss with the students the main points of this parable: the lawyer's question to Jesus, the Samaritan's actions, and Jesus's command at the end. Then have the class as a group formulate a one-sentence theme for the parable.

Henry Vaughan   Text page 411

The Retreat   Text page 411

Objectives

1. To identify images
2. To relate the title to the poem
3. To evaluate tone
4. To write an evaluation of the main idea of the poem

The Poem at a Glance

- **Rhyme:** couplets
- **Rhythm:** iambic tetrameter
- **Significant techniques:** imagery, tone

Teaching Strategies

Providing for Cultural Differences. To prepare students to read this poem, you may want to discuss briefly the concept of sin as a deliberate, conscious choice: either to turn away from what one knows one should do or to do something one knows is wrong or hurtful to others. Allow students to modify the definition according to their own lives and to suggest specific kinds of behavior that may be regarded as sinful.

Providing for Different Levels of Ability. Although average and above-average students will be able to handle the poem on their own, less capable and less mature students will benefit from a guided reading.

Reading the Selection. Have the students suggest some of the positive characteristics that are associated with infancy, such as innocence, peace, and purity. Direct students to discuss how these things change as people mature. Explain that the loss of innocence is one of the things this poem is about. Assign the headnote and poem for independent reading. Plan to work with less capable students, breaking the poem for intermediate discussion after line 20.

Reteaching Alternatives. Have the students compare the ideas in this poem with those in Donne's sonnets "Death Be Not Proud" and "Batter My Heart." Have them consider the ideas of sin and immortality as treated by both poets.

Responding to the Poem

Text page 413

Analyzing the Poem
Identifying Details

1. In lines 1–20, list the images and details that describe infancy. Among the images and details that describe infancy in lines 1–20 are ''angel infancy'' (line 2), ''a white, celestial thought'' (line 6), the image of the infant walking a mile or two (lines 7–10), the gaze on a gilded cloud or flower (lines 11–12), and ''bright shoots of everlastingness'' (line 20).

2. In lines 15–18, list the images and details that characterize adult life. Among these images and details are a wounding tongue (line 15), a guilty conscience (line 16), and sins through sensuality (lines 17–18).

3. What does the speaker long to do? The speaker longs to ''travel back'' and be an innocent child again.

Why does he say he cannot do it? He says he cannot do it because his soul is ''drunk'' and staggers.

Interpreting Meanings

4. What does the title refer to, in terms of the poem? The title implies the backward movement in time that the speaker longs for, so that he can once again be innocent with a pure soul.

5. Who or what is the ''first love'' in line 8? The ''first love'' refers to God.

6. How would you describe this speaker's tone? The tone is full of repentance and regret.

7. What connections can you see between this poem and the account of creation given in Genesis? Student answers will vary. Some students will suggest that the speaker is longing for a happy, Edenic state before his ''fall.'' This state of paradise is symbolized by infancy in the poem.

John Milton

Text page 414

The biography beginning on page 414 provides a thorough summary of Milton's life and accomplishments. You may wish to add that John Milton is generally ranked with Chaucer and Shakespeare as one of the greatest figures in English literature. *Paradise Lost*, in its final form, is cosmic in scope, encompassing all of the Creation and the wonders of the universe, and the fall and regeneration of humankind.

On His Blindness

Text page 417

Objectives

1. To analyze the structure of the sonnet

2. To evaluate the poet's use of the octave and the sestet

3. To write a paragraph extending the dialogue between the poet and Patience

The Poem at a Glance

- **Rhyme:** *abbaabbacdecde*
- **Rhythm:** iambic pentameter
- **Significant techniques:** enjambment, combining octave and sestet

Teaching Strategies

P*roviding for Cultural Differences.* You may wish to remind students that Milton was a Puritan, sharing the religious beliefs of the early settlers of the Plymouth Colony in America. An important tenet of Puritan belief was that a human being's duty was to accept God's will and that human efforts counted as nothing for salvation. This explanation should clarify Patience's reminder in the sonnet: ''God doth not need/Either man's work or His own gifts'' (ie., such gifts from God to man as poetic talent).

P*roviding for Different Levels of Ability.* Slower or less mature students will benefit from your explaining that the metaphor of the proper use of Milton's talent (see Reading the Poem, below) extends through line 6. That is, the poet's ''true account,'' like that of the servant, is that of what he has made of this gift. The response of Patience suggests that it is prideful of the poet to suppose that God has need of his help—even the help of a poet who has written a great epic to ''justify God's ways to man.''

R*eading the Poem.* Since the parable of the talents is the key metaphor in the poem, you may wish to read Matthew 25:14–30 to the class. The poet's concern (in line 6) is that

Jesus will return on Judgment Day and chide him for not having made profitable use of his talent, as the master in the parable chides the "unprofitable servant."

Reteaching Alternatives. To be sure that all students understand the basic meaning of the poem, have them paraphrase it as a short prose dialogue between a deeply religious painter who has been accidentally blinded before completing a masterpiece and a friend, who plays the role of Patience in Milton's sonnet.

Responding to the Poem   Text page 417
Analyzing the Poem
Identifying Details

1. **Who are the speakers in the poem?** The speakers are the poet and a personification of the virtue of patience.

2. **What worries Milton in the sonnet?** Milton is anxious because his blindness prevents him from serving God as much as he would like to.

   How is this worry answered, and by whom? Patience tells Milton tht he will serve God best if he bears God's yoke patiently. Patience also reminds the poet that God has thou-

sands of angels to do His bidding and that, being omnipotent, He does not need the work of men.

Interpreting Meanings

3. **Analyze the structure of this sonnet. How does Milton slightly vary the usual divisions into octave and sestet?** Milton slightly varies the structure by creating the turn of the sonnet in the middle of line 8, rather than at the beginning of line 9.

4. **Suppose the word "sit" were substituted for "stand" in line 14. What difference would that make?** Student answers will vary. The word "stand" carries connotations of respect and attentiveness; these connotations would be lost if the word "sit" were substituted.

5. **If you were in Milton's position, would you have been reassured by the words of Patience?** Student answers will vary. Ask the students to explain their opinions.

6. **To what other situations in a person's life could this famous last line be applied?** Again, students will have various answers. Possible situations might include the loss of a relative or loved one, the loss of a job, or a difficult challenge at school or work. Ask the students to suggest and discuss various possibilities.

On Shakespeare   Text page 418

Objectives

1. To paraphrase the literal meaning of a poem

2. To compare two of Milton's poems in structure and diction

3. To write a tribute to an artist or author using this poem as a model

The Poem at a Glance

- **Rhyme:** couplets
- **Rhythm:** iambic pentameter
- **Significant techniques:** conceit, metaphor

Teaching Strategies

Providing for Cultural Differences. You may wish to expand on the reference in the headnote to the Renaissance practice of including laudatory poems by others in a volume of an author's work.

Providing for Different Levels of Ability. All students will benefit from a review of the glosses before reading the poem; for less able students, such a review is essential. In addition to the words glossed, explain that *unvalued* in line 11 means "invaluable, precious."

Introducing Vocabulary Study. Students will benefit from knowing the meanings of the following words before they read the poem.

    hallowed   sepulchered

Reading the Poem. Explain to students that when Milton wrote this poem, he expected the volume of Shakespeare's plays in which it was to be included to have as its frontispiece a monument to Shakespeare in Stratford. It is this monument that the poet has in mind in lines 1–4. As it turned out, the collection of plays used Shakespeare's portrait as a frontispiece, making these lines somewhat less appropriate than they would otherwise have been. The idea that a poet's work will be his monument goes back at least to Horace in classical times. Milton gives the conceit a new twist by making Shakespeare's readers into the marble monument.

Reteaching Alternatives. Have students compare the conceit in "On Shakespeare" with this similar thought in the epitaph for Sir Edward Stanley, attributed to Shakespeare himself. Ask them to indicate which expression of the thought they prefer. Encourage them to speculate on whether Milton may have had this epitaph in mind when he wrote "On Shakespeare," which was originally entitled "An Epitaph of the Admirable Dramatic Poet W. Shakespeare." The Stanley epitaph by Shakespeare reads in part:

Not monumental stones preserve our Fame
Nor sky-aspiring Piramides our name;
The memory of him for who, this stands grave monument
Shall outlive marble and defacers hands.

Responding to the Poem   Text page 418

Analyzing the Poem

Identifying Details

1. Paraphrase the questions the speaker asks in lines 1–6. A paraphrase of these questions might run as follows:

Why does Shakespeare, whose fame lives on in our minds and hearts, need an impressive monument like a pyramid?

2. According to the poem, what is Shakespeare's true monument? Shakespeare's true monument is his works.

3. What hints does Milton give that Shakespeare was not adequately appreciated in his lifetime? The rhetorical questions of lines 1–6 perhaps hint that Shakespeare's contemporaries did not adequately appreciate him, since they did not in fact build an elaborate monument over his grave when he died.

Interpreting Meanings

4. What qualities in Shakespeare does Milton admire? Milton admires Shakespeare's metrical facility ("easy numbers") and his imaginative powers.

5. What comparison does Milton imply might be made between Shakespeare and himself? He calls the dramatist "my Shakespeare," implying a connection with himself.

from Paradise Lost   Text page 420

Objectives

1. To analyze a metaphor
2. To evaluate characterization
3. To write a paragraph extending the narrative
4. To write a paraphrase of a speech
5. To write a comparison of the biblical account of the Fall with Milton's version
6. To identify and interpret an epic simile

The Poem at a Glance

- **Rhyme:** none
- **Rhythm:** iambic pentameter
- **Significant techniques:** metaphor, characterization, epic simile

Teaching Strategies

Providing for Cultural Differences. As noted earlier, students are likely to lack familiarity with the characteristics of the epic. Be sure that students read the introductory material on pages 420–421 carefully, and remind them that the formality of the language is intended to match the high seriousness of the subject.

Providing for Different Levels of Ability. All students will benefit from hearing at least parts of the selection read aloud by a capable reader or on a recording. Less able readers are likely to need additional help. Read or have a capable reader read to such students the first 83 lines of "The Temptation of Eve." Stop, as needed, to explain the purpose and meaning of the epic simile (line 34ff.). Call students' attention to the marginal glosses, which will help them to follow the main outlines of the narrative.

Introducing Vocabulary Study. Students will benefit from knowing the meanings of the following words before they read the poem.

abject	forelorn
abstinence	guileful
alluring	haughty
burnished	importune
capacious	indignation
comely	inducement
compliance	loath

dalliance	oblique
debased	odious
delusive	omnipotent
diffuse	profane
dialted	recompense
disjoin	reiterated
disport	replete
distemper	resplendent
duteous	satiate
elocution	scruple
emulate	semblance
ennoble	terrestrial
ensue	tortuous
enticing	transgress
exempt	verdant
fluctuate	wily

Before assigning the reading, refresh the students' memories on the properties they associate with epic poetry. Inform them that heroic poems call for heroic measures, and that Milton here makes use of an elaborate simile called an *epic simile*. Direct students to be on the lookout for such devices. Advise them, also, that they will encounter the sort of sentence inversion they first met up with in the excerpts from *The Faerie Queene*.

Reading the Selection. Discuss the preparatory reading section on page 421 with the class before beginning the selection. You may wish to break the selection into short segments at first to make sure the students have understood the action so far. Breaks can conveniently be made after lines 82, 150, and 214. Continue making short assignments if you think this method is advisable.

Reteaching Alternatives. Have students compare this selection from *Paradise Lost* with Spencer's *Faerie Queene* (pages 201–211). Suggest that they pay particular attention to comparing the verse forms used in the two epics, the formality of the language, the use of similes, and the difficulty of vocabulary and sentence structure.

Responding to the Poem   Text page 434
Analyzing the Poem
Identifying Details

1. Where does Satan first catch sight of Eve? Satan first catches sight of Eve in a clump of rose bushes in the garden.

2. What information does Satan give about himself in his first speech (lines 62–82)? Satan says that he has lost all joy except the pleasure of destruction; he says that, since his fall from heaven, he is not "exempt from wound"; and he says he will try to tempt Eve to her ruin by concealing his hatred under the guise of love.

3. What arguments does Satan use to persuade Eve to eat the fruit (lines 263–316)? Satan tells Eve not to believe

any threats of death, because she will not die. He then argues that eating the fruit increased his knowledge and made his life more perfect. He tells Eve that God will probably applaud her initiative if she eats the fruit. Then Satan implies that God has deliberately forbidden Eve to eat the fruit because He wants to keep all His worshipers in lowly submission. He tells Eve that she will be like gods if she eats the fruit, just as Satan, a serpent, now seems human because he has acquired the power of speech. Finally, he asks Eve what harm can exist in a desire for knowledge.

4. How does Eve rationalize her decision to eat the fruit (lines 329–363)? She rationalizes her decision by saying that God's prohibition makes the fruit more desirable. She then argues that prohibitions from good and knowledge are not binding. Eve says that the serpent has eaten the fruit and is not dead; why, then, should she fear death if she eats it? Finally, she relies on the serpent's apparent good will and guilelessness.

5. What is the reaction of earth and nature when Eve eats the forbidden fruit? Earth feels her wound, and Nature sighs.

Interpreting Meanings

6. What does Milton mean when he metaphorically calls Eve the "fairest unsupported flower,/From her best prop so far" (lines 21–22)? He means that Eve is far away from Adam, her strongest supporter.

What storm is nigh (line 22)? The storm of temptation is nigh.

7. How would you describe Milton's attitude toward love, as expressed in lines 79–80? These lines may imply that Milton is suspicious of love, at least as far as love may be inspired by physical beauty.

8. In what ways does Satan flatter Eve? Why doesn't Eve detect his lies? Satan flatters Eve by praising her beauty and comparing her to a goddess. Eve does not detect his lies because she is distracted by the evident miracle that the serpent has the power of human speech.

9. How does Satan prejudice Eve's mind against God? What is his explanation of death? Satan prejudices Eve's mind against God by implying that God is tyrannical and envious. Satan explains death by saying that perhaps Eve will die if she eats the fruit but only to "put on gods"—that is, become immortal.

Are there any inconsistencies in the statements he makes to Eve? Satan's speech, if carefully examined, is full of inconsistencies. For example, if the fruit really has such powers as Satan claims, how can Satan at the same time maintain that eating it will be merely a "petty trespass" (line 277)? Encourage students to identify other inconsistencies in the temptation speech (lines 263–316).

10. How does the fruit affect Eve, both physically and morally? She glories in the taste of the fruit. She then becomes greedy, wondering if she should share the fruit with Adam.

11. Why is eating the forbidden fruit such a serious crime? What do Eve's feelings after eating it tell us about the crime? Eating the forbidden fruit is symbolic of pride and rebellion against God, who has created Adam and Eve and placed them in paradise. Eve's feelings after eating the fruit, which include greed, the lust for power, fear, and envy, shows us that the consequence of this crime is to embroil the human race forever in the passions that lead to unhappiness and destructive behavior towards ourselves and others.

12. It has been said that the sin committed in Eden was the sin not of mere disobedience but of pride. What details in Milton's epic support that view? How would you define *pride*? Student definitions of "pride" will vary. Details that support this view in the epic include Satan's flattery of Eve and her failure to detect it and Eve's wish to become divine.

13. In literature, Satan is often depicted as a shrewd lawyer. From the way he is characterized here, can you explain why? Student answers will vary. Ask the students to explain their opinions.

14. Is Milton's characterization of Eve sexist at all? What universal frailties does Eve manifest? Again, student answers will vary. Among the human frailties that Eve manifests are the following: pride, envy, fear of death, and lust for power.

Andrew Marvell

Text page 435

To His Coy Mistress

Text page 436

Objectives

1. To identify examples of exaggeration and understatement

2. To write a response to the poem

3. To write a comparison of this poem and two others

The Poem at a Glance

- **Rhyme:** couplets
- **Rhythm:** iambic tetrameter
- **Significant techniques:** exaggeration, imagery

Teaching Strategies

Providing for Cultural Differences. The headnote, together with students' previous reading of *carpe diem* poems, should make the meaning of this poem clear to all.

Providing for Different Levels of Ability. Urge all students to consult the glosses as they read through the poem for the first time. Less able readers may need help in recognizing the three major divisions of the speaker's argument: (1) If we had time enough, we could (and should) do these things (lines 1–20); (2) but time is short: old age and death come very soon (lines 21–32); (3) therefore, let us make the most of the time we have in which to be happy (lines 33–

46). You may want to discuss each of these divisions separately, asking volunteers to paraphrase each part of the argument.

Introducing Vocabulary Study. Students will benefit from knowing the meaning of the following word before they read the poem.

languish

Reading the Poem. This is an important poem and all students should hear it read—by you, by an able student reader, or on a recording. Not all of the unfamiliar words need to be discussed before the poem is heard for the first time, but *coyness*, *complain* (line 7), and *vegetable* (line 11) should be briefly explained. (*Vegetable* in the context of the poem has the special meaning of "able to grow without nurture"—in other words, his *vegetable* love would magnify even without the slightest encouragement from her.) Note: The gloss on *make our sun stand still* refers to an event in Joshua 10:13. It is likely that Marvell is here also alluding to the fact that Zeus stopped the sun in order to have a week-long night in which to enjoy the mortal Alcmena.

Reteaching Alternatives. Read Archibald MacLeish's poem "You, Andrew Marvell" to the class. Have students discuss whether this is also a *carpe diem* poem and whether it would be understood as one if it had a title like "On the Beach" instead of one that alludes to Marvell and his famous poem.

Analyzing the Poem

Identifying Details

1. If time were unlimited, how would the lover and his friend spend it? The lover says that they would walk by distant rivers; the lover would complain and his friend would reject him for years; the "vegetable love" of the speaker (alluding to the convention of carving the beloved's name on trees) would grow for centuries, with many years spent in praising her eyes, forehead, breasts, and heart.

2. What does the speaker always hear at his back? He hears "Time's winged chariot, hurrying near."

Interpreting Meanings

3. What is the first word of each major division of the poem? How do these three words indirectly serve to underline the structure and theme of the poem? The first words of the major divisions are "Had," "But," and "Now." The words indirectly underline the structure and theme of the poem because they imply a hypothetical condition (the existence of unlimited time), a challenge to that hypothesis, and a conclusion urging action in the present.

4. The poem contains both exaggeration and understatement. Find examples of each rhetorical device, and explain what they contribute to the poem's effect on the reader. The first major division of the poem displays many examples of rhetorical exaggeration. An example of rhetorical understatement occurs at line 32, where the speaker wryly notes that dead lovers cannot embrace in their graves. Students' opinions about what effect these rhetorical devices contribute to the poem will differ. Ask the students to defend their opinions.

5. Where in the poem does Marvell seem to be making fun of certain kinds of love poems? (Hint: A common conceit referred to love growing like the bark of trees upon which the name of the beloved was carved.) Marvell lightly mocks this conceit in lines 11–20, where he describes how his "vegetable love" would grow.

6. How, according to the poem, can human beings become masters rather than victims of time? By enjoying the present, human beings can become masters of time.

7. Notice that the speaker does not mention—let alone suggest—marriage. Suppose he had proposed marriage to the woman. What difference would that make in the poem? Student answers will vary. Many students will suggest that the mention of marriage would introduce a restrictive or solemn note into a poem that is obviously intended to commend freedom and "sport."

The English Language   Text page 438

This special essay focuses on the development of Modern English during the seventeenth century. Students will read about the emergence of the earliest English dictionaries and grammar books. They will learn about a fundamental dichotomy in English writing—the difference between the *ornate style* and the *plain style*—and how this difference has extended into the modern age. Devote some extra time to the last section of the essay, "Types and Elements of Style," which examines some of the basic choices that determine a particular writing style.

Assign the essay as homework. Encourage the students to think about writing style—not only those they have encountered in the textbook, but also those they have found in newspapers, magazines, and other literature. Encourage them also to think about their personal preferences in writing style. Then have the students answer the questions in the Analyzing Language assignment.

Exercises in Critical Thinking and Writing   Text page 445

This writing assignment will call on the students to perform an analysis of a body of work by one poet. The main point of the exercise is to sharpen the students' skills in characterizing and appreciating a particular writer's work.

Make sure the students understand the idea that poets have distinguishing traits—typical subjects, styles, and themes. After the students have made their choices of poets and poems, have them respond to the questions posed in the

Prewriting section. Encourage them to write their responses in the form of notes. In writing their essays, students should begin with a clear thesis statement that identifies the chosen poet and briefly summarizes the characteristics that make his or her poetry distinctive. Encourage the students to revise and proofread their essays until they feel their writing is concise, logical, errorless, and clear.

Criteria for Evaluating the Assignment. Students' essays should reflect a fairly thorough understanding and genuine appreciation of the chosen poet's work. Check to see that the students have begun with clear thesis statements and that the essays on the whole are coherently organized and accurately documented. Also check to see that the students have carefully proofread their papers.

Suggestions for Teaching and Evaluating the Writing Assignments

A Creative Response

The assignments that fall under this category require students to assemble new work from various materials and inspirations. Through generating work, students are able to demonstrate an understanding and appreciation of the literature they have read. Students are given an opportunity to try their hand at the various forms of literature, both poetry and prose. A typical assignment would have students extend a character, update a scene, or change the outcome of a plot.

Criteria for Evaluating the Assignments. Creative responses to literature require a flexible set of criteria for evaluation. In all cases, students must meet the purposes of the assignment, go into sufficient depth, and produce a cogent piece of writing. Yet, individual differences of style and interpretation should be appreciated.

A Critical Response

The assignments that fall under this category provide students with an opportunity to exercise their higher-level thinking skills. Using the literature as their data base, students perform such operations as analyzing, evaluating, interpreting, and comparing and contrasting. In so doing, students enhance their understanding of specific works as well as literature in general. A typical assignment would ask students to compare one poem to another for the purposes of evaluating the message, imagery, and tone of both pieces.

Criteria for Evaluating the Assignments. Critical responses to literature should demonstrate an understanding of both literal and implied meanings. In almost all cases, it is not enough that students summarize surface meanings. The successful response shows insight into deeper levels of meaning and attempts to bring previous insight to bear on new material. Clarity and organization are attributes to be highly regarded.

Answers to Analyzing Language

Analyzing Language and Style

Text page 211

Spenser's Language

1. Examples include the following: In which my Lord my liege doth luckless lie (line 13), But trembling fear did feele in every vaine (line 29), Missing the marke of his misaymed sight (line 66), So deeply dinted in the driven ciay (line 68), Out of the earth, with blade all burning bright (line 86), Whiles yet his feeble feet for faintnesse reeld (line 124), It dimmes the dazed eyen, and daunts the senses quight (line 135).

2. Answers may include these words: traveiled (line 10, traveled), enchauntment (line 32, enchantment), fyrie (line 48, fiery), bloud (line 89, blood), heavie (line 106, heavy), battell (line 136, battle), myld (line 176, mild), trew (line 225, true,), reliefe (line 270, relief), enimy (line 287, enemy), amazd (line 316, amazed), powres (line 332, powers).

3. Of the following rhyming word pairs, the underlined word is the one that was sounded differently: vaine-

againe (line 31, vain-again), shild-thrild (line 51, shield-thrilled), farre-warre (line 174, far-war).

4. The following are examples of words that are no longer used today. The words in parentheses are contemporary equivalents: trall (line 7, prisoner), wight (line 21, person), weet (line 44, know), engin (line 78, weapon),

glauncing (line 132, shining), stound (line 220, sadness).

5. Some of the final e's are lightly sounded; others are silent. The meter and the rhyme scheme provide clues to pronunciation.

Analyzing Language

Text page 240

1. **a.** humor—whim, proyning—pruning, contemn—condemn, stond—impediment, reigns—kidneys, receipt—remedy, ignorable—little-noticed, physic—purge

   b. (1) Studies are too general and should be limited by experience. (2) Reading makes a person complete; a person who reads little will have to be naturally intelligent to achieve a place in the world. (3) No person thinks as well as him- or herself as a lover thinks of the loved one.

2. Have the students say the words aloud and compare pronunciations.

3. advisor, descendant, caty-cornered, finiky, collectable, mamma, cosy, paraceet

4. Androcles. Never be afraid of an animals, your worship: thats the great secret. He'll be as gentle as a lamb when he knows that you are his friend. Stand quite still; and smile; and let him smell you all over just to reassure him; for, you see, he's afraid of you; and he must examine you thoroughly before he gives you his confidence.

5. balcony—Italian, brocade—Spanish or Portuguese, canoe—Spanish, catastrophe—Greek, landscape—Dutch, mustache—French, scientific—Latin, volcano—Italian

6. indict—c, receipt—p, subtle—b, victual—c

7. Answers will vary. Possibilities include television, films, and radio.

Analyzing Language and Style

Text page 271

Blank Verse

1. Student answers will vary. They should note that the blank verse is affected by the occasional feminine rhyme, or addition of an unstressed syllable.

2. The witches speak in rhymed tetrameter. Shakespeare probably chose this alternative to suggest incantations.

3. Answers will vary. Students should note that the occasional prose passage highlights the information being conveyed. It is thus used for exposition.

Analyzing Language and Style

Text page 334

Imagery and Figurative Language

1. a. Several unnatural sounds and events are reported in Act II, Scenes 2–4. These include the scream of an owl, a severe storm, a falcon being eaten by an owl, and horses breaking from their stalls. The mood is one of doom and gloom. b. Each time the witches appear, the emotional climate becomes extremely foreboding. Many unnatural images appear in these scenes. For example, in Act I, Scene 3, the first witch compares herself to a rat without a tail and claims to have found a pilot's thumb.

2. a. The witch intends to put a curse on the sailor that will

deprive him of sleep. b. Macbeth realizes that having murdered the king, he will no longer be able to sleep undisturbed by guilt c. Figurative language might have detracted from the dramatic tension.

3. Answers will vary. Students who focus on the many images of blood throughout the play may point to Act II, Scene 2, in which Macbeth wonders if the entire ocean could wash the blood from his hands, or if the green sea would instead turn red. The context of this image suggests that Macbeth feels a tremendous amount of guilt over murdering the king. The emotional effect of the speech is to make the reader feel somewhat sorry for Macbeth.

Answers will vary. Below are possible answers. The examples being cited are underlined.

a. And moan <u>th'</u> expense of many a vanished sight (the—line 8, Sonnet 30)

b. Home art gone, and <u>ta'en</u> thy wages (taken—line 4, Fear No More the Heat o' the Sun)

c. O, no! It is an ever-<u>fixed</u> mark (line 5, Sonnet 116)

d. <u>Who</u> loves to lie with me (lines 1–2, Under the Greenwood Tree)

e. O mistress <u>mine</u>, where are you roaming? (instead of "my mistress," line 1, O Mistress Mine)

f. In me <u>thou</u> see'st the glowing of such fire (line 9, Sonnet 73)

g. Thou thy wordly task <u>hast</u> done (line 3, Fear No More the Heat o' the Sun); Nothing of him that <u>doth</u> fade (line 4, Full Fathom Five)

h. As friend <u>remembered not</u> (line 16; Blow, Blow, Thou Winter Wind)

i. O Mistress mine, where are you roaming? (line 1, O Mistress Mine)

j. Rough winds <u>do shake</u> the darling buds of May (line 3, Sonnet 18)

k. The hand that <u>writ</u> it; for I love you so (line 6, Sonnet 71)

l. From <u>sullen</u> earth, sings hymns at heaven's gate (line 12, Sonnet 29)

Context Clues

Answers may vary. Encourage students to determine word meaning from context clues before consulting a dictionary.

perchance—by chance

Catholic—universal
leaves—pages
contention—debate
aright—correctly
intermit—cease for a time
covetousness—wanting what someone else has
bullion—a wedge of gold

Figures of Speech

1. Metaphors include: spring as a box of sweet smells, life as a musical composition.

2. Metaphors that are personfications include: the marriage (bridal) of the earth and sky, the weeping dew, the angry and brave color of the rose.

3. Similes include: the soul like a seasoned timber.

Milton's Poetic Style

Answers will vary. Possible responses include:
1. Lines 34–46: The serpent's pleasure at seeing Eve is compared to the pleasure a person feels upon escaping to the country from the dirty city.

Lines 97–102: The movement of the serpent is compared to the cautious, sideways movement of a ship when it nears the mouth of a river or rocky land.

Lines 218–229: The ability of the serpent to lead Eve to evil is compared to the tendency of a far-off flame to mislead those who try to reach it.

Lines 254–262: The raised up serpent is compared to an orator of ancient times.

2. a. In lines 1–2, the subject is the Fiend and the verb is forth was come, or comes forth.
   b. Words that would make the meaning clearer have been added in italics to lines 2–5: And on his quest *the serpent meets*, where likeliest he might find *them*, The only two of mankind *who exist*, but in them *are* The whole included race, his purposed prey.
   c. Line 13: To his surprise and delight, the serpent found Eve alone in the garden. Line 33: King Solomon frolicked with his beautiful Egyptian wife. Lines 59–61: The more the serpent sees of pleasures not available to him, the angrier he becomes and the more his thoughts turn to mischief. Lines 179–181: With the tempting fruit so near, I picked and ate my fill, and never have I enjoyed myself more.

d. Words that would make the meaning clearer have been added in italics or parentheses.

   Lines 69–71: Then let me not let pass *the* Occasion which now smiles *upon me*, behold alone *is* The woman, opportune to all attempts, Her husband, for I view far round, *is* not nigh (near), . . .

   Lines 134–135: Into the heart of Eve his words made way, Though at the voice *of the serpent she felt* much marveling; at length, . . .

   Lines 139–143: The first (language) at least of these *attributes given by God to people* I thought *was* denied To beasts, whom God on their creation-day Created mute to all articulate sound; The latter (human sense) I demure (or doubt), for in their looks Much reason, . . .

3. Answers will vary. Encourage students to read slowly and clearly so that they can feel the rhythm of the words and comprehend their meaning.

Analyzing Language

Text page 444

1. Most modern dictionaries provide the following information for each word, or entry: spelling, pronunciation, part of speech, origin, definitions, usage in a sentence, synonyms, and related forms (such as the noun form of an adjective).

2. a. companion and helper
   b. caretaker
   c. to be in a foreign place
   d. the promised land
   e. let the punishment fit the crime
   f. one's favorite person
   g. an annoyance; a problem that does not go away
   h. to get yourself together in the eyes of God
   i. to barely escape
   j. place where danger lurks
   k. the weak will be rewarded for their humility
   l. have faith that if you give you will receive
   m. make peace rather than war; turn tools of destruction into tools of creation
   n. self-righteous attitude
   o. something that soothes, relieves, or heals
   p. a weak foundation

3. Answers will vary. Students will conclude that Milton's account of the temptation and fall of Adam and Eve is more ornate in style than the King James account.

Unit Four: *The Restoration and the Eighteenth Century 1660–1800*

Teaching Eighteenth-Century Literature

This period of English literature, encompassing a relatively unwieldy mass of historical/socioeconomic data and literary samplings, can probably best be managed for student comprehension by breaking the material into several subperiods. The Restoration, a relatively short subperiod, dates from 1660, the year in which Charles II returned from France to assume the long-vacant throne of England. Bringing with him a highly developed taste for French theater and life style, Charles, in his accession to the throne, influenced greatly both the life style and literature of his subjects, long under the sway of Puritan thought. This period is one of contradictions. The modern reader is most likely to associate it with the plays of Sheridan and Congreve and with the poetry of the Earl of Rochester. Certainly this perception is accurate in part; there *was* a relaxation of the Puritan legalistic strictures. Nevertheless, there is a tendency to forget that both *Paradise Lost* and *Pilgrim's Progress* were published after the accession of Charles II. Thus, the period must be thought of as one of contrasts, able to encompass both Bunyan and Dryden.

The first half of the eighteenth century might well take its name from its outstanding literary figure; frequently called the Age of Pope, it celebrates a revived interest in what the literary lights of the time thought of as being the "classic" values. This period is also something of a time of contrast. On the one hand, it gives rise to such elegant and classical stylists as Pope, Arbuthnot, and Gay. It is the period of satire, recalling the Roman Age of Juvenal. On the other hand, the new industrialization and the concommittant rise of a new middle class brought forth a popular journalism. This very same period promulgated travel books and instructive tomes of all sorts purporting to instruct these *nouveau riche* burghers: books of etiquette, almanacs, the social essays of Addison and Steele, and myriad other ancestors of the "how to" books. Further, this time also saw the rocketlike rise to popularity of the new prose—the novel, suddenly popular in new middle-class rental libraries and in middle-class family drawing rooms, to say nothing of ladies' morning rooms. Side by side, the modern reader ponders titles as diverse as *Tom Jones* and *The Rape of the Lock* on the eighteenth century bookshelf.

The latter portion of the eighteenth century takes its name from the towering literary figure of the time, Dr. Samuel Johnson. Conversationalist, lexicographer, poet, biographer, social critic, literary critic, and sometime novelist, Dr. Johnson seems almost larger than life. Nevertheless, the rising democratic spirit and the increasing influence of the middle-class values find their voice in writings of this last hurrah of the Age of Enlightenment, shortly to be eclipsed by stresses of the Napoleonic Wars and its attendant political threats.

One of the major goals of the unit is to develop in the students a deep awareness of the classical mind-set. While talking about characteristics of classicism and memorizing lists of typical attitudes will certainly accomplish this goal, it is possible to bring students to a gut-level understanding of these attitudes very quickly. Have the students note that classicism and romanticism are two basic ways of looking out at the world; and although each of us is something of a mixture of attitudes, we tend to lean in one direction or another, which will color many of our ways of reacting to the world.

A second item of major relevance to the American high-school student of English literature is the connection of that thought and culture to the American experience. It is very important for them to come to the realization that their own experience is closely related to the English heritage, whether they claim English blood or not.

Objectives of the Restoration Unit

1. To improve reading proficiency and expand vocabulary

2. To gain exposure to notable authors and works of the period

3. To define and identify significant literary techniques: allegory, apostrophe, autobiography, classicism, Neo-classicism, canto, couplet, heroic couplet, diary, elegy, epic, mock epic, epigram, epitaph, essay, irony, novel, satire, and wit

4. To interpret and respond to fiction, nonfiction, and poetry, orally and in writing, through analysis of its elements

5. To practice the following critical thinking and writing skills:
   a. Evaluating essays
   b. Responding to criticism
   c. Analyzing diary entries
   d. Comparing storytelling techniques
   e. Evaluating a short story
   f. Analyzing a character
   g. Analyzing an elegy
   h. Writing a response to criticism

John Dryden

Dryden, like many other English writers, excelled in more than one genre. During his time, Dryden was not only the critic that the students will see in the selection that heads off the unit, but he was also a noted poet and dramatist as well. Although he was not always paid his stipend in full, he had the public honor of being considered England's master spokesman of literature: appointed Poet Laureate in 1668, he retained that honor until 1688, when he fell afoul of the newly crowned William and Mary.

Shakespeare

Objectives

1. To analyze the technique of argumentation
2. To evaluate opposing viewpoints
3. To write a response explaining an observation

Introducing the Critique

In outline form, for your reference, here are the major elements in the critique:

- **Point of view:** first person
- **Significant techniques:** argumentation, opposing viewpoints

Background on the Critique. This selection, looked at in the light of its time, is far more daring than it would now seem. Shakespeare, at this time dead a mere fifty years, was not yet thought of as the greatest writer of the English language. Indeed, he was not then even considered to be the best of his age. The fact that Dryden discussed Shakespeare in the same breath and with the same seriousness as he did the far more immoderately admired Ben Jonson is an indication of his literary courage. Note that the charges of inadequacy that he laid at Master Will's door are not the result of the Bard's status at the time. Indeed, many more recent authors have found Dryden's words worth reechoing. The whole passage is a tribute to Dryden's cool, reasonable critical mind.

Teaching Strategies

Providing for Cultural Differences. There is not too much that will get in the way of student understanding. If a chronological approach has been used up to this time, the students are already familiar with the subject of the critique. In all probability, they have already encountered other critical views of the playwright. You may very well need only to remind them of some of the truths referred to in the introduction above.

Providing for Different Levels of Ability. Again, the probability is great that most of the students who will be assigned this selection are probably college bound; if this is the case, they should have no learning difficulties with this selection. If this is not the case and the class is a heterogeneous mix, this selection should still present minimum difficulty. As indicated above, the author's style is really quite modern, and with the exception of a few archaisms, the selection is readily accessible.

Introducing Vocabulary Study. Students will benefit from knowing the meanings of the following words before they read the selection.

    bombast   insipid

Reading the Critique. Before students read the selection, you might wish to discuss with them what they would require of a critic. Ideally, you will be able to elicit such answers as objectivity, rationality, balance, and readability. Once the students have set up these criteria, you may then wish to have them critique the critic after a close reading.

Reteaching Alternatives. Although this selection will probably not require it, reteaching can frequently work well through matched-pair review. Have each student who is having difficulty work in a matched pair with one who is not. Have them review the material together in preparation for a brief essay or panel.

Extending the Critique. Suggest that students write a review of a movie or TV show that they particularly admire. Develop the critique in a manner that mirrors at least three elements in the Dryden critique. It is important to praise the production as well as to acknowledge any weaknesses in it. Remind students that it is important to divorce the acting from the actual script. Ask them to examine carefully the writer's ability to develop characters, create an involving story line, and exude in the body of the work a sense of awareness regarding human nature and the human condition in the world.

Responding to the Critique   Text page 461

Analyzing the Critique

Identifying Details

1. What weaknesses of Shakespeare does Dryden acknowledge? Dryden says that Shakespeare is often flat and insipid and that his comic scenes often degenerate into puns. Dryden also says that Shakespeare's "serious swelling" is sometimes so inflated that it becomes "bombast."

Interpreting Meanings

2. In this short critical excerpt, Dryden uses several techniques of *argumentation*. For example, he cites the opinions of a respected poet, of a literary scholar, and of royal courtiers (then considered arbiters of taste). What is the effect of citing these three kinds of authorities? Citing these three different kinds of authorities has the effect of drawing on a representative range of opinion.

Can you think of another kind of authority whose opinion could have lent weight to Dryden's argument? Answers will vary. Possibilities might include actors and theatergoers.

3. Would you have found Dryden's praise more convincing if he had not dealt with *opposing viewpoints*—the opinions of "those who accuse Shakespeare"? Why or why not? Answers will vary. Encourage the students to support their opinions with reasons.

4. What do you think Dryden means by writing that Shakespeare had the "largest and most comprehensive soul"? How does Dryden use this generalization to sway his readers? Dryden probably means that Shakespeare had immense powers of imagination, since "all the images of nature were present to him." This generalization, placed at the beginning of the extract, is meant to influence readers favorably about Shakespeare.

---

from Baucis and Philemon   Text page 462

Objectives

1. To relate a moral to symbolism
2. To identify symbols
3. To analyze a poem's theme
4. To identify tone
5. To write an original version of a story
6. To write a character analysis

The Poem at a Glance

- **Rhyme:** rhyming couplets
- **Rhythm:** iambic pentameter
- **Significant techniques:** moral, symbolism, theme, tone

Teaching Strategies

Providing for Cultural Differences.   Because the poem is set in an ancient time, the students will probably all encounter language difficulties. Nevertheless, at the discussion stage, differences among students are likely to surface. Those coming from other than the Judeo-Christian culture may have some holes to fill in in regard to the Noah story. To minimize this difference, use other flood myths as well as the Noah story to draw comparisons; they abound in most cultures. It is also important to be careful of the sensibilities of your Judeo-Christian constituency. The use of the term *flood myth* can raise many hackles if you do not tread carefully and define your terms.

Providing for Different Levels of Ability.   Because of the artificiality of some of the language, as well as the poetic diction, this selection may be a challenge to many of the students. It certainly is not a once-over-lightly selection. This selection needs to be taught carefully as an in-class experience. Paraphrase frequently, and there should be little likelihood of having to make extra provision for the less literate students. Such provision will automatically occur as you go about presenting the poem to the class as a whole.

Introducing Vocabulary Study.   Students will benefit from knowing the meaning of the following word before they read the poem.

impiety

Reading the Poem.   You may wish to do some preparation for this reading by discussing with the students the flood myths (see above). You may also wish to read this selection in a modern prose translation for the students. Such preparation can lay the groundwork for discussion of comparative mythology and/or the demands on a translator's skill. Further, such an activity will make sure that the students understand the content without talking down to them. In addition, it will lay a groundwork for a later discussion of how much of this selection is Ovid and how much is Dryden. If it is possible, give the students a handout of that prose account so that they can refer to the text.

After sufficient preparation, you might wish to handle this as an in-class oral reading. You might then follow up with an assignment of a close home reading. On the other hand, you might, as the exigencies of time dictate, choose to have the students do a preliminary reading at home, followed by a close reading in the classroom with frequent pauses for commentary and discussion. This decision will be dictated probably in part by time but also by the nature of the class composition. Regardless of how you proceed, you probably need to plan on some class time for either intense follow-up discussion or a close reading.

Reteaching Alternatives. Because the selection requires so much attention as you proceed, you will probably not need to reteach. You will take care of misconceptions and problems as you move through a discussion of the material. Nevertheless, if the necessity arises, you may wish to use a matched-pair review to help the slower students. Nothing is more likely to ensure understanding than to be required to tutor or teach the material to someone else; thus, such a technique, when tactfully employed, can benefit both the slowest and the brightest in a heterogeneous classroom.

Responding to the Poem   Text page 467
Analyzing the Poem
Identifying Details

1. Using details in the poem, describe Baucis and Philemon's house. Among the details students should mention are the following: the low, thatched roof; the small size; the simple benches; the fire; the sooty rafters; the marriage bed and its coverlets.

2. Using details from the poem, describe Philemon's contribution to the successful marriage. Philemon seats the guests and helps with the cooking.

Describe Baucis's. Baucis makes the guests comfortable with cushions and prepares the food.

3. Dryden is very specific about the meal. What did Baucis and Philemon serve for dinner? Baucis and Phile-

mon served boiled cabbage leaves and bacon, olives, berries, salad, eggs, and wine.

4. How do Philemon and Baucis realize they are entertaining gods? At line 106, they observe the bowls magically refilling themselves and dancing around the table. Devotion seizes the couple, and they fall to prayer.

5. What request does the old couple make of the gods? How is it met? They ask to serve at the gods' shrine and to die within the same hour. The gods grant their request and turn them into trees.

Interpreting Meanings

6. Fables frequently provide a moral for the reader. What is the moral of this fable, and who speaks it? The moral, pronounced by the speaker of the poem in the last two lines, is that piety will be rewarded.

7. Why do you suppose Philemon and Baucis were changed into trees? Consider why the gods chose the oak tree for Philemon and the linden tree for Baucis; what do these trees *symbolize*? Answers will vary. In general, the metamorphosis into trees is appropriate because trees symbolize growth and rest (or shade). The oak tree might stand for strength, while the linden might symbolize beauty.

8. Do you think the goose in the story is important? Does it function in any way besides offering *comic relief*? Jove's sparing of the goose perhaps foreshadows the gods' kindly granting of Philemon's request.

9. The metamorphosis of the old couple is just one of the metamorphoses in this story. What are some others, and how do they contribute to the *theme*? Other metamorphoses include the gods changing into mortal form, the bowls refilling themselves, the valley turning into a lake, and the old couple's cottage turning into a shrine. The final metamorphosis, especially, contributes to the theme of piety being rewarded.

10. Does Dryden poke fun at the old couple, or does he admire them? What is the *tone* of the poem? Most students will agree that Dryden seems to admire the old couple and that the tone of the poem, while occasionally light, is predominantly serious.

11. Line 55 mentions the "pleasing chat" that Baucis, Philemon, and the gods had. What do you suppose they talked about? What did the gods tell the couple? What did the couple tell the gods? Answers will vary. Students should support their suggestions from hints in the text.

Samuel Pepys

People have been arguing over the pronunciation of this man's name practically since his writings became public. One of his descendants claims that her family name is pronounced as two distinct syllables; some dictionaries acknowledge a variant pronunciation of "peps"; most usually, however, the name is pronounced "peeps."

However one chooses to pronounce the name, certain characteristics of *The Diary* remain fresh to all readers who encounter his observations for the first time. One of the characteristics most obvious to readers is that this observant man about town could not have kept a diary at a better time.

He is writing at the point when England is emerging from a long Puritan winter. Pepys was a man in and of the Restoration. He enjoyed the influence of the new court life. He enjoyed especially the newly reopened theater life, with a new stage convention that, for the first time, allowed women on stage. He was a man of government. He was one of the movers and shakers, and he was especially endowed with almost boundless energy and curiosity about the world around him. It is indeed fortunate for all of us that he enjoyed the process of recording his impressions of the life and events around him.

---

from The Diary of Samuel Pepys

Objectives

1. To evaluate a diary as a primary source
2. To write a plan for keeping a diary
3. To write a character study of the author
4. To analyze eighteenth-century English orthography

Introducing the Diary

In outline form, for your reference, here are the major elements in the diary:

- **Point of view:** first person
- **Significant techniques:** primary source

Background on the Diary. You might wish to introduce this selection by pondering with the students the nature of the urge to keep a diary. To help students who cannot relate to this manifestation of the impulse, you might wish to compare keeping a diary to taking pictures, video-taping, keeping mementos, or keeping a scrapbook. All of these have, as at least a part of their impetus, a deep desire to capture and savor a moment. Discuss this idea with the students, perhaps getting them to share their own insights. Explore differences between memoirs, diaries, and journals. Finally, discuss the reasons for a public man to keep a journal in a cipher, perhaps drawing parallels with the electronic record keeping of the Oval Office.

You might wish to refer to *Anne Frank: The Diary of a Young Girl*, drawing some conclusions about the character-

istics of a diary and perhaps doing some concept formation about the topic.

Teaching Strategies

Providing for Cultural Differences. Probably there are no cultural differences that will make this work less accessible to one group than another. All of the content will be a historical curiosity for the students.

Providing for Different Levels of Ability. There are no apparent impediments to easy understanding of the material. No special provisions need be made.

Introducing Vocabulary Study. Students will benefit from knowing the meanings of the following words before they read the selection.

combustible proferred
covetous

Remind students that, as the anthropologist-linguist Edward Sapir aptly put it, "languages drift down time." That is, such conventions as spelling and syntax will, in the short space of several centuries, change markedly. Tell them to be on the alert for unusual words and locutions, perhaps keeping a log of the same.

Reading the Selections. This may be a take-home reading assignment, or it may be handled orally. If you choose to make this an at-home assignment, you might wish to have the students keep a double entry journal, taking notes on the left-hand column of the paper and making notes of personal comment on the right-hand column. This is superior to almost any kind of reading check possible to give, and it focuses the students' attention as they read so that they will not indulge in a series of eye exercises passing for reading. In addition, it supplies students with a great deal of supportive material for almost any writing assignment you might choose to give.

Reteaching Alternatives. Insuring that all of the students understand this selection may not require reteaching. If, after home reading, you carry on a detailed discussion, talking not only about what Pepys experienced but about his impressions, you will have compensated for those who did not understand.

Extending the Diary. You may want to suggest that students read an excerpt from another well-known diary. The diaries of Anne Frank and Virginia Woolf are two very different and beautifully written examples. Ask students to list five similarities and five differences between *The Diary of Samuel Pepys* the diary they choose to read a selection from. A diary by a contemporary writer may be particularly interesting to students because it may include references to familiar events in their own lifetime.

Responding to the Diary   Text page 479
Analyzing the Diary
Identifying Details

1. Why was Major General Harrison executed? Harrison was executed because he had participated in the execution of King Charles I in 1649.

2. What happened at the end of the coronation day that caused people to "take great notice of God's blessing"? There was a violent thunderstorm.

3. What fear woke Pepys one night? On July 11, 1664, he was afraid that thieves had broken into the house and were stealing his money.

4. What was Pepys's greatest fear during the Great Fire? During the Great Fire, his greatest fear was that his treasure would be destroyed.

   Name some of the buildings, large or small, that were destroyed in the Great Fire. Among the buildings that were destroyed were St. Magnes Church, most of Fish-street, and hundreds of private houses.

Interpreting Meanings

5. Pepys gives very few details in the *Diary* about the execution that he witnessed. Why do you suppose he didn't devote much space to it? Answers may vary. In general, we may suppose that Harrison, having participated in the crime of regicide, was regarded as an infamous traitor.

6. In the *Diary*, Pepys is surprisingly honest and frank about himself. In which of the entries does he record behavior that is somewhat less than admirable? In the first entry, Pepys records his irritation with his wife because of things "lying about the house." In a fit of anger, he kicks and breaks a fine little Dutch basket that he had given her as a present. In the entry for April 23, 1661, Coronation Day, Pepys records getting so drunk that he vomited and awoke with a terrible hangover the following morning.

7. How is the inauguration of a president in the United States both like and unlike the coronation of the English king? Both occasions are elaborately ceremonial, witnessed by large crowds, and climaxed with parties, fireworks, and so on. Both the president and the king take oaths. However, the inauguration of a president is held in front of the Capitol, rather than in a cathedral, and the president, naturally, does not receive a crown.

8. Of what use would Pepys's account be as a *primary source* for a later historian of the Great Fire? Answers will vary, but most students will agree that this account by an eyewitness would be extremely valuable for a historian. Note that Pepys himself is directly involved in the official efforts to contain the fire.

9. Look at the various places where Pepys mentions his wife Elizabeth in these excerpts from the *Diary*. From these references, what can you conclude about their relationship? Most of the entries where Pepys mentions his wife seem to suggest that they did not have an especially close relationship: note that he scolds her for being untidy, and that he drops her off to sleep at a friend's house one night, while he goes off drinking with male friends.

10. How is Pepys's life like life in your own time? How is it different? Do you think that the attitudes and values of seventeenth-century life, as Pepys describes them, are similar to those of your own time, or different? Explain your answers. Answers will vary. Encourage the students to point to specific parallels and differences, and to support their comments on values.

During his lifetime, Defoe was an incredibly prolific author. The biographical sketch in the student text recounts his struggles both to create literature and to survive. Read the introduction with students, having them note in particular the question mark following Defoe's date of birth. This, you might point out, suggests that we know less about this early figure than scholars of the period might wish.

from Robinson Crusoe

Objectives

1. To evaluate the use of the first-person point of view

2. To analyze and evaluate characterization

3. To write an alternative version of the narrative

4. To write an essay explaining the work's literary appeal

5. To write an analysis of a character's response

6. To write a comparison of two treatments of solitude

Introducing the Story

In outline form, for your reference, here are the major elements in the story:

- **Protagonist:** Robinson Crusoe
- **Antagonist:** nature
- **Conflict:** human vs. nature
- **Point of view:** first person
- **Significant techniques:** first-person point of view, characterization
- **Setting:** a desert island

Background on the Story. It is rather amazing that the present-day reputation of this early journalist rests primarily on *Robinson Crusoe*, which has survived cartoon treatments and children's editions. Almost any time teachers set out to teach this work, or any part thereof, they encounter a good deal of misguided student comment and questioning about the reasons for their reading a "kids' " book. Also, many of them are only too ready to volunteer that "they saw the movie." A further complication is caused by the confusion between this book and the later children's spinoff, *Swiss Family Robinson*; thus, the challenge to the teacher is going to be to get the students to take the book seriously.

You may wish to present Addison and Steele's essay on Alexander Selkirk (page 550) in connection with this excerpt. Since there is considerable critical thought that contends that Defoe was influenced by Selkirk's account, you might wish to read that before you teach *Robinson Crusoe*. Such a reading will provide an interesting way into the Crusoe selection. The student readers will quite likely take the story seriously if they understand what might be a real basis (if only in inspiration) for the novel.

The Plot. In the first excerpts from the longer work, Crusoe has just arrived on the shore of his deserted island after having swum from a shipwreck that only he survived. First he describes his mixed emotions of joy and despair upon realizing his plight. Then he tells of his impressions of the island and his trips to the stranded ship to retrieve what supplies he can.

The second excerpt opens with Crusoe weighing the advantages and disadvantages of his situation. It continues with his building of a shelter and adjustment to his new life style. The third excerpt finds Crusoe fourteen years later, king of his small household, which consists of a few tamed animals and himself. By now he has constructed all the necessary tools for living on the island and can amuse himself with the thought of how frightening he would look to someone back home in England. The last two excerpts describe Crusoe's discovery of other people on the island and his rescue of one, whom he calls Friday, from the brutal hands of others.

Teaching Strategies

Providing for Cultural Differences. There probably are no cultural differences that will be an impediment to understanding this selection. Because it is such an unusual adventure, all of the students will be at the same starting place in understanding.

Providing for Different Levels of Ability. The students in a twelfth-grade class should be able to read this story on their own with no difficulty. Remind the students to use their footnotes and glossaries as necessary.

Introducing Vocabulary Study. Students will benefit from knowing the meanings of the following words before they read the selection.

abate	prodigious
contrivance	ravenous
destitute	regress
discomposure	surly
egress	sustenance
impracticable	unwieldy
inter	

Reading the Story. Once an appropriate entry into the story has been made, the students will encounter very little difficulty in reading this on their own. There are a number of ways you can make an effective entry into the selection. You might wish to have the students, upon first entering the class, do a quick-write journal entry on the subject of what they imagine it would be like to be cast alone on a desert island; if you so intend, you might wish to warn the students that you will ask them to share their quick writes with the rest of the class. This entry assignment will put them in tune with the selection. You might put the students into matched pairs and ask the pairs to come up with as many categories of items as they can think of that would make their lives more bearable on a deserted island. This assignment automatically requires some sorting and quick outlining if the class needs that kind of practice; so it may have a double value.

After the entry has been established, you may wish to use this as an at-home reading assignment. Probably you have already found that most of the literature assignments up to this time have required a good bit of in-class attention. At this point in the class curriculum, the diction that has become modern enough and simplified enough that most or many of the prose selections can be made as home assignments. Since this now is more feasible, it is going to become increasingly important to prepare the students in advance so well that they will read the assignments thoroughly and then to follow through in enough detail to make sure they have profited from the experience.

Reteaching Alternatives. The class discussion, amplified by your additional instruction, should be sufficient to help any student in class to grasp the material. The selection is not so demanding that it should prove inaccessible to very many students.

Extending the Story. Suggest that students write an essay about an imaginary isolated place that they would like to visit. This place can be anywhere—in the city or the country, on an island, on top of a mountain, an iceberg, or a tree. Ask them to describe the surroundings. What does it look like and smell like? How does it feel to be there? What do they eat? Where do they sleep and bathe? What do they think is most beautiful about this place? What is most ugly and unpleasant? What do they do when they wake up in the morning? What do they do for the rest of day? Ask them to describe how it feels to spend several days alone. Suggest that they try to make their imaginary place as vivid to their readers as *Robinson Crusoe* is to them.

Responding to the Story   Text page 495

Analyzing the Story

Identifying Details

1. Though Robinson Crusoe is often thought of as living a primitive life, he actually retrieves from the ship many of the civilized trappings of seventeenth-century England. What items of civilization help him live on the island? Over the course of thirteen days, Crusoe makes eleven expeditions to the ship. Among the stores he salvages from the ship are biscuit, rum, cheeses, corn, carpenter's tools, guns, saws, a hammer, an ax, nails, a grindstone, clothes, ammunition, gunpowder, sails, rope, canvas, twine, sugar, flour, cables, ironwork, razors, scissors, cutlery, and money.

2. When Crusoe finds money on the ship, what is his first reaction? He smiles to himself, recognizing that money is of no use to him and may as well go to the bottom of sea.

His second? He takes the money with him to the island.

3. What companionship does Crusoe have before he rescues Friday? His only companions are a dog and two cats.

Interpreting Meanings

4. *Robinson Crusoe* is told from the *first-person point of view*. What is the advantage of this point of view? The advantage is the immediacy of a personal narrative.

What are its limitations? The limitations are that we, the readers, are restricted to knowing only what Crusoe can observe.

5. What activities show Crusoe to be a man of great patience? Among the activities students may mention are the construction of the rafts, the building and extension of the cave, the making of a chair and a table, and the fashioning of flat boards or planks from trees.

What other qualities, both bad and good, does Crusoe have? How does Defoe make those qualities clear? Student answers may vary. Good qualities might include religious faith, foresight, practicality, and confidence in reason. Bad qualities might include periodic inclinations to despair. Defoe makes these qualities clear through Crusoe's assorted activities and through the first-person narrator's own comments about his situation.

6. Describe Friday. Why do you suppose Defoe characterizes Friday as young, strong, and capable? How would the action have to change if Friday were old, or ugly, or feeble? Crusoe himself describes Friday as a handsome man, about twenty-six years old, quite tall, with a pleasing smile. If Friday had been old or feeble, he would not have been able to outrun the cannibals who were pursuing him.

7. After listing both the good and the evil things in his life, Crusoe concludes that "there was scarce any condition in the world so miserable, but there was something negative or something positive to be thankful for in it." What does he mean by negative and positive? By nega-

tive, he seems to mean unfortunate or unfavorable; by positive, he means favorable or compensatory.

Do you agree or disagree with this conclusion? Give reasons for your opinion. Student answers will vary. Ask the students to support their opinions with reasons.

8. Is Crusoe's behavior plausible to you? In what ways is his behavior like what most people's would be on such an occasion? In what ways is it different? Again, student answers will vary. Most students will probably agree that Crusoe's behavior is plausible, at least in the main: his initial self-pity, his fears, and then his practical, patient actions to come to terms with his condition seem convincing. Ask students to give reasons for any differences they observe between Crusoe's behavior and what students imagine other people's reactions would be.

The Journal of the Plague Year

Text page 497

Objectives

1. To understand the first person narrative

2. To write a narrative drawing on primary sources

3. To write a comparison of Defoe's *Journal* and Pepys's *Diary*

4. To write an essay supporting or attacking a position

Introducing the Journal

In outline form, for your reference, here are the major elements in the journal:

- **Point of view:** first person
- **Significant techniques:** primary sources

Background on the Journal. You might wish to introduce this piece by a discussion of various reactions to the AIDS epidemic. This would not be the first time that that particular comparison has been made. Elicit the various superstitious attitudes that are current. Once you have involved the students, go immediately to this selection.

Teaching Strategies

Providing for Cultural Differences. There is no cultural difference that is likely to impede understanding of this particular piece of literature. It is accessible to almost anyone. Nevertheless, there is a cultural factor worth considering: people living in the twentieth century are likely to feel some

distance from the journal; we are hard put to imagine any catastrophe of the proportions of the plague. There is much of value in helping the students come to a point of identifying with this and understanding how people may be likely to react to wholesale death. Much here depends upon the makeup of your class. Politically aware students may well be reminded here of certain contemporary horrors, especially in third-world environments.

Providing for Different Levels of Ability. Twelfth-graders of all levels should be able to read this selection with little difficulty. Remind the students to use their glossaries. Be sure the students have carefully read the introduction to the text of the journal and understand the nature of the disease.

Introducing Vocabulary Study. Students will benefit from knowing the meanings of the following words before they read the selection.

calamitous	malignity
contagion	mortified
delirious	promiscuously
distempered	scarify

Reading the Journal. This selection is very well-suited to either an in-class or an at-home reading. Have the students set up a double entry journal to keep track of their reactions to the incidents as they encounter them. Such a double entry journal will provide supports for a detailed discussion of the piece after the class meets again. Such a journal has a left-hand column headed Note Taking. This column contains line-by-line notations as the student reads. The right-hand side, labeled Note Making, contains the student's comments about the text. In that column the student may disagree with the text, express surprise, doubt the validity of the observation, or give voice to any other emotion evoked by the text.

Reteaching Alternatives. Such an activity can be pretty informal. An in-depth follow-up discussion to the assignment will ensure that students who may have misunderstood or have missed a point will clarify the error or omission. There should be no need for a wholesale reteaching of the selection.

Extending the Journal. Suggest that students keep a journal over a period of one week. (Some who enjoy this may continue it indefinitely.) Ask them to describe events and the elements around them very carefully. You may want to suggest that they choose a particular social or political or even family matter that they monitor very closely over the week's time. Ask each student to choose an excerpt from his or her journal to share with the rest of the class. Have class members give each other feedback on the effectiveness of their entries and their ability to express themselves candidly and directly.

Responding to the Journal   Text page 504
Analyzing the Journal
Identifying Facts

1. Though the title *A Journal of the Plague Year* implies a daily account of events, the book is written as a narrative years after the plague is over. Where does Defoe let the reader know his *Journal* is being written at a later date? Defoe informs the reader that the *Journal* was written at a later date when he speaks in the first section of "the time of this visitation." In the third section, he introduces an episode by saying "I remember." In the fourth section, he refers to his audience as "those who did not see it," implying that he is writing at a later time.

How does he explain this change in form? The explanation lies in the fact of Defoe's attempting to lend an element of truth to his narrative, which is at least partly stylized.

2. These excerpts from the *Journal* are a series of dramatic scenes introduced by the narrator's general observations of the condition of London's citizens during the epidemic. Who are the four characters that the narrator features? The four characters are the citizen who tries to escape from quarantine, the bereaved husband in the brown cloak, the poor piper, and the man who swam across the Thames and back.

How does each of their situations differ? The citizen who tries to escape from quarantine lies about his condition and is found dead in his garret room at the inn on the following morning. The bereaved husband is shocked at the burial of his wife and children in a common grave. The poor piper wakes up in the dead-cart and asks if he is really dead. The man who swims across the Thames is infected with the plague, but his strenuous exercise apparently causes the swellings to burst, and he recovers after the poison drains from his body.

3. What were the symptoms of the disease? The symptoms included gangrenous swellings, or boils.

4. What attempts were made to cure people? Citizens who had been exposed to the infection were quarantined, and doctors tried to get the swellings to come to a head so that they would burst and run.

Interpreting Meanings

5. What is the *tone* of the *Journal*? The tone of the *Journal* is predominantly sober.

Do you think the tone would have been different if the *Journal* really had been written during the plague? Student answers may vary. Ask the students to give reasons for their opinions.

6. What literary techniques does Defoe use to make his journal seem authentic? Among the techniques that Defoe uses are suspense, foreshadowing, "eyewitness" accounts, direct quotation, and the citation of statistics.

Are these techniques similar to those he uses in *Robinson Crusoe*? Students will probably agree that Defoe uses many of the same techniques in *Robinson Crusoe*.

7. Why does Defoe, or his narrator, say that the manner of burial makes no difference to a dead person? To whom do you think the manner of burial does make a difference? A dead person, presumably, would not care about the manner of his body's burial. But the manner of burial can make a difference to the living, especially to spouses or relatives and friends.

8. Why would the story of the piper be improved if it contained the bit about his playing the pipes while he was in the dead-cart? Why, then, does the narrator refuse to include this bit? This story would be improved because the bit about the playing of the pipes would add an extra touch of ironic humor. The narrator refuses to include it because he insists on the factual accuracy and authenticity of the details he reports.

9. What do we mean by the expression "morbid curiosity"? Student answers will vary. In general, the expression connotes an excessive interest in details involved in violence, illness, death, or an accident.

In which of the incidents recounted here does the narrator appear to be morbidly curious? The narrator seems to be morbidly curious in the fourth section, when he persuades the sexton to allow him to observe the burials at the churchyard.

Where does this kind of curiosity often appear in contemporary life and how do you account for it? (Are people morbidly curious because they enjoy seeing others suffer? Or is there another explanation?) Student answers will vary. Possibilities include violence on television, "rubbernecking" on the highways after an accident, interest in details about executions or murders or other crimes, and so on. Ask students to give reasons for how they account for this type of curiosity.

10. Why does H. F. call his little poem "coarse"? He calls it "coarse" because it is unpolished.

11. If you had been living in London in 1665 and had survived the plague, what would you have done to celebrate? Answers will vary.

12. How would experiencing a plague of this sort change a person's attitude toward life and death? Student answers will vary. Encourage the students to give reasons for their opinions.

Jonathan Swift

Text page 505

Like Defoe, Swift had a serious mission that is often missed by readers, who are trained to focus on the man's misanthropy. Swift's mission was that of the satirist, and his ultimate goal was the reform of a species that he doubtless saw as "having potential." Do not fail to impress this point on students, who, at some later point in their educations, may, thanks to your enlightenment, draw connective tissue between Swift and a much earlier social reformer by the name of Aristophanes.

from Gulliver's Travels

Text page 507

Objectives

1. To evaluate parody
2. To analyze satire
3. To identify instances of symbolism
4. To recognize techniques of characterization
5. To recognize verbal irony
6. To write from an altered point of view
7. To write a variation on the plot

Introducing the Story

In outline form, for your reference, here are the major elements in the story:

- **Protagonist:** Lemuel Gulliver
- **Antagonists:** Lilliputians, Brobdingnagians
- **Conflict:** human vs. human
- **Point of view:** first person
- **Significant techniques:** parody, satire, symbolism, characterization, irony
- **Setting:** the lands of Lilliput and Brobdingnag

Background on the Story. It might be worth drawing for the students a comparison with *Robinson Crusoe.* Both works spring from the contemporary popularity of travel books. Members of the burgeoning middle class were fascinated with all manner of nonfiction that would contribute to self-improvement. Travel accounts were not the least of these literary ventures. Second, Swift, like Defoe, employs the technique of piling detail on detail to achieve the sense of verisimilitude.

The entire work consists of four voyages of one Lemuel Gulliver to Lilliput (the land of the little people), Brobdingnag (the land of the big people), Laputa (the island in the sky inhabited by pseudoscientists and intellectuals), and the land of the Houhynhymns (the horse people). Excerpts from the first two of these are included in the student text.

The Plot. The first excerpt begins as Gulliver awakens from a deep sleep after swimming ashore from a shipwreck. To his surprise, he finds he is tied to the ground. His captors are a tiny people called Lilliputians, who at first attack him but are then reassured that Gulliver means no harm. They bring him food and drink and make him a welcome visitor at the emperor's court. There Gulliver observes customs and political divisions not unlike those in England, though the comparisons are subtle and amusing. The second excerpt finds Gulliver marooned among a different people, the

Brobdingnagians. This time it is Gulliver who is tiny by comparison, ten times smaller than everything and everyone around him. Again, Gulliver becomes a welcome guest at the court, only it is he who amuses his hosts with stories about the politics of England.

Teaching Strategies

Providing for Cultural Differences. Since this entire reading experience is rooted in fantasy, there are probably no cultural factors that would make this obscure to any class members.

Providing for Different Levels of Ability. There may be some problems with this selection. Although the vocabulary is not a major problem, the formality and elevated style of the writing might present some difficulties. This problem might most probably be overcome by doing the reading as an in-class oral reading, stopping at various times to make sure that the students understand what they have been reading. You might wish to plan out the passages where you intend to stop the reading and discuss as you move through the selection.

Introducing Vocabulary Study. Students will benefit from knowing the meanings of the following words before they read the selection.

copious	panegyric
disapprobation	perfiousness
expostulate	scourge
intrepidity	solicitation
ligature	viscous
odious	

Reading the Selection. As indicated above in the section on Providing for Different Levels of Ability, this assignment may best be accomplished through stop-and-go reading and discussion.

Reteaching Alternatives. If you use the stop-and-go approach suggested above, reteaching will not be necessary. You will be able to make sure the students understand as they go along. This would be far better than trying to go back and compensate in some fashion for those who read it alone and did not understand the actual text.

Extending the Story. Ask students to break into several small groups. Suggest that each group write a brief skit satirizing—in a Swiftian manner—something that is politically relevant to them. Subject matter may range from the seemingly insignificant to the seemingly profound. Encourage students to focus narrowly on elements they choose to satirize. You may want to remind them that one way for a satire to be particularly effective is to make the subject matter appear serious, while carefully interjecting the comic elements. Have students act out their skits for the rest of their classmates. The audience may be helpful in pointing

out what works best and what needs extra attention and rewriting.

Responding to the Story   Text page 513
Analyzing the Story
Identifying Facts

1. How large are the Lilliputians? They are less than six inches high—about one-twelfth the size of humans.

Why doesn't Gulliver seize and harm the Lilliputians who come close to his free hand? Gulliver fears that the Lilliputians may renew their attack with the darts; he also begins to feel bound by the laws of hospitality after the Lilliputians have fed him, and he wonders at their courage.

2. What positions do Flimnap and Reldresal hold in this tiny kingdom? Flimnap is the treasurer, and Reldresal is the principal secretary for Private Affairs.

3. Describe the two evils that threaten Lilliput, according to Reldresal. Reldresal identifies the two evils that threaten Lilliput as violent faction at home and the danger of an invasion from abroad by a powerful enemy.

4. Explain how the war between Lilliput and Blefuscu began. The Lilliputians decreed that all eggs must be opened at the small end. But certain rebels disobeyed this edict and continued to open their eggs at the big end. The kingdom of Blefuscu alienated Lilliput by giving sanctuary and aid to the Big-Endians.

Interpreting Meanings

5. In the first episode here, Swift is parodying—imitating and making fun of—contemporary travel books. Such books were notorious for containing two kinds of material: fantastic lies about strange places, and trivial details about the traveler's daily life there. Show how this section parodies both kinds of travel materials. Answers will vary. Students can point to almost any part of the introductory episode as illustrating parody of these two kinds of materials.

6. In the second episode, Swift begins to use the travel book as a medium for satire. He expects his readers to find similarities between what goes on in Lilliput and what goes on at home. The travel book device enables him to comment indirectly on political matters in England. What qualifications are the officials of Lilliput expected to have in order to hold high office? These officials are expected to be able to jump nimbly in rope dancing. They also must leap over or creep under a stick, held by the king or the first minister.

What does Swift's comparison say about English officials? The comparison implies that English officials are servile, inconsistent, unscrupulous, and hypocritical.

7. When people act in a mean, sneaky way, other people say, ''That wasn't very big of them,'' or ''That was a small way to behave.'' What do *big* and *small* mean in these contexts? In these contexts, *big* might be said to mean ''noble,'' ''generous,'' or ''honest.'' *Small* might be said to mean ''dishonest'' or ''mean-spirited.''

List some connotations of *big* and *small* as they are used by Swift. Connotations of *big*: outlandish, threatening, disproportionate, ugly. Connotations of *small*: ridiculous, mean, dishonest, silly.

8. Is there any relationship between the physical size of the Lilliputians and the way Swift wants us to evaluate their behavior? In other words, does their size *symbolize* some other kind of ''smallness''? Explain. Most students will agree that the physical smallness of the Lilliputians also suggests their silliness and pettiness.

9. What does Swift think of squabbles over politics and religion? It is apparent from the passage that Swift thinks that such squabbles are futile and small-minded.

What does he think of the differences that divide people into factions? The passage suggests that Swift thinks that these differences are often overstated and ridiculous.

Do you agree or disagree with his implications? Student answers will vary. Encourage the students to give reasons for their opinions.

10. The critical comment following this selection explains how Lilliputian politics paralleled British politics of Swift's time. Can you detect any parallels between Lilliput and what you know of modern politics, either in this country or some other one? Student answers will vary. Encourage them to make their parallels as specific as possible.

Responding to the Story
Text page 516
Analyzing the Story
Identifying Details

1. To what form of life does the king first compare Gulliver? The king first compares Gulliver to an insect.

2. In comparison, what do English people think of themselves, according to Gulliver? According to Gulliver, English people think of themselves as noble, creative, powerful, virtuous, honorable, and truthful.

3. What feat of dexterity can Gulliver perform that impresses the Brobdingnagians? He can use his knife to cut to pieces the huge flies that annoy him.

4. From Gulliver's defense of England, the king evaluates English officials and institutions. According to the king, what are the qualifications for English legislators? According to the king, the qualifications for English legislators are ignorance, idleness, and vice.

Interpreting Meanings

5. Explain why the king roars with laughter when he asks Gulliver whether he is a Whig or a Tory. The implication is that the king finds that the distinction between the two political factions, taken so seriously in British life, is silly and trivial.

6. Why does Gulliver begin to think of himself as small? He observes that the flies in Brobdingnag are as big as Dunstable larks.

7. How does Swift characterize the king of Brobdingnag? Which actions show the king's personality traits? Swift characterizes the king of Brobdignag as philosophical and reflective. The king is also extremely intelligent and perceptive, as shown by his speeches to Gulliver. The action of taking Gulliver in his hand and stroking him gently may portray the king as kindly, or it may perhaps imply condescension.

8. Point out some instances of *verbal irony* in this section of *Gulliver's Travels*. Instances of verbal irony may include the following: Gulliver's indignation that the reputation of England for honor and virtue is being sullied by the king; the account of the immense flies; and Gulliver's reference to the history of the last century, followed by the king's reaction. Another instance of irony occurs toward the end of the section, where the king supposes that Gulliver's travels have made him wiser than his countrymen: in fact, Gulliver has learned little or nothing.

9. What connections can you make between Gulliver's experience with the Brobdingnagian flies and the king's dismissal of humanity as ''little odious vermin''? These incidents share a common, repulsive motif.

10. What evidence can you find in the text to suggest that Gulliver is learning little or nothing from his experiences in Brobdingnag? The principal evidence is to be found in Gulliver's indignant reaction to the king's comparison of human beings with insects.

11. What do you think of the Brobdingnagian royal family? What faults and virtues do you see in them? Answers will vary. Encourage the students to support their opinions with citations from the passage.

Satire

Ask students to read this essay, paying close attention to the different elements that can be used in satire. Irony, understatement, exaggeration, and sarcasm are a few that are mentioned in this section. Emphasize that satire is used to comment on the wrongs of society or a particular individual without moralizing. *Gulliver's Travels* and "A Modest Proposal" are two excellent examples of satire in this section. To stress the outrageous, foolish, and detestable character-

istics of the satire's target, the subject is often portrayed in contrast to other serious, virtuous, and/or controlled elements (for example, *Artifices in Tragedy*). You may want to ask students to note that satires are often—but not always—comic. Some present criticisms in a subtle and understated manner, while others present observations, character studies, and so on, in an exaggerated style. Some students may be particularly fond of satire, while others prefer a more direct treatment of critical issues.

A Modest Proposal

Objectives

1. To identify instances of characterization
2. To analyze satire
3. To identify the author's purpose
4. To write a newspaper editorial
6. To write an essay relating the selection to current events
7. To analyze diction and connotation

Introducing the Essay

In outline form, for your reference, here are the major elements in the essay:

- **Point of view:** first person
- **Significant techniques:** characterization, satire, author's purpose

Background on the Essay. The shock value is an extremely important part of this pamphlet. Do not spend time preparing the students for what they are going to hear. You might wish to leave the printed introductory remarks until after the students have read the pamphlet. When Swift wrote this pamphlet, he wanted the English legislators to be shocked so that they would seriously consider the plight of the Irish people. The best way for the students to approximate its original effect is for them to encounter the work cold.

You might wish to have the students encounter this as a classroom assignment. Occasionally you will encounter a

literal-minded student who needs to have the verbal reassurance that Swift was not an ogre. This probably needs to be done with as little time-lapse as possible.

When you comment on this selection, after all of the students have been suitably shocked, you will want to explore the situation of the Irish people. Be sure to discuss the impact of the absentee landlord upon them. You can bring the point home by drawing the parallel of what would happen in the students' hometown if most of the local businesses were owned by out-of-towners.

Teaching Strategies

Providing for Cultural Differences. One very real problem with satire is that encountered with exceptionally literal-minded people. They are likely to take such a work at face value and never be able to see the intended point and appreciate the mode by which the point was made. Make special efforts to help students understand that this is sarcastic—that the author did not literally intend what he is suggesting.

Providing for Different Levels of Ability. Immediately after the students have read the selection, you will probably want to carry on discussion. The questions at the end of the text will provide a very good starting point for it. In order to make sure that the students understand that satire is an instrument of social change, you may wish to have students read about this pamphlet and find out whether it had any discernible effect in Swift's day. Ask the students to find out if any legislative change occurred.

Introducing Vocabulary Study. Students will benefit

from knowing the meanings of the following words before they read the selection.

idolatrous   repine

Discuss with students the distinction between denotation and connotation, permitting them to explore the difference in examples. Direct them to look, as they read the selection, for connotative values of words that are highly charged.

Reading the Essay. Have the students read this pamphlet in class. A double entry reading log will be very helpful to the students in understanding this prose work. They are so likely to get caught up in what they are reading that they wind up skimming the material. Have them set up a Note-taking column on the left and a Note-making column on the right. Encourage the students to comment on the text as they go along, recording their initial impressions as they read.

Reteaching Alternatives. If the students do not grasp the factual line, go over the sequence of arguments as they appear. Have the students keep a truly careful log. If the students fail to grasp the meaning of satire and how it operates, you might wish to discuss political cartoons and caricature with them. Talk about other satirical works they have read and have them identify the social problems that those works address. You may wish to have students write a brief satiric skit in which they satirize some school problem.

Extending the Essay. Ask students to read through newspaper and magazine editorials to find a contemporary example of a Swiftian satire. Suggest that students bring in their editorials to share with the class. It may be interesting for them to critique these editorials, using ''A Modest Proposal'' as the source for comparison. How is the current writer more or less effective than Swift? How do they think the public will react to their samples as opposed to Swift's readers at the time that his essay was written?

Responding to the Essay   Text page 524
Analyzing the Essay
Identifying Details

1. Why does the narrator think the food he proposes to be "very proper for landlords"? The narrator says that the landlords should have the first claim on the flesh of the children, since the landlords have already devoured most of the children's parents.

2. Why does the narrator object to the suggestion of selling and eating the twelve to fourteen-year-old children? He says that they are dying off quickly enough in the natural course of events, due to cold, famine, filth, and vermin.

3. Why is the narrator not concerned about old people who are suffering from sickness, poverty, and neglect? He says that they are dying off quickly enough in the natural course of events, due to cold, famine, filth, and vermin.

4. About midway in the pamphlet, the narrator lists the advantages to his proposal. What are the six principal advantages? The advantages are as follows: 1) lessening the number of Papists (Roman Catholics); 2) giving the poorer tenants a tangible asset; 3) increasing the national economy; 4) relieving the breeders of the trouble and expense of raising their children beyond the age of one year; 5) increasing the business of those who own taverns; 6) encouraging marriage.

5. Describe the one objection that the narrator anticipates to his proposal. The narrator anticipates the objection that the proposal, if carried out, would diminish the population; however, he claims that this effect will be one of the proposal's principal virtues, at least as far as Ireland is concerned.

Interpreting Meanings

6. Just as the narrator is about to make his "modest proposal," he says that he hopes it "will not be liable to the least objection." Why does he express this wish? Why does he call his proposal "modest"? Both the expression of the wish and the description of the proposal as "modest" are ironic, given the outlandish, monstrous character of the actual proposal.

7. What impression does the speaker want readers to have of him? The speaker wants us to have an impression of him as restrained, judicious, and constructive.

Find sentences in which the speaker *characterizes* himself favorably and claims to possess certain virtues that—considering the nature of his proposal—he could not possibly have. Among the sentences students may point to are the following: the first sentence of the essay (where the narrator seems to give an impression of himself as sympathetic), the first sentence of the third paragraph (which implies that the narrator has given the matter serious, sober thought), and the first sentence of the last paragraph (which implies that the speaker is dispassionate and neutral, and that he does not offer his proposal in the hope of any personal financial gain).

8. Describe the narrator's purpose in asserting that England will not mind if Ireland kills and eats its babies. What element of *satire* is evident here? This statement illustrates the element of irony in satire. The writer's underlying purpose is to criticize the cruelty and insensitivity of the English.

9. Near the end of the pamphlet the speaker lists "other expedients" that might help lessen the present distress in Ireland. Some of these options are very constructive. Why, then, does the narrator say, "Let no man talk to me of other expedients"? Again, the purpose is ironic; in rejecting the constructive "expedients" and in putting forward his own "modest proposal," the narrator is ironically commenting on the failure of any constructive improvement in Ireland's miserable situation.

10. How would you state the *purpose* of this essay? Students answers will vary. Have them try to state Swift's purpose in a single, clear, and comprehensive sentence.

11. Do you think Swift goes too far in the essay? Why or why not? Answers will vary. Have the students support their opinions with reasons and specific arguments.

Alexander Pope

Text page 525

Pope, probably more than any other eighteenth-century literary figure, is an embodiment of the time. To know and understand this artist is to know and understand this Classical Period, for the two are almost synonymous. Certainly, the classic ideal has been stressed throughout this unit. Nevertheless, a study of Pope, because he is so quintessentially classic, affords a special opportunity for students to grasp these principles with a heretofore unobtainable clarity.

The Age of Reason was one in which artists and thinkers valued balance, rationality, moderation, and good judgment. Rhetorical devices were the order of the day. Again, when one considers rhetorical devices, Pope's work becomes the standard by which one measures. As you move through this section, you will want to allow for a systematic study of the following literary terms and devices: antithesis, epigram, chiasmus, and rhetorical question.

Heroic Couplets

Text page 527

Objectives

1. To recognize heroic couplets
2. To analyze the poetic principles behind Pope's work

The Poem at a Glance

- **Rhyme:** rhyming couplets
- **Rhythm:** iambic pentameter
- **Significant technique:** antithesis

Background on the Couplets.   A high proportion of any list of famous quotations from English literature will be epigrams from the pen of Alexander Pope. Pope had a facility for expressing "What oft was tho't, but ne'er so well expressed." The epigrams in the student text are only a few of the many you would find in any book of famous quotes.

Teaching Strategies

Providing for Cultural Differences.   Although there may be difficulties in understanding some of these couplets, the problems will not be precisely cultural differences. Pope had a propensity for formal poetic diction. He frequently employed a highly Latinate vocabulary and inverted word

order. All of these characteristics will make this particular set of lines very difficult for some students. The only provision one can make is to go over these couplets one by one.

Providing for Different Levels of Ability.   Since these are disjointed little snippets, it would be easy for students to give them the once-over lightly. The questions at the end of the selection will serve to focus students' attention. You may decide to have the students answer these questions after reading the couplets as part of an at-home assignment. If you then go over them in class, the discussion should ensure that all of the students will understand the content.

Introduction to Vocabulary.   Instruct students to be on the alert as they read for poetic devices they have studied and especially for instances of figurative language.

Reading the Couplets.   If the couplets are read in class, have the students paraphrase them as they read. Stop and discuss them individually as you go through them. Handled in this way, there should be no need to reteach the selection. If the couplets are assigned for home reading, assign the students to paraphrase each epigram. This will provide a basis for in-class discussion.

Reteaching Alternatives.   There should be no need for reteaching this selection if you go over the answers to the questions and the paraphrases in class.

Responding to the Couplets   Text page 528

Analyzing the Couplets

Identifying Details

1. List some of the old sayings that you recognized in the couplets. Student answers will vary.

2. Tell in which of the couplets Pope does each of the following:

a. Advocate a mean between two extremes. Couplet 3.

b. Suggest that geniuses are born, not made. Couplet 1.

c. Explain why people are never satisfied with what they have. Couplet 6.

d. Compare writing to putting on clothes. Couplet 3 might be construed as doing so.

e. Show how important education is for the young. Couplet 7.

f. Advise critics to be generous. Couplet 5.

g. Assume that his readers know the Biblical story of creation. Couplet 8, which echoes the first chapter of Genesis, in which God says, "Let there be light."

Interpreting Meanings

3. Give some examples showing how a little learning can be dangerous (Couplet 2). Student answers will vary.

What is the difference between drinking "deep" and drinking superficially from the Pierian spring on Mt. Olympus, Greece, from which the Muses drew their inspiration? On the one hand, drinking "deep" implies a detailed knowledge of a subject; on the other hand, drinking superficially implies a fragmentary, imperfect knowledge that may lead its possessor into error or danger.

4. In the couplet on Newton, explain the difference between what is suggested by the words *night* and *light*. The word *night* suggests obscurity and ignorance; the word *light* suggests intellectual understanding and true reason.

5. Which couplet shows that the pronunciation of a common word has changed since Pope's day? The rhyme in couplet 5 shows that the word "join" was pronounced in Pope's day to rhyme with "divine."

6. Pope compresses a large amount of meaning into the twenty or so syllables of his couplets. Try writing out, in your own words, the idea expressed in any couplet that you find hard to understand. What does Pope gain by compressing his meaning? Answers will vary. Most students will agree that Pope gains the values of pithiness and memorability. Many of the couplets are so compressed and artfully constructed that they might qualify as epigrams.

7. Do you find the advice in these couplets useful, or does it seem out of date? Explain your response. Answers will vary. Encourage students to explain and support their opinions.

---

from An Essay on Criticism   Text page 529

Objectives

1. To analyze a fragment of a verse essay
2. To write lines of verse using euphonious sounds

The Poem at a Glance

- **Rhyme:** rhyming couplets
- **Rhythm:** iambic pentameter
- **Significant technique:** verse essay

Background on the Verse.   The comments made in the student text in the biographical notes on Pope and the introduction to the selection are worth reconsidering. Students may well understand the genius of Mozart as a result of the popularity of the drama *Amadeus*; you might wish to draw a parallel here to Pope's genius. Students are fascinated with the idea of a prodigy, and this will stimulate their imaginations.

You will probably want to review poetic sound devices prior to reading the poem. Review *alliteration*, *onomatopoeia*, and *rhyme* as sound devices.

Teaching Strategies

Providing for Cultural Differences.   As with the heroic couplets and the remainder of Pope's work, the difficulties will not stem from cultural barriers. The difficulties will be for those who have various types of language barriers.

Providing for Different Levels of Ability.   The differences should be met through an oral reading and in-class commentary on this selection. You will want to comment at length about various sound devices utilized in this excerpt.

Reading the Verse. Because this poem deals with poetic technique and sound devices, the selection ought to be read out loud.

Reteaching Alternatives. Have the students attempt to put some wisdom they subscribe to in the form of several lines of poetry. Advise them that their efforts need not consist of rhyming couplets, though students should be encouraged to imitate Pope's style of versification as closely as they are able.

Responding to the Verse   Text page 529

Analyzing the Verse

Identifying Details

1. What, according to Pope, do writing poetry and

dancing have in common? Poetry and dancing both depend on learning and art.

2. **Summarize the advice Pope gives to poets here.** Pope advises that the sound of a poem must harmoniously echo and reinforce its meaning; in other words, a poem's form must be suited to its content.

Interpreting Meanings

3. **In what ways have both poetry and dancing changed since Pope's day? Think of ways in which the changes in these two activities may be related.** Student answers will vary. In gen-eral, most students will agree that both dancing and poetry have become freer, or at least more flexible, in form. A possible reason is that, since Pope's day, the overt expression of emotion in both activities has become more popular. Students will have different opinions on how the two activities might be related. Encourage the students to offer specific suggestions in the class discussion.

from An Essay on Man   Text page 530

Objectives

1. To analyze a fragment of a verse essay
2. To write an illustrative account

The Poem at a Glance

- **Rhyme:** rhyming couplet
- **Rhythm:** iambic pentameters
- **Significant technique:** verse essay

Background on the Verse. The note to the selection will be very helpful in introducing this fragment. Focus on the fact that the essay consists of over one thousand lines in its entirety. Further, reemphasize that this is a synthesis of many of the ideas of all the great philosophers of history. You might wish to have students speculate on what forces in Pope's life conspired to create and encourage his genius.

Teaching Strategies

Providing for Cultural Differences. As with the other of Pope's selections, there will be no particular problems arising from cultural differences.

Providing for Differing Levels of Ability. This selection will need class discussion and teacher-led explication for the

students to understand. Thus, any differences may be resolved by the class work.

Reading the Verse. This selection is a good one for the students to work through as a private lesson. After you have introduced the poem, you may wish to read through it once, giving the students an overview. Establish with them that this fragment will take considerable thought because it is one long *paradox*. Have the students define this literary term if they do not already know it. Suggest that they look at the writing activity presented at the end of the selection and make plans to complete it. Doing the activity will contribute to their understanding of the selection.

Reteaching Alternatives. After the students have submitted their assignments, you will probably wish to go back over their responses to reinforce their learning. You might manage this easily if you plan to present the essay in class and assign the activity as homework to be submitted the following day. Implement a quick check of the responses prior to a discussion.

Responding to the Verse   Text page 530

Analyzing the Verse

Identifying Details

1. **In almost every sentence of this passage, Pope says something flattering about the human race, only to fol-**

low it with something insulting. **What characteristics does he think we should be proud of?** Possibilities include wisdom, knowledge, judgment, and the ability to reason.

What should we be ashamed of? Possibilities include weakness, doubt, error, ignorance, and passion.

2. How many sentences are in this verse? There are two sentences in the verse.

Interpreting Meanings

3. In what ways do you think human beings could be seen as the "glory" of this world? As its "jest"? As its

"riddle"? Student answers will vary. Ask them to explain the specific possibilities that they suggest.

4. What one word would you use to summarize the human condition as Pope describes it? Why do you choose this word? Again, answers will vary. Possibilities might include "ambiguous," "paradoxical," "contradictory," "middle," "wonderful-miserable," and so on. Ask the students to explain and support the word they select.

5. Discuss your opinion of Pope's opening couplet. Encourage students to give reasons for their opinions in the discussion.

---

from The Rape of the Lock
Text page 533

Objectives

1. To identify satire
2. To analyze tone
3. To identify and analyze irony
4. To identify a work's theme
5. To write a prose description using mock-heroic style
6. To write an analysis of a satire
7. To write a comparison of two epics

Introducing the Poem

In outline form, for your reference, here are the major elements in the poem:

· **Antagonists:** Belinda and the Baron
· **Conflict:** human vs. human
· **Point of view:** third-person omniscient
· **Significant techniques:** satire, tone, irony, mock-heroic style
· **Setting:** Hampton Court

B*ackground on the Poem.* Since this is a mock epic, it is important to review the characteristics of an epic as they apply to this work. A good working definition is as follows: an epic is an orally transmitted narrative poem about a larger-than-life hero, whose deeds have captured the imagination of a nation, thus encouraging the repetition of those tales. Through constant repetition, the tales are ritualized; the language is formalized. Detail is lost and exaggeration occurs. Frequently the language becomes elevated to match the hero and the deeds. The Greek epics—*The Iliad* and *The*

Odyssey—both have certain characteristics that are paralleled in Pope's brilliant work. One expects an Invocation to the Muse, in which the poet asks the Muse of epic poetry, Calliope, to bring her blessings to the work of the poet and grant inspiration to the work at hand. One also expects to find an inventory; in *The Iliad*, Homer calls the role of all the Greek leaders and their troops. Further, there is a detailed battle of the troops, followed by a battle between the individual heroes. Of course, these are immortalized in a witty way in the various passages of the poem. Pope, who gained lasting fame in his lifetime for his translations of the Greek epics, did a brilliant job of mocking this literary genre. By elevating a trivial quarrel to the level of a world-shaking epic, all were forced to see the silliness of the quarrel.

T*he Plot.* The story line of this poem begins with the fair Belinda awakening from her slumber. Already the airy spirits that will surround her throughout the day are by her side. One whispers a warning in her ear that she undoubtedly does not hear. With the help of her maid, Belinda dresses and applies her makeup. By Canto III, she has joined friends at a gathering at Hampton Court. There she and other young people of leisure, including the Baron, sip coffee, gossip, and flirt. Upon seeing Belinda, the Baron schemes to shear a lock of her hair. He accomplishes the deed, rousing a scream from Belinda. Using words as weapons, Belinda and the Baron engage in battle. The Baron feels no remorse, and Belinda must accept the situation. Her consolation, the speaker suggests, is that her lock of hair will join the other stars in the heavens.

Teaching Strategies

P*roviding for Cultural Differences.* Cultural differences will be minimal in this poem. The background necessary to make the poem explicable to one student will serve equally well for the next.

Providing for Different Levels of Ability. This poem, to be properly enjoyed and experienced, would best be served by an oral reading. It will assist the students' understanding to have you stop at intervals to explain, question, and discuss, and then resume the reading. Handled in that fashion, the language and literary allusions will not present an insurmountable problem.

Introducing Vocabulary Study. Students will benefit from knowing the meanings of the following words before they read the poem:

bodkin   timorous
consecrate   titillating
pungent

Reading the Poem. This selection should be read aloud. As indicated above in Providing for Different Levels of Ability, an oral stop-and-go reading by the teacher will save time in the long run in reteaching and helping students to understand.

Reteaching Alternatives. If you use the oral reading as a method of presenting this selection, reteaching will not be necessary.

Responding to the Poem   Text page 541
Analyzing the Poem
Identifying Details

1. At the beginning of Canto I, Pope admits that his subject is "slight," or trivial (line 5). What excuses does he give for writing on such a slight subject? Pope gives the excuse that he will think his work well done if his friend John Caryll approves of it, and if it pleases the real-life Belinda (the young and fashionable Arabella Fermor).

2. Why does the guardian sylph Ariel warn Belinda? Ariel warns Belinda that a mysterious, dread event is to occur; she is to beware of Man.

What causes her to forget the warning? Belinda, awakening, happens to notice a love letter, and she forgets all about the sylph's warning.

3. What renders the guardian sylph powerless to defend the lock? The guardian sylph is powerless to defend the lock when he notices that Belinda is thinking about a lover.

4. How does Belinda defeat the Baron in battle? What makes the weapon she chooses seem particularly appropriate? Belinda defeats the Baron "in battle" with a pinch of snuff. The weapon is especially appropriate because taking snuff was a somewhat pretentious habit of the aristocracy in Pope's day.

5. In Canto V, lines 39–44, Pope describes a kind of lunar limbo. What sort of lost objects are found there? The objects include the wits of heroes and beaux (fashionable gentlemen), broken vows, deathbed alms, and lovers' hearts, which are bound with bits of ribbon.

If the stolen lock is not there, where, according to the Muse, is it? If it is not there, the Muse says that it has been transformed into a comet in the sky.

How is this ultimate fate of the lock supposed to soothe Belinda's grief? The ultimate fate of the lock is supposed to soothe Belinda's grief because at least it will confer immortal fame on her.

Interpreting Meanings

6. *The Rape of the Lock* is a famous example of satire. The *tone* of satire can either be angry or good-natured, vicious or mild. Consider the description of Belinda at her dressing table (Canto I, lines 53–80). What is Pope's tone in describing this common human activity? Is he amused or contemptuous? How can you tell? Most students will agree that Pope's tone is one of amusement: the underlying comparison of the lady's toilette to a religious rite is humorous, rather than scornful.

7. Examine the language of this passage and notice all the words associated with religion. What is Pope's purpose in using this language? The purpose is to poke light, satirical fun at the importance that fashionable ladies like Belinda attach to their appearance.

8. Another *satirical* passage is the description of the court at the beginning of Canto III. Again, what is Pope's *tone*—his attitude toward the queen and her courtiers? Is he scornful or tolerantly amused? How can you tell? Most students will agree that Pope is tolerantly amused. The humor is especially evident in the juxtaposition of important and utterly trivial elements in many of the couplets (for example, in line 6, the mention of the fall of foreign tyrants and the fall of nymphs at home, or the mention of counsel and tea in line 8).

9. Belinda's victory at cards (Canto III, lines 23–28) and her cries of triumph are said to be *ironic* because her happiness is so momentary; it's about to be shattered by the rape of the lock. Irony always involves a discrepancy of some kind, here between what Belinda expects—a "victorious day"—and what actually happens, the sad loss of her lock. Explain why Belinda's victory over the Baron (Canto V, lines 13–22) might similarly be considered ironic. Belinda's victory over the Baron might also be said to be ironic because the lock, which Belinda wanted restored, cannot be found.

10. In Canto III, Pope juxtaposes—that is, places side by side—dying husbands and dying lapdogs (line 86). What is the effect of this juxtaposition? The effect of the juxtaposition in this line is humorous.

Find other juxtapositions of this kind in the poem. Students may mention various passages. Among the possibilities are the mention of counsel and tea at III.8, the mention of the British queen and an Indian screen at III.13–14, the mention of hanging judges and jurymen's dinners at III.21–22, and the description of the sylph's being cut in two (but soon uniting again) at III.79–80.

11. In the complete poem, Pope frequently makes *satirical* remarks about the world outside the privileged ranks to which Belinda and her friends belong. An example of such a remark, in the excerpts printed here, occurs in Canto III, lines 21–22 and lines 45–46. Who or what are Pope's targets in these couplets? The targets are cruel, insensitive judges and crafty politicians, respectively.

12. The world outside the poem and the world inside it come together in Canto III, lines 7–8. What is the effect of the three words after the dash? The effect is to "deflate" the solemnity of royal councils of state with the mention of a common, everyday activity—drinking tea.

13. Who, if anyone, is victorious by the end of the action? The narrator implies that Belinda is victorious, since she will have undying fame.

14. How would you state Pope's *theme* in this epic—based on the extracts you have read? Student answers will vary. In general, the theme might be described as poking gentle fun at the silly, petty disputes and vanities that sometimes preoccupy us.

Does the epic apply in any way to any aspects of contemporary life? Can you find passages that could serve as satiric commentaries on people's behavior in the late twentieth century? Most students will have no difficulty in finding such passages. Ask the students to be as specific as they can.

The Elements of Literature

Wit

Have students read the essay and then discuss it in class. As the essay points out in the example of Pope, the meaning of wit has changed over time. This may be somewhat confusing to students. As the first paragraph mentions, wit has been associated with intellectual brilliance and the profound and articulate expression of that brilliance. In the second paragraph, wit is equated with cleverness and compared to dullness.It is then described through Pope's line: "Nature to advantage dressed." "True wit" is then mentioned—which can be compared to false wit (writing that captures the attention of the reader without sufficient knowledge evident in the content). Later in the essay, wit is used to describe a type of individual—a writer, for example. Students may be familiar with the word in relation to humor: something that is witty is funny; a wit, in their minds, may be a comedian. After discussing the essay, ask students to discuss their interpretation of the word. You may want to remind them that the meanings of almost all words change over time.

Sir Richard Steele
Joseph Addison

The goal of Addison and Steele was to educated the *nouveau riche*, who suddenly found themselves with money enough to indulge in society, but who lacked the refinement to match their new station. The key to that goal, if their personal essays were any indication, was gentle satire and a pontificating stance on all matters relating to morals and taste. Readers avidly sought these instructions and read them for purposes of improvement as well as for entertainment. Addison, in the first essay following, attempts the role of arbiter of theatrical taste. Here he instructs the audience upon the subject of what is proper to appreciate in comic theater.

Sir Richard Steele, Joseph Addison   117

Objectives

1. To analyze a personal essay
2. To write an essay describing comic responses
3. To analyze hyperbole, understatement, and sarcasm

Introducing the Essay

In outline form, for your reference, here are the major elements in the essay:

- **Point of view:** first person
- **Significant techniques:** personal essay, hyperbole

Background on the Essay. Prior to beginning this selection, involve the students in a discussion of some present-day journalists. Miss Manners, Ann Landers, Abby, Siskel and Ebert, and Rex Reed would all be worth mentioning. In the same vein, you might wish to see if any of the students recognize Mr. Blackwell, the self-appointed clothing critic who yearly draws up lists of the ten-best dressed and ten-worst dressed men and women. You might wish to inquire into what services these people perform for their audiences. If you can get the students to come up with the idea that these people are all advisers to insecure audiences, you are well on your way to having a good entry into this selection by Addison.

Teaching Strategies

Providing for Cultural Differences. In many parts of the country, students will not have seen much live theater. You may, therefore, need to equate these comments with modern movies and television. If you have students from very different cultures, you may wish to explore with them their sense of comedy and differences in theatrical experiences. If they know anything about this, it can be very instructive to all the students to understand that comedy and drama are different things to different cultures and times. Since this essay is of an instructve nature, there is probably no cultural barrier to understanding.

Providing for Different Levels of Ability. Many of the students will need a great deal of help in understanding the theatrical conventions referred to in the piece. Furthermore, the literary allusions will not enrich the students' understanding, but will be an impediment. Make sure all of the students understand all of the references as you proceed. For that reason, you may wish to deal with this selection as an

in-class reading coupled with oral discussion and explanation. It will require a very strong class to understand this selection completely on their own.

Introducing Vocabulary Study. Students will benefit from knowing the meanings of the following words before they read the selection.

disconsolate   obdurate
extenuate

Explain the notion of hyperbole to students by selecting examples from their daily speech habits. Tell them that the selection makes use of hyperbole that was typical of the period during which the writer lived. You may ask students to compile a running log of examples of this literary device.

Reading the Selection. As intimated above, you might wish to teach this selection using a stop-and-go method, combinining oral reading with pauses to elucidate and discuss the material with students. It will take longer to get through the material the first time, but there will be little or no reteaching necessary.

Reteaching the Selection. If the teaching strategy suggested above is followed, there will be little or no reteaching necessary.

Extending the Essay. Ask students to bring in three different theater reviews. Often reviewers interject satirical comments into their critiques. Have students find at least two examples of satire in their reviews. Ask them to identify what satirical device the writer has used. If there are students who cannot find any elements of satire in their reviews, ask them to assess how a few satirical comments might affect their samples. In what ways would satire enhance the reviews; in what ways would it detract from the established tone?

Responding to the Essay   Text page 549
Analyzing the Essay
Identifying Details

1. According to Addison, what should introduce and accompany the common artifices of ghosts and bells if they are to be used in a tragedy to provoke terror? These artifices should be introduced with skill (as in Shakespeare's *Hamlet*) and accompanied with appropriate sentiments and expressions in the text of the play.

2. What device for provoking pity does Addison say is being overused and made to appear ridiculous? Addison criticizes the device of bringing on stage a disconsolate mother who is accompanied by one or more children.

3. What is the most "absurd and barbarous" of all practices on the English stage? Addison singles out the habit of murdering and butchering characters on stage as "absurd and barbarous."

How is this practice different from practices on the French stage? Addison says that on the French stage murders and executions are always carried out behind the scenes.

4. What does Addison recommend as the correct interpretation of Horace's rule? Addison says that Horace's rule—banning onstage deaths—should generally be adhered to, but not pressed to an extreme, as in some of French dramaturgy (Addison cites a play of Corneille as an example).

What example does he give? To demonstrate the correct application of Horace's rule, Addison gives the example of Sophocles's tragedy *Electra*.

5. Why doesn't Addison provide a detailed treatment of comic artifices? Addison says that this would be an endless task, since "the objects that make us laugh are infinitely more numerous than those that make us weep." In addition, greater indulgence and latitude ought to be allowed to comic poets than to tragedians.

Interpreting Meanings

6. Addison speaks of being delighted and terrified at the same time. How can this be, since delight is pleasant and terror unpleasant? Addison is referring to a common experience of spectators at the theater, particularly of the audience at a tragic play. At the same time as we are terrified by the events of the play, we are "delighted" by the skills of the actors, the artistry of the composition—and, perhaps, by the Aristotelian "catharsis," or purgation, of our emotions that the tragedy provides.

7. Why do people sometimes laugh when they see something that is supposed to inspire feelings of terror or pity? Students may propose several reasons: the action may be ludicrous, improbable, or over done; we may laugh out of nervousness or anxiety, and so on.

Can you think of examples from the contemporary stage or from movies or TV? Have students be as specific as they can in their examples.

8. Do you agree with Addison that "unnatural murders" should be committed out of the view of the audience? Most students will agree with Addison's view, but some may propose that such a practice would compromise realism in contemporary drama. Have the students defend their opinions with arguments.

9. How is such violence handled onstage or on-screen today? What do you think is its effect on the audience? Most students will agree that violence tends to be handled overtly and explicitly on stage and on screen today. Ask the students for their opinions the effects of this violence. Do the students think that such violence tends to jade people or to harden their emotions? Do the students think that violence on stage or on screen may be a factor in delinquency and violent crime? Encourage the students to defend their opinions.

Alexander Selkirk   Text page 550

Objectives

1. To identify the theme in an essay
2. To write paragraphs that examine a conclusion
3. To analyze precise word usage

Introducing the Essay

In outline form, for your reference, here are the major elements in the essay:

- **Point of view:** first person
- **Significant technique:** theme

Background on the Essay. Travel books of one sort or another were exceedingly popular during the eighteenth century, many of them filled with descriptions of monsters and fantastical creatures. Many of these references were, of course, hoaxes, but so eager were audiences for knowledge of the new and original that they would read any traveler's adventure. It was upon this demand that *Gulliver's Travels* and *Robinson Crusoe* were predicated. The straightforward form of this essay, with no regard for exaggeration, is not necessarily the standard for that time, but it is admirable by ours. Since students are going to take objective reporting for granted, since that is our standard, it is important to point this last view out to them.

Teaching Strategies

Providing For Cultural Differences.   There are not likely to be many problems with cultural differences, since Selkirk's situation is alien to everyone's experience.

Providing for Different Levels of Ability.   Unlike Addison's essay, this selection is written in a straightforward, easily accessible prose style. The account should present no problems to student readers.

Introducing Vocabulary Study.   Students will benefit from knowing the meanings of the following words before they read the selection.

irksome   languid

Remind students again that word values shift gradually and imperceptibly over time. Some of the words in this essay, you might caution them, though used precisely by the writer, have acquired entirely different meanings.

Reading the Selection.   There is no reason not to make this a take-home reading assignment. It will be easily accessible to all of the students. Since so many things have to be read in class because of the difficulty level, this will provide a welcome change for the students. Follow up the at-home assignment with a class discussion that will ensure understanding on the part of all the students.

Reteaching the Selection.   There is very little reteaching to be confronted if any misunderstandings are handled through the post-reading discussion.

Extending the Essay.   Suggest that students find a contemporary poem that is particularly moving to them and that deals in some way with the issue of solitude. Some of the poets they might enjoy reading are Galway Kinnell, Sharon Olds, Philip Levine, Ruth Stone, Maya Angelou, Theodore Roethke, Carolyn Forche, Sonia Sanchez, James Wright, and Richard Hugo. All of these poets have written pieces that express a feeling of profound solitude. Ask students to try to identify the element(s) in the poem that speaks to them most acutely.

Responding to the Essay   Text page 522
Analyzing the Essay
Identifying Details

1. **What were Selkirk's two kinds of needs?** He needed food and companionship.

How did he satisfy those needs? He found turtles on the shore to satisfy his hunger, and he read the scriptures to fight off the melancholy caused by his solitude.

2. **What did he do to avoid becoming bored?** After an initial period of dejection, Selkirk began to take pleasure in all his daily activities (such as making his hut and the ornaments for it) and in his natural surroundings.

3. **When the rescue ship arrived, why was Selkirk unwilling to leave his island?** He did not want to surrender the happiness and tranquility he had experienced there.

Interpreting Meanings

4. **How does Steele describe the character of Selkirk?** He describes him as intelligent, devout, determined, and practical.

What personal qualities enabled Selkirk to survive on the island? Students will probably point to Selkirk's physical endurance, his determination, and his religious faith.

5. **What details from this account of Selkirk's experience can you see used in Defoe's *Robinson Crusoe*?** Students may point out a number of details: the making of the hut, for example, as well as the searches for food and the characters' mastery of their natural surroundings.

6. **How well do you think the quotation from Selkirk at the end sums up the theme of the article? State the theme in your own words.** Most students will agree that this quotation adequately sums up the theme. One statement of the theme might be: to be happy, we should confine our desires to natural necessities.

7. **Do you ever feel that you would enjoy being alone for an extended period of time?** Student answers will vary.

Do you think everyone would respond to solitude as Selkirk did? Most students will probably disagree that everyone would respond like Selkirk. The students may suggest that less determined, practical people would give in to despair or suffer a nervous breakdown.

8. **How are Selkirk's means of adjustment to solitude like or unlike the means used by contemporary survivors, prisoners, or hostages?** Student answers will vary. Encourage them to be as specific as possible when they point out similarities and differences.

The commentary in the text on Dr. Johnson is exceptionally thorough. Almost anything one could want to know about the sage is contained in this preface. Bridge the teaching of Johnson's *Dictionary* by noting that the students are very used to taking their own modern dictionaries for granted. You might wish to provoke them to think about where the language and its users would be if no dictionary were available. Through preliminary discussion, try to get the students to realize what a dictionary does for them, regardless of how infrequently they might consult it. Such an introduction may help to give them a respect for the work that Johnson accomplished.

---

from A Dictionary of the English Language

Text page 555

Objectives

1. To interpret a lexicographer's attitudes toward the language

2. To write original dictionary definitions

3. To write a paragraph that draws inferences from definitions

Introducing the Dictionary

In outline form, for your reference, here are the major elements in the dictionary:

- **Significant techniques:** slang, cant

Background on the Definitions. Involve students by procuring and administering to them copies of a good dictionary. Direct their attention to the front matter of the book, which describes the lexicographic principles by which it was developed. Also usually included there are the names of the myriad people who participated in the mammoth undertaking. After a thorough discussion, mention that Samuel Johnson worked entirely on his own in developing his *Dictionary*.

Teaching Strategies

Providing for Cultural Differences. This selection is likely to prove taxing to many students. The word entries, in many cases, use definitions that have undergone a great deal of change. Many of the words and the meanings are now obsolete. The enjoyment of reading some of the entries is in the recognition not only of their obsolescence, but in Johnson's clear biases. None of the subtleties will be obvious to individuals who are not totally comfortable with the nuances of the language. These problems are likely to be most apparent in non-native speakers and in students who have some language difficulties.

Providing for Different Levels of Ability. The problems addressed above and the difficulties implicit in the definitions for slower readers can be mediated through the collaborative learning exercise described below. Jigsawing is a technique for providing detailed and individualized instruction quickly and, usually, in a manner enjoyable to the students. It works very well with material that can be segmented. Once you have mastered the technique, you will find it invaluable in a variety of situations.

To use this strategy, first divide the class into groups; there should be the same number of groups as there are members in the group, five groups of five, for instance. Have these groups go to separate areas of the room to confer. Hand out to each group a segment of the work to be accomplished, in this case a number of word entries and definitions from the text. Instruct the members of each group to cooperate and jointly answer the questions you have listed for them above their entries. At the end of a stated period of time, expect these groups to have finished their work in such a way that each member understands what has transpired. Have the groups now reformulate with one member of each group now assigned to another group. By a gradual rotation, all of the information will be available to every student.

Introducing Vocabulary Study. Students will benefit from knowing the meanings of the following words before they read the selection.

adjudged	lixivium
decoction	ocular
decussated	reticulated
effluvium	serous
interstices	vellicated

Reading the Selection. See the exercise above under Providing for Cultural Differences.

Reteaching Alternatives. No reteaching should be necessary if the exercise described above is used, followed by a class discussion of the experience.

Responding to the Definitions
Text page 558

Analyzing the Definitions

Identifying Details

1. Which words in these excerpts from the *Dictionary* have undergone extensive changes in meaning since Johnson's day? Possibilities include *autopsy, balderdash, companion, dedication, essay, favorite, fillip, jogger, pension, period, vivacious,* and *worm.*

2. Which words did Johnson label as improper that are no longer so regarded? Possibilities include *budge, fun, gambler, immaterial, lesser, lingo, slim,* and *traipse.*

3. Which words do we regard as slangy that Johnson apparently accepted as standard English? Possibilities include *bedpresser, merrythought, mushroom,* and *suds.*

4. Which words are defined by terms that are themselves too strange and complex to be understood? Possibilities include *cant, cough, den, network, smoke, sneeze,* and *soup.*

5. In which definitions does Johnson include moral advice? He includes moral advice when he defines *palmistry* and *slim.*

6. What common words does Johnson define in a sensible, economical way? Possibilities include *bee, blab, pompous,* and *romp.*

Interpreting Meanings

7. What is Johnson's attitude toward slang, which he calls "low words" or "cant"? Johnson displays an unfavorable attitude toward slang.

8. Which definitions show Johnson's sense of humor? Possibilities include the definitions of *hiss, lexicographer, lunch,* and *osprey.*

9. Which definitions show Johnson's political and religious preferences? Possibilities include the definitions of *excise, oats, pension, tory,* and *whig.*

10. Which definitions contain what we would regard as errors of fact? Possibilities include the definitions of *catsup* and *rhinoceros.*

11. From the answers you gave to these questions, what inferences can you make about language, especially about the way it changes? Student answers will vary. Students should include in their discussion some comments about the "living," changing aspects of language. You might want to supplement the discussion with some reference to Johnson's own comments on the *Dictionary,* in which he protested against the concept (then much in vogue with the French Academy) that language was a fossilized, unchanging element that ought to be preserved pure and inviolate.

Letter to Lord Chesterfield
Text page 559

Objectives

1. To identify the author's purpose

2. To analyze the use of irony

3. To identify tone

4. To write a reply to the letter

5. To write a paraphrase of the letter

6. To write an essay explaining satiric elements

Introducing the Letter

In outline form, for your reference, here are the major elements of the letter:

- **Significant techniques:** author's purpose, irony, tone

Background on the Letter. Most students do not know how to vent their frustrations, disappointments, anger, or bitterness in a civilized and socially acceptable fashion. A close reading of this selection can have impact upon the students in the affective domain. First of all, for many, it will be among their first experiences with someone "telling off" someone politely and at the same time making the meaning unmistakably clear. This, in itself, is a superb reason for reading this selection. Many students equate presenting a viewpoint forcefully and clearly with yelling, invective, or profanity; this is a good eye-opener for them; they will quickly understand that this letter was undoubtedly far more effective in making an impact on its recipient than one of another tone might have been. You might wish to get into this selection, therefore, by means of a discussion about how one can express angry feelings effectively. A little prodding will get the students to volunteer ways that this might be done. Have students imagine themselves in a situation somewhat analogous to Johnson's, and have them do a quick-write paragraph prior to the reading. Have them save this entry for later use in the follow-up discussion.

Teaching Strategies

Providing for Cultural Differences. This selection will not cause much difficulty in this area. The position in which Johnson found himself has universal application. You may wish to stress only the relative power of Lord Chesterfield in the aristocratic, class-dominated English society of that period and Johnson's relative helplessness. Modern students do not relate well to the subservience bred in a class-conscious environment.

Providing for Different Levels of Ability. The problems caused by differences in ability will not be ones of content mastery but rather ones of ability to appreciate tone. Sarcasm and irony require sensitivity to the nuances of language. This selection is, of course, very ironic in tone and therefore possibly challenging to some of the students. In a homogeneously grouped class of academic students, this will not present problems. In a heterogeneous class, it might. You could, in addition to the preparation suggested above, divide the students, after they read, into groups for a jigsaw activity in which they paraphrase each paragaph and then see the differences that manifest themselves as a result of that change in language. For details of jigsawing, see Providing for Different Levels of Ability under Johnson's *Dictionary* above.

Reading the Selection. The selection can easily be handled as an in-class reading, with the students perhaps taking notes during the reading, paraphrasing the work after they finish, or working through the selection in one of a number of collaborative ways. Although the letter is short enough that it may not require a home assignment, you might wish to couple the reading with a written response.

Reteaching Alternatives. You might wish to have the students do careful paraphrases of one of the paragraphs under your specific tutelage. When you are sure the students can accomplish this, have them then complete the project on their own.

Extending the Letter. Ask students to write a satirical letter to the editor of your school or local paper addressing an article or editorial. Suggest that students incorporate three elements that Samuel Johnson uses effectively in his letter to Lord Chesterfield. Remind students that they should clearly be making a particular point in their letters. They may or may not choose to use a formal style of writing, but ask them to state why they have chosen their particular style.

Responding to the Letter   Text page 560
Analyzing the Letter
Identifying Details

1. Johnson says that he had asked the Earl for help, but stopped. Why did he stop? He stopped because he received no encouragement or tangible aid from Chesterfield.

2. How does Johnson define a patron? He ironically defines a patron as someone who looks with indifference on a drowning man, and then, once the man has reached ground, "encumbers" him with help.

3. To whom does Johnson give credit for his accomplishment? Johnson says that Providence has enabled him to complete his task himself.

4. What does Johnson say about hope at the letter's end? Johnson says that, at least in this situation, hope was a dream.

Interpreting Meanings

5. What, apparently, was Johnson's *purpose* in writing the letter? To set the record straight? To annoy Chesterfield? To rebuke him? To gloat over him? Most students will probably agree that Johnson's purpose was to set the record straight.

6. Where in the letter does Johnson use *irony*? Johnson uses irony in the first paragraph, where he speaks of not knowing how to receive the "honor" that Chesterfield has paid him. He is also ironic when he defines a patron in the fifth paragraph.

How would you describe the letter's *tone*? The tone of the letter might be described as one of dignified reproach.

7. Johnson refers to himself as an "uncourtly scholar." What traits does such a person typically possess? Student answers will vary.

8. Chesterfield did not take offense at the letter, but kept it lying on a table in his office, where any visitor might read it. Why do you suppose he didn't become angry? Again, student answers may vary. Some students may suggest that Chesterfield, as a cultivated man, knew that he had been in the wrong and that his failure to conceal the letter was tantamount to an admission of fault. Other students may suggest that Johnson had, by this time, gained considerable prominence from the *Dictionary*; Chesterfield may have valued a letter from such an eminent man, even though the letter took him to task.

Objectives

1. To become aware of the individualized nature of approaches to criticism

2. To understand the meaning of universality

3. To write a character analysis

Introducing the Essay

In outline form, for your reference, here are the major elements in the essay:

- **Point of view:** third person
- **Significant techniques:** author's purpose, irony, tone

Background on the Essay.   Upon reading the selection, one of the first things that strikes the reader is the unfailing common sense of Dr. Johnson. This, of course, becomes immediately clear when one compares this piece of criticism with that of Pope and most certainly with the comments of other critics of the Restoration and eighteenth century. So many of them looked to standards outside common sense for judgment that the actual effect of what they saw was lost in theory. Dr. Johnson's work is a signal clarion call to return to good sense and a commentary on what actually *is*.

If you wish to pursue the point about how criticism is formulated, you might wish to show the students a specific video of a television program in class and have the students go home to write a critique of the film. Having the students share their work in some fashion will certainly make the point that people must bring their own individuality to criticism. If you wish to clarify the roles of critics in our own time, you might wish to pursue a discussion of some current critics who influence us—Siskel and Ebert, Rex Reed, Gene Shalitt, and so on. A tightly controlled discussion of the role of critics and how they affect creativity through their influence can be very valid for the students. Such work will provide a good lead into this critic's work.

Providing for Cultural Differences.   This selection will not be easy for any of the students. The difficulties will stem from their lack of familiarity with stage tradition. Fill this cultural gap in their experience by discussing the theater they know. Use current movies to illustrate the points that Johnson makes. There are innumerable examples of all the taboos of which Johnson says Shakespeare is innocent. The problem will be to find examples of the kinds of traits for which Johnson admires the Bard. Such are few and far between. You may need to rely on specific examples from *Macbeth*, which, presumably, students will have read a few

weeks before this time. Depending upon the sequence of curriculum in your school, most of the students may also be familiar with *Romeo and Juliet* and *Julius Caesar*. Plan examples carefully from those works, if applicable, to help the students understand Johnson's comments as they actually apply to a real play.

Providing for Different Levels of Ability.   If you have a heterogeneous class with a wide range of abilities, you might wish, from the very start, to approach this as a jigsaw lesson, parceling out the segments and asking the students to paraphrase. That way, the students who have more difficulty will be able to learn from participating in the group. If one or two students are having difficulty, provide an extra tutorial, in which you or an accelerated peer paraphrases this selection paragraph by paragraph.

Introducing Vocabulary Study.   Students will benefit from knowing the meanings of the following words before they read the selection.

declamation	hyperbolical
depraved	invective
devolve	progeny
exigency	satiety
exorbitant	

Reading the Selection.   You might wish to assign this for at-home or at-desk silent work. If that does not seem appropriate, you may wish to have the students keep a dialectical journal or a reading log as they proceed. This will tend to keep them focused on the selection, and it will also provide them with support for a later writing assignment.

Reteaching Alternatives.   Some of the possibilities for reteaching were covered above in the Providing for Different Levels of Ability section. If you are aware that there are likely to be problems, you might wish to meet the needs in advance; while it is, of course, sometimes necessary to go back, it is better for all concerned to try to anticipate and meet those needs in advance. If you have done all of those things, there probably will be no need to reteach the assignment.

Extending the Essay.   Suggest that students write a one-page essay promoting someone whose work they greatly admire and who they feel has not gotten the attention and respect he or she deserves. This person may be a singer, an actor, a chef, a teacher, a writer, a politician, or another student with a special talent. Ask students to utilize some of the effective elements in Johnson's essay. They may want to compare their subject with someone else who is established and highly regarded in the subject's field. Students will also want to compare their subject with other contemporaries, emphasizing special qualities, insights, and skills their subject has that others do not. Class members may enjoy listening to each other's essays and noting what subjects are depicted in a particularly interesting and enticing manner.

Responding to the Essay   Text page 564

Analyzing the Essay

Identifying Details

1. In the first and second paragraphs, Johnson deals with the reasons why writers may be popular in their own time. Explain in your own words some of his reasons. Among the reasons are the following: personal allusions, local customs, friendship, the championing of popular causes or issues, the taste and manners of the time, prejudice, and fashion.

2. In the third and fourth paragraphs, Johnson explains why writers who have long been dead still remain popular. What is this reason? The reason is the universality of their characters, who resemble species rather than individuals.

3. Having asserted that Shakespeare represents "general nature" in his plays, Johnson (in his fifth paragraph) commends the plays for another important quality. What is this quality? In the fifth paragraph, Johnson praises the memorable quality of Shakespeare's dialogue.

4. For what accomplishments does Johnson commend Shakespeare's plays in the sixth paragraph? In the sixth paragraph, Johnson commends the realism of Shakespeare's plays.

5. In the seventh paragraph, Johnson comments on love as it is represented on the stage and, by implication, in literature generally. What does he think of love as writers portray it? Johnson is highly critical of the manner in which the dramatists of his own time portray love.

Why does he think that love should not be the most frequently treated emotion in literature? Johnson says that love is only one of several passions, and that "it has no great influence on the sum of life." (It should be remembered here that Johnson—a deeply religious and sympathetic man who was devoted to his wife and who often maintained homeless people in his own household—is speaking of ludicrously exaggerated portrayals of romantic love on the eighteenth-century stage.)

6. For what does Johnson commend Shakespeare in the eighth paragraph? In the eighth paragraph, Johnson commends Shakespeare for individualizing his characters and keeping them distinct from one another.

Interpreting Meanings

7. Is it difficult to agree with Johnson's remark, in paragraph nine, that Shakespeare's characters "act and speak as the reader thinks that he should himself have spoken or acted on the same occasion"? Look back at *Macbeth* and see whether you can find a speech that you yourself might have made. Student answers will vary. Encourage the students to give Johnson's statement a broad interpretation that transcends the narrow limits of vocabulary items. What Johnson seems to be saying in this passage is that the *sentiments* expressed by Shakespeare's characters are universal and natural, and that these sentiments are appropriate to the characters' particular situations.

8. What are the present-day equivalents to the "barbarous romances" that Johnson mentions? Student answers will vary. Some students may suggest "romance novels," science fiction novels, television soap operas, and so on.

Why do you think people read "barbarous romances"? Again, students will have various opinions. Possible reasons include escape, vicarious pleasure, and ignorance.

The Elements of Literature   Text page 565

Style

Discuss the essay with students in class. As the Johnson example shows, an analysis of the type of words selected, the structure of clauses and sentences, and the manner of expressing specific thoughts can help to identify a writer's style. The use of metaphors and expressions are also helpful to examine. In addition to looking closely at the Johnson sample, you may want to suggest that students bring in excerpts from their two favorite books. Have them analyze the style of writing, noting the similarities and differences of the authors. This may help them understand—perhaps for the first time—what it is that makes them enjoy their favorite reading material.

Thomas Gray

Text page 566

Elegy Written in a Country Churchyard

Text page 567

Objectives

1. To analyze the effect of imagery

2. To analyze the effect of personification

3. To evaluate a stereotype

4. To write an epitaph

5. To write a meditation that imitates a writer's technique

6. To write an essay comparing and contrasting two poems

7. To identify poetic words

The Poem at a Glance

- **Rhyme:** *abab* in each stanza
- **Rhythm:** iambic pentameter
- **Significant techniques:** elegy, imagery, personification, stereotype

Teaching Strategies

Providing for Cultural Differences.   This poem is an elegy, a ritualized poetic form that has certain expected content and tone. Be sure the students are familiar with this form, either before or after reading the selection itself. A good discussion follows the text and discussion questions for the selection.

Providing for Different Levels of Ability.   This poem deserves to be read aloud. You might wish to read the poem through twice. The first reading gives the students an overall view of the poem and establishes an appreciation for it as a whole. You may then choose to read it aloud again in a stop-and-go style, having the students paraphrase as you finish each unit of thought. Be sure after the discussion is finished to have students go back and read the poem once more as a whole. Such an approach will take care of the problems of those who have trouble comprehending.

Introducing Vocabulary Study.   Students will benefit from knowing the meanings of the following words before they read the poem:

circumscribed   sequestered

Tell students that this elegy contains what are often thought of as *poetic words*—expressions such as *e'er*—as well as inverted word order. The last of these properties they have encountered twice before in this course. By now they should be able to approach it with little trepidation.

Reading the Poem.   Begin by reviewing the information on Thomas Gray on page 566 in the student text. Then move on to the poem. As indicated above, you will probably wish to read the poem aloud. The first five stanzas are full of imagery. At the end of those lines, you might wish to ask the students to pick out more memorable images. (Some very sensitive student may point out that silence itself can be heard in contrast to the specificity of the lowing in the distance and the hum of the beetles.) You might also wish to discuss the fact that the opening is panoramic. If one were to describe this in cinematic terms, the poem opens with a long shot at a valley scene, pans slowly around the vista, and shortens its scope, moving into the immediate environs of the poet, who is sitting on a bench under a tree by the bell tower in the Stoke Poges churchyard. Thus, the poet/camera draws the listener/viewer into the scene. As you move through the poem, you will wish to cite the various movements of the ideas; in stanzas 6 and 7, the poet contemplates the state of the humble dead buried at his feet and of the earthly joys to which they are now insensible. In stanzas 8–11, the poet becomes protective of the humble nature of these burial sites and in apostrophic fashion addresses would-be mockers, pointing out that death comes to all, regardless of their estate, and magnificent tombs and sepulchers cannot alter the reality of that fate. Stanzas 12–19 concern themselves with "what might have been." The poet speculates on the nature of these rude folk here laid to rest and hazards that perhaps the only difference between famous heroes and villains and these ordinary folk is that the former had opportunities, where the latter did not. Stanzas 20–24 ruminate on the human impulse to erect monuments to the dead. Stanzas 25–29 contain the poet's fantasy about his grave and some curious passerby who might inquire about the fate of this young man who used to hang about the graveyard. The Epitaph contains three quatrains in celebration of the shy, simple life of the individual buried therein (who might or might not be intended to be understood as Gray himself).

Reteaching Alternatives.   If you have read, paraphrased discussed, and then reread the poem, there is not much more reteaching to be done.

Analyzing the Poem

Identifying Details

1. Where is the speaker and what time of day is it? The speaker is in a country churchyard at dusk.

What, according to the *images* in stanzas 2 and 3, does he hear? He sees the glimmering landscape at dusk and the beetle's flight; he hears the tinklings of bells from the sheepfolds and the hooting complaint of the owl.

2. In the fourth through eighth stanzas, the speaker describes the poor people in the churchyard. Name the various things they will never again experience. Among the things that the poor people will never again experience are the twittering of the swallow, the crowing of the cock, the sound of the hunting horn, the sight of the blazing hearth, the sight of the housewife, the greetings of their children, the experience of driving their team to the fields, and the labor of planting and harvesting.

3. The poet *personifies* Ambition and Grandeur in lines 29 and 31. What does he warn them not to do? The poet warns Ambition not to mock the people's toil or their homely joys and obscure destiny; he warns Grandeur not to smile disdainfully at these people's short and simple history.

What does he warn the proud about in lines 37–40? He warns the proud not to blame the humble people if they did not have elaborate funerals or monuments erected on their graves.

4. What other examples of *personification* can you find in the poem? Among the examples of personification are the following: Honor (line 43), Flattery (line 44), Knowledge (line 49), Penury (line 51), Luxury and Pride (line 71), Forgetfulness (line 85), Nature (line 91), Earth (line 117), Science (line 119), Melancholy (line 120), and Misery (line 123).

5. What questions does the speaker ask in lines 41–44? He asks rhetorically whether monuments, honor, or flattery can bring the dead back to life.

6. What does the speaker imagine these humble people might have become, if they'd had the opportunity (lines 45–60)? The speaker imagines that one might have become an emperor, another a poet, and another a soldier.

What do the details in lines 53–56 have to do with this idea? The details of the neglected gems and flowers show that excellence and virtue often go unrecognized or are unfulfilled. Just as the gems lie neglected on the ocean floor and the flowers bloom, unappreciated, in the desert, the potential distinction of the humble people buried in the churchyard was never achieved.

7. What did their "lot" or place in life forbid the poor people to experience, according to lines 61–72? Their place in life forbade them to experience high political office and commemoration in their nation's history. Their lot also "circumscribed," or limited, both their virtues and their crimes: none of them, at least, became tyrants, slaughterers, or worshipers of luxury and pride.

8. According to lines 77–92, what evidence on their gravestones shows that the humble also wish to be remembered? According to these lines, the simple, crudely unlettered epitaphs on the graves show that the humble people also wish to be remembered. The poet reflects that such a wish is universal among humankind.

9. What does the speaker imagine an old man (the "hoary-headed swain") might say of him one day (lines 98–116)? He imagines that the swain may remember him after his death as a humble and good man, just as he is now remembering the other dead who are buried in the churchyard.

Interpreting Meanings

10. Many readers of the "Elegy" have assumed that Gray himself is the poet whose epitaph is given in the final lines. Is it necessary to make this assumption to understand the poem? Why does the assumption seem attractive? Most students will agree that it is not necessary to make this assumption in order to understand the poem. On the other hand, the assumption is attractive, since it provides an elegant structural parallel between the speaker's own situation and the situation he is describing in the poem.

11. Suppose that Gray is being autobiographical. What defense does he give of his life? He offers the defense that he was generous, sincere, and pious.

12. From Gray's time almost to the present, many people have thought of poets as possessing the characteristics described in lines 98–112. Gray established a *stereotype* that the public long accepted as genuine. Does this stereotype fit any of the poets you have so far studied in this book? (Think particularly of Chaucer, Shakespeare, Donne, Milton, Pope, and Swift.) Student answers will vary. Most students will agree that the stereotype of the poet as a dreamy, melancholy, and intensely reflective person hardly fits the facts of these poets' lives as we know them. Encourage the students to offer their own opinions and to support them with examples.

13. In one sense, most neoclassical writers thought the purpose of literature was to convey ideas; most Romantic writers, by contrast, thought the purpose of literature was to convey emotions. Judging by his "Elegy," in which group does Gray seem to fit? Gray's purpose in the "Elegy" seems to involve a bit of both. However, most students will agree that, on balance, the poem is seeking to establish a certain mood and to prompt an emotional response in the reader; in this respect, the "Elegy" is more "Romantic" than "neoclassical."

14. The poem contains at least two statements that are still frequently quoted:

a. **The paths of glory lead but to the grave. (line 36)**

b. **Full many a flower is born to blush unseen, And waste its sweetness on the desert air. (lines 55–56)**

How do these lines relate to the message of the poem? The quotations relate to the poem's message by underscoring the sentiments that life is transient and that excellence may easily be ignored or remain unfulfilled.

The Elements of Literature

Text page 573

Elegy

Ask students to read the essay. It will be interesting for them to know the difference between the original definition of elegy—which refers to any poem written in a *distich* form— to the present definition, which most often refers to a contemplative and often laudatory piece of writing that ad-dresses or deals with the death of someone whom the writer has cherished. As the essay points out, elegies have not always dealt with mournful and somber subjects. It may be interesting and helpful for students' grasp of the meaning of elegy to ask them to write a brief elegy. The subject matter might focus on the death of a relative, a public figure, or a pet.

James Boswell

Text page 574

It is worth pointing out to students that Boswell's biography of Johnson is as much a portrait of the biographer as it is of the subject. Scholars, you might mention, have long been fascinated by this aggressive young Scotsman who managed not ony to gain audience with the foremost sage of the era but to form a lasting friendship with the man.

from The Life of Samuel Johnson

Text 576

Objectives

1. To identify eccentricities
2. To write a biographical sketch that includes dialogue
3. To write a paragraph expressing a personal opinion

Introducing the Biography

In outline form, for your reference, here are the major elements in the critique:

· **Point of view:** first person
· **Significant technique:** biography

*B*ackground on the Biography. This biographical selection is more a character study than a biography. Boswell shows the reader the operation of Johnson's personality. He does not create a history of the life of the great man. Thus, the reader comes to see the great man through Boswell's eyes. Student readers need to be aware that, in this fashion, they are also gaining a picture of the biographer, as was pointed out in the introduction to Boswell above.

Teaching Strategies

*P*roviding for Cultural Differences. This selection is fitted with cultural references that ought to be explained to the students. If it is possible, find pictures of The Chesire Cat, the pub around the lane from Johnson's home. Discuss with the students the social patterns of the time. For instance, they are unlikely to understand that many shop proprietors lived on the premises, as did the Davies. The students ought to know who Sir Joshua Reynolds was. The fact that so famous a painter did a portrait of Johnson is a measure of the greatness of the man, in spite of his constant pecuniary embarrassment. The students ought to know who David Garrick was and why Johnson might be gossiping with Davies about that person. Finally, the students would be very interested in the dress standards of the time, so that they can draw conclusions from Boswell's details about Johnson's inattention.

Providing for Different Levels of Ability. A jigsaw exercise would provide for the eventuality that some of the students might have difficulty understanding this excerpt. Divide the material into manageable units and use the jigsaw grouping to have the students read, discuss, and paraphrase the material. Teaching the selection this way might take two class periods: one day for the first group conference and the second day for the second group sharing. By employing the jigsaw collaboration, you will ensure that all of the students gain a full understanding the first time around.

Introducing Vocabulary Study. Students will benefit from knowing the meanings of the following words before they read the selection.

abasement	noxious
animadversion	slovenly
discomfited	tremulous
ejaculation	vociferation
jocularity	waggish

Reading the Selection. As indicated above, you might wish to split the material into easily manageable segments. Have the students deal with this as a jigsaw, discussing the material as they go. Prepare a set of questions specific to the group's segment, including the vocabulary word in their section.

Reteaching Alternatives. The jigsaw provides for the understanding of all of the students. No reteaching should be necessary.

Responding to the Biography Text page 581
Analyzing the Biography
Identifying Details

1. How did Boswell feel as he was about to meet Johnson? Boswell felt awed and apprehensive.

2. How was Johnson dressed when Boswell first visited him in his study? Johnson was dressed in a rather disorderly brown suit and had on an unpowdered wig that was too small for his head; his clothes did not fit well; and he wore a pair of unbuckled shoes for slippers.

3. What superstitious habit did Johnson have? Johnson had the peculiar habit of passing through a doorway or passage with a particular number of steps.

4. Describe the peculiar mannerisms Johnson exhibited when he was talking. He held his head toward his right shoulder and spoke in a tremulous manner; he moved his body backward and forward and rubbed his left knee; and he made various unusual sounds and movements with his tongue. When he had ended what he had to say, he blew out his breath like a whale.

5. Why, according to Boswell, did Johnson sometimes express opinions that he did not really believe? According to Boswell, Johnson did this to exercise and display his ingenuity.

Interpreting Meanings

6. Before meeting Johnson, Boswell thought that he lived in "a state of solemn elevated abstraction." Explain how the actual experience of meeting and talking with Johnson differed from Boswell's expectations. When Boswell actually met Johnson, he found the celebrated man to be down-to-earth, rather slovenly, and far less awe-inspiring than he had expected.

7. Why didn't Boswell or any of Johnson's other friends ask him about his eccentricities, or attempt to make him more conventional? Student answers will vary. Johnson's friends may have found his eccentricities refreshing, and they were very probably afraid to risk his ire by trying to persuade him to become more conventional.

8. What defense does Boswell offer for describing Johnson's eccentricities in the *Life*? He says that he has the goal of being accurate.

Do you think the defense is valid? Student answers will vary.

9. Was Johnson an impolite person, or did he only seem rude? Discuss. Student answers will vary. Most students will agree that Johnson was not really impolite.

10. What do we mean when we call someone an "eccentric"? How is *eccentricity* different from *insanity*? We mean that someone departs—in an unexpected or amusing or somewhat trivial way—from the usual or conventional norms of social behavior. The word *Insanity* denotes true madness, rather than individual foibles or quirks.

11. Would Johnson have been more or less interesting had his behavior been more conventional? Most students will agree that Johnson would have been less interesting if his behavior had been conventional.

Why is eccentricity of behavior important to society? How do you think eccentricity is regarded in society today? Student answers will vary. Ask the students to discuss and defend their opinions in class.

Extending the Biography. Suggest that students practice the art of storytelling in its original oral form. Have students develop a character together. Before they begin their description, you may want to establish the character's profession or pasttime and name. This will help to focus their imaginations a bit, and the elements of their stories should feed into each other. You may want to ask one particularly creative student to start the biographical sketch, and after a few minutes move to another student and another until you have gone completely around the room. Encourage students to be as detailed as possible in their descriptions of their character and the character's activities and involvement with other people.

John Bunyan

Text page 582

from The Pilgrim's Progress

Text page 584

Objectives

1. To interpret an allegory
2. To write a version in which a character is altered
3. To write an outline of an allegory
4. To write a recasting of a sermon

Introducing the Story

In outline form, for your reference, here are the major elements in the story:

- **Protagonists:** Christian and Hopeful
- **Antagonists:** indifferent humans
- **Conflict:** human vs. self
- **Point of view:** third-person omniscient
- **Significant technique:** allegory
- **Setting:** a mythical land

Background on the Story. A proper understanding of this excerpt from *The Pilgrim's Progress* can best be ensured by exploring with the students the nature of an allegory. The student text presents a very complete exploration of this literary device. Plan to discuss this device with the students prior to reading. You might wish to suggest that, just as a conceit (which students no doubt formally encountered in their study of John Donne), is an extended metaphor, so an allegory is rather like an elaborated and extended personification. For students fully to appreciate the ramifications of this literary form, you might wish to have them do a preliminary writing task in which they are to develop a personification and then to go the second step and extend it into an allegory. Nothing will give them an appreciation of the form faster than trying to write one themselves.

Teaching Strategies

Providing for Cultural Differences. In most classrooms the primary impediments to understandng will be those involved with spiritual matters. Since the religious commitments of a modern American public schoolroom will probably be varied from agnostic to exotic, with all ranges of conventional Christianity in between, understanding the Puritan mind is of the greatest importance. Students appreciate that Puritanism was more than the Founding Fathers sitting down to turkey with native Americans. You might wish to make the connections for the students between the mind-set of Bunyan and that reflected in Jonathan Edward's sermons ("Sinners in the Hands of an Angry God," for instance), or that reflected in almost any of Hawthorne's works, but most specifically *The Scarlet Letter*. The mere mention of these titles should evoke a flood of student memories locked up from their eleventh-grade year, and this parallel will build some connections for them between their American heritage and their English heritage. If great numbers of students in the class remain unable to relate to this piece because of religious chasms, you might wish to deal with the idea of depression and despair on a nonreligious basis. It is entirely possible to explore the truth of the allegorical meaning of this selection without encountering the spiritual teachings intended by the author. The characteristics of depression and despair are the same, regardless of their origins.

Providing for Different Levels of Ability. Most students taking an English literature survey in a twelfth-grade setting are probably pretty firmly college-bound. Nevertheless, one place where individual differences will show up is in the literal mind-set of some of the very bright "left-brain" types of students. These are the students who are very intelligent, but sometimes lack either the verbal skills or the creative

130   Unit Four: The Restoration and the Eighteenth Century

imagination that brings literature, along with the other arts, to life. This difference can be very frustrating for all concerned, first, because these students are used to learning easily and quickly, and second, because these students tend to prefer answers which are straightforward. They are very uncomfortable with the more abstract, intuitive conclusions so typical of humanities. Many of these frustrations may well manifest themselves when such students encounter a selection requiring as much abstract interpretation as an allegory does. Be sure to lay a careful foundation for this aspect of the selection, making sure that students understand that the interpretation of prolonged symbolism is not based on the reader's whimsy, but on the actual intent implicit in the author's art.

Introducing Vocabulary Study. Students will benefit from knowing the meaning of the following word before they read the selection.

doleful

Reading the Selection. Although the selection may be assigned for home reading, the students will find it not only more comprehensible but more enjoyable to read in class as an oral exercise. You might wish to prepare a rather detailed prompt sheet for the students to use as they follow the selection. The archaic diction may be off-putting to some of the less motivated students, so you may wish to employ extraordinary means to keep the students focused.

If you choose not to use the prompt sheet, you may wish to employ a variety of reading log. The dialectical journal works well for a selection like this. In this type of log, you have the students draw a line vertically down the middle of a sheet of binder paper, labeling the left-hand column "Note-taking" and the right-hand column "Note-making." The left-hand column is used for the actual noted entry (for example, a word, a phrase, or a cited idea), and the right-hand column contains the student's comment about the significance of that entry, the meaning of the word, the reason for citing the phrase, and so on. Such a log will keep the student reader focused and will also provide ample detail for support material for later writing.

Reteaching Alternatives. If you used the prompt sheet for the first reading, you might wish to use the dialectical journal as a reteaching strategy. If, for any reason, fairly large numbers of the students seriously missed the point of the selection, you may wish to go back and have the students do a modified jigsaw. Break the students into four or five groups. Assign a segment of the selection to each group, telling the members of the group to come to an understanding of that segment in a given amount of time. Then reconstitute the groups, having one member of each group now reporting the findings to a new group. In that manner, the entire selection will have been covered in some detail.

Extending the Story. You may want to suggest that students write a brief story about a journey they have taken. As *The Pilgrim's Progress* illustrates, a journey can be internal or symbolic as much as it might be actual and "realistic." Try to encourage students to be as free as possible in their interpretation of a journey. Ask them to describe a journey during which their feelings changed between the moment of departure and the moment of arrival. This may be a dreamed or imagined journey or an actual one. Remind them that including as many details as possible will help to make it as important and powerful for their reader as the experience is for them.

Responding to the Story   Text page 589
Analyzing the Story
Identifying Details

1. What is Christian's problem? Christian's problem is that he feels an intolerable burden on his back.

How does he set about resolving it? He obeys the Evangelist's command and sets out on a pilgrimage.

2. Why do Christian and Hopeful go with the giant? Why don't they resist? The giant is stronger than they are.

3. How long are Christian and Hopeful held captive? They are held captive for four days, from Wednesday to Sunday.

Why does the giant beat them? The giant beats them because his wife, Diffidence, advises him to do so.

4. How, and on what day, do they escape? They escape on Sunday morning, using a key called "Promise."

Interpreting Meanings

5. What do you think the book is that so upsets Christian? The book is probably the Bible.

6. Most commentators on this story agree that such realistic details as the rags Christian wears are to be interpreted spiritually: the rags signify the desperate condition of Christian's soul, not the desperate condition of his pocketbook. What would be a spiritual interpretation of the heavy burden on Christian's back? A spiritual interpretation might equate the burden with sin or guilt for sin.

7. In the account of the giant and his wife, which details do *not* seem to have spiritual meaning? Student answers will vary. Ask the students to support their responses in class.

8. Christian abandons his wife and children to go on his pilgrimage. How do you know that Bunyan approved of Christian's values? We know that Bunyan approved of Christian's values because he describes the family rather unsympathetically and because he obviously identifies with Christian's quest for salvation.

9. In thinking about Doubting Castle, remember that doubt is the opposite of faith. How, then, should the place be interpreted *allegorically*? Why are Christian and Hopeful shut up in Doubting Castle? Their enclosure in the castle perhaps symbolizes a crisis of faith and a temptation to give in to despair.

What helps them escape? The key called "Promise" helps them to escape.

10. What do you think of the way Christian and Hopeful escape the giant? Is it psychologically realistic that Christian would have forgotten his "key" for so long? Why or why not? Student answers will vary. Ask the students to support their opinions in class.

The Elements of Literature

Allegory

Ask students to read the essay and discuss it in class. The essay deals primarily with *The Pilgrim's Progress* and the way that Bunyan has developed an allegory with the characters and journeys of Christian and Christiana. Through the allegory, Bunyan is able to relate two different stories simultaneously. You may want to ask students if they find it effective or confusing to read an allegory. A well-written allegory maintains a very special balance and tension between the underlying story and the surface story. To clarify their understanding of allegory and the allegorical meanings of the characters in *The Pilgrim's Progress*, it might be helpful to have students name each character in class and discuss the appropriateness of the names in regard to the characters, their action, and behavior.

To introduce students to allegory, you might first make them aware of an everyday use of allegory in the way that we assign nicknames to people we know and want to characterize in a particular way because of their actions and personality. You might want to use the example of how the names of characters in many fairy tales are allegorical—Snow White and the Seven Dwarfs, for instance. Ask the students if they or other people they know have given or received allegorical nicknames, and have the students explain how and why the names are allegorical.

The English Language

Just as it is interesting to almost every child to learn something about his or her family background, it is interesting to almost every native English speaker to learn something of the history of English. This special essay provides an overview of the developments in the language throughout the course of the eighteenth century. The first section addresses the question: should change in language be considered degeneration or growth? The next section describes the efforts of some English speakers during the eighteenth century to refine, explain, and stop further changes to the language. Following sections treat the creation of dictionaries in Great Britain and America, and the many ways that a language evolves. The essay concludes with a thoughtful discussion of the difference between good and bad English.

Assign the essay for homework. Then have students break into groups and discuss particular sections. Encourage students to debate the question posed by the essay, such as should language be allowed to change? or what constitutes "good English"? Have each group also take responsibility for one of the questions in Analyzing Language. At the end of the discussion period, allow groups to share their findings and conclusions with the class.

Exercises in Critical Thinking and Writing

Using Logical Reasoning to Write a Persuasive Essay

This assignment calls upon students to write a persuasive essay refuting one of the five generalizations about the literature in this unit. Students are reminded of the nature and purpose of a persuasive essay and are instructed about the pitfalls of hasty generalizations and circular reasoning. Students are then encouraged to research their positions by reading what the critics have said about the works and by finding out the meaning of political, religious, and literary allusions. One of two approaches to writing is suggested: beginning with facts and reasons that support a conclusion (inductive reasoning) or beginning with a general statement that is then supported by specific details (deductive reasoning).

Read through the assignment with the students, discussing with them the logical fallacies they want to avoid. Ask them for examples of facts and reasons that would correctly support one of the assigned arguments. For instance, a student might offer as evidence that *Robinson Crusoe* is *not* simply an adventure story for very young readers the fact that he or she found the story quite fascinating.

Criteria for Evaluating the Assignment. A commendable essay will present a convincing, well-stated argument. It will open or close with a general statement of opinion and will present, in an organized fashion, facts and reasons to support the general statement.

Suggestions for Teaching and Evaluating the Writing Assignments

A Creative Response

For assignments that ask students to create an original piece, have students work with partners to brainstorm ideas. If, for instance, students are narrating a different outcome to the story of Robinson Crusoe, partners could take turns elaborating on each other's leads. Once students have ideas, they can go about the task of writing individually or continue to collaborate. Advise students to gather many ideas before writing and organize those ideas in a way suitable to the type of writing they are doing.

Criteria for Evaluating Assignments. An effective creative response should show a blending of new ideas with concepts gleaned from the reading. Point of view should be thoughtfully chosen and maintained throughout. In cases where a response revises or extends a selection, the transition from the old to the new should be smooth.

A Critical Response

When students are asked to respond critically to a work, encourage them to think analytically. Explain that analysis requires one to gather information, look for patterns in the information, and then come to conclusions about the findings. For instance, students who choose to draw inferences about the personality of Samuel Johnson based on his dictionary entries should be encouraged to notice his tendency to poke fun at himself, his eagerness to reveal his political views, and his snobbish attitude towards certain things. Inferences about his personality will flow naturally from these observations and categorizations.

Criteria for Evaluating Assignments. Successful responses will show analytical thinking, familiarity with the topic, and careful organization. Paragraphs should contain topic sentences and supporting details. Students should follow rules of grammar and punctuation and demonstrate a willingness to proofread and correct their work.

Answers to Analyzing Language

Eighteenth-Century Usage

1. The modern spellings of the entries are as follows:

bonfires	turn	altar
music	themselves	noise
frolic	show	loaded
tipple	Franklin	ruin

2. Examples of archaic diction include: wife doth expect his coming, from thence, did give them some oysters, did get up, the very fiddlers, he did give him, these two days have held up fair, it fell a-raining and a-thundering, which is a foolery, how these ladies did tipple, fell down stark drunk and lay there spewing

3. Archaic verb forms: doth, My Lord of Albimarles going and eat, when he is come, there was three gallants, I fell asleep and sleep till morning

---

Diction and Connotations

1. ". . . there may be about two hundred thousand couples whose wives are breeders . . ." (p. 519).

   ". . . because it is very well known that they are every day dying and rotting by cold and famine and filth and vermin . . ." (p. 521).

   ". . . I compute that Dublin would take off, annually, about twenty thousand carcasses . . ." (p. 522).

   All of these examples demonstrate the dehumanizing effect of Swift's language. The breeders, Popish infants, and carcasses are presented as animals or objects worthy of absolutely no concern or pathos. Filth is used in a disdaining, and again, inhuman manner.

2. Other words that could have been used to create different emotional effects are helpless, professed beggars, rudiments, flesh, nutriment, love.

Satirical Techniques and Tone

An example of *hyperbole* is used in the description of "venice Preserved": "the sounding of the clock . . . makes the hearts of the whole audience quake." An example of *understatement* is when Addison says: "To delight in seeing man stabbed, poisoned, racked, or impaled is certainly the sign of a cruel temper." An example of *sarcasm* is evident in the ocmment about handkerchiefs: "Far be it from me to think of bandishing this instrument of sorrow from the stage; I know a tragedy could not subsist without it . . ."

1. These techniques provide a satirical tone for the essay.

2. The tone begins to become evident at the mention of a ghost appearing onstage with a bloody shirt. It is entirely clear when Addison says, "There may be a proper season for these several terrors; and when they only come in as aids and assistances to the poet, they are not only to be excused, but to be applauded."

3. The tone shifts in the discussion of Orestes and Horace and then resumes in the conclusion.

Precise Meanings

1. "... the different *revolutions* in his own mind ..."
"A complete or radical change of any kind" [Webster's New World Dictionary, Second Collede Edition]. *Revolutions* here implies thoughts and the development of his thoughts or ideas.

2. "... the *generality* of mankind ..."
"The bulk; main body" [Webster's New World Dictionary ...]. Generality here suggests the word most.

3. "... perform all *offices* of life ..."
"Service" [Webster's New World Dictionary ...]. Today the word *offices* would most likely be replaced by the word *duties*.

4. "... The most delicious *bower* ..."
"A place enclosed by overhanging boughs of trees or by vines on a trellis; arbor" [Webster's New World Dictionary ...]. The word *bower* may actually be used in just this same manner today. Or perhaps the word *arbor* might be used. It suggests a hideaway made of vines and branches.

5. "... gentle *aspirations* of wind ..."
"A blowing or breathing" [Webster's New World ...]. *Aspirations* here suggests the contemporary use of the word *breath*; a breath of wind or a breeze.

6. "... familiar *converse* ..."
"Social intercourse" [Webster's New World ...]. Today the word might be replaced by *neighborliness*.

Poetic Style

1. Other poetic words in the elegy are *o'er* (line 2), which today might be replaced with the word *over*; *ne'er* (line 50), which would be replaced by *never*; and *yon* (linc 116), which would probably be replaced with *that*.

2. Because the words are dated, thay may make the reader feel removed from the poem.

3. Another example is "The plowman homeward plods his weary way" (line 3).

4. One reason might be that he took poetic liberty in wording his thoughts to fit his meter and rhyme scheme in the poem.

5. Answers will vary. One may read: They are not permitted to insist upon the arrival of listeners. They cannot despise, and therefore reject, the threats of pain and destruction. They cannot distribute wealth over a rich and happy country, and they cannot possibly understand and know their history—their past—in an entire nation's eyes. They cannot understand their virtues without their crimes. They are forbidden to reach the throne, or highest position, by passing through slaughtered bodies and destruction. They may not remove mankind from mercy. They are not permitted to hide their knowledge of truth or to cover the marks of so-called innocent shame. They may not add to or create a shrine of Luxury and Pride with praise and tributes from other poets when that shrine has been started and fed by their Muse.

Unit Five: *The Romantic Period 1798-1832*

Teaching Romantic Literature

The Romantic Period, spanning the years 1798 to 1870, was actually a movement from one way of thinking to another. Inherent in the movement were several issues important to writers of the time. The main tenets of Romanticism included a shift from faith in reason to faith in the senses, feelings, and imagination; from interest in urban society and its sophistication to an interest in the rural and natural; from tradition to originality; from the expression of accepted moral truths to the discovery of beauty that is truth; from the use of satire to the use of myth; from impersonal poetry to subjective poetry; from concern with the mundane to interest in the mysterious and infinite; from a belief in God and evil to a belief in man and goodness; from formal correctness to individual expressiveness and variety; from a preoccupation with human nature to a preoccupation with spiritual and aesthetic values of external nature; and from faith in established religions and philosophical creeds to faith in individual speculations and revelations. The most important tenets of Romanticism, however, were the belief in the individual, the importance of imagination, and intuition.

The Romantic Period had its beginning in the publication of Wordsworth's *Lyrical Ballads* in 1798. However, the era entailed more than just a new slant on poetry in particular and all literature in general. It was a time of optimism. It was also a time of historic turbulence in England. It began during the Napoleonic Wars but fostered a general belief in humanity. In its early years, Romanticism reflected the renewed interests in possibilities. In its later years, it found itself opposed to the ugly sides of a ultilitarian society changing too rapidly for the Romantic writers. The movement was at odds with the Industrial Revolution, the corruption and pollution of large cities, and the sheer capitalistic motives of many businessmen. Out of its opposition to such changes, the literature of the movement reflected the conflicts of its contemporary society. The Romantic Period saw the resurgence of revolt and radical political thought that chose to change the status quo.

Before beginning a study of Romantic poets and their works, students may need to review such underpinnings of the genre as purpose, structure, diction, and imagery. Make sure that your discussion of these elements focuses on general comments and opinions regarding each element. You might also want to present a definition of poetry and contrast the genre with those of fiction and nonfiction.

As with previous units, you may elect to choose only some of the selections included here for class consideration. Bear in mind the wisdom of preserving the chronological order of the works you select. This will ensure that students develop an appreciation for what precisely sets the Romantic Period apart from other key periods in English literature.

*O*bjectives of the Romantic Unit

1. To improve reading proficiency and expand vocabulary
2. To gain exposure to notable authors and works of the period
3. To define and identify significant literary techniques: imagery, rhyme, meter, theme, mood, and tone
4. To interpret and respond to poetry, orally and in writing, through analysis of its elements
5. To practice the following critical thinking and writing skills:
   a. Analyzing a poet's purpose
   b. Analyzing a poem's theme
   c. Analyzing the structure of a poem
   d. Evaluating the point of view chosen by a poet
   e. Analyzing the use of imagery
   f. Analyzing the use of symbolism
   g. Imitating a poet's technique
   h. Analyzing metrics
   i. Responding to criticism

Robert Burns

Text page 611

To a Mouse

Text page 613

John Anderson, My Jo

Text page 616

Objectives

1. To consider Burns's use of dialect in some poems

2. To determine probable reasons for Burns's use of standard English in other poems

3. To determine the theme or message of each work

4. To evaluate the structure of each of Burns's poems

Introducing the Poems

Ask students to focus on the theme of each poem. "To a Mouse" concerns how even the best plans go awry; "John Anderson, My Jo" concerns the speaker's continued love for John Anderson.

Background on the Poems. As students read the two poems, ask them to consider Burns's use of dialect. For what reason does the poet rely on dialect here?

You may want to read and discuss Burns's own comments, in David Daiches's in *A Critical History of English Literature* (New York, 1960). Burns wrote that he "never had the least thought or inclination of turning Poet till [he] got once heartily in love and then rhyme and son were, in a manner, the spontaneous language of [his] heart." Burns wrote not only of what he knew but also often in the dialect he knew. Many critics have said that his poems written in dialect are his best.

Teaching Strategies

Providing for Cultural Differences. Burns's language, particularly in "To a Mouse," may present a fair amount of difficulty to students. His use of dialect may cause students to feel as though they are reading a foreign language. It will be particulary helpful for you to read the poems aloud to students. The music of the language is beautiful and should be felt by the listeners. And as is evident in "To a Mouse," the play on words is especially important. It will be extremely helpful to present the poems to students in a manner so that the dialect may appear more as a puzzle than as a blockade to their understanding of the poem.

Providing for Different Levels of Ability. These poems will probably present some difficulty to even the best students. Try to approach the poems in an interesting way, so that the language is not forbidding. "To a Mouse" should be approached with humor as well as pathos. Encourage students to relate their own experience to the experience that Burns describes in both poems. The feeling of appealing to nature for help, as is evident in "John Anderson," and the feeling of conflict regarding the destruction of nature for our own gain, as is evident in "To a Mouse," should provide room for interesting discussions among students, which will help to make the poems accessible and more interesting to them.

Reading the Poems. It is very important for these poems to be read aloud by the teacher or an exceptional student. Burns's language may seem obstructive to students, but try to make the poems intriguing rather that intimidating. Reading the poems aloud a few times, and then having students read the poems silently to themselves two or three times, may aid the students' comprehension. During all readings, suggest that students look for and keep their ears tuned to specific elements in the poems.

Reteaching Alternatives. Ask students to focus on the positions of human beings and the elements of nature in these poems. How do they relate to each other in each poem? What element is in a position of power? How does that power affect the separate parties in each case? Can students think of other literary references to these situations?

Responding to the Poem

Text page 615

Analyzing the Poem

Identifying Details

1. What has happened to the mouse that engages the speaker's sympathy? His plow has destroyed her nest.

2. What comparisons between the mouse and himself does the speaker make in the last two stanzas? For both mice and men, plans are not always fruitful, and for all the happiness they seem to assure, they may only amount to discomfort. The mouse, however, only deals with the present, and man is less fortunate because he can look backward to failure and forward to the fear of failure.

Interpreting Meanings

3. Where does the speaker's *tone* change? What does the speaker imply about his own past and his prospects for the future in the last stanza? The tone changes in the last two stanzas. The speaker's past seems to be filled with misfortune, and his future is bleak.

4. The best-known lines of this poem are lines 39–40. Do you agree with the philosophy expressed in these lines? Does the speaker seem to be saying that it makes no sense to make plans for the future at all, or is he simply commenting on what another British writer, Thomas Hardy, was to call "the persistence of the unforeseen"? (Do you recognize in these lines the title of a famous novel by American writer John Steinbeck?) Answers may vary, but most students will probably agree with the philosophy. He is commenting on Hardy's term. These lines are the origins of Steinbeck's *Of Mice and Men*.

5. Paraphrase the meaning of the second stanza. What are the meanings of the words *dominion* and *union* here, in your view? What attitude about man and nature does the use of these words imply? The speaker is sorry that his power as a man has destroyed the mouse's home—Nature's social union. He understands why the mouse is afraid of him and is sorry for being responsible for that fear. Dominion and union infer rule and cohesion. Answers may vary, but the answer may be summed up thus: Generally, man tries to rule over nature.

6. Identify some uses of alliteration in the poem. How does Burns combine alliteration with dialect? Are any of the poem's sound effects comical? He uses alliteration in line 4, line 29, and line 33. He emphasizes the sounds of the dialect with alliteration sound effects that are often very comical.

Responding to the Poem   Text page 616

Analyzing the Poem

Identifying Details

1. Who is addressing whom in the poem? John Anderson's lover is addressing John Anderson.

2. According to the speaker, what did the lovers used to do? What must they do now? The lovers used to climb up the hill together. Now they must climb down and return to sleep at the base of the hill again.

Interpreting Meanings

3. What symbolic meaning might be suggested by line 15? The line symbolizes that the lovers will die together.

4. What attitude toward old age seems to be held by the speaker, in your view? Do you think this attitude is prevalent today? Answers may vary. In general, the speaker is accepting old age and dying after having spent many joyous years with John Anderson. This reflects a personal sense of life, aging and dying. Many people today are happy to die peacefully with the one they love. Others are resistant to death and to aging, and try anything in their power (with the help of modern medicine, cosmetics, and so on) to retard the aging process.

William Blake   Text page 617

Objectives

1. To determine the depiction in poetry of the two contrary natures of humans

2. To determine the narrator's viewpoint in each poem

3. To analyze the imagery in Blake's poems

4. To consider the irony or paradox in Blake's poems

Introducing the Poems

Students should view Blake's poems as reflective of his two distinct ways of looking at the world. The poems coming from *Songs of Innocence* reflect the innocence of childhood and the idealism children often convey. *Songs of Experience*, on the other hand, reflect the disillusionment of the adult world. As Daiches writes in *A Critical History of English Literature* (New York, 1960), Blake asserted that the *Songs of Experience* do not "simply represent the corruption of innocence by the immoral forces of society, but show the inevitable distortion and sadness that systematized empirical philosophy imposes on life, and through which the road to the ultimate wisdom lies. The true vision cannot come to the innocent, for innocence by its very nature is easily led astray, nor can it come to those who acquiesce in the distortions of experience; those distortions must be known and transcended." Ask students to be aware of these comments as they read Blake's poetry.

Background on the Poems. In addition to the previous comments attributed to Blake, students will do well to review the headnote prefacing the Blake poems included in their text. You will want to emphasize the contrary nature of the poetry students will be reading. In particular, you will need to explain that poetry reflects changing views or philosophies Blake held at various times in his life. Thus, the two contrary natures reflected in the poetry did not necessarily coexist in Blake's mind.

Teaching Strategies

Providing for Cultural Differences. Students who are not steeped in Christian teachings may be unsure of the meaning of many of Blake's religious references and allusions. Suggest that these students pay particular attention to the glosses. You might also make reference books available that will clarify meaning. Finally, encourage students to share insights and information with one another.

Providing for Different Levels of Ability. All students, especially the less advanced, may benefit from varying the modalities of learning. For example, the weaker students may better understand the poems if they are read aloud with expression by the teacher. The stronger students may find the assignments more stimulating if they are required to analyze the accompanying art and photos as well.

The Tyger   Text page 620

Reading the Poem. Be sure students realize that "tyger" is an old-fashioned spelling of "tiger," so that the literal as well as the figurative meaning of the poem can be appreciated. Ask for a restatement of the question in line 20, "Did he who made the Lamb make thee?" In particular, clarify to whom "he" and "thee" refer and what "the Lamb" represents.

Reteaching Alternatives. The poem lends itself to being read aloud. Discuss the meaning of the poem with students and then allow them to "stage" the reading as they see fit.

Responding to the Poem   Text page 621
Analyzing the Poem
Identifying Details

1. What questions does the speaker ask the tiger? In essence, the speaker asks who would dare create such a fearful creature. He asks the tiger where the idea of the tiger may have existed previous to its creation. He asks where were its eyes and heart forged. He asks if the maker was pleased with the work, and whether the same "immortal" who made the lamb made the tiger.

2. Where in the poem does the speaker wonder if the tiger may have been created by God? What *imagery* tells us that the speaker also suspects that the tiger could be a demonic creation? What images suggest a human creator-like a blacksmith or goldsmith? The information is found in line 3 of stanza 1: immortal hand or eye; in line 5, in reference to distant skies; and most specifically in stanza 5, when he asks if the same creator of the lamb made the tiger. The images are those in line 5, in reference to distant deeps, and in line 10, in the reference to twisting the heart into an aberrant shape. The images of the tiger being forged in stanza 4 suggest possible human creation. The suggestion is that such a human creation is itself demonic.

Interpreting Meanings

3. What do you think is meant by the tiger's "fearful symmetry"? Student answers will vary. The likely answer will be that the tiger is perfectly shaped for its being, which is fearful, bright, pulsing with energy.

4. The last stanza of the poem virtually repeats the first. In your view, what is the significance of the one word that is changed in the last stanza? Student answers will vary. The word *could* is replaced by *dare*. The answer is that, in the first stanza, he simply asks who might have made the tiger; in the last stanza the speaker is in a state of wonder or perplexity of who could have made this creation.

5. What *imagery* suggests that the tiger could be a force of enlightenment? Of violence? The "enlightenment" imagery is in lines 6-7 and 17–18, in which the fallen angels give up their arms. The most salient image of violence is in line 16. In response to this question you might lead students into a discussion of the power of imagination and experience, for in many aspects this seems to be the underlying theme of the poem. The tiger can be seen as representative of both attributes.

6. The poem has always appealed to children, as well as to adults. What reasons can you think of for the poem's appeal to younger as well as older readers? Student answers will vary. Possible answers will include reference to the simplicity of the meter and directness of rhyme, as well as the vivid and unusual description of the tiger. Teachers may want to note the indirect technique of describing the tiger.

7. How does the poem testify to the simultaneous attraction to and repulsion of evil? Student answers will vary. The speaker is attracted to the power and repulsed by the destructive capability.

The Lamb
Text page 622

Reading the Poem. Point out how careful Blake is to establish the image of the little lamb—soft, wooly, and gentle—before expanding the meaning of the poem to metaphoric, even spiritual, dimensions. Ask the students to describe the effect of the speaker questioning the lamb, as opposed to simply stating his impressions and ideas.

Reteaching Alternatives. Ask students to review the sections about Romanticism in the introduction to the unit. Have them write short essays explaining why "The Lamb" is a good example of a Romantic poem.

Responding to the Poem
Text page 622
Analyzing the Poem
Identifying Details

1. What did its creator do for the lamb in the first stanza? The creator gave the lamb life, food, clothing (fleece), and a "tender voice."

2. How does the second stanza respond to the question posed in the first? It tells the lamb who made it.

3. What do you know about the speaker of the poem? The speaker's viewpoint is incomplete. He usually regards Christ as a fighter rather than as a lamb.

4. How is the lamb both a literal object and a symbol in this poem? It is both a lamb and a symbol of innocence.

5. Christ called himself a lamb because, like the Passover lamb slain to save the people of Israel, he sacrificed himself for the people. What might this imply about the fate of the young speaker in this poem? The speaker identifies with the lamb and with Christ and may expect to die soon, perhaps to be martyred. You might refer students to Blake's arrest at this time.

6. Blake wrote a two-line poem called "An Answer to the Parson" in which the parson (or preacher) asks, "Why, of the sheep, you do not learn peace?" The narrator replies, "Because I don't want you to shear my fleece!" How would the narrator of this poem disagree with the narrator of "The Lamb"? Student answers will vary. This narrator would not submit (react meekly or mildly) to any act affecting him, but would instead react against such an act.

The Chimney Sweeper (Songs of Innocence)
Text page 623

Reading the Poem. You might turn attention to the point of view in the poem. Ask students if the optimism of the young chimney sweeps is shared by the narrator. Allow students to explain the appropriateness of the words "weep

weep weep weep.''

Reteaching Alternatives. Students will recognize the ironic tone of the poem. Have them write a statement that conveys the speaker's real opinion of the situation.

Responding to the Poem   Text page 624
Analyzing the Poem
Identifying Details

1. What do we learn about the speaker in the first stanza? His mother died when he was young and his father sold him off as a chimney sweeper. The speaker sweeps and sleeps in the soot.

2. In the second stanza, how does the speaker try to reasurre Tom Dacre? He tells Tom that it is better to have a shaved head, for he will be spared the discomfort and ugliness of sooty blonde hair.

3. Describe Tom's dream. How does the angel reassure him? Tom dreams that sweepers locked in coffins are set free by angels. They wash in a stream and play on clouds. The angel tells him that if he's a good boy, God will be his father and he'll always be happy.

4. What moral lesson does this speaker draw from his dream? He determines that if a person willfully performs earthly duties he ''need not fear harm''—i.e., God will care for him.

Interpreting Meanings

5. How does Tom's dream of heaven contrast with the actual conditions of his daily life? In the dream he is clean, plays in heaven, trouble free. In actuality, he exists in the narrow, filthy, and harmful confines of chimneys.

6. Why would the angel's promise that Tom (and presumably any ''good'' boy) can ''have God for his father'' be especially significant for this speaker? He is without a parent. Most significantly, the idea of God as the ''good father'' directly contrasts with the speaker's earthly father.

7. Reread line 3 carefully. How is the child's mispronunciation of the chimney sweep's cry at once poignant and ironic? Is it possible, in your view, that the irony here establishes a certain tone for the entire poem? What is the tone? The mispronunciation is poignant because the speaker means to say ''sweep'' but unknowingly reveals his spiritual and physical condition with the word ''weep.'' It does establish an ironic tone, for although the speaker is upbeat and comforts Tom, his cry ''weep'' pervades the entire scene.

8. Where in this poem does the speaker try to make the best of a degrading situation? Does his reasoning convince you? This occurs in the final line, in which he derives his moral from the dream. Student answers will vary.

9. How does the final line affect you? Student answers will vary.

The Chimney Sweeper (Songs of Experience)   Text page 625

Reading the Poem. Ask students, if they had to guess, which chimney sweeper seems older—the one in this poem or Tom in the previous poem? Be sure students understand the term *irony* and are able to make use of the concept to explain the poem's message.

Reteaching Alternatives. Point out that the first chimney sweeper poem is from *Songs of Innocence* while the second is from *Songs of Experience*. Have students use the two lines to expound on the idea that ''innocence is bliss.''

Responding to the Poem   Text page 625
Analyzing the Poem
Identifying Details

1. How does the speaker of the first three lines describe the young chimney sweeper? He describes the sweeper as a miserable and pitiful thing in the snow.

2. What does the child say his parents did to him, and why? The child's parents clothed him in the ''clothes of death'' and taught him to sing sad notes, because he was happy in the country.

Interpreting Meanings

3. How do the first two lines of the poem help you to realize that the chimney sweeper's statement in line 9 must be *ironic*? The first lines establish the child's negative attitude to his situation.

4. What are the ''clothes of death'' (line 7)? They are the soot-blackened clothes of the chimney sweeper.

5. What are the different meanings of the phrase ''to make up'' (line 12)? How do these different meanings of the phrase affect your interpretation of the final line of the poem? The phrase can mean to ''make up,'' as in a child making up a game. It also means that the three elements in line 11 combine to make up a new element, i.e., "a heaven of our misery." You might point out the reference to the Holy Trinity to students. The phrase also suggests the monetary aspect of the situation. The meanings combined create a most ironic, sardonic, and bitter conclusion.

6. How do you imagine the sweeper's story affected the narrator of the poem? Student answers will vary.

7. What do you think was Blake's purpose in writing this poem? Blake probably wanted to share his philosophy of life. He sees contradictions in that his parents pray for the "chimney sweeper" and, at the same time, sell him into a life of labor.

London

Text page 626

Reading the Poem. Students should note that the speaker, who is probably the poet, observes the tragic aspects of his society as an insider. He wanders the streets of London and then chooses to speak out, quietly yet directly, in hopes of causing others to face reality.

Reteaching Alternatives. Encourage students to write their own versions of the poem, discussing today's social problems and using a tone they feel is appropriate. Some students may prefer to share their ideas in the form of a letter to the editor.

Responding to the Poem Text page 626

Analyzing the Poem

Identifying Details

1. What specific images describe what the speaker sees in London? The images include "chartered street," "chartered Thames does flow," faces of woe, weakness, fear, "blackning church," "blood down palace walls."

Interpreting Meanings

2. Blake uses specific, concrete images to stand for larger concepts and institutions. Identify figures or images of war; of oppression and restriction; of religion; of prostitution; and of anger. Such figures are found respectively in lines 11–12, lines 1–2, 8, 14–16, line 9–10, lines 14–16, and lines 5–9, 16.

3. What do you think the "mind-forged manacles" are

(line 8)? Student answers will vary. The metaphor refers to the institutions that create and condone the oppressions and injustices of the poem as well as to the people themselves, whose minds are shaped by the circumstances of life. The manacles syntactically refer to the preceding three lines, but are more specifically described in the succeeding stanza.

4. Where does Blake use images of darkness in this poem? What do you think darkness symbolizes? These images occur in lines 10, 13, 16. The image of the "blackning church," line 10, is difficult. Most obvious is that the church is unclean (note "Chimney Sweeper," line 11). Midnight in line 13 implies the hidden unseen life that takes place in the city, most specifically the pathetic life of the prostitutes and their customers. The "marriage hearse" symbolizes the spiritual destructiveness of marriage, which may lead men to prostitutes. More specifically, it may represent the literal death of children and spouse through venereal disease.

5. In Blake's time, sexually transmitted diseases were often incurable. If the husband had previously been infected by a prostitute, he infected his wife and the disease "blasted" (infected) their children's "tear" (the disease caused infants to be blind from birth). In Blake's time, the word *hearse* could mean both a carriage and a funeral bier. Given all this information, how would you explain the poem's final line? It refers to venereal disease transmitted to the husband, infecting both wife and children (plague), and thus blighting the marriage. Marriage itself may be interpreted as a carriage carrying its inhabitants to death. The implication of venereal disease can also be interpreted spiritually.

Jerusalem

Text page 628

Reading the Poem. Have the students think about the way the poem divides into two parts-one about Christ and the other about the poet. Help them to see that the poem's

structure draws attention to the comparison of Christ's inspiration to poetic inspiration.

Reteaching Alternatives. The introduction to this poem mentions that it has been set to music and has become a popular English hymn. Suggest that students try to find the music, compose their own music, or have a group discussion about why the poem was set to music and became popular.

Responding to the Poem Text page 628

Analyzing the Poem

Identifying Details

1. What ancient legend does the speaker recall in the first two stanzas? The stanzas refer to the legend that Christ visited England.

2. What does the speaker call for in the third stanza? He calls for arms of glory or righteousness.

3. According to the last stanza, what is the speaker resolved to do? He is resolved to build a new Jersusalem or holy land in England.

Interpreting Meanings

4. What is the tone of the third stanza? In line 13, how does Blake clarify the kind of battle he is talking about here? The tone is passionate, emphatic, imperative. He makes specific reference to a mental or imaginative battle.

5. What do you think Jerusalem symbolizes in the poem? It symbolizes redemption or heaven on earth.

6. How would you describe the speaker's attitude to- ward the present state of society? How would you compare this attitude to the attitudes of the narrators of the *Songs of Innocence* and to those of the *Songs of Experience*? The speaker sees society as fallen from innocence, comparable to a hell. His attitude is comparable to both the *Songs of Innocence* and *Songs of Experience*—with the significant difference that the speaker here proclaims a will to alter the state of affairs. In the other poems, the speakers either accept their condition and/or put their faith in God.

7. What is there about the poem, in your view, that makes it especially suitable to an adaptation as a hymn? Student answers will vary. Possible answers are that the poem is a lyrical poem and appears easily adaptable to music and song. It also contains elements of the traditional hymn, such as religious fervor or righteousness, and the basic generally religious tone of the poem. Hymns generally call for a change of heart of some kind, usually for belief in God. This is where Blake's poem differs. His is a religion of earth.

Primary Sources Text page 630
"Blake is a real name . . ."

Read this brief commentary aloud to students. Inform them that Lamb, whose own work they will be encountering in coming weeks, was an important familiar essayist of the age. Based on Lamb's remarks, ask students what parallels they can draw between the poetry and paintings of Blake, both in the areas of style and subject matter. Elicit, further, the general consensus of Blake by his contemporaries, if Lamb's views were representative. Have students support their views with specific passages from the reading.

William Wordsworth Text page 631

George Sampson's *The Concise Cambridge History of English Literature* (Cambridge, England, 1970) offers the following comment about Wordsworth: ". . . no one has ever surpassed him in the power of giving utterance to some of the most elementary, and, at the same time, obscure, sensations of man confronted by the external spectacle of nature. These sensations, old as man himself, come to us as new, because Wordsworth was the first to find words for them." Wordsworth's poetry proclaims the Romantic notions of a love of nature and a bittersweet remembrance of things past.

Objectives

1. To analyze Wordsworth's theme of recalling past experiences and places

2. To consider Wordsworth's references to nature

3. To analyze Wordsworth's references to the imagination

4. To compare Wordsworth's view of city life with that of William Blake in his *Songs of Experience*

Introducing the Poems

In William Vaughn Moody and Robert Morse Lovett's *A History of English Literature* (New York, 1964), the following statement is made regarding Wordsworth's poetry: "... the growing sensibility to natural phenomena ... reached its height. [Wordsworth] was gifted by nature with an eye and an ear marvelously sensitive to those slight and elusive impressions which most persons pass by without noticing at all." Perhaps this ability above all others has caused Wordsworth's poems to be among the most impressive of the Romantic Period. As students begin a study of Wordsworth, they should watch for the poet's "slight and elusive impressions" represented in the written word.

Background on the Poems. George Sampson's *The Concise Cambridge History of English Literature* (Cambridge, England, 1970) refers to the years during which Wordsworth wrote the majority of his best-known poems: "The certainty that he had found his true purpose in life sustained and exalted Wordsworth through the years from 1798 to

1805. This was a period of plain living and high thinking, a period, too, of careful reading intensely devoted to the older English poets; and to it belongs nearly all that is supremely great in his work."

As Moody and Lovett correctly state, what is correct in Wordsworth's poetry is his sensitivity toward nature, his sense of truth, the breadth of his poetry, his treatment of human nature, and the introduction of the mystical. In teaching Wordsworth's poetry, ask students to look for these traits. Doing so will aid them in focusing on important aspects of Wordsworth's writing.

Teaching Strategies

Providing for Cultural Differences. Some students may have difficulty visualizing the England Wordsworth describes in his poems. If possible, bring in travel books or other sources of material about England that show the countryside and London. Art books are another source of visual information, especially those that include reproductions of paintings from the same period in which Wordsworth was writing.

Providing for Different Levels of Ability. Less advanced students may at first find "Lines Composed a Few Miles Above Tintern Abbey" overwhelming. To assist these students, you might begin the study of Wordsworth with a few of the shorter and more accessible poems, such as "I Wandered Lonely as a Cloud." More advanced students should be allowed to read the first poem uninterrupted, then encouraged to respond to the poem in writing before it is discussed in class.

Reading the Poem. As a prelude to reading the poem, you might ask students to think of one of their happiest memories. After students have had an opportunity to read the poem, call on individuals to read favorite parts aloud. Discuss the mood that the poem evokes.

Reteaching Alternatives. The beauty of this poem would be highlighted by having students rise and read verse paragraphs aloud. Give students time to prepare before reading, so that they are familiar with the words and ideas and have coordinated the transitions from one reader to another.

Responding to the Poem   Text page 637
Analyzing the Poem
Identifying Details

1. Briefly sketch what the speaker hears and sees as he beholds "once again" the scene in the first verse paragraph (lines 1-22). He hears the murmur of springs and sees the steep cliffs, quiet sky, sycamore tree, orchard thickets, and hedgerows that mark the boundaries of small farms.

2. Why are these "beauteous forms" not, for the speaker, "As is a landscape to a blind man's eye" (line 24)? Unlike the blind man, the speaker has experienced the landscape firsthand and has been able to reexperience it emotionally and reorganize it through memory.

3. What has the speaker lost since he first "came among these hills" (line 67)? He has lost the purity and innocence of his youth, when he "bounded o'er the mountains." He is older and responds to nature meditatively rather than spontaneously.

4. What does the speaker see in his "dear Sister" that makes him more aware of what he "was once" (line 120)? He sees the passion of the "shooting lights/Of thy wild eyes" (line 119)—her spontaneous joy of nature.

5. Describe the *meter* of the poem. Pick out at least four instances of *run-on lines* that keep the poem from sounding mechanical and singsong. The meter is unrhymed iambic pentameter, or blank verse. Instances of run-on or enjambed lines are numerous. Some notable instances are in lines 3, 9, 17, 34, 39, 45, 47. (To assist students you might instruct them to read the poem aloud. Also look for lines that appear to conclude but are then forced to turn over to the next line with an additional word or phrase.)

Interpreting Meanings

6. What do you think is meant by "the burden of the mystery" (line 38)? Do you think Keats understood this phrase in the same way? (See Keats later in this unit.) The reference is to the mystery of an "unintelligible world." Based on such poems as "When I Have Fears" and "Ode to a Nightingale," it seems evident that Keats shared Wordsworth's understanding of this idea.

7. What "gifts" (line 86) and "abundant recompense" (line 88) does the speaker believe he has received for his "loss" (line 87)? How important is the theme of loss and gain in this poem? The gifts are the gifts of understanding and maturity. He continues to perceive nature with joy, but not with the rapture of the past. He now sees nature as a reflector of humanity or the self. He understands that the experiencing of nature is "half-created," that is, projected by the person. Nature is seen as a moral guide. The themes of loss and gain are of prime importance.

8. What role does the speaker's sister play in the poem? Compare this role with that of the silent figures in Coleridge's "This Lime-Tree Bower My Prison" (page 652). Do you think that Dorothy's presence here seems more or less contrived than the presence of the silent figures in Coleridge's poems? The speaker's sister is used as a window or mirror into the speaker's past. Her role as an intermediary between the speaker and nature is a contrivance. It can be argued that, in this sense, she becomes a mere vehicle for the progress of the poem. The counter argument is that she was with him at the second experience of the landscape and that her response to it may indeed have been the inspiration for the poem. The figures in Coleridge's poem are natural inhabitants of it, as their presence, or lack of it, is the occasion that inspired the poem. Coleridge responds spontaneously and directly to them.

9. Summarize and comment on the significance of the speaker's conclusion, beginning with line 102. Have you ever been in a situation where you felt you wanted to have some reassurance and recompense for the sense of losing part of your past? The speaker retains love of nature. He recognizes that what is taken in through the senses is half-created by a person's sensibility or imagination (lines 106–107). He addresses his sister, commenting on her youthful or innocent reaction to nature. He comments on nature's role in life, its guarding and healing effect. He addresses the "maturing years," when responses are more sober. He asks his sister to remember him and his love of nature when she is alone, in fear, in pain, even if he himself has forgotten this love. He concludes with two lines that encapsulate the poem, when he expresses his equal love for both her and nature. The significance of these lines is that the speaker learns to separate nature and human beings, but also sees the moral and emotional response of people to nature. Nature takes on the role of religion.

Strange Fits of Passion Have I Known

Text page 638

Reading the Poem. Help students to see the connection between the image of the moon dropping behind the cottage and the speaker's premonition of death. Discuss the speaker's assessment of the experience, as suggested by the first stanza of the poem.

Reteaching Alternatives. Students might enjoy turning this poem into a short story. Guide them to discover the characters, setting, plot, and theme already present in the poem. Help them to understand and make use of the poem's suspense.

She Dwelt Among the Untrodden Ways

Text page 639

Reading the Poem. Too often, students learn about similes and metaphors from trite examples. Take advantage of the wonderful metaphors (lines 5-8) that the speaker uses to characterize Lucy to impart an appreciation of figurative language. Point out how much is said in so few words.

Reteaching Alternatives. Students might enjoy an opportunity to read this poem aloud. Encourage each reader to apply his or her own interpretation of the poem through tone of voice, tempo, and emphasis. Discuss the various ways the poem is read.

A Slumber Did My Spirit Seal

Text page 640

Reading the Poem. After students have read this short poem, you might pose this question: Were you surprised by the last two lines? Bring out the idea that the description does not romanticize death, but rather deals with it in very concrete terms.

Reteaching Alternatives. You might use the poem as a springboard for a discussion of alliteration. Ask students to find the lines that repeat sounds. Have them read the lines aloud, savoring the effect of the alliteration.

Responding to the Poems   Text page 640
Analyzing the Poems
Identifying Details

1. Who is the intended *audience* of "Strange Fits of Passion Have I Known"? The reader or humankind is the intended audience.

2. What does "difference" in the last line of "She Dwelt Among the Untrodden Ways" refer to? Lucy's death has a strong effect on the speaker.

3. What has happened to the woman in "A Slumber Did My Spirit Seal"? She has fallen asleep, thereby escaping earthly problems.

Interpreting Meanings

4. Explain the role of the moon in "Strange Fits of Passion Have I Known." The moon's movement corresponds to or directs the speaker's mood. He projects his fears onto the moon. Its movement becomes potentially symbolic of the death of the speaker's beloved.

5. What two contrasting metaphors does the speaker use to characterize Lucy? How could one person be both of these very different things? In "She Dwelt Among the Untrodden Ways" she is still fair but now only when compared to negatives: "mossy stone," "a star, when only one/ Is shining." Student answers will vary. The most likely answer will be that the speaker's relationship is intimate and emotional, subject to change.

6. Why does the speaker of "A Slumber Did My Spirit Seal" specify that the "fears" he refers to are "human"? He does so in order that readers might understand that there is something greater and more meaningful than these "earthly years."

7. What connections among themes and recurring images do you note in these three poems? Do you think the poems should be read together as a unit? Recurring themes are love and death. Recurring images are of night: moon, star; of flowers: rose, violet. The subject matter and themes link the poems into a unit.

8. Why is "Lucy" special to the speaker? How much do we learn about her in the poems? Is this information enough on its own to justify the speaker's concern for her? In one poem, Lucy is his lover, and in the others, a similar relationship is suggested. We learn of her fundamental nature, which is loneliness. She lives alone, is not known, little loved. Students may differ in their view of whether the speaker's emotional attachment justifies his concern.

9. Do the poems offer any consolation for the sadness they explore? The poems offer no consolation. Instead, they offer pity, fear, and pain.

Why do you think the speaker has said what he has? Student answers will vary. Answers should revolve around the speaker's love and fear for Lucy's well-being.

London, 1802

Text page 641

Reading the Poem. Be sure that students understand why the poem is addressed to John Milton. Discuss each of the attributes the speaker hopes to recover for England (manners, virtue, freedom, power).

Reteaching Alternatives. You might have students find pictures of and factual information about England at the turn of the nineteenth century. Suggest that they use this information to elaborate on the message in the poem.

Responding to the Poem Text page 641
Analyzing the Poem
Identifying Details

1. To whom is the poem addressed? It is addressed to Milton.

2. According to lines 2-6, why does England need Milton now? England is stagnating and has forfeited her attributes.

What striking metaphor characterizes the country? The metaphor is in lines 2–3.

3. What does the speaker ask Milton to do? He asks Milton to return from death and, with the strength of his pen and voice, revive the strength, beauty, virtue, and freedom that was once England's.

4. According to the speaker, what kind of man was Milton? Milton was pure and godlike.

Interpreting Meanings

5. What would a "voice . . . like the sea" (line 10) sound like? Answers will vary. The voice might be described as deep, resounding, inspiring, and powerful.

6. What does each of the following objects in lines 3-4 symbolize: "altar, sword, and pens/Fireside, [and] the heroic wealth of hall and bower"? They symbolize respectively religion, military strength, freedom, comfort or warmth, abundance of life, and culture in city and country life.

7. What do you think the "lowliest duties" are in the last line? The line might refer to Milton's treatment of his daughters or to other things resulting from his blindness. Knowledge of Milton's life is necessary to answer the question.

I Wandered Lonely as a Cloud

Text page 642

Reading the Poem. Be sure to discuss the commonality of this theme with the theme of "Lines Composed a Few Miles Above Tintern Abbey."

Reteaching Alternatives. After discussing the poem, allow students to experiment with personification. Call out names of objects or living things and ask for spontaneous responses that describe the items in human terms. Give students the option of writing a poem using personification.

Responding to the Poem Text page 643
Analyzing the Poem
Identifying Details

1. Describe the speaker's *mood* in the first stanza. It swings from lonely or melancholic to delighted.

2. What does the speaker compare the daffodils to in the second stanza? He compares them to stars.

What word in this stanza personifies the flowers? *Heads* is the word.

3. What does the speaker not realize at the end of the third stanza? He does not realize the potential change of mood brought on both by the cheerful play and beauty of the flowers, as well as by his imaginative involvement in them.

4. How does the speaker describe the effect of memory in the last stanza? Memory can bring back experience when a person is in a pensive mood or in solitude.

Interpreting Meanings

5. What details in the last stanza echo the word "lonely" in line 1? What might this echo suggest about the speaker's personality? The details are: "Vacant . . . pensive mood/. . . bliss of solitude." The echo suggests the speaker's general loneliness and brooding thoughtfulness.

6. What word is repeated in each stanza? What could be the significance of this repetition? Dance is repeated. The word keeps the image in the reader's mind, thus continually emphasizing dance. The poem then takes on the mood or movement of a dance.

7. What do you think the speaker means by the "inward eye" (line 21)? Why can the inward eye be called the "bliss of solitude"? The reference is to the mind's eye: memory and imagination. Only in solitude can one recollect experience so purely and fully.

8. Would you describe that faculty known as "the inward eye" as an eye, or as something else? Student answers will vary.

Composed Upon Westminster Bridge, September 3, 1802

Text page 644

Reading the Poem. Point out to students that the poet is always aware of his role as poet. Have them find the lines that gently suggest that not everyone is sensitive enough to appreciate the simple beauties life has to offer (lines 2–3).

Reteaching Alternatives. You might have students search for or draw pictures that seem to illustrate the poem. Suggest that students work in small groups, first to discuss the imagery in the poem and then to describe how best to illustrate the cityscape described.

Responding to the Poem Text page 644
Analyzing the Poem
Identifying Details

1. What details and features of the city are noticed by the speaker? He describes the early morning glow, silence, buildings, surrounding fields, and sky.

2. What details *personify* the city? The main personification is that the city wears "like a garment" the elements that make it a city. In addition see lines 10, and 12–14.

Interpreting Meanings

3. What seems to be the *mood* of the speaker in the poem? The mood might be described as deeply moved yet tranquil.

4. What *paradox* do you find in the poem's last line? The paradox is the idea that, when the city is asleep and unaware of itself, it is beautiful.

5. What quality or characteristic of the scene seems to move the speaker most? The quality is the tranquility of the sleeping city. The speaker is astonished at this quality.

The Solitary Reaper

Text page 645

Reading the Poem. After discussing the literal meaning of the poem, you might ask the students to think about the poet's way of viewing the world. For instance, is the singing woman really an individual or does she exist as a piece of the landscape, a natural wonder more like the daffodils of "I Wandered Lonely as a Cloud" than like a real person?

Reteaching Alternatives. Students will probably appreciate the musical quality of the poem itself. Suggest that they set the poem to music. As an alternative, have students select a song to be played as background to a reading of the poem.

Responding to the Poem   Text page 646
Analyzing the Poem
Identifying Details

1. **What is the Highland lass doing?** She is reaping and singing.

2. **Is the girl's song happy or melancholy? How do you know?** The song is melancholy. Lines 6 and 18–24 state that she either sings of old woes or of recent loss.

3. **What shift in verb tense occurs in the fourth stanza? How does the speaker alter the** *rhythm* **in the second and fourth lines of this stanza?** The tense shifts from present to past. The rhythm is altered by the addition of the unstressed syllable ''ing'' at the end of both lines.

Interpreting Meanings

4. **Why do you think the speaker wanted to recapture this brief experience in a poem? (Is there any significance in the fact that the girl and the speaker are both** *singers***?)** Student answers will vary. A possible answer is that although it was a brief experience, it contained eternal themes of melancholy and longing. It has deeply affected the speaker (lines 29–32).

5. **How does this poem, and others in this selection from Wordsworth, comment on the problem of experiences that too quickly fade away?** Student answers will vary. Have students support their answers with details from the poem.

The Elements of Literature   Text page 646

Romantic Lyrics

This special section reviews the various forms of lyric poems students encounter in this unit. It focuses on the sonnet, the ode, and the meditative poem and discusses the distinguishing characteristics of each form. Emphasis is on how these forms were used and adapted by the Romantic poets. Students are encouraged to pay particular attention to the speaker in each of the lyric poems they read.

Before students read the section, you might want to explain that the term *lyric poem* is generally used to describe any fairly short, nonnarrative poem presenting a single speaker who expresses a state of mind or a process of thought and feeling. After students have read the section, call on them to find examples in the unit of each type of lyric poem and discuss its characteristics.

Samuel Taylor Coleridge   Text page 647

Perhaps Charles Lamb's comment about Coleridge best describes him: ''Never saw I his likeness, nor probably the world can see again.'' Coleridge's genius is unique because of his talents in several different areas. He was not simply an excellent poet, a fine critic, or an interpreter of others' writings. Rather, he was all of these things, as well as a religious philosopher and a psychologist.

Coleridge's talents in various areas have pleased many and irritated probably just as many. In doing so many things and contributing so much to the world of letters and philosophy, Coleridge perhaps did not achieve as much as he might have had he worked in one or two fields exclusively.

Some of his harsher critics complain that he gave posterity only a small part of what he actually was capable of achieving.

However, Coleridge's interests did lie beyond just the writing of poetry. Still, for all his endeavors in various fields, Coleridge may be studied and interpreted as a fine poet whose philosophies of the genre are reflected often in the lines of his creations. As students read ''Kubla Khan,'' ''This Lime-Tree Bower My Prison,'' and ''The Rime of the Ancient Mariner,'' they should watch for the poet's interpretation of imagination, a concept central to Coleridge's philosophy.

Objectives

1. To consider Coleridge's use of opposites

2. To determine the narrative or lyric nature of each respective poem

3. To determine and analyze the various uses of imagery in the poems

4. To locate and analyze the theme of imagination in the poems

Introducing the Poems

In his book titled *Critical Approaches to Literature* (New York, 1956), David Daiches discusses Coleridge's comments on the unique qualites of a poem and his definitions of "poem" and "poetry." This material, presented in summary form for high-school seniors, should be very helpful to them as they begin their study of Coleridge's works. Students may find interesting Daiches's comments about Coleridge's own views of the similarities and differences between poetry and prose.

Background on the Poems. Few, if any, other poets have provided readers with as comprehensive an insight into their own personal beliefs about poetry and the imagination as Coleridge has left for us. As time permits, you may wish to review sections of *Biographia Literaria* (1817) particularly apropos of the study of the four poems in the text. In particular, consider reviewing Chapter 13 on the imagination and Chapter 14 on Coleridge's definitions and discussions of poetry and prose. I. A. Richards's *The Portable Coleridge* (New York, 1950) includes this important material and includes an introduction to Coleridge's life and works.

Teaching Strategies

Providing for Cultural Differences. The language, and the vocabulary in particular, in these three poems may present students with some difficulty. It is extremely important that students look up all confusing and unfamiliar words. This may seem overwhelming because there are so many, but for an understanding of the poem, it is essential.

"Kubla Kahn" is basically a projection of a fantasy and vision, and should in that sense be familiar to students from all backgrounds. The subject matter of "This Lime-Tree Bower My Prison" should not present students with a problem of comprehension. It is likely that they have all been left behind, due to illness or injury, at some point in their lives. "The Rime of the Ancient Mariner" may be confusing because of the references to the sea, and to the dramatic experiences and strange and terrifying feelings that the Mariner describes. It might be helpful for you and students to discuss the confusing elements in the poem and then summarize events in the poem, so that a clear comprehension of the narrative is reached.

Providing for Different Levels of Ability. You might suggest that students compare a fantasy of their own with the vision presented in "Kubla Kahn." This may help to make the poem more meaningful to students who read it as an expression that is completely removed from their own lives. "This Lime-Tree Bower My Prison" may be a bit confusing for students if they are unfamiliar with the circumstances under which it was written. Explain to students that Coleridge wrote the poems after his foot was burned and he could not walk with his friends through the countryside. He was forced to sit in the lime-tree bower and spend the day alone, awaiting the return of his companions. As with "Kubla Kahn," you might suggest that students compare this experience with one they have had of being sick or injured and having to stay put while their friends go off for an afternoon of fun.

"The Rime of the Ancient Mariner" is a poem that will probably present some confusion to all students. Suggest that students read Bruce Chatwin's essay from *In Patagonia* on page 1066. This fascinating essay describes the true story on which Coleridge based the poem. Summarizing the events of the poem will be helpful. You may also find it extremely useful—for an overall comprehension—to discuss the philosophical elements presented in the poem. The death of the albatross is brutal and especially important because of its randomness—it was never provoked. Because the Mariner has killed what loved and protected him, he is forced to live through the horrors at sea and then live through the horrors repeatedly by telling the story for the rest of his life. Encourage the students to discuss the Mariner's fate and to state whether or not they believe it is justified.

Introducing Vocabulary Study. Students will benefit from knowing the meaning of the following word before they read "The Rime of the Ancient Mariner."

unslaked

Reading the Poems. It may be helpful to ask different students to read "Kubla Kahn" and "This Lime-Tree Bower My Prison" aloud in class. After students have listened to the poems, ask them to read the poems silently to themselves, focusing on one or two of the questions at the end of the sections. When reading poems aloud and listening to them, encourage students to pay close attention to the music of Coleridge's language. "The Rime of the Ancient Mariner" is too long to be read aloud by a single person. You might want to go around the room, asking each student to read a section out loud. It will be necessary for them also to read the poem silently to themselves at least twice, so that they reach a full level of comprehension.

Reteaching Alternatives. It will be helpful for students to summarize the events and feelings conveyed in each of the poems. Ask students to focus on how emotions are depicted through the events. How does the speaker in "Kubla Kahn" express feelings? How does the speaker in "This Lime-Tree Bower My Prison" convey his sense of loneliness, resolution, and so on? How does Coleridge present the events and the Mariner in the last poem? What feelings affect students at the end of the poem? Who do the students empathize with? What knowledge do the depicted events and emotions leave them with?

Responding to the Poem   Text page 651
Analyzing the Poem
Identifying Details

1. **What *images* recreate the earthly paradise that Kubla Kahn decrees in the first stanza?** The images include the pleasure dome, sacred river, fertile ground, gardens, streams, blossoming fragrant trees, and sunny spots of greenery.

2. **Why is the "deep romantic chasm" of line 12 called a "savage place"?** Within it ceaseless turmoil seethes.

What ominous note is introduced toward the end of the second stanza? Amid the tumult are ancient voices prophesying war.

3. **What does the speaker see in a vision in the third stanza?** He sees a damsel with a dulcimer.

How does the speaker imagine himself in the stanza? He imagines himself listening to her and creating, as she creates song with her dulcimer.

4. **Describe the *rhyme scheme* and *meter* of the poem. Can you find examples of *alliteration* that add to the poem's music?** The rhyme scheme is *abaabccdbdb*. The

meter is iambic with varying syllabic measure. Examples of alliteration may be found in lines 19, 27, 33, and 50.

Interpreting Meanings

5. **Who is the speaker of the poem? Compare him with Kubla Kahn.** The speaker is a third-person narrator. He wants to create, like Kubla Kahn. Kubla Khan is the alter ego of the narrator.

6. **Why is the "damsel with a dulcimer" important to the speaker?** She is important because she is his muse.

How could the speaker "build that dome in air"? What could the "pleasure dome" *symbolize*? The dome could be built with artistry. It may symbolize heavenly creation or fertile creativity.

7. **Many ancient cultures regarded poets as seers who had a special relationship with the gods and were thus to be treated with special reverence. How may Coleridge be alluding to such beliefs in the closing lines of the last stanza?** The narrator is being perceived as godlike and visionary; he is treated with reverence and awe.

8. **Where does the poet use contrasting *images* (of greenery and ice, of tranquility and turmoil, etc.)? In your view, does he offer any synthesis of these images in the concluding stanza?** Examples occur in lines 14, 36, et al. Student answers will vary.

Does the poem seem to you to bear out Coleridge's own description of it as a "fragment"? Or do you think that these lines were all the poet really intended to write? Explain. Students should note that Coleridge stated unequivocally that this was a fragment, implying that he intended or hoped for the poem to have been written on a larger scale.

Responding to the Poem   Text page 654
Analyzing the Poem
Identifying Details

1. **What is the situation at the beginning of the poem? Describe the scene the speaker imagines his friends will see when they "emerge/Beneath the wide wide Heaven" (lines 20–26).** The speaker has been left by his friends, who have gone for a walk without him; Coleridge had hurt his foot and could not walk. The friends will see the beautiful landscape of fields and villages, the sea and the two islands off the coast.

2. **What time of day is it in lines 32–37?** It is sunset.

Can you tell approximately how much times passes in lines 43–59? The passage of time is from daylight to nightfall.

3. Describe in your own words the scene the speaker sees from his bower in lines 43–59. He sees brilliant light shining through the leaves, and then the dappled light beneath the leaves. He sees the walnut tree and the bright ivy climbing up the elms. He sees the twilight lighten the dark branches and the bat begin to fly silently, and the swallows stop their song.

4. Whom does the speaker address by name in the poem? He addresses Charles—specifically, Charles Lamb.

5. Why does the speaker bless the "last rook" in lines 68–70? What consolation does he suggest the rook brings? He blesses the rook because it was going home, which suggests that his friends will be returning home as well. This also may refer to Lamb's tragic family situation—and the idea of accepting loss.

Interpreting Meanings

6. In what sense is the bower a prison? The speaker is trapped there.

What other prisons, literal or figurative, are alluded to in the poem? How does the poem suggest that one can escape from them? Cities, age, and grief are other prisons alluded to. One escapes them by recognizing the beauty around us in nature.

7. Paraphrase what the speaker seems to have learned from his own experience. Look carefully at the statement beginning, "Henceforth I shall know . . ." (line 59). He has learned that nature frees and cares for those who open themselves up to her beauty.

8. How does the speaker's tone change in different sections of the poem? Look again at these four sections: lines 1–9, 32–43, 59–67, and 68–76. Lines 1–9 have a mournful sense; lines 32–43 are joyful and celebratory; lines 59–67 are contemplative; lines 68–76 are gentle and comforting.

9. How do you respond to these statements from the poem?
   a. **"Nature ne'er deserts the wise and pure"** Answers may vary. The statement reflects the Romantics' sentiment: cities are corrupt and evil, while the country is filled with goodness and beauty. Those in the country will be protected by Nature.

   b. **"No plot so narrow, be but Nature there, No waste so vacant, but may well employ Each faculty of sense, and keep the heart Awake to love and beauty!"** Answers may vary. Rural students may disagree; students from urban areas may agree.

   c. **"No sound is dissonant which tells of life."** All is beautiful in life. Again, answers will vary. Students who have experienced tragedies may disagree.

Responding to the Poem Text page 675
Analyzing the Poem
Identifying Details

1. Who is presented as the *narrator* of the ballad? To whom is he telling his story? The narrator is an all-knowing overseer. The story is told to the listener/reader/audience (man to mankind).

Summarize the Mariner's story. The Mariner killed an albatross—the embodiment of love and good fortune. Because of his act of irrational destruction, he is punished with a life of permanent alienation. The crew of the ship dies, yet maintains the power—even in death—to deem him an outcast. The Mariner's journey at sea continues, as a placement for his suffering and penance, and he eventually returns home, where he is fated always to travel. In his travels he must tell and retell (as he does to the Wedding Guest) his story (thereby reliving his horrors and shame), and through his story he must teach love and the necessary reverence of all living things.

2. According to Part II, what consequences follow the Mariner's killing of the albatross? The ship is becalmed. The Mariner and his crew are ensconced in silence, heat, and water that they cannot drink.

3. Explain the Wedding Guest's fear at the opening of Part III. He fears the Mariner is a spirit.

How does the Ancient Mariner reassure him? The Mariner assures him that he is made of flesh and blood—a real live man.

4. Who are the occupants of the strange ship that appears in Part III? A woman and her Deathmate are the occupants.

What results from their appearance? The men die one by one as a result.

5. In Part IV, why is the Mariner unable to pray? He is filled with self-hatred for his act. His heart is "as dry as dust" and he sees only the looks and curses in the dead men's eyes.

What happens that enables him to pray? When he shifts his focus away from himself and his circumstances, he sees the beauty of the watersnakes, and he begins to feel love for what is outside him. With the acknowledgement of love and beauty, he is at last able to pray.

6. What is the reaction of the Pilot and the Hermit to the Mariner's homecoming? They are afraid of the Mariner. They think he is the devil.

What does the Mariner plead with the Hermit to do? The Mariner asks the Hermit to shrive him—to release him from his guilt of killing the albatross.

7. At the end of the ballad, how does the Mariner

describe his current life? He says he is destined to travel from land to land telling his tale. His is the life of the permanent outcast in constant penance for the wrongs he has done in his act of destroying what loved and protected him.

What lesson does he draw for the Wedding Guest from this tale? He tells the Wedding Guest to love ''man and bird and beast.'' One who loves well will live well is the lesson from the tale.

Interpreting Meanings

8. **Where in the poem is the wedding mentioned? How does this context for the ballad affect your response to it?** The wedding is mentioned in the beginning of the poem and at the end. The Mariner's story is symbolic of what happens when love (in the form of the albatross) is destroyed. The wedding, in contrast, symbolizes the celebration of love. The Mariner's message is that loving all beings—not exclusive love—is essential for a happy life.

9. **Describe in detail the changing states of the Mariner in Part IV.** He changes from seeing himself as cursed and his surroundings as ugly—dry and rotting—and shutting his eyes to protect himself from the horrors around him, to opening his eyes and viewing the watersnakes ''in tracks of shining white,'' coiling and swimming in tracks of golden fire. In recognizing the beauty he begins to acknowledge and celebrate life. In the acknowledgement of life outside of himself, he begins to love, and the weight of the albatross falls from him.

Given the circumstances, are these changes believable? Yes, the changes are believable. In his complete isolation he recognizes his need for other living beings; focusing only on himself—his regret and his shame and guilt—is deadly. Focusing on others outside himself offers him life, which is symbolized by his ability to pray.

10. **After he shoots the albatross, the Mariner experiences both shame and guilt. What is the difference between these two emotions? Where in the poem does he experience each emotion?** The difference is knowing you are responsible for having done something wrong and feeling regret for having done it. He experiences guilt after he kills the albatross. He experiences shame when he acknowledges the harm he has caused to the albatross and the crew, regrets his actions, and accepts the penance he must do for the remainder of his life.

11. **What is the Mariner's ''penance'' (line 408)?** His penance is having to be alone on his ship, forced to live with the consequences of his act.

What penance does he have left to do? Does it seem fair that he should have to do any sort of penance? Explain. He still has penance—to live as an outcast, traveling from land to land telling his story. It should seem fair

that he does penance. He has randomly and irrationally killed what offered him complete love. Many have died for his act.

12. **Explain in your own terms the Mariner's moral (lines 612–617). Does the story indicate that he ought to have added something to his moral conclusion? Explain.** Answers will vary. Generally, one who loves generously and completely will live happily and therefore well. Nothing needs to be added to the conclusion. Prayer, here, implies life in general.

13. **Why is the Wedding Guest sadder but wiser after hearing the Mariner's tale?** He is sad because he knows the fate of one who must spend his life in penance, alone. He is wiser because he has learned the importance of loving others.

What other figures in Coleridge's poems in this selection are also listening to a speaker? No other figures in the other poems are listening to a speaker, although speakers do address others—such as Charles in ''The Lime-Tree Bower My Prison.''

14. **What do you think of Coleridge's side notes to the poem? Do you think reading them alters the meaning of the poem? Should they be consulted in a careful reading of the poem? Why or why not?** Answers may vary. Students might feel that the side notes are helpful in summarizing the main events of the story. Reading them should not, however, alter the meaning of the poem. The notes should be consulted while reading the poem because the poet included them and therefore intended that they be read.

15. **This ballad is famous for its use of vivid *imagery* and memorable sound effects. Pick out and comment on several especially effective examples of simile, metaphor, personification, alliteration, assonance, and internal rhyme.** The following effects might be noted. Simile: lines 33–34 describe the radiant beauty of the bride. Personification: line 112 describes the sun's heat and parallels both the death of the albatross and suggests the nature of anger against the destructible force of man. Alliteration: liens 171–173; the *w*'s create a faster rhythm and even suggest through the pronunciation the breeze that is absent. Internal rhyme: line 381; the sound evokes the tune that is left. Metaphor: lines 280–281 reflect the brilliance of the snake's tracks. Assonance: lines 521–522 emphasize the stump and add to the lyrical quality of the stanza.

16. **For the most part, the form of the poem is the regular ballad stanza. Occasionally, however, Coleridge varies the meter of the lines and the length of the stanzas. Pick out several examples of such variations and comment on the effect of each.** Answers will vary. Lines 45–50, 91–102, 111–122, 589–590 exemplify the effect of breaking the rhythmical pattern. The shifts in pace call attention to the events described as well as to the lyrical elements of the poem as a whole. The varied meter and

length of the stanzas also help to avert a singsong quality that could, if uninterrupted, lull the readers into a daze rather than keeping them spellbound through the story.

17. There was a time in American history when almost every schoolchild could recite "The Rime of the Ancient Mariner," or parts of it. Find some stanzas that strike you as particularly quotable. What situations in life could you apply the lines to? Answers will vary. Sections cited may include the following. Lines 115–118: The feeling of being completely isolated from everything and everyone around you. Lines 287–291: The feeling of overcoming a terrible burden and beginning to find happiness in life again.

18. Do you think that this poem has something universal to say about human conduct? Explain. The poem suggests that human beings must avert destructive behavior or prepare to carry the burden of violence for life. To live fully and happily as a part of society, as a part of this world, we must love all living beings and recognize the beauty of life in its many forms.

Primary Sources Text page 677
Coleridge Describes His Addiction

Before students read this supplemental behind-the-scenes glimpse of the author of "Kubla Khan," review some of the facts of Coleridge's life as treated in the introduction to the poet beginning on page 647 of their text. Have students read the letter for homework, directing them to look up in a dictionary any words with which they are unfamiliar, such as *vitriol* in the second line. At the beginning of the following class, ask students to write a brief essay that discusses what differences, if any, Coleridge's revealing self-portrait makes in their regard for his life and works.

George Gordon, Lord Byron Text page 678

In *The Story of English Literature* (New York, 1947), R. F. Patterson states that "Much of Byron's writing, indeed, is rhetoric rather than poetry" Patterson refers also to Byron's lack of correct diction and grammar, as well as his errors in rhyme and syntax. However, Patterson also states that "Byron's poetry was received with rapture on its first appearance, and his poetic reputation continued to grow during his lifetime." Today, Byron's reputation proceeds from *Don Juan* and *The Vision of Judgment* more than from his other works. In *A Critical History of English Literature* (New York, 1960), David Daiches speaks of that reputation:

"Modern criticism prefers the latter Byron . . . Yet the histrionic, narcissistic, attitudinizing Byron cannot simply be sliced off from the ironic Byron and ignored; the two Byrons represent different sides of the same medal, and to see the poet whole we must look at both sides." Ask them to watch for these two sides of the poet.

In addition, students should be aware of Byron's poetic use of satire. Before students begin a study of *Don Juan*, they should have a clear understanding of the nature and purpose of satire.

Objectives

1. To analyze the distance between speaker and person spoken about in the first three poems

2. To determine the mood of each poem

3. To determine Byron's reliance on epic conventionality in *Don Juan*

4. To compare Byron with Wordsworth and Coleridge

Introducing the Poems

A. C. Ward, in *English Literature: Chaucer to Bernard Shaw* (New York, 1967), writes of Byron: "His words say what they say, and they say no more." Some critics feels that Byron's poetry, because of this lack of suggestion and mystery, does not contain the poetic genius of Wordsworth or Coleridge; however, possibly more than any other writer of the period, Byron typifies the Romantic poet. Ask students to begin their study of Byron and his works by paying particular attention to the poet's use of language, his recollections of past experiences, and his satire found in *Don Juan*.

Teaching Strategies

Providing for Cultural Differences. "She Walks in Beauty" and "So We'll Go No More A-Roving" should not present students with a problem regarding cultural difference. The first poem is one of admiration and the second is a poem that describes the speaker's need for reformed behavior. "The Destruction of Sennacherib" and the excerpts from *Childe Harold's Pilgrimage* and *Don Juan* will be more confusing for students. "Sennacherib" requires a historical understanding so that the students will comprehend the events of the poem. *Don Juan* requires an understanding of the mores that existed at the time in which it was written. It also requires a knowledge of Cervantes's character Don Juan. Discussions of these important elements will help to clarify the students' understandings of the events, ideas, and implications expressed within these poems.

Providing for Different Levels of Ability. Any problems encountered by students with respect to the works of Byron will exist independently of differences in native ability.

Introducing Vocabulary Study. Students will benefit from knowing the meanings of the following words before they read the excerpt from *Childe Harold's Pilgrimage*.

palpably   protracted

Reading the Poems. It will be helpful and enjoyable for students to read these poems aloud during class. The poetic elements of the poems—rhyme, meter, etc.—will become evident to them through an oral presentation. Due to the length of the excerpt from *Don Juan*, you may want to ask several students to read passages aloud. Encourage students to read the poems silently and aloud at home, as well. This will aid their comprehension and their appreciation of the musical quality of Byron's language.

Reteaching Alternatives. It will be helpful for students to create character studies of each of the subjects in the poems. Understanding the subjects of the poems will assist them in comprehending the situations evoked and the ideas expressed within each of the poems. In the case of *Childe Harold's Pilgrimage*, you might suggest that students pick out one particularly powerful image from each stanza and explain the reason for their choice.

Responding to the Poem   Text page 680
Analyzing the Poem
Identifying Details

1. What *simile* does the speaker use to describe the woman in the first stanza? She is like the night.

2. What aspects of the woman's physical appearance does the speaker mention? He mentions her hair, eyes, cheek, brow, and her smile.

3. What does the woman's appearance suggest to the speaker about her character and personality? It suggests that she is good, sweet, innocent, and at peace.

Interpreting Meanings

4. What does the speaker imply about day when he calls it "gaudy"? The implication is that it is garish, compared to the night.

5. "Dark and bright" in line 3 suggests a balance of opposites. How is this idea developed in other details? See line 7, lines 13–14, and lines 15–16.

6. What does the speaker mean by "below" in line 17? He means earth.

7. This poem sometimes has been criticized for being oversentimental and dependent on cliches. Tell whether or not you agree and why. Answers will vary for each student.

Responding to the Poem   Text page 681
Analyzing the Poem
Identifying Details

1. What decision has the speaker made in the first stanza? He has decided to cease roving.

What are the reasons for that decision, as given in the second stanza? He is worn out.

Interpreting Meanings

2. What do you think the speaker means by "roving"? He means carousing.

3. What single point is the speaker driving at with his examples of the sword, the soul, and the heart in the second stanza? He is saying that each needs its rest.

What do you think the sword and the sheath stand for? They stand for lust and passion.

4. What attitude toward time does the speaker imply in this poem? Do you agree or disagree with this attitude? Night is paralleled with love and sensual indulgence, and day with more somber behavior. Answers will vary.

Responding to the Poem — Text page 683

Analyzing the Poem
Identifying Details

1. What are the Assyrians doing in the first stanza? They are attacking.

What has happened to them in the second stanza? They have died.

What *similes* describe the army in these two stanzas? Similes that describe the army are "wolf," "leaves of the forest in summer," "fallen leaves in the autumn."

2. According to stanza 3, who or what is credited with the victory? The Angel of Death is so credited.

3. What does the field look like after the battle is over? It looks terrible and silent.

4. What is "the Gentile" in the last stanza? Sennacherib is the Gentile.

What *simile* describes how the Gentile was conquered? He was melted like snow.

Interpreting Meanings

5. Describe the *meter* of the poem. The meter is anapestic.

How does the movement of the meter help reinforce the action of the poem? It is fast and bouncy.

Responding to the Poem — Text page 690

Analyzing the Poem
Identifying Details

1. How does the speaker describe the setting in lines 1–8? He describes a ragged coast with a guarded sandy shore. The ocean is usually very rough, except in summer, when it appears calm as a glittering lake.

2. Who is Haidée's only companion? Zoe is the only person mentioned.

Where has her father gone? Her father is on an expedition.

3. What exaggerated *figures of speech* are used to describe the kiss beginning on line 49? Adjectives, metaphors, and similes are used.

4. According to line 79, what is nature's oracle and what best interprets it? First love is the oracle. It is best interpreted as: no fear of other people, no terror of the elements, all passion found in one sigh.

5. In what ways is Haidée, lines 81–82, described as totally innocent? She had never heard of plight or peril, or promises in love; she didn't speak of scruples.

Why doesn't she ask her lover for a vow of constancy or faithfulness? She had never dreamt of falsehood—she didn't know it could exist.

6. What does the narrator say Haidée should have remembered, but did not (lines 110–112)? She should have remembered the Stygian River, Hell, and Purgatory.

7. Identify all the exaggerated *similes* in lines 121–126. See lines 153–158. The infant, child, devotee, Arab, sailor, and miser are among those students might mention.

8. In lines 129–136, what does "it" refer to? It refers to what women love.

9. According to lines 145–168, what do women do when their love is lost? They take revenge, take a lover, drink, or pray; some look after their household, others turn to dissipation; some run away, play the devil, and write novels.

Why, according to the poem, are women correct in behaving this way? Woman are correct in behaving this way because men treat them unjustly.

10. Describe the nuptials that Haidée and Juan celebrate in lines 185–191. The priest was solitude. The nuptial torches were stars. The witness was the ocean. Their bed was the cave. They were hallowed and united by their feelings.

Interpreting Meanings

11. Why does the speaker link Haidée with "pure ignorance"? (What is the difference between "ignorance" and "innocence"?) She is untouched in knowing about falsehood. Innocence implies freedom from sin and actions that are morally wrong; it also suggest naivete. Ignorance implies lack of knowledge.

12. In what way could this story be analagous to the account of Adam and Eve? Is there evidence in the poem that Byron intended it to be? Answers may vary. The two are alone in "Paradise." It is as if they are the only beings on earth. Innocence and downfall are alluded to. There are several other Biblical references. Yes, Byron intended an analogy between the lovers and Adam and Eve.

13. Describe the stanzas' *rhyme scheme* and find examples of *alliteration*. Where does Byron use sound devices to create humor? The rhyme scheme is *ababcc*. For examples of alliteration, see lines 107–109, line 119, and line 122. Students may suggest others. Humor is created in the end rhymes of the final couplets in each stanza.

14. Which of Byron's *figures of speech* do you think are comically exaggerated? The verbs and adjectives are exaggerated.

15. Where does Byron say things that surprise you, in that they catch you off guard and make you laugh? For example, what about his description of Zoe, the servant, in lines 20–24? She only works during the day, and she asks Haidée for hand-me-down dresses.

16. What seems to be the speaker's *tone* as he describes Don Juan and Haidée falling in love? The tone is exaggerated and satirical.

17. If *Don Juan* is in part witty *satire*, who or what are Byron's targets? Answers may vary somewhat. Some of Byron's targets are the characters of men and women and the love between them, indulgence, lust, morality, and religion.

Can you find some barbs directed at the whole Romantic tradition, as exemplified by Wordsworth and Coleridge? Explain. There are many barbs directed at the Romantic tradition. In general this is evident by the exaggerated sincerity, the relationship between man and nature, and the discussion of love. Line 157 suggests Coleridge's ''Rime of the Ancient Mariner.'' Lines 153 and 154 suggest Wordsworth's evocation of purity of infancy and youth.

Responding to the Poem   Text page 692
Analyzing the Poem
Identifying Details

1. According to the first stanza, how does the speaker feel about nature? The speaker loves nature.

2. In stanza 2, what does the speaker say man does to earth? Man destroys the earth.

What can man do to the sea—or the sea do to him? Man cannot destroy the sea, but the sea can destroy man—causing shipwrecks and death.

3. What experience from his childhood does the speaker recall in the third stanza? He recalls playing in the ocean.

What *figure of speech* describes the sea as a horse here? ''Mane,'' a noun, describes the sea as a horse.

4. What does the speaker say about himself and his poem in the fourth stanza? The speaker describes himself as tired and old, and he describes the poem as finished but not as worthy—as fine—as he would like it to be.

5. What does the speaker hope for in the last stanza? He hopes that he will be remembered.

6. Describe the *rhyme scheme* of each stanza. How does the last line of each stanza differ in *rhythm* from the preceding eight lines? The rhyme schemes for all the stanzas are: *ababbcbcc*. The last line in each stanza has two extra syllables.

7. What single aspect of the ocean does the speaker repeatedly emphasize in these stanzas? He emphasizes its depth and boundlessness.

8. In spite of the ocean's destructive aspects, the speaker professes that he loves it passionately. What might this tell you about the speaker's personality? It seems to reveal his love of nature. Students should recognize this adoration to be a basic trait of the Romantic spirit.

9. What link does the speaker imply between himself and the pilgrim in the final two stanzas? The two are about to embark on the final journey—that is, die.

10. From the little you have read, what would you guess the speaker's pilgrimage was in search of? Student answers will vary. Most would recognize that, as a Byronic hero, the speaker was perhaps in quest of fame, immortality, or a spiritual level of being.

11. Can the fierce identification and rapture experienced by this speaker in the presence of nature be felt today? Student answers will vary. Some will contend that there is so little unspoiled natural beauty left that a quest to discover nature would be frustrated from the outset.

Do any of these lines strike you with particular irony, considering what has happened to the environment in some places in the twentieth century? Student reactions to the blight exacted by modern society will vary. Be sure students support their claims with sound arguments.

Primary Sources   Text page 693
Byron Writes to Shelley

Have students note, as they read this letter, the use of italics for emphasis. When they have finished reading, ask them to assess the tone (which appears, for the most part, to be almost mocking). In general, the letter, insofar as it is a response to the passing of one of the great poets of the day, will strike them as rather callous and uncaring. Ask students to evaluate the letter in a brief paragraph, noting in what ways the document seems consistent with the personality of Byron as revealed in the brief biographical passage in their text and in his poems. Is Byron's reaction to a contemporary's death atypical of reactions in the present day? Can students think of twentieth-century or other notable figures who have expressed an outward dislike of their peers? Might such a dislike be discernible in Byron's letter?

Percy Bysshe Shelley

Text page 694ment>

Critics and others of Shelley's generation have called Shelley everything from a genius and prodigious child to an unrepentant atheist and demon. Some applauded his unique ability to make profound pronouncements about the evils in society, while others considered him a supreme egotist, intent only on having himself heard. In *English Romantic Writers* (Great Neck, New York, 1958), Nehry M. Battenhouse writes of Shelley: "He was, in the last analysis, an aristocratic humanist and not a Christian humanitarian." This notion is reflected in Shelley's pamphlet titled *The Necessity of Atheism*. As a result of this early work of Shelley's, he was expelled from Oxford. This is only one example of the poet and writer who felt he must put onto paper what he actually believed, no matter what the cost.

Perhaps a description of Shelley, the writer, found in *The New Century Handbook of English Literature* (New York, 1956), provides a succinct determination of the poet's place in British literature: "As a lyric poet Shelley is perhaps unrivaled in English literary history. He was an idealist, a philosopher, rebel, and reformer, and both in prose and verse expressed with singular completeness the revolutionary and more progressive aspects of his time. His belief in humanity and its ultimate approach towards perfectibility through truth and love is a constant theme that finds its fullest expression in *Prometheus Unbound*."

Ask students to consider the quotation and its validity as they read Shelley's poems.

Ode to the West Wind — Text page 697

To a Skylark — Text page 701

England in 1819 — Text page 705

Ozymandias — Text page 706

Objectives

1. To gain insight into the poet's view of the world

2. To determine Shelley's use of symbolism

3. To evaluate Shelley's attempts to convey abstractions in his poetry

4. To determine Shelley's effectiveness in using "framing devices"

Introducing the Poems

First, review what we know of Shelley, the man. Ask students to be particularly cognizant of Shelley's own intellectual philosophies concerning life in general and politics and religion specifically. Also, have students consider Carlos Baker's comments in *Shelley's Major Poetry: The Fabric of a Vision* (Princeton, 1948): "There is hardly a poet in the history of English literature who has been the victim of so many attacks and so many defenses." As students read Shelley's poetry, they should look for justification of Baker's comment. For instance, do students find Shelley's poetry objectionable in terms of literary merit? Do they find it better than other Romantic poetry?

Background on the Poems. Perhaps more than his fellow Romantic poets, Shelley was a poet of anarchy. You may need to discuss the term *anarchy* with students and ask them to characterize the word. You also may want students to read Shelley's "The Mask of Anarchy." Doing so will give students a good foundation for studying a poet whose works reflect his personal philosophy in a very meaningful way.

Students should also know, as Angela Leighton explains in *Shelley and the Sublime: An Interpretation of the Major Poems* (Cambridge, England, 1984), that Shelley was influenced by two major forces or traditions in Britain of the eighteenth century. The first is that of empirical philosophy.

Percy Bysshe Shelley   159ment>

Leighton mentions that Shelley was interested in Lock, and Hume's description of "the mind's relation to the outside world." The second influence was the tradition of the sublime. The term *sublime* refers to grandeur. In natural grandeur we may see the divine presence. Thus, "the mind susceptible to natural grandeur is also the mind able to achieve religious ecstasy." The sublime "point[s] beyond the visible distances of nature to the invisible presence or power which they manifest." Students should remain alert to Shelley's poetic representation of these two influences.

Teaching Strategies

Providing for Cultural Differences. It will be helpful for you to encourage students to come to terms with all unfamiliar vocabulary words in these poems, and to pay attention to the footnotes. The use of unfamiliar language will present the most immediate cultural problem for students. The subject matter itself in "To a Skylark" and "Ode to the West Wind" should not present difficulties. It is, however, important to have students refer to the headnotes in their text to "England in 1819" and "Ozymandias." In studying these two poems, students will need at least background information provided there to comprehend the occasions of the poems and the events and descriptions in them.

Providing for Different Levels of Ability. As stated in the previous section, vocabulary is likely to present problems for most students. In addition to having students look up the definitions of unfamiliar words, you might assign each student a different problematic word and have them present full definitions of those words to each other in class. To encourage a full comprehension of the new words, you might suggest that students write a paragraph using two of their new words and two words from another student's list.

If students have trouble understanding the descriptions and events in the poems, it may be helpful for you to go through the poems, asking students to paraphrase the meaning of each stanza (or each few lines in the last two poems).

Introducing Vocabulary Study. Students will benefit from knowing the meanings of the following words before they read the poems.

crystalline	languor
despoil	profuse
impetuous	visage
incantation	

Reading the Poems. All of Shelley's poems should be read aloud in class. You might ask for volunteers to read the five sections of "Ode to the West Wind." "To a Skylark" is long enough for you to go around the room and have different students each read a stanza. "England in 1819" and "Ozymandias" are short enough to assign to two individual students to read aloud. In addition to these in-class

readings, have students read each of the poems at home, so that they get a full sense of the music of the poems as well as a complete comprehension of the subject matter of each piece.

Reteaching Alternatives. You might want to ask students to choose their favorite images from the poems. Ask them to read aloud the passages containing those images and explain why they find the words powerful and evocative. This will encourage a close reading of each poem. Listening to classmates' selections, moreover, will increase their appreciation and understanding of the poems.

Responding to the Poem   Text page 700

Analyzing the Poem

Identifying Details

1. What does the speaker ask the wind to do at the end of sections 1, 2, and 3? He implores the wind to listen.

2. What does the wind do to the leaves, the clouds, and the sea? The leaves are blown or "driven" (line 3). The clouds are spread over the sky (lines 19, 25–27). The sea grows grey and begins to roll or "tremble" (lines 41–42).

3. How is the speaker like the wind, according to section 4? He is "tameless, and swift, and proud."

4. In the final section, what does the poet pray the wind to do? He prays the wind to make him its instrument, to drive his "dead thoughts over the universe," and to scatter his wind-inspired words "among mankind."

Interpreting Meanings

5. How is the wind both a "destroyer and preserver" (line 14)? It serves the final death to autumn leaves and preserves seeds by carrying them to earth.

Why does the sky become a "vast sepulcher" (line 25)? How do lines 24 and 25 hint at the time the poem may have been written? The clouds form a blanket over the sky, thus closing in the earth. Line 24 mentions the dying or waning year. Line 25's reference to a tomb also hints at coming winter.

7. What are the "level powers" of line 37? They are the single level of the ocean.

8. What are the "thorns of life" in line 54? The reference is to the pain, suffering, and the sorrows of life.

9. What is an *incantation* (line 65)? It is a ritual, often using words, designed to produce some effect.

How is it related to a prayer? As in prayer, an incantation requests something from a force outside and greater than the person.

10. Does the ode argue that poetry cannot come into being unless the poet is inspired by a force greater than himself or herself? Explain. Student answers will vary. Although the answer is subject to interpretation, the poem does on its surface state that the speaker needs the power of the wind to make poetry, or, more specifically, a poetry of transformative power. It can be argued that the speaker feels as lifeless as one of the leaves without the power of the wind behind him and in him. However, nowhere in the poem is it suggested that poetry needs an outer inspiration. And in specific reference to this poem, the west wind is commonly interpreted as inner inspiration itself. Still, it is more powerful than the speaker, who wants most of all to be torn from his grief, the occasion of the poem.

11. How do the fourth and fifth sections of the poem differ in their approach and emphasis from the first three sections? The first three sections describe the wind's effects. The fourth and fifth sections ask or invoke the wind to drive, shape, and rattle the speaker as it did the leaves, seeds, and clouds. The sections also ask the wind to empower the speaker with its own power.

12. In line 67, the speaker describes his words as "ashes and sparks." How can you explain this *paradox*? An unextinguished hearth contains both ashes (comparable to dead leaves) and sparks (comparable to seeds). The speaker contains both elements of life and death within him. Both are emblematic of the poet's being and therefore appropriate.

13. What do you think lines 68–70 of the ode mean? The speaker continues to ask the wind to speak through him, to give him the voice of prophecy. But more than this, he seems to desire to divest himself of his soul or to share it with mankind. He wants more than anything the power of expression. He is in a dormant state-winter-and concludes by asking rhetorically if spring (poetry, expression, life) will come after winter (grief, silence).

The Elements of Literature

Text page 700

Apostrophe

This special section examines the literary device of apostrophe, especially as it was used by the Romantic poets. Apostrophe is defined as a figure of speech in which a writer directly addresses an absent person, a personified inanimate object, or an abstract idea. It is suggested that apostrophe may have its origins in the invocations of prayer.

After students have read the section, you might have them discuss in detail and even debate the question raised in the last paragraph: Did the Romantic's notion of "empathy" somewhat blur their use of apostrophe?

Responding to the Poem Text page 704
Analyzing the Poem
Identifying Details

1. Identify the different *similes* that the poet uses to describe the skylark. The similes occur in lines 15, 20, 21–22, 28–30, 32, 36, 41, 46, and 51.

2. What questions does the speaker ask the bird? What does he ask the bird to teach him? He asks it what the objects of its song are (lines 71–75). He asks how it could sing so purely without knowledge of life and death (lines 81–85). He asks the bird to teach its thoughts (lines 61–62), its gladness, its rapture, its knowledge (lines 101–105).

3. What kinds of songs would be an "empty vaunt" (line 69) compared to the song of the skylark? Wedding songs and chants would be empty.

4. Why are humans' "sweetest songs" (line 90) not the same as the song of the skylark? The skylark's song is happy; humans' songs are sad.

5. What, according to lines 91–95, would be necessary for "harmonious madness" to flow from the speaker of the poem? He must know the gladness (knowledge) that inspires the song of the skylark.

Interpreting Meanings

6. What do we learn about the skylark and its song from the following words used to describe it: "unpremeditated" (line 5), "unbodied" (line 15), "unbidden" (line 38), "unbeholden" (line 48), "ignorance" (line 75), "ne'er knew love's sad satiety" (line 80), and "Scorner of the ground" (line 100)? We learn that its song is spontaneous (5), unhindered, free, flowing (15); it sings for itself (38). It is rarely seen (48), is untouched by pain (75). Its song is free of love's melancholy, therefore of desire, restraint, vacillation; it is unattached (80). It is free of earthly concerns, and sings of cosmic themes (100).

7. What details of this poem do you think suggest the special quality of the skylark's music? Student answers will vary. Following are a few details, listed by line number. Lines 21–24, 27–30, 35, 46–50, 55, 56–60.

8. What passages in the poem seem to reflect the Romantics' esteem for spontaneity in poetry? Such passages are in stanza 1, in lines 326–45, 61–70.

9. Lines 86–90 of this poem are among the most quoted lines in English poetry. Do you agree with what this stan-

za says about humans? What examples can you provide that support line 90? Student answers will vary. Lines 41–44, 66–70, and 91–95 might be suggested

Responding to the Poem — Text page 705
Analyzing the Poem
Identifying Details

1. **What does the speaker say about kings and rulers of England? What *figures of speech* are used to describe them?** He says the king is old, mad, and despised. The royalty are a dull race, scorned by the people; they are leech-like; "dregs of their dull race," "mud from a muddy spring," "But leechlike . . . cling."

2. **What does the speaker say about the people, the army, the laws, and religion?** The people are starved and killed; the army whose job is protection, rather inflicts pain or oppression; the laws are corrupt, written to protect finances of England rather than the lives of the people; religion Christless, Godless, as well as dead: "a book sealed."

Interpreting Meanings

3. **Why are the "princes" described as "dregs of a dull race" (line 2), and the "rulers" as "leechlike" (line 5)?** Princes are the last of an incompetent and dying institution: royalty. Rulers feed off the people.

4. **Analyze the effectiveness of Shelley's choice of adjectives that describe King George III in line 1.** Student answers will vary. The words describe a most despicable and pitiful man. Note the similarity to King Lear.

5. **Explain the *paradox* in line 13: that "graves" might give birth to the glorious Phantom.** The oppressive statue, which is a spiritual grave, would cause (give birth) the people to react with a revolution.

6. **Can you think of any other periods in history to which Shelley's invective might apply?** Student answers will vary. The American Revolution, French Revolution, Russian Revolution, and ongoing struggles in Africa and South America are possibilities.

Responding to the Poem — Text page 706
Analyzing the Poem
Identifying Details

1. **Explain in your words what the traveler has seen.** He sees legs of stone, the head of the sculpture, a pedestal with an inscription, and the great expanse of the desert.

2. **What words are on the pedestal? What works remain?** The words are in lines 10–11. The only works that remain are the severed sculpture of the king.

3. **Even in the brief space of a sonnet, Shelley suggests a number of *narrative frames*: how many speakers do you hear in this poem?** There are three speakers: the narrator, the traveler, and the inscription bearing the words (voice) of Ozymandias.

Interpreting Meanings

4. **What do you think are the passions that the sculptor read and embodied in the "visage"?** The passions are the king's bitterness and contempt for others.

5. **What kind of pride is condemned by the poem?** Disdain and haughtiness are condemned.

6. **Explain the fundamental *irony* of the sonnet.** The inscription suggests the king's vast riches; the irony is that the inscription now relates only to the shattered visage of the king.

7. **Could this poem apply to any contemporary figures that wield political power?** Student answers may vary. Former President Nixon might be cited.

John Keats — Text page 707

In general, critics acclaim Keats as being more of a "modern" poet than his contemporaries. Douglas Bush expresses this belief in the following comments: ". . . he carries relatively little excess baggage in the way of mediocre writing or 'dated' ideas from which, in various ways and degrees, Wordsworth, Coleridge, Byron and Shelley must be cut loose. Keats speaks to us directly, almost as one of ourselves; we do not need to approach him through elaborate reconstructions of dead philosophies or dead poetical fashions. The romantic elements in him remained, so to speak, central, sane, normal . . . It is one of Keats's essential links with some poetic leaders of our own age that he, alone among the romantic poets, consciously strove to escape from self-expression into Shakespearean impersonality" (Walter Jackson Bate, ed., *Keats: A Collection of Critical Essays*, Englewood Cliffs, New Jersey, 1964). Students may find helpful a discussion of possible reasons for Keats's unique place in British Romantic poetry. Ask them to read Keats's works with this question in mind.

Objectives

1. To determine Keats's variety of rhyme schemes

2. To analyze Keats's use of imagery

3. To determine Keats's reliance on legend

4. To determine the tone of each poem

5. To evaluate the figures of speech in Keats's poems

6. To consider Keats's perspective about nature as represented in his poems

Introducing the Poems

As students begin their study of Keats's poetry, they should take advantage of reviewing two opposing critical views of the poet and his work. In *Keats and His Poetry: A Study in Development* (Chicago, 1971), Morris Dickstein states: "On the one hand certain critics since Northrop Frye have stressed the visionary tendencies of the Romantics, their prophetic independence not only from received wisdom moral or theological, but from the dross of the empirical world. To these critics Romanticism is more a new confrontation with literature than with reality: a revival of the myth-making power and imaginative freedom of Spenser and Milton and a "modern" renewal of the archetypes of pastoral and romance. They see self-consciousness not as an end in itself for the Romantics but only as a necessary and temporary burden, the negative moment that demands the higher harmony and reintegration of the autonomous imagination. Keats, with his recurrent skepticism about the imagination, does not fit well into this pattern, but at least Professor Wasserman, in his influential book *The Finer Tone*, has contrived to see his whole *oeuvre* as tending toward some condition of self-transcendence, a 'realm of pure spirit,' from which the mortal poet, mired in a 'sense of real things,' is unfortunately always falling away.

"The most consistent opposition to such a view, at least as it concerns Keats, has come from a distinguished group of present or former Harvard scholars, who have emphasized Keats's skepticism and moral growth . . . One of them, Professor Stillinger, has brilliantly ransacked even Keats's romances for undermining notes of irony and realism, and has gone so far as to find in the very arrangement of the 1820 volume 'a progressive abandonment of the ideal and acceptance of the natural world.' . . . With their great editions and extensive writings the Harvard Keatsians have taught us an immense amount about Keats and his circle; their image of the poet is far more accurate than Wasserman's, and they have firmly and finally interred the nineteenth-century view of him as a sensitive aesthete."

Students will want to make their own evaluations of Keats, the poet, from a careful study of the poems included in the text.

Background on the Poems. After focusing on the two opposing views mentioned previously, you may want to review figures of speech and ask students to locate them in Keats's poems. If you do so, make certain also to ask students what effect these devices have on the overall tone of the works.

Also, in the poetry of Keats, as in other Romantic works, nature is an important image. Review with students on the comments about imagery and nature found in Holman's *A Handbook to Literature*. As you teach each work, ask students to determine Keats's use of nature, the extent of that use, and the ultimate effect on the overall message and tone of each work.

Teaching Strategies

Providing for Cultural Differences. Students who are not familiar with classical and medieval literature may find it difficult to appreciate various of Keats's poems. As time permits, expose these students to examples of art and literature from the classical and medieval periods. For example, you might assign a selection from *The Iliad* or show pictures of medieval tapestries.

Providing for Different Levels of Ability. Some students may find it difficult to read Keats. These students may be helped by a careful review of unfamiliar vocabulary before a selection is read. Students who are advanced in their reading and understanding of Keats might benefit from doing outside reading of literary criticism on his work. These students could prepare summaries of their reading.

On First Looking into Chapman's Homer

Reading the Poem. Through discussion, help students to appreciate the comparison being made in the poem between adventure and new discovery and the reading of poetry. Ask them to restate the main idea of the poem in their own words.

Reteaching Alternatives. You might allow students to uncover the levels of meaning in this poem on their own. Suggest that they look up a summary of *The Iliad* and that they think carefully about the various metaphors Keats has used to describe the experience of reading Chapman's translation of Homer.

Responding to the Poem
Text page 709
Analyzing the Poem
Identifying Details

1. What does the speaker say he had already experienced before he read Homer? He has read many great poets, but has only secondhand knowledge of Homer.

2. How does the speaker say he felt on reading Homer? He feels as though he has had a breath of fresh air.

3. Describe the *rhyme scheme* of the sonnet. The rhyme scheme is *abba abba cdcdcd*. The sonnet is therefore Italian or Petrarchan rather than English or Shakespearean.

Interpreting Meanings

4. What do you think "realms of gold" are (line 1)? "Realms of gold" are imaginative lands in the travels of poetry.

5. What significance can you find in those two famous similes that tell how the speaker felt on reading Homer? (By implication, what is he comparing the experience of reading poetry to?) The speaker feels like an astronomer or an explorer, both of whom search for the undiscovered. Poetry is compared to a search of either the heavens or the earth for what has been hitherto unknown.

Bright Star, Would I Were Steadfast as Thou Art
Text page 710

Reading the Poem. Be sure students understand the meaning of the word *steadfast* as it is used in this poem (immovable, not subject to change). Ask for interpretations of the poem. For example, one could read the poem as a statement of Keats's awareness of his impending death and his longing to have a more lasting hold on life, especially a life shared with someone else.

Reteaching Alternatives. It might be interesting to students to keep a running list or chart of the similes and metaphors Keats uses in his poems. They are sure to notice his frequent references to stars, clouds, and so on, and can form

their own conclusions about Keats's reasons for thinking in these terms.

Responding to the Poem
Text page 710
Analyzing the Poem
Identifying Details

1. What characteristics of the star does the speaker want to resemble? Which ones does he *not* want to emulate? He wants to have the star's quality of steadfastness or permanence. He does not, however, want to be alone in such splendid permanence.

2. What does the speaker really want? He wants to live forever (or to die) with a beloved.

3. How is the star *personified*? How are the waters personified? The star is personified as a hermit; the waters are personified as agents of absolution or spiritual cleansing.

Interpreting Meanings

4. How does the octet (lines 1–8) define the meaning of *steadfast*? **How does the sestet clarify further what the speaker means by the wish in line 1?** The speaker defines *steadfast* in the octet as "absolute watchfulness"; in the sestet, he clarifies his meaning by adding the virtue of faithfulness to amplify his sense of steadfastness.

5. What is ominous about the mention of death as an alternative in the last line? For the speaker, death is the only alternative to permanence; because permanence like the star's is impossible, the presumed alternative is, by definition, ominous.

When I Have Fears

Text page 711

Reading the Poem. Give students a chance to read this poem twice, perhaps once silently and once aloud. Allow students to focus immediately on the feelings expressed by the poem and be sure to encourage them to talk about their own feelings as they read it. Then turn to an analysis of individual lines and the poem's structure.

Reteaching Alternatives. You might suggest that students write their own poems using the same title Keats used here. After writing their poems, students may want to compare and contrast their fears with those shared by Keats.

Responding to the Poem Text page 711
Analyzing the Poem
Identifying Details

1. What experiences that he may never have make the speaker stand "on the shore/Of the wide world" alone?
He may never experience either the fulfillment of his work or the companionship of his beloved.

2. What *simile* describes the books the speaker hopes to write? The simile is the comparison of such books to harvests of grain.

3. Whom is the speaker addressing in this poem, and what line tells you? He is addressing his beloved (line 10).

Interpreting Meanings

4. What do you think the last line signifies? The last line suggests that the achievement of the ideals of love and fame are both dependent upon the speaker's mortality.

5. Describe the speaker's tone. Does it remain constant or become more intense? Explain. The tone might be described as anxious, rattled, Students should note an abating of the tone as the sonnet progresses.

La Belle Dame Sans Merci

Text page 712

Reading the Poem. Students may need help articulating their understanding of the subtle shift in the speaker's identity. Ask them why the ending is ironic (the speaker has become the knight he had been viewing with such sympathy) and them go back and find the moment of change in the speaker's identity (stanza 4).

Reteaching Alternatives. Students might enjoy telling the same story from the point of view of the lady. Allow them to work in small groups to write a ballad in which she is the speaker (or a letter if ballad form seems difficult).

Responding to the Poem Text page 714
Analyzing the Poem
Identifying Details

1. Who are the two speakers in the poem? Where does the first speaker stop and the other start? What is the first speaker's question? The first speaker is the poet; the second is the knight-at-arms of whom he speaks. The second speaker begins in the third stanza. The first speaker asks the night what is troubling him.

John Keats   165

2. At the opening of the poem, what time of year is it? The time of year is late autumn or early winter.

3. What *images* help you visualize the knight? The images of loneliness, pallor, aimlessness, fatigue, depression, and feverishness help the reader visualize the knight.

4. According to the knight's story, what happened when he went off with the enchantress? What did he learn from his dream? He and the enchantress seemed to fall deeply in love. The knight learns from his dream that he has been enchanted—deluded, deceived—into such a belief.

Interpreting Meanings

5. What do you infer happened to the pale kings and princes? They, too, were enchanted and had the same experience as the knight-at-arms.

6. Where does Keats vary the *meter* of each ballad stanza? What is the effect of this change in rhythm? Keats changes the meter in the last line of each stanza; the effect is one of pulling the reader up short, breaking the lulling rhythm of the first three lines of each stanza—much as the knight's enchantment is broken when he awakens from his dream.

Keats's "Great Odes"

During the late spring and early summer of 1819, Keats wrote five odes—to Psyche, to a nightingale, on a Grecian urn, on melancholy, and on indolence. A sixth ode, "To Autumn," was written in September of 1819. All are "regular" odes in that they have their own uniform stanzas with uniform lengths. As is usually the case in an ode, in Keats's odes the speaker addresses himself in a formal yet passionate manner to an object of some sort. Though this object can be understood to exist independently of the poem, in other ways the poem itself invokes, or brings into vivid being, the object. This accomplished, the poem explores the speaker's relationship to the object and what the speaker comes to experience and understand as a result of this relationship.

The phrase "great odes" is sometimes applied to all of Keats's odes of 1819, and sometimes to only three or four of them, since they vary in quality and interest. The six poems are usually understood to comprise a sequence thematically and stylistically—from the most subjective and personal ("Psyche" and "Nightingale") to the most disinterested or distanced ("Autumn") attitudes of their speakers. In each ode, the speaker has a particular role to play. In "Ode to a Nightingale," the speaker is a poet who wants (in vain) to achieve the "full-throated ease" of the singing bird. In "Ode to a Grecian Urn," he is a lover of beauty who finds through his gradual absorption into the object, and much to his excitement, a preserved yet stunning experience of human passion. In "To Autumn," the speaker is much less dramatized than in the other odes and plays the part of a quiet observer and appreciator of what he experiences. Each ode displays its particular speaker's special emotional experience, rising and falling in the first two odes and maintaining an apparently level serenity in "To Autumn."

Keats's reputation as a major poet rests most securely on his odes. And rightly so. But as we admire their beauty, we should also remember that if he had lived longer, he might have surpassed them—not so much in their finished quality (there are few poems in English that have their "perfectness")—but in the range, length, and probing that are suggested by the unfinished works Keats left behind.

Ode to a Nightingale

Introducing Vocabulary Study. Students will benefit from knowing the meanings of the following words before they read the poem.

    lustrous   plaintive

Reading the Poem. You might ask students to hypothesize about Keats's reasons for writing the ode. For example, it was clear that he wanted to pay tribute to the lovely song of the bird. In addition, he may have wished to explore—through imagination—different ways of letting go of both the strains and the pleasures of human life.

Reteaching Alternatives. Students might enjoy finding a creative way to respond to this poem. Some may wish to draw or paint scenes as suggested by the poem's imagery. Others may wish to write their own odes, either to Keats or to something beautiful in nature. Still others may like to collaborate on a reading of the poem, perhaps with the song of a nightingale played in the background.

Responding to the Poem   Text page 718
Analyzing the Poem
Identifying Details

1. Describe the outward *setting* and the emotions of the speaker as they are portrayed in the first stanza. The setting is one in which the poet is to be found under a tree listening to the nightingale that sings from its branches. His emotions are depression and lethargy.

2. According to the second stanza, what state of feeling does the speaker want to have? The speaker wants to let go of himself and feel at one with nature.

3. What misfortunes does the speaker want to escape in the third stanza? What means of escape are considered in the fourth stanza? In the third stanza, the speaker wants to escape from worldly worry, aging, and ugliness. In the fourth stanza, the speaker thinks of poetry as a means of escape.

4. What thoughts about death does the speaker have in stanza 6? How does he resolve these temptations? The speaker is tempted by the prospect of death. He resolves the temptation by realizing that even death would not be equivalent to the bird's song; his symbolic ideal of sustained unconsciousness of pain—the nightingale—would remain nonetheless alive, and he would be unable to relish it.

5. Where does the speaker imagine the song of the nightingale has been heard in the seventh stanza? The nightingale's song has been heard throughout history—in ancient empires, in the Bible, and in fairy tales.

6. What is happening in the final stanza? In the final stanza, the nightingale flies away, beyond the speaker's sight and hearing, and the speaker is left alone.

Interpreting Meanings

7. Why is the night already "tender" (line 35) for the nightingale? What time of year is it? The night is "tender" because it is spring-time; more precisely, it is "mid-May."

8. Why would the speaker become a "sod" to the bird's "high requiem" (line 60)? The speaker would become a "sod" because he imagines himself as dead—part of the earth—in stanza 6.

9. Why does the speaker want to capture or imitate the nightingale's "ease"? Why is he "too happy in thine happiness"? The speaker wants to capture the nightingale's "ease" because it represents a unity with nature and the unconsciousness of worldly trouble that he desires. He is, however, "too happy" in the bird's "happiness" because he comes to realize that his identification with it is illusory, not real.

10. What differences does the poem emphasize between the realm (or experience) of the nightingale and those of the speaker? The speaker's is a realm of time, awareness, and decay; the nightingale's is presumably a realm of eternity and happy unconsciousness.

11. What does the speaker realize by the end of the poem? By the end of the poem, the speaker realizes that there is an absolute difference between the world of the nightingale—whether real or imagined—and his own human world; when the nightingale flies away, he is left with the lonely sense of self with which the poem began.

12. What are the different *moods* of this speaker? Does he seem to be more, or less, exalted at the end than at the beginning? The speaker's moods shift back and forth from despair to hope; he sees himself bereft, then imagines a series of escapes from his pain, each one of which turns out to be deceptive in its promise. At the end of the poem, he is perhaps a bit more exalted than at the beginning—while he is still trapped within his "sole self," he has at least had the experience of the symbolic transcendence the nightingale represents.

13. How would you answer the speaker's question at the end of the poem? The question at the end of the poem is best answered either affirmatively or negatively. A combination of dream and reality is exactly what the speaker's symbolic experience has been in the poem, and what the reader's has been reading the poem.

Ode on a Grecian Urn   Text page 719

Reading the Poem. Guide students to see that the poem is really a meditation on the passage of time. In observing that time does not pass for the figures on the urn, the speaker contrasts their experience with his own. Discuss the wistfulness of the tone and the sensuality of the imagery (especially stanza 3) and what both aspects bring to mind about the poet (his impending death and unfulfilled love affair with Fanny).

Reteaching Alternatives. Make available to students several art books that contain pictures of antique Greek vases. Some students may like to draw scenes from the urn as they imagine them to look based on the descriptions in the poem. Others may simply like to work with partners to find pictures of urns that, in one feature or another, resemble the one immortalized by Keats.

Responding to the Poem   Text page 721
Analyzing the Poem
Identifying Details

1. The urn is called a "sylvan historian" in line 3. What does the speaker say about its ability to tell a tale? The urn can tell a tale "more sweetly than our rhyme"—that is, "more sweetly" than poetry itself.

2. Describe the details represented on the urn according to the first and second stanzas. What actions are "frozen" in time on the vase? In the first stanza, the poem describes an idyllic Grecian scene with "men and gods" in "mad pursuit" of "maidens loath," who try to escape a festive din; in the second stanza, it describes a lover under a tree about to kiss his beloved. Though all the actions described are, of course, "frozen" because all are parts of a sculptured scene, the lover about to kiss his beloved in the second stanza is the scene "frozen" most prominently and at greatest length.

3. What is suggested about the speaker's state by the last three lines of the third stanza? The speaker has reached a state of high excitement not unlike those states he beholds on the urn.

4. Describe the picture on the urn according to the fourth stanza. The fourth stanza describes a pagan sacrifice—a priest sacrificing a calf in the sight of the citizens of a nearby village, the latter situated by water, and, nearby, hills or mountains.

5. According to stanza 5, what will happen to the urn when the speaker is dead? The urn will remain, just as it is, even when the speaker is no more. The urn represents a perpetually frozen moment of desire just prior to its satisfaction. This tension may be representative in turn of beauty, truth, or both, depending upon how you wish to define them. As to the urn's message, responses will vary.

Interpreting Meanings

6. Why are "unheard" melodies (line 11) sweeter than heard ones? How does this relate to the poem? How could this idea be said to be typically Romantic? The "unheard" melodies of which the poem speaks are sweeter than the heard ones because they appeal to "the spirit" rather than to mere sense. In the poem as a whole, this notion suggests the eternal tension between striving ("the spirit") and satisfaction (the senses) that is the subject of what the urn represents. This unfulfilled striving is typical of the Romantic depiction of unattainable grandeur or perfection.

7. How would you respond to the criticism that the third stanza is badly written because Keats used "happy" and "forever" too many times? The words "happy" and "forever" are used often in order to produce a strong, repetitive rhythm that conveys the depth of the speaker's ardor when contemplating the urn.

8. If the urn could "tease us out of thought," what state would we be in? Would this state be better than thinking? Explain. The state would be one of lifelessness—ironically, the very opposite of the vivacity both the urn and its contemplation represent. This state is presumably not better than thinking because it is the equivalent of death.

9. How would you paraphrase the last five lines of the final stanza? In what sense are truth and beauty the same? The urn has an immortality that man does not have because it is art—concrete yet eternal, full of feeling and yet inanimate. The equation and reversal of beauty and truth are ways of trying to express these tensions or paradoxes. It is best to offer a series of definitions or alternatives for each of the terms in order to explore their similarities and differences.

10. There is a famous textual difficulty surrounding the last two lines of this poem. Based on the manuscripts, some critics suggest that the quotation marks should enclose the entire couplet, rather than simply "Beauty is truth, truth beauty." Explain what differences in meaning the different punctuation would cause. The difference is whether or not it is the urn that, figuratively, speaks the entire couplet, or whether the speaker of the poem speaks the final line and a half. If the former, the urn speaks for itself; if the latter, it is the speaker of the poem who must draw a conclusion from it, and thereby insist on the urn's distance rather than on its ability to signify without the aid or mediation of commentary or interpretation.

Reading the Poem. Help students to appreciate the connection between the language of the poem and its subject. For example, ask them to support or refute this statement: The poem is as heavy with imagery as the fruit trees of autumn are heavy with fruit.

Reteaching Alternatives. Direct students' attention to the question in the third stanza: "Where are the songs of spring?" Ask them to explain why the speaker would address this question to autumn and then say not to think about them (line 24). Guide students to see the association the poet is making between spring and youth and autumn and declining years.

Responding to the Poem   Text page 723
Analyzing the Poem
Identifying Details

1. Where is the speaker of this ode? Describe the landscape. The speaker is in an apple orchard adjacent to other harvest fields; it is a beautiful autumn landscape.

2. How many sentences are there in the poem? To whom are these sentences addressed? There are five sentences (this includes the questions at the beginning of the second and third stanza as separate sentences). The sentences are addressed to autumn itself, which is personified throughout the poem.

3. What details personify autumn in each stanza? In stanza 1, autumn is personified as a friend of the equally personified sun; in stanza 2, autumn is personified as some-

one happily sitting amid a grain and fruit harvest; in stanza 3, autumn is personified as a maker of music.

4. According to stanza 3, what are the songs of autumn? The songs of autumn are "wailful" and mournful songs.

Interpreting Meanings

5. What might the "songs of spring" be? The "songs of spring" are presumably cheery.

How would they differ from the songs of autumn? They differ because they represent the opposite of autumn's mournful, wailing songs.

6. How does the speaker feel about autumn? Do you think by extension the speaker is also talking about a human season? Explain. The speaker feels an attraction to the luxuriant bounty of autumn despite its mournfulness. The speaker is also referring to the last stages of human life; the harvest of fruit and grain are like the end of human productiveness.

7. Does this poem give too mellow and pleasant a picture of this season of harvest and the beginning of decay and loss? How would you characterize autumn? How do most people regard autumn, and why? The poem gives both a pleasant picture of autumn (it is the time of ripeness) and a vaguely ominous sense of it because it also begins a time of decay. Autumn is, of course, both. Most people regard autumn as a time of both fruition and of the onset of cold and darkness; responses, however, will doubtless vary, including the sense that autumn is a beginning because it is the beginning of the traditional academic calendar.

The Eve of St. Agnes   Text page 724

Introducing Vocabulary Study. Students will benefit from knowing the meanings of the following words before they read the poem.

ethereal   sumptuous
sagacious

Reading the Poem. Be sure students read the introduction before reading the poem. As discussion of the poem begins, call on students to summarize the plot developments. Also focus attention on the other major elements of a narrative: characters, setting, and theme.

Reteaching Alternatives. It might be worthwhile to ask students to write plot summaries. Suggest that they prepare

to write their summaries by making a note of what is happening in each of the stanzas. Then they can group their notes into related events and trace the plot.

Responding to the Poem   Text page 734
Analyzing the Poem
Identifying Details

1. Describe the opening *setting* of the story. The opening setting is the chapel of an old castle on a bitterly cold night.

2. What do we learn at once about "one lady," Made-

line, in lines 42–44? What have the old wives told her must be done in order to have visions that night? Madeline is brooding upon love. The old wives have told her that proper ceremonies are required to have visions which include fasting before bed and lying in bed horizontally with eyes facing upward.

3. Explain what keeps Porphyro and Madeline apart, according to lines 82–89. What keeps them apart is an old feud between their families.

4. Describe Porphyro's strategem. Porphyro's strategem is to find a way to see Madeline without being seen.

5. What role does Angela the nurse play in bringing Porphyro and Madeline together? Angela conducts Porphyro to Madeline's room and hides him there where he cannot be seen.

6. What sight of Madeline in her room makes Porphyro grow faint? The sight of her eyes opening makes him grow faint.

7. Describe what happens in Madeline's room. Porphyro appears to Madeline as though he were in her dream, even though he is actually present; he serves her a feast, as the legend requires, and proclaims his love.

8. Describe the elopement. Who are the "sleeping dragons" all around? Porphyro and Madeline sneak out of the castle. The "sleepy dragons" are Madeline's family and its guests.

What does the last stanza suggest happens to those who are still in the castle? It suggests that Madeline's father the Baron, and his guests become haunted and bewitched; the Beadsman and Angela are said to die.

Interpreting Meanings

10. What do you think the castle in this love story might symbolize? The castle might symbolize either the institution of the family or, more generally, tradition, including its confinements and prejudices.

11. Do you think it is a weakness of the poem that Keats does not show us what happens to Madeline and Porphyro after they leave the castle? Do you think the storm they flee into has any symbolic significance? No, the storm symbolizes the world of adventure and imagination that are beyond the gates of the traditional, and which is, by definition, indescribable in advance.

12. What particular elements of this story remind you of old fairy tales and legends? Reminiscent of old fairy tales and legends are the castle, the old woman, the enchanted lovers, the conjuring of visions, and the figure of the dangerous father.

Primary Sources   Text page 735
Keats's Last Letter

Point out to students that this letter was penned a mere three months before the poet succumbed to tuberculosis. Ask them what sorts of thoughts they would expect to run through the mind of an individual weakened by illness. How well does Keats's letter conform to that impression? Ask them also to review this letter in light of the one by Byron to Shelley on page 693. Does Byron's image of Keats two months after the latter's death seem to describe fairly the man who presents himself in the present letter? Remind students that Byron, by his own admission, was not one of Keats's admirers. Despite his protestations to the contrary, might Byron's reaction to news of Keats's death have been one of relief, or at least indifference?

Charles Lamb   Text page 736

Dream Children: A Reverie   Text page 737

Objectives

1. To analyze Lamb's use of pathos
2. To evaluate Lamb's interweaving of reality and illusion
3. To determine the tone and theme of the essay

Introducing the Essay

Background on the Essay. Charles Lamb was unlike other Romantics in his love for—rather than disdain of—city life. His admiration of other Romantics was based on their depiction of human experience and emotional response rather than their workship of natural elements and their sublime contemplations. His own life was, in general, fairly quiet. He was not, however, spared tragedy. When he was in his early twenties, his sister, who was responsible for the care of his sickly parents, killed their mother in a state of insanity. When she was released from the asylum, Lamb devoted the rest of his life to her comfort and well-being. ''Dream Children: A Reverie'' is one of the many personal essays he wrote. He also wrote poems, a novel, a farce, many critical essays, and together with his sister Mary, the children's book *Tales from Shakespeare.*

Teaching Strategies

Providing for Cultural Differences. The writing style and content of this essay should not present students with any cultural difficulties. The only element of possible confusion might be the reference to the ballad of the Children in the Wood, and as long as students read the footnote that provides information about the story, they should have a clear understanding of the contemplation that Lamb evokes.

Providing for Different Levels of Ability. After an initial reading of the essay, many students may be confused. You may want to discuss with students that this is an essay about reminiscence, regret, and imaginings. To help make the essay relevant to students' own experiences, ask them to think about times when they have, in a daydream, changed events and circumstances in their own lives. The last several lines—beginning with ''We are not of Alice . . .''—may be particularly confusing to students. Explain to them that this is the reader's moment of realization—the children are imagined children and wished-for children—they exist only in the reality of Lamb's dream. One way in which this essay is special is in the evocation of how dreams can hold a hodgepodge of the real and the unreal. It will be particularly helpful for you to encourage students to relate this basic quality of the essay to their own lives.

Reading the Essay. First ask students to read the essay silently in class or at home. Discuss any specific questions that students have about the essay, and then read it aloud to them. The essay is presented in a contemplative storytelling fashion, and it will be enjoyable and true to the mood of the essay for students to listen to Lamb's reverie read aloud.

Reteaching Alternatives. It would aid students in their comprehension of the essay to spend time discussing the way that Lamb intermingles memory and fantasy within his reverie. You may want to suggest that students imagine the way the essay might be presented if it were performed on stage or on film. How might the scenes of memory be evoked? How might the fantasy of the children be depicted? How would students create a visual distinction between the speaker's memory and the fantasy of children he expresses? Would the children appear to be real until the very end—in the same way that Lamb depicts them—or would they appear ghostlike and unreal through the use of a trick lense or theatrical device?

Responding to the Essay   Text page 740
Analyzing the Essay
Identifying Details

1. Describe the situation at the beginning of the essay. The speaker describes a past evening when his children sat around him and he told them about their great-grandmother.

2. What qualities of their great-grandmother Field does the narrator single out to tell the children? What does he say to the children about their Uncle John? He tells how great-grandmother Field was religious and good, respected and beloved by everyone, even though she took care of and did not own the huge house she lived in. She knew the Psalter by heart and much of the Testament. She was tall, upright, and graceful. She was a fine dancer until she became sick—and even then she kept up her good spirits. She was good to her grandchildren and wasn't afraid of the ghosts of two infants who visited her house.

Uncle John is described as having been handsome and spirited, whom everyone looked up to because he was brave, daring, and loved adventure. He was also considerate and caring, and he carried the speaker when he could not walk.

3. How do the children respond to the father's story of the ''old days''? They become involved with the stories: Alice taps her feet at the mention of her dancing great-grandmother; John becomes afraid of the infant ghosts, but tries to act courageous and strong; they cry at the death of their Uncle John and the loss and sadness his death brings to their father.

4. What do the children say as they disappear? They say that they are ''less than nothing.''

Interpreting Meanings

5. According to the writer, where are all the people who might have existed but weren't born? They are on the shores of Lethe.

6. Tell what the essay's title and subtitle mean. The title and subtitle refer to the fact that the narrator is relating a dream and the children within the dream are not his own, but rather a dream of the children he might have had.

7. What do you infer happened between the speaker and Alice W.? Answers may vary slightly. The two were apparently in love, but parted ways: he remained a bachelor, and she married someone else.

8. What significance can you find in the fact that the stories Lamb is telling the children are stories about his grandmother? (What would have been lost if he had been telling them about King Arthur, or the history of England? Answers may vary. He tells the stories about his grandmother so that he may reminisce about his own childhood. Telling stories about King Arthur obviously would not permit that. The speaker seems to need to meander through his past while mourning the loss of his brother.

9. How does the first sentence of the essay establish *tone*? How would you describe this tone? Through mention of stories and children, elders, and imagination, the first sentence sets a tone of nostalgia and yearning. It suggests the comfort and solace people create in imagining relatives they have never seen. It suggests the basic importance of feeling connected to others, and that that connection for most people exists through families. The narrator's need to speak and be understood by people close to him suggests a sadness, a sense of longing and solitude that is carried through the essay.

10. What impression do you have of the ending? Is it over sentimental? Clever? Touching? Given Lamb's life story, how did the essay make you feel? Answers may vary. The ending is sad. It suggests that the speaker's life is not as full as he would like it to be. It suggests his sense of solitude. Given the tragedies of Lamb's life, it is particularly moving and sorrowful.

Mary Wollstonecraft Shelley

Text page 741

from Frankenstein

Text page 743

Objectives

1. To evaluate the structure of the passage from *Frankenstein*

2. To evaluate the nature of the major character

3. To determine the theme of the selection

4. To analzye the tone of the selection

5. To analyze Shelley's representation of the terrifying and the magnificent

Introducing the Novel

Students should be aware that what they read is only a fragment of Mary Shelley's novel. This excerpt should present many subjects for lively class discussion. The notion and depiction of evil in the novel is a subject addressed by Robert Kiely in *The Romantic Novel in England* (Cambridge, England). He comments: "The Shelleys . . . were fascinated by the correspondence between the terrifying and the magnificent, the proximity of ruinous and constructive forces at the highest levels of experience." Another element addressed by feminist critics Sandra Gilbert and Susan Gubar in their book *The Madwoman in the Attic* (New Haven, 1984) is the notion of Frankenstein representing woman in her "fallen" Eve-like state. You may want to suggest to students that Frankenstein may take on the role of woman in his act of creating a living being. You might also remind them that Shelley was the daughter of the very famous feminist, Mary Wollstonecraft, whose work she studied carefully. It is not, therefore, surprising that Shelley might use the novel as an expression of her own sense of femaleness and motherhood—or lack of motherhood (her own mother died shortly after her birth).

In Gilbert and Gubar's description of the intellectual birth of the monster, they say: ". . . what this crucial section of *Frankenstein* really enacts is the story of Eve's discovery not that she must fall but that, having been created female, she is fallen, femaleness and fallenness being essentially synonymous. The discovery that one is fallen is in a sense a discovery that one is a monster, a murderer. . . ." It might be very interesting for students to read the excerpt from a feminist perspective. What or who do they feel the monster represents? Who do they feel Frankenstein represents? Perhaps Shelley uses both the monster and Frankenstein to represent her sense of self and/or all women.

Background on the Novel. It may be interesting for you to tell the students about the origin of the novel. It began as a group challenge to write a ghost story during a rainy period on a summer holiday in Switzerland when Shelley, her husband, Percy Shelley, Lord Byron, and another visitor were confined indoors. Everyone but Mary Shelley was able to write a story quickly. After many days of labored thought, she chanced to listen to a conversation between Shelley and Byron concerning Darwin and the reanimation of corpses. Mary Shelley went to bed, and before sleep overtook her, she developed the idea of the story of Frankenstein and his monster.

Teaching Strategies

Providing for Cultural Differences. The characters of Frankenstein and the monster should be well-known to students. Aside from the fact that the novel is not written in contemporary English, the language should not present difficulties to the students. Encourage them to look up any unfamiliar words in the dictionary, and to refer to the footnotes included in the text.

Providing for Different Levels of Ability. Most students should not have difficulty comprehending the basic narrative of the novel. Who and what Frankenstein and the monster may represent may pose a bit of confusion, however. Suggest that students read through the passages, paying close attention to the way that Shelley describes both characters. What do they look like? Are they appealing or likable on any way? Does Shelley create a sense of empathy in her descriptions? If students feel for the characters in some way, ask them to describe how and why. It may surprise them to feel any sense of kinship with Frankenstein or the monster, but try to help them understand that the characters are not intended to be simply ugly and horrifying; they are meant to be human and representative of different elements of human nature.

Introducing Vocabulary Study. Students will benefit from knowing the meanings of the following words before they read the excerpts.

delineate   lassitude
incipient

Reading the Novel. Suggest that students take their time reading these passages. Because the character of Frankenstein will be familiar to students, many may feel certain that they already know the story, and they may skim through it quickly. Point out that the film versions with which students are acquainted are quite different from Shelley's original story. Encourage them to allow enough time to read through the excerpts twice.

Reteaching Alternatives. Focusing on how Frankenstein changes in these passages, it might be helpful for students to make a list of several early and later descriptions of him. What does he look like? How does he act? How do his reactions to the monster shift? You may want to ask students why they think he does change. It may be helpful to personalize the story by asking students if they have ever participated in a scheme or project that began in an excited and ambitious manner and then got completely out of control—so that the end product was nothing like the anticipated result when the endeavor was first begun.

Extending the Assignment. You may want to ask students to write a short story from the monster's point of view, describing what it was like to come to life, and how it felt when Frankenstein reacted in such a horrified manner upon realizing what he had created. Encourage students to be precise in their depictions and to use as many details as possible so that they convey their thoughts and ideas in a powerful and provocative manner.

Responding to the Novel   Text page 747

Analyzing the Novel

Identifying Details

1. Summarize the overall steps that Frankenstein took in order to discover the secret of human life. First he studied anatomy, and then he studied the decay of the human body after death.

2. Once Frankenstein has gained knowledge, what does he want to do with it? Why does he hesitate? What finally moves him to carry out his plan? He wants to give life to the inanimate. He hesitates because it was an enormous task to find a suitable frame to give life to. He decides, at last, to create a being like himself, because impressed with his initial success, he is sure of his ability to create a creature as complex as man. At first the huge undertaking was intimidating, but he decides that even if his attempts fail, they would "lay the foundations of future successes." He is also thrilled with his potential godlike position as creator of a new species.

3. Describe how Frankenstein changes physically during the two years he works on his creation. He becomes pale and thin, sickly and extremely nervous.

4. What is Frankenstein's first response as the monster begins to breathe? He is horrified.

   Describe his next response. He runs out of the room and spends the night pacing in his bedroom.

5. What does Frankenstein's monster look like? Describe how it moves, talks, etc. The monster's limbs are in proportion; his skin is yellow. His hair is black; his teeth are "pearly" white. His eyes are watery; his complexion is shriveled and his lips are black. He makes inarticulate noises and he grins. His hand stretches out to Frankenstein.

6. Briefly describe the scene that is taking place as the selection ends. Frankenstein is frantically walking through the streets, afraid that his creation might appear before him at every turn he makes. He seems terrified, and to articulate his agitation, he quotes an ominous passage from Coleridge's "Rime of the Ancient Mariner."

Interpreting Meanings

7. Frankenstein begins his study with the rational curiosity of a scientist. However, as his project develops, Frankenstein's motives and behavior change. Explain whether you believe his behavior warrants the adjectives "mad" or "morbid." Student answers will vary. One striking element of Frankenstein's behavior is his growing sense of autonomy, which parallels his delight in viewing himself as the omnipotent creator. Mad and morbid do not necessarily describe him at all. Studying the human body—even the decaying body—is not morbid; it is essential in advancing scientific knowledge of living creatures. It is through this knowledge that Frankenstein actually does create life.

He is not necessarily mad at all; he is living out the fantasy of many men—to assume women's natural power of giving birth. And, godlike, he hopes to create his own species.

8. What feeling does Frankenstein expect to be left with when his creation comes alive? What do you think Shelley was trying to express about human nature? Student answers will vary. Frankenstein expects to feel thrilled, joyous, and powerful. Shelley was perhaps exploring human beings' desire for power and creativity and their ultimate fear of that power, and their subsequent sense of alienation from the very thing they create.

Dorothy Wordsworth

Text page 748

from The Journals

Text page 749

Objectives

1. To evaluate Dorothy Wordsworth's perceptions regarding nature

2. To evaluate the author's unassuming style

3. To determine the author's likely intent in writing the journal entry

Introducing the Journal

Background on the Journal. In teaching these selections from Dorothy Wordsworth's journals, tell students that the writings of Dorothy Wordsworth have been enormously overshadowed by the attention given to her brother, William. As these excerpts illustrate, she was a very fine writer in her own right. Her ability to observe astutely and depict her observations clearly and richly are evident in these selections, which have been excerpted from the journals she kept from 1798 through 1828. Before students read the selections, it might be interesting for them to know that Dorothy and Mary Hutchinson, William's wife, were very dear friends from childhood on, and that Dorothy in fact encouraged the courtship and eventual marriage of the two. In a letter to William Wordsworth, Coleridge described Dorothy Wordsworth as follows: "Her manners are simple, ardent, impressive. . . . Her information various—her eye watchful in minutest observation of nature—and her taste a perfect electrometer—it bends, protudes, and draws in, at subtlest beauties & most recondite faults."

Teaching Strategies

Providing for Cultural Differences. For students of all backgrounds to place Dorothy Wordsworth's writings in a proper perspective, they should understand that very little attention and seriousness were given to women's writings during Wordsworth's lifetime. That may be a reason why her writing took the more private, and therefore acceptable, form of journal entries. It will also be helpful for students to know that it was socially expected of women to marry, have children, and focus their complete attention on their wifely duties.

Providing for Different Levels of Ability. These journal excerpts should not present difficulties for many students. Encourage students to view these writings as brief accounts of a woman's life in 1802 and 1803. If a few students do have difficulties in comprehending Wordsworth's journals, it may be helpful to have them summarize the main events that occur in each excerpt.

Introducing Vocabulary Study. Students will benefit from knowing the meaning of the following word before they read the excerpt from Wordsworth's *Journals.*

diffidence

Reading the Journal. Suggest that students read the journal entries carefully to themselves. While they are reading, encourage students to pay close attention to the descriptions of nature and the way that the speaker conveys her feelings and reactions. For each reading, you might ask students to look for one or two particular elements within the entries (weather in the first, distress in the second, excitement and descriptions of people in the third).

Reteaching Alternatives. You may want to ask students to visualize the scenes that are described. Ask students to list six memorable details from each entry. This will help them appreciate Wordsworth's striking ability to depict her observations so precisely that they become almost tangible to the reader.

Responding to the Journal
Text page 751

Analyzing the Journal

Identifying Facts

1. What did William and Dorothy see on April 15, 1802, in the woods beyond Gowbarrow Park? What *figures of speech* does Dorothy Wordsworth use to describe the sight? The two saw an amazing quantity of daffodils. To describe the flowers, she uses effective personification.

2. Tell what Dorothy did as her brother was married to Mary Hutchinson. She stayed quietly at home.

Interpreting Meanings

3. Describe the writer's attitude toward what she observes in nature. Does she seem ''Romantic'' in spirit or more like an objective observer? Explain your answer with specific references to the journal entries. The speaker does seem Romantic in spirit. She becomes involved with what she observes in nature, and there is an emotional content within her descriptions and evocations of it. The morning of April 15th is ''threatening'' but ''mild.'' The wind is ''furious.'' She uses a great deal of personification, which reflects her own identification with Nature.

4. What do Dorothy Wordsworth's entries on the day of William's wedding suggest about her relationship with her brother? What do you think her emotions were as her brother was married? The entries suggest that she was extremely close to her brother. It seems that she was very disturbed and saddened by her brother's marrige, and that it presented an overwhelming sense of loss.

5. What do these journal entries reveal to you about life in eighteenth-century England, in the Highlands? Answers may vary. In general the entries reflect that for many life was very simple and that the people in rural areas—especially in the Highlands—seemed content and unaffected by the industrialization of England.

Primary Sources
Text page 751

Dorothy Wordsworth Describes Coleridge

Tell students it is rare that we have so frank and detailed a description of a writer who lived in a century that predated electronic media coverage. Permit them to read the passage from Wordsworth's letter purely for pleasure. Point out that the reference in the next-to-the-last sentence to the ''poet's eye in a fine frenzy rolling'' is from Shakespeare's *A Midsummer Night's Dream*.

The English Language
Text page 752

The essay treats the phenomenon of dialects, singling out several of the vagaries endemic to regional speech. Mention is made of the principal dialectal regions recognized by scholars. Finally, the concept of ethnic dialects is discussed, with specific examples of pronunciation and vocabulary drawn from the black English dialect.

The essay will prove entertaining to most students, who will doubtless identify with several of the generalizations made in the piece. If you have students of immigrant families in your class, you might ask them to volunteer particular locutions that they find common among their adult relatives.

Exercises in Critical Thinking and Writing
Text page 757

Interpreting Poetry

This assignment asks students to write an essay interpreting one of the poems in the unit. As background, students are told that interpretation requires a reader to determine the literal meaning of the poem, analyze the poetic elements used, and respond on a personal level to the ideas and techniques of the poet. Students are encouraged to gather ideas for their essays by asking themselves questions, such as: Who is the speaker? What is the situation? What poetic elements are used by the poet and to what effect? They are then provided with a general plan for writing that they can adapt for their own purposes. A model of part of an essay is included to demonstrate how these suggestions may be implemented.

Have students read the assignment. Then read through the Background and Prewriting sections with them, pausing to discuss the concepts and eliciting examples. Encourage students to complete an outline similar to the one shown and discuss it with a partner before writing the actual essay as homework.

Criteria for Evaluating the Assignment. A successful essay will accurately summarize the literal meaning of the poem. It will also examine deeper levels of meaning and analyze poetic elements, such as meter and imagery. It will begin with a paragraph that introduces the topic and will end with a statement of personal response.

Suggestions for Teaching and Evaluating the Writing Assignments

A Creative Response

Many of the writing assignments in this unit ask that students respond to the poem in a creative way. To do so, students must use the form and content of the poem as the inspiration for original thought. A typical assignment is the one following "Lines Composed a Few Miles Above Tintern Abbey," which asks students to describe a scene from nature that prompts a strong emotional response in them. A sound approach to this assignment would be for each student to recall feelings about nature, select a particular experience, and freewrite notes about it until as many sensory details have been recorded as possible. The student then needs to shape a description either in poetry or prose.

Criteria for Evaluating the Assignments. Effective creative responses will show concern for both content and form. If a response is a description, it will begin or end with a statement of overall impression and will include sensory details that support that impression.

A Critical Response

For assignments that require a critical response to a poem, you can help students by encouraging them to ask the right questions. For example, the second assignment that follows "Lines Composed a Few Miles Above Tintern Abbey" asks students to analyze the structure of the poem. To do so, students must ask themselves "How is the poem organized? Why would the poet have used this structure?" In this case, you want to direct students' attention to the discussion of verse paragraphs in Analyzing Language and Style. A student who reads that section, answers the questions above, and traces the progression of thought in the poem (as suggested in the assignment) will find it easy to write a meaningful essay.

Criteria for Evaluating Assignments. Commendable essays will address questions of how and why a poem is structured in a particular way. First the structure will be described and then it will be evaluated for its success in achieving the poet's purpose.

Answers to Analyzing Language

Analyzing Language and Vocabulary

Text page 627

Puns

1. In addition to the usual meanings of the word *appalls*, Blake may also intend a pun on the words *a pall*; that is, the churches are both appalled (dismayed) and turned into palls (shrouds) by the chimney sweepers' cries of misery.

2. With the word *curse*, Blake intends us to think about the harlot's oppression by society, about her loud, angry condemnation of society, and also about the venereal disease that may "curse" the harlot herself and be transferred to her newborn infant as well.

Parallelism

1. Examples of parallelism in "Little Lamb" include the beginning of lines 1, 9, 11, 12, 19, and 20 with *Little Lamb*; the beginning of lines 3, 5, and 7 with *gave*; and the repetitions of *he* and *he is* in lines 13, 15, and 16.

2. Examples of parallelism in "The Chimney Sweeper" (*Innocence*) include the beginning of lines 2, 9, 13, 14, 16, 19, 21, and 22 with *and*; the beginning of lines 15 and 17 with *then*; and the conclusion of both the first and last stanza with lines beginning with *so*.

3. Examples of parallelism in "London" include the repetition of *marks* of in line 4; the repetition of *in every* in lines 5–7; and the repetition of *how the* in lines 9 and 14.

Verse Paragraphs

1. Answers will vary, depending upon which verse paragraph the student chooses; tell your class to use as a model the comments on the first and second paragraphs given in the instructions to this exercise. You might divide students into five groups and assign one paragraph to each group.

2. Again, answers will vary depending on the paragraph chosen, but students should be able to write a statement of each paragraph's main idea. The main idea of the second paragraph, for example, might be stated: Memories of beauty are spiritually uplifting.

Archaic Words

1. Modern synonyms (or synonymous phrases) for these words are as follows: a. *Eftsoons*: *immediately afterward* b. *Swound*: *swoon* c. *Uprist*: *rose* d. *Wist*: *knew* e. *Gramercy*: *Thank God* f. *clomb*: *climbed* g. *wont*: *accustomed* or *used* h. *corses*: *corpses* i. *rood*: *crucifix* or *coss* j. *shrieve*: *absolve* k. *trow*: *believe*

Substituting modern synonyms for these archaisms makes the poem sound more contemporary and less quaint and exotic; some students may feel the synonyms make the poem sound less romantic.

2. The word *wont* is still used today, especially as a noun meaning "habit or custom." The word *Gramercy* will be familiar to some students as a name (as of Gramercy Park in New York).

3. *Jargon* today means the specialized vocabulary of a particular subject or field. Contemporary jargon is like bird twittering in that both are mere incomprehensible noise to most listeners. (The dictionary says that jargon in its original sense was onomatopoeic.)

Connotations

Words from the sonnet that students might cite include *mad*, *despised*, *dying*, *dregs*, *dull*, *scorn*, *muddy*, *leechlike*, *sanguine*, and *tempestuous*. Ask them to volunteer their substitutions orally, and assess the results with them in a round-table discussion.

Imagery

1. Most students will probably feel the color of silver dominates, because of such images of sight as *silver . . . trumpets, argent revelry, a little moonlight room,/Pale, latticed, silver taper's light, silver cross, dim, silver twilight,* and *baskets bright/Of wreathed silver.*

2. Images presenting contrasts include *silver, snarling trumpets*; *the sound of merriment and chorus bland*; *Porphyro on her face doth look,/Like puzzled urchin on an aged crone*; *soft and chilly nest*; *wakeful swoon*; and *sleeping dragons all around,/At glaring watch.*

3. Images presenting a sense of menace include *The sculptured dead . . . Emprisoned in black, purgatorial rails*; *already had his deathbell rung*; *a little moonlight room,/Pale, latticed, chill, and silent as a tomb*; *more fanged than wolves and bears*; *Whose passing-bell may ere the midnight toll*; *the frost wind blows . . . Against the windowpanes*; *the iced gusts still rave and beat*; *In all the house was heard no human sound*; *the besieging wind's uproar*; *the door upon its hinges groans*; and *shade and form/Of witch, and demon, and large coffin worm.*

4. The images of the outdoors and the chapel create an atmosphere of chilly gloom; those of the party create an atmosphere of brilliant frenzy; those of the dark house create an atmosphere of mystery and foreboding; those of Madeline's bedroom create an atmosphere of beauty and lush sensuality.

Analyzing Language   Text page 756

1. Answers will vary, depending on students' dialectal regional orientation.

2. If possible, make a copy of *DARE* available to students, and carry out the assignment as an in-class project.

3. Before undertaking the assignment, which, again, will require a copy of *DARE*, ask black students in your class, if any, to volunteer meanings they may know of for the terms listed.

4. Answers will vary. Students might note that dialects tends to be shibboleths in a society, branding speakers as provincial or learned. Thus, some Romantics will have celebrated dialects as having ''natural'' roots, while others will have deplored them as stultifying.

Unit Six: *The Victorian Period 1832-1901*

Teaching Victorian Literature

Most teachers would agree that the Victorian Period provides the richest array of selections of interest to secondary school students and that it is the most easily, and happily "mineable," of all the periods of English literature.

The sentiments and themes of Tennyson's poetry combined with its musical quality and poetic diction will provide students with a source of British poetry more easily enjoyed than any so far. Until now, with a couple of exceptions, the poems they have studied have been veiled by language problems (Anglo-Saxon, Middle English), complicated by scholarly context, dulled by pedantry, or made strange by simplicity and unpoetic language. Tennyson builds on the sonnets of Shakespeare and the lyrics of Gray and Keats. There are elegies and narratives that recall forms, ideals, and stories introduced in earlier periods. Some of Tennyson's poems are easy to memorize and others will be echoed in the poetry of later poets.

Browning introduces the dramatic monologue. This is not an easy poetic form, but it is intrinsically interesting, as drama is always interesting. Browning also uses a diction that will open up for students a whole range of poetry, British and American, reaching into modern times. His poetry dismisses once and for all any idea students may have about poetry being effeminate. Also, Browning deals with real, flesh-and-blood people—murderous dukes, separated lovers, insane lovers.

If your students are going to love poetry, they will find poems to love—and remember—in Kipling and Housman. They will learn about modern poetry, its language, intricacy, and tone (crisp, pessimistic at times, ironic) from Hopkins and Hardy. They will encounter poets who are forthrightly religious and they will encounter poets who are forthrightly patriotic. Finally, the Victorian poets deal more clearly and deeply with everlasting themes—faith (or lack of it), nature, wisdom, loss, absence, fear, and death.

In the Victorian Period, prose became popular as a literary form for the first time in the history of the English language. Poetry, as each preceding unit in the text will attest, was the language of literature, of the written word as well as spoken word, for centuries. Prose entered through criticism, essays, history, philosophy—not very popular forms of literature. Stories were told in poetry (*The Odyssey*, Chaucer), and in drama (Shakespeare's plays). Earlier in the nineteenth century, British fiction took shape and became a major—often the most important—form of literature, as Jane Austen, Mary Shelley, and the Brontës produced popular novels. But it was not until the Victorian Age that prose of high literary quality and lasting value captured the interest of the mass market. Charles Dickens, writing inexhaustibly, it seemed, novel after popular novel, led the movement, reaching out beyond London and the British Isles, especially to the United States. Robert Louis Stevenson, a poet, essayist, and short story writer, as well as novelist, also held an exciting popularity, at home and abroad, as did the equally versatile Rudyard Kipling. This was a new world for British literature, wide, welcoming, and profitable, at least to publishers. The poet Thomas Hardy also brought the British novel to new ground, using setting and country characters to introduce his own sense of pessimism and inevitability. George Eliot, a woman following in the footsteps of the earlier women novelists, advanced the novel as a means of introducing new and important ideas.

Nonfiction prose also reached new popularity, as the brief selection of popular history, Macaulay's "London Street," exemplifies. This blaze of new glory owed something, we must admit, to new ways of printing and distributing literature and to the existence of a rising middle class with money and social ambition.

Playwrights since the days of Shakespeare have, with a few exceptions, written for a limited wealthy and discriminating market. Presenting a play is a quite different task than publishing or reading a poem. The Victorian public loved good stories, but they got them in magazines and new, mass-produced novels. The telling and enjoying of stories in drama form, for a mass market, had to await the advent of the motion picture and then TV. The writing of plays continued beyond Shakespeare chiefly in the form of comedies of manner, like *The Importance of Being Earnest*. It is in plays like this one by Oscar Wilde that a tradition of drawing room comedy developed. This tradition carried on in the United States, modifying into musical comedies and combining writing talents with the long if sleeping tradition of tragedy. From this live theater came, of course, modern drama in the form of movies and TV drama.

Objectives of the Victorian Unit

1. To recognize the changes that occurred in British poetry following the Romantic Period, including
   a. changes in diction
   b. changes in themes, including different views of nature
   c. changes in form, including the introduction of the dramatic monologue

2. To make comparisons among poets and their poetry, between literary periods, within the Victorian Period, and even within the works of a single poet

3. To recognize the new diversity in the forms and uses of prose

4. To make comparisons among the styles and themes of

Victorian novelists

5. To compare the aims of the selections of prose in the Period

6. To recognize the craftmanship of the playwright in creating drawing room comedy

Thomas Babington Macaulay
Text page 773

London Streets
Text page 774

Objectives

1. To draw inferences about Macaulay's views as a historian

2. To evaluate the style and appeal of the essay

3. To conduct an interview that will reveal historical changes in the student's community

4. To present an oral report contrasting the physical appearance of the student's present-day community and the way it used to be

Introducing the Essay

In outline form, for your reference, here are the major elements in the essay:

- **Point of view:** third person
- **Significant technique:** formal essay

Background on the Essay. In clear, measured, well-balanced sentences, Macaulay presents an array of detail, full of human interest, even dramatic. These are the specifics from which the reader receives vivid impressions and, with no prodding by the author, can form generalizations about a specific city, London, at a specific time, 1685. The selection shows how effective good narrative can be in the writing, and reading, of history.

Teaching Strategies

Providing for Cultural Differences. To visualize the activities that Macaulay describes, students may need help with vocabulary. Some of the items named are no longer part of our culture, except perhaps on a regional basis, for example, *fruit women*, *rabble*, *mountebanks*, *liveries*, *grandee*, *stalls* and *roisters* (in addition to footnoted words).

Providing for Different Levels of Ability. The narrative quality of the selection carries along readers of varying ability. All students approach the vocabulary on an equal basis because only certain concrete nouns, not abstractions and concepts, may cause difficulty.

Reading the Selection. After a review of the Macaulay biography on page 773 and a first reading of the entire selection, start with the second paragraph of "London Streets" and have students generalize about the specifics cited in each paragraph. What areas of human activities are involved? Literacy? Noise control? Animal Welfare? Sanitation? Crime?

Reteaching Alternatives. To emphasize the point that Victorians, or at least those who were well-off, were especially pleased with the progress that England had made in the world of material things, point out that Macaulay just assumes that his readers will recognize that London is now an ideal city. Point out that some historians believe in Progress with a capital "P" and others do not. In which group do we place Macaulay? Then ask students to choose teams and debate the proposition that, were Macaulay alive today, his belief in progress would remain unshaken.

Responding to the Essay   Text page 765
Analyzing the Essay
Identifying Details

1. What statistics does Macaulay offer to measure the importance of London as a city under Charles II and under Queen Victoria? He offers populaton statistics: In Charles II's time, London's population was six times that of Manchester or Liverpool. In 1685, London was the most populous European capital, with little more than half a million people; in Macaulay's day it had at least nineteen hundred thousand.

2. What are some of the "insupportable grievances" that the population of London suffered in the seven-

teenth century, according to Macaulay? Residences were close to the filthy, noisy market of Covent Garden and the rabble gathered in Lincoln's Inn Fields every evening. The streets were full of rubbish and dead animals, and residents dumped their chamber pots into the streets. Beggars, thieves, and gangs of young ruffians bothered people walking in the streets.

3. In the seventeenth century, why would it have been useless to place numbers on the houses? Many of the residents, especially workers who had to locate houses, could not read.

Interpreting Meanings

4. What would you guess Macaulay's politics to have been? Student answers will vary. Some may conclude from the words he uses to describe the seventeenth-century poor (rabble, *the ignorant*, *noisy* and *importunate*, *impudent squatter*) that Macaulay was hardly a liberal reformer in sympathy with the poor, but was instead allied with maintaining the status quo for the wealthy, privileged, and educated upper classes.

5. Given this sample of it, why do you think that Macaulay's *History* was so popular? Students may mention the many specific details about everyday life not usually given in a history text and Macaulay's clean and easy-to-read prose style.

Alfred, Lord Tennyson

Text page 777

Inasmuch as your students are probably motivated by anecdotes relating to genius, supplement the biographical material on this leading Victorian poet with the following infor-

mation. Tennyson, who studied the classics at his father's knee, was so motivated as a student that by the age of eight he had memorized the entire collection of Horace's odes.

Tears, Idle Tears

Text page 779

Objectives

1. To identify the pairs of similes in each of the stanzas 2–4 and tell what contrast in feeling each pair creates
2. To interpret and analyze imagery

The Poem at a Glance

- **Rhyme:** none
- **Rhythm:** iambic pentameter
- **Significant techniques:** simile, imagery, refrain

Teaching Strategies

Providing for Cultural Differences. The scenes that moved Tennyson may be quite different from those that students today, especially those living in urban areas, may look back on with joy. Students can be helped to transform these scenes into urban settings.

Providing for Different Levels of Ability. The language of the poem may sound dated, but only one or two words create diffculty: *verge* (edge); *feigned* (lured).

Reading the Poem. Read the biography with the students. To prepare them for the poem, you might introduce pictures of the landscape surrounding Tintern Abbey and ask them to think of their own favorite spot and of the memories it brings back to them. Try to help them to see that the more they think about their own memories of days that are no more, the sadder and more profound their thoughts become.

Reteaching Alternatives. Have students compare this poem with Wordsworth's "Lines Written Above Tintern Abbey."

Responding to the Poem   Text page 779
Analyzing the Poem
Identifying Details

1. What does the speaker gaze on in the first stanza? He is looking at "the happy autumn-fields."

What memory prompts his tears? The memory of the days that are no more prompts his tears.

2. Stanzas 2–4 present a series of comparisons that attempt to make concrete the abstract memory of "days that are no more." What are these comparisons? Stanza 2 compares the fresh sunrise and the sad sunset with the days that are no more. Stanza 3 compares a summer day to days gone by. Stanza 4 compares the days that are gone by to lost or hopeless loves.

Interpreting Meanings

3. How does the sequence of images in this poem result in an increasingly darker tone? Students may observe that the second stanza only hints at death, while the third and fourth stanzas speak of dying and then the remembrance of something after death has come.

4. Explain and comment on the meaning of the poem's last line. Students should recognize that the line is an expression of extreme loss and the emotional climax of the poem. "Death in Life" may be grief over the loss of friendship and love, or it may refer to our knowledge that, even as

we live, we inevitably must die. Students may have other interpretations of "Death in Life."

5. Analyze the structure of "Tears, Idle Tears." What is the scene of each stanza? The poem begins with a statement of an emotion (lines 1–3) and moves to an analysis of the cause of that emotion. Stanza 1 mentions a specific scene (the speaker gazing on happy autumn fields) in the present. The "scenes" in succeeding stanzas are not real but, rather, thoughts and memories: sunrise and sunset of the birth and death of souls, discussed in terms of sea imagery (stanza 2); a summer dawn experienced in a bedroom (stanza 3); stanza 4 is entirely abstract and has no setting.

Why do you think Tennyson arranges the scenes and events in the order he does? Students may mention that the poem moves from the present to the past, from the concrete to the abstract, and from the real experience of stanza 1 to the memories of stanzas 2–4. In terms of the feeling it expresses, the poem moves from quiet sadness to an intense emotional expression in stanza 4.

6. What do you think the "divine despair" is in line 2? Do you think Tennyson is alluding to the account of the fall of Adam and Eve in Genesis here? Would that account explain the poet's existential sadness? Student answers will vary.

Now Sleeps the Crimson Petal

Text page 780

Objectives

1. To identify instances of repetition
2. To identify parallel syntactic structures
3. To analyze the role of images in the poem
4. To compose music to accompany the lyric
5. To write an analysis of images in the poem

The Poem at a Glance

- **Rhyme:** none
- **Rhythm:** blank verse
- **Significant techniques:** image, repetition, syntax

Teaching Strategies

Providing for Cultural Differences. Even those unfamiliar with palaces and water lilies will have little trouble

understanding what is happening as night descends in this poem—at least after the mythological allusion is explained in the footnote.

Providing for Different Levels of Ability. The images are clear, involving simple objects. No one should have trouble after the allusion is explained.

Reading the Poem. To prepare students for reading the poem, you might have them talk about the actions that occur among plants and animals, as well as in the skies, as night falls. Have them select a natural action that could occur every night or any night. Even the simplest action is worth noting. Then you might have the students discuss the best verb that can be used to describe these actions. You might explain to the students that the selection of words like these by the poet helps us to think about them in a fresh light.

Reteaching Alternatives. Have the students walk down the path with the lovers, following the speaker's comments, noticing what he notices and thinking about what he has to say.

Responding to the Poem

Analyzing the Poem
Identifying Details

1. **What time of day is described in the poem?** Night is described in the poem.

2. **Who is the speaker talking to?** The speaker is talking to his beloved.

What does the speaker ask in the last two lines of the poem? He asks his love to slip into his bosom and be lost in him, to make herself a part of him.

Interpreting Meanings

3. **Various details in the poem hint at the setting, or at least at the social position or rank of the speaker. What are these hints?** The poem describes a beautiful garden with a "palace walk," a decorated fountain, and a peacock (an exotic bird imported to decorate the estates of the wealthy). These details suggest that the speaker is a wealthy man.

4. **Explain the meaning of line 7. How can the Earth lie "all Danaë" to the stars?** The light of the stars "showers down" upon the Earth. The Earth, although distant and in a sense "hidden," is open to receive starlight.

5. **Identify the instances of *repetition* and *parallel syntax* in the poem.** Each stanza presents at least one vivid image of something occurring at the present moment. Both the first and final stanzas end with a command to the person being addressed in the poem. Each stanza begins with the word *Now* followed by a present-tense verb; each stanza ends with a prepositional phrase ending in *me*.

6. **Pick out two or three lines whose *images* and sound you think are especially remarkable. How do these lines help create the mood of the poem?** Answers will vary. Students may note that, except for the commonplace firefly, the images in stanzas 1 and 2 are exotic and ornate; those in stanzas 3 and 4 are of heavenly objects. Some may say that the mood of the poem is mysterious and sensuous.

Break, Break, Break

Objectives

1. To identify atmosphere
2. To recognize tone
3. To analyze the role of images in the poem
4. To write an analysis of the poem's structure

The Poem at a Glance

- **Rhyme:** *abcb* in each stanza
- **Rhythm:** predominantly antapastic
- **Significant techniques:** atmosphere, tone, imagery

Teaching Strategies

Providing for Cultural Differences. Someone who has never seen a ship slide slowly over the horizon may need help in visualizing the image in the second stanza.

Providing for Different Levels of Ability. The poem speaks eloquently to students of varied levels of ability.

Reading the Poem. To prepare for the reading of the poem, you might ask students to think about sounds and sights that bring back memories. Bells, for example, evoke memories—campfires, songs, sunsets, train whistles. Have students think of other examples and then think about the memories, happy and sad, that the sounds and sights evoke.

Reteaching Alternatives. You might ask students to place themselves in a situation similar to the one the speaker was in—by the edge of the sea, a lake, or on a mountain looking out at a landscape, or on a city rooftop. Have them imagine happy sights that might take place in such a setting, sights that would today take the place of a sailor singing in a rowboat and children at play. Then ask the student to imagine how such a sight could bring back a sad thought about days gone by, lost friends, for example.

Responding to the Poem

Analyzing the Poem
Identifying Details

1. **Where is the speaker as the poem begins?** The speaker is standing at the seashore, watching the waves break on the shore.

2. **In the third stanza, what does the speaker grieve for?** He grieves for the touch of a vanished hand and the sound of a voice that is still.

Interpreting Meanings

3. The words of the title are repeated twice; at the beginning of the first and fourth stanzas, when the speaker calls on the waves of the sea to "break, break, break." Considering the *atmosphere* and *tone* of the poem, what else might we imagine to be "breaking" in this lyric? It appears that the speaker's heart is breaking.

4. What moods are suggested by the *images* of the fisherman's boy (line 5), the sailor lad (line 7), and the stately ships (line 9)? The images of the fisherman's boy and the sailor's lad suggest the joy of life and youth. The ships sug-

gest serenity.

How do these moods contrast with the speaker's emotions? Far from being happy or at peace, the speaker is full of grief and despair.

5. Has the speaker's sorrow changed in any way from the beginning of the poem to its end? If so, how? Some may say that the sorrow remains the same, endless as the image of the waves breaking on shore. Others may feel that, after having voiced his feelings, the speaker seems to be somewhat more resigned to his loss. Students may have other responses.

Crossing the Bar

Text page 782

Objectives

1. To identify the basic metaphor of the poem

2. To describe the effect of the rhythm of the poem

The Poem at a Glance

- **Rhyme:** *abab* in each stanza
- **Rhythm:** mixed iambic and dactylic
- **Significant technique:** extended metaphor

Teaching Stategies

Providing for Cultural Differences. Those familiar with the sea and ships will see the metaphor most clearly and easily. For others, an examination of words associated with the sea would help.

Providing for Different Levels of Ability. The ability to grasp the whole idea of metaphor varies from student to student. For some students, a discussion of the concept of comparison in language, comparing the sun to a balloon, for example, would be helpful.

Reading the Poem. You might explain that the poet was standing on the deck of a ship crossing the English Channel when this poem came to him. Then read through the poem for its literal sights and sounds. What did the poet actually see and hear?

Point out to students that the poem is one extended metaphor. The speaker compares his own approaching death with the act of setting out to sea. One can go through the poem, from the first word to the last, and find parts of the overall metaphor. Sunset suggests the end of a day, and, in

this context, the end of a life. The bar is the dividing line between the known, well-traveled harbor and the deep, unknown sea. May there be no sorrow when I cross it, the speaker says. He says that he is turning home. Notice that he does not say that he is facing the dark (although, the word would rhyme with *embark*), only dusk—an uncertainty. He does not know the pilot of his ship, but he hopes to see him face to face. This is obviously a religious poem or a poem of faith, or at least hope, in a life after death. The pilot, to a Victorian poet, could only be God.

Reteaching Alternatives. To help students understand the metaphor, ask them to try to transpose the journey idea to a plane trip. There are obvious parallels—taking off, space, and so on.

To help them understand the thoughts about death that the speaker expresses, ask students to give brief oral summaries of the speaker's ideas. Does he fear death? What is his hope?

Responding to the Poem   Text page 782
Analyzing the Poem
Identifying Details

1. What does the speaker wish in the first stanza? He wishes that there will be no moaning of the bar when he puts out to sea.

2. What hope does the speaker express in the final stanza? He hopes to see his Pilot when he has crossed the bar.

Interpreting Meanings

3. Who might the "Pilot" (line 15) be? The "Pilot," or someone who acts as a guide, refers to God.

4. What is the speaker's sea voyage a *metaphor* for? The voyage is a metaphor for the journey from life to death.

5. Analyze the rhythm of the poem and comment on how it affected you. Student responses will vary. They should note that the rhythm is basically iambic with a pattern of shorter lines (3 feet) followed by longer lines (4 and 5 feet). The soothing rhythm seems to imitate the ebb and flow of the tide, or wave action.

The Lady of Shalott

Text page 784

Objectives

1. To describe musical effects created by rhythm and rhyme
2. To explain the use of foreshadowing
3. To identify images
4. To write a screenplay based on the poem's action
5. To write an essay comparing and contrasting endings

The Poem at a Glance

- **Rhyme:** *aaaabcccb* in each stanza
- **Rhythm:** iambic tetrameter with a fine tag line in trimeter
- **Significant techniques:** rhythm, rhyme, foreshadowing, imagery

Teaching Strategies

Providing for Cultural Differences. Most students will have some background knowledge of feudal England, the days of chivalry, of knights and castles, and of Camelot and King Arthur. Many will have read a poem or two from *Idylls of the King* and sections from Malory's *Morte Darthur*.

Providing for Different Levels of Ability. The footnotes clear away the problems of vocabulary. The lines are, indeed, short and simple, even though the details of the story may be a little murky here and there. A straight narrative approach is the simplest and is, itself, rewarding, even to literal-minded students.

Reading the Poem. To prepare students for the poem, you may want to develop some visual understanding of the setting. Pictures of castles and the English countryside may not be necessary, but a map, even of the chalkboard variety, will help students to see what the Lady saw from her window and to follow her journey down to Camelot. Explain that the poem is a ballad, but not, of course, a folk ballad like the ballad "Lord Randal." This is a literary ballad, created by a masterful poet. It is an example of narrative poetry, telling, like all ballads, a story, usually a sad one,

but it is also an example of lyric or love poetry, filled with melody and images. Narrative and lyric often go hand in hand in this way. The repetition is characteristic of the ballad, as is the short, simple line. Tennyson's rhymed couplets keep the poem moving along. The poem also has allegorical aspects, the Lady symbolizing the secluded artist as set against the outside world of reality.

Reteaching Alternatives. Contrast, or more accurately, *contrasts* are the key to understanding the allegorical aspects of the poem and to appreciating Tennyson's great poetic talents. The contrast between the images and figures of speech that surround Lancelot with light and happiness and the shadows and shelters that surround the doomed young maiden are mentioned in the text. Another contrast can be found in the daily activities of the Lady, the knights, and the common people. Notice also contrasts in the setting outside the castle, between town and countryside. Finally, look for contrasts in emotions, again using Lancelot as the starting point.

Responding to the Poem Text page 789
Analyzing the Poem
Identifying Details

1. How does the poet describe the *setting* for the ballad in Part I? The setting is a castle ("Four gray walls, and four gray towers") on an island in a river that leads to Camelot. On either side of the river are fields of barley and rye; lilies, willows, and aspens surround the island castle.

2. In Part II, what is the Lady of Shalott said to do? She "weaveth steadily" by night and day.

What does she see in the mirror? Reflected in the mirror are the shadows of the world. The poet mentions specifically the highway to Camelot, the river, the village people, knights, a funeral, and two newlyweds.

3. What is the lady's reaction to the appearance of Sir Lancelot in Part III? She stops weaving and sets off to Camelot by boat.

According to Part IV, what are the consequences of her reaction? She dies mysteriously (her blood froze) on her journey to Camelot. When she arrives, everyone comes down to see her. The royal celebration ends, the knights cross themselves in fear, and Lancelot utters a blessing for her.

Interpreting Meanings

4. Describe the *rhythm* and the *rhyme scheme* of the poem. The poem is written in iambic tetrameter (four feet in each line), with many irregularities in accent. The final line in each stanza has three iambic feet. The rhyme scheme is *aaaabcccb*. Students should notice that the *b* rhymes (the fifth and final lines in each stanza) are either Camelot, Shalott, or Lancelot.

How do both rhythm and rhyme produce an especially musical quality in this lyric? The short, rhythmic lines and the three lines of consecutive rhyming words, plus the repetition of Camelot, Shalott, and Lancelot, create a very regular, musical, almost hypnotic effect.

5. Explain why lines 69–72 might be said to *foreshadow* the whole second half of the poem. What yearning do you think the Lady expresses when she exclaims, ''I am half sick of shadows'' (line 71)? In these lines, the Lady notices two young lovers, and she is envious of them. When she says she is ''half sick of shadows,'' she means she is tired of living her solitary life and wants to interact with real people and exist in the real world. Later, she acts on these feelings when she falls in love with Lancelot and leaves her tower.

6. What do you think the Lady's curse is? Student answers will vary. Clearly, though, the Lady must die if she leaves her weaving and her isolated existence and tries to live an ordinary life in the real world.

Explain how the poem as a whole can be interpreted as Tennyson's comment on the role and the life of the artist in relation to society. Like the Lady of Shalott, the artist observes the world and weaves his or her thoughts and feelings into a poem, a story, a painting, or a song. Tennyson seems to be saying that the artist cannot lead a ''normal'' human life, but must instead observe and record others' lives from afar. Artists are totally dedicated to their work and cannot be happy in the way most people define happiness.

7. Find examples of *images* used to describe Lancelot in Part III that are associated with bright, shining light. The sun flames on the ''brazen greaves'' of Lancelot; his shield sparkles, his bridle glitters like a branch of stars. Also, his saddle leather shines with jewels, his helmet and its feather burn like flame, and his brow glows.

What is this dazzling imagery contrasted with in other parts of the poem? Lancelot's glowing image contrasts with the dim world of shadows the Lady dwells in. Even her castle is described as gray. It is also a contrast with the image of the pale, dying Lady floating down the river at dusk.

8. In what ways does Tennyson contrast the Lady's life with that of the village churls and of the court in Camelot? The Lady lives alone in a world of shadows, seeing the world only as a reflection in a mirror. The churls, the market girls, the abbot, and the court go down the road to Camelot, where they interact with others and experience the real world.

Do you think that Tennyson indicates any preference for any of these ways of life? Student answers will vary.

The Eagle: A Fragment

Text page 790

Objectives

1. To describe setting in a poem
2. To write a paragraph extending the poem
3. To write stanzas imitating the poet's technique
4. To write a paragraph interpreting the poem

The Poem at a Glance

- **Rhyme:** *aaa* in each stanza
- **Rhythm:** iambic tetrameter
- **Significant technique:** setting

Teaching Strategies

Providing for Cultural Differences. No special considerations apply.

Providing for Different Levels of Ability. Except for the word *azure*, the vocabulary and concepts can be easily understood by students of varying ability.

Reading the Poem. To prepare students for reading the poem, you might give some time to the study of eagles in paintings and in photographs and read aloud an article about eagles. Point out that here the poet makes us see the eagle as lonely, imperious, watchful, not very attractive, and not the least bit in repose. His clasping, crooked claws give us a sense of tension. The majesty and vastness, and somehow the color, of the setting lull us into contemplation. We are not ready for the suddenness and force of the action in the final line. We sense that some victim lies at the end of the eagle's fall. We have left a world of splendor for a wrinkled sea where disasters and death are instantaneous and unavoidable.

Reteaching Alternatives. To help students understand the effectiveness of the final line of the poem and how it creates action that changes the world, have them try to create other similes—using, for example, a meteor or bomb.

Responding to the Poem Text page 790
Analyzing the Poem
Identifying Details

1. Describe the physical *setting* in the poem. The eagle is perched on a high mountaintop, looking down on the world below.

2. What movement or action takes place in stanza 2? In stanza 2, the sea crawls along, and the eagle leaves his perch and falls "like a thunderbolt."

Interpreting Meanings

3. Tennyson uses no adjectives to describe the eagle. What two or three adjectives would you use, and why? Students may describe the eagle as lonely, isolated, majestic, powerful, and so on. The eagle is all alone, looking down on the rest of the world from above.

What happens in the poem, and what ideas about eagles do you bring to it, that make your adjectives appropriate? Student answers will vary. They should note that the eagle's setting and sudden movement make the eagle seem powerfully in command of its life.

Ulysses Text page 791

Objectives

1. To identify audience
2. To analyze elements of character
3. To write a reply by a character in the poem
4. To write an analysis of an epic hero

The Poem at a Glance

- **Rhyme:** none
- **Rhythm:** iambic pentameter
- **Significant techniques:** character, epic
- **Figures of speech:** simile (a famous one, line 31), metaphor (lines 19, 59)

Teaching Strategies

Providing for Cultural Differences. By now, all students will have some knowledge of the sea, at least as Tennyson saw it.

Providing for Different Levels of Ability. Poor readers, of poetry especially, will benefit from help in seeing the dramatic aspects of the poem—for example, where the speaker changes tone and diction.

Reading the Poem. To prepare students for the reading, you might remind them of their exposures to *The Odyssey* in earlier grades and review it with them. A time chart and map relating Homer's time and territory with Tennyson's would also be helpful.

The idea of assuming the voice of Ulysses, making him the speaker of the poem, was in Tennyson's time new and from a literary viewpoint a step forward. This idea is carried a step further by having the speaker bring in elements of drama—setting a stage, shifting scenes, and pretending to address other actors in the drama. Robert Browning, who shared top honors with Tennyson as a poet in this period, is noted for his dramatic monologues. When you reach Browning you might compare his pithy, complex monologues, with brief lines of conversation, with this more poetic than dramatic poem by Tennyson.

Reteaching Alternatives. Have a student read the poem aloud, indicating by tone of voice and gesture the dramatic turns in the poem.

Responding to the Poem Text page 792
Analyzing the Poem
Identifying Details

1. In lines 1–5, how does Ulysses describe his life in the present? He and his wife are old, and he considers himself an ''idle king,'' making and enforcing unequal laws for a savage people, who do not even know him.

How does his present life contrast with his past adventures? Ulysses's present life is boring and unfulfilling (''How dull it is . . . ,'' lines 21–22) compared with his past adventures and world travels (''Much have I seen and known . . . ,'' lines 13–14). He has in the past ''enjoyed/ Greatly, have suffer'd greatly . . .'' (lines 7–8) and refers specifically to the ''delight of battle'' during the Trojan War.

2. What does Ulysses claim about ''all experience'' in lines 19–21? He says that all experience is just an arch through which he can see a boundless (''whose margin fades/For ever and for ever'') untraveled world.

3. How does Ulysses describe his son Telemachus in lines 33–45? He says Telemachus is his well-loved heir, who will take over his duties. Telemachus is discerning, prudent, and decent. (Telemachus seems to have a quiet, plodding personality in contrast to Ulysses's tempestuous nature.)

4. Whom does Ulysses address in the second half of the poem? He addresses ''My mariners'' (line 45), the loyal old sailors who sailed with him in the past. Supposedly, these are the sailors who accompanied him home from Troy (though in Homer's *The Iliad*, Ulysses returned alone to Ithaca; all of the sailors perished).

In the concluding lines of the poem, what qualities does he emphasize that he shares with his mariners? Though they are weaker than in the old days, Ulysses and the mariners have heroic hearts and are strong-willed, determined ''To strive, to seek and not yield.''

Interpreting Meanings

5. In *The Odyssey*, Homer lays great stress on the hero's powers of endurance and his insatiable curiosity. Where does Tennyson emphasize these characteristics of Ulysses? Students should cite the following: lines 6–7, line 12, lines 30–32, lines 45–48, lines 51–52, lines 56–57, lines 59–64, lines 65–70.

6. What seem to be Ulysses's underlying feelings toward his son? He says he loves Telemachus well, but in distinguishing himself from Telemachus, he seems to show negative feelings for him. The phrases ''slow prudence,'' ''soft degrees,'' ''centered in the sphere/Of common duties'' have somewhat negative connotations. Ulysses finds Telemachus well suited to do the kind of tedious work that he cannot stand: ''He works his work, I mine'' (line 43).

Find and comment on the speaker's sole reference to his wife. How does he feel about her? In line 3, he mentions her as ''aged.'' His feeling seems to be ambivalent.

7. How would you *characterize* Ulysses? Student answers will vary. Many will see him as self-centered and selfish. He has already decided to abandon his wife, son, and kingdom to satisfy his own desires; and he is determined to lure the old mariners to their certain death. Others may view him more positively as a faded hero, unwilling to face old age and death passively. He is determined to ''die with his boots on,'' like the Western hero.

8. Ulysses knows that his journey is like pursuing the horizon. Do you think he is foolish for setting out on a journey in which he cannot arrive at the destination he pursues? Explain. Student answers will vary. Have them support their views. Discussion may touch on their views on old age, death, and the purpose of human life.

---

from In Memoriam   Text page 794

Objectives

1. To describe the setting

2. To analyze the effects of rhyme

3. To write an essay addressing the reader's expectations in poetry

The Poem at a Glance

- **Rhyme:** *abba* in each stanza
- **Rhythm:** iambic tetrameter
- **Significant techniques:** setting, rhyme scheme

Teaching Strategies

Providing for Cultural Differences. There are no new or special problems here, unless we consider that students especially interested in science may be better prepared for the discussion in lyrics 55 and 56.

Providing for Different Levels of Ability. The stanzas have few difficult words, and the lines are short. The concepts in all but lyric 95 are difficult, however. With students who are not good with abstractions, you might want to concentrate on lyric 95.

Introducing Vocabulary Study. Students will benefit from knowing the meaning of the following word before they read the poem.

    fluctuate

Reading the Poem. Before reading the first two lyrics in class and assigning the balance for homework, point out that the *abba* rhyme scheme of these lyrics is famous. The lyrics taken together are regarded as one of the famous elegies in English literature. An elegy that is probably familiar to your students is Gray's "Elegy in a Country Churchyard." The comparison is informative, with respect to the subjects that interest the poets—views of nature, for example.

Reteaching Alternatives. You may want to discuss lyric 95 from the viewpoint of activities and thoughts that Tennyson shared with his friend Hallam. These also give us an interesting view of university life in Victorian England.

Responding to the Poem   Text page 797

Analyzing the Poem

Identifying Details

1. In lyric 55, why does the poet envision the possibility that God and Nature may be "at strife"? What complaint does the speaker voice against Nature in his poem? The speaker wishes to believe in life after death but finds no evidence of it in Nature. Nature has no regard for the individual life but is only "careful of the type."

2. How does Nature answer this complaint in lyric 56? Nature claims not even to be interested in the type. She says that a thousand types come and go and that she cares nothing for them. All that she does is bring life and death. To Nature, there is no spirit that survives after death: "The spirit does but mean the breath."

3. Describe the *setting* at the beginning of lyric 95. The setting is the lawn of a house on a summer night in the country, where a group of people linger to talk and sing.

How does this setting contrast with that at the end of the poem? At the end of the poem, the speaker is alone in the same setting. A breeze moves the flowers and trees, scattering their smells. The final stanza describes the light of dawn.

4. Of what is the speaker confident in lyric 130? He feels confident that he is in some way forever united with Hallam: "I shall not lose thee though I die."

Interpreting Meanings

5. Describe the *rhyme scheme* of these lyrics. The rhyme scheme is *abba*.

6. What is the difference between the aspects of nature described in lyrics 55 and 56 and in lyric 130? In the earlier lyrics, Nature is portrayed as a force at strife with God, a cold unfeeling force that denies the possibility of a soul or of life after death. In lyric 130, Nature is seen as a positive force no longer in conflict with God ("though mixed with God and Nature thou"). The speaker feels and hears his friend Hallam's soul diffused throughout Nature; and the images of air, water, sunrise, sunset, star, and flower are positive images.

7. Consider the structure of lyric 95, its move from a particular, local sense to "empyreal heights of thought" and then its return to the original scene. How is this movement related to the speaker's mood in lyrics 55 and 56? In lyric 130? Student answers will vary; this is a difficult question. Help them to see that lyrics 55 and 56 express the speaker's anguish, doubt, and despair. Lyric 130 expresses his joyful celebration of faith in life after death. In a sense, lyric 130 expresses the "empyreal heights of thought"—the existence of eternal life—as experienced and affirmed by Nature and everyday reality.

Robert Browning   Text page 798

In reviewing the introductory material with students, emphasize that Browning was an individual who truly believed in the adage "Never say die." This view is certainly suggested by his late start as a poet, a career, it might be added, that followed his relative failure as a playwright. Point out also the irony attending Browning's having married an established poet whom, in retrospect, he far outshines as a writer of the period.

Objectives

1. To identify the natural effects of rhyme and rhythm
2. To recognize elements of characterization
3. To write an original dramatic monologue
4. To write an essay analyzing the poem's theme

The Poem at a Glance

- **Rhyme:** rhyming couplets
- **Rhythm:** iambic pentameter
- **Significant techniques:** rhyme, rhythm, characterization, dramatic monologue

Teaching Strategies

Providing for Cultural Differences. Some acquaintance with Renaissance art and life in Renaissance Italy (and the location of Ferrara) would help to give students a glimpse of the world they enter as they read this poem.

Providing for Different Levels of Ability. Attention to the scene, the position of the actors, their gestures, and the props will help to give shape to the reading.

Introducing Vocabulary Study. Students will benefit from knowing the meanings of the following words before they read the poem.

   officious   munificence

Reading the Poem. After the first reading, have a student or two read the poem to the class as a piece of drama. Before they read, inform students that, because Browning is telling a fabricated story about a real duke in a period of history, we can expect to learn something not only about the duke and his last duchess (and maybe a little about the person addressed) but also about life among the rich and powerful during the Italian Renaissance. Browning, by the way, would have assumed that his Victorian readers knew all about the historical setting: that it produced some of the greatest painting and sculpture of all time (thanks, in part, to art patrons like this duke), and that rich nobles lived ruthlessly beyond the power of any law.

Reteaching Alternatives. In addition to having the poem read aloud as a kind of drama, permitting rehearsals with comment and criticism by the class, you might have students keep a list of clues that the Duke gives out about his character, and the character of his last duchess.

Responding to the Poem   Text page 801
Analyzing the Poem
Identifying Details

1. **Describe the occasion for this monologue. Who is speaking to whom, in what circumstances, and for what purpose?** The Duke of Ferrara is the speaker, and he is addressing a representative of an unnamed Count. They are working out the terms of a marriage agreement between the Duke and the Count's daughter.

2. **How does the Duke describe the personality of his "last Duchess"?** In lines 21–24, he says that she had a heart "too soon made glad" and that everthing she looked upon delighted her. She treated everyone alike—with smiles and courtesy.

3. **What happened to the last Duchess, according to the Duke?** He "gave commands" (line 45), and her smiling stopped altogether; in other words, he had her killed.

Interpreting Meanings

4. **Describe the *rhyme* and *rhythm* of the poem.** The poem is written in iambic pentameter couplets (pairs of rhyming lines) with occasional variations.

   Pick out a few passages that seem to you to be especially striking examples of colloquial, natural speech. Student choices will vary, but note with them the lines in which the Duke interrupts himself (for example, lines 22 and 31–32).

5. **What impression of himself do you think the Duke intends to create in his remarks to the Count's emissary?** Students may remark that the Duke presents himself as cultured, confident, and wealthy—unwilling to haggle over money.

   Why would he choose so to present himself? Answers will vary. Some may feel that the Duke is trying to make himself as attractive as possible to the Count so that the marriage with the Count's daughter will take place.

6. **What kind of man do you think the Duke really is? Which lines reveal his true character?** Students may mention that the Duke is malevolent, amoral, jealous, and insecure—so preoccupied with his own needs and power that he had his last wife killed because she didn't pay enough attention to him. Lines 13–15 and 19–45 reveal the Duke's true character.

7. What is the effect of having the Duke's monologue begin and end by referring to works of art? The references to works of art give an ironic note to the poem. We find it horrible that the Duke could, in the same breath, confess to his wife's murder and brag about his possessions. Students may suggest other effects.

Porphyria's Lover

Text page 802

Objectives

1. To evaluate the importance of setting in a poem
2. To write a composition based on the poem explaining the relationship of Porphyria and her lover
3. To write an essay comparing themes and techniques to two poems

The Poem at a Glance

- **Rhyme:** *ababbcdcdd . . .*
- **Rhythm:** iambic tetrameter
- **Significant techiques:** setting, metaphor

Teaching Strategies

Providing for Cultural Differences. The sentimentality of the language may put off readers.

Providing for Different Levels of Ability. The vocabulary level is not difficult, but the sentiment and madness of the speaker can create a veil that obscures the action and the clues. You might move through the poem slowly, getting students to list direct actions and clues of any sort.

Reading the Poem. The poem can be handled as homework with some preparatory advice. To prepare students, you might tell them that this is about a murder and that they should read closely and weigh the words. Tell them to imagine that they will have to sit in judgment on this case.

Reteaching Alternatives. You may want to introduce the poem in the ways that have been suggested here, and then, once the students have answered the questions in the text, hold a class discussion in which you try to reach some conclusions about this tragedy. As a final step, have the class, working jointly, go back and read the poem aloud, looking for signs that point to the speaker's condition.

Responding to the Poem

Text page 804

Analyzing the Poem

Identifying Details

1. What is the speaker's mood at the opening of the poem? He is very sad and irritable. His heart is "fit to break."

How does his mood change when Porphyria comes to him? Students may say that he seems to cheer up, but this is never stated directly in the poem. The emotion that the speaker does mention is surprise (line 33) when he realizes that Porphyria worships him.

2. What reasons does the speaker give for strangling Porphyria? In lines 36–37, he says that in the moment that he strangled her, "she was mine, mine, fair,/Perfectly pure and good: . . ." Apparently, he wished to preserve that moment forever. Also, he complains in lines 21–24 that Porphyria is too weak to give herself to him forever.

3. What leads the speaker to assert that Porphyria "felt no pain"? After she was dead, when he opened her eyelids, her blue eyes laughed again "without a stain" (lines 44–45); and her cheek blushed bright again when he kissed her (lines 47–48).

Interpreting Meanings

4. "And yet God has not said a word!" Why do you think the speaker expects God to say something? What does this line tell you about the speaker's character and awareness of what he has done? The speaker seems to realize the awfulness of his deed. He is not directly repentant, but a part of him must feel that he will be struck down or punished by God for murdering Porphyria. This implies that the speaker is not totally insane.

5. Browning first published this poem, along with another dramatic monologue, under the general title of *Madhouse Cells*. How does a knowledge of that *setting* affect your response to and interpretation of the poem? Knowing that the speaker is telling his story from a madhouse makes the speaker's action a bit more understandable, a bit less shocking. The title also tells us what happened to the lover—how he was punished—after Porphyria's death was discovered. Students may have different responses.

Where did you think the poem was set before you knew about Browning's original title? Students will probably say that they thought it took place in a country house, the place in which the crime occurred.

6. What do you think Browning was saying about the relationship of crime to madness or mental instability? Browning is definitely showing a relationship between this crime and the murderer's insanity, but he is not saying that all such crimes are committed for this reason.

Do you agree or disagree? Explain why. Student answers will vary.

Meeting at Night
Text page 805

Parting at Morning
Text page 805

Objectives

1. To compare the rhythms of the two poems

2. To explain the reason why the beloved is not mentioned in the second poem

3. To write an extension of the poems by filling in details about the lovers

4. To write a poem from an alternate point of view

Understanding the Human Elements. Many of Browning's poems are about love affairs. This pair expresses simply a relationship, from the man's point of view. In the first poem, we travel over sea and land and read eight lines of a twelve-line poem before we realize what the poem is about. Then, like the flash of the match, we find two lovers united. At the end of this poem, we look back and realize the effort of the man and the waiting and anxiety of the woman. It is a common enough event, but Browning makes us understand its importance in terms of time and space and human emotion. He has carved it in poetry. In the second poem, we are surprised at first by the abrupt change of mood, the complete neglect of the woman, and the man's honesty. After a moment of thought, we realize that the speaker is returning to the world he left the night before, a world of men, a city. It seems to be the sun that calls him back to work. This is a natural rhythm, then: an age-old rhythm of love and work. It is just that Browning has seen the drama in it.

The Poems at a Glance

- **Rhyme:** ("Meeting at Night") *abccba* in both stanzas
- ("Parting at Morning") *abba*
- **Rhythm:** iambic tetrameter
- **Significant techniques:** metaphor, rhythm

Teaching Strategies

Providing for Cultural Differences. Nothing serves as a cultural barrier.

Providing for Different Levels of Ability. The poems are simple in their vocabulary, but quite sophisticated in their ideas. You may want to warn students that they are about to read two poems that seem very simple but that deal with a quite sophisticated idea, the love of a man and woman.

Reading the Poems. Remind the students that the speaker of the poems is alone in a lonely but beautiful area. Have them trace his journey, trying to visualize the beauty of what he sees and to think about the effort he must make. In assigning the two poems, note that comparison of length is important. In rhyme and rhythm the poems are related.

Reteaching Alternatives. The poems clearly tell one side of the story. The woman's point of view, the drama in her waiting, and her reaction to her lover's departure need to be discussed.

Responding to the Poems
Text page 805
Analyzing the Poems
Identifying Details

1. Describe the speaker's journey in "Meeting at Night." Where does he finally meet his beloved? The speaker rows a boat on the ocean to a cove, then crosses a mile of the beach, three fields, and finally meets his lover at her farm and taps on her window.

2. Why does the speaker leave his love at the end of "Parting at Morning"? The speaker says that he "has need of a world of men."

Interpreting Meanings

3. In "Meeting at Night," what words underscore the speaker's restless anxiety to gain his destination? Students may mention the following: "As I gain the cove with pushing prow, ..." and "two hearts beating each to each." Also, the speaker's naming each obstacle ("a mile of . . . beach," "three fields to cross") suggests his eagerness to reach his destination.

What words emphasize the anxiety of his beloved? The phrase "the quick sharp scratch" in response to his tap on the window suggests that she is waiting anxiously for him. Her voice is "less loud, through its joys and fears" than a heartbeat.

4. Compare the rhythms of the second stanza of "Meet- ing at Night," especially lines 9–12, with those of "Parting at Morning." How do the rhythms of each poem create and fit the mood of each episode of the love story? Ask students to comment on the overall effect of the rhythms instead of having them scan the lines. The rhythm in "Meeting at Night" seems hurried and anxious, with many irregularly stressed syllables that give a harsh sound, as in "the quick sharp scratch." "Parting at Morning" seems to have a lighter, easier, much less tense rhythm, in keeping with its relaxed mood.

5. Why do you think the beloved is not explicitly mentioned in "Parting at Morning"? The speaker is no longer so obsessed with being with her but is focusing on his own need to leave.

6. Do the episodes of the love story described here ring true to you? Explain. Student responses will vary.

Prospice

Text page 806

Objectives

1. To identify images
2. To interpret differences in images and rhythms
3. To write a comparison of Browning's and Tennyson's attitudes toward death

The Poem at a Glance

- **Rhyme:** *ababcdcd . . .*
- **Rhythm:** alternating iambic tetrameter and dimiter
- **Significant techique:** imagery

Teaching Strategies

Providing Cultural Differences. The language, the religious viewpoint, and the concept of death itself will all be alien to your students. A discussion of death and the afterlife will help in some classes.

Providing for Different Levels of Ability. Perhaps the simplest way to explain this poem is to compare it, in detail, with "Crossing the Bar," an allegory of death that is easier for students to understand.

Reading the Poem. Have students read with the idea that this is an athlete, an old boxer, or soldier talking at least through line 20. Then ask, "Who is the speaker fighting?" A discussion of death, led by students, may also help to lead into a difficult poem.

Reteaching Alternatives. For students of every level of ability, Tennyson's simple, allegorical poem about death, "Crossing the Bar," may be a good introduction to this poem, as well as a basis for comparison.

Responding to the Poem   Text page 807
Analyzing the Poem
Identifying Details

1. What concrete images does the poet use in lines 1-6 to suggest the approach of death? The speaker mentions feeling fog in his throat and mist in his face. He describes a storm with snowy blasts. The "blasts" in line 3 may also be interpreted as a sound, as in trumpet blasts.

What images later in the poem suggest a battle? The speaker mentions barriers that fall and a battle to fight before the reward can be gained. He talks about the heroes of old, who "Bear the brunt" and feel "pain, darkness, and cold" in their battle.

2. Why does the speaker want to be conscious at the moment of his death? He wants to "taste the whole of it" like the ancient heroes who were brave at the moment of their death.

3. What does Browning look forward to after death? He looks forward to being reunited with his dead wife (lines 26-27).

Interpreting Meanings

4. What is the effect of the abrupt, colloquial beginning of this monologue, in your opinion? Students may suggest

Robert Browning   193

that it sets up a dramatic situation similar to those in other dramatic monologues they have read: It implies that there is a listener whom the speaker is addressing who has just asked, "Do you fear death?" Others may say that the beginning not only announces the subject of the poem, but also suggests that the speaker is about to reveal his innermost, secret thoughts.

5. Consider the images and rhythms of lines 1–10, the fight with death, and lines 21–28, the results of the battle. How are these passages different? Lines 1–10 contain images of fog, mist snow, darkness, and storm. These lines contain many heavily stressed syllables, beginning with the first two words of line 1. In contrast, the imagery in lines 21–28 is of the storm's cease; darkness turns to light and reunion with the soul of the beloved in God's presence. The

rhythm at the end of the poem is lighter and more regular, with fewer heavily stressed syllables.

How do the differences affect the poem's point and feeling? The differences reflect the movement from battle, anguish, and night to peace, love, and light. The poem suggests that life after death is beautiful, peaceful, and desirable.

6. What is your interpretation of the last line, "And with God be the rest"? Students should consider that *rest* may have two meanings in this line: "relaxation from toil" and "all that is left over." The line suggests that the speaker will give up his burdens to God and enjoy a peaceful existence.

7. What do you think of the speaker's attitude toward death? Student answers will vary.

Elizabeth Barrett Browning
Text page 808

Remind students that the life shared by this poet and her poet/husband was one characterized by both an intense love and a genuine flair for romance. This love affair became very famous and has been dramatized both on stage and on the screen under the title *The Barretts of Wimpole Street*.

from Sonnets from the Portuguese
Text page 809

Objectives

1. To analyze the use of pauses in the sonnet

2. To write an extension of the poet's description

3. To write an analysis of concrete and abstract words

Teaching Strategies

Providing for Cultural Differences. Help the students find evidence of the differences between the culture of Browning's time and that of today. One difference is the lack of electricity (references in the sonnet to sun and candle light).

Providing for Different Levels of Ability. Some of the lines in the sonnet are easily understood. Other are not. The slow reader may need help with lines 3 and 4 and 9 and 10.

Reading the Sonnet. Before reading the sonnet, help the students understand that Elizabeth Barrett Browning is revealing a great deal about herself in the lines she writes: her faith both as a child and an adult, her Victorian belief in

righteousness, and her modesty. Tell them to look for examples of these revelations as they read the sonnet.

Reteaching Alternatives. Remind students that this poem is a sonnet. Have them compare the structure, language, and rhyme scheme with other sonnets in this text.

Responding to the Poem Text page 809
Analyzing the Poem
Identifying Details

1. How many distinct ways does the speaker say that she loves her beloved? Have students identify each separate way. Not counting the future love (after death in lines 13–14), the speaker mentions seven different ways.

2. Which lines indicate the speaker's religious faith? Students may mention lines 9–12 and 13–14.

Interpreting Meanings

3. How are the pauses in the last three lines different from those in the rest of the poem? The pauses through line 11 indicate the end of a thought or a natural pause within a thought. (Note the many places where commas indicate a modifying adverbial clause.) The pauses in lines 12 to 13 indicate an emotional interruption as she announces her most all-encompassing way of loving.

What do you think is the effect of these differences? The emotional pitch of lines 12–13 contrasts strongly with the quiet of the preceding lines and with the final image: her calm announcement of loving after death.

4. **Compare the ending of this poem to that of Robert** Browning's "Prospice." **How does each speaker treat the movement from life to death?** Elizabeth Barrett Browning does not suggest that the movement from life to death is a struggle, a "black minute," as Robert Browning does in "Prospice." Both suggest that there is a life after death and that it is a desirable state in which one continues loving a beloved person.

Do you find one ending more attractive that the other? Explain. Answers will vary.

Matthew Arnold

Remind students that, although Tennyson and Browning produced poety with dramatic differences, in language and tone the two were similar. Both, that is, were concerned with serious matters, essentially trying to reach a conclusion about the meaning of life. Arnold had the same concerns. Ask students to keep an eye out for similarities in content and for differences in treatment as they read three poems by the last of the three giants of Victorian poetry.

Dover Beach

Text page 813

Requiescat

Text page 815

To Marguerite—Continued

Text page 816

Objectives

1. To determine setting
2. To identify mood
3. To explain an allusion
4. To explain a metaphor and a simile
5. To describe rhyme and rhythm
6. To write an extension of the narrative in a poem
7. To write a character sketch
8. To write an essay contrasting two poems
9. To write an extended metaphor
10. To write a comparison of two poems

The Poems at a Glance

- **Rhyme:** ("Dover Beach") irregular rhyme
  ("Requiescat") *abab* in each stanza
  ("To Marguerite—Continued") *ababcc* in each stanza
- **Rhythm:** ("Dover Beach") mixed iambic
  ("Requiescat") iambic trimeter
  ("To Marguerite—Continued") iambic tetrameter
- **Significant techniques:** allusion, rhyme, rhythm, characterization, extended metaphor

Teaching Strategies

Providing for Cultural Differences. Although Arnold's poetry is low-key and generally clear, understanding it depends upon an ability to handle metaphor, in some cases extended metaphor, and allusion (to Sophocles, for example). To some extent, at least, this ability depends on cultural background.

Providing for Different Levels of Ability. Readers will vary in their ability to handle metaphors and allusions. You can give help to those who need it, explaining the figurative use of language and filling in cultural gaps.

Reteaching Alternatives. Plan two readings of the three poems. In the first, carry out the writing exercises in the text and the ideas mentioned above. Then, ask the class to list three or four themes or ideas that are central to the poems and read each poem over to determine how these themes are manifest in them.

Dover Beach

Reading the Poem. Explain in advance that the poem depends upon two extended metaphors—the sea and armies.

Requiescat

Reading the Poem. Have students look for and list the characteristics of the woman.

To Marguerite—Continued

Reading the Poem. Prepare students for the island-continent metaphor.

Dover Beach

Responding to the Poem   Text page 814
Analyzing the Poem
Identifying Details

1. What is the *setting* of the first stanza? Who is the speaker, and whom is he addressing? It is night. The speaker is standing in a room in Dover, England, overlooking the cliffs, the straits, and the French coast. All that we can tell about the speaker is that he is an educated man because of the classical references to Sophocles and Thucydides. We do not find out whom the speaker is addressing until the final stanza (line 29); he is addressing his beloved.

2. What contrast does the speaker draw in the third stanza? He contrasts the way the Sea of Faith once was with the way it is now.

3. What does the speaker urge in the last stanza, and why? He urges that he and his love be true to one another because, he says, the world has "really neither joy, nor love, nor light,/Nor certitude, nor peace, nor help for pain."

Interpreting Meanings

4. What is the mood evoked by the first six lines? It is a calm and peaceful, even joyful mood.

How does Arnold begin to change this mood in the second half of the first stanza? He begins line 7 with the word *Only*, suggesting that a contrast will follow, and he uses the imperative *Listen!* in line 9, further suggesting a change. Lines 9–14 describe the sound of the waves, which he says is an "eternal note of sadness."

5. How does Arnold make the speaker's mood at the end of the first stanza seem timeless and universal? Arnold says that the same sound could be heard centuries ago and in a different place: "Sophocles long ago" heard the same "eternal note of sadness" in the sound of the sea.

Explain the literary *allusion* in the second stanza. The allusion is to the works of the ancient Greek playwright Sophocles, whose plays, such as *Oedipus the King* and *Antigone* (though Arnold does not name any of Sophocles's plays), deal with "the turbid ebb and flow/Of human misery."

6. Explain the *metaphor* and *simile* in lines 21–23. These are the most difficult lines of the poem. The Sea of Faith (religious belief) was once at its fullest point (the metaphor). It surrounded the earth, encompassing it like the folds of a bright belt (the simile) that enclosed and decorated the earth.

How do lines 24–28 relate to the sound the speaker hears at the end of the first stanza? The "melancholy, long, withdrawing roar" of the Sea of Faith—the disappearance of religious belief—is similar to the sound at the end of the first stanza. In stanza 1, the sound of the waves and the pebbles is called a "grating roar" and a sad sound. In stanza 3, the sound is called a "withdrawing roar" and a melancholy sound. Pebbles (shingles) are also mentioned in stanza 3.

7. Describe the *rhyme scheme* and *rhythm* of the poem. What is the effect of their irregularity? Students will find that the lines in each stanza rhyme but not in a repeated pattern. The rhythm, too, is irregular in its number of feet per line and beats. Student opinions about the effect of these irregularities will vary. Perhaps Arnold is reinforcing his assertion that the world does not have certitude; you cannot depend on recurring actions. Perhaps he is also trying to imitate the sound of the sea's waves, which hit the shore irregularly.

8. What is the speaker's view of his world as it is presented in the last stanza? He sees the world pessimistically as a chaotic, painful place without joy or peace. Students should note the irony of his telling his beloved that they must "be true/To one another," followed immediately by the statement that there is no love. The poem ends with a powerful simile: we live our lives as if we are "ignorant armies" clashing by night, killing friend and foe alike.

Do you think this view is relevant to today's world?

Explain why or why not. Answers will vary. Many students will say that this poem expresses a view of human life that is widespread today.

Requiescat

Responding to the Poem   Text page 815
Analyzing the Poem
Identifying Details

1. What appears to be the occasion for this poem? The woman described in the poem has just died.

2. What contrast between the woman's inner world and the outer world does the poet emphasize in the second and third stanzas? She gave the appearance of being merry, but she really was not: at heart she was tired. She was always busily involved with others in circumstances so difficult or hectic that they were "mazes of heat and sound," but she yearned for peace.

Interpreting Meanings

3. Explain the *metaphor* in line 6. How does the poet echo this metaphor in line 12? She bathed the world in smiles of glee; that is, she faced every person and event with a happy smile. In line 12, the bathing metaphor is used again: The woman herself is bathed in peace ("peace laps her round").

4. What makes the use of the word *inherit* appropriate in line 15? *Inherit* has two meanings: "to come into possession of" and "to receive something of value from a person who has died." In line 15, the word has both meanings. The dead woman herself has inherited the peace, rest, and quiet of death.

5. The poet uses *repetition* in each of the first three stanzas. Identify the instances of repetition. In each stanza, the poet repeats a word in one of the lines (see lines 1, 7, 9).

Why do you think the poet does not continue this pattern in the last stanza? Answers will vary. The poet may have wanted to emphasize the seriousness and finality of death, so he abandoned the singsong repetition. Or perhaps he wanted to emphasize that the woman's soul was finally at rest: two of the repetitions (*tired, tired* and *turning, turning*) describe the exhausting quality of her life.

6. The bouncy pace of the first three stanzas makes them sound much like the verses on greeting cards found in drugstores and supermarkets. How does the poet's *tone* change in the fourth stanza? The images of death (the spirit "fluttered and failed for breath") and of the "vast hall of death" create a serious tone.

7. What attitude toward death emerges from this brief elegy? What do you think of this attitude? The speaker believes that death brings rest and peace after the exhaustion of life. Student opinions about this attitude will vary.

To Marguerite—Continued

Responding to the Poem   Text page 818
Analyzing the Poem
Identifying Details

1. To what are human beings compared in the first stanza? They are compared to islands.

2. What is the "longing like despair" of line 13? The islands long to touch each other, to be joined: "Oh, might our marges meet again!"

3. In the last stanza, whom or what does the speaker identify as the cause of human isolation? The speaker says that "a God" ruled that humans should be isolated.

Interpreting Meanings

4. What *extended metaphor* runs throughout the entire poem? Human beings are islands separated by a sea.

5. How does the poet establish two contrasting *moods* in the second and third stanzas? The beautiful, calm, romantic images of the second stanza create a mood of peace and beauty. In the third stanza, the interjection *Oh*, the two exclamatory sentences, and the word *despair* sharply break the tranquil mood of the preceding stanza.

6. Comment on the three adjectives for the sea in the last line of the poem. What are the *connotations* of each adjective? Some students may feel that *unplumbed* has negative connotations (something unexplored is potentially dangerous), while others may feel that the word has positive connotations (the unexplored is glamorous and exciting). Although *salt* is really a neutral word, it is necessary to animal life (positive), but it also stings when it touches an open wound (negative). *Estranging* has negative connotations, suggesting arguments and dissensions.

Why do you think the poet chose this particular order for these three words? If students view *unplumbed* as positive, then there is a progression from positive through neutral to negative. Students may also suggest that *unplumbed* is vast while *salt* is more specific, and that *estranging* is the only adjective that has to do with human beings.

7. Is Arnold's view of human isolation and estrangement relevant to today's world, in your view? Support your answer with reasons. Answers will vary.

Matthew Arnold   197

Objectives

1. To interpret the mood and atmosphere of the poem and to identify details that create them

2. To imagine providing an illustration for the poem

3. To write an analysis of the poet's use of metaphor, archaic diction, and symbolism

Teaching Strategies

Providing for Cultural Differences. The poem is based on a traditionally Christian view of heaven, quite literally interpreted and full of graphic details. The details are subjective and mystical to some extent and also borrowed from religious art. The key religious figures in heaven, all students need to know, are God, Jesus (in the Christian view, one with God), and the Virgin Mary, the mother of Jesus. Paintings from Early Italian art, the Renaissance, and the nineteenth-century pre-Raphaelite period would help bridge the cultural gap.

Providing for Different Levels of Ability. Slow readers will benefit from help in keeping separate the three "voices" in the poem: (a) the speaker when he recounts the narrative, (b) the speaker when he turns aside—in parentheses—to tell us what he thinks, and (3) the voice of the blessed damozel, enclosed in quotation marks.

Introducing Vocabulary Study. Students will benefit from knowing the meaning of the following word before they read the poem.

abashed

Reading the Poem. Remind students that, in addition to watching for the change of voice, they should try to visualize the images as if they were going to paint them. You might also tell students that the poet is telling a story that he finds heartbreaking and see if they agree with him that there is nothing sadder than the thoughts of two lovers who are separated forever.

Reteaching Alternatives. You might compare the poem with several other poems of this period. Consider introducing a love poem (perhaps Browning's "Meeting at Night"), a dialogue poem ("My Last Duchess" would be a good one), and a narrative about a maiden (Tennyson's "The Lady of Shalott").

Responding to the Poem

Text page 824

Analyzing the Poem

Identifying Details

1. **Where is the blessed damozel?** She is in heaven.

   How long has she been separated from her lover? She has been separated for ten years.

2. **To what is time compared in line 50?** Time is compared to a pulse that shakes the world.

3. **For what does the damozel pray?** She prays that her lover will join her in Heaven.

Interpreting Meanings

4. **How would you describe the *mood*, or *atmosphere*, of this poem?** Student answers will vary. They may describe the mood as melancholy, ethereal, mysterious, sensuous.

   What details in the first three stanzas help to establish this mood? The three lilies and seven stars establish a mood of mystery. The description of the damozel is sensuous. Students may suggest other details, depending on how they identify the mood.

5. **What is the reason for the lover's doubts expressed in lines 97–102?** The lover worries that he and the damozel will not be eternally united in heaven because the only way in which they were alike was that they loved each other while she lived. He questions whether that is enough for God to grant them "endless unity."

6. **Describe the structure of the final stanza. What is especially effective about this structure?** The first and last words in the stanza are those of the earthly lover, who is so "in tune" with the damozel that he is aware of her emotions ten years after her death. His comments on her smile and tears reveal the power of his love for her and suggest that, despite his doubts in lines 97–102, the two will be joined in "endless unity" once he dies.

7. **Victorian critics sometimes complained of the sensualism of "The Blessed Damozel." Do the relationship of the lovers and the damozel's condition in heaven support a description of the poem as sensual, in your view?** Answers will vary. Though the definition of *sensual* is surely different today from what it was in Victorian times, most students will guess that the poem was sensual to the Victorians. Ask them to find details in the poem some Victorians might have found shocking.

Christina Rossetti

A Birthday

Objectives

1. To identify similes
2. To distinguish between types of imagery
3. To evaluate the poet's use of subject and tone

The Poem at a Glance

- **Rhyme:** *abcbdefe* in each stanza
- **Rhythm:** iambic tetrameter
- **Significant techniques:** simile, imagery, tone

Teaching Strategies

Providing for Cultural Differences. Students of varying cultures should have no difficulty with the first stanza of the poem. It might help the students understand the second stanza if you talk to them a bit about medieval art. If possible, show them a picture of a medieval throne room.

Providing for Different Levels of Ability. Either read the poem aloud or have a good reader read it aloud so that students will be aware of the rhythm of the poem. Be sure to go over the footnotes, and make sure that all students know the meaning of *dias*.

Reteaching Alternatives. To help the students understand the speaker's feelings, initiate a discussion about some event in their life that made them very happy.

Responding to the Poem   Text page 826

Analyzing the Poem

Identifying Details

1. What three *similes* describe the speaker's heart in the first stanza? She says that her heart is like a singing bird (lines 1–2), an apple tree (lines 3–4), and a rainbow seashell (lines 5–6).

2. How does the last line of the second stanza echo the last line of the first? Both lines end with "my love is come

to me," which in each stanza ends an adverb clause beginning with *Because* (lines 8 and 15) that explains why she is happy.

Interpreting Meanings

3. How would you interpret the phrase "birthday of my life"? Answers may vary. Students may say that it is her actual birthday—the anniversary of her birth. Others may feel that it marks some kind of new beginning—the beginning of a love relationship or some kind of religious turning point.

4. What is the difference between the kinds of *images* used in the first and second stanzas? The first stanza contains images of nature—common, everyday images. The second stanza contains exotic images of rare, expensive things.

5. How can the lyric be read as both a conventional love poem, and as a religious lyric? None of the images or statements in the poem contradicts its interpretation as a conventional love poem. The cause of the speaker's happiness may well be the arrival of her lover or the beginning of her love. However, we also know that Christina Rossetti was deeply religious and wrote religious poetry, and nothing in the poem contradicts its interpretation as a religious lyric.

When read as a religious lyric, who is the "love" referred to so often? The love is Jesus Christ.

What "birth" is anticipated? Student answers will vary. The birthday might be interpreted as the beginning of the speaker's religious faith (her being "reborn"); her participation in a religious ritual, such as baptism; or even the ceremony of conversion to a different religion.

6. How does this poem compare with Donne's "Batter My Heart" (page 373) in *subject*, *imagery*, and *tone*? Depending on student interpretations of the meaning of "A Birthday," they may argue that both poems share the subject of preparedness for a major change and a tone of willingness. The imagery differs between the two.

Reinforce the information provided in the biographical sketch of the poet in the student text by highlighting Hopkins's skill and sophistication as a poet and his devout Catholicism. The combination, you might stress, produced some interesting and important poetry that, in many ways, was both ahead of and behind its time. That is, Hopkins's experimental verse form at once anticipates modern (read: twentieth-century) trends in poetry and recalls the Romantic poets' fascination with nature.

Spring and Fall
Text page 828

Felix Randal
Text page 830

Pied Beauty
Text page 832

Objectives

1. To identify sonnet conventions
2. To evaluate imagery
3. To identify theme
4. To explain the poet's synthesis of alliteration and antithesis
5. To analyze the effectiveness of rhythm
6. To write a prose paraphrase of a poem
7. To write an extension of a poetic catalog
8. To write an analysis of the poet's diction

The Poems at a Glance

- **Rhyme:** (''Spring and Fall'') rhyming couplets
  (''Felix Randal'') *abba*, *abba*, *ccd*, *ccd* (Petrarchan sonnet)
  (''Pied Beauty'') *abcabc*, *abcac*
- **Rhythm:** sprung rhythm in all poems
- **Significant techniques:** sonnet, imagery, theme, alliteration, sprung rhythm

Teaching Strategies

Providing for Cultural Differences.   Unlike the poetry of the pre-Raphaelite Rossettis, which is filled with religious symbols based on traditional Christianity, Hopkins's poetry does not use Christian symbols as a key.

Providing for Different Levels of Ability.   Readers who are slow to comprehend poetry will have difficulty with certain words of Hopkins's invention. Instruct the students to use the footnotes, and not just read them. You may want them to write out the sentences in a short poem, inserting their own translations. You may also want these students to rewrite each sentence, using standard syntactic order.

Introducing Vocabulary Study.   Students will benefit from knowing the meaning of the following word before they read the poems.

  fallow

Spring and Fall

Reading the Poem.   These days young girls do not weep at the sight of falling leaves perhaps, but they do have moments of sadness that they cannot explain. You may want to tell the class that this poem begins with such a moment. The rest of the poem may fall into place as the speaker tries to explain the girl's sorrow and how it will change as she grows older.

Reteaching Alternatives.   The poem is written in rhymed couplets, and you might want to point out that, in the second and final couplet, Hopkins simply repeats the same word. You may want to examine a couplet at a time, making sure students understand its meaning before going on to the next. You may want to summarize the meaning of each couplet in writing and then put them together in a general paraphrase of the poem. Some students may want to reconvert their paraphrase into poems of a more normal persuasion.

Felix Randal

Reading the Poem. You may want to remind students of the work of the village blacksmith (perhaps few students have seen one at work, but the work of shoeing horses still goes on) and the work of a village priest—the anointing of dying or very ill people.

Reteaching Alternatives. You may want to have the students read this first as a narrative. What has happened? What has the speaker, the priest, done in response? Finally, what thoughts and words of the speaker seem unusual?

Pied Beauty

Reading the Poem. You may want to make certain that every student knows the meaning of *dappled* and *pied*, perhaps by asking each student to give an example.

Reteaching Alternatives. You may want to have students make lists, first of the "things" in the poem, then of the words that Hopkins uses to describe these things.

Spring and Fall

Responding to the Poem   Text page 828
Analyzing the Poem
Identifying Details

1. **What is Margaret grieving for at the opening?** She is grieving for the autumn leaves fallen from the trees.

2. **What does the speaker predict about Margaret's feelings when her "heart grows older"?** The speaker predicts that Margaret will grow "colder" and not even spare a sigh for the fallen leaves.

3. **Whom does the speaker say she is really grieving for?** He says that she is grieving for herself (line 15).

4. **Identify at least four examples of *alliteration* and *assonance* in the poem.** Make sure students understand what they are looking for. Alliteration is the repetition of similar consonant sounds at the beginning of words that are close together. Assonance is the repetition of similar vowel sounds in words that are close together.

Interpreting Meanings

5. **Discuss the multiple meanings of *spring*, *fall*, and *leaves* in the poem.** *Spring* and *fall* in the title refer to the seasons of the year. *Springs* in line 11 are the sources or

origins of water or, in this case, sorrow. Though the word *fall* appears only in the title, the season is referred to again in lines 1–4. The *fall* of man is also suggested in line 14: "the blight man was born for." *Leaves* are the fallen leaves of trees mentioned in lines 2–3 and again in line 8. *Leaves* also suggest the verb: Innocence, youth, and life are transitory and *leave*.

6. **What does the speaker mean by saying "sorrow's springs are the same" (line 11)?** All kinds of sorrow in life (Margaret's sorrow over the leaves; the speaker's sorrow over the loss of youth and the death of loved ones) have the same source.

7. **What is the "blight man was born for" in line 14?** The blight refers to the Biblical fall of man. All human beings are destined to struggle, to experience pain and sorrow, and to die.

8. **Explain how the speaker's attitude toward Margaret and her grief shifts in the course of the poem.** In lines 1–8, the speaker suggests that Margaret will outgrow her sensitivity to such losses as the falling leaves and that she will no longer care ("nor spare a sigh") because her heart will have grown "colder." In the middle of the poem (lines 10–12), the speaker's attitude changes. He realizes that Margaret's sadness is an unconscious, innate grief for much larger losses in her future.

How would you interpret the poem's last line? Margaret is grieving for the loss of her own innocence and youth, for the prospect of her own death and the death of those she loves.

Felix Randal

Responding to the Poem   Text page 831
Analyzing the Poem
Identifying Details

1. **How does the speaker say that he took care of Felix Randal?** He anointed him and gave him Holy Communion, confession, and absolution.

What were the stages of Randal's reaction to his illness? Students should mention the following stages, although their sequence is not altogether clear: He was impatient at first and cursed (line 5). Later he had a "heavenlier heart" and took Holy Communion (line 7). He wept (line 11) and was comforted by the speaker. Finally, he was "mended" by being anointed (line 6).

2. **What prayer does the speaker offer for Felix Randal?** In line 8, he says, "Ah well, God rest him all road ever he offended!"

3. How is Felix Randal described in lines 12–14? He is seen at the height of his good health, "powerful amidst peers," at work in his forge putting horseshoes on a large gray horse.

Interpreting Meanings

4. Hopkins here uses a conventional, fourteen-line sonnet form. What is the topic of each of the four sections of the poem? Section 1: the news of Felix Randal's death, the speaker's thoughts of Felix during his last days. Section 2: the course of Felix's illness, how the speaker tendered to him, the blessing. Section 3: thoughts about comforting the sick, about comforting Felix. Section 4: Felix whole and healthy at the forge.

What is the "turn" of the poem, the difference between the subject of the first eight lines and the subject of the last six lines? Answers will vary. The first section begins with the news of Felix's death and ends with the speaker's (priest's) blessing. He talks in this first section of his priestly duties to Felix. The second section deals with emotions about illness and death in general and about Felix's and the speaker's emotions specifically. The second section ends not with thoughts of death but with the triumphant image of the healthy Felix at work in his forge.

5. Why does Hopkins refer to the farrier as "child" in line 11? Student answers will vary. Some may say that "child" refers to Felix as a child of God; others may say that he is like a child because he weeps in fear and needs to be comforted.

What is the effect of this reference? It is very moving and makes us identify with Felix. Like Margaret's grief in "Spring and Fall: To a Young Child," Felix's illness and fear of death is universal and inescapable.

6. It is clear enough how "seeing the sick endears them to us" (line 9). What does Hopkins mean by saying that "us too it endears"? Visiting the sick endears us to them; they are grateful for our visits.

7. Why do you think that Hopkins decided to end the sonnet with images of Felix Randal whole and healthy at his forge? What is the effect of this ending? Answers will vary. It is a powerful, triumphant image that emphasizes life, not death. Students may suggest other reasons and responses to the ending.

Pied Beauty

Responding to the Poem Text page 832
Analyzing the Poem
Identifying Details

1. What specific examples of pied beauty does the poet mention in lines 2–6? He mentions skies, a brinded cow, rose-colored spots on trout, roasted chestnuts, finches' wings, landscapes divided into fields and plowed, the gear and tackle, and trim of all trades.

2. How does the poet describe God in line 10? He describes God as the creator whose beauty is unchanging.

3. Why does the poet offer praise and beauty to God? He praises God because God has created all of the beauty that he mentions and because God's beauty is unchanging.

Interpreting Meanings

4. What phrases and *images* do you think serve to reinforce the poem's title and its *theme*? Give at least four specific examples to support your answer. Student examples will vary. Ask students for a statement of the poem's theme. One possible statement: We must praise God for the great beauty he has created on earth in even the homeliest, most ordinary objects and creatures.

5. What do you think the poet means by "all things counter" (line 7)? All things counter are all things that are strange, unlike the norm, opposite to what we expect to see.

6. In line 10, what contrast does the poet suggest between the "pied beauty" of the physical world and the beauty of God the creator? The pied beauty on earth is changing and transitory; the beauty of God is unchanging and eternal.

7. Explain how the poet combines *alliteration* with *antithesis* (opposites) in line 9. The line contains three pairs of words with opposite meanings. In each pair, a consonant sound is repeated at (or near) the beginning of the word. The first two pairs (*swift*, *slow*; *sweet*, *sour*) repeat the *s* sound; two repeat *sw* sounds. The *d* sound is repeated in *adazzle*, *dim*.

8. How does the *rhythm* of the last line make it especially effective? This short line consists of one spondaic foot (two accented syllables) whose effect is that of a final chord, bringing the poem to a definite close and emphasizing the most important words in the poem.

9. How is this poem like the psalms from the King James Bible—which are ''praise songs''? Answers will vary. Students should point out that this poem, like the psalms, praises God and gives reasons for that praise. ''Pied Beauty,'' like the psalms, is written in heightened language.

Thomas Hardy
Text page 833

The Darkling Thrush
Text page 834

Channel Firing
Text page 835

The Convergence of the Twain
Text page 836

Objectives

1. To identify details of setting
2. To identify examples of irony
3. To explain the poem's title
4. To explain the poem's main idea
5. To write an essay summing up hopes
6. To write a comparison of two poems
7. To write an editorial
8. To write an analysis of the poem's point of view
9. To write a commentary on a real event
10. To write an essay evaluating two approaches to an event

The Poems at a Glance

- **Rhyme:** (''The Darkling Thrush'') *ababcdcd* in each stanza
  (''Channel Firing'') *abab* in each stanza
  (''The Convergence of the Twain'') *aaa* in each stanza
- **Rhythm:** (''The Darkling Thrush'') mixed iambic
  (''Channel Firing'') iambic tetrameter
  (''The Convergence of the Twain'') mixed trochaic
- **Significant techniques:** setting, irony, main idea

Teaching Strategies

Providing for Cultural Differences. Students may have problems with the language. Although Hardy set out, like Wordsworth, to use the language of the common people, the common people were North Country farmers. A good use of the footnotes will bridge this gap.

Providing for Different Levels of Ability. In all of these poems there is a simple narrative or situation that the slow reader can be helped to understand.

The Darkling Thrush

Reading the Poem. You may want to ask your students what they want to do, not next New Year's Eve, but next century's eve. If there is drama in a passing year, there is one hundred percent more in a passing century. Students might try to remember what Thomas Hardy was doing when the last century ended. He was alone in a barren, cold landscape, taking courage from the beautiful song of a frail and aging thrush. Ask your students if they think the thrush was right.

Reteaching Alternatives. You may want to see if the students understand why Hardy found ''such little cause for caroling'' by the thrush (line 25). He is clearly not speaking of the dreary landscape and time of year (which serve only as a kind of extended metaphor). Then, why is he almost hopeless? Has the whole nineteenth century, now ending, been such a disaster? He has nothing like nuclear arms to worry about, as we do. Is it that he has lost his faith in the traditional Christianity of the Church of England or of the Roman Catholic Church, the bulwarks of faith as the century opened? Is it that he personally has a harrowing life? Has his faith in humanity—on every level—been destroyed, simply through his observation as a poet and novelist? Perhaps the other poems of Hardy that students read here will help them to reach a conclusion about Hardy's pessimism. You may want to come back to this poem.

Channel Firing

Reading the Poem. Some background on World War I may help to orient your students. You may want to remind them that it was a war of big guns, on ground and sea, and that the English Channel is narrow.

Reteaching Alternatives. Hardy's Christian heritage and love of England—the last two lines show his sense of history—provide a key to his bitterness and fear. You may want to ask your students what they worry about losing, in addition to their lives, as they hear "channel firing" today.

The Convergence of the Twain

Reading the Poem. The story of the *Titanic* is a familiar one. You may want to ask your students to guess, before they read the poem, what the title means—and at the end to go back and discuss it.

Reteaching Alternatives. The prose source of this poem, and other retellings of the *Titanic* sinking that students may have been exposed to, provide a way to illustrate the difference between poetry and prose. You may want to ask, "What does the poem tell you about the *Titanic* that was not in the prose version, or that you had not thought of before?" This is also a way to teach the importance of structure in a poem, as the poem switches at stanza 6. You may also want to use the title as a key to the poem.

The Darkling Thrush

Responding to the Poem   Text page 834
Analyzing the Poem
Identifying Details

1. What details in the first stanza establish the *setting* for the poem? The poem is set in the country (coppice gate) during the winter (Frost, Winter's dregs) in late afternoon or twilight (weakening eye of day). It is very cold outdoors (everyone is indoors near the household fires).

2. Where in the poem is the thrush first introduced? How does the bird first come to the attention of the speaker? The thrush is introduced in the third stanza. The speaker hears the thrush's joyful song before he identifies the bird.

3. What does the speaker say about the "air" of the thrush in the last stanza? He says that the thrush's "happy good-night air" suggests that the thrush may know of "Some Blessed Hope" of which the speaker is unaware.

Interpreting Meanings

4. What is the significance of the word *darkling* in the poem's title? *Darkling* is an amalgam of *dark* and *sparkling*. The two ideas suggest both gloom and hope.

   Do you think the thrush's song seems hopeful or hopeless? Explain. Student answers will vary.

5. Does the speaker's mood change significantly in the course of the poem? If so, how? Most students will agree that the speaker's mood does change. In the first two stanzas, words like *Winter's dregs*, *desolate*, *death-lament*, and *fervorless* suggest his despondent, hopeless mood. But his mood changes in the second half of the poem as he listens to and thinks about the thrush's joyful song. In the last two lines, the speaker imagines that the thrush's song indicates that there exists "Some Blessed Hope" of which he is unaware.

Channel Firing

Responding to the Poem   Text page 835
Analyzing the Poem
Identifying Details

1. Who is the speaker? Who are *we* in line 4? The speaker is one of the dead (the *we* in line 4) who are buried in or near a church somewhere near the English Channel.

2. In the first stanza, why are the people afraid? They hear the noises of the guns and think that the Judgment Day has come.

3. What does God say about the Judgment Day in the fifth stanza? He says that it is a good thing that it is not the Judgment Day for some of the living, who would be doomed to scour the floors of Hell.

Interpreting Meanings

4. What do you make of God's irritation at those who fire the guns? Student answers will vary.

5. Point out at least three examples of *irony* in the poem. Students may need some help with this question. Have them recall the definitions of *verbal irony* (saying the opposite of what you mean), *situational irony* (having things turn out the opposite of what you expect), and *dramatic irony* (knowing something that the characters in a literary work do not know). Here are some suggested answers: (1) The gunnery practice wakes the dead and disturbs ''dumb creatures,'' even the worms, but does not disturb the living who are engaged in the practice. (2) People have not changed, and the world is ''Just as before you went below,'' God tells the dead. (3) Parson Thirdly looks back on his life and wishes that, instead of forty years of preaching, he had ''stuck to pipes and beer.'' (4) The sound of the guns and their ''readiness to avenge'' seem entirely out of place in such timeless, legendary places as Camelot and Stonehenge.

6. What do you think this poem says about war? Hardy clearly expresses his negative attitude: that war is foolish, mad, unjustifiable; that it is an eternal human activity.

The Convergence of the Twain

Responding to the Poem   Text page 837
Analyzing the Poem
Identifying Details

1. What physical details does Hardy use in his description of the *Titanic* in the first four stanzas? Hardy mentions that the ship ''stilly couches'' deep in the sea; that its steel chambers were recently pyres; that the seaworms crawl over its mirrors; that its jewels are lightless and blackened.

2. What does the poet ask in line 15? ''What does this vain gloriousness down here?''

Where and how does he answer this question? He answers the question in all of the remainder of the poem. He says that the Immanent Will (also called the Spinner of the Years) fashioned an iceberg at the same time that the ship was being built and determined that the two should collide.

Interpreting Meanings

3. How does Hardy divide the poem into two halves? How does the structure reinforce the poem's meaning? The first half of the poem is devoted to a description of the sunken *Titanic*. It ends with a question (line 15). The second half of the poem answers that question.

4. According to Hardy's poem, was the sinking of the *Titanic* an accident? Explain. According to the poem, it was no accident, but a predetermined ''august event.''

5. Who is the ''Spinner of the Years'' (line 31)? The Spinner of the Years is the same force that Hardy calls the Immanent Will in line 18. It is also an allusion to the Fates in Greek mythology, who controlled human destiny and life. Clotho was the one who spun the thread for each person's life, Lachesis determined the length of the thread, and Atropos cut the thread of life.

6. How would you explain the poem's *title*? The twain are the *Titanic* and the iceberg. Their convergence is their collision.

7. What is your response to Hardy's *main idea*? Student responses will vary, depending on their notions of free will, chance, and destiny or fate.

Primary Sources   Text page 838
The Sinking of the *Titanic*

This prose selection is from a general work of history. It provides students with a chance to make a broad comparison between prose and poetry treating the same event, between the historian and the poet. Ask students to list as many ways as they can find in which this example of a prose selection differs from this example of a poem. Ask them also how the poet has used the primary source, possibly his only information on the topic. As a general inspiration? As a source of detail? Does the poet take issue with the writer or try to support or supplement the prose?

The historian in this passage says that the disaster raises certain questions about progress as it had been thought of up to that point in history and about the existence of a ''just'' and ''wrathful'' God. How does Hardy respond to these questions? You may want students to select three favorite quotes from each work and defend their selection in class. Finally, the class might find it interesting to try to prepare a time number line using solid lines for the prose and broken lines for the poem and taking as their center the moment of impact.

Ah, Are You Digging on My Grave?   Text page 839

Drummer Hodge   Text page 840

Objectives

1. To evaluate anticlimax in a poem

2. To analyze tone

3. To write a character sketch

4. To write an analysis of the poet's use of irony

5. To write a comparison of two poems

The Poems at a Glance

- **Rhyme:** ("Ah, Are You Digging on My Grave?") *abcccb* in each stanza
  ("Drummer Hodge") *ababab* in each stanza
- **Rhythm:** alternating iambic tetrameter and trimeter in both poems
- **Significant techniques:** anticlimax, tone

Teaching Strategies

Providing for Cultural Differences. In approaching "Drummer Hodge," some of your students may require more information on the Boer War, which is provided in the headnote on page 840. Remind students that the conflict described in this note has continued to exist through the present time.

Providing for Different Levels of Ability. Both of the poems are straightforward and metrically easy to read. Be sure that students note the use of the alternating quotation marks in "Ah, Are You Digging on My Grave?"

Ah, Are You Digging on My Grave?

Reading the Poem. You may want to set the rural scene for your students. You might also remind them that they are used to following dialogue in poetry. This is a commentary on what Woodward would call "man's inhumanity to man," although the irony is strictly Hardy's. Tell students, if you wish, to be prepared for a dog story of a special kind.

Reteaching Alternatives. You may want to have students read this poem as a dialogue.

Drummer Hodge

Reading the Poem. You may want to develop the background of this poem in some little historical detail. It is another war poem, going back to the Boer War, and it is another poem about death. The fact that the British fought for possession of African colonies in Southern Africa against other white Europeans may prove of interest to students aware of the heritage of the whites in South Africa.

Reteaching Alternatives. Once you have set the stage—the setting of the poem—you may want to have students see this in graphic terms—a triangle: the stars above England, the stars above South Africa, and a grave.

Ah, Are You Digging on My Grave?

Responding to the Poem   Text page 839
Analyzing the Poem
Identifying Details

1. The dead woman who speaks part of the dialogue in this poem tries three guesses about the identity of the person digging her grave. Whom does she guess? She guesses that the person is her husband (or lover), her "nearest, dearest kin," and her enemy.

2. In the last stanza, what reason does the dog give for digging on the grave? The dog was digging on the grave to bury a bone.

Interpreting Meanings

3. *Anticlimax*, or *bathos*, is the deflating effect we feel when our lofty expectations are let down. Comment on how Hardy employs the device of *bathos* in each of the first three stanzas. For each guess the dead woman hopefully makes, the person or persons are far from devoting themselves to grief and the dead woman's memory. Her husband or lover has immediately wed a bright, healthy, beautiful, wealthy woman. Her kin dismiss as useless the idea of tending her grave or planting flowers, for it will not bring her back to life. Her enemy does not even deign to think of her.

4. How would you characterize the *tone* of this poem? Students should agree that the tone is wry, ironic, perhaps even bitter. Some may suggest that it is also humorous.

Which two or three passages do you think are most important in establishing this tone? Student answers will vary. Some may feel that the last three establish the tone most powerfully, for once the identity of the speaker is established, we are as surprised as the dead woman at the dog's heartless reason for digging on her mistress's grave.

Drummer Hodge

Responding to the Poem   Text page 840
Analyzing the Poem
Identifying Details

1. How was Drummer Hodge buried? He was thrown into a grave without a coffin on a small hill somewhere in South Africa.

2. Find three phrases that the poet uses to describe the stars of the southern hemisphere, which are different from the stars visible in England. He calls them ''foreign constellations'' (line 5), ''strange stars'' (line 12), and ''strange-eyed constellations'' (line 17).

Interpreting Meanings

3. Which lines suggest that, in a sense, Hodge has not died? Lines 13–16 suggest that Hodge has become part of the earth and its foliage.

Do you think the poem suggests that this is a consolation? We know that all humans die and return to the earth, but Hardy implies that Hodge's manner of dying, his burial, and his resting place are unnatural and strange.

4. What is the effect of Hardy's contrast of the strangeness of South Africa with Drummer Hodge's Wessex home and ''homely Northern breast and brain''? The contrast emphasizes the idea that Drummer Hodge was far from home, that he did not belong in the place where he was killed.

from The Return of the Native   Text page 842

Objectives

1. To analyze the mood of a novel
2. To identify imagery that contributes to mood
3. To write an analysis of the writer's style

Introducing the Chapter

In outline form, for your reference, here are the major elements in the chapter:

- **Protagonist:** Estacia Vye
- **Antagonist:** disenfranchisement
- **Conflict:** person vs. human nature
- **Point of view:** third-person omniscient
- **Significant techniques:** mood, imagery

Background on the Novel. This is a novel in which the sense of time and place is very strong. Here also is the sense that Hardy gives in his poetry—that humans are trapped by an uncaring universe represented by uncaring nature. In this novel, that nature is a heath. Evil with a capital ''E'' exists for Hardy. It lurks in the shadows of the heath and in the curl of Eustacia's lips.

The Plot. The heroine, Eustacia Vye, a beautiful and rebellious young woman, entraps and marries Clym Yoebright, recently returned to his native Dorchester from Paris. Eustacia hopes to escape the Heath and live with Clym in Paris. Her hopes are dashed when Clym, against her and his mother's wishes, decides to stay on the Heath and open a school. When Clym, almost blind from too much reading, decides to become a woodcutter, Eustacia feels degraded and cheated. She resumes a relationship with a former lover, Damon Wildeve, who in turn deserts the girl he is planning to marry.

One day, Mrs. Yoebright, Clym's mother, walks across the Heath in the hope of seeking a reconciliation with her son and daughter-in-law. Resting on a knoll some distance from the cottage, she sees a man whom she mistakes for her son entering the house. It is Wildeve, coming to see Eustacia. When no one answers Mrs. Yoebright's knock on the door, she thinks that her son has rebuffed her and starts back home across the hot Heath. Overcome by exhaustion and grief, she stops to rest and is fatally bitten by a snake. Clym, who has been asleep inside the cottage, starts across the heath to see his mother and stumbles over her dead body. His bewilderment over his mother's presence on the Heath is solved when he discovers that Eustacia was with Wildeve in the cottage. Clym orders Eustacia out of the cottage, and she goes to her grandfather's house nearby. One night, on the way to a meeting with her lover, she falls into a lake and is drowned. Wildeve, in an attempt to save her, is also drowned. Eustacia's death is regarded as suicide.

Teaching Strategies

Providing for Cultural Differences.   Students will probably have difficulty in relating to this chapter. It contains descriptions with no dialogue and with many allusions with which the students will be unfamiliar. It might be illuminating to have students write descriptions of settings with which they are familiar—a city street, the seashore, the mountains—and then compare their efforts with Hardy's.

Providing for Different Levels of Ability.   The chapter will prove difficult for many students. You may want to stop and explain each footnote.

Introducing Vocabulary Study.   Students will benefit from knowing the meanings of the following words before they read the chapter.

nomalous	inviolate
congruity	opacity
factitiously	swarthy

Reading the Chapter.   Use the subtitle at the beginning of the chapter to stimulate the student interest. You may want to try reading parts of the chapter aloud.

Reteaching Alternatives.   To help students understand the depth and breadth of the chapter, you might help them to outline the chapter, chiefly trying to reveal the many ways in which Hardy approaches the subject.

Responding to the Chapter   Text page 845
Analyzing the Chapter
Interpreting Meanings

1. What do you think the chapter title means? Answers will vary, for the subheading "Queen of Night" is never clearly explained. The text refers to Eustacia's dark hair,

dark eyes, her "pagan eyes full of nocturnal mysteries," "the only way to look queenly without realms or hearts to queen it over. . . ." Hardy also mentions her "sudden fits of gloom, one of the phases of the night side of sentiment which she knew too well for her years."

2. Describe the *mood* of the chapter. Which *images* help to create this mood? The mood of the chapter is one of restless uneasiness, of disaster about to happen. Hardy's description of Eustacia's isolation on the wild moors, his description of her dark beauty, her deigning to be like others in the community help to create the mood.

3. How does Hardy convey the impression that Eustacia is goddesslike? He begins the chapter by saying that she "was the raw material of divinity" and goes on to talk about how she would have fared on Olympus. He says that her appearance, with some slight rearrangements, could have been that of Artemis, Athena, or Hera.

   What specific phrases associate her with the devil or underworld? Students may mention "Queen of Night," "Egdon was her Hades," "A true Tartarean sat upon her brow, . . ."

4. Explain why Eustacia Vye is unhappy. She longs for a passionate love affair. She seems to consider herself better than the natives of Egdon Heath. She misses the social activity of Budmouth.

   In what kind of setting or circumstances might she be happy? Student answers will vary. She clearly needs a strong man. Some may suggest she would be happy in an elegant, cultured society, where she could be the dominant, admired figure.

5. Is there anything "modern" about Eustacia? Student answers will vary. Insist that students support their views with details from the selection.

Extending the Chapter

Discuss with the students the effect that their surroundings have on them. Some students may have lived in different states and different countries. Ask them to think about whether their behavior was different when they were in strange surroundings.

Further Reading

English literature is full of novels, stories, and poetry that have the moor or heath as a setting. Students who have not already done so might enjoy reading *The Hound of Baskervilles* by Sir Arthur Conan Doyle.

A. E. Housman

Housman said that a poem should have an actual physical effect on the reader—like a punch in the stomach. You may want to tell students to expect a "punch" at the end of Housman's poems, not to be ashamed of a reaction, and to try to find out what line or idea creates it. (George Orwell, by the way, calls all of Housman's themes "adolescent." If so, so much the better!) You can also tell students that in each of Housman's poems there is usually a "situation." Finding it will also give focus to the reading.

When I Was One-and-Twenty

The Night Is Freezing Fast

With Rue My Heart Is Laden

On Moonlit Heath and Lonesome Bank

Objectives

1. To analyze the connotative effect of the titles of poems

2. To determine the themes of the poems and apply them to life today

3. To determine the tone and mood of the poems

4. To analyze the structure of the poems

5. To recognize and extended metaphor

6. To recognize a parable in a poem

7. To evaluate the effect of repetition

8. To write a comparison of several poems of the author

9. To write a paraphrase of a poem

10. To write an essay on setting

The Poems at a Glance

- **Rhyme:** ("When I Was One-and-Twenty") *abcbdefe* in both stanzas
  ("The Night Is Freezing Fast") *abcabc* in both stanzas
  ("With Rue My Heart Is Laden") *abab* in both stanzas
  ("On Moonlit Heath and Lonesome Bank") *abab* in each stanza
- **Rhythm:** ("When I Was One-and-Twenty") iambic trimeter
  ("The Night Is Freezing Fast") iambic trimeter
  ("With Rue My Heart Is Laden") iambic trimeter
  ("On Moonlit Heath and Lonesome Bank") mixed iambic
- **Significant techniques:** repetition, theme, connotation, rhyme, extended metaphor, rhythm

Background of the Poems. Although Housman has dramatic situations in his poems at times, he is essentially a lyric poet, the best since Tennyson. His pessimism is, like Hardy's, new to Victorian poetry. Whereas earlier poets had doubts, Housman felt that life was poisonous. His ironic reaction to life is not as modern as Hardy's but certainly can be appreciated by modern readers.

Teaching Strategies

Providing for Cultural Differences. Attention to the footnotes will help students with unfamiliar vocabulary. The situations in the poems are often dated (Victorian), but they are not difficult to grasp.

Providing for Different Levels of Ability. The poetry is tight, charged with meaning, but most of the poems are short. You may want to read aloud the longer poems.

When I Was One-and-Twenty

Reading the Poem. This poem is easily memorized and eminently quotable. You may want to suggest this as a way of getting into the poem.

Reteaching Alternatives. Ask students to identify the situation in this poem and to tell it as a prose story. Also ask them to look for Housman's use of repetition.

The Night Is Freezing Fast

Reading the Poem. You may want to ask students to find the "situation" of this poem, as it is set forth in the first stanza and as it applies to Dick and his friend the speaker.

Reteaching Alternatives. Ask students to read this poem as a seasonal poem and to be ready to talk about the different moods the seasons create in humans. Suppose the action had occurred in the midst of an English springtime. Would Housman feel any different?

With Rue My Heart Is Laden

Reading the Poem. Suggest that students memorize this poem as well.

Reteaching Alternatives. The theme of lost friends and days that never will be again is found, students may recall, in the poems of Tennyson ("Tears, Idle Tears," for one). You may want to have students reread the Tennyson poem and make comparisons.

On Moonlit Heath and Lonesome Bank

Reading the Poem. You may want to tell students that this is a poem about a way of dealing with crime.

Reteaching Alternatives. What is the situation here? What does the poem say about Housman's view of progress and the past? How might students apply these ideas to their own feeling for the way things were six or seven years ago? Was life, in general, better?

When I Was One-and-Twenty

Responding to the Poem   Text page 847
Analyzing the Poem
Identifying Details

1. **In the first stanza, what advice did the wise man give the speaker?** He tells the speaker not to give his heart away and to keep his "fancy free."

2. **How much time has passed between the first and the second stanza?** A year (or part of a year) has passed.

Interpreting Meanings

3. **What has the speaker learned, in your opinion?** He has learned that love relationships can be painful.

4. **What do you think of the wise man's advice that it is better to pay money than to fall in love? Explain.** Student answers and reasons will vary. Most will agree that the experience of having been in love is worth whatever pain may occur if/when the relationship ends.

5. **What is the effect of Housman's use of *repetition* in the last line of the poem?** The repetition of " 'tis true" emphasizes the speaker's agreement, suggests the pain of the experience he has had without giving any information about that experience, and brings the poem to an emphatic close.

What other kinds of repetition do you find in the poem? Students should note the repetition of whole lines (1 and 9), similar lines (lines 2 and 10), syntax in the two stanzas (introductory adverb clause, followed by the imperative sentences of the wise man). Students should also point out examples of alliteration and assonance, and should note the repetitions in rhyme and meter.

6. **What do you think is the poem's *theme*, or message? Do you think Housman is being serious or ironic or humorous in his attitude toward falling in love?** Student opinions will vary. Ask them to point to details in the poem, if they can, to support their answers.

The Night Is Freezing Fast

Responding to the Poem   Text page 848
Analyzing the Poem
Identifying Details

1. **According to the evidence of the first stanza, what day is it?** It is November 30th ("Tomorrow comes December").

2. **What has happened to Dick?** Dick has died.

3. **Describe the *rhyme scheme* of the poem.** The rhyme scheme is *abcabc*.

Interpreting Meanings

4. **What are the *connotations* of the poem's title?** The connotations of icy cold and darkness are unpleasant and uncomfortable. Humans yearn to escape such darkness and cold to be indoors where there is light and warmth.

5. Explain the *extended metaphor* that dominates the second stanza. The earth, which covers the body of Dick, is Dick's clothing: his winter robe, his overcoat. Dick has become one with the earth and ''wars'' the whole planet.

6. What do you think *winterfalls* (line 3) means? The phrase may have more than one meaning. Winterfalls suggests the beginnings of many winters as nightfall suggests the beginning of night. It also suggests that period of the year when the weather feels like winter but it is not yet officially winter, which begins on December 21st; it is some combination of winter and fall.

How do you interpret the phrase ''Fall, winter, fall'' (line 7)? It suggests the quick passing of years. Students may also suggest that fall be interpreted as a verb in this phrase: Winter no longer causes Dick any discomfort for he is clothed in the earth.

7. What would you say is the poem's *theme*, or message? Is it about winter, or Dick, or something else entirely? Student answers will vary; it is difficult to state this poem's theme. If students seem baffled, begin by having them discuss this statement of theme: The troubles and discomforts that plague us soon disappear, for our life on earth is short, and nothing troubles us in the grave.

With Rue My Heart Is Laden

Responding to the Poem   Text page 849
Analyzing the Poem
Identifying Details

1. Why is the speaker mournful? He is mourning for the friends of his youth who have died.

2. According to the second stanza, where are the boys laid to rest? Where do the girls lie? The boys are laid to rest beside ''brooks too broad for leaping.'' The girls lie in ''fields where roses fade.''

Interpreting Meanings

3. Given the burial places where the boys and girls are said to lie in the second stanza, what is appropriate about the adjectives used to describe them? The boys are ''lightfoot'' and are buried beside brooks too broad for leaping; we can imagine that they enjoyed leaping over many brooks when they were alive. The girls are ''rose-lipt'' in contrast to the living roses that fade in the fields where they lie. In the speaker's memory, the boys are forever light-footed and the girls forever rose-lipped.

4. The *rhythm* of the poem is perfectly regular, even in the variations of lines 1, 3, 5, and 7, where Housman adds an extra final syllable to create a weak *rhyme*. **What is the effect of this regular variation of strong and weak rhymes?** Answers will vary. Students may suggest that the regular variation of strong and weak rhymes adds to the musical quality of the poem. Lines 1, 2, 5, 7 rhyme two syllables instead of one, and these lines move very musically into the succeeding lines. In contrast, the one-syllable rhymes that end the even-numbered lines suggest a kind of finality.

On Moonlit Heath and Lonesome Bank

Responding to the Poem   Text page 850
Analyzing the Poem
Identifying Details

1. What differences between the past and present does the speaker remark on? Criminals sentenced to be hanged were once hanged at the crossroads; now they are hanged in Shrewsbury jail. Today men waiting to be hanged can listen to passing railroad trains.

2. What does the speaker say will happen to the young man in Shrewbury jail? He will be hanged in the morning sometime between eight and nine.

3. In the final two stanzas, what does the speaker say he will do? He will stay awake on the heath waiting for morning and wish his friend in jail a sound night's sleep.

Interpreting Meanings

4. What seems to be the speaker's *attitude* toward the past, as compared to the present? Answers will vary.

5. What is the speaker's relationship to the condemned man? The condemned man is the speaker's friend, someone the speaker likes and respects.

6. How are the sounds of the fifth and sixth stanzas different from those of the stanzas the precede and follow them? The differences are subtle, and students may have trouble recognizing them. Suggest they read the poem aloud. They should notice the harshly accented syllables in lines 19 and 21. They may also notice the sixth stanza is the only stanza made up entirely of one-syllable words.

Explain the purpose and effect of this difference. These two stanzas are set off from the story that the speaker tells. In these stanzas, the speaker expresses his strong negative feelings about the injustice of this particular execution and perhaps of capital punishment in general.

7. Do you think this poem has any contemporary applications, given what you know about crime and punishment in our society? Student answers will vary.

Amplify the introduction to Dickens in the student text by telling students that the Dickensian characters who have become literary immortals have managed to do so through their own destinctive voices, plus a few well-placed comments by their creator. No two characters in Dickens, that is, speak the same. Each has a unique manner and an often-amusing viewpoint on life. We can recognize their voices and their words in total darkness and say to ourselves, ''Ah, that must be Peggotty, or Betsey Trotwood, or Oliver Twist, or the prisoner on the moors in *Great Expectations*!'' Dickens also often sets two completely different characters off against each other, as here Miss Betsey is juxtaposed against a complete opposite, Mr. Chillip.

from David Copperfield

Text page 852

Objectives

1. To identify characterization through imagery

2. To evaluate an author's point of view

3. To write a synopsis of an episode from the work

4. To write an analysis of a character

Introducing the Chapter

In outline form, for your reference, here are the major elements in the chapter.

- **Protagonist:** David Copperfield
- **Antagonists:** the Murdstones
- **Conflict:** person vs. person
- **Point of view:** first-person limited
- **Significant techniques:** characterization, dialogue
- **Setting:** a house in Suffolk

Background on the Novel. Every page of a Dickens novel characterizes Victorian England in some respect—its law courts, inns, transportation, and so on. Victorian schools and education are frequently the butt of Dickens's satire. He found the schools inadequate and the people who managed them cruel. (Murdstone's ''lesson'' to David in this selection is typical.) The Victorian attitude toward women (resulting in complete subservience, as we see here) may not have been recognized by Dickens as a major flaw in Victorian society, but it did not escape his eye for absurdities in human affairs.

The Plot. The plot is rather loose because of its autobiographical nature. It describes the adventures of David from the viewpoint of an adult David looking back on his childhood and the many characters who inhabited his youthful world.

Teaching Strategies

Providing for Cultural Differences. Students should have no trouble in identifying with David.

Providing for Different Levels of Ability. Dickens is easy and amusing to read aloud. Parts can be assigned.

Introducing Vocabulary Study. Students will benefit from knowing the meaning of the following words before they begin the chapter.

compunction	torpor
indolence	vindictive
portentous	

Reading the Story. If the story is read aloud, ask the students to watch for examples of the ways in which the author uses humor.

Reteaching Alternatives. The essential problems of growing up do not change much across the years. Some children must still live with hateful and irresponsible adults. There is still wide disagreement about discipline and methods of education. The medical profession is still the butt of scrutiny by novelists. Single aunts are still arrogant. Changes have taken place, however, in many areas—from ways of thinking to institutions to technical advances—to such an extent that the scenes depicted here would simply not be possible today. You may want to have students go through this selection creating two columns of notes, one headed ''Repeatable Today'', the other ''Changes That Make This Impossible.''

Responding to the Chapter   Text page 862

Analyzing the Chapter

Identifying Facts

1. **Name several changes that occur in the household as a result of Clara Copperfield's marriage to Mr. Murd-**

stone. Students may mention any of the following: David's bed is moved to a new room. Mr. Murdstone's sister Jane moves in with them and takes control of the household. Peggotty no longer accompanies David and his mother to church. David notices that his mother's appearance seems changed, the gaiety of her beauty almost worried away. Mr. Murdstone and his sister preside over David's lessons, which become a torture to him.

2. Describe a typical lesson for David. Students should mention the following essentials: Mr. Murdstone and his sister are present and make David so nervous that he invariably falters and cannot remember his lesson. David's mother does the actual "teaching" and is caught by Miss Murdstone whenever she tries to help David. At the end of each lesson, Mr. Murdstone invents a difficult arithmetic problem that David cannot do.

3. How does David's mother respond when Mr. Murdstone is about to flog David? She bursts into tears and runs toward David and Mr. Murdstone as they are leaving the room.

What does David do? He entreats Mr. Murdstone not to beat him, and after the first blow bites Mr. Murdstone's hand.

Intererpreting Meanings

4. By the end of Chapter 4, how do you feel about each of the following characters: David's mother, Peggotty, Mr. Murdstone, Jane Murdstone? Student answers will vary somewhat. Most will express sympathy for David's mother; some will think she has little backbone and should have stoood up to the Murdstones more. Peggotty is all positive, a good and loving force in the novel. The Murdstones are despicable; it is difficult to determine which one is worse.

How has Dickens managed to make you feel this way? (Discuss the *images* associated with each character as well as Dickens' methods of *characterization*.) Only one new character—Jane Murdstone—is introduced in this chapter, and Dickens describes her appearance in detail. (Have students reread the "metallic" description of Miss Murdstone.) Except for Miss Murdstone, Dickens develops his characters by telling what they say and do (or don't do) and letting us draw our own conclusions. In this chapter Dickens does not use any *direct characterization*; that is, he does not directly describe any of the characters' traits.

5. Discuss the advantages and disadvantages of the *point of view* Dickens uses for this novel. How does Dickens overcome the limitations of a child-narrator? The first-person narrator is the adult David Copperfield, looking back at his life. In the early chapters the child-narrator reports his experiences and thoughts, and the point of view makes us feel much sympathy for him. The limitation of this point of view is that we can know only the thoughts and feelings of the narrator: we cannot know the minds and hearts of other characters. Thus, we do not know why Mr. Murdstone and his sister are so diabolical nor why David's mother is so weak. Dickens takes some liberties with the point of view. Occasionally the narrator will comment in his adult voice: ". . . I knew as well that he could mold her pliant nature into any form he chose, as I know, now, that he did it."

6. Why do you think the Murdstones are so insensitive to David? Are they simply hard and cruel people, or is there some additional reason for their behavior toward him? Student opinions will vary.

Extending the Novel

Have a class discussion of the advantages and disadvantages of living in David Copperfield's time.

Further Reading

Guide students who are interested in Dickens to other novels by the author.

Lewis Carroll

Text page 863

from Through the Looking Glass

Text page 865

Objectives

1. To evaluate setting, events, character, and structure
2. To identify the target of satire
3. To write paragraphs imitating the author's style
4. To write an essay supporting an opinion
5. To analyze portmanteau words

Introducing the Story

In outline form, for your reference, here are the major elements in the excerpt.

· **Protagonist:** Alice

· **Antagonists:** March Hare, Mad Hatter, Doormouse, Humpty Dumpty

· **Conflicts:** Alice's rationality vs. the irrationality of the others

- **Point of view:** third-person limited (Alice)
- **Significant techniques:** dialogue, comment, portmanteau words
- **Setting:** a tea table under a house (The Mad Tea Party) and a high narrow wall (Humpty Dumpty)

Background on the Story. *Through the Looking Glass* is the result of stories that the author told the three little daughters of the Dean of Oxford University as they rowed down a river. Although the settings of the stories are those of a dream world, Alice is a very real little girl.

The Plot. In *Through the Looking Glass* Alice dreams that she jumps through a mirror and enters into a world on the other side of it. This world is largely inhabited by live chess pieces, and Alice's object is to move across a landscape laid out like a chessboard until she becomes a queen. She wakes up when she succeeds.

Teaching Strategies

Providing for Cultural Differences. The humor and characters in *Through the Looking Glass* should be universal enough to appeal to all students. However, Alice is an English Victorian child, and it might be helpful to remind students that English children are accustomed to afternoon tea. Mention, too, that Victorian parents were very concerned with good manners.

Providing for Different Levels of Ability. All students should be able to read these excerpts in a single sitting. However, because the stories were originally told aloud, students will benefit from hearing them read aloud. You might assign the parts of different characters in the excerpts to readers.

Reading the Story. Before students read the excerpts, have a class discussion about dreams. Ask for volunteers to describe a dream of theirs to the class. Then have the class try to analyze what part of the dream is based on fantasy and what part on reality. Ask the class how familiar they are with the book and in what form they first became familiar with it. As a children's book? A cartoon? A play? Have they ever read the original?

Reteaching Alternatives. You may want to accept, at least as a teaching device, the theory that Lewis Carroll is satirizing ideas and aspects of life in Victorian England. Then ask students to try to detect at every step just exactly what it is that Carroll is poking fun at. That is, what is the rational situation that he is treating?

Responding to the Novel   Text page 870
Analyzing the Novel
Identifying Facts

1. What is the one clear idea that Alice makes out in "Jabberwocky"? She finds it clear that somebody killed something.

2. According to Humpty Dumpty, why can glory mean "there's a nice knock-down argument"? Humpty Dumpty says that when he uses a word, it means just what he chooses it to mean—"neither more nor less."

Interpreting Meanings

3. Describe Alice's response to the irrationality and rudeness she encounters. Alice seems untroubled by the irrationality and ignores Humpty Dumpty's rudeness and insults. To avoid arguments with him, she frequently changes the subject. She tries not to hurt Humpty Dumpty's feelings, but she does become indignant and sometimes challenges what he says. She doesn't express her dissatisfaction with Humpty Dumpty until after she has left him.

4. In what ways are the *setting*, *events*, *characters*, and *structure* of the episodes like those of a dream? Student answers will vary. They should mention that the setting is unreal, Alice floats rather than walks, and scenes dissolve. The characters are fantastic: a nursey rhyme character and an old Sheep that knits and runs a grocery store. The "Jabberwocky" poem and much of Alice's conversation with Humpty Dumpty seem almost to make sense but don't.

   What elements of a nightmare can you find? Students may mention that the laws of gravity don't work, language doesn't communicate in the expected way, and ordinary civility doesn't get the expected results.

5. Some critics have said that the Alice books are satirical. (A *satire* uses ridicule, sarcasm, and irony to criticize specific faults, vices, or stupidities.) In the episode you have just read, who or what do you think Lewis Carroll might be satirizing? Students may suggest poets, linguists, dictionary writers, history writers, politeness.

6. What do you think Lewis Carroll seems to be saying in these excerpts about language and the difficulties of communicating? Student answers will vary.

Extending the Novel

Bring in a copy of *Alice in Wonderland* with the original Teniel illustrations and compare them with the works of a more modern illustrator. Have a discussion on the importance of illustrations. Have students bring in examples of nonsense rhymes and read them aloud to the class.

Further Reading

Guide students who are interested in reading other books by Lewis Carroll to *The Hunting of the Snark* and *Sylvie and Bruno*.

Rudyard Kipling

Text page 872

The Miracle of Purun Bhagat

Text page 873

Objectives

1. To identify and analyze the humor in the story
2. To write a personal narrative about a time of contemplation and reassessment
3. To write an essay supporting an opinion

Introducing the Story

In outline form, for your reference, here are the major elements in the story:

- **Protagonist:** Purun Dass/Bhagat
- **Antagonists:** Bristish culture; materialism; the destructive forces of nature
- **Conflict:** person vs. another culture; person vs. material values; humans vs. nature
- **Point of view:** third-person omniscient
- **Significant techniques:** tone and stylistic conventions of fable, humor, atmosphere
- **Setting:** India, nineteenth century

Background on the Story. Indians who are Hindu believe in a caste system in which each person belongs to one social class throughout life. Each class has an elaborate code governing the behavior of its members. The highest caste is that of the Brahmins, scholars and priests, whose purpose is to preserve national ideas. Just below come the Kshatriyas, the warriors and rulers, and below them the Vaisyas, merchants and artisans. The Sudras, servants and laborers come at the bottom. Excluded from caste are the untouchables and pariahs.

The Plot. Purun Dass is a very Anglicized Brahmin who achieves great power and honors as the prime minister of an Indian state. At the height of his fame and power, he gives up everything to wander through his country as an anonymous mendicant and seeker of truth. When he settles in a deserted shrine in the hill country, he is revered by the local villagers. His death, as the result of exerting himself to warn the villagers of a landslide, establishes him as a kind of saint.

Teaching Strategies

Providing for Cultural Differences. The story's ending, in which Purun Bhagat dies after saving the lives of the villagers, is a product of Kipling's western imagination and is less true to Indian culture than the earlier parts of the story. Responsibility for one's fellow humans is an alien concept as far as Hindu culture is concerned, and achieving holiness is thought to consist not of doing good works but of renouncing the material world and living a detached, contemplative life. Students may be interested in comparing the Hindu view of spiritual superiority with the views of their own culture.

Providing for Different Levels of Ability. The slow pacing of the story and lack of dramatic incident throughout much of it may discourage less patient readers. In order to stimulate their interest, you may wish to divide the story into sections and have students pause after each to make comments or predictions after the speech of Purun Bhagat, for example.

Introducing Vocabulary Study. Students will benefit from knowing the meanings of the following words before they read the story.

brindles	mendicant
cavalcade	piebald
lionized	unrelenting

Reading the Story. Before reading the story, you might have the students discuss the impressions of India they have gotten from books, movies and television programs. Record their observations on a semantic map on the chalkboard or on chart paper. Whenever possible, encourage students to compare and contrast Indian culture with their own. You might have students take notes while they read on what they learn about Indian life and culture and afterward use this information to expand the map.

Reteaching Alternatives. Have students working in small groups draw up what they believe might be the code for the Brahmin way of life, basing it on facts in or inferences drawn from the text.

Responding to the Story

Analyzing the Story

Identifying Facts

1. What improvements does Purun Dass make when he is Prime Minister? He establishes schools for little girls, builds roads, starts dispensaries (health clinics) and shows of agricultural tools. He endows scholarships for the study of medicine and manufacturing.

2. Name the animals that share the mountain shelter of Purun Bhagat. Use both the English and the Indian names. He shares his mountain shelter with *langurs*, gray-whiskered monkeys; *barasingh*, red deer; *mushick-nabha*, musk deer; *Sona*, a Himalayan black bear; *minaul*, the Himalayan pheasant.

3. How does Purun Bhagat find out about the catastrophe that is about to befall the village? He is awakened by a *langur*, who pulls at his hand and runs to the door. A *barasingh* comes to the shelter and pushes Purun Shagat toward the door just before the floor of the shelter gives way.

4. Make a list of the Indian words and customs that you have learned by reading this story. Lists will vary.

Interpreting Meanings

5. Explain and comment on the meaning of the story's title. Clearly, the miracle is the holy man's saving all of the villagers' lives. Ask students if they can name any other miracle in the story. A villager says that it is "a miracle after a miracle" that Purun Bhagat dies in the very attitude in which Sunnyasis must be buried. Students may also suggest other "miracles": Purun Bhagat's ability to communicate with the animals; his transformation from a powerful government official to a simple holy man.

6. Why would no English person "have dreamed of doing" what Dewan Sir Purun Dass, K.C.I.E. does? Student answers will vary, and some may even disagree with the statement. Certainly, few Westerners would voluntarily give up wealth, power, and fame to lead a holy life of isolation and poverty. Most Westerners are too tied to their families to "disappear" as Purun Dass does in the story.

7. Why does Purun Bhagat feel at home when he reaches the hill country? His mother was from the hill country, and he remembers how she was always homesick for it. When he stops at a deserted shrine to the goddess Kali, it is because he has decided that there he will find peace.

How is this feeling of being at home related to his reception by the villagers and the animals? The villagers make him welcome, treat him respectfully as a holy man, and bring him food each day. The animals, too, seem to welcome him and trust him readily.

8. What do you think is the story's theme? Student statements of theme will vary.

9. The Hindu goddess Kali, who represents time, is both a creator and destroyer. Why is she an appropriate figure in this story? Purun Bhagat leaves the hurry and rush of civilization to settle in a mountain shrine, where he finds peace in the timeless landscape. In such a setting the animals and people live by the natural time of night and day and the changing seasons. In her role as creator, Kali enables the villagers, plants, and animals to thrive and grow. As destroyer, she causes the landslide that would have destroyed the village but for Purun Bhagat's quick action.

Extending the Story

Discuss how the story of a man like Purun Dass might be retold from the points of view of writers from several different cultures. Encourage students to draw on their own cultural backgrounds and on their readings about other cultures.

Further Reading

Students who like this story might enjoy *Plain Tales from the Hills* or other anthologies of Kipling stories. Those who saw the movies *Heat and Dust* based on the Ruth Prawer Jhabvala novel or *A Passage to India* based on the E. M. Forster novel may enjoy reading these books. Those interested in reading about India from an Indian point of view might look for the fiction of R. K. Narayan or Rabindranath Tagore.

Introducing Victorian Drama

The short essay provides students with a background glimpse of the drama of the period in preparation for their reading of the sole drama in the text, Wilde's *The Impor-* *tance of Being Earnest*. Help students to develop an understanding of the playwright's intent to portray triviality seriously and to depict issues of a serious nature in a completely trivial and absurd fashion. By using comedy in this way, Wilde conveys—and laughs at—human beings' obsession with appearance. In his use of epigrams, Wilde also conveys his belief that art should not preach morality. Everything in the play—characters, plot, events, and circumstance—is very funny. Wilde does not preach to the audience. He addresses serious social, political, and personal issues in an hysterical manner, so that he makes his points while listeners or readers laugh their way from the first line of Act One to the last line of Act Three. This play is a farce in form and a comedy in spirit and in the treatment of characters and interactions. It has been termed a psychooglical farce—a farce that deals with ideas. The action and character development are not primary concerns. What is most important and what contributes to the constant hilarity of the play are the often contradictory and unbelievable things the characters are saying. The action in the play is not the literal movement of the characters or the psychological development of the characters; it is the movement from one comic remark to the next.

Oscar Wilde

Text page 882

Preface to The Importance of Being Earnest

Text page 883

The Importance of Being Earnest, subtitled *A Trivial Comedy for Serious People*, was described by Wilde as "Exquisitely trivial, a delicate bubble of fancy, and it has a philosophy . . . that we should treat all the trivial things of life seriously, and all the serious things of life with sincere and studied triviality." (*The Importance of Being Earnest*, Bard, Avon, 1965, p. 18) The play is filled with several characters, none of whom elicits any sense of pathos. Algernon, Jack, Cecily, Gwendolen, Lady Bracknell, Miss Prism, Lance, and Dr. Chasuble were all outlets for epigrams. The play explores the importance of appearances and the silliness of seriousness. The chaotic and absurd events are portrayed in a somber and "respectable" fashion, while the underlying content of the play (the class system, marriage, love, identity, knowledge, and morality) is presented under the guise of complete frivolity. The setting of the play is Victorian England, but much of the action and sentiments expressed could be focused on American culture and society today. The characters create no sense of empathy; they serve as instruments with which Wilde can both voice and illustrate his philosophy of life and his criticisms and observations of human nature and society. The play is not, however, moralizing, and the characters are never judgmental. They play entertains from its first moment to its last. As uncomfortable as many of the brilliantly posed epigrams have made some people feel, everyone reading or watching the play performed will find it very difficult to stop laughing at the very serious actors and the inane chaotic action.

The Importance of Being Earnest

Text page 884

Objectives

1. To identify and define the terms comedy, farce, irony, and satire

2. To analyze the functions of dialogue and action in the play

3. To analyze the characters, their interaction, setting, and purpose

4. To analyze the mechanics and function of the jest

5. To understand the use and structure of the epigrams in the play and to write several on chosen topics

6. To understand the function and importance of the plot

7. To analyze the importance of the themes of the play and how they are evoked

8. To write an additional act for the play, evoking the weddings of Cecily and Algernon and Gwendolen and Jack

9. To write and analysis of the play, relating it to the time in which it was written and discussing how something like it might be written and received today, relating to the current American scene

Introducing the Play

In outline form, for your reference, here are the major elements in the play:

- **Protagonist:** Jack (alias Earnest Worthing)
- **Antagonist:** his own deceit and self-doubt
- **Conflict:** person vs. self
- **Significant techniques:** foreshadowing, tone, epigram, satire, motif, repetition, irony, farce, deus ex machina, plot
- **Setting:** England, nineteenth century

Background on the Play.   Understanding the importance of the delivery of the lines will help the students acquire a sense of the tone of the play. Explain that the crux of a good farce depends on the seriousness of the actors' delivery and the silliness and triviality and truth of their concerns and activity. The plot and the character development are intentionally chaotic and shallow. The lines themselves (specifically the epigrams) provide the comic tension and relief, and hence the true action in the play.

The Plot

Act One.   The morning-room of Algernon Moncrieff's apartment in London is the setting for the first act. It begins with a dialogue between Algernon and his manservant Lance. This conversation introduces the farcical tone of the play, the underlying them (Art as sentiment, Life as science), as well as two of the overt themes: the British class-system and the institution of marriage. Jack (alias Ernest Worthing) enters and with him comes another theme: the issue of false identity. The concept of Bunburying a la Algernon and its equivalent a la Jack is presented, and soon Algernon's cousin Gwendolen enters with her mother, Lady Bracknell, Jack (as Ernest) proposes to Gwendolen, Lady Bracknell inspects his elligibility and refuses the proposal because of Jack's insufficient parenting. Gwendolen, however, assures him her affections because she loves and trusts the name Ernest. The act ends with Algernon commenting to Jack on the frivolity of scrapes and contemplating the next day's Bunburying excursion—with Jack and his ward Cecily's country address safe in his pocket.

Act Two.   The setting of the second act is the garden of the Manor House. Cecily and her governess, Miss Prism, are discussing the seriousness of Jack's nature and the elements of writing diaries, three-volume novels, and fiction in general. In Miss Prism's comment about the meaning of fiction, Wilde again proposes his disdain for art as a tool for moralizing. Dr. Chasuble arrives and goes for a walk with Miss Prism just as Alergnon, calling himself Ernest Worthing, Jack's deviant younger brother, arrives to examine the wooing potential of Cecily. Miss Prism and Dr. Chasuble are in the midst of tedious flirting when Jack arrives in a suit of mourning, claiming that his brother Ernest just died from a severe chill in Paris. He immediately arranges with Chasuble to be christened later in the day.

Cecily quietly appears and informs Jack that his brother is in the dining room. After Jack and Algernon meet and Algernon is told to leave, but decides (with Cecily) to stay, Cecily informs Algernon (alias Ernest) that they have been engaged for the past three months. She tells him she loves him because of his name, and he goes off (like Jack) to find Chasuble to be christened. Gwendolen arrives from London to see her fiance, and she and Cecily get along very well until both claim to be engaged to Ernest. Jack, and then Algernon, enter after Cecily and Gwendolen have been quarrelling over tea, and the identities of the Ernests are unveiled. The scene ends with Jack and Algernon bickering over muffins and christenings and stuffing themselves until only one muffin is left.

Act Three.   The drawing-room at the Manor House is the scene for Act Three. Gwendolen and Cecily console each other until Algernon and Jack enter and begin to explain themselves. Lady Bracknell arrives to retrieve her daughter, Gwendolen, and after approving of the social standing and financial stability of Cecily, consents to her marriage to Algernon. Because of her disapproval of Jack, he threatens to obstruct Cecily's marriage until she legally comes of age. Chasuble enters prepared for the christenings, and he mentions Miss Prism, whom Lady Bracknell quickly and disdainfully recognizes. Lady Bracknell and Miss Prism reveal Miss Prism's mix-up years ago, when she checked a baby in a handbag into a cloakroom of Victoria Station and left her three-volume novel in a baby carriage in a remote corner of Bayswater. Jack produces the handbag in which he was found as an infant, and his family background is remarkably recovered: He is the nephew of Lady Bracknell and the cousin of Gwendolyn, and the older brother of Algernon. With the exception of Algernon's assumed name, the aliases of Algernon and Jack are revealed as their true identities, in spite of their false intentions. The marriages are then acceptable for all of the parties involved, and Jack realizes, at last, "the vital Importance of Being Earnest."

Teaching Strategies

Providing for Cultural Differences.   The Victorian period—in which the play was written—will probably be unfamiliar to the students. Much of the jesting is targeted at the British class-system, which is particularly important for the students to understand. Another concept that will be extremely helpful in discussing as background material for reading the play is the Esthetic Movement and Wilde's strong belief in art for art's sake. Placed in the context of moralistic Victorian society, the play is a denunciation of every level of its contemporary social stratas, as well as being a critique of human nature in general. As mentioned earlier, it is not, however, moralizing. Wilde, unlike many of his contemporaries, refrained from preaching right and wrong, good and bad. A discussion exploring elements of Victorian England—cultural as well as social—will help to illuminate the humor of the play and the stance that Wilde takes through it. The discussion may also encompass the similarities and the differences between the period in which the play was written and the period in which we are living today. Drawing a parallel between 19th-century society and the 20th century will make the play more relevant and accessible to the students.

Providing for Different Levels of Ability. To help students who are having difficulty understanding the play, have students break up into small groups and read the play aloud together. Ask them to describe their favorite comic shows or books or movies, and help them compare the play's differences and similarities (in technique and subject matter) to these favorites. Try to relate and help the students relate the subjects of the play (love, marriage, appearances) to the students' personal experiences and feelings.

Introducing Vocabulary Study. Students will benefit from knowing the meanigs of the following words before they read the play.

celibacy	indiscretion
equanimity	misanthrope
expurgation	superciliously
immaterial	utilitarian
indecorous	

Reading the Play. Plays are intended to be read aloud, if not in fact acted on stage, and this play is certainly no exception. Because of the wonderful humor in the play, this should be extremely entertaining. As the students read the play out loud, a momentum will build due to the comic tension developed, and it is often a good idea to keep questions and discussion to a minimum until the end of the play reading. If you have particularly funny students in your class, you may want to assign them the roles in Act One. This may help to break the ice and relax the student listeners so that they fully enjoy the humor in the play. Switch student roles from time to time. It is always a good idea to get as many students as possible involved in reading the play aloud—without allowing the role turnover to become too distracting. After the class has read the play through, discuss it together and answer and pose questions for the students.

Reteaching Alternatives. To illustrate the comic-profound nature of the play and the irony with which Wilde fully conveys his themes, have a group of students act out the second half of Act Three. After the piece is performed, discuss the many elements that the final catch in the story reveals. What does the scene suggest regarding the importance of family heritage and social standing? Ask the students if they have had any personal experiences—or know other people who have—that deal with similar issues. What does the act relate about the importance of naming? What does Wilde imply is the true nature of love and marriage? Whom do each of the characters seem to love the most?

Responding to the Play   Text page 896

Analyzing Act One

Identifying Facts

1. What does Jack reveal to Algernon about his name? Jack tells Algernon that his real name is Jack and that he is known as Ernest in town and Jack in the country. Jack explains further that in order to come to town, he has invented a younger brother named Ernest, who lives in town and gets into terrible scrapes. Jack uses Ernest as an excuse to leave the country frequently.

2. Who is Bunbury, and what is "Bunburying"? Algernon has invented a permanent invalid called Bunbury, who lives in the country, as his excuse to get out of engagements he doesn't want to keep. Bunburying is Algernon's telling people that he is going to the country to take care of Bunbury when he is really doing something else.

3. What questions does Lady Bracknell ask Jack in her inquisition of him? She asks him whether he smokes, how old he is, whether he knows everything or nothing, what his income is, whether it is in land or investments, whether he owns a house in town, and where it is. She asks who Lady Bloxham is, what Jack's politics are, whether his parents are living, who his father was, how his father made his money, and where Jack was found.

What does she advise him to do if he wants to marry Gwendolen? She advises him to acquire some relations as soon as possible and to produce one parent before the season is over.

4. At the end of Act One, what are the *obstacles* that Jack must overcome in his pursuit of Gwendolen? He must convince Lord and Lady Bracknell that he is an acceptable husband for their daughter. Lady Bracknell has informed Jack that he must produce some relatives and at least one parent. He must also get rid of his fictional brother Ernest and tell Gwendolen about his ward Cecily.

What is the first step he intends to take? He intends to kill off his brother Ernest.

Interpreting Meanings

5. In what ways does the brief opening scene with the butler *foreshadow* the *tone* of the play? The dialogue is witty, and the pace is quick. "Serious" topics, such as marriage and class differences, are made light of, as they are throughout the play.

6. Comedies often include a *blocking* figure who opposes the wishes of the young lovers. Who is the blocking figure here, and what is her *motive*? Lady Bracknell is the blocking figure. She is looking out for her daughter's welfare.

7. Give some examples of Wilde's use of *epigrams* in Act One. Which epigrams strike you as the cleverest? Are they only throwaway lines, or do some of them contain a grain of truth? Student answers will vary.

8. What do you look forward to happening next? How has Wilde piqued your curiosity about future events? Student answers will include their eagerness to find out whether Jack and Gwendolen manage to get together and whether Jack's true identity is revealed.

Responding to the Play   Text page 911
Analyzing Act Two
Identifying Facts

1. Where does the second act take place? The second act takes place in Jack's country house, the Manor House.

2. Describe Miss Prism and Dr. Chasuble. Answers will vary. Miss Prism is Cecily's governess, a serious and very wordy woman. Dr. Chasuble is a somewhat addle-brained country rector, her obvious admirer.

3. When Jack arrives, what does he say about his brother Ernest? He announces to Miss Prism and Dr. Chasuble that Ernest is dead.

    How does this soon lead to difficulties? Algernon has already arrived, introducing himself to Cecily as Jack's brother Ernest. Jack is forced to accept Algernon as Ernest, and Algernon soon announces that he is in love with Cecily.

4. What do Gwendolen and Cecily argue about? They argue about Ernest, for both claim to be engaged to him.

    How is their argument swiftly and comically reversed? Their respective lovers come in and are identified. When it is revealed that neither of them is named Ernest, the young women are repulsed and sympathize with each other at their having been deceived. When Jack is forced to admit that he has never had a brother named Ernest, the two women are further united against men.

Interpreting Meanings

5. Name some of the targets of Wilde's *satire* in this act. Among other things, Wilde satirizes the popular literature of his day (three-volume novels), the rector's adaptable sermons, the relationship between men and women, and the notion of falling in love at first sight. Students may have other responses.

6. How does Wilde incorporate the age-old comic *motif* of the "battle of the sexes" in this act? Answers will vary. Students may note the following: Miss Prism seems bent on trying to entrap Dr. Chasuble, while Algernon and Cecily and Jack and Gwendolen move in and out of love very

quickly. Obstacles prevent the lovers from being united, and misunderstandings occur. The young women are depicted as empty-headed and unreasonable.

7. What echoes, or *repetitions*, of the first act occur near the end of the second? Students may note Jack's and Algernon's muffin-eating orgy, which echoes the cucumber-sandwich scene in Act One. Also, at the end of Act One new obstacles arise to prevent the lovers from being united. Students may also point out that identity becomes important. Much of the act is about mistaken identity; both Algernon and Jack are determined to change their identity by being baptized as Ernest.

    What could be the reason for these echoes? Student answers will vary.

Responding to the Play   Text page 920
Analyzing Act Three
Identifying Facts

1. What does Jack reveal that causes Lady Bracknell to change her mind about the proposed marriage of Algernon and Cecily? He reveals that Cecily has about a hundred and thirty thousand pounds in the Funds.

2. What chance remark leads to the revelation that Jack and Algernon are, indeed, brothers? Dr. Chasuble remarks that Miss Prism has been waiting for him in the vestry. Lady Bracknell, overhearing the remark, asks to see Miss Prism.

3. What weddings do we look forward to at the end of the play? Algernon and Cecily, Jack and Gwendolen, and Miss Prism and Dr. Chasuble will marry.

Interpreting Meanings

4. Explain the *irony* of the play's title. There is, of course, a play on the name Ernest and the word earnest. Students should note that instead of demonstrating the importance of being earnest (hard-working, sincere, serious, and intense), the play celebrates wit, idleness, and deception.

5. What clues might have led you to expect, especially from their behavior, that Jack and Algernon were brothers all along? Student responses will vary; they have already noted many similarities in Question 5, Act One. Both young men have invented a fictional character that lets them do as they please. Both are prone to devour cucumber sandwiches and muffins.

6. As an actor or actress, which role would you like to play in *The Importance of Being Earnest*? Which role seems to offer the best comic possibilities? Answers will vary. Ask students to give reasons for their choice.

7. In a *farce*, the situations become so entangled and complicated that the ending is often purely arbitrary or a trick. In ancient Greek and Roman drama, the ending was sometimes brought about by a god descending from the heavens in some kind of device or machine. Hence, these arbitrary endings are called *deus ex machina* endings. Who is the deus ex machina in this play, and were you disappointed in the ending? Miss Prism is the character who enables the play to come to a sudden suprise resolution. Her revelations about Jack's parentage make everything end happily. Student responses may vary as to whether or not they were disappointed.

Was it in keeping with the *tone* of the rest of the play? Explain. Students should agree that the ending is in keeping with the ironic, humorous tone of the play. Their explanations may vary.

The Play as a Whole

1. Look back over the characters' proper names. What is significant about some of them? Responses will vary. Jack is certainly not very Worthy (Worthing). Algernon Moncrieff sounds very upper-class. A *chasuble* is a sleeveless outer garment worn by priests during Mass, an appropriate last name for Dr. Chasuble. Miss Prism's last name suggests that she is very prim or prissy, which she is.

2. Certain strands in Wilde's *plot* are so often found in comedy that they might be called elements of comedy. How does Wilde use these comic motifs: disguise; mistaken identity; mysterious parentage; triangle of boy-girl-and-obstinate-parent? In what ways are these motifs used today? Responses will vary. Students should note that these devices are typical of much of comedy. The series of

obstacles that separate the lovers are finally overcome, and the play ends in the lovers' impending marriage—in this case, three marriages.

3. Wilde hints several times that the play is not to be taken seriously. What are these hints? The play's subtitle is *A Trivial Comedy for Serious People*. Students may point out passages, such as the dialogue between Jack and Algernon near the end of Act One, that begins with Jack saying, "I am sick to death of cleverness. Everybody is clever nowadays . . . ."

In spite of them, do you think the play may have a serious message, or theme? What might it be? Student responses will vary.

Extending the Play

During the Victorian era, the "beard" regained popularity. This seems appropriate when one asseses the contrast between the private behavior and the public facade that the time was known for and the play takes issue with. The beard, like appearance in general, often serves as disguise. Ask students to discuss the various ways that appearances can serve as masks. The subject of masks and appearance is a wonderful one for classroom interaction. Suggest that the students paint or describe in an essay a mask they have used in a particular situation and the self that was safely (or not so safely) hidden behind the mask. Encourage students to discuss the many different reasons that people use facades. Often we act differently with friends, parents, siblings, teachers, and bosses. Why do we do this? Is it ever necessary, or should we always present ourselves in the same way?

The English Language

After your students read "The English Language: One Language—Many Nations," ask them to discuss their perception of English as a universal language. If there are students in your class who have traveled outside the United States, ask them what language they spoke in the countries they visited. Was it necessary for them to learn the language of the countries? Where in their travels did people speak English? Cities? Towns? Rural areas? In shops? Restaurants? Airports? Train stations?

It has been proposed that a special international language, Esperanto, be used worldwide. This language, invented by Russian physician, Dr. L.L. Zamenhof in 1887, is based on many European languages and is intended to be relatively

easy to master. People from all over the world have debated whether or not Esperanto would be a positive move away from English as the major international language. Ask students how they feel about the idea of Esperanto. How do they feel it would affect the political power play around the world? How would it effect Americans?

Dialects of English exist between and within countries. In fact, dialects exist within states and even within counties. Expressions and pronunciations popular in one area may be unfamiliar several miles away. Students who have moved to your school district from different counties, states, and countries will be especially helpful in this area. Ask students if they notice different accents and ways of speaking among their friends and classmates. Can students determine where other students grew up because of the way they speak? Emphasize that there is no one way of speaking that is better than another. Mention that we often pick up expressions and speech mannerisms from the people around us; in fact, that is how language changes through time. Ask each student to give an example of a way of speaking that they picked up from someone who grew up outside of their home.

Exercises in Critical Thinking and Writing

Text page 925

Before having the students begin their work on this exercise, discuss with them the idea of generalizations. Point out that generalizations are often easy to make—and are therefore somewhat dangerous. It is important always to examine assumptions and question generalizations; otherwise, we run the risk of believing and espousing ideas that may be dishonest or false.

Tell the students that the exercise deals with *valid* generalizations made in response to literature. Tell them that their task will be to develop and write an argument that states and supports a valid generalization about a work they have read in this unit.

Go over the material in the Background section, making sure that the students fully understand what a valid generalization is. As they begin the prewriting process, have them study the model essay that is provided; this will give them a good idea of how to organize their own essays. Encourage the students, as always, to think through their arguments and to take the time to outline their thoughts, even if only in rough form. After they have finished writing a first draft, have them read it over and make any necessary corrections or adjustments in spelling, punctuation, and style. Then have them prepare a clean final copy.

Criteria for Evaluating the Assignments. Student essays should open with a clear thesis statement that gives the generalizations that the rest of the essay will develop and support. The generalizations themselves should take the form of a personal opinion or response to the work. From there on, the essays should be logical and coherently organized. Each subsequent point or statement should be supported by specific evidence from the text. Quotations should be precise, relevant, and as brief as possible. Check to see that the students have quoted accurately and have taken care to reread and proofread what they have written.

Suggestions for Teaching and Evaluating the Writing Assignments

A Creative Response

In this unit, students will be asked to respond creatively to their reading in numerous different ways. Activities range from extending poems and narratives to imitating styles and techniques to composing a melody, drawing illustrations, and writing a screenplay. In general, be sure that the students understand the primary objectives of the assignments and their relation to the selections they have read. Where an extension or an imitation is called for, you might first go over with the students some of the distinguishing characteristics of the writing they have studied. For the more creative assignments (such as writing a screenplay or composing a melody), you should encourage the students to be as fanciful as they like to be: after all, the point of these assignments is to be creative, and the work should be fun.

Criteria for Evaluating the Assignments. Student responses should be genuine and imaginative and should reflect an understanding of the purpose of the task and the nature of the material to which the students are responding. Effective creative responses should demonstrate an effort at originality and sound preparation.

A Critical Response

Students will be asked to respond to their reading by analyzing language, structure, character, setting, point of view, and theme. For several assignments, they will be called on to write a full analysis of a selection or to compare and contrast two selections or writers. Go over each assignment with the students before they begin to write. Make sure that they understand the purpose of the assignment and its connection to the piece they have studied (especially where a particular element or technique has been introduced). Encourage them to write at least a rough outline that organizes their thoughts, so that they will have something to refer to as they write.

Criteria for Evaluating the Assignments. Student responses should, in general, be logical and well organized. They should open with a clear thesis statement and move fluidly from there on. Where students are working with a particular literary technique or element that has been introduced, their essays should reflect comprehension of that element and of its use in the selection. Where students are asked to make specific references to a text, their quotations should be accurate, and rules of proper documentation should be followed. Finally, student papers should show that care has been taken to reread and proofread the copy.

Answers to Analyzing Language

Analyzing Language and Style

Text page 871

Portmanteau Words

Smog is a combination of *smoke* and *fog*.
Moped is a combination of *motor* and *pedal*.
Motel is a combination of *motorist* and *hotel*.

Galumph is a combination of *gallop* and *triumph* and was coined by Lewis Carroll.
Chortle is a combination of *chuckle* and *snort* and was coined by Lewis Carroll.
Splurge is a combination of *splash* and *surge*.

Analyzing Language and Style

Text page 920

Puns and Paradoxes

After the class discussion on epigrams (described above in Creative Response), relate to the class that in general epigrams arc not only witty remarks. Epigrams first originated in Ancient Greece, where they were used for epitaphs and eulogies. They were short poems used to summarize a feeling or observation in a permanent manner. During Shakespeare's time, Ben Jonson was the master of the epigram in the English language, and he used them to express a philosophical idea, friendship, and satire, as well as for epitaphs and eulogies. It is the classical epigram, from the Elizabethan period, that is known for its satirical content usually embodied in a short two-part poem. Wilde's use of the epigram certainly carries on this tradition. They are filled with puns and paradoxes that constantly call attention to language itself and the meaning of things. What is spectacular about the play on words and the seemingly contradictory remarks is that they are filled with such honesty and truth.

Describe and discuss the meanings of puns and paradoxes with the students. Wilde once said, "A Truth in Art is that whose contradictory is also true. The Truths of metaphysics are the Truths of masks." (*Oscar Wilde*, edited by Richard Ellman, Prentice-Hall, 1969, p. 115) How does Wilde's use of paradoxes in the play exemplify this belief?

1. paradox
2. pun
3. paradox
4. paradox

Have students read aloud the other puns and paradoxes they have found.

Unit Seven: *The Twentieth Century*

Teaching Twentieth-Century Literature

Modern British Literature actually had its genesis in the last decade of the nineteenth century. From that time on, writers came to be concerned with the individual and society as a whole. Many pieces of literature focused on the lonely, isolated, and thoughtful individual, fighting to find peace and security in a world that often offered neither. Literature seemed to turn away from the idealism nurtured by the Romantic movement and refocused instead on social and moral issues. Much literature began to deal with the psychological nature of human beings. With the early 1900s also came the first so-called "World War," and with it the desire and need to look inward in the hopes of securing some understanding of human nature. Thus, the literature of this period mirrors that need as well.

In technique, the early twentieth century was a period of experimentation. Such devices as stream of consciousness, advanced by writers like James Joyce and Virginia Woolf, came into currency. The character's psychological makeup was elevated to a level of pre-eminence in fiction previously enjoyed by plot and story line. Disenfranchisement from a world that was uncaring to start with began to turn up regularly as a thematic strand.

The poetry of the twentieth century plays on the same theme. In the works of poets such as Dylan Thomas and T. S. Eliot, one can discern the writer's dissatisfaction with his place in society. Yet, the ultimate goal of the twentieth-century writer should not be construed as an acceptance of societal evils but—as was more often than not the case—a search for solutions.

Students should be made aware early on that twentieth-century British fiction follows the same basic criteria established for all fiction; thus, you may wish to begin with a good definition. *The Handbook to Literature* explains that fiction is "narrative writing drawn from the imagination of the author rather than from history or fact." It also explains that the pupose of fiction is to entertain, or be interesting. It also may be written to instruct, to edify, to persuade, or to arouse. As you teach this unit, ask students to determine the likely purpose of each selection they read.

Before beginning a study of literature, be sure to have students read the introductory essays regarding twentieth-century British literature. These essays provide clear, succinct insights into important events in British history and into the writers of importance during the modern period.

Objectives of the Twentieth-Century Unit

1. To improve reading proficiency and expand vocabulary

2. To gain exposure to notable authors and works of the period

3. To define and identify significant literary techniques: elements of the short story (plot, character, setting, point of view), theme, mood, and tone

4. To interpret and respond to fiction and poetry, orally and in writing, through analysis of its elements

5. To practice the following critical thinking and writing skills:
   a. Extending a short story beyond its ending
   b. Analyzing a story's theme
   c. Analyzing a character in a story
   d. Comparing and contrasting characters
   e. Evaluating the point of view chosen by a writer
   f. Writing a comparison of poems
   g. Imitating a writer's technique
   h. Analyzing dialogue
   i. Analyzing an adaptation
   j. Responding to criticism

Joseph Conrad
Text page 935

The detail that ought to be stressed as you review the introductory material on Conrad with the students is that English was *not* the writer's first language. Impress the point on students by asking for a show of hands of those students who believe themselves to be fluent, or at least capable of sustaining a conversation, in a second language. Ask those students to imagine themselves attempting a piece of fiction in that language, keeping in mind the many demands that the writing of an effective short story carries with it—the development of character through subtle nuances, the use of vivid imagery, and so on. Then proceed to the reading.

Objectives

1. To explain a character's motivation

2. To analyze symbolism

3. To identify allusions

4. To identify and analyze point of view

5. To describe atmosphere and mood

6. To write an extension of the story

7. To write analyses of theme, character, and imagery

8. To write an essay interpreting the story's ending

Introducing the Novel

In outline form, for your reference, here are the major elements in the novel:

- **Protagonists:** The captain, Leggatt
- **Antagonist:** The tribulations induced by a secret, self-doubt
- **Conflict:** person vs. self
- **Point of view:** third-person omniscient
- **Significant techniques:** motivation, symbolism, allusion, point of view, atmosphere, mood
- **Setting:** aboard a ship

Background on the Novel.   Before reading *The Secret Sharer*, students should know that the story is a study into the psychological makeup of two men: the captain and Leggatt. The captain's main problem is his inability to believe in himself and in his capabilities. When he assumes command of the ship, he is full of self-doubt. When Leggatt appears, the captain looks to him as someone who will have empathy for him. He comes to view Leggatt as a secret sharer, seeing him as an idealized version of himself. However, the captain begins assuming actual command of the ship as time passes. When Leggatt insists that he must leave for the captain's own good and for his own, the captain finally agrees, seeing Leggatt as a proud swimmer striking out for a new destiny. In both men, readers see examples of humans outside the boundaries of traditional society.

The Plot.   *The Secret Sharer* is a story offering psychological insight into the nature of isolated, alienated individuals. Leggatt appears mysteriously on the captain's ship, makes the captain face himself and his own abilities, and leaves before authorities overtake him for a murder he once committed. By the end of the story, Leggatt has become a more sympathetic person, and the captain has overcome self-doubt.

Teaching Strategies

Providing for Cultural Differences.   Your students may not have had experiences on the sea, but they will have experienced self-doubt. You may wish to discuss the setting of the story, but explain that the physical setting is not nearly as important as the emotional setting. In one way, though, the nautical aspect of the story may be a thematic representation of the captain's struggles in finding himself.

Providing for Different Levels of Ability.   If you have several slow readers, you may wish to have the story read aloud. For better students, you may wish to spend time discussing critical approaches to the story. Wilfred L. Guerin's *A Handbook of Critical Approaches to Literature* (New York, 1979) offers a fine discussion of the psychological approach. In any case, you will want to discuss changes that occur in both the captain and in Leggatt and the causes for those changes.

Introducing Vocabulary Study.   Students will benefit from knowing the meanings of the following words before they read the excerpt.

arduous	impassive
cadaverous	incredulity
confabulation	pestiferous
evanescent	superfluously
felicitous	tenacity
immaculate	urbanely

Reading the Story.   If possible, students should read the story in one sitting, in order to notice easily the changes in the captain's nature. Make sure to emphasize that the story contains a story line, rather than a plot.

Reteaching Alternatives.   Holman's *Handbook to Literature* (Bobbs-Merrill, 1972) discusses conflict in literature. You may wish to read and discuss that passage with students, pointing out excerpts from the story that support the conflict of person versus self.

Responding to the Novel   Text page 962
Analyzing the Novel
Identifying Facts

1. The captain (the ''I'' of this story) tells us that he ''had been appointed to the command only a fortnight before.'' What is the captain's relationship with the rest of the crew, especially with the chief mate and the second mate? The captain feels like a stranger to them. He suspects that the chief mate and the second mate are privately chuckling over his inexperience.

How does the captain feel about himself and his new career? The captain feels diffident and tentative as he confronts the "novel responsibility of command." At the same time, he feels excited and looks forward to this new stage of his career.

2. Outline the details of Leggatt's story. What, if any, are the excruciating circumstances of his crime? Leggatt served as a chief mate on the *Sephora*. In the middle of a terrific storm, he was struggling to set a reefed foresail when one of the crewmen, who had been habitually impudent, started an altercation with him. Leggatt hit the insubordinate sailor, who then rushed to attack him. In the struggle, Leggatt throttled the man to death. The captain then dismissed him from his post as chief mate and confined him in his quarters, saying that Leggatt would have to be put off the ship and surrendered to the authorities. Leggatt, however, slipped overboard, and managed to swim to the captain's ship.

3. Why is Archbold seeking Leggatt, when Leggatt really saved the ship? Archbold is a stickler for the law, and he is also afraid of a blot on his own career.

4. How do the captain's thoughts and feelings toward his crew change after he has hidden Leggat on board? He comes stealthy, secretive, and apprehensive.

How does the crew perceive the captain? The inexplicable oddities and eccentricities of the captain's behavior cause the crew to be suspicious of him. He reflects that some of them probably think he has been drinking.

Interpreting Meanings

5. The captain risks his ship and his career to help Leggatt. What are his *motivations* for taking these risks? Student answers will vary. In general, the captain is motivated by his compassion and his feeling of kinship with Leggatt. He thinks that both he and Leggatt are "strangers" and outsiders. He is struck by their remarkable physical resemblance. And he admires Leggatt's courage.

What does he gain in the end? Has he lost anything? Explain. Again, student answers will vary. The captain gains the satisfaction of knowing that he has succeeded in helping Leggatt. Since Leggatt is repeatedly described as the narrator's "double," the captain has also, in some sense, helped himself. The end of the story, featuring Leggatt's hat, also implies that the captain has achieved a new-found confidence in his handling of his ship: he now knows much more precisely than before what the ship is capable of and how to maneuver her. Students may suggest, however, that with the disappearance of Leggatt into the unknown, the captain has symbolically lost a part of himself as well: his innocence, perhaps.

6. A meeting with one's double is a recurring motif in literature. What passages indicate that Leggatt is the captain's double? How is Leggatt like the captain, and how is he different? There are numerous passages in the story that indicate that Leggatt is the captain's double. First, the two men are both young, dark, and remarkably similar in their physical appearance. The captain dresses Leggatt in a sleeping suit that is identical to his own. They occupy the same quarters, eat the same food, and sleep in the same bed. The captain says at one point that he felt "more dual than ever." The narrator refers to Leggatt several times as the "secret sharer" of his life, echoing the title of the story. Finally, the captain senses a kinship in their position vis-a-vis the crew as the "only two strangers on board." However, Leggatt is unlike the captain in that the captain is a figure of authority, whereas Leggatt is a fugitive. The captain's admiration for Leggatt's long swim implies that Leggatt may be athletically superior to the captain.

When a character meets his double, he usually gains a new perspective; the meeting often changes his life, for better or worse. How do these aspects of the "double" motif apply to *The Secret Sharer*? Students may suggest that, as a result of his experience with Leggatt, the captain has grown in maturity and achieved more profound understanding, both of his ship and of the moral factors involved in Leggatt's "crime."

7. Leggatt is an excellent swimmer, so there was no need for the ship to go so dangerously close to land. Why, then, do you think the captain sailed his ship so near to the black hill of Koh-ring? The story implies that the captain had to take the risk so that he could prove to himself that he was capable of sacrifice and of confronting danger.

8. One famous critic of Conrad, H. W. Stallman, writes that "everything in *The Secret Sharer* is charged with symbolic purpose." What *symbolic* significance can you find in the captain's floppy white hat? The hat is a symbol of pity and salvation.

In Leggatt's sleeping suit? The sleeping suit symbolizes the "double" motif, since it is identical to the captain's own.

In the sea itself? The sea may be held to symbolize danger and the unknown.

9. Locate in *The Secret Sharer* the several *allusions* to the Biblical story of Cain and Abel. Is the "brand of Cain" a punishment worse than death, or is it also a blessing? What do these allusions contribute to your understanding of Conrad's story? The first allusion to Cain and Abel occurs toward the end of section I of the story, when Leggatt explains to the captain why Archbold's wife would have been only too glad to have him (Leggatt) off the ship. The second allusion occurs when Leggatt refers to the Biblical words about Cain, "driven off the face of the earth" (see Genesis 4:12), and says that he wishes to be marooned at night: he would rather take his chances at starting a new life than having to face an English jury. Students will differ in their reactions to the significance of the "brand of Cain" in the story. Conrad perhaps intends these references to be ambiguous. Ask the students to support their opinions in class.

10. In his letter to Richard Curle (see Primary Sources, next page), Conrad complains that the classification of his stories as "sea yarns" causes readers to overlook the stories' true subject matter. He worries that Americans, especially, will fail to see past the nautical settings. *The Secret Sharer* **is, of course, set on board a ship, yet it is not primarily about ships or the sea. How would you state the theme of** *The Secret Sharer*? **Did you find the theme easy to overlook, or do you think Conrad made it obvious?** Most students will agree that Conrad has deliberately conveyed the theme in an oblique fashion, perhaps in an effort to parallel the captain's gradual maturation process. One statement of the theme might run as follows: It is only by confronting the danger of our dark side and of the unknown that we can achieve a fully mature moral sense in life.

11. From what *point of view* **is The Secret Sharer told?** The novel is told from the first-person point of view of the captain.

How does this point of view affect the impact of the story? The point of view adds vividness and immediacy to the story.

Does it have any limitations? Explain. The limitations are that we cannot know for sure what Leggatt and the other characters are thinking and how they are reacting. The result is to reinforce the impression of Leggatt in the story as something of a "mystery" figure.

12. The first three paragraphs of this story have often been analyzed. How would you describe the *atmosphere* **or** *mood* **created by these paragraphs?** The mood might be described as exotic, mysterious, and disturbing.

What details contribute to that mood? Among the details students may cite are the following: the "incomprehensible" lines of fishing stakes, the barren islets, the setting sun, the description of the Paknam pagoda, the image of the "impassive earth" swallowing the tug, the immense stillness, the breathless silence, the sudden tide of darkness, and the "disturbing sounds" heard by the captain.

Extending the Novel

You may ask students to find information concerning Conrad's own experiences on the sea. Among other books, *British Writers and Their Works No. 10* (Lincoln: U of Nebraska P, 1966) offers such information.

Primary Sources   Text page 963

"I wish that all those ships of mine were give a rest."

Before having students read these comments by Conrad, ask whether they feel it would be accurate to describe *The Secret Sharer* as a sea story. After they do the reading, discuss why Conrad might have been so irritated that his works were categorized this way. What headings might Conrad have preferred to see on the press notices for his books?

Hector Hugh Munro (Saki)   Text page 964

Sredni Vashtar   Text page 965

Objectives

1. To understand the development of characterization, both direct and indirect

2. To identify theme

3. To analyze dramatic irony in the story

4. To determine aspects of situational and dramatic irony in the story

5. To write a new beginning or end to the story

6. To write a response to a critical comment

Introducing the Story

In outline form, for your reference, here are the major elements in the story:

- **Protagonists:** Conradin
- **Antagonist:** Mrs. De Ropp
- **Conflict:** person vs. person
- **Point of view:** third-person omniscient
- **Significant techniques:** characterization, theme, irony
- **Setting:** the home of Mrs. De Ropp

Background of the Story. You may wish to discuss acts of desperation. Ask students to consider times in which they have not had a clear, simple answer to a problem. You may also wish to discuss the concept of faith and its importance in worship. Further, you may discuss reality and imagination and how we separate the two. This discussion can lead your students into talks about the nature of the two main characters: Conradin, who represents imagination and escape from reality, and Mrs. De Ropp, who represents the real world which Conradin hates violently.

The Plot. Conradin, a ten-year old boy, comes to realize that his guardian, Mrs. De Ropp, does not like him and even enjoys tormenting him. She actually thwarts him for his own good, which she considers "a duty which she did not find completely irksome." In order to escape reality, Conradin goes often to a woodshed, where he houses a hen and a large polecat-ferret named Sredni Vashtar. Conradin leaves the hen alone, but offers prayers and worship to the polecat, whom he views as being strong against Mrs. De Ropp. After having taken away the hen, Mrs. De Ropp tells Conradin that she will also take away whatever he has housed in the cage. Conradin watches the door to the barn, seeing his guardian go inside and Sredni Vashtar come out. The story is one of triumph of imagination over reality, as we see the "underdog" win against what he has considered heavy obstacles.

Teaching Strategies

Providing for Cultural Differences. You may wish to obtain a guide to the practices of religions that worship animals, in order to provide a background for students unfamiliar with such practices. Further, you may discuss Saki's writing in general, which often tells of animals righting the wrongs perpetrated by humans. For instance, in his novel, *When William Came*, Saki has one of his characters make the following statement: "Animals . . . accepted the world as it was and made the best of it, and children, at least nice children, uncontaminated by grown-up influences, lived in worlds of their own making."

Providing for Different Levels of Ability. Slower classes may find it helpful to see the roles of Conradin and Mrs. De Ropp acted out before them. Then you may discuss with them the motivations that lead each character to act in the manners related in the story.

Introducing Vocabulary Study. Students will benefit from knowing the meanings of the following words before they read the story.

furtive   wistful
paean

Reading the Story. Slower classes may find it helpful if you assign the role of narrator to one student, while others take the parts of Conradin and Mrs. De Ropp. Whether you choose this strategy, ask students to read the story in one sitting; it is short enough to do so, and this will help create and maintain suspense and interest.

Reteaching Alternatives. Able students may read other short stories by Saki, and you may lead discussions about the juxtaposition of realism and imagination in these works. Or you may ask those students to discuss Saki's use of animals in each respective work. Further, you may wish to secure a copy of *When William Came* and read the extended passage in which the previously-stated comment about animals is made. You may discuss with students that character's own perceptions about animals. Then, determine from your discussions what general statement can be made regarding Saki's own views of animals and their relationships to humans.

Responding to the Story   Text page 968
Analyzing the Story
Identifying Facts

1. Praying to a wild animal seems an act born of desperation. What desperate circumstances in Conradin's life have led up to this behavior? Conradin is lonely and alienated from his aunt, who regiments his life. He has also been told by the doctor that it would be surprising if he lived for five years. The imaginative, sensitive child has no friends or playmates.

2. What prompts Mrs. De Ropp to offer Conradin toast at teatime? She feels guilty about having told Conradin that the hen has been taken away and sold.

What is her excuse for not making toast more often? She thinks that toast is bad for Conradin; she also thinks that making toast "makes trouble."

3. What does Conradin do after he sees Sredni Vashtar emerge from the doorway and vanish into the undergrowth? He makes himself a piece of toast and enjoys eating it.

Interpreting Meanings

4. Saki develops his characters by using both *direct characterization*, in which he states directly what the characters are like, and *indirect characterization*, in which he lets the characters' actions speak for themselves. Find examples in the story of both kinds of character description. Students should be able to find copious examples of both methods of characterization.

How would you summarize the aunt's character? The aunt is cruel and insensitive.

5. What would you say is Saki's message, or theme, in telling this strange story? One statement of the theme might be: you corner a person or animal at your peril.

6. Munro's sister (see Primary Sources, next page) says that people detect an element of cruelty in his stories. Do you see any cruelty in this story? If so, at whom is the cruelty directed, and what is its nature? Many students may agree with this comment, suggesting that the aunt's behavior is cruel and that the boy's "prayer" for her death is also cruel. Saki's cruelty is really directed, however, at the insensitivy of the aunt.

7. *Situational irony* refers to a twist of events—a contradiction between what is expected and what happens. Why is there such irony in Conradin's worship of an animal in a locked cage? The behavior presents "religion" in a ludicrous, unexpected context.

What other situational ironies exist in "Sredni Vashtar"? It is ironic that the aunt is actually killed by the ferret, and also that Conradin is presented as eating toast with such evident pleasure at the end of the story.

8. Find in the story an example of *dramatic irony*, in which an event reveals something to the readers that a character does not realize. Explain how your example shows dramatic irony. The conclusion of the story, in which we learn of the aunt's death but Conradin remains ignorant of it, is an example of dramatic irony.

9. An expert on modern British literature once said that the mark of an excellent critic is knowing how to ask the right questions. List the questions that you would ask readers of this story. Student answers will vary. Ask the students to explain the reasons for the questions on their lists.

Extending the Story

You may wish students to write their own story that involves the juxtaposition and/or merging of reality and imagination. Also, you may wish to locate and read in class one of Saki's other short stories, discussing its theme and structure as you did those aspects in "Sredni Vashtar."

Further Reading

Students desiring further information on Saki should be directed to Charles H. Gillen's *H. H. Munro (Saki)* (New York, 1969). The book provides background information on Saki's life and discusses his "acid wit, his singular fantasies, his highly unsusual viewpoint."

James Joyce

Text page 970

To help students appreciate the contribution of Joyce to English fiction, it might be instructive to have them reread a short story or other short piece of fiction by a writer of much earlier vintage. Have them discuss, afterwards, any differences between the two styles that were particularly noteworthy. If possible, you might also wish to obtain a videocassette of the film version of Joyce's short story *The Dead*, to show and discuss with your students.

Araby

Text page 973

Objectives

1. To describe setting and atmosphere
2. To identify connotations of the title word
3. To identify the theme of the story
4. To identify irony
5. To describe the writer's tone
6. To identify details of plot and setting
7. To rewrite the story with a new setting
8. To write an analysis of the story
9. To write an analysis of a character and of theme

Introducing the Story

In outline form, for your reference, here are the major elements in the story:

- **Protagonists:** a preadolescent boy
- **Antagonist:** his crush on the girl next door
- **Conflict:** person vs. self
- **Point of view:** third-person omniscient

- **Significant techniques:** theme, irony, setting, character
- **Setting:** a community in Dublin, Ireland

Background of the Story. Students should be aware that "Araby" is one of several short stories that comprise *The Dubliners*. You may wish to read aloud the following passage from David Daiches's *A Critical History of English Literature* (New York, 1960): "Joyce began, in the collection of short stories he called *Dubliners* (1914), with carefully etched pictures of Dublin life which were meticulously realistic in detail and atmosphere and at the same time had a symbolic relation to the other stories, the whole constituting not only (as he claimed) a picture of 'the centre of the paralysis' but a projection of the basic crises of human experience and the archetypal rituals with which men confront them." Thus, you may help students realize that, in "Araby," they are seeing only the smallest sampling of Joyce's overall efforts in writing short stories. In the character-narrator of "Araby," we come to discern a human crisis in the eyes of a youth.

The Plot. Because a boy's uncle has stopped at a bar on the way home from work, the youth cannot arrive at a bazaar in time to buy a gift for a girl he likes. After arriving at the bazaar, he determines that he is too late to purchase a gift and looks at the closing through the disillusioned eyes of a youth given little consideration by his adult relative.

Teaching Strategies

Providing For Cultural Differences. Because this story transcends the Dublin of Joyce's day, students should be able to identify with the youth's disillusion and frustration. Still, you may wish to provide some background concerning Ireland and its customs and people.

Providing for Different Levels of Abililty. For better classes, you may wish to discuss narrative focalization more fully. If so, refer to the annotated bibliography at the end of this discussion, which refers to Magill's critical studies. For weaker students, you must be aware that Joyce can provide difficulties as readers look for action and find little. Thus, you may need to emphasize the fact that depiction of character sometimes, especially in British literature, can be more important than action. Ask students to consider just what Joyce was trying to convey to his readers. What important events have occurred in the youth's life, and what effect are these events likely to have?

Introducing Vocabulary Study. Students will benefit from knowing the following words before they read the story.

chalice	imperturbable
derided	litany
garrulous	

Reading the Story. You may wish to read the story aloud or have a student do so. For students unfamiliar with Joyce's unique style of writing, hearing the story and reading it simultaneously may help in reader understanding.

Reteaching Alternatives. You may wish students to relate times in which they have had experiences similar to the one had by the youth in "Araby." Ask them to discuss how they felt at the time and what their experiences taught them. They may choose to compare themselves to the narrator, or to contrast their experiences with his. You may also choose to discuss question 12 under Responding to the Story in their text.

Responding to the Story   Text page 978
Analyzing the Story
Identifying Facts

1. Who is the narrator of the story? The narrator is an adult who remembers an episode from his childhood.

Is the narrator the same age as the hero? Find evidence to support your answer. The narrator is older than the hero, This fact is indicated by the narration of the story in the past tense.

2. The first two-and-a-half paragraphs describe the *setting* and establish the story's *atmosphere*. List the specific sensory adjectives in these paragraphs. (You should be able to find at least thirty, excluding such adjectives as two, former, few, its, all.) Sensory adjectives include: quiet, square, brown, imperturbable, musty, old, curled, damp, yellow, wild, straggling, rusty, short, somber, feeble, cold, silent, dark, muddy, rough, dripping, odorous, buckled.

What colors are named? Colors include yellow, brown, and violet.

Which adjectives paint a gloomy scene? Among the adjectives painting a gloomy scene are brown, somber, rusty, musty, old, damp, wild, rough, muddy, silent, dark, and feeble.

Which adjectives are repeated? Among the repeated adjectives are silent and dark.

3. Describe the object of the hero's "quest." What are the obstacles that keep him from getting to the bazaar on time? The object of the "quest" is to buy a gift at the bazaar for Mangan's sister. The obstacles include the uncle's lateness, Mrs. Mercer's visit, the train's delay, and the narrator's failure to find a sixpenny entrance to the bazaar.

4. Cite the sentence that tells you what *connotations* the word Araby had for the hero. The sentence is "The syllables of the word Araby were called to me through the silence in which my soul luxuriated and cast an Eastern enchantment over me" (page 975).

In your own words, describe in detail what he actually discovered the bazaar to be like. He found the bazaar to be a great dark hall, with most of the stalls closed. Only a few people were there, and the hall was eerily silent.

Interpreting Meanings

5. Has the main character changed by the story's end? Use details from the story to support your answer. Most students will agree that the main character has changed, because he has recognized his romantic dreams to be illusions. He feels a sense of burning shame for having indulged this "vanity."

6. How often have the hero and Mangan's sister spoke to each other? How would you describe the hero's relationship with her? The narrator has spoken only a few casual words to Mangan's sister. The relationship might be described as a case of unrequited "puppy love."

7. In what ways are the lives of these characters narrow or restricted? Student answers will vary. Students may point out that the elders control the children strictly, and that the children's only recreation seems to be playing on their street in the city.

8. How does the hero deal with intrusions of reality into his fantasy—at the market, for example, or at school? At the market, the hero imagines that he bears his "chalice" safely through a throng of foes. At school, his thoughts wander, and he considers the classwork "child's play" because it stands between him and his desire.

9. What do you think is the purpose of including the dead priest in the story? The inclusion of the dead priest further accentuates the gloominess of the hero's house and the drabness of the surroundings.

List all the other religious references you can find in the story. What do you think they contribute to the significance of the boy's quest? The boy imagines himself bearing a "chalice" in the market; the aunt says that the narrator may not be able to go to the bazaar because he will have to stay in on "this night of our Lord," and she hopes that the bazaar is not a "Freemason affair"; Magnan's sister cannot go to the bazaar because of a retreat at her convent. Students will differ in their opinions about what these references contribute to the significance of the boy's quest.

10. In what ways could the story be seen as presenting a conflict between romance and reality? Ask students to defend their opinions. Many students may suggest that the boy's vision of Mangan's sister and his concept of *Araby* represent romance, while his disappointment at the bazaar and his failure to buy the gift represent reality.

How would you state the *theme* of the story? (In your statement of theme, use the word *Araby*.) Statements of the theme may vary.

11. What do you see as the central *irony* in this story? The central irony is that the boy's vision of a beautiful, intriguingly exotic place (*Araby*) turns out to be reversed: the bazaar is quiet, dreary, and disappointing.

How would you describe the writer's *tone*—his attitude toward the characters and what happens to them? Student answers will vary. On the whole, the tone might be described as sympathetic and melancholy.

12. The story is set many years ago in Dublin. Does it relate to American life today? If it were set in America in the 1980's, would any details of *plot* have to change? Would the *characters* have to be different, or would they remain the same? Explain. Student answers will vary. Most students may agree that the central motif of "Araby" as an exotic bazaar would have to be changed.

Extending the Story

Students may consider the following quotation made by Lillian Hellman at the end of her last memoir: "I have written here that I have recovered. I mean it only in a worldly sense because I do not believe in recovery. The past, with its pleasures, its rewards, its foolishness, its punishments, is there for each of us forever, and it should be.

"As I finish writing about [the McCarthy era], I tell myself that was then, and there is now, and the years between then and now, and the then and now are one."

Ask students whether the older narrator of "Araby" feels as Hellman states she does, or if the narrator in Joyce's work differs from Hellman. Discuss reasons students have for their beliefs.

The Elements of Fiction   Text page 978

Irony

This passage offers a clear, careful review of the principal forms of irony, as well as a thorough and illuminating explication of the story "Araby." If students find the Respond-

ing to the Story questions particularly difficult, have them read this passage before answering them. To check your students' comprehension of the concept of irony and of the story's central meaning, ask them to explain what irony of situation and what dramatic irony "Araby" contains.

Ezra Pound Reviews *Dubliners*

Pound's provocative statements are likely to challenge many of your students' assumptions. Ask them to summarize the arguments Pound makes in Joyce's favor. By contrast, what kind of literature does Pound object to? Pound describes "Araby" as a "vivid waiting"; what does he mean by this phrase? Do students agree that such a thing is preferable to a "story"? (Explain the allusion to Guy de Maupassant, the nineteenth-century French writer famous for short stories with ironic plot twists; students may be familiar with his tale "The Necklace.")

From A Portrait of the Artist as a Young Man   Text page 980

Objectives

1. To understand the "stream-of-consciousness" technique, the reasons for its use, and its effect

2. To determine the point of view of the selection

3. To describe and analyze tone

4. To write a passage using the stream-of-consciousness technique

5. To write a comparison of two characters

Introducing the Story

In outline form, for your reference, here are the major elements in the story:

- **Protagonist:** Stephen Dedalus
- **Antagonist:** his struggles at adjusting to a new environment
- **Conflict:** person vs. self
- **Point of view:** third-person omniscient
- **Significant techniques:** point of view, tone
- **Setting:** a schoolyard, County Kildare, Ireland

Background on the Novel. Before students begin reading the excerpt from *A Portrait of the Artist*, it is imperative that you explain the three literary terms detailed below under Reading the Story. Without such explanation previous to their study, most students will not be able to understand Joyce's writing.

Also, it is important to note the symbolic meaning of both Stephen's home town and his school. In Joyce's novel, the two represent a stifling existence for the artist living in Ireland. Stephen, the six-year-old, represents Joyce as he attempted in his own life to cope with his differences from those about him.

The Plot. You should point out to students that Joyce's masterpiece emphasizes characterization much more than external action. To understand the implications of this statement, please refer to the section below that explains the psychological novel. The passage included in the student text follows Stephen first on a day in his own neighborhood, trying to cope with others about him. The action then moves to the playground of Clongowes Wood College, an elementary school where Stephen tries to interact with other boys and encounters numerous problems.

Teaching Strategies

Providing for Cultural Differences. Most of your students will have had little experience reading stream-of-consciousness fiction. Some may have read Faulkner's *The Sound and the Fury*. If so, you may wish to read a section of Quentin's interior monologue and discuss the narrator's representation of the thought processes in the character's mind. However, even if students have read *The Sound and the Fury*, they will have had little or no other contact with such novels. You then may wish to discuss the fact, as Holman states it, that "In the twentieth century, with the advance of psychology as a science, [the psychological novel and its reliance on interior monologue] has come into popular use. Freudianism particularly gave impetus to the type." If you can locate a brief, general description of Freud's beliefs in this area, students may find the tangential information interesting and possibly helpful in understanding Joyce's work.

Providing for Different Levels of Ability. Slower students may have serious difficulty in understanding *A Portrait of the Artist*, especially if you assign the reading of the selection on their own. You may wish to spend time on a class reading, rather than delving into the more intricate concepts inherent in the stream-of-consciousness technique and the psychological novel in general. For more able students, the latter approach may provide an impetus toward learning more about writers such as Joyce, Woolf, Faulkner, and others.

Reading the Novel. Refer students to the three terms that follow and, as the ability of your students permits, discuss the explanations of the terms, relating each to a *Portrait of the Artist*. The explanations originated with C. Hugh Holman and may be found in *A Handbook to Literature* (New York, 1972).

Psychological novel. Prose fiction in which heavy emphasis is placed on "interior characterization." The narrator considers not only external action, but the motives, circumstances, an internal action of a character. "The psychological novel is not content to state what happens but goes on to explain the why of this action." Some psychological novels rely on the narrator-character's use of interior monologue, explained below.

Interior monologue. A technique of the narrator that allows the recording of "internal, emotional experience of the character on any one level or on combinations of several levels of consciousness, reaching downward to the nonverbalized level where images must be used to represent nonverbalized sensations or emotions." It is important to note in addition Holman's comment that "It assumes the unrestricted and uncensored portrayal of the totality of interior experience on the level or levels being represented." Holman comments that such a portrayal may give the appearance "of being illogical, associational, free or auctorial control."

The stream-of-consciousness novel. Concerned with presenting "the uninterrupted, uneven, and endless flow of the stream of consciousness of one or more of its characters." Concentrates on "the pre-speech, nonverbalized level, where the image must express the unarticulated response and where the logic of grammar belongs to another world." Holman provides a very fine summary of the "common assumptions" that writers of stream-of-consciousness novels hold to be true: (a) "the significant existence of man is to be found in his mental-emotional processes and not in the outside world"; (b) "his mental-emotional life is disjointed, illogical"; (c) "a pattern of free psychological association rather than of logical relationship determines the shifting sequence of thought and feeling."

The selection presented from *A Portrait of the Artist* may be read in one sitting. In doing so, the continuity of Stephen's problems will be more clearly evident.

Reteaching Alternatives.   You may wish particularly able students to act out the roles of Stephen and the other boys at the school. You may also choose for your classes to locate instances of the repetitive sentence structure and discuss Joyce's possible motives for providing such repetition. Ask students to determine what would happen to the passage and its effectiveness if Joyce had avoided all repetitions.

Responding to the Story   Text page 982
Analyzing the Story
Identifying Details

1. What details show how Stephen is different from his classmates? Stephen is sensitive and easily picked on; one of the classmates shoves him into a ditch, and some of the boys tease him about kissing his mother every night.

2. Why is Stephen "sick in his heart"? He is lonely, homesick, and confused about the boys' remarks and behavior toward him.

3. What topics do Stephen's thoughts touch on? Among the topics students may mention are the following: being bullied, kissing, the sounds in the refectory (dining room), the appearance and habits of the other boys, learning geography, poetry, the universe, and God.

Interpreting Meanings

4. How would you describe the *point of view* from which these experiences are narrated? The experiences are narrated from a limited third-person point of view, focusing on Stephen.

How would the effect have been differerent if a different point of view had been used? Student answers will vary. Ask the students to discuss what effect a first-person or omniscient third-person point of view would have on the story.

5. In what ways is identity one of the key topics in this selection? Again, student answers will vary. Most obviously, Stephen's identification of his name and location on the flyleaf of his geography book indicates a concern, subconsciously at least, with his identity. More consciously, he displays a concern with his identity when he tries to understand the behavior and remarks of the other boys. He is painfully shy and anxious about fitting in at school.

6. Do you think that Joyce tries to show how the artist is present in young Stephen? Explain. Student answers will vary. His self-consciousness, sensory perceptions, and reflective personality might be indicators of the budding "artist" within Stephen.

7. What examples of *free association* do you find in this recreation of the child's thoughts? Students should be able to supply a number of examples of free association: for instance, the series of comments about the noise of the refectory and the comments on Wells's face, which lead in to the memory of Wells's shoving Stephen into the ditch.

Did you find the narration convincing? Student answers will vary. Encourage the students to support their opinions with reasons.

8. How did you feel about Stephen as he's presented in this extract? How would you describe Joyce's *tone* toward his young hero? Answers will vary. In general, the tone is gentle and affectionate.

Extending the Novel

You may have able students consider other portions of *A Portrait of the Artist*. They may then analyze the continuity of Joyce's writing style. Of particular assistance in this matter is *Persona: A Style Study for Readers and Writers* by Walker Gibson.

The Stream of Consciousness

Explain to your students that the stream-of-consciousness technique, pioneered by Joyce, has become a staple of contemporary literature. The passage first defines and analyzes this technique, then goes on to discuss the evolution of the stream-of-consciousness technique in Joyce's later work. Your students will probably follow the writing in *A Portrait of the Artist as a Young Man* with relative ease, but they may need your help in getting through the excerpt from *Ulysses*, which makes greater associational leaps, and the playful but tricky passage from *Finnegans Wake*.

D. H. Lawrence

Text page 985

The Rocking-Horse Winner

Text page 987

Objectives

1. To analyze character

2. To understand symbolism

3. To analyze the theme of the story

4. To identify tone and a possible satiric target

5. To write a new outcome to the events of the story

6. To write an analysis of a character

7. To write an essay applying a quote from the story

8. To write an essay about characters from different stories

Introducing the Story

In outline form, for your reference, here are the major elements in the story:

- **Protagonist:** Paul
- **Antagonist:** the inner struggle to win
- **Conflict:** person vs. self
- **Point of view:** third-person omniscient
- **Significant techniques:** symbolism, theme, tone, satire
- **Setting:** London

Background on the Story. Ask students to discuss the nature of fairy tales. You may then wish to give them Holman's definition from his *Handbook to Literature*. In it, he states that a fairy tale is "a story relating mysterious pranks and adventures of supernatural spirits who manifested themselves in the form of diminutive human beings." After this discussion, consider the title. Ask students to determine their preconceived ideas about a story with this title. Although many students will not have been to a race track, they will likely have knowledge of horse racing and betting.

The Plot. Paul, a young boy, realizes that his parents' relationship with one another is a failure. To make up for this circumstance, Paul decides to help his mother by providing her with the income her husband does not give her. He begins betting on horses, always after riding his own rocking horse to determine the winner of a race. As Paul gives his mother more money, the walls of the house keep telling him "There *must* be more money!" Paul is so driven that he finally falls off his horse, a brain fever having overtaken him. At the end of the story, Paul says to his mother, just before dying, "I can ride my horse, and get there . . . Mother, did I ever tell you? I am lucky!" The mother answers no, and watches her son die.

Teaching Strategies

Providing for Cultural Differences. You may wish to discuss the nature of fairy tales, offering examples and briefly discussing their plots. For slower classes, you may engage students' interest by building suspense. In almost all cases, students will have some knowledge of horse racing, but they may find it interesting to learn the background of racing and betting.

Providing for Different Levels of Ability. For slower classes, you must explain initially that the story relies on a supernatural influence. More able students will recognize

easily this reliance and adapt their expectations accordingly.

Reading the Story.   Before students begin the story, you
may wish to elaborate on D. H. Lawrence's life and especially on his personal relationship with his mother. See both
the introduction to Lawrence and the headnote for "The
Rocking-Horse Winner," which allude to this relationship.
Also, you may wish to discuss the fact that the theme of
parent-child relationships occurs in Lawrence's other
works, among them *Sons and Lovers* and *The White Peacock.*

Reteaching Alternatives.   You may wish to teach "The
Rocking-Horse Winner" as a study in cause-and-effect relationships. Ask students what motivates Paul, what motivates his mother, and what each ultimately achieves from
acting on the motivation. Discuss whether the serious nature
of the effect is warranted from the cause.

Responding to the Story   Text page 995

Analyzing the Story

Identifying Details

**1. In the style of a fairy tale, the opening of the story
tells about a woman who "had no luck." How had she
been unlucky?** The woman's love had turned to dust; she
had found herself unable to love her children; and she felt
flawed.

**What else does the writer tell us directly about the
mother's *character*?** Lawrence tells us that the woman was
ambitious and eager for social position; she was not as rich
as she hoped, and was thus continually disappointed and
dissatisfied; and she had expensive tastes.

**2. How does Paul's mother define luck when Paul asks
her what it means?** She says that luck is what causes people
to have money.

What is Paul's confusion about the word luck? Paul
cannot understand why God doesn't reveal the reason why
one person is lucky and another is not.

**3. What step does Paul take to ease his mother's anxiety
over the family debts?** He asks his uncle to make an anonymous birthday present to his mother of a thousand pounds a
year for five years.

**How does she react when she learns of her birthday
surprise?** Disappointed that she has not received the whole
amount, the mother appears cold and indifferent.

4. Who is Bassett? Bassett is the gardener and Paul's partner at the races.

Why does he keep Paul's secret? Bassett respects the
boy as a "young sport."

5. Does Paul solve his mother's problem? Why or why
not? Paul fails to resolve his mother's problem, because her
receipt of the money leads only to the desire for more
money.

Interpreting Meanings

**6. Why do you suppose only Paul and his sisters hear
and react to the whispering of the walls?** The fact that
only the children hear and react to the whispering under-
scores the parents' obliviousness to their own materialism.

How would you describe what has happened to Paul?
Student answers will vary. Some students will suggest that
Paul goes into some psychic trance, the pressures of which
eventually kill him.

7. What might the rocking horse *symbolize*? Again, student answers may vary. Possibilities might include escape
or desire.

**8. What do you think the story means? Do you agree
that the *theme* has something to do with an inability to
love? How would you state the story's theme?** Student
answers will vary. Some students will suggest that the mother's inability to love is the central thematic strand of the
story and that this inability symbolically results in Paul's
death. Other students may suggest that the theme of the
story centers on the futililty of materialism.

**9. How would you describe the *tone* of Lawrence's
story?** The tone might be described as ominous.

**If you detect a *satiric* tone, who or what is Lawrence's
target?** Materialism and greed may perhaps be the targets of
Lawrence's satire.

**10. In what ways is the story's ending a distortion of the
usual fairy-tale ending?** The conclusion of the typical fairy
tale is "They all lived happily ever after." But in Lawrence's story, Paul dies, and the uncle somberly comments
that "he's best gone out of a life where he rides his rocking
horse to find a winner."

**What do you think of Lawrence's decision to end it as
he did?** Student answers will vary. Encourage the students
to defend their opinions.

Extending the Story

You may ask students to find in other works by Lawrence
examples of mother-son relationships. In particular, you
may ask them to consider sections of *Sons and Lovers* in
which Paul interacts with his mother, Gertrude. Also ask
students to determine Paul Morel's relationship with his
father, Walter.

D. H. Lawrence on Money

In these comments Lawrence virtually suggests a moral lesson for ''The Rocking-Horse Winner.'' Ask the students to explain how the story demonstrates the tenets regarding life and money Lawrence expresses here. Does anyone in the story appear to learn the lesson Lawrence is trying to teach Gardiner?

Further Reading

Students may learn more about Lawrence's relationships with others in his life by reading T. O. Beachcroft's collection of essays, *British Writers and Their Work No. 10*, (Lincoln, Nebraska, 1966).

Katherine Mansfield   Text page 997

Miss Brill   Text page 999

Objectives

1. To determine the basic situation of the story

2. To discern the author's use of dramatic irony

3. To determine the use of symbolism

4. To analyze the writer's use of ambiguity

5. To write a continuation of the events in the narrative

6. To write an analysis of the writer's chosen point of view

Introducing the Story

In outline form, for your reference, here are the major elements in the story:

- **Protagonist:** Miss Brill
- **Antagonist:** her discovery of her antiquity
- **Conflict:** person vs. self
- **Point of view:** third-person limited
- **Significant techniques:** dramatic irony, symbolism
- **Setting:** a public park

Background on the Story.   Before students read ''Miss Brill,'' you may need to discuss with them the notions of sympathy and empathy. Ask students what kinds of circumstances elicit sympathy in them. Then ask them to watch for circumstances in Miss Brill's life and in her nature that elicit this response. You will want students to focus on the shifting disposition of Miss Brill toward the end of the story.

The Plot.   Plot is far less important in this story than is characterization. The narrator's emphasis on the latter and

the exclusion of the former cause us to discern how inactive Miss Brill really is. The only action of Miss Brill's is to watch others and listen to them. She actually enjoys living vicariously. Her outlook changes abruptly as she realizes the young couple consider her stupid and out of date.

Teaching Strategies

Providing for Cultural Differences.   Although many students may not have known someone just like Miss Brill, they very likely have known older individuals who seem out of touch with life and reality. You may wish to have them think of these individuals, recall exactly why they seem this way. You may also wish them to place themselves in Miss Brill's life. How would they feel, and what would cause them to feel that way?

Providing for Different Levels of Ability.   This story is not difficult to read. Some students may be unfamiliar with certain vocabulary, so you may wish to address those few terms in class. You may also choose better students to review other authors' use of story line—for instance, Virginia Woolf's

Reading the Story.   Students should be able to read the story easily in one sitting. Ask them to focus their attention on the shifting tone.

Reteaching Alternatives.   You may wish to focus on Mansfield's view of aging and dying, as represented in ''Miss Brill.'' If you wish, you may ask students to read another of Mansfield's short stories, considering the same theme in it.

Responding to the Story   Text page 1003

Analyzing the Story

Identifying Details

1. The story takes place in a public park, where Miss Brill is in many ways an outsider. In what country is this park located? The park is located in France, in Paris.

What clues reveal Miss Brill's nationality? Her name suggests that she is not French; the fact that she has ''English pupils'' suggests that she is English.

2. ''Miss Brill'' is a story without much plot or action; rather, it focuses, as do many of Mansfield's stories, on the small human dramas within an ordinary situation. What is the *basic situation* in this story? The basic situation is one of Miss Brill's regular Sunday outings to the park, where she sits on a bench and observes her surroundings.

Describe some of the human dramas the reader is permitted to see. Among the examples students may mention are the following: the English couple discussing spectacles, the two girls in red meeting the soldiers, the beautiful woman dropping her violets and then throwing them away after the small boy picks them up and returns them to her, the woman in the ermine togue and her meeting with the elderly man, and the rich young boy and girl making fun of Miss Brill's fox collar.

Interpreting Meanings

3. Miss Brill is unmarried and getting on in years. What evidence indicates that she is set in her ways—a creature of habit? Her regular expeditions to the park, always at the same hour on Sundays, is one bit of evidence that she is set in her ways. Another piece of evidence is the comment about her customary purchase of a slice of cake on the way home (sometimes with an almond, sometimes not).

What evidence indicates her kind heart? Her delight in the park, her pleasure in the band music, and her reading to the elderly invalid gentleman might be cited as evidence of Miss Brill's kind heart.

4. What is *ironic* about Miss Brill's observations of the ''other people'' who sit on the benches and chairs every Sunday? She does not realize that she, too, is part of the ''show.''

5. In *The Secret Sharer*, by Conrad, the narrator's hat takes on *symbolic* meaning. What symbolic meaning is given to Miss Brill's fox collar? Pay close attention to its description at the beginning and end of the story. Miss Brill's fox collar is a precious, beloved possession that she has cherished. The callous mockery of it by the young girl causes Miss Brill deep sorrow.

6. In her critical comment, Eudora Welty maintains that a great deal happens in ''Miss Brill,'' even though ''its plot is all implication'' and the action ''consists nearly altogether in sitting down.'' What happens in ''Miss Brill''? Basically, the protagonist of ''Miss Brill,'' who had always thought of herself as an amused, detached spectator of the people around her, is rudely confronted by an unpleasant aspect of the outside world; she herself is ''observed,'' and her prize possession is roughly mocked.

How would you state the story's *theme*? Student statements of the theme may vary. In general, the theme has to do with human vulnerability and the harm that a casual, thoughtless remark may inflict.

7. Note that the last line of the story does not, as it easily might have, tell you exactly who or what is crying. Who do you think is crying? Most students will agree that it is Miss Brill who is crying.

What is the effect of the *ambiguity* here? The ambiguity reinforces the motif of ''observing'' in the story; by having Miss Brill think that ''she heard someone crying,'' Mansfield refers once again to the ambiguous situation of Miss Brill as a spectator and, in turn, as the subject of observation herself.

8. How did this story make you feel about Miss Brill? Do you think there are characters like Miss Brill in the world as you know it? Student answers will vary. Urge the students to support their opinions.

Extending the Story

Ask students to study the following quotation from William Vaughn Moody and Robert Moriss's *A History of English Literature* (New York, 1964): ''The type of story [Mansfield] practiced is the plotless variety of Chekhov, whose work Miss Mansfield admired inordinately. Dealing less than he with universals and more with fragile moods of tenderness and irony, she too was primarily an impressionist. The significant moment in a human relationship, the curious and subtle spiritual adventure, the poignant ironies of contrasting human emotions, she strove to mirror with increasing objectivity. Her painfully developed insight into human experience led her to deal almost exclusively with inner rather than outer events. . . .''

Ask students to discuss this quotation, paying particular attention to the concept of impressionism in writing. Holman's *A Handbook to Literature* (Bobbs-Merrill, 1972) offers a fine explanation of this subject, and you may want to apply its general principles to ''Miss Brill.''

Primary Sources   Text page 1004

Letters and Journals

These three excerpts provide insight into Mansfield's view of her role as a writer. Ask students whether they can detect any hints here that part of the character of Miss Brill may be Mansfield herself. In addition, have them analyze a paragraph of "Miss Brill": Does it meet the exacting criteria to which Mansfield holds herself in her letter of January 17, 1921?

The Elements of Fiction

Text page 1004

The Modern Short Story

These comments provide a review of the history of the short story, and a brief analysis of the aims and techniques of modern short fiction. These elements are illustrated through discussion of "Miss Brill." Encourage students to use this material as a guide to reading, appreciating, and understanding the succeeding short stories in the text.

Elizabeth Bowen

Text page 1006

The Demon Lover

Text page 1008

Objectives

1. To identify setting as a creation of mood
2. To determine images that contribute to mood
3. To determine instances of foreshadowing in the story
4. To analyze the use of the omniscient narrator
5. To determine dramatic irony in the story
6. To identify the use of flashback
7. To write a character description
8. To write a proposal outlining a film version of the story
9. To write a comparison of the story to a ballad

Introducing the Story

In outline form, for your reference, here are the major elements in the story:

- **Protagonist:** Mrs. Drover
- **Antagonist:** a former lover, the threat of his memory
- **Conflict:** person vs. person, person vs. self
- **Point of view:** third-person omniscient
- **Significant techniques:** setting, mood, foreshadowing, dramatic irony
- **Setting:** a bombed-out area of London during World War II

The Plot. A forty-year-old woman returns to her abandoned city house to pick up a few belongings. She begins to recall a previous autumn day during World War I, twenty years before. She sees a letter, opens it, and realizes that this day is the anniversary of a day twenty years before when she promised to remain faithful to a soldier with whom she had fallen in love. When she leaves the house rather hurriedly, all the while thinking that a ghost of the past lover might come to the house, she enters a taxi and encounters the demon lover she was attempting to avoid.

Teaching Strategies

Providing for Cultural Differences. You may wish to discuss with students the possible psychological effects of war on people who live through it. Also, discuss the nature of memory—the fact that sometimes we recall circumstances, events, people, and places because of something that reminds us of them. So it is with Mrs. Drover. It is, therefore, important to discuss the "emotional backdrop" of the story, explaining that the present exists in terms of the past.

Providing for Different Levels of Ability. Slower classes may enjoy completed the assignment listed under "A Creative Response"—number 2. As they become involved with the production and directing, they may gain more pleasure in analyzing the story. Stronger classes may even enjoy considering the psychological nature of Mrs. Drover. You may wish such students to refer to the analytical approaches discussed in Guerin's *A Handbook of Critical Approaches to*

Literature (New York, 1979). Of particular interest may be the Rhetorical Approach found under "Other Approaches."

Introducing Vocabulary Study. Students may benefit from knowing the meanings of the follow words before they read the story.

    intermittent   precipitately

Reading the Story. This kind of story, which builds suspense as it progresses, may be enjoyed if the class hears it read by a very good student or by the teacher. Ask students to consider the effect of plot on characterization and how the latter develops as the story progresses.

Reteaching Alternatives. Ask students to rework Bowen's short story into a narrative poem in which the character of Mrs. Drover is also the narrator. Have students pay particular attention to the interweaving of past and present time and place. As they prepare to write their poems, you may want them to consider the follow authorial preface to Lillian Hellman's second memoir, *Pentimento*: "Old paint on canvas, as it ages, sometimes becomes transparent. When that happens it is possible, in some pictures, to see the original lines: a tree will show through a woman's dress, a child makes way for a dog, a large boat is no longer on an open sea. That is called pentimento because the painter 'repented,' changed his mind. Perhaps it would be as well to say that the old conception, replaced by a later choice, is a way of seeing and then seeing again. That is all I mean about the people in this book. The paint has aged now and I wanted to see what was there for me once, what is there for me now."

Responding to the Story   Text page 1012
Analyzing the Story
Identifying Details

1. **In some stories, the *setting* is much more than a description of physical background—it also creates a particular *mood*. In "The Demon Lover" an atmosphere of foreboding is established immediately. List the *images* in the first paragraph that help create this strong sense of foreboding.** Among the images students may list are the following: the shut-up house, the "steamy, showery day," the batch of clouds that pile up "ink-dark," the broken chimney and parapets, the references to the unwilling lock, the warped door, and the dead air inside the house.

2. **Why has the Drover family been dislocated from their home? Cite two places in the text that make the reason clear.** The family has been dislocated because of the wartime bombings of London. Two places in the text that make this clear are the mention of the part-time caretaker and the mention of the family's growing used to their country life. One might also add the detail of the cracks in the wall, caused by the recent bombing.

For what purposes has Mrs. Drover returned? She has returned to pick up some things from the house.

3. **Explain the circumstances surrounding the arrival of the letter. Before Mrs. Drover reads the letter, how does she feel about its being in the house?** Mrs. Drover spies the letter on the hall table. She cannot understand how it got there, since the caretaker has not been in the house because of his holiday, and, even if he had returned, he would not have known of Mrs. Drover's visit, which was planned as a surprise. As she picks up the letter, Mrs. Drover feels mystified.

How do her feelings change after she reads the letter? She becomes terrified.

4. **A tale that begins with the promise of a meeting between two former lovers could easily lead the reader to expect a sentimental love story. But the reader of "The Demon Lover" never for a moment expects this. What details in the description of the lovers' last meeting *foreshadow* a sinister, threatening reunion?** Among the details that students may mention are the following: the lack of kindness with which the lover presses Mrs. Drover's hand, the spectral glitters that she imagines in place of his eyes, and the ambivalence with which the lover says, "I shall be with you sooner or later."

What does Mrs. Drover tell us about her fiance that explains why she is terrified of him? She feels that she promised herself to him unnaturally; she also says that he has threatened to come back sooner or later to reclaim her, and that he was not kind to her.

5. **The use of *omniscient narrator* allows Bowen to give her readers information about Mrs. Drover's psychological makeup that Mrs. Drover herself is not consciously aware of. Find several such passages in the text.** Among such passages are the references to Mrs. Drover as a "prosaic woman," the explanation of her "intermittent muscular flicker," and the descriptions of her reactions to her fiancé.

Interpreting Meanings

6. **World War I and World War II bracket this story like bookends. During each war, Mrs. Drover experiences confusion, dislocation, and disorientation. During each war, the demon lover is part of her life. Yet the demon lover doesn't appear during the intervening twenty-five years. Use these strands of the story (the war, Mrs. Drover's inner turmoil, and the appearance of the demon lover) in a statement of the theme of the story.** Student answers will vary. Encourage the students to use all the elements listed in their statement of the story's theme.

7. **Dramatic irony* occurs when the audience is aware of a situation that a character in the story is not aware of.**

What is the dramatic irony of the story? The dramatic irony of the story consists of the fact that the reader suspects that the taxi driver cannot be the demon lover; Mrs. Drover (who cannot remember her lover's face) is, nevertheless, so unnerved by the letter and by her fear of her fiance's return that she screams in horror.

8. One aspect of "The Demon Lover" that contributes to its richness and depth is the interplay between present and past. Locate the place in the story where Bowen uses a *flashback* to tell what happened earlier in Mrs. Drover's life. Note that Bowen does not provide a smooth transition into the flashback. Do you think the abrupt shift into the past is effective in this story, or merely confusing? Why? The flashback begins with the sentence, "The young girl talking to the soldier in the garden had not ever completely seen his face." The abrupt shift is perhaps appropriate, given Mrs. Drover's disorientation and excited frame of mind.

9. One possible, decidedly psychological, interpretation of "The Demon Lover" is that Mrs. Drover's experience is an hallucination. Another way of looking at the story is to consider it a frank ghost story. Which interpretation do you favor, or do you have another? Support your interpretation with evidence from the text. Student answers will vary. Ask the students to support their interpretations with citations from the story.

Extending the Story

After students complete the poems discussed under Reteaching Alternatives, you may wish to discuss with them their motives for creating their respective poems as they did. In what ways have they been faithful to Bowen's concept, and in what ways have they not?

Frank O'Connor
Text page 1015

My Oedipus Complex
Text page 1017

Objectives

1. To understand the use of a child narrator
2. To explain irony
3. To identify and analyze conflict
4. To describe a character
5. To identify the theme of a story
6. To write a scene using an alternate point of view
7. To write a comparison of two characters
8. To write an essay analyzing the writer's intent

Introducing the Story

In outline form, for your reference, here are the major elements in the story:

- **Protagonist:** Larry, a five-year-old boy
- **Antagonist:** his father
- **Conflict:** person vs. person
- **Point of view:** first person
- **Significant techniques:** conflict, character, theme, point of view
- **Setting:** just after the war

Background on the Story. This story is a good introduction to the sometimes understated, sometimes sarcastic and ironic British humor. You will want students to understand fully the concept of the Oedipus complex. Make sure to review with them the headnote, and elaborate on it if you wish. The story may be seen as an analysis of two opposing forces—at first, apparently the child and his father. Ask students to watch the shift in the members of each force.

The Plot. "My Oedipus Complex" is a successful short story through the author's expert use of humor. This humor, resulting from the dramatic irony present in the naive child, pervades the entire story and aids in story unity.

Teaching Strategies

Providing for Cultural Differences. As the headnote states, "In psychoanalytic theory, the Oedipus complex is an important part of normal human development, lasting from about age three to age five or six. . . ." Thus, all of your students should come to understand its universality, which transcends cultural differences.

Providing for Different Levels of Ability. Your slower classes may be motivated by efforts to locate humor throughout the story, and you may wish only briefly to discuss Freud and his theory. On the other hand, better students may find a somewhat more in-depth study of Freud very interesting. Such a study may aid students in gaining a meaningful analytical tool for research.

Introducing Vocabulary Study. Students will benefit from knowing the meanings of the following words before they read the story.

cajole   intercession

Reading the Story. Students can gain faster insight if they read this story in one sitting, watching for the narrator's shifting views regarding his father and mother.

Reteaching Alternatives. Students may find a dramatic interpretation of this story amusing and helpful in realizing motives for character actions.

Responding to the Story   Text page 1023
Analyzing the Story
Identifying Details

1. How far into the story must you read before you can identify the *narrator* and determine his age? By the end of the second paragraph, it is clear that the narrator is a five-year-old boy.

2. Larry describes the war, ironically, as the most peaceful period of his life. Outline the details of Larry's peaceful morning ritual during the war. Larry awakens with the first light, feeling liberated from the previous day's responsibilities. He puts his feet out under the clothes, which he calls Mrs. Right and Mrs. Left, and invents dramatic dialogues for them about the problems of the day. Then Larry settles his plans for the day, looks out of the window, and goes to his mother's room, where he climbs into bed with her.

How does his life change when his father comes home? His mother pays much less attention to him, and she scolds him for interrupting his father when the father is talking, reading, or trying to sleep.

3. At one point in the story, Larry realizes that he and his father are conducting a "series of skirmishes against one another, he trying to steal my time with Mother and I his." What details justify Larry's conclusion that his father is really jealous of him? Students might point to Mick's ill-tempered resentment of Larry's talking and of his visits to their bed in the morning.

4. What event finally resolves the *conflict* between Larry and his father? The birth of Sonny, and the mother's attention to the baby, makes Larry's father feel neglected; the father experiences a feeling of kinship with Larry, and crawls into bed with the boy. Larry decides to forgive his father.

Interpreting Meanings

5. The story is full of comic *irony*, including Larry's rueful remarks about sharing his mother with his father. Find some of Larry's comments about his mother and his father and explain what it is that Larry doesn't understand in each case. (Include his remarks about the cost of a baby.) Larry does not understand how babies are born, and assumes instead that they are purchased for "seventeen and six." He also doesn't understand why his parents share the same bed, since his mother has told him that it would be "unhealthy" for her and her son to sleep in the same bed. When Larry decides to make his father jealous by saying that he is going to marry mother one day and have many children with her, the results are hilariously ironic.

6. How would you describe Father's *character* as the young narrator sees it? As the young narrator sees Father, he is somewhat gross and unrefined. Larry says that he thinks his father is selfish and tyrannical with both him and his mother.

7. How does the end of the story indicate that the Oedipal stage of the narrator's development is over? Larry becomes friends with his father and "forgives" him; Sonny occupies the mother's attentions; and Father buys Larry a model railway for Christmas.

But what new problem has arisen in the household? The birth of Sonny has made Father jealous.

8. How would you state the *theme* of the story? Student answers will vary. Many students may suggest that the story, which is really a humorous series of "take-offs," or burlesques, of the Oedipal theme, has no serious theme, but is rather intended simply as an entertaining sketch of the zaniness of family life.

Extending the Story

You may choose to read to your classes O'Connor's short story "The Drunkard" which also is told through the eyes of a child. You may then ask students to compare the two works, either by an oral discussion in class or by a written assignment.

Further Reading

Students who found the story entertaining may wish to read more by Frank O'Connor. Suggest *The Stories of Frank O'Connor* (New York, 1970). An introduction by the author discusses his own efforts at writing.

Graham Greene

The Destructors

Objectives

1. To analyze a character's motivation

2. To explain irony

3. To identify connotations of words integral to the story

4. To identify the theme of the story

5. To rewrite the story from an alternate point of view

6. To write an essay explaining the relevance of selected imagery

Introducing the Story

In outline form, for your reference, here are the major elements in the story:

- **Protagonist:** Trevor
- **Antagonist:** his conscience, his social class
- **Conflict:** person vs. self
- **Point of view:** third-person limited
- **Significant techniques:** irony, theme, point of view
- **Setting:** wartime England

Background on the Story. You should provide students with some background on Graham Greene's life and time. Many students will not be familiar with a writer such as Greene, who depicts life with such unnerving and unusual accuracy. Greene is particularly good at depicting evil within modern society. Ask students to review the major details of Greene's life, keeping in mind his often-used theme of moral or philosophical decay.

Teaching Strategies

Providing for Cultural Differences. By their senior year, students will likely have taken a course in world history, including information about England's role in World War II. However, for students to have a clear picture of the time depicted in "The Destructors," you should review this particular aspect. You may wish to locate texts that contain pictures of England immediately after the war. Such pictorial representaion will serve students who have never before seen the physical results of war.

Providing for Different Levels of Ability. Slower students may do well to complete the activity assigned under

Writing About the Story: A Creative Response. You may wish better students to consider other short stories by Greene, determining similarities of theme and symbolism in them. Again, Guerin's *A Handbook of Critical Approaches to Literature* (New York, 1979) will aid students a great deal.

Introducing Vocabulary Study. Students will benefit from knowing the meanings of the following words before they read the story.

altruistic   impromptu
implacable

Reading the Story. If time does not permit a class reading of the story, you will want to read and discuss passages in which the motives of the boys and the decay of the situation are considered. In particular, you will want someone to read aloud the last passage in which the driver laughs and Mr. Thomas reacts.

Reteaching Alternatives. Consider discussing "The Destructors" by applying the following quotation, which appears in the biographical sketch of Graham Greene on page 1025 of the student text: "In his autobiography, *A Sort of Life*, Greene reveals his motive for writing fiction. It is, he writes, 'a desire to reduce the chaos of experience to some sort of order, and a hungry curiosity.' "

Responding to the Story

Analyzing the Story

Identifying Details

1. Assuming Blackie is about the same age as Trevor, what clues in the story would help you approximate the year the story takes place? The narrator says that Blackie would have been a year old at the time of the bombings (in 1940); he also mentions that Trevor is in his fifteenth year. From this evidence, we can deduce that the story takes place around 1954

2. The first two paragraphs of this story are remarkable for the amount of information they communicate. The writer manages (a) to convey the flavor of the gang's interactions, (b) to explain how Trevor is different from the rest of the gang, and (c) to hint at the reasons for the difference. List the details that supply these three kinds of information. The flavor of the gang's interactions is suggested by the brusque treatment of Mike; the difference between Trevor and the rest of the gang is suggested by the comments about his name; and the reasons for the difference are hinted at in the comments about Trevor's background.

3. Why is Old Misery's house valuable? It was built by the renowned seventeenth-century architect Christopher Wren.

Why was Old Misery able to restore certain parts of the house inexpensively? Since Old Misery used to be a builder and decorator, he was able to buy materials for the restoration at cost.

4. Who is the leader of the gang at the opening of the story? At the opening of the story, Blackie is the leader of the gang.

At what point does the leadership change hands? The leadership of the gang changes hands when Trevor proposes the destruction of Old Misery's house and all that Blackie can come up with as an alternative is pinching free rides.

When is the new leadership almost lost? The new leadership is almost lost when Summers mocks Trevor and Trevor stands undecided about a plan for the final phase of destruction.

What criterion determines who leads the gang? The criterion that seems to determine leadership is the boldness of the leader's proposals.

5. How does the gang go about their destructive project? On the first day, they destroy the banisters, slash the beds and pillows, smash the dishes and glasses, break the bath and washbasin, and tear up the papers. On the second day, they proceed to more structural demolition.

What do they do to Old Misery himself? Tricking him, they manage to lock him up for the night in the shed that he uses for a lavatory.

Interpreting Meanings

6. Trevor's *motives* for destroying Old Misery's house are important. Several details shed light on what these motives are *not*. What motive do you rule out based on the way the boys treat Old Misery? The boys are not trying to harm him physically, and they are not out for revenge on him personally.

What motives do you rule out based on what the boys do with the money? Since they burn the money, the boys are not interested in robbing Old Misery.

7. What do you think Trevor's motives *are* for destroying Old Misery's house? Student answers will vary. Greene never explicitly reveals Trevor's motives. Some students may suggest that Trevor takes perverse pleasure in the complete destruction of beauty, as beauty is represented by the house.

8. It is *ironic* that the abilities Trevor exhibits in destroying the house are highly prized by society. What are Trevor's talents? Trevor is talented at organization and leadership. He also displays considerable technical knowledge.

9. Why is it *ironic* that Trevor's father was once an architect? The fact that the father was an architect, or builder, sharply contrasts with the son's talent for destruction.

In light of the history of Old Misery's house, what is ironic about its destruction? It is ironic that this house, which has survived the German bombings in the blitz of World War II, is destroyed by a gang of boys while the owner is away.

What is ironic about Old Misery's horoscope reading? The horoscope reading predicts a ''serious crash''; this comes about unexpectedly (and literally) when the house crashes to the ground in a heap of rubble.

10. What significance does the name *Wormsley Common* have in the story? The gang is known as the ''Wormsley Common'' gang.

What are the *connotations* of these two words? What details in the story back up your answer? The name ''Wormsley'' suggests worms, and, by extension, destruction and corruption. It is interesting to note that Trevor uses the following simile for the gang: ''We'd be like worms, don't you see, in an apple.'' The word ''common'' perhaps suggests vulgarity; perhaps this word hints at the lower-class origins of the boys.

11. When Blackie asks Trevor whether Trevor hates Mr. Thomas, he answers, ''Of course I don't. . . . There'd be no fun if I hated him.'' How would you explain Trevor's answer? Student answers will vary. They should point out that the answer makes Trevor's actions even more ominous; devoid of even the passion of hatred, his destructiveness is randomly and frighteningly malicious.

12. The gang is an entity, and as such has its own set of values. What are its values? Is the gang's antisocial stance merely one of poor versus rich, or does it spring from something deeper? Explain. Student answers will vary. Ask them to support and defend their opinions. Possibilities might include: boredom, petty malice, alienation, and so on.

13. Consider the following excerpt from the story:

Streaks of light came in through the closed shutters where they worked with the seriousness of creators—and destruction after all is a form of creation. A kind of imagination had seen this house as it had now become.

How close do you think this statement comes to expressing the theme of ''The Destructors''? Explain. Many students will agree that this quotation is closely related to the paradoxical *theme* of the story: that destruction, just like creation, requires planning, organization, and effective implementation. Ask the students to explain their interpretations of the quotation and then to relate it to the story as a whole.

14. Some people feel that the story should have ended differently, so that the destructors are punished. Do you think this would have been a better ending, or is the story more powerful as is? Explain. Students who want to see poetic justice served may suggest that the boys ought to have been punished. But some students may argue that the story's ironic tone and effect would be damaged if the boys had been punished.

15. Do such acts of destruction, for similar motives, take place today in the world as you know it? Who or what might be today's "destructors"? Student answers will vary. Encourage them to offer specific examples and illustrations.

Extending the Story

Reading portions of a biography of Graham Greene may be helpful in students' understanding important details of his life that affect his writing. Such a title appears below in Further Reading.

Further Reading

In John Atkin's biography of the writer, *Graham Greene* (London, 1957), the author provides an analysis and discussion of Greene's novels, the plays, and the journals. Suggest this title to students interested in learning more about this twentieth-century luminary.

Doris Lessing

Text page 1035

No Witchcraft for Sale

Text page 1036

Objectives

1. To determine action that sets the plot in motion

2. To identify irony

3. To write paragraphs that build upon a character from the story

4. To write an analysis of the story's conflict

5. To write an analysis of the writer's point of view

Introducing the Story

In outline form, for your reference, here are the major elements in the story:

- **Protagonist:** Gideon, representative of native Africa
- **Antagonist:** the outside civilized world, represented by the scientist, and to a lesser degree Mr. and Mrs. Farquar
- **Conflict:** person vs. person
- **Point of view:** third-person omniscient
- **Significant techniques:** plot, irony, character, conflict, point of view
- **Setting:** Africa

Background on the Story. You may need to discuss with students the tension they will come to discern in the story. The nature of that tension is important: It is nothing that the

Farquars wish to occur. It simply occurs as the byproduct of two societies that understand one another very little. The young boy, Teddy, may represent innocence, for he is not involved in the struggle between the scientist and the Farquars, and Gideon. Gideon represents native African customs and beliefs. The scientist and the Farquars represent the capitalistic world of the West.

The Plot. The plot centers on differences in perceptions or philosophies. Its action purposefully begins after Teddy's eyes are injured and continues as the separation between Gideon and the Farquars increases.

Teaching Strategies

Providing for Cultural Differences. Most of your students will have little knowledge of native African customs. If you have a student who has come from such a society, you may wish him or her to explain Gideon's motivation in keeping the plant from the Farquars and the scientist. You may wish also to discuss the capitalistic notion of "buy and sell."

Providing for Different Levels of Ability. A review of the regional terms listed below will be necessary if students are to understand the story more fully. Review these terms with them either before they read the story or as they are reading it: *kraal, piccanin, baas, permanganate, veld, puff adder, kaffir, salting the tail, mealie, verandah.*

Introducing Vocabulary Study. Students will benefit from knowing the following words before they read the story.

annul   protuberance
efficacy

Reading the Story. Ask students to read the story in one sitting, being careful to note the shift in mood or atmosphere after Gideon realizes outsiders want the plant for material purposes.

Reteaching Alternatives. Students may rewrite the ending of the story, so that Gideon allows the Farquars and the scientist to take the plant. Ask students to keep in mind the cause-and-effect relationship that must result in the story, and how it will be different from the one Lessing describes.

Responding to the Story   Text page 1041
Analyzing the Story
Identifying Details

1. Describe the relationship between Gideon and Teddy at the start of the story. What incident signals a change in their relationship? At the start of the story, Gideon and Teddy are great friends. The cook plays with the child and teaches him to walk. The incident that signals a change in their relationship occurs when Teddy, riding his scooter, frightens Gideon's son out of the way. When Gideon reproaches the boy, Teddy answers that ''he's only a black boy.'' After this exchange, Gideon's attitude toward Teddy grows more distant.

2. Mrs. Farquar and Gideon share a sense of sadness about the reality of their children's future lives. What is the reality that gives these two characters, and this whole story, a feeling of sadness? The reality is the compulsory separation of the races (*apartheid*) in South Africa.

3. What happens to Teddy that sets the action of the *plot* in motion? A venomous tree snake sprays him in the eyes.

4. What does Gideon do for Teddy? Gideon chews a root, and then rubs the spittle in the boy's eyes. Within a short time, his eyes are cured.

5. Although Lessing makes it clear that the Farquars feel close to Gideon, when the ''Big Doctor'' arrives from the city, it also becomes apparent that they do not really understand Gideon at all. Cite the sentences that express their puzzlement over Gideon's behavior. The Farquars cannot understand why Gideon would not want to share his knowledge as a benefit for humanity. They feel he is unreasonable (see pages 1039–1040).

6. What happens to the scientist's quest for the plant? The quest fails, after Gideon leads the scientist and the Far-

quars six miles from the house, only to hand the scientist some common blue flowers at the end of the trek.

7. How does Teddy's relationship with Gideon change as he grows up? As he grows up, the relationship becomes more formal, polite, and guarded.

Interpreting Meanings

8. How do you think Lessing feels about the Farquars: Does she really feel that they are people of good will, or is there some *irony* in her attitude? How did you respond to them? Most students will agree that, even though Lessing does not condemn the Farquars, there is some irony in her attitude toward them. Students will have differing opinions in their response to the Farquars.

9. What implicit criticism can you detect in the fact that while Teddy is riding on a scooter, Gideon's son of the same age is a herdsboy? This passage vividly points up the economic disparity between the races in South Africa.

10. Why do you think Gideon refuses to share his wisdom with the Farquars? Students may suggest a variety of motives, including secretiveness, fear, stubbornness, and pride.

11. Describe how you feel about the ''Big Doctor.'' Did you find yourself identifying with him, with the Farquars, or with Gideon? Explain your responses. Student answers will vary. Ask the students to explain their responses.

12. In what ways is this story about a clash of cultures? Reread Gideon's comment at the end of the story. What does it tell us about Gideon's understanding of the relationship between the two cultures? The comment tells us that Gideon, better than anyone else in the story, understands the sad realities of apartheid and the human divisions and suffering that the practice causes. Students will differ in their opinions about the story's interpretation as a portrait of a clash of cultures. Ask the students to defend their opinions with reasons.

13. How would you state the *theme* of this story? One statement of the theme might run as follows: All too often, social prejudice and social institutions—even apparently beneficial ones—erect insuperable barriers between people.

Extending the Story

One critic has stated that Doris Lessing's ''short stories, even more than her work in other literary forms, perhaps, display her ability to observe and record her characters and their actions with a realism that is both pitiless and compassionate. Lessing believes that human beings are dogged by 'the hound of repetition,' endlessly crossing and recrossing the same small territory, committing the same errors again and again.''

Ask students to write a five-paragraph essay in which they discuss ''No Witchcraft for Sale.'' They may wish to emphasize their own reactions to the idea that Lessing is both ''pitiless and compassionate,'' or they may choose to discuss her notion that human beings make the same errors, over and over again. In any case, students should find examples that support their thesis very clearly.

Nadine Gordimer

Text page 1042

The Soft Voice of the Serpent

Text page 1043

Objectives

1. To identify details about the protagonist
2. To identify similes
3. To analyze the story's title
4. To identify the story's theme
5. To write paragraphs using similes
6. To write an analysis of a character

Introducing the Story

In outline form below, for your reference, here are major elements of the story:

- **Protagonist:** the man who lost a leg
- **Antagonist:** self-doubt and fear
- **Conflict:** human vs. self, human vs. human nature
- **Significant techniques:** protagonist, simile, theme
- **Point of view:** third-person omniscient
- **Setting:** a couple's garden

Background on the Story. You may choose to discuss with students the kind of inner conflicts people experience in their lives—whether those conflicts occur because of a tragic death of someone close, the loss of a limb, the loss of employment, the defeat that comes in an important game. This story exists because of such a defeat—one that, by the end of the story, the protagonist has yet to conquer or overcome. Refer students, before they begin the story if you wish, to Question 9 under Interpreting Meanings.

The Plot. The plot is almost nonexistent here. Emphasis has been placed on the character of the protagonist. The narrator explains in detail the man's interest in a hurt locust and the man's realization that the two are very alike. The mood shifts as the man sees the locust fly away and realizes that, at least in that one way, he is very much different from his counterpart.

Teaching Strategies

Providing for Cultural Differences. Almost every student will have experienced some kind of defeat or deep hurt. Thus, you should focus on the universality of the man's emotions and his final reaction to the locust's flight.

Providing for Different Levels of Ability. This story may easily be read during class. You may then discuss with students, as their experiences and maturity allow, the psychological nature of humankind in trying to cope with that which is irreversible and final. The initial paragraph of the story should entice students to want to know more about the protagonist and his unique circumstances. Then ask students when they began having empathy for the injured man.

Introducing Vocabulary Study. Students will benefit from knowing the following words before they read the story.

efface   lugubrious

Reading the Story. The story is brief, so you may take advantage of this fact by having the students read it during the first part of the class period. The remainder of class time may be spent discussing important literary details.

Reteaching Alternatives. You may wish to begin a study of Gordimer's story by considering the following definition of empathy, found in *A Handbook to Literature* (New York, 1972): ''The act of identifying ourselves with an object and participating in its physical and emotional sensations, even to the point of making our own physical responses as, standing before a statue of a discuss-thrower, one flexes his muscles to hurl the discus.''

Ask students to determine if they believe they have empathy for the protagonist in this story and, if so, what has caused this emotion to occur.

Responding to the Story   Text page 1046
Analyzing the Story
Identifying Facts

1. Describe the *protagonist's*, **or main character's, daily routine.** His wife wheels him into the garden, where he takes the air and reads.

What is his plan for coping with the loss of his leg? Whenever he becomes consciously aware that he has lost his leg, he quickly turns back to his book. He thinks that if he can get into the habit of ignoring the reality of his amputation, he will soon grow to feel as if he has always been one-legged.

2. In the fourth paragraph of the story, what adjectives let the reader know the kinds of things the protagonist is trying to avoid? Among the adjectives students may mention are ''dark'' and ''crushing.''

3. What discoveries does the man make about the locust? The man discovers that the locust is also missing one leg (the left one); he feels that the locust is like himself.

Interpreting Meanings

4. At the end of the first paragraph, the narrator compares the garden in which the story takes place to the Biblical Garden of Eden. How do you think the *protagonist* **is like Adam?** The protagonist is like Adam in that he is situated in a comparatively safe, cocoon-like, Edenic atmosphere in the garden, preparing himself to go out into the ''stare of the world.''

5. What ''understanding'' does the man hope he'll come to? He hopes that he will come to the ''understanding'' that he has suffered no real loss by having his leg amputated.

What knowledge does he actually achieve by the story's end? By the story's end, the man actually realizes that the comparison he made between himself and the locust, however seductive, was false, since the locust can fly and since he is still one-legged and earth-bound.

6. Find the details which imply that the husband and wife do not want to hurt each other. Such details include

the wife's sympathetic interest in the locust, despite her initial repulsion, and the husband's not suggesting that the nurse would wheel him better.

7. The description of the locust contains a number of *similes*. **List the similes and then discuss their significance in the story.** Among the similes that students may mention are the following: The locust looked like a little person out of a Disney cartoon; its body was like a small boy's homemade airplane; its back legs were like the parts of an old crane; its front legs were like one of the wife's hairpins, bent in two; it passed a leg over its head, just as a man might wipe his brow with his handkerchief. Student opinions on the significance of the similes in context will differ. In general, it is clear from the similes that the man is trying to personify the locust and to draw a parallel between the situation of the insect and his own situation.

8. The *title* **of the story refers to the serpent's temptation of Eve in the Garden of Eden. Who or what plays the tempter in this story? What is the temptation?** Student answers will vary. Most obviously, the locust plays the tempter, and the temptation is the seductive idea that the man has never really lost his leg—or at least that an analogue in nature can make up for his pain and loss. At the end of the story, this temptation is exposed as false, when both the husband and wife realize that the locust, unlike the man, can fly. Ask the students to propose other suggestions and to defend their opinions.

9. ''The Soft Voice of the Serpent'' raises a question about human nature in its attempt to cope with personal tragedy. What question is raised, and what answer is implied? Try to combine this question and answer in a statement of the *theme* **of the story.** Student answers will vary. In general, the story asks how capable we really are at coping with personal tragedy, and implies that most people, like the husband in the story, really need the assistance of illusions in doing so. Student statements of the theme of the story will vary.

Extending the Story

You may ask students to refer to notes they took concerning the various aspects of tragedy. (See Aristotle's definition of tragedy and the seven things we expect of tragedy, found in the *Macbeth* section of Unit III in this Teacher's Manual.) Then ask students to determine whether the protagonist is a tragic hero, providing reasons for their answers.

Virginia Woolf   Text page 1047

Stress, in approaching the introductory data on page 1047 of the student text, that the Bloomsbury Group was characterized by a rich and stimulating intellectual climate that has rarely known a peer in western civilization. Explain, further, that Woolf was violently opposed to war and that witnessing the devastation of one global conflict, proved to be her limit. It is generally held by scholars of her life that a depression brought on by the outbreak of World War II is what ultimately drove her to suicide.

Objectives

1. To analyze the tone of the essay

2. To evaluate the theme of the essay

3. To write an analysis of what the writer discovers

4. To write an essay contrasting an insect's natural environment to the one in which you observe it

Introducing the Essay

In outline form, for your reference, here are the major elements in the essay:

- **Point of view:** first person
- **Significant techniques:** epiphany, theme

Background on the Essay. Students should understand that Woolf's theme of struggle and decay underlies not just this essay, but many of her serious, longer works. Her obsession with death and dying is evident, though not always explicit, in *The Voyage Out*, *To the Lighthouse*, and *Mrs. Dalloway*.

Teaching Strategies

Providing for Cultural Differences. A review of the nature of analogy may assist students in understanding the essay more fully. In written and oral communication, analogies often are used to help explain something unknown or unfamiliar to an audience, by means of comparing it to something known or familiar. In Woolf's essay, she implicitly compares a human's struggle in living to that of a moth.

Providing for Different Levels of Ability. In addition to teaching this essay by considering its construction, you may also explain its emphasis on epiphany. David Daiches, in *A Critical History of English Literature* (Ronald, 1960), explains epiphany as "the sudden realization that some quite ordinary incident or situation or object encountered in daily experience has an intense symbolic meaning." In Woolf's essay, epiphany occurs as she realizes that "nothing. . . had any chance against death. . ." and that, in the moth, ". . . somehow, one saw life, a pure bead." Students should consider the narrator's epiphany as the gradual realization of a woman quietly, but deeply, in thought—and not as a rapid realization coming quite unexpectedly.

Reading the Essay. After students read the essay, they also should consider their responses to the second question under Interpreting Meanings. A class discussion should follow the reading, during which an explanation should be given concerning Woolf's own philosophy of life as a struggle.

One other important consideration is tone. Students should be aware that Woolf's tone is one of detachment and calmness—a reflection of her own resignation concerning life's difficulties. Ask students to consider how the effectiveness of the essay might have changed if Woolf had not remained so detached.

Reteaching Alternatives. In a discussion, have students identify Woolf's tone—her attitude toward her subject. Then have students make a list of the words and details in the essay that contribute to this tone.

Responding to the Essay   Text page 1050
Analyzing the Essay
Identifying Details

1. At what time of year does Woolf make her observations? It is the middle of September.

   What activities are going on around her? The ploughmen are notching the fields and the rooks are flying.

2. How is the moth different from other species of moths? He is a day moth.

3. How does she compare the moth's environment to the environment at large? The moth's environment seems pathetic and confined, compared to the spacious environment at large, which is full of "possibilities."

4. What changes come over the landscape when the moth begins to die? Stillness and quiet replace the animation of the landscape.

Interpreting Meanings

5. How does Woolf's description of the September morning as "mild, benignant, yet with a keener breath than that of the summer months" help to prepare the reader for the experience she is going to relate? The phrase "keener breath" foreshadows the moth's death.

6. When she sees that the moth is turned on its back, Woolf reaches out a pencil to turn it over again. But then she lays the pencil down. Why does she do this? She hesitates to interfere with its dignity and peace at the moment of its death.

7. The moth is described as both marvelous and pathetic. What characteristics generate this ambivalent attitude on Woolf's part? The moth is marvelous because it suggests a graceful, simple form of energy, a ''tiny bead of pure life.'' It is pathetic because of its feebleness and vulnerability.

Extending the Essay

Don Marquis' poem ''The Lesson of the Moth'' presents the death of a moth from a very different point of view: that of an imaginary cockroach named archy. Have students read this poem (available in collections of Marquis's ''archy and mehitabel'' poems). Then, in a discussion, have students compare and contrast the tones of the two works, their messages about life, and their overall effects.

Dylan Thomas

Text page 1057

A Child's Christmas in Wales

Text page 1057

Objectives

1. To determine the theme of the work
2. To analyze the mood and tone of the work
3. To write an analysis of the writer's style
4. To write about the sensory pleasure afforded by a scene

Introducing the Essay

In outline form, for your reference, here are the major elements in the essay:

- **Point of view:** first person
- **Significant techniques:** theme, tone

Background on the Essay. Explain that ''A Child's Christmas in Wales'' is an informal essay—that is, its purpose is to entertain rather than instruct. In this work, Thomas's prose tends toward poetry, especially in its incorporation of imagery. As students read the essay, ask them to locate specific instances in which Thomas's use of imagery transforms what might have been, at the pen of another writer, a dull essay into one that is unique and interesting.

Teaching Strategies

Providing for Cultural Differences. While most of the unfamiliar customs and words in this account of an early twentieth-century Welsh Christmas are explained in the footnotes, you may want to point out that the ''Christmas box'' referred to on page 1052 is a holiday tip or present for the postman, and that the traditional Christmas ''pudding'' is actually similar to a fruit cake. Help students see that, despite some unfamiliar details, there is much for them to identify with in these recollections of the excitement of childhood holidays.

Providing for Different Levels of Ability. Slower students may have some difficulties with Thomas's wide-ranging vocabulary and his sometimes unorthodox use of words. Point out the similarity of his compound words to kennings, to which students were introduced during their study of Anglo-Saxon literature in Unit One. If time permits, reading the story aloud in class will allow you to help with any comprehension difficulties.

Introducing Vocabulary Study. Students will benefit from knowing the meanings of the following words before they read the essay.

   forlorn   strident

Reading the Essay. The introductory comment which prefaces the essay in the student text refers to the musical nature of this work. Part of that musicality lies in the rhythm of the sentences, and part by Thomas's reliance on the senses. Ask students to locate Thomas's uses of the senses in this essay. They then should determine what effect such sensory descriptions have on the work as a whole. Another important issue is Thomas's view of the past and its place in the present. You may want students to evaluate this view as it is expressed in the essay.

Still another teaching strategy is the analysis of a paragraph in terms of its stylistic content. Students may analyze, for example, the first paragraph in terms of its incorporation of metaphors. In effect, the paragraph is an extended metaphor, built on Thomas's reaching into past years, circumstances, and experiences. Thus, students may locate each metaphor and then determine the overall effect of such a comparison.

Reteaching Alternatives. Discuss the narrator's tone in this essay. Then have students trace images throughout the essay that create and maintain this tone. In addition, have students locate passages that help create the impression (despite our knowledge that the essay was written by an adult) that we are seeing the world from a child's point of view.

Responding to the Essay   Text page 1056

Analyzing the Essay

Identifying Facts

1. What happened in the home of Mr. and Mrs. Prothero on Christmas Eve? There was a fire in the dining room.

How did the boys react to this event? The boys threw snowballs into the smoke. They then went to a public telephone box and alerted the fire brigade.

2. What are some of the Useful Presents Thomas lists? Among the Useful Presents are: mufflers, mittens, a tam o-shanter, a nose bag, and books.

What are some of the Useless Presents? Among the Useless Presents are: bags of jelly babies, a celluloid duck, a painting book, candy, tin soldiers, a whistle, and a pack of cigarettes.

Which does he remember more fondly? How can you tell? Thomas remembers the Useless Presents more fondly; one can tell his preference both from the gusto with which he describes them and from the fact that they are exactly the sort of things that little boys would like.

3. What kind of people are the Uncles, who were always around on Christmas? The Uncles smoked cigars and sat in front of the fire after dinner and slept.

4. What do the boys do in front of Mr. Daniel's house? They sing *Good King Wenceslas.*

What response do they get? A small dry voice joins their singing.

How do they react? They think the voice may have been that of a ghost or of trolls.

5. Thomas writes of a fire gong that was "bombilating" and snow that came "shawling" up from the ground. The first is an invented word, and the second is an unusual use of the word *shawl*. Find at least two more examples in the essay of invented words and of ordinary words used in a startling way. Among the invented words are "white-ivied," "tea-tray-slithered," and "tug-o'-warred." Among the ordinary words used in a starling way are "whooed," "rasping vests," and "wind-bused cheeks."

Interpreting Meanings

6. Thomas writes, ". . . I can never remember whether it snowed for six days and six nights when I was twelve or whether it snowed for twelve days and twelve nights when I was six." How does this statement affect your reaction to the entire essay? Why? Answers will vary. In general, most students will agree that the statement playfully suggests that the essay is probably part imagination, part fact.

7. Compare Thomas's depiction of his aunts with that of Mr. Prothero. What impression does he want to give in each case? What details in the descriptions support your answer? Mr. Prothero and the aunts are lethargic and somewhat given to the bottle. The impression given in each case is that they are rather comic, eccentric figures.

8. In the middle of the essay, a small boy says, "It snowed last year, too." What other comments does the boy make? How does the writer respond to each comment? The small boy asks if there were postmen; he asks the speaker to identify the presents; and he asks if there were uncles. The writer responds to each comment by giving his reminiscences.

Why did Thomas include this imaginary conversation in his essay? What is he suggesting about the past? Thomas's purpose may have been to suggest that, however disordered and "unfactual" his memories of Christmas may be, there is in fact a common core of nostalgic memories for Christmas that is pretty much the same for everyone. These memories have more to do with emotional feeling and a certain atmosphere than with specific details of time and place.

Extending the Essay

Have students read Thomas's poem "Fern Hill" on text page 1129. Discuss how the use of language in this poem compares to that in the essay students have just read.

Objectives

1. To determine the mood of the work

2. To write an essay about a social problem

3. To write an essay analyzing the writer's technique

Introducing the Essay

In outline form, for your reference, here are the major elements in the essay:

· **Point of view:** first person
· **Significant techniques:** mood, tone

Background on the Essay. Students very likely will be familiar with satire and its purpose to effect change in the status quo. They may not, however, be as famililar with the novel of social criticism. Ask them to recall works by American writers such as Sinclair Lewis, Upton Sinclair, and Mark Twain, who often depicted circumstances reflective of problems within their society. In much the same way, English writers of social criticism attempted to effect changes within their society. Orwell was such a writer. Students should have heard of his masterpiece, *Nineteen Eighty-Four*, a novel about the evils of totalitarianism. They may not be as aware of his other works of social criticism, among them *The Road to Wigan Pier*. You may introduce this selection, then, by comparing it to well-known works of the genre and reviewing with students the characteristics common to such works.

Teaching Strategies

Providing for Cultural Differences. While coal remains important in manufacturing processes, it is no longer the primary fuel for heating homes and powering transporation. Help students see, however, that Orwell's main point remains valid: that many material comforts we take for granted depend on the hardship of others.

Providing for Different Levels of Ability. Slower students may at first be overwhelmed by the enormous amount of detailed description this essay contains. To help them absorb this material, encourage them not merely to picture the job of coal mining but to imagine, as much as possible, that they are actually experiencing it.

Reading the Essay. Compile several works by American authors representative of the genre of social criticism.

Review these works with students, asking them to attempt to state the major themes. Guide students in focusing on the writer's perceived notions regarding necessary changes and on his or her attempts in writing to effect such changes.

Next, ask students to read the Orwell selection, keeping in mind not only the depiction of coal miners but also what Orwell seems to be saying of their jobs and lives. Ask students to locate Orwell's attempts at expressing the disillusionment and discontent of the miners. Further, students should analyze the essay in terms of what parts reflect the telling of facts and what parts reflect the narrator's own intrusion into the essay.

Reteaching Alternatives. To help students focus on the message and tone of the essay, ask them to imagine that Orwell's last paragraph were replaced with one beginning something like this: "How dare the owners and operators of coal mines exploit their workers in this fashion? These working conditions are a scandal that should not be permitted! Responsible citizens should join me in denouncing these atrocities . . . ." Discuss how the tone and the overall effect of the essay would be changed by such a conclusion.

Responding to the Essay   Text page 1065
Analyzing the Essay
Identifying Details

1. **According to Orwell, why is it difficult to get a good view of coal miners at work?** It is difficult to get a good view of the miners at work because visitors to the mines are not encouraged, and also because the ubiquitous coal dust makes it difficult to see.

2. **In what way is getting into the mine "a job in itself"?** Orwell describes the vertical descent in the cage, as well as the immense horizontal distances—often several miles— that must be traversed once one is at the bottom of the shaft. A visitor must travel hunched over, which is excruciatingly painful. The heat, smell, and noise add to the difficulty of getting into the mine.

3. **Why did Orwell have trouble telling whether a particular miner was young or old?** He says that all miners must have a young man's body in order to do their work.

4. **What comparisons does he use to describe the distance the miners must travel before they begin their work?** He uses the comparison of the distance between London Bridge and Oxford Circus.

5. What two reasons does he give for considering the return trip even worse than going into the mine? First, the men are extremely tired after their day's work. Second, the return journey is uphill.

6. What comparison does Orwell use to emphasize the amount of coal each miner produces every day? He compares the shifting of two tons of coal an hour to a gardener shifting two tons of earth in his garden.

7. What recently discontinued practice does he mention in his final paragraph? He mentions the practice of employing pregnant women as miners.

Interpreting Meanings

8. Reread the first paragraph. How does the *tone* of this paragraph contrast with the conditions described in the rest of the essay? Why do you suppose Orwell used this tone as an introduction to the essay? The first paragraph displays a relatively upbeat tone. In contrast, the tone of the rest of the essay is serious, even depressing.

9. What opinion of the miners does Orwell express when he is describing their physiques? He evidently admires the miners.

Find at least three other places in the essay where he expresses a similar opinion. Places where Orwell expresses a similar opinion include his description of the miners' ''traveling,'' his description of the amount of coal moved by the fillers, and his description of the men in the heat of the mines.

In what way are these opinions a preparation for the last paragraph of the essay? These opinions prepare us for the stark juxtaposition in the last paragraph of the ignored, but herculean, work performed by the miners and the superficialities of cultural and political activity mentioned by Orwell.

10. Reread the paragraph beginning, ''It may seem that I am exaggerating, though no one . . . .'' The word *traveling* is enclosed in quotation marks several times in that paragraph. One common use of quotation marks is to suggest a sarcastic tone of voice. Explain why you think Orwell is or is not using the word traveling sarcastically. Students will have different opinions. On the whole, Orwell seems to be employing understatement rather than sarcasm.

11. Reread the sentence beginning, ''In order that Hitler . . .'' in the second-to-last paragraph. What is the effect of Orwell's joining together the particular activities he mentions? Is he after the same effect, or a different one, when he gives a similar list in his last sentence? Explain. Student answers will vary. In general, the effect is ironic because of the contrast between the serious work of the miners and a) political rantings (Hitler) and b) superficial representatives of ''culture'' and ''society'' (the Nancy poets and the cricket crowds at Lord's). Many students will agree that the effect is the same in the last sentence. Ask the students to defend their opinions in class.

Extending the Essay

Have students find and read some investigative stories from contemporary newspapers and magazines. Discuss how these compare in tone, point of view, and purpose to Orwell's essay.

Bruce Chatwin

Text page 1066

from In Patagonia

Text page 1066

Objectives

1. To describe the narrator's characterization of himself
2. To identify tone
3. To write a reminiscence of a childhood event
4. To write an essay comparing two works

Introducing the Essay

In outline form, for your reference, here are the major elements in the essay:

- **Point of view:** first person
- **Significant techniques:** characterization, tone

Background on the Essay. It is important to begin students in their study of Chatwin's work by explaining the nature of impressionism as opposed to realism. Whereas the goal of realism is to depict events, circumstances, and people as they actually are, the goal of impressionism is to present ''characters or scenes or moods as they appear to [the author's] individual temperament at a precise moment and from a particular vantage point . . . .'' (Holman). In the passage from *In Patagonia*, Chatwin relies on the merging of past and present, actually presenting the two in juxtaposed passages. If students view the selection as being comprised of individual brushstrokes that, together, create a whole, they may understand the uniquely impressionistic nature of Chatwin's writing.

Teaching Strategies

Providing for Cultural Differences. On a globe, help your students locate the places mentioned in the essay, and trace the routes of the voyages taken by Charley Milward and John Davis. Explain that "Puerto Deseado" is Spanish for "Port Desire."

Providing for Different Levels of Ability. Slower students may need your help in understanding the chronology of John Davis's life and voyages, as Chatwin uses flashbacks and foreshadowing in recounting Davis's story.

Introducing Vocabulary Study. Students will benefit from knowing the meanings of the following words before they read the essay.

blighted   putrified
disconsolate   resonant

Reading the Essay. You may ask students to locate instances of associations Chatwin makes in his work. You may wish to locate one such association and discuss it, then have students find other examples and analyze them.

In additon, you may have students locate instances of sensory detail Chatwin includes in the selection. Ask students what effect the inclusion of such details has on the work as a whole. Then discuss the impressionistic nature of the work aided by Chatwin's sensory details.

Reteaching Alternatives. The most obvious connection between the three sections of Chatwin's essay is that they all have to do with Patagonia. Help students trace other images and subjects that link the three sections; examples include the ideas of exploration and investigation, the images of putrefaction, and the references to killing and death.

Responding to the Essays Text page 1071
Analyzing the Essays
Identifying Details

1. What does the "brontosaurus skin" turn out to have actually been? The "brontosaurus skin" turns out to have been skin from a mylodon, or Giant Sloth.

2. What other factor contributed to Chatwin's interest in Patagonia? This factor was the author's passion for geography, spurred on by Stalin, the Cold War, and the threat of the cobalt bomb. The author and his classmates wanted to identify a place of refuge where they would be safe if the bomb were ever used.

3. What was the result of the slaughter of the penguins on Penguin Island? Worms, which bred in the carcasses of the penguins, ate everything on board the ship.

4. Why, according to Chatwin, was Coleridge interested in the travels of real or imaginary wanderers? According to Chatwin, Coleridge had what Baudelaire called "The Great Malady," or "Horror of One's Home."

Interpreting Meanings

5. How does Chatwin *characterize* himself as a young boy? He characterizes himself as imaginative, curious, and observant.

How would you describe the *tone* he uses in descriptions of himself as a boy? Student answers will vary. Ask the students to support their opinions with specific references to the text of the essay.

6. What connection does Chatwin imply between penguins and travelers, such as himself and the ornithologist in Puerto Deseado? Is there any connection between this and his description of Coleridge? Penguins, travelers, and Coleridge all are described as being migratory.

7. The sentence "Albatrosses and penguins are the last birds I'd want to murder" is rather confusing at first, since it doesn't seem to bear much relation to what has preceded it. How does what follows it make the sentence clear? The sentence is clarified by the subsequent account of the slaughter of the penguins by Davis's crew and the references to Coleridge's poem, "The Rime of the Ancient Mariner," in which the shooting of an albatross is the pivotal event.

8. Chatwin has a skillful way of using a single detail or two to provide a complete and telling description of something. For example, he describes the inside of his grandmother's home: "Inside it smelled of church." Find two other examples of Chatwin's use of a surprising detail to give the reader an especially vital sense of something or event. Student answers will vary. The students should be able to pick out a number of vivid, telling details in the essay.

Extending the Essay

Have students use their imaginations together with the vivid details supplied in the essay to write some entries for a journal that might have been kept by John Davis on his catastrophic Patagonian voyage.

Twentieth-Century Poetry

Text page 1072

This passage provides a historical overview of British poetry of this century, with analysis and commentary. Your students will be introduced to the century's important movements: the Trench Poets, the English Group, and Dylan Thomas and the New Apocalypse. In addition, poets representing no major movement but possessing striking individual merit are discussed: Thomas Hardy, D. H. Lawrence, Robert Graves, and John Betjeman. The passage repeatedly contrasts the relative conservatism of twentieth-century British poetic forms with the high degree of innovation in American poetry of the same period. Encourage your students to recall some of the experimental poetry they have read by such American writers as Stevens, Pound, Williams, Eliot, and E. E. Cummings. Then have your students discuss possible reasons why British and American poetry of this century took such divergent paths. They might also enjoy arguing whether an individual writer, however great, can ever make as deep a mark on his or her culture as a major literary movement can.

Wilfred Owen

Text page 1078

As students prepare to read the first of the so-called trench poets, note that Wilfred Owen shares with several other British poets of this era—most notably Rupert Brooke—the unfortunate distinction of having died at a tender age. Note, in the case of Owen, the particular irony of his having died a mere week before the armistice was achieved.

Anthem for Doomed Youth

Text page 1079

Dulce et Decorum Est

Text page 1080

Strange Meeting

Text page 1082

Objectives

1. To explain and discuss the themes of the poems
2. To identify metaphors, extended metaphors, and other figures of speech used in the poems
3. To recognize the tone of the poems
4. To identify the uses of alliteration, assonance, consonance, and half rhymes in the poems
5. To write a paraphrase of a poem
6. To write an essay analyzing imagery in a poem
7. To write essays comparing poems

Introducing the Poems

Ask students to think of the poems they have read that deal with war. Hardy's irony and bitterness in "The Man He Killed" come to mind. Ask students to think about the ways a poet can deal with war. It is easy to see how poets deal with death and absence and with fear, but war involves weapons and wounds and enemies—unpoetic material. Ask students to prepare themselves for the manner in which Owen deals with the grimmer aspects of war. Note that he introduces some of the noises and names weapons in "Anthem for a Doomed Youth," creates a nightmare of horrific scenes in "Dulce et Decorum Est," and takes on the problem of killing other human beings in "Strange Meetings."

Background on the Poems. The Civil War in America introduced poets to some of the ills of modern warfare, but to British poets, World War I brought an unimagined horror, a completely new kind of reality, shocking in its unavoidable, undismissable evil. Owen was a talented young poet who found himself in the midst of death. His poetry, thus, raises some new questions: What does a young poet write about when his own life is in danger and he is in the midst of evil? How are British poets in general going to react to a new world (one that Hardy saw coming in "Channel Guns")? One of the fascinating aspects of Owen as a poet is that he never seems to have forgotten that he was, first and foremost, a poet. He shapes every experience, however chaotic, into a poetic form. Every word he writes, however new and ugly, becomes a part of a poem with images, figures of speech, and even new rhyming techniques and familiar techniques such as alliteration. He also shows the depths of his learning. In many ways, therefore, we have reached a new turn in British poetry, one that looks back at least as far as the Roman poet Horace and that introduces an unvarnished view of life that will come to be called Naturalism.

Anthem for Doomed Youth
Text page 1079

Teaching Strategies

Providing for Cultural Differences. "Anthem for Doomed Youth" may introduce details with which some students may be unfamiliar—the details associated with a Christian burial service.

Providing for Different Levels of Ability. Some students will need help understanding the extended metaphor in "Anthem." You may want to stress the narrative in the poems for some students, having the class outline the events in each.

Reading the Poem. Outline the comparisons in the extended metaphor.

Reteaching Alternatives. Ask students to find examples of pity in the poem.

Responding to the Poem
Text page 1079

Analyzing the Poem

Identifying Details

1. How does Owen answer the questions that open his two stanzas? In the first stanza, Owen asks what kinds of bells mark the deaths of the dead soldiers. He answers that the guns and rifles commemorate their deaths. In the second stanza, he asks what candles appear at the soldiers' funerals. He answers that the only "candles" he can find are in the glimmering of their eyes.

2. What weapons of war does the poet name in the first eight lines? The poet speaks of guns, rifles, and shells.

How are these weapons juxtaposed with elements associated with a funeral service? The guns are juxtaposed

with passing-bells; the rifles are juxtaposed with orisons, or prayers; and the sound of shells is juxtaposed with "shrill, demented choirs" (line 7).

3. Explain the *metaphor* in line 12. In the metaphor of line 12, the pallor of the girls' brows is implicitly compared with the "pall," or cloth covering on the coffins of the soldiers.

Interpreting Meanings

4. Comment on the poem's use of sound effects, especially *alliteration*, *assonance*, and *consonance*. How do they reinforce the poem's meaning or emotional effect? Among the sound effects students may mention are: alliteration in lines 8, 11, 12, 14; assonance in line 11; and consonance in lines 3, 4, 7, and 12. Student opinions on how these sound effects reinforce the poem's meaning and emotional effect will differ; encourage the students to give reasons for their opinions.

5. Explain the *extended metaphor* of the poem as a whole. The extended metaphor underlying the poem as a whole ironically equates the dead soldiers' funeral service with the actual sound and sights on the battlefield.

6. What do you think is the effect of the poem's final line? The effect of the final line is to fuse the violent destruction and the deaths of the young men on the battlefield with the routine, everyday falling of dusk and the mourning of the bereaved families at home.

7. Do you think this poem has something universal to say about war? Tell why or why not. Student answers will vary. Encourage the students to support their opinions with reasons.

Dulce et Decorum Est
Text page 1080

Teaching Strategies

Providing for Cultural Differences. Talk a bit with students about Latin and the Ancient Roman.

Providing for Different Levels of Ability. Some background on Latin as a language and about Ancient Rome will help some students.

Reading the Poem. Have students concentrate on following the story line, the narrative in the poem, and then fill in the details. Get students to try to focus on what Owen sees in the men at war. Tell students that this is a nightmare but a real one, introduced by the use of poison gas. There may still be people in your community who know of men who suffered from such assaults in World War I. The question of what is happening to the issue of chemical warfare and gas warfare may be one that can be researched and discussed after reading the poem.

Reteaching Alternatives. You might want to ask students to retell in their own words what is described in the poem.

Responding to the Poem — Text page 1781
Analyzing the Poem
Identifying Details

1. Describe the condition and actions of the men in the first stanza. In the first stanza, the exhausted men, bent double and coughing, march on, even though many of them have lost their boots and are lame.

2. What are "the mighty panes" in line 13 through which the speaker glimpses the dying man? The panes are the panes of the gas mask that the speaker wears.

3. What experience does the speaker refer to in lines 15–16? He refers to a nightmare, in which he sees one of his fellow soldiers choking to death in a gas attack.

4. Who is addressed in the final stanza? In the final stanza, the speaker addresses a "friend," who may be assumed to be the reader of the poem.

5. Analyze the *rhyme scheme* of the poem. Can you find any *half rhymes*? The rhyme scheme is as follows: *ababcdcdefefghghijijklklmnmn.* Half rhymes include "in" (line 18) and "sin" (line 20) and "glory" (line 26) and *mori* (line 28).

Interpreting Meanings

6. Explain the *figure of speech* in lines 23–24. How is this *metaphor* relevant to the *theme* of the poem? The figure of speech compares the tainted blood that pours from the damaged lungs of the gassed soldier to a cud chewed by a cow; this cud, in turn, is chewed with a cancerous, sore-ridden tongue. The figure of speech reinforces the theme of the poem: that war and its destructive ruin are a vile disease of humanity.

7. This poem uncompromisingly contrasts the high-minded ideals of patriotism with the reality of war. What is your personal reaction to this contrast? Student answers will vary. Urge the students to support their reactions with reasons.

8. Could this poem describe the conditions of any modern war? Most students will agree that the poem could apply to the conditions of modern war, although some students may suggest that changing technology would lead to a modern war being more impersonal and mechanized.

How would you describe the speaker's *tone*? Is it a tone that you sense in war stories today or even in war movies? Many students will describe the tone as tormented and angry, or as brutally realistic. Students will vary in their opinions on analogues for this tone in contemporary war stories or war movies.

Strange Meeting — Text page 1082

Teaching Strategies

Providing for Cultural Differences. Students should encounter no problems here.

Providing for Different Levels of Ability. You may want to help some students follow the dialogue and narrative aspects and then list details.

Reading the Poem. Tell students that this is an important poem in which the poet takes up the question of what one should feel about an enemy. Then ask the students to look for Owen's answers to this important question.

Reteaching Alternatives. Hold a discussion about the issue raised by the poem. Instruct students to look for examples of what Owen calls the "pity of war."

Responding to the Poem — Text page 1084
Analyzing the Poem
Identifying Details

1. Describe the speaker's experience in lines 1–10. It seems to the speaker that he escapes from battle down a long, dark tunnel. He sees people who look as if they are asleep. One of these persons springs up, staring and smiling at the speaker. The speaker imagines that he is in hell.

Where is the poem *set*? The poem is set figuratively in hell; literally, it is set on a battlefield in wartime.

2. What "causes to mourn" does the stranger identify? Among the causes to mourn that the stranger identifies are his wasted years, his premature death, his sense of hopelessness, and the pit of war.

3. What "truth" does the speaker refer to in line 24? In line 24, he refers to the "pity of war," by which he means the boundless destruction that war causes.

4. What surprising revelation occurs in line 40? The stranger reveals that he is the "enemy" whom the speaker had killed on the previous day.

5. List the examples of *half rhyme* you find in the poem. Virtually every pair of lines in the poem contains a half rhyme.

Where are the half rhymes combined with *alliteration*? Such combinations occur in virtually every pair of lines.

Interpreting Meanings

6. What points of kinship between two speakers does the poem suggest? The poem suggests that both speakers are tormented by the grim experience of warfare. In line 40, the stranger addresses his killer unexpectedly as "my friend," and says that he knew him in the dark. The stranger says in the final line that both men should sleep. Hints in the poem imply that the stranger may, ironically, be the speaker's "double," or a product of his tormented imagination.

7. What do you think is the *theme* of this poem? Student answers will vary. One possible statement of the theme might be that war is grueling, nightmarish, and ruinous.

Siegfried Sassoon

Text page 1085

The Rear-Guard

Text page 1086

Objectives

1. To locate examples of onomatopoeia in the poem
2. To explain aspects of the setting of the poem
3. To explain the irony in the poem
4. To compare the poem with respect to structure and sound devices with Owen's "Strange Meeting"

Introducing the Poem

The study of Wilfred Owen and the introduction to his poetry will serve to introduce this poem of a close friend of Owen. You might remind students that Sassoon, born to the highest level of English society, was of a distinctly different class from Owen. Ask if they can detect this difference in Sassoon's poem. Usually, the class difference did matter. There may be a trace of arrogance in the speaker's attitude in "The Rear-Guard," but students will discover that in general World War I was a great "leveler." Ask students to look for similarities in Sassoon's and Owen's reaction to the setting in which they found themselves—the trenches.

Background on the Poem. Sassoon won public acclaim for his actions in speaking out against the war and against its leaders in his prose and poetry. His poetry in particular places him as one of the "war poets" of World War I.

Teaching Strategies

Providing for Cultural Differences. Students will encounter no special problems here.

Providing for Different Levels of Ability. The slow reader or a student who has trouble with poetry will always benefit from both drawing a "stage set" of the poem's setting and a narrative outline of the speaker's path.

Reading the Poem. Ask students to pay attention to the objects that the speaker encounters and to the changing light. Sassoon has had things his own way all his young life. He is not necessarily more fearless and, perhaps, is less sensitive than Owen. He simply has had no reason to think before he speaks—at least out of some sense of caution or self-protection. Have students notice that he apparently does not live in the trenches and that he is able to leave them at will. He still concentrates pretty much on himself, at least in this poem.

Except for the metaphor in the last line, Sassoon seems content to let the episode speak for itself, concentrating on details, without trying to stylize the episode in the traditional manner of poets. His language is the language of prose, strong prose at that. It is clear that he used it as a weapon to shock the "Establishment."

Reteaching Alternatives. You may want to have students, on a second reading, use the poem to set the stage for a play. Have them list props, plan lighting effects, and position the speaker and the dead man he discovers.

Responding to the Poem   Text page 1087

Analyzing the Poem

Identifying Details

1. What is the man looking for in the tunnel? In line 11, he says that he is looking for headquarters.

Unit Seven: The Twentieth Century

How deep is it? The tunnel is fifty feet below ground.

2. Why does the man tug at the sleeper's arm in line 10? The man tugs at his arm because he wants the sleeper to guide him through the tunnel.

3. What does the man discover about the sleeper? He discovers that the sleeper is dead.

4. What does the man do in the final three lines? Horror-stricken, the man climbs up through the darkness to the twilight on the battlefield.

5. What words in the poem use *onomatopoeia* to help you hear the sounds in the tunnel? Examples include: "winked" (line 2), "smashed" (line 5), "tripping" (line 8), "humped" (line 9), "tug" (line 10), "stagged" (line 19), "muttering" (line 21), "boom" (line 22), "muffled" (line 22).

Interpreting Meanings

6. Why is the air "unwholesome"? The air is unwholesome because the tunnel contains the bodies of dead soldiers.

7. How is the officer's behavior simultaneously brutal and pathetic? Students may suggest that his behavior is brutal because he curses and kicks the sleeper. His behavior is pathetic because of his evident shock at finding that the sleeper is dead and his horror at being lost in the tunnel.

8. Look at the present and past participles in the poem—words such as *groping*, *prying*, *smashed*, and *tripping*. What effect do these words have on the poem? These words establish a vivid sense of immediacy; they also hint at the officer's desperation and powerlessness.

9. Explain the *irony* of the quotation in line 13. The irony derives from the fact that the officer is asking a dead man to be his guide.

10. What does the speaker mean by saying he is "unloading hell"? Students may suggest that the speaker means that, by ascending to the surface of the earth out of the dark tunnel, he is escaping from an inferno.

William Butler Yeats

Objectives

1. To recognize the poem's setting

2. To identify the tone of a poem

3. To identify the feelings of the speaker in a poem

4. To make inferences from clues about the speaker's past experience

5. To recognize and interpret symbols in a poem

6. To state the theme of a poem

7. To find images in a poem

8. To interpret certain lines in a poem that have become famous

9. To perform research into the background of a poem

10. To write an elegaic poem

Introducing the Poems

Tell students that in Yeats they will no longer be reading a "war poet." Yeats's interests are far broader. He was too old to share the experience of being a young poet in the trenches of France, although he lived almost long enough to experience the beginning of World War II. His age was not the only significant factor. Yeats was also a native of Ireland, an island that had its own problems and interests and never felt itself a part of England. Students can expect to find that these poems deal with subjects that remind them of Wordsworth and Tennyson and the sensitivity of those poets to time and nature. But, like all truly great poets, Yeats adds his own stamp to these subjects and adds a major interest of his own—a concern for art. Finally, his Irishness is revealed in a sense of the magic of nature.

Background on the Poems. Yeats, like a number of other top poets of the day, owed much to the American poet Ezra Pound, who was not only a fine poet but was an excellent teacher. Yeats and Pound were close friends and for a time shared a house. As students will learn from the introduction in their text, Pound succeeded in getting Yeats to move from the dreamy, pretty language that we find in the early poems into language that is highly charged, sharp, almost breathtaking in its impact. Ask students to notice this change in the use of language, as they move from "The Lake Isle of Innisfree" with its "glimmer" and "purple glow" (line 7) to "The Second Coming" and "A shape with lion body and the head of a man, a gaze blank and pitiless as the sun."

Teaching Strategies

Providing for Cultural Differences. "The Second Coming" calls for a simple understanding that the first "coming" was, according to Christian belief, the birth of Jesus at Bethlehem, which is celebrated each year at Christmas. Some background notes on the city of Byzantium and an example of its art would help in the understanding of "Sailing to Byzantium."

Providing for Different Levels of Ability. The two earlier poems are easier to understand and provide a good introduction to Yeats.

The Lake Isle of Innisfree Text page 1090

Reading the Poem. Ask students to consider how Yeats creates a sense of what we call "peace and quiet." Ask them to look for the way in which Yeats creates a sense of space and a sense of quietness.

Reteaching Alternatives. Ask students to find poems about a similar scene in nature by Wordsworth and Tennyson and to compare the language in the works of all three poets. Ask students to recall a place they have loved and to think about how they would write about it.

Responding to the Poem   Text page 1090
Analyzing the Poem
Identifying Details

1. In the first stanza, what does the speaker say he will do? The speaker says that he will go to Innisfree, build a small cabin there, and live alone.

2. What sounds does the speaker describe in the poem? In line 4, the speaker refers to the sound of the bees in the glade. Line 6 refers to the singing of the cricket. Line 10 mentions the sound of the lake water lapping the shore.

3. How do the surroundings of the lake island contrast with the speaker's actual location? The lake island is beautiful, natural, and tranquil. The speaker's actual location, by contrast, is urban and dreary (line 11).

Interpreting Meanings

4. Why do you think the speaker cannot find peace in the city setting? The speaker is evidently a lover of nature. He finds the city setting grim and dreary.

5. How would you describe the *tone* of this poem? Possible descriptions might be: lyrical, escapist, nostalgic, yearning, quiet.

Do you think it could be called a Romantic poem? Explain why or why not. Because the speaker evidently values the tranquility and beauty of natural surroundings, many students will agree that the poem could be called a Romantic work.

The Wild Swans at Coole Text page 1092

Reading the Poem. Tell students that this is a poem in which each line adds new information of some kind. Get them to look out for this information and to see whether it adds to the setting, the movement of the swans, and the poet or speaker.

Reteaching Alternatives. Have students trace the actions of the swans and list each motion. Then ask students to explain what it is about the swans that Yeats envies.

Responding to the Poem   Text page 1093
Analyzing the Poem
Identifying Details

1. Describe the scene depicted in the first stanza. How does the time of year correspond to the time of day? In the first stanza, the speaker describes trees by a lake or pond in the autumn. On the pond, fifty-nine swans swim in the water. After a while, they mount into the sky. Autumn (the season) corresponds with twilight (the time of day).

2. How is the speaker feeling as he gazes at the swans? He feels melancholy.

How did he feel nineteen years earlier when he heard the beating of their wings? Line 18 indicates that he then "trod with a lighter tread."

3. In what ways have the swans remained unchanged? They are unwearied and their hearts have not grown old. They seem unaffected by time.

4. What question does the speaker ask in the last stanza? He wonders where the swans will have gone, and where they will have built their nests, when the speaker realizes that they have flown away.

Interpreting Meanings

5. The second, third, and fourth stanzas offer some hints about the speaker's personal experience that underlies the poem. What are these hints? Why do you think the speaker's heart is "sore" (line 14)? Answers will vary. Students may suggest that the speaker rues his advancing age, or possibly a disappointment in love. In general, the stanzas suggest that the speaker has undergone a sobering, sad set of experiences.

6. What qualities of the swans do you think the speaker envies? Why? What might the swans *symbolize* to the speaker? He envies their brilliance, their timelessness, their mystery, and their ability to delight men's eyes. Perhaps the swans symbolize beauty and changelessness to the speaker.

7. The word *awake* in the next-to-last line is mysterious at first reading. Do you think it signifies that the poem has all been a dream? Or could it mean something else? How might this word offer a clue to the *theme* of the poem? Students may suggest that the word implies that the speaker's life is as fleeting as a dream—thus, the word *awake*, paradoxically, would connote the speaker's death.

8. How are the time of year and the time of day appropriate to the theme of the poem? The theme of the poem, which relates to the speaker's contemplation of his own mortality, is indirectly reinforced by the setting of ancient twilight in the autumn, a symbol for old age or decline.

The Second Coming   Text page 1094

Reading the Poem. The first stanza can be read a prose—with the aid of the footnote and an understanding of the falconer image. The second stanza makes sense only in the context of the Christian belief that Jesus will return to earth again in the Second Coming. Many students will not have heard of the Second Coming, including those who are professed Christians. Today few people dwell on the vision, but the full force of Yeats's irony will be lost if it is not set against a scene such as many people know—the manger scene in the stable at Bethlehem, the First Coming, with a human impact, innocent animals, and a great hope for the future.

Reteaching Alternatives. You may want to suggest that Yeats is reacting here to the events of the new century—as did the Trench Poets. He expresses his concern much differently from the younger men who went to war. Yeats's concern is wider, deeper. Ask students if Yeats or the World War I poets succeed in making readers concerned about the future.

Responding to the Poem   Text page 1095
Analyzing the Poem
Identifying Details

1. In your own words, describe the picture of the world that the speaker offers in the first stanza. The speaker offers a bleak picture of a world of anarchy, warfare, loss of traditional values, and strife.

2. What *image* of the Second Coming troubles the speaker in the second half of the poem? Name some of the specific words that make this image especially vivid. The speaker offers a frightening image of a violent beast emerging from the desert, half lion and half man, with a blank and pitiless gaze. Students may mention the following words: "blank," "pitiless," "reel," "indignant," "stony," "rough," and "slouches."

Interpreting Meanings

3. What do you think the poet means by the word *center* in line 3? He probably means "moral center," or that scheme of civilized values that helps to stave off anarchy and chaos.

Why, in this poem's context, is the image of the falcon especially appropriate? The image of the falcon is appropriate because the falcon flies in widening circles around the falconer. The fact that the bird can no longer hear its master corresponds to the fact that humanity has lost its moral "center" and has raged out of control with warfare, sin, and violence.

4. Comment on the force of the words *mere* in line 4 and *slouches* in line 22. In line 4, the word *mere*, used to describe anarchy, has the ironic force of understatement. In line 22, the verb *slouches* carries ominous connotations.

5. What might the "blood-dimmed tide" in line 5 refer to? The "blood-dimmed tide" probably refers to warfare.

What could the "ceremony of innocence" in line 6 mean? Student answers will vary. Ask the students to support their suggestions. Some students may suggest that the phrase might obliquely refer to Christian baptism.

6. How does the idea of the Second Coming become frighteningly ironic in the second half of the poem? The idea becomes frighteningly ironic because Yeats is suggesting that the Second Coming—traditionally thought of as the day of the Last Judgment—may actually turn out to be the advent of a cruel, sinister "god" who will preside over the loss of civilization as we know it.

7. Like some monster in a horror movie, Yeats's "shape with lion body and the head of a man" begins to move "its slow thighs" and start upon a path of destruction that human beings are helpless to halt or stall. What hints in the poem indicate that this creature has the power to paralyze its enemies and overcome their defenses? The mention of the creature's gaze, "blank and pitiless as the sun" (line 15), implies that the creature is merciless and powerful. In line 18, the mention of the darkness dropping carries menacing undertones.

8. If you know enough about the history of the twentieth century, tell who might be counted among "the best" and among "the worst." Student answers will vary.

Sailing to Byzantium   Text page 1096

Reading the Poem. The first two lines of each stanza serve as a topic sentence to the stanza as a whole. One way to get into the poem is to read only first two lines of the first three stanzas, and then the final stanza. The most beautiful lines in the poem and those that support the "topic sentences" are the remaining six lines in the first, second, and third stanzas. They must be read and relished, word for word.

Reteaching Alternatives. Ask students to think of the speaker in the poem as an old man who has loved the world described in stanza 1, to understand his explanation in stanza 2, his hope in stanza 3, and his final refuge in Art, expressed in stanza 4.

Responding to the Poem   Text page 1097
Analyzing the Poem
Identifying Details

1. In the first stanza, what is the speaker's complaint about the young? He complains that the young have no regard for anything except sensual pleasure.

What happens to people caught in "that sensual music"? They neglect "monuments of unaging intellect," or the products of the intelligence and the imagination.

2. In the second stanza, what does the speaker say are the alternatives that confront the old? The old can give in to physical decrepitude, or they can celebrate the inner life of the mind and the imagination.

Why is he sailing to Byzantium? He is sailing on an imaginary voyage to Byzantium to celebrate the power of art and the imagination.

3. Paraphrase the speaker's prayer to the sages, or wise men, and saints in the third stanza. He prays that the sages and saints will take him out of his aging, physical body and transmute him into the eternal realm of art.

4. How does the speaker imagine himself in the fourth stanza? He imagines himself transformed into a bird, fashioned from gold and enamel, who will sit upon a golden bough and sing of the past, present, and future to the court of Byzantium.

Interpreting Meanings

5. What is the "dying animal" in line 22? The "dying animal" refers to the speaker's physical body.

6. Explain how the *image* of singing helps to unify the poem. References to song and singing occur in each stanza at lines 3, 11, 13, 20, and 30. This image helps to unify the poem because it is drawn from the realm of art, creativity, and the imagination.

What do you think this song symbolizes? The spiritual song of the speaker/bird (as opposed to the "sensual music" of the first stanza) perhaps symbolizes wisdom, art, or timelessness.

7. What values does the speaker seem to uphold in the poem? He seems to uphold spiritual and artistic values, as opposed to sensual, physical, or worldly values.

8. Is this poem primarily a protest against the ravages of time, or is it a celebration of art, or does its major *theme* lie elsewhere? Explain your answer. Student answers will vary. Urge the students to support their opinions with reasons.

Objectives

1. To interpret significant details and allusions in the poem

2. To analyze the poetic techniques used in the poem and to explain their effect in developing the theme of the poem

3. To identify the tone and theme of the poem

4. To prepare and perform a choral reading of the poem

5. To write an essay explaining the relationship of the poetic techniques used to the theme of the poem

Introducing the Poem

Tell students that this is another war poem, the first one on World War II, occurring twenty years after the war of the Trench Poets. Explain that war is now out of the trenches and that bombs are falling on civilians in cities across England. Ask students to look for comparisons—the view of the enemy, or lack of it, and the uses of religion in facing the war.

You may also want to point out that Sitwell is the first woman whose poetry they have studied since Elizabeth Barrett Browning. If you make a comparison across the century, you can not only do so with the content (less innocent) and techniques of the poems (less traditional in structure than Browning's sonnet) but also with the backgrounds of the two poets. You may want to read some of Edith Sitwell's early, rebellious poetry, and with it some examples of French Symbolist poetry. You might also display some French post-impressionist painting.

Finally you might want to prepare the students for the religious references used throughout the poem—from Cain and Abel and the Garden of Eden through the Crucifixion and including the message that Christians believe Jesus brought to the world.

Background on the Poem.   When Adolph Hitler, the dictator of Germany, started World War II and began overrunning neighboring European states with his fast-moving mechanzied armies and air force, the trench warfare of World War I became a memory. When the English armies were forced to withdraw from the Continent and Hitler's forces were facing England across the English Channel, England was in peril. Hitler, the Allies knew, might invade with paratroops from the sky and tanks rolling off landing craft, or he might try to bomb England, especially its industrial cities and London. Indeed, in 1940, he chose the latter course. No longer would civilians merely read about the horrors of war, for the horrors rained on them nightly. By then Edith Sitwell was a convert to Christianity, and she saw the immense new evil of war in terms of the historical evil of humanity, which had roots in the Garden of Eden.

Teaching Strategies

Providing for Cultural Differences.   Although students who have not been exposed at all to the story of Jesus and the details of his death upon the Cross will be especially at a disadvantage in understanding this poem, you should not assume that the details mentioned in the poem are well-known to any students.

Providing for Different Levels of Ability.   The repetition of the line, "Still falls the Rain," as students think of weapons of death falling from the sky, will have an effect on all students if the poem is read aloud.

Reading the Poem.   As suggested above, reading the poem aloud may serve as a good introduction before tackling each of the allusions. You might also want to tell your class that, to the speaker in this poem, each allusion, however far removed it may seem, is to the same message: we should love one another.

Retaching Alternatives.   You may want to pay attention to the title and subtitle—to the word *still* and, of course, the word *rain*. Students may see significance in the words *night* and *dawn* as expressing some hope for a new dawn based on peace.

After an introductory reading, as suggested above, you may want to mount a head-on attack on the references, Biblical and otherwise, so that in future readings the meaning of each stanza will become clear.

Responding to the Poem   Text page 1100
Analyzing the Poem
Identifying Details

1. How many nails does the speaker mention in the first stanza? What is the significance of that number? She mentions 1940 nails, a number that corresponds to the year during World War II in which she wrote the poem.

2. Upon what various items or places does the rain fall? The rain falls on the Potter's Field, the Field of Blood, and at the feet of the Cross.

3. What is the *rhyme scheme* of each stanza of the poem? First stanza: *abcb*. Second stanza: *abbcaaa*. Third stanza: *abcca*. Fourth stanza: *abbccded*. Fifth stanza: *abcdeab*. Sixth stanza: *abc*.

4. Each stanza but the last one begins with the same *refrain*. What would you say the *rain* symbolizes? Does it refer to more than one thing? The rain might be held to symbolize human sin, violence, war, cruelty, or departure from God's will.

Interpreting Meanings

5. Who is Cain (line 11)? What does he have to do with the subject of the poem? Cain, in the Bible, was the first murderer, who killed his brother Abel. His mention is appropriate in the poem because the subjects of the poem are warfare and killing, and, by extension, human cruelty.

6. Why does the poet mention the "baited bear" and the "hunted hare"? These references help to expand the chronological field of reference of the poem; the poet emphasizes that cruelty and inhumanity have, tragically, been part of human nature in all of history.

7. The last line is enclosed in quotation marks. Who is the speaker? The speaker of the last line is the crucified Christ.

What is the meaning of the speaker's words? Christ means that, despite man's unworthiness and violence, he still loves humanity and is still willing to shed his own blood for man's redemption.

8. Examine the *meter* of the poem, especially the meter of the refrain. What effect does this meter help to create? The meter of the poem alternates between rising and falling structures (trochees and anapests), producing an irregular, strained effect. The meter of the refrain (two stressed syllables, followed by an iamb) suggests the steady falling of rain.

9. Do you think this is an optimistic poem or a pessimistic one? Student answers will differ. Ask them to support their opinions with reasons.

D. H. Lawrence

Text page 1102

The Snake

Text page 1102

Objectives

1. To identify the setting of the poem and the scenes that form the setting

2. To interpret the speaker's attitude

3. To interpret an inner conflict of the speaker in the poem

4. To recognize and interpret the theme of a poem

5. To write a memoir relating the effect of music or some form of art to poetry

6. To recognize the symbolic quality of some images

7. To compare poems and the setting of poems

8. To identify allusions

9. To recognize free verse and poetic techniques

Introducing the Poem

Suggest that students will find in Lawrence another new change in the style and subject matter of British poetry.

Suggest that they will find his poetry more straightforward in both style and content. His sentences are usually straightforward, as in prose. He depends on the reader finding poetry in what he says rather than in how he says it. You can point out later that there is artistry in the lines of poetry, chiefly in the selection of sounds. Point out that Lawrence is honest about himself and his feelings. Some earlier poets might be embarrassed to write about fear in encountering a snake.

The Background of the Poems. Lawrence's background—a childhood in which he watched his mother suffer through poverty and the harsh working conditions of a coal-mining town—probably made him less hesitant to speak out unashamedly on a number of subjects, especially where his own feelings were involved. Whereas upper-class Britishers at this time were usually taught to be self-restrained, keeping their feelings to themselves, Lawrence put great stock in emphasizing feelings.

Teaching Strategies

Providing for Cultural Differences. Students will have no special problems with this poem.

Providing for Different Levels of Ability. "Snake" can be introduced for slower readers by concentrating on the animal strictly as an animal, as the poet does through line 21. Lines 22–40 are introspective and present the speaker's ruminations. You might examine these lines with students to ensure their grasp of the literal meaning.

Reading the Poem. The process suggested for slower readers above may suggest a pattern for reading the poem with all students.

Reteaching Alternatives. After setting up the setting of the poem—a village square with water fountain in a country town in Sicily—and following the actions of the snake, almost camera shot by camera shot—concentrate on what is going on in the mind of the speaker. List all the emotions that he expresses. Ask students why he thinks that the snake comes from the "bowels of the earth."

Responding to the Poem   Text page 1103

Analyzing the Poem

Identifying Details

1. Where did the speaker find the snake? He found the snake by his water trough.

What is the speaker's reaction? The speaker was pleasurably fascinated by the snake.

2. What *internal conflict* does the speaker experience? Even though he liked the snake, the speaker was warned by the "voice of his education" that the reptile might be poisonous.

How does he resolve it? He throws a log at the snake.

3. Why does the speaker throw the log at the snake? The speaker is horrified at the idea that the snake may disappear down the hole into the earth.

Why does he regret having done so? He regrets the act because it suddenly strikes him as mean and vulgar.

4. At the close of the poem, what does the speaker compare the snake to? He compares the snake to a king of the underworld.

Interpreting Meanings

5. What *images* describing the snake seem to you especially realistic? Among the images students may mention are: the snake's "yellow-brown slackness" (line 7), the flickering of the snake's tongue (line 17), the snake licking his lips (line 44), and the snake writhing like lightning (line 50).

What aspects of the description seem mostly *symbolic*? The concluding simile, comparing the snake to an exiled king of the underworld, seems especially symbolic.

6. What does the poem imply about the dichotomy, or split, between culture and nature? Student answers will vary. In general, the speaker seems to come down on the side of nature, since he calls his human education (the symbol of culture in the poem) "accursed" in line 60. The poem implies that human civilization has involved man in a dangerous split between his "natural" instincts and pleasures and his "civilized" or "educated" inclinations.

Does the poem suggest any resolution of this split? Again, student answers will vary. Ask the students to support their suggestions with references to the poem.

7. Do you find any *allusions* in this poem to Pluto or Hades, the king of the Underworld in Greek and Roman mythology? The simile in lines 68–70 might refer to Hades.

Do you detect any allusions to the account of the serpent in Genesis? Explain. Some students may suggest that the speaker's fascination with the serpent's beauty is an oblique allusion to the tale of the temptation in Genesis.

8. Can you think of occasions when the voices of one's "human education" might make one do something that later would be cause for shame or regret? Student answers will vary.

Robert Graves   Text page 1104

Warning to Children   Text page 1105

Objectives

1. To explain the repetition in terms of the poet's theme

2. To evaluate the poem's rhythm in terms of its tone

3. To write a reply and description of what a child might find if he or she pulled the string

Introducing the Poem

Explain to students that Robert Graves was one of the most serious and intellectual writers in modern British literature but that he was used to writing simple stories. Add that Graves seemed to think that very serious, perplexing matters could be best dealt with when presented in simple stories or poems like this one.

Background on the Poem. You might want to remind students that children's pastimes and play were quite different back in the days when this poem was written, even though human imagination has not changed.

Teaching Strategies

Providing for Cultural Differences. The mystery in this poem is not a matter of culture.

Providing for Different Levels of Ability. Rather than ask all students to try to solve the mystery of reality versus imagination, you may simply want to let some students compare the poet's imagination with their own. What playthings would young children today imagine in place of slates, nets, and dominoes?

Reading the Poem. Tell students that they will find out in this poem what Robert Graves thinks about the role of imagination in our lives. How real is it? How important is it? How does it work?

Reteaching Alternatives. You may want to ask students how they would go about trying to think about the "greatness" and "rareness" of the world. What are some of their thoughts? Where does reality end and imagination take over? Is, in fact, the imagination the greatest force in the world?

Responding to the Poem   Text page 1105

Analyzing the Poem

Identifying Details

1. To whom is the poem addressed? The poem is addressed to children.

What "warning" does the speaker deliver? The speaker tells the children not to undo the parcel, for they will then find themselves trapped inside it.

2. What is inside the parcel? Inside is a small island with a fruit tree.

3. Why shouldn't the children undo the parcel? They should not undo the parcel because, if they do, they will find themselves inside it.

Interpreting Meanings

4. Identify the *repetitions* in the poem. Given the poem's *theme*, what makes the use of repetition especially effective? Lines 2–5 are repeated in lines 34–37, and lines 6–9 are repeated in lines 17–20 and 26–30. The repetitions are especially effective because they reinforce the "puzzle" of the poem and the theme that it is self-defeating, or illusory, to try to unravel the uniqueness and mystery of human life.

5. Comment on the poem's use of *rhythm*. Do you think it gives the poem a somber, serious tone, or does it create a sense of fun and playfulness? The rhythm is predominantly trochaic tetrameter. Many students will suggest that this rhythm creates a sense of fun and playfulness.

6. What do you think this poem is really all about? What could it be saying about the imagination? In general, the poem seems to be saying that the imagination cannot be analyzed the way a parcel could be unwrapped and inspected. The human imagination, and human life itself, should be enjoyed, not dissected.

John Betjeman   Text page 1106

Death in Leamington   Text page 1107

Objectives

1. To infer the speaker's attitude toward dying and death

2. To retell the narrative from the nurse's point of view

3. To write an essay analyzing the theme of the poem

4. To compare the poem to the short story "Miss Brill"

Introducing the Poem

Because Betjeman mourned the passing of the Victorian and Edwardian eras, you can point out to students that they may regard this poem as belonging in a sense to these eras. The twentieth-century poets they have been studying so far have been concerned with war, storytelling, or religion—not with the passing of a long and impressive period in British society. Here Betjeman says farewell reluctantly and perhaps with a certain ill grace. He has little to say for those who watch the passing of the period and who, like the nurse in the poem, may not even realize that the days of gentility and class stability are no more. Students may wonder why he finds the nurse to be lacking in soul (see line 11). Explain that she, like the caretakers of the society in which the poet now finds himself, simply goes through the motions of her job without regard for what has been lost.

Background on the Poem. Betjeman, as an architect and self-appointed custodian of a society that was dead or dying, has an eye for details of decay in the upstairs bedroom. He clearly intends the room to symbolize the decay that he finds about him in the modern world.

Teaching Strategies

Providing for Cultural Differences. Students who have read novels set in British seaside resorts and health spas will recognize more quickly than others the setting of this poem and the atmosphere that pervades it.

Providing for Different Levels of Ability. Attention to detail is called for, but otherwise there are no special problems.

Reading the Poem. You may want to have students read the poem as if they were going to create a stage set from it.

Reteaching Alternatives. You may want to remind students that Tennyson in ''Crossing the Bar'' asked for a death by the light of an ''evening star.'' Is the old lady's death the kind of death Tennyson would have welcomed? Do students find the nurse's behavior defensible?

Responding to the Poem Text page 1108
Analyzing the Poem
Identifying Details

1. Why does the nurse come into the sickroom? She comes into the sickroom to bring the tea things.

2. What does the nurse do in the room? She bolts the window, unrolls the blinds, lights the coal fire, and tells the woman to wake up for tea. Then, realizing that the woman is dead, the nurse tiptoes out of the room.

Interpreting Meanings

3. What is the significance of the nurse's last action? By turning down the gas in the hall, the nurse acknowledges the death of the woman with a practical gesture: the heat is no longer needed at such a high level, as in a sickroom.

4. How does the poem connect the woman's death to her surroundings? The poet mentions the ''crotchet'' near the woman's fingers in the second stanza; the room is described in the first three stanzas; and references are made to the town of Leamington in the first and seventh stanzas.

5. Why do you think the poet does not give the characters' names? Student answers will vary. Many students will suggest that the reason is that the poem is intended to comment on death in general, and on the human reaction to it.

6. Is the poem's focus primarily on the dead woman, or is it on the nurse and her reactions? Explain your answer. Many students will suggest that the poem is primarily about the nurse and her reactions.

7. What *attitude* towards dying and death do you think is implied by this poem? Does this viewpoint have anything to teach us in the contemporary world? Student answers will vary. Ask the students to support their answers with reasons.

W. H. Auden Text page 1109

Objectives

1. To identify and analyze the themes of the poem

2. To interpret the significance of the titles of the poems

3. To identify and explain the tone of a poem, including irony

4. To identify images

5. To identify and explain figures of speech

6. To write a description of a painting

7. To relate an ancient myth to a modern poem

8. To write an essay analzying the satire in a poem

9. To imitate the poet's technique

Introducing the Poems

At just what point British poetry left behind the nineteenth and entered, intellectually and emotionally, the twentieth century is difficult to say. The bombing of London was certainly a twentieth-century event, but Edith Sitwell viewed it against the ageless story of Christianity, almost as if she were in the Middle Ages. Robert Graves also gave us an ageless poem, but the allusions are Edwardian. John Betjeman keeps us looking backward a little. Auden brings us, in his "The Unknown Citizen," not only into the twentieth century but into the 1930s. He has come almost to the computer age. Ask your students to see if they can recognize this coming event.

Background on the Poems. As the introduction to Auden in the student text suggests, Auden was a well-educated, well-traveled, sophisticated person. If jet airplanes had existed in the years before World War II, Auden would have been a member of the jet set. He combines the scholarship of Oxford and Vienna with the modern American experience of the "Bureau of Statistics." Have students consider what he might have said elsewhere in his writing about TV and computers.

Teaching Strategies

Providing for Cultural Differences. Background in some famous myths, and, particularly in the legend of Mount Olympus, will bridge the cultural gap for all students.

Providing for Different Levels of Ability. Auden's language is generally simple, but students who have difficulty with poetry can be instructed to concentrate on the narrative structure in each poem—the story of Icarus, the walk through London, and the life that the "unknown citizen" seems to have led.

Musée des Beaux Arts   Text page 1110

Reading the Poem. After the first reading, you might try having students read the second stanza first so that it becomes a comment on what Auden saw in the painting.

Reteaching Alternatives. Ask students if they question Auden's conclusion about human suffering. For example, would they have acted as the plowman did? Would a farmer today turn away unconcerned from the sight of a boy drowning? Ask students to find news items that support and refute Auden's view of how people react to the suffering of others.

Responding to the Poem   Text page 1111
Analyzing the Poem
Identifying Details

1. **Who are the "Old Masters" (line 2)?** The "Old Masters" are the masters of European painting in the Renaissance.

What examples does the speaker provide to show how they understood suffering? The examples from Brueghel's paintings show human indifference to great events.

2. **What examples of his theory does the poet offer in lines 14–21?** In these lines, the poet refers to Brueghel's painting *Icarus*.

Interpreting Meanings

3. **What is the meaning of the title?** The title means "museum of fine arts."

4. **Lines 5–13 describe two other paintings by Brueghel. What do you think are the events that Brueghel portrays? What is the attitude of the bystanders to those events?** In the first painting, the subject is probably the birth of Christ; the indifferent children skate on a pond at the edge of a wood. The subject of the second painting may be the crucifixion or the martyrdom of one of the saints; dogs and horses are pictured as an ironic counterpoint.

5. **Identify and comment on what you think is the overall *theme* of the poem.** One statement of the theme might run as follows: human beings are indifferent to each other's suffering. Student comments will vary.

6. **Do you agree with Auden's view of the "human position" of suffering? Explain.** Student answers will vary. Ask the students to support their opinions with reasons.

Song: As I Walked Out One Evening
Text page 1112

Reading the Poem. Ask students to note all that the speaker in the poem sees and hears. Ask them if they would have the same reaction as he does, or whether the speaker is more sensitive and more pessimistic about life.

Reteaching Alternatives. Ask students to study the life that the speaker seems to live. Why is he so pessimistic about life? Is it simply that he is a poet and sees life more clearly than the average human being?

Responding to the Poem Text page 1113
Analyzing the Poem
Identifying Details

1. What does the lover declare to the beloved in lines 8–20? He says that he will love her forever.

2. How do the clocks of the city respond to the lover's declaration? The clocks warn the speaker that he cannot conquer the deceits of time.

Interpreting Meanings

3. What does the *metaphor* in lines 3–4 reveal about the lover's mood as the poem opens? This metaphor, comparing the crowds to fields of wheat, suggests that the lover is in an upbeat, romantic mood; perhaps it also implies that he is inclined to hyperbole.

4. List the *images* and *figures of speech* in the clocks' response that contrast with this metaphor. Among the images and figures of speech students may mention are the following: the image of naked justice buried in a nightmare (lines 25–26), the figure of speech of life "leaking away" (line 30), the "appalling snow" (line 34), the glacier and the desert (lines 41–42), the beggars (line 45), and the mention of scalding tears (line 54).

5. What do you think the poet means by the glacier that knocks in the cupboard and the desert that sighs in the bed? The first figure of speech may suggest poverty, while the second figure of speech probably refers to lovelessness or the waning of passion.

How would you explain the significance of the crack in the tea cup and where it leads? (See lines 41–44.) The crack in the tea cup may be a metaphor for the wrinkles, or "cracks," of old age; since the crack leads to the land of the dead (line 44), the poet is probably referring to two inevitable facts of human existence: old age and death.

6. What other *reversals* of romantic expectations does the clocks' response give us? The clocks suggest that justice is often thwarted (lines 25–26), that human life is beset by anxiety (lines 29–30), and that children are often immoral or promiscuous (lines 47–48).

7. How would you explain the central *irony* of the poem? The central irony is that time inevitably reverses some of our youthful, optimistic expectations about life and romance.

What is the *tone* of the poem? Student answers may vary. Many students may suggest that, although playful on the surface, the poem is actually quite somber.

8. Does a new dimension of love emerge from the clocks' statement? Explain. In lines 55–56, the clocks suggest that, despite human beings' "crookedness" and all their imperfections, they are still capable of love.

9. What effect does the form of the poem—its *sounds* and *metrics*—have on its message? Student answers will vary. The relatively light form of the poem—quatrains that resemble the ballad stanza, with rhyme scheme *abcb*—ironically contrasts with the somber message, just as the romantic lover's expectations contrast with the clocks' response.

10. What do you think of the poet's feelings about love, as expressed by the clocks? What experiences might make a person feel this way? Student answers will vary.

The Unknown Citizen Text page 1114

Reading the Poem. Ask students to read the poem for clues to the personality and character of the "citizen" and to the kind of life he led.

Reteaching Alternatives. Have students think about the facts that the poet mentions and to imagine a typical day in the life of the citizen. What additional information about the citizen would a computer record?

Responding to the Poem Text page 1115
Analyzing the Poem
Identifying Details

1. What did the unknown citizen do for a living? The unknown citizen worked in a factory.

What facts are reported on his conduct? He satisfied his employers, held "normal" views, paid his Union dues, liked a drink, was well liked by his "mates," bought a paper every day, took out insurance policies, had one stay in the hospital, bought appliances on the installment plan, served in the war, married and had five children, and never interfered with his children's education.

2. What agencies or groups contribute to this report? Among the agencies and groups contributing to the report are: the Bureau of Statistics, the Union, the Social Psychology workers, the press, Producers Research and High-Grade Living, the researchers in Public Opinion, and the Eugenist.

3. Who is the speaker in the poem? The speaker purports to be a government official who has compiled all the reports of the agencies and groups, and who has erected a marble monument on the grave of the unknown citizen.

Interpreting Meanings

4. What do you think a saint is in the "modern sense" of an old-fashioned word (line 4)? This ironic turn of phrase implicitly contrasts the "old-fashioned" sense of the word "saint"—piety and an exemplary life—with the "modern" sense—normalcy and conformity.

5. Who do you think might have asked the questions in line 28? The questions might have been asked by an unconventional person in the "government" that the poet envisions as background for the unknown citizen's life. Note that the speaker brusquely rejects the questions as absurd.

6. What do you make of the inscription under the title? What other "monuments" are you reminded of? Student answers will vary.

7. The poem seems to depict the "unknown citizen" as a colorless stereotype. Did you, however, sympathize with the citizen? Explain your response to him. Again, student responses will vary. It is possible that some students will sympathize with the citizen, claiming that the notion of rigid conformity, rather than the citizen, is Auden's real target in the poem.

8. Although the poet does not directly state his opinions in this poem, they clearly emerge from the poem's *tone*. How would you describe this tone? The tone is satirical.

9. What is the effect of the poet's free verse? What does it make the poem sound like? The effect of the free verse is perhaps to make the poem sound like a eulogy, or speech at a funeral.

10. What is the message or *theme* of this poem? One statement of the theme might be: Life in the modern world has emphasized rigid conformity at the expense of individuality, freedom, and happiness.

11. Do you think this poem gives a true depiction of contemporary society, or where society is heading? Explain what details of the poem are or are not paralleled in reality. Student answers will vary. Ask the students to comment on specific details.

12. Could this poem have been written in any other time of history but the twentieth century? Why or why not? Most students will agree that the mention of various social institutions and the references to the appliances and automobile make this a uniquely twentieth-century poem.

Louis MacNeice

Text page 1116

Prayer Before Birth

Text page 1117

Objectives

1. To identify the point of view in the poem

2. To summarize the poem

3. To explain an epigram

4. To identify the tone of the poem

5. To relate two poems by different poets

6. To identify and explain the use of techniques of poetry, especially those used in free verse

7. To interpret the importance of setting in a poem

8. To interpret the themes of poems

Introducing the Poem

MacNeice, like Auden, was responsible for some of the best intellectual poetry of the 1930s. The tone and subject matter, selected by the two poets, are worth comparing. Both use irony, and both are bitter, even despairing. MacNeice's view of human existence is made obvious in his prayer poem. Fear seems to be the pervasive element. This is not satire like Auden's "Unknown Citizen."

Background on the Poem. MacNeice found much to fear and dislike in the 1930s. Fascism was on the rise in Europe—Hitler in Germany, Mussolini in Italy. Communism, apparently working in Russia, was reaching out, intellectually at least, casting doubt on all the institutions that Western society had lived by, especially religion. England and the United States were in the midst of the Great Depression. Finally, the shadow of a new world war hung over England, as Hitler announced his plan to conquer the world.

Teaching Strategies

Providing for Cultural Differences. The setting and the language are quite clear and generally understandable.

Providing for Different Levels of Ability. For literal-minded students, you may want to concentrate at first on the specific fears expressed in ''Prayer Before Birth,'' asking students to list the fears.

Reading the Poem. Read the poem aloud, in class, much as you would a psalm.

Reteaching Alternatives. Do students share MacNeice's fears? Spend some time discussing certain of the fears. Ask students to compile lists of their own collective fears for the future of the human species. Then have them write their own class prayer, with each student contributing one stanza that reflects his or her profoundest doubt or concern.

Responding to the Poem   Text page 1118
Analyzing the Poem
Identifying Details

1. From whose *point of view* is the prayer uttered? The prayer is uttered from the point of view of a speaker who is an unborn child.

2. Summarize the speaker's prayer in each stanza. In the first stanza, the speaker prays for protection from the physical threats of the bat, the rat, the stoat, and the ghoul. In the second stanza, he prays for consolation. In the third, he asks that he may enjoy the beauties of nature. In the fourth, he asks for forgiveness of the sins he may commit. In the fifth stanza, he asks for emotional patience and forebearance. In the last stanza, he asks for the courage to preserve his own individuality.

Interpreting Meanings

3. What repetitive structures in the poem can you identify as typical of other prayers you are familiar with? The repetitive structures (for example, the phrases ''I am not yet born'' at the beginning of each stanza, the use of ''O,'' and the use of the word ''let'') have many parallels in prayers from a variety of cultures and time periods.

4. Why do you think the stanzas of the poem grow gradually longer? They gradually grow longer because the speaker's requests grow more complex as he progresses from prayers for physical protection to requests concerning his emotional, intellectual, and moral nature.

How and why does the last line clash with this pattern? The last line, consisting of only three words, clashes shockingly with this pattern, as the speaker asks for death if the other requests cannot be fulfilled. The implication is that in this case life would not be worth living.

5. MacNeice's poem is rich in unusual figurative language. Pick out some especially striking examples of *simile* and *metaphor* in the poem. Among the examples of simile and metaphor students may mention are the following: ''tall walls wall me,'' ''water to dandle me,'' ''sky to sing to me,'' ''me death when they live me,'' ''mountains frown at me,'' ''dragoon me into a lethal automaton,'' ''blow me like thistledown,'' and ''like water held in the hands would spill me.''

6. What is the significance of the *epigraph*? The quotation from George Herbert refers to the fact that even the most obnoxious elements of God's creation—symbolized by ''poisons''—are brought by His will to praise Him. The poet may be implying that human beings, evil as they may sometimes be, still praise God and pray to Him for the strength and courage to be good.

7. How would you describe the overall *tone* of the poem? Student answers will vary. Most students will agree that the tone is serious.

8. If you could have uttered a ''prayer before birth,'' what might you have asked for? Student answers will vary. Encourage the students to give reasons for their ''requests.''

C. Day Lewis   Text page 1119

Departure in the Dark   Text page 1120

Objectives

1. To recognize and explain the main idea of the poem

2. To identify details that relate to the main idea of the poem

3. To paraphrase part of a poem

4. To compare and analyze poems

5. To recognize and explain the significance of titles

6. To imitate poetic techniques used by the poet

7. To recognize and interpret images

8. To recognize connotative words and phrases

Introducing the Poem

This poem is about death, like Tennyson's "Crossing the Bar," Browning's "Prospice," and Betjeman's "Death in Leamington," among others. Before comparing the Lewis poem with these others, it might be best to have students read "Reconciliation," which is Lewis's sequel of sorts to "Departure in the Dark." Does the journey of life have a happy, or at least peaceful, ending, as Tennyson hoped for?

Background on the Poem. As one of the Oxford group, Lewis was more of an activist, both in politics and in his participation at administrative levels of World War II. That he wrote detective stories may be more than merely interesting. With this in mind, we may be inclined to credit him with a more narrative type of imagination (thinking in terms of journeys rather than gardens). For one who, like most young scholars of the time, was intellectually intrigued by Marxian philosophy, Lewis surprises us with his concern with life after death, presenting an image that is almost traditional. The war is obviously a more direct concern to Lewis than, say, to Auden. This poem clearly reflects his concern with the British war against German tanks in the African desert in the early days of World War II.

Teaching Strategies

Providing for Cultural Differences. The passover mentioned in the poem can be easily explained as a celebration of the Jewish faith commemorating the deliverance of the Jews from bondage in Egypt. There are two journeys involved in this allusion, the stories of which are shared by both Jews and Christians: the journey of Joseph and his family into Egypt and then the return journey to the Promised Land, led by Moses as God divided the waters of the Red Sea.

Providing for Different Levels of Ability. The idea of a journey, around the block or to the moon, provides a simple approach to the poem.

Reading the Poem. Almost everyone will have had the experience of starting off, perhaps just to school, before the sun is up. Is not the poet here simply putting into words thoughts and images that we have all experienced?

Reteaching Alternatives. A reading of a prose version of the exodus of the Jews from Egypt will help to reveal the poetic aspects of the poem and to show how Lewis relates a journey to an idea—in this instance, the idea of death.

Responding to the Poem Text page 1121

Analyzing the Poem

Identifying Details

1. What experience described in the first stanza reminds a person of mortality? The experience that reminds a person of mortality is leaving a familiar place, such as his own home, on an early winter's morning.

2. What details in the third stanza add a vivid dimension to this scene? Details adding a vivid dimension are the timetable, the scrambled meal, and the bag that stands packed by the door.

3. How does the poet sum up his main point in the last stanza? The poet sums up his point by saying that the experience of leaving a place, like human life and death, is paradoxical: it contains both release and torment.

Interpreting Meanings

4. Paraphrase the second stanza in your own words. What does this stanza contribute to the poem as a whole? A paraphrase of this stanza might run as follows: Life in the world is restricted and full of dreariness; freedom has withered; and we are prisoners of an uncertain future.

5. How does the word *passover* in line 17 foreshadow the extended *allusion* in the fourth stanza? The word *passover* refers to God's decision to spare the children of the Israelites (but not those of the Egyptians) when Moses was pleading with the Egyptian Pharaoh to let the Israelites go.

6. Comment on the poet's use of *rhyme* and *half rhyme*. How would you describe the effect the half rhyme has on you as you read the poem? Half rhymes occur at lines 1, 4, and 8 ("mortal," "metal," and "nettles"), at lines 9, 12, and 16 ("age," "passage," and "presage"), at lines 17, 20, and 24 ("passover," "lover," and "ever"), and at the corresponding places in the remaining stanzas. The half rhymes help to reinforce the poem's paradoxical, bittersweet theme about the nature of life.

7. Do you think this poem has anything in common with the Anglo-Saxon poems "The Wanderer" and "The Seafarer" (see Unit One)? Explain. Student answers will vary. Ask the students to support their responses with specific points of similarity (for example, the uncertainty of life, the melancholy aspects of voyaging or wandering, etc.).

Stephen Spender

The Express

Objectives

1. To recognize figures of speech in the poem, including personification

2. To recognize the use of poetic techniques

3. To analyze the speaker's choice of words

4. To compare a poem with another like it

5. To write a poem or short paragraph on a machine

Introducing the Poem

Although the machine has been crucial to English life since the eighteenth century, here a major British poet treats one in poetic terms. Why, we might ask, does Spender pick a train rather than a plane? Realizing that Spender was the most politically motivated of the so-called English Group, we might wonder whether this poem is his belated ode to the new world of the machine. We might ask what political implications are in the poem. The word *manifesto* is associated with the phrase "Communist Manifesto" that proclaimed the Russian Revolution. Yet Spender may have seen the "Express" as declaring an entirely different kind of new, mechanized world. Finally, there is the possibility that Spender, for all his political orientation, was simply enchanted with the image of a long, winding train.

Background on the Poem. We might wonder why it has taken British poets so long to turn their imaginations to something as dramatic as a train. Certainly the poets that we have been considering in this section had more reason to think about the mechanized world than did Emily Dickinson decades before in a small New England village. Have students compare this poem with her "I Like to See It Lap the Miles."

Teaching Strategies

Providing for Cultural Differences. Students will encounter no special problems in this poem.

Providing for Different Levels of Ability. The poem is short, and the language is fairly simple.

Reading the Poem. Have students notice that the train in the poem moves slowly through the city limits, passing the gasworks (always offensive to poets) and a graveyard (al-

ways tempting to poets) and then comes to life around line 9. The poem is most effective when read aloud. Entrust this task to a skilled student reader or undertake it yourself, making certain in either case to emphasize the poet's use of rhythm and careful diction to suggest the blinding speed of the locomotive.

Reteaching Alternatives. Have student select a modern analogue to the train in Spender's poem and write their own tribute. Possible subjects, of course, include late twentieth-century modes of transportation, though students might be encouraged to turn their creativity to other high-speed wonders such as the digital computer.

Responding to the Poem   Text page 1123
Analyzing the Poem
Identifying Details

1. **Name the sights the train passes in lines 1–7.** The train passes houses, the gasworks, and the cemetery.

2. **Explain the *simile* in line 20. What two things are being compared?** The speaker compares the moving train with the trajectory of a bullet from a gun.

3. **What *metaphors* are combined in lines 21–27?** Students should mention the following metaphors: the "crest" of the world, the arrival of the train at "night," the "tossing hills," the "streaming brightness of phosphorous," the simile of the comet moving through flame, the image of the express train as "entranced," and the metaphor "wrapped in her music," and the image of the bough "breaking with honey buds."

Interpreting Meanings

4. **Why do you think the poet chose the word *manifesto* in line 1? What are the connotations of this word?** The connotations of the word are philosophical and political, as in Karl Marx's *Communist Manifesto*. Spender may have chosen the word to set a philosophical tone at the outset of the poem.

5. **The poem makes constant use of *alliteration* to achieve *onomatopoeic* effects. Which lines do you think most clearly show the poet's attempt to fit the sound to the sense?** Among the lines students may mention are line 3 ("gliding like a queen"), line 5 ("She passes the houses

which humbly crowd''), line 14 (''deafening tunnels, brakes, innumerable bolts''), line 16 (''retreats the elate meter of her wheels''), and line 24 (''phosphorus on the tossing hills''). Urge the students to suggest and defend other possibilities as well.

6. Even when they have masculine names, ships are always referred to by sailors as though they were female. Why do you suppose the poet uses the feminine pronoun to refer to a railroad train? Line 10 might be a clue. The poet may be suggesting that the train is, in its own way, as majestic and marvelous as the ship was in an earlier era.

7. On the evidence supplied by this poem, what does speed do to perception? At what point does mechanical propulsion cease being a convenience and become a mystery? Beyond a certain point, speed warps perception and becomes mysterious.

8. This poem was written long before the countryside became so altered by the presence of railroad tracks and superhighways. Do you agree with Spender's romantic view of the train and her music? Explain. Student answers will vary. Ask the students to support their opinions with reasons.

Henry Reed

Text page 1125

Naming of Parts

Text page 1126

Objectives

1. To distinguish between spoken and unspoken dialogue in the poem
2. To recognize repetition in the poem
3. To recognize and explain ambiguity
4. To identify the tone of the poem
5. To write an imaginative dialogue based on the poem
6. To analyze the use of language in the poem

Introducing the Poem

This is a World War II poem, written by a participant. The poem explains the reaction of a sensitive recruit to a wartime reality. Although the ''reality'' that Reed writes about is quite harmless and compared with the horrors of life in World War I trenches, Reed, like Wilfred Owen, uses peacetime experiences to achieve a striking contrast with wartime reality. Reed's poem deals with a much softer, subtler assault than anything to be found in the experiences of Owen or Sasson, and Reed would be the first to admit this. He handles a subtle experience with sophistication, and even wit, in a manner that we might expect from Auden.

Background on the Poem. This poem reveals a reaction that one might expect from a trainee in a wartime ''civilian'' army. Often these early assaults on civilian sensitivity, though relatively harmless, are recalled with as much trauma as a later battle-zone encounter with death. That may be one of the purposes of boot camp, and, ultimately, of the

drill instructor in the poem—to ''help'' sensitive civilians to form emotional calluses.

Teaching Strategies

Providing for Cultural Differences. Students will encounter no special problems in this poem.

Providing for Different Levels of Ability. To help poor readers over the problem of exactly where the voice of the instructor ends in each stanza, you may want to make a real dialogue out of the poem, with two students reading aloud. You can expect students to recognize the sexual implications in line 24.

Reading the Poem. As suggested above, after a first reading, you may want to have pairs of students try dramatic readings.

Reteaching Alternatives. Ask students to write the dialogue in each stanza in the form of two parallel columns—the instructor's words and the trainee's thoughts side by side. Then have the students analyze (a) the length and complexity of sentences and (b) the use of adjectives and adverbs. You also may want to have pairs of students try to imitate this poem using another example of machinery. Have them read their efforts aloud.

Responding to the Poem Text page 1127

Analyzing the Poem

Identifying Details

1. Identify the lines spoken by the principal speakers in

the poem. What details describe the *setting*? The drill instructor speaks the first three and a half lines of each of the first four stanzas; the recruit silently answers in the last two and a half lines. The whole last stanza represents the thoughts of the recruit.

2. List the "parts" that are named as the poem goes on. The parts include the lower sling swivel, the piling swivel, the safety catch, the bolt, the breech, and the spring.

3. How do the first and second halves of stanzas 1–4 contrast with each other? The first half of each of these stanzas is a dry, mechanical recital by the instructor; the second half is the recruit's lyrical, imaginative daydream about a beautiful sight in spring of a garden.

4. In the last stanza, what phrases are repeated or echoed from the preceding four stanzas? "Easing the Spring" (line 25) repeats part of line 24; "it is perfectly easy/If you have any strength in your thumb" (lines 25–26) repeats phrases from lines 15–16; the list of parts in lines 26–27 picks up some of the parts mentioned in the fourth stanza; the phrase "Which in our case we have not got"

(line 28) echoes line 10 and line 12; and line 30 repeats lines 1 and 6.

Interpreting Meanings

5. What different meanings does "easing the spring" have in the poem? The phrase could refer to slowly releasing the spring on a weapon. It could also carry the meaning of "making the spring come easily."

6. Among the poem's elements are irony, bitterness, mockery, humor, and sorrow. Which *tone*, in your opinion, is the dominant one? Explain your answer. Student answers will vary. Ask the students to support their opinions about the poem's tone.

7. What do you think the poet is protesting against? Is the protest valid, in your view? Many students will suggest that the poet is protesting against warfare and mindless regimentation. Students' opinions on the validity of the protest will differ.

Dylan Thomas
Text page 1128

Fern Hill
Text page 1129

A Refusal to Mourn the Death, by Fire, of a Child in London
Text page 1132

Do Not Go Gentle into That Good Night
Text page 1134

Objectives

1. To recognize the point of view of the speaker in a poem

2. To identify and explain allusions in a poem

3. To identify examples of personification in a poem

4. To recognize paradox in a poem

5. To recognize the poet's use of repetition

6. To identify the techniques used by the poet, including syntax and figurative language, especially metaphor

7. To evaluate a line of poetry

8. To analyze the theme or main idea of a poem

9. To recognize examples of wordplay in a poem

10. To imitate a poet's technique

11. To identify and explain ambiguity in a poem

12. To analyze a villanelle

Introducing the Poems

If one can hear the melody of Ireland in Yeats's poems, one will hear the special rhythms and melodic use of the language of Wales in the poems of Dylan Thomas. Wales, like Ireland, is set apart from the mainstream of English culture in which the other key poets of this period grew up. Dylan Thomas did not go to Oxford, although Oxford would have been glad to have him. His childhood in a beautiful countryside and the temperament that made him choose journalism over scholarship are revealed in his poetry. He is more interested in feelings than in intellectual ideas. One feels that he would like to sing his poems, and he was, indeed, famous for reading them aloud.

Background on the Poems. Probably because Thomas grew up in a land that we associate with natural beauty, harsh poverty, and melodious language, we are inclined to think of Thomas as a natural genius, more naturally at one with nature than earlier poets, one more openly rebellious against the unfairness of life, and one less studious in his crafting of poems. We should also recall that he spent a good part of his adult, productive life in the post-World War II world. Although no one can say that his poetry speaks in any way for the postwar world or even touches on the major themes of the day—fear of nuclear disaster in particular—Thomas lived at the edge of this world. With no profession or economic base, he seemed cast adrift in its rising affluence and jet-age rhythms. Overwhelmed by these, he seems to have turned back to the concerns of his early days in Wales, to his family, his village, and his remarkable gift of poetry.

Teaching Strategies

Providing for Cultural Differences. The language, bucolic setting, and unfamiliar customs will challenge many students. You will be able to find lines, however, that cut through to common ground and that move students of all backgrounds.

Providing for Different Levels of Ability. Read the poems or parts of them aloud. This kind of poetry speaks for itself and provides an understanding of some of the characteristics of poetry even when detailed meaning is not instantly apparent to most students.

Fern Hill   Text page 1129

Reading the Poem. You may want to take this poem stanza by stanza, after an introductory reading, preferably aloud, and see what kind of paraphrases, even partial ones, your students can create.

Reteaching Alternatives. Have students search for sounds and sights and try to place each in a setting.

Responding to the Poem   Text page 1130
Analyzing the Poem
Identifying Details

1. **From whose point of view is the poem told?** The poem is told from the point of view of an adult who is nostalgically remembering his childhood and youth.

2. **What details tell how the speaker felt when he was "young and easy"?** Among the details students may men-

tion are: "prince of the apple towns" (line 6), "singing" (line 11), "sang to my horn" (line 16), and "ran my heedless ways" (line 40). These details all contribute to a feeling of carefree happiness.

What did he do on the farm? Among the activities he mentions are singing in the yard, hunting and herding, sleeping under the stars and listening to owls, and running.

3. **What did the boy fail to realize about time, according to the fifth stanza?** He failed to realize that time would pass and that his happy childhood would soon be over.

4. **How do the statements about time in the second stanza differ from those in the sixth stanza?** In the second stanza, time is said to let the child play; the speaker refers to time as "golden" in line 14. But in the sixth stanza, it is implied that fleeting time has deceived the speaker, who refers to himself as "green and dying" in line 53.

5. **What lines in the poem seem to refer to the Biblical account of paradise, of the Garden of Eden?** These lines (29–36) occur in the fourth stanza.

Interpreting Meanings

6. **Find where time is *personified* in the poem. Describe the different kinds of intentions Time seems to have in regard to the boy.** In lines 4 and 13, Time is obliquely personified as an indulgent parent who allows the boy the freedom to be happy. But in line 53, Time is personified as a parent who holds a dying child in his arms. Thus, Time seems at one point to have intented for the speaker to be happy. However, Time passes inevitably, and so intends for the boy to grow up, lose the paradise of childhood, and eventually die.

7. **In what specific ways was the speaker's childhood "Edenic," that is, like the life Adam and Eve led in Eden?** Student answers will vary. They may mention the speaker's carefree happiness and his joy in nature (represented, for example, by the references to river, stars, calves, foxes, owls, pheasants, the hay, etc.).

In what ways is the boy's "waking" in the last stanza like the "waking" of Adam and Eve as they left the Garden? The boy's "awakening" into the reality of adulthood, with all its disappointments, commitments, and responsibilities, may be compared to Adam and Eve's loss of Eden because of their disobedience.

8. **How would you explain the *paradox* in the next-to-last line?** The phrase "green and dying" is paradoxical because it suggests innocent freshness and mortality at the same time.

9. **Find where the word *green* occurs in each of the seven stanzas. For a craftsman as meticulous as Thomas, these recurrences are certainly not accidental. Why do**

you suppose Thomas repeats the word so often? What associations and feelings are connected with the word *green*? Thomas evidently wants the word *green* to connote freshness, youth, and innocence.

10. Where is *gold* used in the poem? This word is used in lines 5, 14, and 44.

What associations do you have with *gold*? Students may suggest associations like "perfection," "preciousness," "valuable," "warm."

11. Read the poem aloud, or listen to a recording of it. How does its *rhythm* match its subject and mood? Students may suggest that the poem's lilting rhythm and the variation of long and short lines reinforce the happy mood and the subject matter of the carefree attitude of youth.

Where does Thomas use *alliteration* and *onomatopoeia* to provide the sound effects? Examples of alliteration and onomatopoeia occur in lines 2, 3, 7, 14, 15, 19, 20, 26–27, 34, 41, and 51.

12. Is the experience described in this poem universal? Explain. Most students will agree that the impulse to look back on one's youth nostalgically and to recognize time as fleeting is universal. Some students may point out, however, that not everyone has experienced as idyllic a childhood as Thomas describes here.

13. Years after this poem was first published, Thomas told a friend that one line continued to bother him because it was "bloody bad." "What line is it?" asked the friend. " 'I ran my heedless ways,' " said Thomas, and he winced as though he had made a mistake from which he would never recover. Why do you think Thomas felt so strongly about a line that most people accept and even quote as part of his most celebrated poem? How do you feel about the line? Student answers will vary. Some students may suggest that this line, which is so well-known that it has now become almost a cliche, did not satisfy Thomas because it does not contain an original metaphor or figure of speech.

A Refusal to Mourn the Death, by Fire, of a Child in London

Text page 1132

Reading the Poem. Guide the students carefully through the poem line by line. Like "Fern Hill," this one will deserve at least a second reading if students are to grasp the full import of the poet's words and the richness of his language. After a second reading, have students comment on the poet's selection of an atypically long and highly specific title for a poem that operates on a chiefly nonliteral level.

Reteaching Alternatives. Ask students to compare this poem with Betjeman's "Death in Leamington." The old lady is made more "alive" to us by the specific details with which Betjaman creates a setting. The maid also serves to humanize the death.

Responding to the Poem   Text page 1133
Analyzing the Poem
Identifying Details

1. How many sentences are in the poem? Where does each one begin and end? There are four sentences in the poem. The first runs from line 1 through line 13, the second runs from line 14 through line 18, the third runs from line 19 through line 23, and the last is line 24.

2. In stanza 3, what does the speaker say he will not do? In this stanza, he says that he will not "blaspheme" the child's death by offering a cliche about death or by composing an elegy mourning her youth and innocence.

Where does he violate his promise? He violates the promise in the last stanza.

3. What is the "salt seed" in line 11? The "salt seed" is a tear.

What is the "mother" in line 21? The "mother" is the earth.

4. Where, according to the speaker, does "London's daughter" lie now? She lies with the "first dead"—that is, with all who have died before her.

Interpreting Meanings

5. What do you think the last line means? Student answers will vary. Literally, the line may mean that "we only die once." But Thomas may also mean that all deaths are finally identical, in the sense that after our death, we join all those who have inevitably met the same fate.

6. Does Thomas' poem minimize the tragedy, or does it endow it with a larger dimension? Explain. Student answers will vary. Most students will agree with the notion that Thomas, who seems genuinely affected by the girl's death, "minimizes" the tragedy; it is only on the surface that he "refuses to mourn." Ask the students to explain the "larger dimensions" they suggest for the poem.

7. How does the *tone* of this poem differ from the tone of "Fern Hill"? The tone of "Fern Hill" is lyrical and bright for the most part; the tone of this poem is somber.

Do Not Go Gentle into That Good Night
Text page 1134

Reading the Poem. You might wish to approach the lesson in reverse, beginning with the Analyzing Language and Style exercise on page 1135 of the student text, which offers a detailed explanation of the villanelle. Point out that, next to the sestina, the villanelle is perhaps the most challenging verse form in the English language. To deliver the point home, you might ask students to attempt to write two lines that are sufficiently important to bear four repetitions each. Conclude by noting that this is precisely what Thomas has done in this poem.

Reteaching Alternatives. Make copies of the villanelle "written by" Stephen Dedalus in *A Portrait of the Artist as a Young Man*. Have students comment on the similarities between this poem and Thomas's, attempting to arrive at a generalization about what sorts of topics seem suitable to treatment in this highly specialized poetic form. You may wish to ask students to attempt their own villanelles and set aside some class time for a consideration of their efforts.

Responding to the Poem
Text page 1135

Analyzing the Poem

Identifying Details

1. To whom is the poem addressed? The poem is addressed to the speaker's father.

What does the speaker say old age should do? The speaker says that old age should "burn and rave" at the close of day—namely, that old people should protest angrily against the coming of death.

2. What four types of people are described in stanzas 2–5? These stanzas describe wise men, good men, wild men, and grave men.

How do all these people respond to the dying of the light? The wise men are angry because their counsels failed to convince others; the good men deplore the inefficacy of their deeds; the wild men learn too late that time is fleeting; and the grave men resent their previous failure to be gay and enjoy life.

3. What does the speaker pray for in the final stanza? He prays his father both to curse and to bless him.

Interpreting Meanings

4. What is the "good night"? The "good night" is death.

What *pun* on the phrase does Thomas intend for you to catch? He intends us also to catch the meaning of a casual farewell.

Given Thomas's feelings about the "good night," do you see anything contradictory in his use of the word *good*? The use of the word is paradoxical, since Thomas obviously wants his father to protest against death.

5. Why would any son beg his father to "Curse, bless me now with your fierce tears"? What might this strange request indicate about the relationship between this father and son? Student answers will vary. The phrase hinges at a complex relationship, involving both love and dislike, or estrangement.

6. Identify at least three *metaphors* in the poem. Among the metaphors students may mention are the following: the notion of old age burning and raving (line 2), the idea of the wise men's words forking lightning (line 5), the metaphor of "frail deeds" dancing in a "green bay" (line 8), the singing of the sun in flight (line 10), and the blazing of blind eyes (line 14).

7. Soon after this poem was finished, Thomas sent it to the Princess Caetani in Rome, hoping that she might publish it in a literary magazine of which she was editor. In an accompanying letter, he wrote: "The only person I can't show the enclosed little poem to is, of course, my father, who doesn't know he's dying." Given the fact that the poem has become one of the most famous elegies of this century, do you think Thomas's reluctance was justified? Student answers will vary. Urge the students to support their opinions.

Objectives

1. To recognize details and their significance
2. To identify the rhyme scheme
3. To interpret the meaning of the title
4. To compare the poem with the poetry of earlier poets
5. To write a character sketch of the speaker

Introducing the Poem

Here is another poet who studied at Oxford, albeit a decade after Auden and the English Group. Notice that Larkin is a conservative in politics, whereas the earlier Oxford scholars were attracted to Marxism. Also, Larkin is more direct and specific about religion: he comes face to face with the Church of England and he talks about it in specific terms. Yeats in "The Second Coming," with which this poem will be compared, seems to take the question of the "Second Coming" out of the religion entirely. The beast that lurches toward Bethlehem "to be born" seems to have little to do with religion. Larkin, on the other hand, faces up to the question of the future of traditional religion and even sees a time when churchgoing will become passe.

Background on the Poem. The problem, faced by Dylan Thomas and many others, of being able to write poetry in England or America without starving to death, was solved by Larkin, who became a librarian. Ask students to imagine Dylan Thomas as a librarian. Elicit from them that this preposterous idea demonstrates not only the renegade spirit in Thomas but perhaps a practical side of the present poet that should not be discounted in an analysis of his work.

Teaching Strategies

Providing for Cultural Differences. Little in this poem is alien to the background of most students. Artifacts and architecture mentioned in the poem should not prove beyond the experience, or at least the grasps, of a high-school senior.

Providing for Different Levels of Ability. The length of the poem may hamper student appreciation. Reading it in manageable sections—first to see what the speaker does, then what exists in the church—may be the best way for students to approach the reading.

Reading the Poem. Enter the poem as though it were a report on a bicycle sightseeing trip. Then have students explore the theme.

Reteaching Alternatives. There are questions that you can raise to stimulate student understanding. Why does the poet not mention the graveyard, as Gray does in his "Elegy"? Where does the speaker get the idea that religion is dying in England? What thoughts enter your head when you stand in an empty building of any sort?

Responding to the Poem   Text page 1139
Analyzing the Poem
Identifying Details

1. What concrete details does the speaker notice in the church? Among the concrete details he notices are the matting, seats, stone, little books, flowers, brass, the font, the organ, and the lectern with the Bible.

What does he do there? He pauses to make sure that there is no service in progress. Then he steps inside, takes off his cycle clips, runs his hand around the font, and mounts the lectern, where he says a few verses of the Bible. Then he signs the book and donates an Irish sixpence before he leaves.

2. What questions does the speaker ask in the third and fourth stanzas? He wonders what will become of churches when they fall out of use and no one uses them anymore for religious services. Perhaps, he reflects, we will keep some cathedrals on show as symbols of the past. Perhaps churches may become superstitious gathering places for women and children.

3. According to stanza 5, what might become of the church in the future? The church might become a sort of antique curio, examined eagerly by "ruin-bibbers" like a sort of archaeological site.

4. According to the final two stanzas, why does it please the speaker to visit the church? The speaker says that even though he has no idea of the value of the church, he is still pleased to stand there because it is "a serious house on earth." The church is a meeting place for human beings, where their "compulsions" blend. It is a proper place to "grow wise in."

5. What is the *rhyme scheme* of the poem? The rhyme scheme is as follows: *ababcadcd.*

Interpreting Meanings

6. What are the two possible meanings of the title? The title could mean "attending church" or "the disappearing, or fading, church."

7. In the last two lines of the last stanza, there is an example of humor that some people might find offensive. Why is the church a good place to grow wise in? The church is a good place to grow wise in because the adjacent cemetery, filled with the dead, reminds us of death, our ultimate destiny.

How would you justify the poet's wry comment to someone who finds it distasteful? Student answers will vary.

8. What does the speaker seem to be saying about the place of the church, or of faith, in the contemporary secular world? The speaker seems to be saying that people in the contemporary secular world are steadily abandoning the church as irrelevant, hollow, and "antique." All the same, the speaker suggests that he derived pleasure, consolation, and perhaps a sense of wisdom from visiting the church, even though he cannot account for its specific "worth."

How do you think this outlook might be related to the speaker's own religious faith, or lack of it? Student answers will vary. Many students will suggest that the poem, for all of its expressions of skepticism and its wry humor, is still deeply religious.

9. Can you think of reasons why the speaker might like to stand in the old church? Students may suggest that he derives a feeling of consolation and tranquility.

10. Can you seen any connection between the *tone* of this poem and that of Matthew Arnold's "Dover Beach" (Unit Six)? Student answers will vary. Students should point out that, in both poems, the speaker notes a general decline of religious faith.

Derek Walcott

Text page 1140

The Virgins

Text page 1141

Objectives

1. To explain an example of irony
2. To identify images and their associations
3. To write an essay analyzing a poem's use of irony and double meanings

Introducing the Poem

Both this poem and its poet will, at first blush, strike students as removed from most of the poetry they have read thus far in this unit. Point out, therefore, that Derek Walcott, like numerous of the British poets students have encountered thus far, makes use of allusions in his work and uses the medium of poetry as a platform for addressing social grievances. Walcott, then, like the members of the Oxford group before him, is a champion of change.

Background on the Poem. Most of what students will need in preparation for a reading of the poem is provided in the introductory material on pages 1140–1141 of the student text.

Providing for Cultural Differences. In order to grasp the poem's central meaning, students will need some understanding of how the lively, colorful activity of Caribbean port cities has changed. Discuss how changing from an economy based on agriculture and export to an economy based on tourism would affect the vitality of street activity. How might it affect the daily life of an average inhabitant of St. Croix?

Providing for Different Levels of Ability. Slower students are likely to need your guidance as they work through the poem's long, complex sentences. Help them see that the poem is not—as it might first appear—merely a description; it is an ironic, even bitter commentary on the dying of a way of life.

Reading the Poem. Students will need to read this poem several times to grasp its meaning. First have them read it silently. Discuss the poem's tone, and have students point to words and details that create this tone. Then ask volunteers to read it aloud; encourage readers to convey the poet's emotion as they read, and tell listeners to be alert for alliteration, consonance, and other sound echoes. Finally, discuss the meaning of the title; help students see that, while on one level, it simply refers to the Virgin Islands, it takes on ironic resonance when we realize that, in the poet's view, these "virgins" are anything but unspoiled.

Reteaching Alternatives. To help students grasp the overall contrast the poet is making—between the vitality of former life in St. Croix and its current moribund state—have them contrast the connotations of the words in the preceding lines. Then have them point to details that reveal the poet's feelings about this contrast.

Responding to the Poem Text page 1141
Analyzing the Poem
Identifying Details

1. What is the tourist reminded of as he strolls the streets of Frederiksted? He is reminded of "life not lost to the American dream" (line 4)—in other words, the simplicities of a natural life that have not been blighted by greed and commercialism.

2. According to line 9, what, *ironically*, is the result of "the good life"? The result is that the crime rate is on the rise.

Interpreting Meanings

3. List all the *images* in the poem that suggest emptiness and decay. Among the images the students should list are the following: the dead streets (line 1), "funeral pace" (line 3), "streets blighted with the sun" (line 10), "plazas blown dry" (line 11), the condominium drowning in vacancy (lines 12–13), the reference to dust (line 13), and the rusty spinning of the roulette wheels (lines 15–16).

4. How would you explain line 2? This line contains the paradox that the "free port" has died of tourism, which is a metaphor for a fatal disease. Students might explain the line as indicating that, paradoxically, the commercial exploitation of the town has led to the decline of its basic values.

5. Why are the condominiums drowning in vacancy? They are decaying because no one lives in them or visits them. They are empty shells.

6. What images remind you of what life was once like in Frederiksted? Among the images students should mention are the references to the vigorous trade around the pierhead in the last lines of the poem. They may also refer to line 5, where the speaker evokes the "simplicities" of a vanished way of life.

Who or what is responsible for the change? Commercial greed and a "selling out" to tourism are the culprits.

Is it a change for the better or worse? Most students will agree that the change is a destructive one.

Ted Hughes Text page 1142

Hawk Roosting Text page 1143

Objectives

1. To define the setting of the poem
2. To explain key lines in the poem
3. To paraphrase a poem
4. To write a poem similar to this one
5. To write an analysis and response to the theme of the poem

Introducing the Poem

Tennyson's "The Eagle" makes a good introduction to this poem. Setting aside the fact that the two poems deal with different species, this Hughes poem could be almost an "instant replay" of the Tennyson poem—without running comment and philosophical background notes by the bird itself. Tennyson recognized the violent, inhuman aspect of nature and of natural things, and it may be that he came close in his poem to suggesting the kind of world Hughes here makes explicit. Tennyson's imagination did not run in the same direction that Hughes's does, but you can point out that in their poetry and descriptive techniques the two poets are not far apart. Point out that "Hawk Roosting" has another Victorian precedent—in the dramatic monlogues of Browning.

Background on the Poem. Hughes, like Dylan Thomas, spent his childhood roaming the English countryside, and by the age of fifteen was writing poetry that often treated animal subjects. Hughes's poetry also resembles Thomas's in its preoccupation with death. Hughes himself admits Thomas's influence, but his own verse style is more disciplined—reminding one of Yeats's poetry after Ezra Pound had urged him to cut and tighten the lines that came naturally in his early poems.

Teaching Strategies

Providing for Cultural Differences. The poem presents no special problems for students.

Providing for Different Levels of Ability. The poem is short and the language simple.

Reading the Poem. Ask students to concentrate on the setting while reading the first three stanzas. Then remind them of Tennyson's poem when they reach the fourth stanza. Here they may imagine Hughes's hawk explaining, graphically and as a bird of prey, the act of killing and the justification for the act.

Reteaching Alternatives. You may want to go back to Blake's poem "The Tyger" to help students appreciate the ambivalence that, for some poets at least, exists in nature.

Responding to the Poem   Text page 1143
Analyzing the Poem
Identifying Details

1. Where is the hawk speaking from? The hawk is speaking from perch at the "top of the wood."

2. Why does he like his roost? He likes his roost because of the air's buoyancy and the sun's ray, and because he can inspect the face of the earth.

3. What are his actions? He kills where he pleases, he flies in a straight line, the sun is behind him, he is changeless.

How does he describe his "manners"? In line 16, he says that his "manners" are "tearing off heads."

Interpreting Meanings

4. What does the hawk mean by saying he holds Creation in his foot? He means that he has the entire world at his mercy.

How is this different from the notion that God has "the whole world in His hands"? Each expression has an entirely different effect; the hawk's boast evidently comes from a brutal, amoral sense of power, while the notion that God has the whole world in His hands is generally associated with the benevolent care and protection of an all-powerful God.

5. How would you *paraphrase* lines 18–19? One paraphrase might be: I am so powerful that I am above the level of rational argument.

6. What two meanings can you propose for the line "the sun is behind me"? One meaning might be that "the sun supports me." Another meaning might be that "I am more powerful than the sun; it must take second place to me."

7. What is the hawk's attitude toward the world it surveys? What does it think of itself? It surveys the world like a powerful master or lord. It thinks that it is omnipotent.

8. In what ways is the hawk's philosophy inhuman, or even nonhuman? In what ways does it resemble the philosophy of some people? Student answers will vary. Ask the students to support their opinions.

Seamus Heaney   Text page 1144
Digging   Text page 1144

Objectives

1. To describe the setting of the poem
2. To identify images
3. To interpret figues of speech
4. To write an original poem or prose piece

Introducing the Poem

This poem reveals a tendency that has become increasingly pervasive in poetry of our own age—that of targeting the versifier's craft at quite ordinary and common subjects and experiences. At the same time, it might be pointed out to students that "Digging" belongs to a long poetic tradition—tracing back certainly as far as Wordsworth—of treating a recollection from childhood. Have students contemplate the degree to which the experiences described in "Digging" might have been those of Dylan Thomas. Urge them to look also at the language of both this poet and his Welsh predecessor, perhaps even tallying up the number of sensory images in "Fern Hill" and those in "Digging."

Background on the Poem. As students read the introductory material on Seamus Heaney on page 1144 of their text, direct their attention in particular to the Robert Lowell comment at the top of the second column. Determine what they know of the struggles of Northern Ireland, and ask them to consider what differences in nationalistic outlook might be evident between Heaney and Yeats.

Teaching Strategies

Providing for Cultural Differences. Some words may be unfamiliar, but as the exercise in the text indicates, the meanings of these can be guessed from context.

Providing for Different Levels of Ability. Slower students may need to take a preliminary pass through the poem and note problematic words. Instruct such students to develop familiarity with these words before approaching the poem's content.

Reading the Poem. Owing to the richness of its language, the poem will have its greatest impact on students if they hear it read aloud. Assign this task to a better student reader, or undertake it yourself.

Reteaching Alternatives. Ask the students whether they believe Wordsworth would find Heaney's childhood recollection to be recalled in "tranquility." Before they answer the question, students should be instructed to reread the introduction to Wordsworth in their text, along with his ode "Intimations of Immortality."

Responding to the Poem   Text page 1145
Analyzing the Poem
Identifying Details

1. **Describe what the speaker sees from his window.** He sees his father digging with a spade in a vegetable garden.

2. **What scene does the speaker remember involving his** grandfather? He remembers taking his grandfather some milk in a bottle, watching him drink it, and then seeing the old man digging the turf.

3. **What *images* in the poem help you to share what the speaker hears, feels, and smells?** Among the images students may mention are the following: the mention of a "clean, rasping sound" (line 3), the sight of the father's "straining rump" (line 6), the cool hardness of the potatoes (line 14), the cold smell of the potato mould (line 25), and the squelch and slap of soggy peat (lines 25–26).

4. **At the end of the poem, what does the speaker intend to do?** He says that he will "dig" with his pen—namely, use his writing ability to create literature.

Interpreting Meanings

5. **What *figures of speech* compare the speaker's pen to other things? What significance can you find in these comparisons, particularly the last one?** In line 2, the pen is "snug as a gun." In the last line, a metaphor compares the pen to a spade. The first figure of speech implies the power of the pen, since it is compared to a weapon. The second figure of speech is especially appropriate, for in context it emphasizes the notions of creativity and continuity.

6. **What do you think the speaker wants to "dig" for?** He wants to "dig" for memorable incidents that can be turned into poetry or other literature.

7. **Why do you think the father comes up "twenty years" away in line 7? (What word did you expect to find here?)** One expects to find a word like "feet" or "yards." The effect is to emphasize the time span of the speaker's memory of his father.

8. **How would you say this speaker feels about his father and grandfather and the work they did?** Most students will agree that the speaker feels respectful and admiring, even though the work the two men did seems humble and quite different from being a writer.

Bernard Shaw   Text page 1146

You may want to ask students what they think of when someone says, "modern drama." Shaw's plays are an excellent introduction to almost any aspect that they may mention. Shaw is modern in his ideas—about women, about language, about social hypocrisy. His plays have been transformed into the forms of drama that we think of as "modern"—musical drama (*My Fair Lady*) and movies. Shaw's wit is modern as well—sharp, satiric. His characters do not follow social conventions. They surprise you by acting intelligently, but not as a typical Edwardian theater audi-ence would have expected. Shaw wanted, above all, to interest his audiences. He goes out of his way not to be boring. Accordingly, few people are bored by Shaw.

Shaw, an Irishman by birth, carried on the Irish tradition of light comedy of which Wilde's *The Importance of Being Earnest* is an example. Both the Wilde play and *Pygmalion* satirize conventions and manners. Both depend on amusing, brilliantly written dialogue. A comparison of the plays will be interesting and informative to students.

Objectives

1. To identify the themes of the play

2. To recognize and explain the satire

3. To analyze the author's use of stage directions

4. To analyze the ending of the play

5. To write a sequel to the play

6. To write a modern version of the play

7. To adapt a myth to the stage

8. To support an opinion about the author's dialogue

9. To analyze a musical adaptation of the play

10. To write an essay on the author's attitude toward women

11. To write an essay responding to a critical review of the play

Introducing the Play

In outline form, for your reference, here are the major elements of the play.

- **Protagonist:** Eliza Doolittle
- **Antagonist:** Henry Higgins
- **Conflict:** person vs. person
- **Significant techniques:** satire, humor, foreshadowing, stage directions
- **Settings:** a portico outside St. Paul's church, Covent Garden, Eliza's room on Drury Lane, Henry Higgins's house on Wimpole Street, Mrs. Higgins's drawing room in Chelsea

Although Shaw's wit seems biting and at times cold-blooded, *Pygmalion* reveals Shaw as warmhearted and sensitive to the feelings of people. The device of a "created" woman gives Shaw a chance to comment on social and economic conditions, to be sure, but chiefly it provides him with his main theme: It is morally wrong to treat people as if they were objects. (The original myth of Pygmalion makes very much the same point as the creator falls in love with the woman: Love, not superiority, is the conquering force.)

Early on in the play, Shaw has several people express concern about Liza Doolittle's future. In his Epilogue, he shows sympathy and understanding for all his characters, including Higgins. He is not a sentimentalist, but he reveals a shrewd understanding of human conditions, up and down the social ladder.

Background on the Play. Students should realize how skillfully Shaw uses the drama form to entertain and at the same time to present sophisticated ideas. How Shaw does this can best be seen by comparing *Pygmalion* with Wilde's *The Importance of Being Earnest*. In almost every scene, Wilde seems to say, "Now I am going to drop a gem of wisdom." Shaw, on the other hand, integrates his social comment into his dialogue and action. In the first scene, for example, Shaw enlists our sympathy for the Flower Girl and our contempt for The Daughter. In deference to Wilde, it will be noted that Shaw does a lot of explaining in his stage directions (not much help when one is seeing the play on stage!), and even provides the reader with a long prose epilogue.

The Plot

Act I. A cockney flower girl, a British matron and her grown son and daughter, and two professors of linguistics are all thrown together when they take shelter from a rainstorm outside Covent Garden. Henry Higgins (labeled The Note Taker in this act) is busy noting the speech of the various people surrounding him and takes delight in telling them exactly where they live by listening to their pronunciation. Eliza takes offense at his noting her cockney speech, and Higgins boasts that he could pass her off as a duchess or as a shop assistant by teaching her how to speak. Colonel Pickering (labeled The Gentleman in most of the act) and Higgins meet and discover their mutual admiral admiration. Eliza goes home in her first taxi ride with money given to her by Pickering, and the two new friends plan to meet the next day.

Act II. Eliza appears at Higgins's house and asks to be given speech lessons so that she can become an assistant in a flower shop. Pickering challenges Higgins to make good his boast of the night before that he could pass Eliza off as a duchess at a garden party with the proper speech lessons. They agree on a six-month period of lessons with Pickering paying for the lessons if Higgins succeeds. In this act we are also introduced to Mrs. Pearce, Higgins's wise, sensible, and compassionate housekeeper, and to Alfred Doolittle, Eliza's rascally father, a garbage man who is not above selling Eliza for five pounds. Doolittle's dialogue reveals many of Shaw's ideas on middle-class morality.

Act III. This act takes place in the drawing room of Henry Higgins's mother, an elegant, wise woman in her sixties, who is about to entertain friends at an "at home." Higgins, who has been teaching his pupil for some months, chooses this setting for the first test of his experiment. Mrs. Higgins reluctantly agrees and the Eynsford-Hills arrive as guests. We met them in the first act as the mother and daughter and son waiting in the rain for a taxi outside Covent Garden. Eliza's learned behavior patterns break down under the pressure of questions, resulting in an amusing scene. Freddy, the son, is enchanted with Eliza's beauty, and Clara, the daughter, is impressed with her "modern small talk." Higgins and Pickering are pleased with their pupil, and only Mrs. Higgins worries about what is to become of Eliza once the experiment ends.

Act IV. It is six months later. The bet has been won by Higgins. Eliza has passed the test at a garden party, at the opera, and at a dinner party. Back at Higgins's house after the triumphs, both men congratulate themselves, taking little notice of Eliza's resentment at being passed off an as "interesting experiment" instead of as a person who helped win the bet by her hard work. Higgins shows little interest in Eliza's future, but does show that he has become accustomed to having her around to fetch his slippers and carry out his orders. Eliza decides to run away after Pickering and Higgins have retired for the night. She meets Freddy Eynsford-Hill outside her house, where he has been waiting for a lovesick glance of her. They embrace and leave in a taxi to ask Mrs. Higgins's advice.

Act V. The next morning Higgins and Pickering arrive at Mrs. Higgins's house very disturbed by Eliza's disappearance. Doolittle also arrives, dressed for a wedding, and reveals that he has received an unexpected inheritance as a result of Higgins's attentions, which have made him respectable, a situation that he resents in some typical Shavian dialogue. Mrs. Higgins reveals that Eliza is upstairs in her bedroom and berates Higgins and Pickering for their unfeeling treatment of Eliza. Eliza joins them and rejects Higgins's offer to return to his house, announcing that she will marry Freddy. All but Higgins go off to see Alfred Doolittle marry his seventh wife.

Teaching Strategies

Providing for Cultural Differences. There are references to parts of London and to some Edwardian customs such as Mrs. Higgins's "at-home" that might be puzzling to American students. Perhaps you might bring a map of London to class and point out the location of such places as Covent Garden, Wimpole Street, Chelsea, Charing Cross, Trafalgar Square, and Drury Lane.

Providing for Different Levels of Ability. This play, like all plays, benefits from reading aloud. Assign parts to various members of the class and let them enjoy the rhythms of Shaw's speech.

Introducing Vocabulary Study. Students will benefit from knowing the meanings of the following words before they read the play.

bravado	nomenclature
brusquely	oblivious
cogitation	opulence
congeniality	perfunctorily
deplorable	peremptorily
deprecate	petulance
derisive	placidly
didactic	prodigal
disquisition	quietude
imprecation	remonstrance
incarnate	repudiate
incorrigible	stolid
ineptitude	straightened
inscrutable	sumptuous
inveterate	unassailable
magnanimous	verbatim
mendacity	voluble
modulation	vouchsafed
morosely	zephyr

Reading the Play. Before reading the play, ask the students if they are familiar with the play in any form—that is, with the movie, the stage play, or the album of *My Fair Lady*. Tell them that certain scenes had to be omitted from the movie, such as the garden party, because they were too expensive to produce. Have students look for this type of scene as they read the play.

Plan to devote a week of class work to the teaching of the play, assigning an act per day. If time permits, you will want to have students act out portions of the acts, encouraging those with a flair for accents to attempt to read in dialect where appropriate. Slower students may be given additional opportunity to prepare at home for each of the acts. Direct all students to maintain a running log of unfamiliar terms or ideas for later discussion.

Reteaching Alternatives. Explain that Shaw was among the first to make a popular point about language as a function of social status and to note some strange aspects of our alphabetical system. Have students find examples of how letters and sounds are not consistently related.

Alternatively, use the songs from *My Fair Lady* to introduce situations and insights into character. List the song titles on the board and asks students to explain where in the play each song fits, what situation suggested the song, what imagination Lerner and Loewe added to the situation. Finally, what do the songs add to our understanding of Shaw's character or idea?

Responding to the Play   Text page 1158
Analyzing Act One
Identifying Details

1. Where does the first act take place? Most of the act takes place on a street near St. Paul's in London.

2. The *exposition* in a play consists of background information about the locale and the principal characters who will be involved in the action. Shaw handles the exposition brilliantly by inventing an amusing incident that tells us all we need to know. What is the incident, and what do we learn from it about the flower girl, the note taker, and the gentleman? What are these characters' names? The incident is the effort of Eliza, the flower girl, to sell flowers to the Eynsford Hills and Pickering, who are trying to get a cab in the rain. When the flower girl loudly protests her right to be there, a small crowd gathers—including Higgins, who is the note taker. It turns out that Higgins is a professor of phonetics and that Colonel Pickering is the author of a book on Sanskrit.

Interpreting Meanings

3. Usually, an opening scene will in some way *foreshadow* the coming *conflict*. Is there any clue as to what action might arise from what has happened so far? Student answers will vary. In general, students may suggest that Higgins's comments about the way he makes a living and the focus on Eliza at the end of the act combine to suggest that Higgins will try to teach Eliza the pronunciation of standard English.

4. Shaw says in the Preface, ". . . it is impossible for an Englishman to open his mouth without making some other Englishman despise him." What evidence of this statement occurs in Act One? Evidence of this statement in Act One includes the suspicion and hostility of the bystanders, and also Higgins's comments on the prevalence of social climbing.

Do we also judge people by their speech and accent in America? Students will probably agree that such judgments are also made in America, despite the fact that most people would consider such judgments "snobbish."

5. What does Shaw seem to think of the "society daughter" in this scene? How does her manner contrast with that of the flower girl? What might Shaw be trying to tell us by this counterpoint? The society girl is spoiled and haughty and contrasts pointedly with the flower girl. Student interpretations of this contrast will vary.

What further developments might he be preparing us for? Shaw may be preparing us for a surprise: a romantic plot involving the superficially unattractive flower girl.

6. What do you think the set of Eliza's room reveals about her background and her *character*? In general, the set reveals that Eliza comes from a humble background. The detail of the bird cage hints at tenderness in her character; the portrait of the popular actor and the fashion plate of ladies' dresses perhaps suggests romantic yearnings.

Responding to the Play   Text page 1173
Analyzing Act Two
Identifying Details

1. Why does Eliza come to Higgins's laboratory? Eliza comes to Higgins's laboratory because she hopes he will give her speech lessons so that she can work in a genteel flower shop.

How does Higgins treat her? He treats her peremptorily.

How does Pickering treat her? He treats her like a lady.

2. What is the bet made between Pickering and Higgins? Describe the plan set in action as a result of the bet. Pickering and Higgins bet on whether Higgins will be able to pass Eliza off as a duchess at the ambassador's garden party. Pickering will for the moment assume all the costs of the lessons. This bet leads to Higgins's order to Mrs. Pearce to take Eliza upstairs and clean her up, dressing her in some decent clothes.

3. What reasons does Higgins give for remaining a "confirmed old bachelor"? Higgins says that the moment he makes friends with a woman, she becomes jealous and he becomes selfish.

4. Why does Doolittle visit Higgins? He visits Higgins to retrieve Eliza.

What are his problems as a member of the "undeserving poor"? He says, amusingly, that he can't afford to have morals because they are too expensive.

Interpreting Meanings

5. Point out some of the *paradoxes*, or apparent contradictions, between Doolittle's speeches and his behavior. Where does he vacillate between moral indignation and rascally wheedling? Among the paradoxes that students may point out are the contradiction between Doolittle's demand for his daughter and his apparent willingness to allow Eliza to stay if he is paid five pounds for his part in the "arrangement." Although he is greedy for money, he stubbornly refuses when Higgins offers him ten pounds, saying that so much money might make him feel "prudent" and then his happiness would be ruined.

6. What *satiric* point might Shaw be making in his characterization of Doolittle? Shaw might be making the satiric point that the poor have been ground down so often by middle-class attitudes of contempt that they have grown to believe that their inferiority and poverty are inevitable.

7. Mrs. Pearce several times expresses the major question of the play. What is it? The major question of the play is: What is to become of Eliza?

What is Higgins's attitude toward the question? Does he have a point? Higgins has an indifferent attitude. Student interpretations will vary.

8. The *character* of Higgins could be a monster, but obviously Shaw does not see him as such. How does Shaw describe Higgins, and what keeps him from being unbearable? Shaw describes Higgins as very amusing. Underneath his apparently callous exterior, we suspect that he is really quite kind.

What is Higgins's view of himself? He views himself as an expert at what he does.

9. What is the function of Colonel Pickering in the action? The function of Colonel Pickering is as a sensible, kindly "uncle" figure who helps to moderate Higgins's sharpness towards Eliza and serves as something of a "straight man" for Higgins's amusing patter.

10. Eliza is a tough street girl, but Shaw goes to great lengths to establish her innocent nature. How does he do this? He shows her pathetically misinterpreting words such as "grammar," and he also has her confidently speak up about her good morals.

11. What is the basic *conflict* of Act Two? The basic conflict of this act is whether or not Eliza will stay at Higgins's house and start her training.

What means does Higgins use to gain his end? He bribes Eliza with chocolates and tempts her with visions of her future life.

What does the *resolution* of the conflict lead us to expect about what will happen next? The resolution of the conflict leads us to expect that Higgins and Pickering will indeed take Eliza in hand and try to "present" her as a duchess at the garden party.

Responding to the Play Text page 1185
Analyzing Act Three
Identifying Details

1. Who are the other guests at Mrs. Higgins's at-home, and where have we seen them before? The other guests are Mrs. Eynsford Hill and her daughter, whom we have seen on the rainy London street at the opening of Act One. Later, Colonel Pickering and Freddy Eynsford Hill enter.

2. Eliza's accent and manners are perfect. But what does she say that shocks the other guests—at least some of them? She says that she thinks that her aunt was "done in" and that her father was addicted to gin.

How does Higgins explain Eliza's slang? He says that it is the new small talk.

How does Freddy feel about Eliza? Freddy is romantically attracted to Eliza.

3. According to Mrs. Higgins, what "problem" walks in the door with Eliza? She says that the problem is "what is to be done with her afterwards."

4. What role does Nepommuck have in the play at this point? Nepommuck, who was Higgins's first pupil, now speaks thirty-two languages. He serves as an interpreter at the embassy entertainment. Higgins is afraid he may be able to unmask Eliza because of his knowledge of languages and phonetics.

5. Describe Eliza's triumph at the ball. How is Pickering's bet with Higgins resolved? Eliza enters, beautifully dressed with diamonds, flowers, and a fan, and escorted by Higgins and Pickering. Everyone stares at her in admiration, and the Hostess sends Nepommuck to find out all about her. Because of her perfect English, Nepommuck comically makes the assumption that Eliza must be a foreigner, and he pronounces her to be a Hungarian princess. Higgins wins the bet.

Interpreting Meanings

6. *Characters* can be revealed to us by physical activity, by what they say and by what they do, and by the way other characters respond to them. In this act, how does Shaw use physical activity to reveal Higgins's personali-

ty? Higgins reveals his absent-mindedness and impatience by flinging himself around the room, stumbling over various objects of furniture.

What do his mother's actions in particular reveal about Higgins's nature? His mother reveals Higgins's absent-mindedness and lack of manners by taking his hat off and presenting it to him at the beginning of the act.

7. How is Eliza changing—in *appearance*, *speech*, and *character*? Eliza is becoming more and more attractive physically, and her English speech has become so perfect that she scores a triumph at the embassy. In character, she is portrayed as more and more romantic and sensitive, especially in the speech where she refers to herself as "in a dream."

8. What does Mrs. Pearce mean by her comment to Higgins, "You, don't think"? She means that he is absent-minded and insensitive.

9. What do Higgins and Pickering mean when they assure Mrs. Higgins that they take Eliza seriously? They mean it in the sense that they are working hard to meet the new challenges in her training that pop up each week.

What, on the other hand, is Mrs. Higgins really talking about? Mrs. Higgins is really referring to taking Eliza seriously as another human being.

10. How do you feel about Higgins and Pickering at this point in the play? Student answers will vary. Ask the students to discuss and support their opinions.

11. What do you predict is going to happen next? (What are the possibilities?) Student answers will vary. Among the possibilities students may mention are a romance between Freddy and Eliza (hinted at in Act Two) and an unhappy resolution, in which Higgins might turn Eliza out, now that he has won his bet.

12. In *My Fair Lady*, the musical comedy made from *Pygmalion*, the scene at Mrs. Higgins's at-home is a comic triumph. What incongruous elements in that scene would contribute to its comedy? (*Incongruity* refers to the joining of two opposites to create a situation that we don't expect.) Students may mention the following incongruous elements: Higgins flinging himself about the room, his bad manners to the guests, Mrs. Higgins's ironic remarks about her son, and Eliza's hilarious remarks about her father and her aunt.

Responding to the Play   Text page 1191
Analyzing Act Four
Identifying Details

1. During this act, Eliza stands on stage saying nothing for a very long time, yet we begin to pay more attention to how she is reacting than to what is being said. In his stage directions, how does Shaw show us Eliza's mood and prepare us for what she will eventually say? The stage directions show that Eliza is angry and hurt at the fact that Higgins and Pickering do not give her any of the credit for her "triumph."

2. From Eliza's point of view, what has Higgins done that is wrong? Higgins has been selfish and cruel to raise her hopes in life.

3. Who "rescues" Eliza as she is about to "make a hole in the river"? Freddy rescues her.

Interpreting Meanings

4. What small indications does Higgins give in Acts Three and Four that he has become attached to Eliza? He says that she keeps his appointments, that he can't find any of his possessions without her help, and that she has "wounded him to the heart" by causing him to lose his temper.

5. Plays often move through a series of *reversals*. At the end of this act, a reversal makes us feel that Higgins has in some way been toppled and that Eliza has gained the upper hand. How does she do this? Why is she so happy that Higgins loses his temper? Eliza infuriates Higgins by handing back all the things he had given her, including a ring he had bought for her. She is happy that Higgins has lost his temper because she has gotten a little of her own back on him.

6. A *crisis* in a play is a turning point—a moment when the action begins to move toward either a happy ending or a tragic one. What is the crisis in this brief act? The crisis in this act is Eliza's angry departure from the house, together with the hint that she is so unhappy that she may commit suicide in the river.

7. The long game is over, and Higgins has won his bet. Why do we continue to be interested in the play? What questions has Shaw put in our minds? We continue to think about the question of Eliza's future and of what will come of the romance between her and Freddy. We also wonder if Higgins really is attached to Eliza.

8. How do you feel about Higgins's behavior in this act? Student answers will vary. Ask the students to discuss and support their opinions.

Responding to the Play   Text page 1209
Analyzing Act Five
Identifying Details

1. At the end of Act Four, Eliza leaves Higgins's house. At the beginning of Act Five, how does Shaw let us know where Eliza is? From the dialogue at the end of Act Four, we suspect that Eliza and Freddy have ridden around all night in the taxicab and that Eliza is now at Mrs. Higgins's house.

2. How has Doolittle been transformed? Doolittle is now a respectable-looking, nicely dressed gentleman. He has inherited a trust fund yielding three thousand a year as a result of a bequest by a wealthy American.

Why is he miserable with his new station in life? He chafes under the restrictions of his new "respectability."

3. How does Eliza turn the tables on Higgins when she tells Pickering what really turned her into a lady? She turns the tables on Higgins because she says she learned more about being a true lady from Pickering's gentlemanly example than from Higgins's speech lessons.

4. Though Higgins is not about to humble himself when he and Eliza are finally alone together, Shaw reveals how vulnerable Higgins is through certain stage directions. Cite examples of these. Among the examples students may cite are Higgins's sitting down on the ottoman near Eliza, his bouncing up on his knees, and his thunderstruck reaction when Eliza reveals that she will marry Freddy.

5. Explain in your own words Higgins's theory of how people should behave toward each other. He says that people should treat everyone in exactly the same way.

6. As Eliza and Higgins argue, they seem to slip from subject to subject. What are they really arguing about? They are really arguing about their relationship to each other.

What is Eliza's main point? Eliza's main point is that she wants a little kindness.

7. In Act Two, Mrs. Pearce tells us how Higgins can turn on his charm. How does he do it in Act Five? What does he offer Eliza if she comes back? Higgins turns on his charm by telling Eliza that he depends on her. He says that he will adopt her as his daughter and settle money on her.

8. Higgins and Eliza finally do have passionate physical contact. How is it shown? Infuriated at the suggestion that Eliza may marry Nepommuck and reveal Higgins's professional secrets, Higgins lays hands on her as if to shake her.

Interpreting Meanings

9. Are you convinced by Eliza's transition from someone who wants to be cared about to someone who is independent? Explain. Student answers will vary. Ask the students to support their opinions in class.

10. Do you see any evidence that Higgins has also changed? Explain. Again, student answers will vary. Ask the students to explain their interpretations.

11. What do you think about the ending of the play? Is Shaw's intent ambiguous, or do you think it is perfectly clear? Many students will agree with the theory that Shaw's intent is ambiguous, since the futures of Eliza and Higgins are left up in the air. Ask the students to discuss and support their interpretations of the final scene.

The Play as a Whole

1. What kind of ending did Shaw lead you to expect? How does Shaw defend the outcome of his play in the epilogue? Most students will probably say that Shaw has led us to expect a romantic ending. In the epilogue, Shaw defends the outcome of the play by saying that a romantic conclusion would have been a capitulation to stale conventions. He says that a marriage between Higgins and Eliza would have been inconsistent with both of their characters as these characters are portrayed in the play. Student responses to Shaw's arguments will differ. Encourage the students to discuss and support their reactions in class.

2. In your view, who emerges as the play's most important character, or *protagonist*: Eliza or Higgins? Defend your opinion. Since the play is entitled *Pygmalion*, many of the students will argue that Higgins is the play's most important character. On the other hand, some students may suggest that Eliza is portrayed as a more dynamic character than Higgins and that she is therefore the real protagonist. Other students may suggest that, since the basic conflict of the play hinges on the relationship between Higgins and Eliza, the two characters are of equal importance. Ask the students to support their responses with arguments and specific references to the text.

3. Look up the myth of Pygmalion in Ovid's *Metamorphoses* or in a reference book. How has Shaw altered the myth? Why might Shaw have made these changes? Among the alterations are Shaw's making the "metamorphosis" of Eliza include her speech, rather than just her physical appearance; the fact that Higgins does not really fall passionately in love with Eliza; and the outcome of the play. Student speculations on why Shaw might have made these changes will differ.

4. Look back over the roles of the minor characters in the play. Explain the dramatic function of each of the following characters: Doolittle, Mrs. Eynsford Hill, Mrs. Pearce, Freddy. How are some of these people representative of *character types*? Which type does Shaw approve of? Doolittle functions as a vehicle of comic relief and social commentary; Mrs. Eynsford Hill functions as a middle-class stereotype; Mrs. Pearce functions as a kindly "housekeeper" stereotype; and Freddy functions as the type of the romantic, handsome, young hero. Shaw probably approves most of Mrs. Pearce's kindness and good sense.

5. What has Eliza gained as a result of her experience with Higgins? What, if anything, has she lost? She has gained self-respect. Some students will suggest that she has lost a certain quality of innocence and naivete, which were two of the traits that made her originally so attractive.

6. Try to state Shaw's *theme***, or underlying message, in two or three sentences. What do you think of his theme?** Student statements of the theme and responses to it will vary.

7. If we think of *Pygmalion* **as a** *satire***, who or what would you say are Shaw's targets? What is your response to his satire? Do you think it has application to society as you know it today?** Among the targets that students may suggest are hollow or insensitive social conventions, snobbishness, posturing, and the attitudes of the rich (or the middle class) toward the poor. Student reactions to the satire will vary, but most students will agree that the satire might still have application to society as we know it today.

Modern British Drama

Text page 1211

This historical overview encompasses a good deal of material, much of which will be unfamiliar to your students. Be sure to allow plenty of time to read and discuss the material, preferably section by section. After students read the five introductory paragraphs, assign separately the sections on the Irish dramatists, on English comedy, on the Angry Young Men, on the Theater of the Absurd, and on Pinter. Students should enjoy reading the excerpts from the plays, especially the three longer dialogues, aloud in class. Interesting discussions might be generated by considering first the quotation by Synge on page 1213, and second the distinction made on page 1220 between Naturalism and Naturalist dialogue. It would be greatly enriching to show your class videotapes of productions of some of the works mentioned; Pinter's *Betrayal*, for example, has been made into a movie.

The English Language

Text page 1223

Your students may be surprised at how entertaining they will find this survey of types of etymology. Encourage them to think of additional examples to illustrate the various ways English words are formed: onomatopoeia; borrowings from other languages; compounds; affixes; acronyms and other shortenings; back-formations; blends; and shifts in meaning.

Some students may require additional explanation to clarify the concept of folk etymology. This might be a good opportunity to make the point that there is a degree of speculation in virtually all etymologies and that even expert opinions as to a word's origin are often variable.

Exercises in Critical Thinking and Writing

Text page 1229

This assignment calls on the students to draw together all they have learned about style, to select a strong passage from a story they have read in this unit, and to write an analysis of the writer's style. The Background section includes a discussion of the basic elements of prose style and emphasizes the idea that, in good writing, style and content are unified. The questions in the Prewriting section will help the students both to analyze the style of the passage and to organize their ideas before beginning to write. The Writing section provides students with additional suggestions for how to approach the assignment. Finally, encourage the students to study the sample analysis of James Joyce's "Araby."

Criteria for Evaluating the Assignments. Student essays should begin with a clear thesis statement that concisely describes the writer's style in the passage being analyzed. Check to see that student essays are coherent and well organized and that they reflect a good understanding of the basic elements of style. Any quotations should be accurate and pertinent. Finally, check to see that the students have taken care to revise and proofread what they have written.

Suggestions for Teaching and Evaluating the Writing Assignments

A Creative Response

In this unit, students will be asked to respond creatively to their reading in various ways. These range from adopting different points of view to imitating writers' styles to describing the setting and character to performing a choral reading and writing a movie version of a story. Before beginning to write, students should have a firm grasp on the main objectives of each assignment. If the students are asked to work with a particular element or technique that they have studied, you may want to go over that element with them first. If the assignment is purely creative—as in composing a poem or a screenplay—enourage the students to be free and imaginative as they work.

Criteria for Evaluating the Assignments. Student responses should demonstrate comprehension of the material they have studied and of the purpose of the assignments. The best creative responses will be those that are most imaginative, original, and well prepared.

A Critical Response

Students will be asked to respond critically to their reading in several different ways. These range from comparing and contrasting authors and their works and styles to analyzing character, conflict, imagery, point of view, and theme to discussing allusion and symbolism. As with the creative assignments, you may find it helpful to go over each of these assignments with the students before they start writing. Be sure that they understand the nature of the task and its relation to the writing they have read, particularly where a new technique or element has been introduced. Encourage the students to devise at least a rough outline as a way of organizing their thoughts.

Criteria for Evaluating the Assignments. Check the student responses for coherence, logic, and organization. Essays should always begin with a clear statement of the topic and should flow smoothly from there on. Where a particular element or technique has been covered, the student essays should show an understanding of that element and the way it is used in the given selection. Where research or reference is required, check to see that the students have quoted accurately and concisely. Finally, look for evidence that the students have taken the time to proofread their papers.

Answers to Analyzing Language

Analyzing Language and Style   Text page 1034

Slang

1. *Lav* is slang for lavatory, or toilet. The word lavatory originally referred only to the washbasin. It comes from the Latin *lavare*, "to wash."

2. To *pinch* is to steal, it comes from the word's basic meaning, dating back to Middle English: "to squeeze between two fingers." *Bleeding* is a variant of the expletive *bloody*, probably originally from *s'blood* (for *God's blood*). A *funk* is a state of depression; it probably comes from the Flemish *fonck*, meaning "dismay."

3. *Haw-haw*, an onomatopoeic imitation of laughter, refers to an affected, superior manner of speech.

4. *Jug* is slang for jail. Students may not be able to find any discussion of the word's etymology, but should be able to make the connection that both jugs and jails are used to keep something or someone closed inside.

5. A *bob* is a shilling; the word may come from the name Bob.

   Your students should be able to think of many parallel American slang expressions. Examples include *john*, *rip off*, *stinking*, *the blues*, *stuck-up*, *the slammer*, and *buck*.

Assonance and Alliteration

1. The long *e* sound dominates the first stanza, through the rhymes *Innisfree* and *honeybee*, and the words *bean* and *bee-loud*. Some students may note that the long *o* sound is also prominent.

2. The rhyming words repeat the long *e*, *a*, and *o* sounds.

3. In line 10, the repeated *l* and *w* sounds echo the sound of lake water.

4. The repeated vowel sounds make the poem musical, haunting, and languorous. More hard consonant sounds would have made it guttural and harsh.

Free Verse

1. Examples of onomatopoeia include *dripped*, *sipped*, *lick*, and *clatter*.

2. Examples of alliteration used to create onomatopoeia include *slackness soft-bellied . . . stone trough . . . rested . . . stone bottom*; *dripped from the tap*; *Softly . . . straight gums . . . slack . . . silently*; *two-forked tongue*; take a stick and break him; *flickered . . . like a forked night*; *lick his lips*; and *slowly drew up, snake-easing his shoulders*.

3. Key images and events in the poem are emphasized by being described both in unusually short, even one-word, lines (such as line 13) and in unusually long lines (such as line 43). Contrast often heightens this emphasis; for example, line 13, a single word, follows an unusually long line.

4. Parallelism, a type of repetition, creates rhythm in lines 8–10, 17–19, 31–33, 42–51, and 66–67. In addition, the repetition of words and phrases creates rhythm in lines 2, 4, 11–12, 20, 37, 46–48, and 52.

Free Verse

1. Internal rhymes in the poem include *bat/rat*, *tall walls wall*, *wise lies*, *black racks rack*, and *hither/thither*. Other rhymes include *hear me/near me*, *console me/roll me*, *provide me/guide me*, *forgive me/live me*, *rehearse me/curse me*, and *fill me/spill me/kill me*. In addition, the many near or slant rhymes include *speak/think* and *lecture/hector*.

2. The abundant examples of alliteration include *blood-sucking bat*, *bat/rat/stoat/club-footed*, *drugs dope*, *with wise lies lure*, *black/bloodbaths*, *grass/grow*, *trees/talk*, *sky/sing*, *birds/back*, *world/words*, *thoughts/think*, *treason/traitors*, *murder/means*, *parts/play*, *bureaucrats hector*, *lovers laugh*, *white waves*, *desert/doom*, *thistledown/hither/thither*, *held/hands*, and *stone/spill*. An example of onomatopoeia is *blow*.

3. The poet makes the poem's last line very short for dramatic effect.

Connotations

1. Answers will vary, but associations with *departure* might include sadness and ending; with *dark*, nighttime and fear; with the phrase as a whole, apprehension, mystery, cold, and loneliness.

2. Other words in the poem that contribute to these associations include *unkind*, *goodbyes*, *numb*, farewell, suicide, *gloomed*, *clemmed*, *ice age*, *dead end*, *sleep*, *drear*, *extinct*, *part*, *fugitive yearnings*, *blind*, and *ruins*.

3. Most students will probably cite *arrival* and *light* as the opposite of *departure* and *dark*. Associations with these words will vary, but might include, for *arrival*, happiness and relief; for *light*, warmth and friendliness.

Word Play

Cliches turned upside-down include "happy as the grass was green," "once below a time," "All the sun long," and "fire green as grass." Puns include "the sun grew round" and "morning songs." The many surprising uses of modifiers include "lilting house," "I lordly had the trees," "windfall light," "simple stars," "walking warm," "whinnying green stable," "sky blue trades," and "lamb white days." Old sayings with new twists include "honored among wagons," "the calves sang to my horn," and "honored among foxes and pheasants."

1. *Easel* comes from the Dutch *ezel*, meaning "ass," as a result of the original French word for the objects, *chevalet*, or "little horse." *Escalate* is a back-formation from *escalator*, which was coined as a trademark in 1895. *Gas* was invented by a chemist as a variant of the Greek word *chaos*, meaning "air." *Hiccup* is onomatopoeic. *Jeep* originally came from a comic-strip character, Eugene the Jeep; a false etymology later associated it with *G.P.*, for "General Purpose Car." *Kitty-cornered* was formerly *cater-cornered*; however, *cater* did not mean "cat," but was Middle English for "four." *Motel* is a blend of the words *motorist* and *hotel*. *Pep* was originally short for *pepper*. *Scarecrow* is a compound for a thing that scares crows away. *Lengthwise* is composed of *length* and the suffix *-wise*, meaning "ways."

2. Answers will vary, but students would be correct in guessing that *business* once meant "busy-ness," or "a state of being busy"; that *doff* was once "do off"; that a *cupboard* was once a board on which cups were stored; that a *bonfire* was a "bone fire," or funeral pyre; and that *disease* meant "dis ease," or discomfort.

3. Answers will naturally vary.

4. Students should have no trouble finding one of these sources. Have each student share his or her list of new words with the class.

Writing About Literature

Relating composition to the study of literature produces numerous benefits for both students and teachers. In order to write about a literary work, students must read it closely and must formulate their thoughts about it clearly: They gain a deeper understanding of what they have read and of how it applies to their own lives and values. At the same time, they practice essential critical thinking and composition skills as they use the basic forms of discourse: narration, description, persuasion, and, primarily, exposition, the form they will use most frequently throughout their lives.

Having students write about their reading provides advantages for you as well. When students write on the same topic, you can evaluate their essays more equitably, and when they write on different topics, their common knowledge of the literary work makes collaborative writing, evaluating, and revising especially fruitful. Students' written work can also alert you to individual problems in reading comprehension or to a general need for reteaching: If many essays evidence a similar difficulty, you will know where to clarify the analysis of a selection.

Draw students' attention to the "Writing About Literature" section early in the term, explaining that it provides strategies for answering the text's essay questions and for choosing and writing about their own topics for essays on literary works. Throughout the year, remind students to refer to this section when they are writing or preparing for an essay test.

If you want to teach the section in one or two lessons, some suggestions for presentation follow. This is also a good time to explain whether you will regularly set aside class time for writing, how often you will give timed essay tests, and how you will grade students' papers.

Writing Answers to Essay Questions

You probably cannot overemphasize to students the importance of understanding exactly what an essay question is asking. What are the mental tasks required? What specifics of the literary work are to be dealt with? What kind of support, and how much, is stipulated? Suggest that students read a question more than once as they work, to make sure they are following all of the directions.

In discussing the key verbs that are listed in the text, whenever possible use examples from selections the class has already read. As a further illustration of *analyze*, for example, you could ask students how they would proceed to analyze the theme of Nadine Gordimer's story "The Voice of the Serpent." As they answer, emphasize that they are *isolating* elements (foreshadowing, details that create ambiguity or doubt, vivid descriptions of physical and emotional states): They are "taking apart" the suspense in order to understand it.

When you discuss *compare* and *contrast*, remind students of the two methods for organizing this type of paragraph or essay. Using block organization, students write about one work (or element) and then the other; using point-by-point organization, they alternate between two works or elements as they cover each point of comparison or contrast. Be sure to emphasize that a direction to compare may mean to look for both similarities and differences. Suggest that students check with you when they are not sure whether *compare* has this comprehensive meaning in a particular question.

Few students are likely to misinterpret a direction to *describe*; however, you might spend a few minutes reviewing spatial order as a method for organizing details of physical description. Also emphasize the importance of using precise words and of including a variety of sensory details.

Students may have more difficulty with a question that requires them to *discuss*. Explain that this direction allows a broader response than do some other key verbs, but that it does not permit superficiality or vagueness. If the generality of *discuss* confuses your students, stress the alternate verb *examine,* and also point out that, in order to discuss, one must almost always first analyze.

Another way for students to think of *evaluate* is as a judgment of how well a literary element or technique "works"—how effectively it creates a desired effect. Emphasize that evaluation is not merely an expression of personal preference: It is a test against certain criteria, or standards. For evaluation questions, suggest that students first clarify the criteria they will apply. They can then specify how the work fulfills or falls short of those standards, providing the required "proof" for their positions.

For the next verb, *illustrate* (similar verbs are *demonstrate* and *show*), stress that students must always provide examples from the work (details, dialogue, figurative language, etc.) to support their ideas; otherwise, even good ideas appear as mere opinions, lacking force.

Students should see that such support is especially important when a question asks them to *interpret* meaning or significance. Explain that *interpret* implies that no single, or absolute, statement of meaning exists; students must therefore carefully explain what has led them to their interpretation.

Finally, point out that a direction to *explain your response* does allow students a purely personal reaction to a work but that, again, support is required, this time in the form of reasons. Offer an example: The statement "'The Woman Wanderer' is the most beautiful poem in the book" is acceptable—but not by itself; the student must tell why he or she thinks so.

Be sure students see that a question may contain or imply more than one key verb. For example, in *discussing* the use of irony in "Get Up and Bar the Door," a student might use *illustration* and *description* to develop the essay's thesis. In every case, however, the question will provide a clear purpose on which to focus.

The next step, item 3, is crucial for students and should be stressed: Write a brief, direct, and specific thesis statement. You could ask students to rephrase actual essay questions from the text as thesis statements, following the example. Then note that in gathering supporting ideas and evidence, students usually can draw from class discussion of a selection. In fact, class work on the "Analyzing the [Selection]" questions can be thought of as prewriting: Explain that active participation and note-taking will yield ideas and data for later writing.

In discussing items 4 and 5, be sure students see that an essay's main ideas will come from the information gathered to support the thesis statement. Emphasize that each paragraph should contain a single idea, buttressed with evidence, and suggest that students draft a thesis statement and a topic sentence for each paragraph before writing the complete answer.

Make clear that all of this thinking, note-taking, and organizing is essential no matter what form the rough outline takes. It is not time wasted, *especially* when time is restricted. If students begin writing without planning, their essays will be incomplete or unorganized no matter how correct the grammar and mechanics. Emphasize that, in timed writing, students must set a schedule for themselves, allowing time for all major stages of the writing process: prewriting, writing, evaluating and revising, and proofreading. (On occasions that seem to warrant it, you may want to consider allowing students who run out of time to turn in their prewriting notes along with their papers. The notes may demonstrate that a student understood the question and had planned a sound answer but simply did not have time to execute it.)

Writing and Revising an Essay About a Literary Work

Students should recognize the significance of choosing a limited topic, one narrow enough to cover in detail in a fairly brief essay. If they are afraid they won't find enough to say about a narrow topic, assure them that developing a specific idea is actually easier than thoroughly supporting a broad generalization. Suggest that they find limited topics

by asking further questions about information discussed in class. They might look at *why* a character changed in attitude, *which* conflict or conflicts revealed a major theme, or *how* word choice set a particular tone. Students should skim a selection they want to write about and review their reading and class notes. Encourage them to take more notes as they reread, even if they haven't yet settled on a topic; the notes can help them define their thesis and gather supporting evidence.

Go over each of the remaining prewriting steps with the students, illustrating how formulation of the thesis statement will control, or direct, the subsequent steps. Remind students to write a plan or outline, even if informal; you might refer them to the discussion of outlines in their composition and grammar text.

The text's outline of essay form is a good general reference. Emphasize that students should write their first drafts by working steadily through to the end, referring as needed to their outlines and notes. You may want to take this opportunity to warn against overusing direct quotations to pad the body of an essay. Tell students to ask themselves whether the precise wording of the quotation is important to their point or whether a shorter reference or paraphrase will suffice.

When you discuss revision, note that this final step presupposes evaluation: Students must first read a draft to evaluate its strengths and weaknesses; then they can make the changes—adding, deleting, replacing, or reordering words and phrases—that will improve the draft. Suggest that students go through their drafts once for content and organization, a second time for style (wordiness, monotonous sentence structure, etc.), and a third time for mechanical errors (spelling, punctuation, etc.). Explain that learning the proofreader's symbols can streamline this part of the process. Also encourage the use of peer evaluation, illustrating appropriate constructive criticism if your students do not regularly exchange work.

You might guide the class through the model essay twice, to focus attention on different aspects. First have students concentrate on content and organization, using the side-notes that highlight development of the thesis. The second time, they can focus on the writer's revisions. Ask the class why the changes were made and how they improve the essay. For example, in the first paragraph, the first change corrects the citation of a short story, the second change corrects a reference, and the remaining changes on the same page smooth out a wordy, choppy style.

Documenting Sources

Specify for students the style you prefer for documenting sources, and be sure to make available a reference containing several examples of citations, whether a published style book, your own information sheet, or the students' composition and grammar text. Students could also use good essays from your previous classes as models of correct documentation.

Model Students Essays

The following papers were written by twelfth-grade students in response to four of the "Exercises in Critical Thinking and Writing" sections in *Elements of Literature: Sixth Course*. They are included here as samples of the writing you can expect from twelfth-graders using the text. The names of the student and school are listed after each model.

The central themes of D. H. Lawrence's short story "The Rocking-Horse Winner" have to do with love, respect, and, most importantly, money. The mother in this story is the character who is most deeply affected by these three things.

The woman has three children and a husband, none of whom she loves. ". . . when the children were present, she always felt the center of her heart go hard." The mother buys her children presents and toys so that they will not notice her lack of love toward them.

The mother would like everyone to believe that her family is wealthy. They used to be, but now they often borrow money and are in debt. She blames the father for their lack of wealth, because he can't make enough money to support the extravagant lifestyle to which she was accustomed. Once, as a birthday present, she received five thousand pounds, which was to be given to her in one thousand-pound installments over a five-year period. The mother convinces the family lawyer to give her the entire sum at once. Instead of using the money to pay overdue bills and help her family financially, the mother uses the five thousand pounds to buy flowers and other decorative things that the family cannot afford. She doesn't want everyone thinking that she is poor, so she puts up a front. The mother cannot limit her spending habits, and, in turn, she is harming her family.

Her son Paul realizes how important money is to her. Once, in a discussion about luck, the mother tells her son that if he had luck he would have money. Paul knows that his mother doesn't love him, and he also knows that the only thing she cares about is money. He comes to the conclusion that if he had money, not only would he be able to buy his mother everything she wanted, but he feels sure that she would love him. Paul dies trying to win his mother's love.

The mother learns the hard way that money cannot buy everything, especially not love. In her fight to acquire money, she suffers many losses, the greatest of which is the death of her son. Maybe now, after this tragedy, the mother will realize how important love is and how unimportant money is.

—Natasha Claro

Benjamin N. Cardozo High School

Bayside, New York

In the essay "The Death of the Moth" by Virginia Woolf, the "true nature of life" as revealed by Woolf through her examination of the moth is that all creatures, no matter how insignificant and useless, must pass away when their time comes.

Woolf uses the moth, an insignificant creature, to make her point clear. She describes the moth as having a zest for his meager opportunities. But, as his life slowly comes to a close, he loses the spark of life, his zest, and he dies. I feel that the author is trying to convey that one cannot, no matter how hard one prays, escape death. Everyone and everything will eventually pass away. The little moth struggles with all his energy against death, as do most people who know that they are about to die. They fight to hold on just a little while longer. No one has any chance against death. Death is stronger than all mankind. I think once you've experienced death by having someone close to you die, you have a different outlook on it. You begin to realize that life is precious and should not be wasted by worrying about petty matters. You should enjoy life while it is still fresh, for it is precious.

—Randy Duryea

Lindenhurst Senior High School

Lindenhurst, New York

The conflict in the story between the scientist and the Farquars and Gideon results when Gideon refuses to share his knowledge. The conflict is not between right and wrong; it is a result of cultural differences. All three sets of people, Gideon, the scientist, and the Farquars have different points of view although they share some similarities as well.

The Farquars wish Gideon to share his knowledge for a universal purpose, to save lives. They feel that making the substance known world-wide would save countless people from blindness. The scientists' view is similar to the Farquars except that his also has an ulterior motive. The production of this drug would make the scientist both famous and rich. The scientist wishes to achieve both those goals under the guise of "the advancement of science."

Gideon's point of view is much different. Though he would be happy to give to the world the knowledge that could save many lives, Gideon refuses for a very valid reason. Gideon feels that this knowledge is part of the customs of his people and that it would be exploited by the profit-seeking scientist. In a sense, Gideon refuses to sell out his tribe for fame and fortune.

As we can see, there are differences between the Farquars and the scientist and Gideon, with the conflict in the story arising over cultural differences.

—Richard Lisi

Lindenhurst Senior High School

Lindenhurst, New York

In the short story "No Witchcraft for Sale" by Doris Lessing, a conflict caused by cultural differences occurs when Gideon is asked to reveal one of the healing secrets of his tribe. Gideon refuses: his point of view is different from that of Farquars and the scientist.

I feel that Gideon refuses because he sees his homeland and his people being exploited by the white "baases" whose only wishes are to fulfill their own imperialistic desires. He wants to preserve from exploitation whatever bit of his own culture he can. Although he is a kind, loyal servant, he sees the disrespect and degradation dealt out to his people who are practically slaves living in poverty, working in their own homeland to fill the pockets of the foreign white "baas." He sees the low opinion of his race even in the eyes of the children. When young Teddy frightens a black boy with his scooter and he is asked why he did it, he laughs. "He's only a black boy," and won't even bring himself to apologize. The white man even took away Gideon's religion and domesticated him. Gideon shows this by saying, "Ah, missus, these are both children, and one will grow up to be a baas, and one will be a servant. It is God's will." This quote is taken right from the beginning, showing what the white men have led Gideon to believe. I strongly feel that Gideon refuses to turn over the herb in order to preserve a piece of culture from becoming the property of the insincere, mocking "big baas."

I feel that both the scientist and the Farquar believe that the medicine could serve a great purpose to all humanity, but in other ways their attitudes are different. The Farquars are "kind, simple people, who liked to think of something good coming about because of them." They think the medicine is some kind of miracle and aren't interested in money, only in the advancement of humanity. I think Gideon senses this, and this is why he is loyal to them. The scientist, on the other hand, is very cocky and shows disbelief when he "sat back and sipped his coffee, smiling with skeptical good humor," and he "was being polite, even though there was an amused look in his eyes," when he thanked Gideon. I believe that these examples show the three different points of view over the plant.

—Michael Burren

Lindenhurst Senior High School

Lindenhurst, New York

In the short story "No Witchcraft for Sale" by Doris Lessing there is a conflict between the scientist and the Farquars and Gideon. This story takes place in Africa and the Farquars are part of the British ruling class who have a son named Teddy. Gideon is the Farquars' black cook and servant and is very close to Teddy. One day Teddy comes into the house screaming with his hands over his eyes after a tree snake spat on him in the eyes. Gideon quickly runs to the boy and gets help. He seeks out a plant and strips it; he then chews it and spits it into the crying boy's swollen eyes. He is confident that the plant will cure Teddy, and it does.

Now begins the conflict. The Farquars and the scientist and Gideon have different points of view about this so-called miracle. The scientist thinks that the whole story is nonsense. He wants Gideon to show him the plant he used, but Gideon refuses. The Farquars believe Gideon should help the scientist so this plant's medicine can help save the sight of other Africans. Gideon feels betrayed by his friends because these are his people's customs and secrets and he doesn't want the world to know about them. The Farquars don't understand why Gideon is being so stubborn, but they finally accept it. The scientist goes away to study a plant which the servant poins out as the plant he used (but it isn't).

There are quotations in the story which emphasize the similarities and differences of each character's point of view. For example, the scientist says to one of the townspeople, "Nonsense, these things get exaggerated in the telling. We are always checking up on this kind of story and we draw in blank every time." After the Farquars tell Gideon about the scientist, Gideon, feeling angry and betrayed, says "The big baas want to know what medicine I used?"

—Kelly Behnken

Lindenhurst Senior High School

Lindenhurst, New York

Between my finger and my thumb
The squat pen rests.
I'll dig with it.

I'll dig a trench in time
Recording the labors of my ancestors,
How my family has been digging for decades,
    and will continue to do so.

Betwen generations custom change,
Values change, people change.
But curiosity remains.

I'll dig with my pen, rooting out words,

Nicking and slicing phrases,

Heaving stanzas and paragraphs.

I'll explore new horizons, saving the family

   memories on paper,

Explaining our heritage,

   as I dig the plastic point of a bic onto pure white paper.

                 —Toni Cassara

                     Lindenhurst Senior High School

                     Lindenhurst, New York

The squat pen rests.

I'll dig with it.

My memory remind me

Remind me each day,

Of the way,

The harsh way,

She was treated each day—

My grandmother

Was a slave to her work

And to her children.

She waited on tables

And when she came home

Nothing changed,

Seven kids to feed

All on her own.

The war had taken all she had.

They dug a place for him to rest.

He was the lucky one.

She's been digging.

Constantly, ever since.

Digging for some means of survival.

And I look at her now

I see all her suffering,

In every wrinkle

Upon her face.

And I smile—

I smile for I know

That although I hope

My future is nothing like her past,

I want to be so different from her,

But yet just like her.

   —Tracey Gibbons

     Lindenhurst Senior High School

     Lindenhurst, New York

Underneath my fingers

The keys lay.

I will dig with them.

In the next room

I hear the tapping of her typewriter:

My mother typing.

She stops to think for just one moment.

But when the moment is gone

Her head drops and she types.

I bring her a cup of tea

As she works furiously to get the job done.

She thanks me and then goes on.

Late at night I go to bed.

As my mother finally finishes her job,

The tapping stops and she rests.

I wish someday to be just like her,

So here I sit at my computer.

And I will dig with it.

   —Lisa Eisner

     Lindenhurst Senior High School

     Lindenhurst, New York

The squat pen rests.

I'll dig with it.

I will dig a new place,

Not far from yesteryear.

A passage reaching to the future.

With my pen, a new song can be sung.

A brilliant story uncovered,

Or a poem unfolded.

The squat pen that has descended

Down from above,

Shall not rest in mine eyes

Till the peat has long gone.

This pen shall dig a deep, dark hole.

A hole that is full of words made of gold.

The gold will glitter and gleam,

As plenty of eyes look down.

Not only to read, but experience.

   —Heather Meacham

    O. H. Cooper High School

    Abilene, Texas

Between my finger and my thumb

The squat pen rests

I'll dig with it.

Out on the farm, I stop for a while,

With my grandfather I talk and walk for miles.

The things that he tells me are familiar...unchanged,

Only the names and places seem the same.

Between my finger and my thumb

The squat pen rests; snug as a gun.

   —Kevin Smith

    O. H. Cooper High School

    Abilene, Texas

Between my finger and my thumb

The squat pen rests.

I'll dig with it.

    But where do I begin?

    Do I dig on one side of my body

    to the seed that controls my mind?

      Or, do I dig

      on the other side to the seed

      that controls my heart?

Down the middle I decide.

    As

      I

        Weave

          Down

I find beautiful lilacs with cool

Water droplets that sooth my mind.

    I dig deeper and find old thorned

weeds that make my heart bleed.

    I reach the bottom.

Between the weeds and the flowers

I find that there are no seeds after all.

I'll plant one.

      —Lydia Buettemeyer

        O. H. Cooper High School

        Abilene, Texas

Assessing Students' Mastery of Subject Matter and Concepts

Students' writing is an excellent measure of their understanding of literary works and concepts. Whether writing compositions or answers to essay questions, students must organize and apply the knowledge they have acquired through reading, note-taking, and class discussion. They must demonstrate their understanding of particular selections as well as their understanding of literary genres and techniques.

With the aids in this manual, you can plan your evaluation strategies carefully and reduce the time needed for grading or reviewing papers. For example, for each writing assignment in the text, the manual provides "Criteria for Evaluating the Assignment," two or three major points to guide your assessment of students' work. In addition, the model responses that follow the criteria for some of the assignments and the sample essays that appear in "Writing About Literature" can serve as assessment aids. Finally, you can make use of the following evaluation methods, which include checklists, written comments, self-evaluation, and peer evaluation.

Holistic Scoring

For some writing assignments, you may want to use holistic scoring, a method in which you read each paper quickly and respond to it as a whole, making no comments or corrections. With a carefully prepared scoring guide, holistic evaluation is an efficient and consistent means of judging students' work. Even though it does not provide students with your personal comments, it is not superficial or vague: Students receive an evaluation of key features of their papers. Two types of holistic scales you may find useful are the analytic and the general impression.

Analytic Scales

Using an analytic scale, you rank each of several features of a piece of writing from high to low. Here is one scale that lists features common to all writing and uses a numerical ranking.

Analytic Scale				
	Low	**Middle**	**High**	
Ideas	2	4 6 8	10	
Organization	2	4 6 8	10	
Word choice	1	2 3 4	5	
Tone	1	2 3 4	5	_____
Usage, grammar	1	2 3 4	5	
Punctuation, capitalization	1	2 3 4	5	
Spelling	1	2 3 4	5	
Legibility	1	2 3 4	5	_____
			Total	_____

Adapted from Paul B. Diederich, *Measuring Growth in Writing* (Urbana, IL: NCTE, 1974).

In other analytic scales, the features are specific to a form of writing (description, narration, etc.). Such scales can be adapted for many different assignments; in fact, the revision checklists in the text's critical thinking and writing exercises are excellent for this purpose: For example, you can use the revision checklist on text page 286 to develop an analytic scale for comparing and contrasting poems, and you can adapt that scale for comparison and contrast papers in other genres.

The scales that follow cover four common writing tasks, each applied to a different genre. These examples use the dichotomous, or yes–no, scale.

Fiction: Summarizing a Plot Analytic Scale	Yes	No
The story's title and author are cited.		
The summary includes the story's most important events.		
The events are summarized in the order in which they occur.		
The summary explains how one event causes or leads to another.		
The setting is briefly described.		
Extraneous details are omitted.		
The student primarily uses his or her own words.		
Word choice is precise and appropriate.		
Sentence structure is varied.		
Grammar, usage, and mechanics errors do not interfere with reading.		

Poetry: Responding to a Poem Analytic Scale	Yes	No
The poem's title, author, and subject are stated.		
The student describes his or her general response to the poem.		
At least two details about the poem's content are used to explain the response.		
At least two details about the poem's construction are used to explain the response.		
Quotations from the poem are exact and are cited correctly.		
A concluding or summary statement ends the composition.		
Word choice is precise and appropriate.		
Sentence structure is varied.		
Grammar, usage, and mechanics errors do not interfere with reading.		

Nonfiction: Analyzing a Report Analytic Scale	Yes	No
The report's title and author are cited.		
The main idea of the report is stated.		
A sufficient number of the strongest facts supporting the main idea are cited.		
The facts in the report are distinguished from the author's opinions.		
Any appeals to emotion are identified and discussed.		
Significant narrative techniques are identified and discussed.		
Organization is clear and coherent.		
The conclusion summarizes main points of the analysis.		
Word choice is precise and appropriate.		
Sentence structure is varied.		
Grammar, usage, and mechanics errors do not interfere with reading.		

Drama: Analyzing and Evaluating a Theme Analytic Scale	Yes	No
The play's title and author are cited.		
A clear theme statement is presented.		
The theme statement is supported with at least three examples of action and dialogue.		
The student expresses an evaluation of the theme.		
The student presents at least two reasons for the evaluation, supported by evidence from the play.		
Quotations are exact and are cited correctly.		
The conclusion summarizes or restates the statement of theme and the student's evaluation.		
Word choice is precise and appropriate.		
Sentence structure is varied.		
Grammar, usage, and mechanics errors do not interfere with reading.		

General Impression Scales

A general impression scale is also keyed to the form of writing, but the individual features of the paper are not ranked separately. Instead, the paper as a whole is judged high, average, or low. In this case, developing a scoring guide entails outlining the general characteristics of high, average, and low papers for the assignment. For example, you could use the following general impression scale to evaluate a descriptive paragraph:

There is no one prescribed format for writing the general characteristics for this type of scale. What is important—whether you use complete sentences, a series of phrases, or even a list of items—is that you cover the key features of the writing assignment and that you address the same features in each ranking. Here is a second example of a general impression scale, one for use in evaluating an essay comparing and contrasting elements in two poems.

Descriptive Paragraph General Impression Scale

Assignment: To write a subjective description of a person, place, or object

4   The topic sentence expresses a main impression of the topic; many concrete and sensory details create a vivid picture; each sentence supports the main idea in the topic sentence; organization is clear; ideas flow smoothly, with effective transitions; sentences are varied and diction fresh; grammatical and mechanical errors are minimal.

3   The topic sentence expresses a main impression of the topic; concrete and sensory details are used, but the description could be fuller and more vivid; organization is clear; some transitions could be added or improved; sentences are varied and diction accurate but unoriginal; occasional grammatical and mechanical errors appear.

2   The topic sentence is vague or inexact; details are not specific or are insufficient; organization is flawed but can be followed; few transitions are provided between ideas; sentences are correct but often awkward or monotonous, with some inexact wording; occasional grammatical and mechanical errors interfere with reading.

1   The topic sentence is missing or does not clearly identify the topic; details are not specific and are insufficient to develop the description; organization is unclear; ideas are missing or irrelevant; word choice is often inaccurate, frequent syntax and mechanical errors interfere with reading.

0   The paragraph does not develop a description.

Comparison and Contrast Essay General Impression Scale

Assignment: To compare and contrast the messages and tones of two poems

4   The essay addresses both similarities and differences, insightfully interprets the poems' messages and tones, supports main ideas with appropriate details, is well organized (with a clear thesis statement in the first paragraph, a main supporting idea in each body paragraph, and a concluding paragraph), flows smoothly, and contains few errors in grammar and mechanics.

3   The essay addresses both similarities and differences, interprets the messages and tones thoughtfully, and is well organized, but it provides less support for main ideas, displays occasional awkwardness or monotony, and contains occasional errors in grammar and mechanics.

2   The essay does not address (or address equally) both similarities and differences, interprets the messages and tones sketchily, omits some needed supporting detail, is difficult to follow in places, and contains errors in grammar and mechanics that occasionally interfere with reading.

1   The essay does not address both similarities and differences, lacks insight into or misinterprets the messages and tones, does not support main ideas with sufficient evidence, is disorganized, lacks clarity of expression, and contains errors in grammar and mechanics that frequently interfere with reading.

0   The essay does not follow the assignment or does not develop its thesis.

When you use a general impression scale, be sure to provide students with your scoring guide so that they know the specific criteria that determined their score. If possible, provide each student with a copy; students with lower scores should use the guide to identify the errors and weaknesses in their papers, and all students can use the guide when developing similar papers in the future.

Remember that holistic scoring, while allowing you to evaluate many papers rapidly, does not preclude your giving more personal attention to students who need help. For example, you can invite students to consult with you individually when they cannot pinpoint the errors in their papers. You can also ask students to submit their revised papers; the revisions will show you exactly where they need further instruction.

Comments and Corrections

Some papers you will want to mark thoroughly, commenting on students' ideas and writing style and indicating where errors lie. You cannot afford to do this for all assignments, but you should do it for some: Students respond remarkably well to such personal attention and specific guidance.

Only with written comments can you react to a student's individual thoughts and use of language. Whether you are agreeing or disagreeing, praising or finding fault, your comments show that you are paying attention to students' ideas and that you care about students' skills. Always include some praise or encouragement. Even when a student has written poorly, you can often offer encouragement by referring to real strengths: "You used some fresh, original words in last week's character sketch. I *know* you have the vocabulary to go beyond the trite expressions I've marked in this essay. I'll be looking for your vivid wording in the next assignment."

Keep in mind that a heavy marking of a paper is not a rewriting. Even if you suggest some specific content revisions, students must decide how to make the changes. Even though you isolate errors in grammar, usage, and mechanics, students must correct them. (Don't hesitate occasionally, however, to show students how to rework or correct a passage; students need models when they are acquiring skills.)

Using correction symbols will speed your marking of papers. You may want to distribute a list such as the following one with students' first marked papers. After students have worked with the list, you can ask for questions about particular symbols and writing problems.

Correction Symbols

Symbol	Meaning	What to Do
Content		
concl	conclusion missing, weak, or unrelated to main idea	Add or rephrase summarizing statement or paragraph.
irr	irrelevant detail	Delete or replace phrase or sentence.
spec	needs to be more specific	Clarify a detail, or add supporting details.
ts	thesis statement or topic sentence missing or not clear	Add or revise main idea.

Symbol	Meaning	What to Do
Organization		
org	organization not clear	Rearrange ideas in a more logical order.
tr	transition between ideas missing or confusing	Add or replace connecting words or phrases.
¶, no ¶	paragraphing problem	Begin new paragraph (¶), or join paragraphs (no ¶).
Style		
agr	agreement error	Make a subject and verb or an antecedent and pronoun agree in number.
awk	awkward sentence or passage	Rephrase sentence or section.
cap	capitalization error	Add capital, or lower-case capital.
frag	sentence fragment	Add subject or verb, or attach fragment to nearby sentence.
gr	grammatical error	Determine type of error, and correct it.
p	punctuation error	Add, replace, or delete punctuation.
pv	unnecessary shift in point of view	Eliminate shift in person.
ref	pronoun reference error	Clarify reference of a pronoun to its antecedent.
ro	run-on sentence	Correct with needed punctuation and capitals.
sp	misspelled word	Correct spelling.
t	tense error	Correct verb tense.
var	sentences lack variety	Vary structure and length of sentences.
wc	word choice problem	Replace with correct, more exact, or livelier word.

Grading

In grading students' writing about literature, you will want to focus on the quality of their ideas. Without diminishing the importance of mechanics and style, let students know that *what* they have to say is of first importance in their grades: An error-free paper that is either shallow or incomplete should not receive an *A.*

Some teachers use a double grade on papers, for example *B + /C,* to distinguish between content and mechanics. Whatever system you use, explain clearly to students how your marking relates to their grades. Sample papers are especially helpful for this purpose. From previous classes, accumulate a file of marked and graded papers that students may examine, and review in class *A, B, C, D,* and *F* papers for a typical assignment. These papers will illustrate for students exactly what you expect.

Self-Evaluation

Students help both themselves and you by evaluating their own papers. Good writers evaluate automatically, although usually not in writing; most students, however, skip this essential step altogether. By assigning even brief and informal evaluations, you can show students the importance of this writing stage and instill a habit of lasting benefit. What you gain is not only improved papers but also insight into the students' ideas about writing. You may uncover misconceptions (a student is more concerned with correct spelling than with organization) and problems in composing (a student is a perfectionist and writes and rewrites an opening sentence). You can then help individual students or plan class sessions on particular aspects of the writing process.

One self-evaluation assignment is to have students rank the papers they are submitting as either high, average, or low and to explain their criteria for the ranking. Stress that you are not grading the evaluations and simply want honest, thoughtful responses to this question: What do you think of your paper and *why?* It will be most helpful if you combine this self-evaluation with your own evaluation, of whatever method; when you return the papers, students will see how their judgments compare to yours and can use the discrepancies to improve their evaluation skills. You can also use a simple form, such as the following one, for a self-evaluation of this type.

Self-Evaluation Comments

Name _____   Date _____

Assignment or Title of Paper _____

1. I think one strength of this paper, or one thing that works well, is _____

_____.

2. The weakest aspect of this paper is _____

_____.

3. One problem I faced and was not sure how best to solve was _____

_____.

Students should evaluate and revise the first draft of every paper: No first draft is ever perfect. If students evaluate and revise for themselves—rather than submitting first drafts—they will take a great step toward improved writing and better grades. Students can use the following general checklist to evaluate and then revise their writing about literature. (If you use holistic scoring guides, also alert students that the guides may be reused as evaluation checklists for particular assignments.)

Self-Evaluation Checklist for Writing About Literature	Yes	No
1. Have I followed all of the directions for the assignment?		
2. Have I understood the literary terms and used them correctly?		
3. Have I clearly expressed a main idea in a strong topic sentence or thesis statement?		
4. Have I included enough details from the literary work to support my ideas?		
5. Are all the details accurate and directly related to the main idea?		
6. Does my paper have a clear beginning, middle, and end?		
7. Have I used precise words and avoided clichés and repetitious phrases?		
8. Have I correctly punctuated quotations and dialogue?		
9. Have I checked other punctuation, spelling, and use of capitals?		
10. Have I read the paper aloud to listen for missing words and awkward phrasing?		

Peer Evaluation

When properly prepared for, peer evaluation can be highly rewarding and enjoyable for both writers and evaluators, producing new insights about the literary work and about the writing process. Unguided, though, peer evaluation can be ineffective or unpleasant; irrelevant comments merely confuse, and heavy-handed criticisms wound. What is required is sensitivity, objectivity, and a common understanding of the evaluation criteria.

For successful peer evaluation, provide students with evaluation forms, and demonstrate constructive criticism. First conduct a class evaluation of a paper from a previous class. Explain the writer's assignment, read the paper aloud, and offer samples of the comments you would make. As students enter the discussion, point out off-target comments or negative comments that serve no purpose; help students redirect or rephrase these criticisms, and remind them always to point out a paper's good features: Evaluation identifies both strengths and weaknesses. You may want to go through two or three papers in this way before students work on their own.

At least for initial peer evaluations in small groups, use some type of prepared form. After students hear or read a paper, they can complete the form and then base group discussion on their written responses. Using a form need not limit discussion; always encourage students to react to each other's comments and to brainstorm solutions for writing problems. After the discussion, the writer can use the completed forms for revising.

Depending on your students' abilities and maturity, you can use a highly structured checklist or a form that elicits a more general impression. For example, you could adapt the preceding self-evaluation checklist for peer evaluation, providing room for the evaluator to explain every No response. A sample of a less-structured evaluation form follows.

Peer Evaluation Comments

Reader _____   Writer _____

Assignment or Title of Paper _____   Date _____

1. What I liked best in this paper was _____

_____.

2. The most effective sentence was _____

_____.

3. Good word choices were _____

_____.

4. Ideas that I felt needed clarification or further support were _____

_____.

5. Other positive comments are _____

_____.

6. Other suggestions for revision are _____

_____.

Reading Development in the *Elements of Literature* Program: *The Student as Reader/The Teacher as Facilitator*

Nancy E. Wiseman Seminoff

Elements of Literature is a comprehensive program of literature study for grades 7–12. Each anthology includes a wide range of significant literary works, as well as supporting instruction that helps students become more proficient readers and writers as they learn to analyze, interpret, and evaluate literature. The twelfth-grade anthology is organized into units by period—Emergent, Middle Ages, Renaissance, Restoration and Eighteenth Century, Romantic, Victorian, and Twentieth Century. Often, selections are grouped to facilitate comparison and contrast of theme, structure, or style and technique. The list of the selections organized by themes (text page 1261) allows teachers the flexibility of using a thematic approach.

The instructional materials include background information for understanding the genres, the selections, and the writers' lives; factual and interpretive discussion questions; and creative and critical writing assignments. The questions and assignments, designed to stimulate critical thinking, emphasize reading and writing strategies in which students use their own experience and knowledge to comprehend and appreciate literature. For twenty selections in the anthology, the *Connections Between Reading and Writing* worksheets provide further intensive reading and writing practice.

Additionally, exercises throughout the text use specific linguistic features of the selections as springboards to language and vocabulary instruction in some sixty skills. The exercises cover literary terms and techniques, such as allusions and figures of speech, as well as word-study skills important in all reading, such as context clues, dictionary use, and word roots. For a listing of all skills taught in the program, see the index on text pages 1257–1260 and the scope and sequence chart in the front of this manual.

Elements of Literature provides you with excellent materials and tools with which to help your students become better readers. Naturally, your role in the classroom is pivotal to students' success; by understanding the reading process and basing your teaching strategies on it, you can draw out the anthology's full potential for reading development.

Understanding the Reading Process

Educators in the past viewed reading as a series of discrete skills, sequential and hierarchical in nature. They increasingly found, however, that students who learned these skills in the elementary grades did not necessarily develop into proficient readers in the higher grades. Something was missing in the traditional view of the reading process: the interaction between the reader and the author.

According to recent research, reading is a dynamic process that involves the reader, the author's text, and the situation in which the reading takes place. The assumption behind previous reading theory was that the author bore sole responsibility for conveying meaning; educators now recognize that readers must actively expect and seek meaning as they read and must be able to modify their approach to a text if the approach doesn't yield meaning. The reader's characteristics and background (linguistic, social, cultural, and psychological) and the author's characteristics (as evidenced in the text) necessarily influence the reader's understanding.

Students actually *construct* meaning as they read; they do not simply absorb it. They bring prior experience and knowledge (which includes expectations about the type of literature) to the work, drawing tentative conclusions as they begin to read and modifying those conclusions as they continue; the reading process is thus one of accumulating meaning.

The development of schema theory by cognitive psychologists during the past decade has helped illuminate this process, showing how people approach new information by setting it against a known framework. In reading, schemata (frameworks) enable a student to recall relevant facts and experiences, to anticipate what will happen next, to fill in missing information, and to know when an author's meaning is not clear. Important to a student's schemata, therefore, is experience not only with the topic of a reading selection but also with the genre. In reading about ravens, for example, a student's comprehension is aided by prior knowledge of the bird's physical appearance and behavior, no matter what the genre of the writing. But a student cannot approach the reading of "The Three Ravens" and the reading of a scientific explanation of the raven's eating habits in the same way. To obtain (construct) full meaning from "The Three Ravens," the student must be familiar with poetic conventions and techniques, as well as with stylistic variations within genres; the student must have appropriate expectations against which to gauge understanding.

Teachers, in turn, must be alert to gaps in students' experience and knowledge that will prevent them from being "active" readers, supplying (or guiding students in finding) necessary background in the many ways suggested in this manual and in the text. If students face a literary work that seems thoroughly unfamiliar, the reading will seem a difficult chore; students will not read, or continue to read, with interest—and interest is another fundamental element in the dynamics of reading.

The purpose for reading a selection, either self- or teacher-imposed, is an additional variable in the reading situation. A student uses quite different reading skills to gain an initial impression of an essayist's position and to read a dramatic soliloquy; for the first task, the student reads in "chunks," with wide eye sweeps, while for the second, the student reads closely, ideally aloud, with attention to specific phrasing and detail. ("Teaching Students to Vary Reading Rates" in this manual provides a discussion of different reading strategies as well as genre-specific guidelines for close reading.)

Reading involves adapting to each reading situation as it is encountered. The selection (topic, genre, structure, and author's style), the purpose for reading, and the student's interest (conditioned by prior experience) all affect comprehension. The successful reader is able to "shift gears," to approach differently each encounter with a literary selection. It is important that your students recognize the need for this variation and know appropriate strategies to apply in different situations.

The conscious awareness and control of cognitive processes is termed *metacognition*; in reading, metacognition is the adjustment of reading strategies to control comprehension. You should encourage students to monitor their own comprehension: to pause and raise questions when they do not understand, to reread a section to seek clarity, to use context clues to determine meaning, and so on. You should help students see, in short, that the response to difficult reading is not to stop reading. Students can learn techniques to become flexible, strategic readers—a necessity if they are to understand and enjoy literature.

Using the Instructional Materials

The instructional materials that accompany the selections in the anthology provide a framework for your classroom activities, which can be considered in three phases: preparation for reading the selection, an encounter with the selection, and extension beyond the selection. Before deciding on the specific activities you will use in these phases, you have two key tasks: establishing content and deciding on approach.

The "content" of your instruction is both your own analysis and interpretation of the literary work and the aspects of the work you choose to highlight. Arriving at a personal understanding of the work's meaning in no sense means that you will prescribe a single interpretation to the students, but that your own thoughts about the work are organized and focused; in this way you will better lead students to their own understandings. When you clarify for yourself a selection's possible meanings, you can then choose, or create, questions and assignments that will move students toward meaning, not simply test their recall.

Another part of your planning is deciding on your teaching emphasis: historical background, symbolic interpretation, analysis and evaluation of theme, language exercises, and so on. The objectives in this manual show at a glance the text's instructional emphases; they can guide you in choosing those "Responding" items that meet your specific teaching goals.

Finally, all your initial judgments of what and how to teach involve your students' particular needs. In preparing to teach a selection, you not only master content; you also consider how best for your class to bring about the interaction at the heart of the reading process. This manual provides many suggestions for accommodating different ability levels and cultural backgrounds.

An overview of using *Elements of Literature* in the three phases of teaching a selection follows.

Before Reading—Moving into the Selection

Students' preparation for reading a selection often determines the success of their reading and therefore cannot be left to chance. The unit and section introductions, the selection headnotes, and the "Focusing on Background" features supply background information, relate the selection to contemporary life, and help students anticipate topics and themes. This manual offers additional information and ideas for introducing the selections.

Also important are activities to bridge the gap between students' prior knowledge and an unfamiliar literary work, activities that will motivate them to want to begin reading. The teaching guides in this manual present many hints for stimulating interest in individual selections. Remember, however, that students do not need exhaustive introductions to begin reading, understanding, and appreciating a selection. Reading preparation should be stimulating and revealing, not oppressive. When students must learn many new facts, concepts, and terms, the introduction should be a separate lesson.

During Reading—Moving Through the Selection

The questions in "Analyzing the [Selection]" are intended to assist students in understanding the literary work. They are instruction, not testing, and students should refer freely to the selection when answering them. (You may on occasion select some questions for closed-book reading checks or essay tests.)

Good reading questions help students organize information by leading them to identify facts and an author's salient points, to draw inferences, to combine the facts and inferences with their prior knowledge, and to consider the author's suggested meaning in light of the broader context of life and other literature. Questions should lead readers to *accumulate* understandings of the selection while encouraging them to think on their own. The "Identifying Facts" and "Interpreting Meanings" questions are therefore not linear and hierarchical. As students answer the questions, they are continually gathering information, interpreting, and raising their own questions in a process that causes them to refine their understandings and to confirm or reject initial predictions. Cognitively, they move between and among the questions as they build comprehension and understanding.

Consequently, you should encourage students to answer questions as fully as possible but to be open to revising their responses in light of new evidence. In this process of deepening comprehension, other students' responses also play an important role. It is particularly effective to have students discuss questions, or compare their written answers, in small groups. In this way, students can refine, reconsider, reject, revise, or confirm their understandings as a consequence of others' ideas.

Keep in mind that while all reading questions should guide students to find meaning and contribute their own ideas, the amount and type of guidance can vary. Debate exists among reading experts about how structured the guidance should be, but your students' needs should be the determining factor. For some students and in some situations, a highly structured question may be best. In other cases, you may be able to use open-ended questions and provide minimal guidance. For further discussion of questioning strategies, particularly to provoke critical thinking, see "Using Literature to Teach Higher-Level Thinking Skills."

After Reading—Moving Beyond the Selection

Activities after reading serve two purposes: assessing students' understanding of a selection and helping students apply what they have learned to a new situation or selection. Culminating small-group discussions—following your instruction and guided class discussion—are one simple but effective way for you to determine students' comprehension. As students express and explain their final thoughts about the work, you should move among the groups, listening for problem areas. You can determine how many students still have not read successfully and how best to help them.

Exercises in "Writing About the [Selection]" and "Analyzing Language and Vocabulary" require students both to demonstrate comprehension and to go beyond the selections. Many of the writing assignments encourage students to use their insights about a work to explore a literary element more deeply, to compare and contrast another selection, or to relate the work to other life situations. The language and vocabulary exercises, while assessing students' mastery of selection-related skills and terms, usually extend and apply the language study to other areas. Thus the students' schemata, the frameworks available to them, increase as they complete each exercise.

Discussing one or more selections in relation to each other also broadens students' schemata. You may ask students to consider theme, style, genre, historical period, or another element or combination of elements. You may ask them to apply what they have learned through study of a selection to the creation of an original work. (This manual provides many "Extending the Selection" suggestions.) In these activities, students are synthesizing; they analyze the selections, but they arrive at understandings (comparisons, contrasts, original works) that are external to the selections. In applying elsewhere what they learn from a literary work, students learn how to use past reading to approach new reading. They extend the schemata that make them proficient, strategic readers.

In summary, the study of literature can be a means for students to become proficient readers, capable of varying their reading strategies to meet the demands of the task, but the teacher must be the facilitator of this accomplishment. The decisions you make for moving students into, through, and beyond a literary work are important in helping them both appreciate literature and monitor their own reading

methods. *Elements of Literature* provides excellent materials to assist you in this important process.

Further Reading

Alvermann, D. E. "Metacognition." *Research Within Reach: Secondary School Reading*. Eds. D. E. Alvermann, D. W. Moore, and M. W. Conley. Newark, DE: International Reading Association, 1987. 153–168.

Anderson, R. C., et al. "Frameworks for Comprehending Discourse." *American Educational Research Journal* 14 (1977): 367–381.

Armbruster, B. "The Problem of 'Inconsiderate Text.'" *Comprehension Instruction: Perspectives and Suggestions*. Eds. G. Duffy, L. Roehler, and J. Mason. New York: Longman, 1984. 202–217.

Baker, L., and A. L. Brown. "Cognitive Monitoring in Reading." *Understanding Reading Comprehension*. Ed. J. Flood. Newark, DE: International Reading Association, 1984. 21–44.

Langer, J. A. "Examining Background Knowledge and Text Comprehension." *Reading Research Quarterly* 19 (1984): 468–481.

Meyer, B. J. F. "Organizational Aspects of Text: Effects on Reading Comprehension and Applications for the Classroom." *Promoting Reading Comprehension*. Ed. J. Flood. Newark, DE: International Reading Association, 1984. 113–138.

Mosenthal, P. "Reading Comprehension Research from a Classroom Perspective." *Promoting Reading Comprehension*. Ed. J. Flood. Newark, DE: International Reading Association, 1984. 16–29.

Paris, S. G., M. Lipson, and K. K. Wilson. "Becoming a Strategic Reader." *Contemporary Educational Psychology* 8 (1982): 293–316.

Pearson, P. D., ed. *Handbook of Reading Research*. New York: Longman, 1984.

Pearson, P. D., and R. J. Spiro. "Toward a Theory of Reading Comprehension Instruction." *Topics in Language Disorders* 1 (1980): 71–88.

Rosenblatt, L. M. *The Reader, the Text, the Poem*. Carbondale, IL: Southern Illinois University Press, 1978.

Rumelhart, D. E. "Toward an Interactive Model of Reading." *Attention and Performance*. Ed. S. Dornie. Hillsdale, NJ: Erlbaum, 1977. 573–603.

Using Literature to Teach Higher-Level Thinking Skills

Because human life is its subject, imagination its method, and words its medium, literature is rich and subtle in both meaning and form. Critical thinking is inherent in its study. In order to discuss and write about literature, students must use the very skills that define critical thinking, including analysis, inference, interpretation, comparison and contrast, hypothesis testing, argumentation, evaluation, and synthesis. Moreover, they must use these skills on a subject matter that requires them, as few other subjects do, to confront ambiguity and relativity; to comprehend irony; to arrive at moral and aesthetic judgments; and to make connections on many levels—the concrete and the abstract, the personal and the impersonal, the literal and the figurative. These are the sophisticated, but essential, mental processes that are increasingly recognized as the realm of higher-order thinking.

Critical Thinking in the *Elements of Literature* Program

The *Elements of Literature* program not only thoroughly exercises students' critical thinking skills in the interpretive questions and composition assignments following each selection, it also uses literature to teach thinking skills. At the end of each unit or division of a unit, a critical thinking and writing exercise isolates an important cognitive skill to be applied to a writing assignment. (For a complete listing of these exercises, see the "Index of Skills" on text page 1257.) The "Background" material defines and explains the skill; then the student is given detailed instruction—prewriting, writing, and revision—on using the skill in writing.

The importance of this feature for students' intellectual development is great. Students are not simply being put through the paces of an exercise; they are being shown how to think, how to approach problems, how to transfer cognitive skills from one setting to another, how to make critical thinking a habit of mind.

As you use the *Elements of Literature* program to develop students' critical thinking, the following teaching strategies, derived from educational theory and cognitive psychology, will assist you.

Three Basic Teaching Strategies

First, continually lead students to relate literature to their own lives. This approach has several connected benefits: It makes unfamiliar material less threatening or alien; it helps students find ways to discover writing and project topics of particular interest; and it enables students to make connections between an external reality and their personal experience—an important criterion of higher-level thinking. The text and manual demonstrate many ways to elicit these personal relations.

Second, take every opportunity to help students perceive the ambiguities, ironies, multiple meanings, and contrasting points of view that abound in literature. Emphasize exploration of a number of positions and supporting arguments, rather than the search for a single right answer. This attempt to see several sides of an issue is what philosopher Richard Paul calls dialogical, or dialectical, thinking; a related concept is Jean Piaget's ideal reciprocity, the ability to empathize with other people, ideas, and values.

Collaborative activities foster dialogical thinking, as do questions that require students to choose a position and assignments that concentrate on point of view. Especially important is the atmosphere you create in your classroom: When you communicate your willingness to entertain alternatives, to consider differing interpretations, students will respond in kind. They will learn to listen more open-mindedly to their classmates' conclusions, as well as to examine their own more carefully.

Students' assessment of their own reasoning is related to the third basic teaching strategy: Make students *conscious* of their critical thinking; make them think about their thinking. (The term for this awareness is *metacognition.*) The text establishes this method in the critical thinking and writing exercises. You can extend it to daily classroom work in several ways: by calling students' attention to their cognitive processes during discussion; by asking them how they arrived at an idea or opinion; by insisting that they justify interpretations with textual evidence; by requiring them, when they disagree with a classmate's conclusion, to explain how the argument is flawed. When you build students' awareness of how they think, students' thinking improves.

These three teaching strategies—guiding students to relate literature to their own lives, to think dialectically, and to consider their own thought processes—underlie the questions and exercises in the text and manual, and additional teaching ideas follow. Using them, you can make critical thinking a central focus in your students' study of literature.

Questioning Strategies

To make students think, you must ask questions; to make students think in particular ways, you must ask the right questions. These pedagogical truths bear reexamination as you use literature to teach critical thinking. By planning the questions you ask and when you ask them, you will be rewarded not only with more enthusiasm for literature but also with keener thinking about it.

Initial Questions

First, simply question frequently: Use questions to stimulate discussion, not just to check comprehension. For example, begin the discussion of a selection with a question: Do you think "Sredni Vashtar" is really a short story? How does "Sredni Vashtar" make you feel? Why? Rather than presenting your ideas about a work, let students offer theirs first. An initial question immediately creates an atmosphere of inquiry, frees students to form their own hypotheses (or to voice feelings) without reference to your ideas, and provides focal issues around which they can organize new information (Meyers 59–60). (See "Teaching Students to Vary Reading Rates" for a discussion of using predictive prereading questions to provoke critical thought.)

Dialogue Questions

Remember, too, that you can respond to students with questions, not statements. Meet a question with a question; turn a statement into a question; throw a problem back to the student who raised it or to the rest of the class. Whenever possible, do not "give" answers; help students find them.

A student may offer, for example, that "The Importance of Being Earnest" isn't very realistic. Rather than disagreeing (or agreeing) and offering your own examples, draw out the student's thoughts: Why do you say that? Compelled to go beyond the vague statement, the student may reply, "The characters are too shallow. Real people have more values and are more sincere than Wilde's characters." You can of course press the student further (Which characters are you thinking of?), but even at this point, the class has a specific judgment to explore (the characters are unrealistic), and other students may want to jump in.

As the discussion unfolds, continue probing with questions (What examples from real life support your opinion? Do you think Wilde intended his audience to find these characters realistic?), so that students define their criteria for judgments, offer examples and evidence, generate hypotheses to explain inconsistencies, and so on. Such questions create group dialogue and also put students in dialogue with themselves: Pushed to elaborate, reflect, or defend, students will learn more about both the content of their

thought (what they "really mean") and its quality (how they arrived at a position).

Structured Questions

When choosing or creating discussion questions, you can structure them to call forth particular types of critical thinking, but another approach is to focus on three areas: the literary work, the student's personal experience, and the external world (Christenbury and Kelly 12–15; Swope and Thompson).

About *Macbeth*, for example, you could ask: Why does Macbeth feel he has to murder Banquo's sons? (The question elicits facts and inferences solely about the work.) What do you think of the tradition of rule by heredity? What are its strengths? Its weaknesses? (The question calls for the student's personal opinion.) What was the lineage of the Scottish kings at the time of *Macbeth*? (The question seeks information external to the work.)

Each type of question can provoke critical thinking, but questions that combine two or three of the areas will lead students to more complex reasoning. A question that simultaneously elicits textual facts, opinion or personal experience, and outside information—what Christenbury and Kelly call a "dense question"—can be the focus of a class discussion, presented to the students in advance. (For example: If you were Malcolm, would you have taken a different course of action after your father was murdered?) The single- and two-area questions that you ask during the discussion will help students approach the complex question, clarifying its issues and guiding students to a more fully thought-out response. (For example: What do the witches tell Macbeth? How does Macbeth respond to their predictions? Do you think Macbeth would have acted as he did if he had never met the witches? Do you think they are real witches, or do they symbolize the evil part of Macbeth's character?)

Classroom Activities
Collaborative Interpretation

Collaborative activities are especially conducive to critical thinking because they necessarily involve dialogue and exchange. Many teachers find, in fact, that lively whole-class discussions are greatly aided by initial small-group work. Dragga suggests the following collaborative-learning method for discussing interpretive questions.

Assign each group the same question, one that will generate different answers and require reference to the selection. Give each group about fifteen minutes to devise a collective answer, with textual justification, to be reported by a group spokesperson. (Change speakers during the term so that each student serves in this role.) Because each group must arrive at a single answer, every group member is drawn into the discussion. Each student must offer, if not an original idea, at least a reasoned judgment of any suggested answer and evidence. As the groups work, you can move among them, monitoring the content and process of the discussions and aiding students through impasses.

When the time limit is reached, have each spokesperson report the group's answer, explaining reasons for main ideas and citing support from the text. (For early collaborations, speakers may report from notes; later, you may want groups to write collective essays, which the speakers will read.) In the ensuing discussion, students will challenge each other's interpretations, defend their own arguments, build on another group's position by offering overlooked evidence, and attempt an evaluation of the differing interpretations.

The critical thinking benefits of this collaboration and discussion are manifold: Students model their thinking processes for one another; examine literary works closely to find logical supporting evidence; synthesize their thoughts into a coherent spoken or written answer; and evaluate divergent interpretations of literature.

Courtroom Trials

A more structured collaborative activity is a courtroom trial about a compelling conflict in a literary work (Segedy). The trial format captivates students' imaginations as it challenges their reasoning power; it keeps students' interest high not only because of its inherent drama but also because of the variety of activities required: close reading, research, debating, role-playing, and composition.

For this project, choose a narrative containing a conflict appropriate to courtroom investigation, plan how you will delineate the actual ''case'' (who is bringing suit against whom for what), and decide the roles students will play. Stories, novels, and plays that focus on crimes are of course excellent choices, but any work that raises questions of social, ethical, or moral injustice may yield issues for prosecution and defense.

Generally, you will appoint a team of three or four lawyers for each side of the case and will choose students to play characters who must appear at the trial. (For some cases, you might need to involve some students as expert witnesses, such as psychologists or scientists.) The attorneys must work together to develop the best possible cases to represent their clients, without contradicting the literary work in any way. They must prepare strong logical arguments, support their arguments with compelling evidence, plan their questioning of witnesses, create persuasive rhetoric, and practice their public speaking. The students playing characters must do in-depth character analyses, gleaning from the text all facts about the characters and making inferences about feelings, motives, and experiences not explicitly described. The expert witnesses must research

their areas sufficiently to be able to offer sound and relevant testimony. Any students not playing roles are paired with either a lawyer or a character as research aides; they actively participate in case preparation or in character analysis and can thus substitute for their partners during the trial if necessary.

After both sides have presented their cases, every student prepares a written summation to the jury. Students should be preparing for this persuasive composition during all pretrial work; they must also attend keenly during the trial itself, for the proceedings may yield new ideas or arguments. For the essay, all students assume the persona of an attorney, address themselves to an imagined jury, and argue for conviction or acquittal as persuasively as possible.

Thus a courtroom trial project uses a variety of methods to improve students' critical thinking. Working in small groups and pairs to prepare for their trial roles, students analyze, interpret, and synthesize many elements of a literary work. Participating in the trial, students think on their feet to present and defend logical arguments in dynamic, unrehearsed exchanges. Listening to the trial, students observe and evaluate others' thought processes and refine their own positions accordingly. Writing the summations, students work individually to synthesize all of their experience into strong persuasive compositions.

Expert Groups

In addition to having groups of students research and report on particular aspects of a literary work (see ''Varying Teaching Techniques'' in this manual), you can have them take complete responsibility for presenting—teaching—one of the text selections (Bonfiglio). This more sophisticated collaborative activity should be reserved for later in the term, after students have worked through many selections with you, and assigned only to students capable of independent work: The expert groups must devise an entire project plan, not simply follow directions, and must accomplish their plans without supervision.

Assign an appropriate text selection, and explain that the group's charge is to serve as teacher: They must decide how to present the work (classroom methods and teaching focus), conduct necessary research, and delineate divisions of labor. Stipulating the use, or creation, of visual aids enriches the activity, and you can also require a written outline of the presentation. Encourage students to use their imaginations, to think of innovative ways to engage their classmates' interest while presenting sound insights into the literary work.

This activity requires critical thinking on two levels: Students analyze, interpret, and evaluate the literary work, and they propose, prepare, and execute a teaching plan. Throughout the project, they must make judgments both about the selection and about their presentation; they must solve problems of interpretation and of group interaction, compare and contrast teaching methods, organize their presentation into a coherent sequence, and so on. The task is challenging but extremely beneficial, and satisfying, particularly for advanced students: They use higher-level reasoning not only to investigate literature but also to communicate their findings to others.

Oral Composition

Oral composition is a collaborative activity that specifically develops metacognition. Again, students need some preparation for this technique; you should attempt it only after students have completed several of the text's critical thinking and writing exercises or after you have accustomed students—through comments and questions during discussion—to reflecting on their own and their classmates' reasoning processes. Vinz describes an effective paired-student approach to oral composition.

Give each student in the pair a different interpretive essay question about a selection. Select or create questions that do not have clear right and wrong answers, such as those requiring decision making or problem solving. (Do you think the title "The Demon Lover" is appropriate for Bowen's short story, and do you have any suggestions for alternative titles? What explanations for the eerie events of the story do you think Bowen had in mind when she wrote the story?) You may use the same two questions for all pairs in the class.

For this open-book activity, students take turns as speaker-writers and listeners. The speaking-writing student is to compose *aloud* an answer to the question. The listening student is to take notes on the speaker's composition process. Explain that the composers are simply to say aloud exactly what they are thinking as they plan and draft their essays. Remind them of what they do normally during prewriting: brainstorm, consider and reject ideas, articulate a possible thesis, look for supporting evidence, contemplate how best to arrange their main points. Students should now verbalize these processes, writing down important prewriting notes and then beginning to draft their essays.

The listeners are to observe, interpret, and record the composers' thought processes; they do not comment aloud. They might note how much time their partners spend on different processes (free-associating ideas, searching for supporting facts, evaluating their own thoughts, rereading and revising a draft paragraph); how often good ideas come from chance associations; what seems most often to stop the flow of the composer's ideas; whether the composer is methodical, completing each line of thought before starting another, or more unstructured, willing to leave a difficulty unresolved and move on to something else.

You may want to set aside portions of two class periods

for each composer to generate a first draft (students can work alone to write final versions of their essays). Then have the pairs exchange and discuss their listener-notes. As a summarizing activity, both students should write, perhaps as a journal assignment, what they learned about their own thinking processes. The oral composition process itself, as well as the listener's written observations, should lead to some insight for all students. They may ask themselves: Exactly how, and how well, do I think my way through problems? What could I change, improve? What did I learn from my partner's reasoning and composing process that I could adopt?

References and Further Reading

Bonfiglio, Joseph F. "Collection, Connection, Projection: Using Written and Oral Presentation to Encourage Thinking Skills." NCTE 93–96.

Christenbury, Leila, and Patricia P. Kelly. *Questioning: A Path to Critical Thinking*. Urbana, IL: ERIC Clearinghouse on Reading and Communication Skills and National Council of Teachers of English, 1983.

Dragga, Sam. "Collaborative Interpretation." NCTE 84–87.

Educational Leadership 42 (1984).

Lazere, Donald. "Critical Thinking in College English Studies." Urbana, IL: ERIC Clearinghouse on Reading and Communication Skills and National Council of Teachers of English, 1987.

Meyers, Chet. *Teaching Students to Think Critically*. San Francisco: Jossey-Bass, 1986.

NCTE (National Council of Teachers of English) Committee on Classroom Practices. Chair Jeff Golub. *Activities to Promote Critical Thinking*. Urbana, IL: NCTE, 1986.

Parker, Walter C. "Teaching Thinking: The Pervasive Approach." *Journal of Teacher Education* 38.3 (1987): 50–56.

Segedy, Michael. "Adapting the Courtroom Trial Format to Literature." NCTE 88–92.

Swope, John W., and Edgar H. Thompson. "Three *R*'s for Critical Thinking About Literature: Reading, 'Riting, and Responding." NCTE 75–79.

Vinz, Ruth. "Thinking Through Dilemmas." NCTE 107–111.

Teaching Students to Vary Reading Rates

The ability to read flexibly, that is, at different rates according to purpose and subject matter, is a valuable skill for students of literature. If students learn to adjust their reading habits, they are likely both to improve their comprehension and to increase their enjoyment of literature.

To introduce the concept of flexibility, draw on students' experience with recreational reading. Suppose they have just acquired a new novel by a favorite author. Ask what they read first, how many times they read all or part of the novel, and what they look for as they read. Responses might run along these lines: They first read the title and any other information on the cover and may glance at any illustrations or chapter titles, all to get an idea of the subject and the plot. They may also read a few pages quickly to see whether the setting, characters, tone, and style are familiar. Then they probably settle on a comfortable pace to read the whole story, perhaps stopping occasionally to think about what a character says or does. Later they may come back to the story, rereading certain pages quickly to locate a character's exact words or more slowly to recapture the feeling of a favorite scene; they may even reread the whole story to see more clearly how early events led to the climax. Use the example to show students that (1) they usually read something more than once to get the most out of it, (2) they do sometimes vary the speed at which they read, and (3) they choose a pace based on their purpose for reading.

Setting a Purpose

Students often mistakenly believe that studying literature and enjoying literature are two mutually exclusive purposes. Some may argue that their main purpose in reading the anthology's excellent selections should be pleasure—having to "appreciate" each selection through study spoils the fun. These students don't realize that enjoyment is built on understanding. They cannot take pleasure in the irony of a story if they do not recognize it; they cannot articulate a personal response to a work if they do not possess the tools of evaluation—the literary concepts and reading skills that lead to understanding. Full enjoyment, then, requires study, or, more specifically, reading for several purposes: to get an overview, to analyze and evaluate ideas and literary techniques, to locate details, to refresh the memory, or to generate new ideas.

Naming one of these purposes for a particular reading is just the first step; an active reader takes another: formulating intitial questions to be answered while reading. For example, to get an overview, a reader might ask: What type of work is it? What is the topic? When was it written, and

by whom? To locate particular details, a reader might ask: What key words or phrases will help me find the details? Am I likely to find them near the beginning, the middle, or the end of the work? Such questions not only further define the purpose but also provide an active reading plan.

With a definite purpose in mind, students should more easily identify a suitable reading rate. In general, they should use an average, or "most comfortable," rate when reading for pleasure; faster rates when reading to get an overview, locate details, refresh the memory, or generate ideas; a slower rate when reading to analyze and evaluate the writer's ideas and language. Students can apply this approach to literature by using the following reading techniques.

Skimming

Skimming is reading quickly for main ideas—just how quickly, in terms of words per minute, will vary from person to person. A rule of thumb is that the skimming speed should be twice as fast as the individual's average reading rate (Fry). To achieve the higher speed, the reader skips some sentences, or details, concentrating instead on reading just enough of each paragraph to get its main idea. Since the reader does not consider every detail, the level of comprehension necessarily decreases somewhat. Some teachers like to describe skimming as a "prereading" or "rereading" activity; this distinction often helps students decide when to use the technique.

As a rereading activity, for example, skimming is an efficient way to review main ideas of a work and mentally summarize a personal response to it. A student might quickly go over a selection with questions such as these in mind: What did the writer say about life or about people? What literary devices did the writer use? Did the piece end as I expected it to? How did it make me feel, and why? If skimming reveals a point of confusion, the student can slow down for a more careful rereading. Note that students may also use skimming to review their class discussion notes.

Skimming is useful, too, for generating writing topics. To questions like those above, a student searching for a topic might add these: Why was I drawn to a particular character, passage, or scene? Which literary element of the work seemed most effective? Does this work have something in common with another I have read? How does the theme of the work relate to my own life?

Perhaps most important is the use of skimming as a prereading activity. Explain to students that the common habit of simply opening the book to the right page and reading straight through once at an average rate is not the most efficient—or rewarding—reading approach. When they open the book to read a selection, they should first skim the title, the headnote, background information about the writer and the work, chapter or section titles, the questions and assignments that follow the selection, and their own notes from preliminary class instruction. The intent is to obtain an overview of the work; this skimming is an exercise in orientation that will help students prepare specific questions to be explored in a close reading.

Close Reading

A close reading is a slow and careful reading for the purpose of analyzing and evaluating a literary work. For class discussion and many assignments, mature readers may need to read at this "thoughtful" pace only once: others, more than once. When reading a difficult or lengthy work and when writing comprehensive essays, almost all students should do two or more close readings, at least of portions of the work. All of your twelfth-graders should begin to realize that in reading literature closely, they are seeking three levels of understanding: literal, inferential, and critical. Put another way, they must read the lines, read between the lines, and read beyond the lines (Poindexter and Prescott). You no doubt have found students to be most comfortable, and most practiced, at the literal level—understanding directly stated details. They usually need more help at the inferential level—understanding implied ideas—and at the critical level—understanding a writer's purposes and making value judgments about a piece of literature. As "coach" for a close reading, you can guide students toward full comprehension in several ways.

Posing Questions

Before students begin a close reading, have them list a few questions about the selection to guide their initial reading. Use the text's headnotes and the teaching suggestions in this manual to prompt appropriate and specific questions. The headnote introducing each selection directs attention to a particular aspect of the work, often by raising issues that will require higher-level comprehension. Several sections in this manual, in particular "Introducing the [Selection]" and "Reading the [Selection]," will give you additional ideas for elements that students can look for and consider as they read. Posing initial questions sets a precise purpose for close reading, activates students' prior knowledge of both literature and cultural values, and arouses personal interest in a literary work.

Predicting Outcomes

For several selections, the text and this manual suggest a stopping place in the reading, a point at which students are

asked to predict what will [...] their opinions. Take full advan[...] it for other selections whenever p[...]ive reasons for have found that predicting outcomes [...]tegy, and use rich exchange of ideas in the classroom[...]ny teachers comprehension, more so than would a tra[...]not only a what has been read so far (Nessel). In order [...]ultilevel resolution of events, students must recall esse[...] [...]iew of details, draw inferences about the situation crea[...]t the evaluate the writer's intent; thus, the class gains a revie[...]ral well as practice in critical thinking. Evaluate the prediction[...] not on how close students come to the writer's conclusion but rather on how logically they form and support their hypotheses.

Responding Personally

Suggest to students that their ultimate goal in reading closely is to understand their own intellectual and emotional responses to a literary work—what they liked or disliked and why. They should think about their reactions as they read and when they discuss the work in class. Alert them to the design of the "Responding" sections in the text: The questions and assignments will help guide them, during a close reading, through the three levels of comprehension and will lead them, after the reading, to an organized expression of their personal responses through creative and critical writing.

Following Guidelines

Certain close-reading techniques apply generally to literature; others are important to particular types of literary works. You may want to duplicate and hand out the following guidelines, which are addressed to students.

Guidelines for Reading Literature Closely

1. Write down a few questions you would like to answer as you read the selection. The skimming you did to get an overview of the work will help you pose questions, as will your teacher's introduction.

2. Take brief notes as you read. Jot down answers you find to your initial questions as well as any further questions that come to mind. Note your impression of the characters in the selection. Note passages that seem to hint at the writer's purpose or theme, passages that are particularly vivid to you, and passages that seem confusing. Identify the emotions you feel when reading different parts of the work.

3. Stop occasionally to think about what you have read. Ask yourself these questions: What main ideas or events have been presented so far? What do I think will happen next?

4. Look up unfamiliar words and allusions. First check for a special note on the page that explains the word or phrase; then see whether the context gives you clues to its how each scene moves the plot along and reveals character. Determine when the action of the play "turns" and begins moving toward resolution (the crisis), as well as the most intense or emotional moment (the climax). Be sure to read the stage directions as carefully as you read the dialogue. They will give you clues to the setting and the action and to the appearances and emotions of the characters.

meaning. Refer to a... ...t your teacher has provided, and chec... ...n in the textbook's Glossary. Rememb... ...also use "A Handbook of Literary Terms" ...the text. Keep your diction- ary handy fo... ...ined in the text. Add the word or phrase to y... review its meaning.
later and ...d the type of literature you are reading. The

5. K... you ask and the understanding and pleasure you queom a work often relate to the writer's chosen form. ...re are some specific hints:

Fiction. Look for the elements of narration: What is the point of view? The narrator's tone? What conflict or conflicts does the writer create? What complicates the problem? What are the main events of the plot? How does the setting affect the story? What passage marks the climax of the tale? How is the main conflict resolved? What is the theme of the story? Be careful not to identify the central conflict solely on the basis of which character you feel closest to or like best. Decide which character sets out to do something (the protagonist) and who or what works against the attempt (the antagonist).

Poetry. Read a poem several times, at least once out loud. (If the poetry is in an epic or a play, read each section or scene several times.) Pay particular attention to the punctuation; it will help you follow the writer's ideas and help you "hear" the emphasized words. Paraphrase any lines or passages that are not immediately clear to you. Make a note of figures of speech and sound effects, and look for the writer's main idea. Is a central thought or emotion expressed? Or is a theme presented by telling a story? Try to state the main idea in one or two sentences. When the poetry tells a story, apply what you know about plot and character development.

Nonfiction. Be alert for the writer's attitudes toward the topic and toward the people described. Is the writer's tone humorous, serious, sympathetic, hostile, or some combination of these feelings? Is the work objective, or is it written from a subjective, or personal, point of view? Does the writer use narrative techniques, such as foreshadowing or suspense, to hold your interest? Decide what the writer's main purpose is: to tell a story, to explain or inform, to describe, or to persuade. Notice how the writer organizes information, and make an informal outline of the main points. Then determine the main idea of the work. Is it directly stated? Implied?

Drama. Identify the mood of the play (Serious and sad? Light and humorous?). What do you see and hear happening on the stage? Remember that you are "overhearing" conversations: What tones of voice and facial gestures would actors use in saying their lines? Think about the personalities of the main characters, and predict how they will react to each other's comments and actions. Decide

Scanning

Scanning is reading very rapidly to locate details. Students unfamiliar with the term are likely to recognize the technique when it is explained: They use it to find a name and number in the telephone book, a listing in the television program guide, or a definition in the dictionary. Scanning is faster than skimming, because the reader is searching for key words rather than reading sentences or phrases to isolate ideas. The reader focuses the mind and eye by moving a finger rapidly across and down the page, not stopping until the key word or phrase is found.

In the study of literature, scanning is most useful as a rereading activity. When students have already read a work and know its organization, they can use scanning to answer certain kinds of follow-up questions, usually ones of literal comprehension (Who? What? Where? When?). For example, you may ask a student to identify Homeric similes that help describe a certain episode in an epic. The student would first locate the episode and then find the similes by scanning for key words such as *like* and *as*.

Essential to the process are having a sense of a work's organization (Should I look first in the beginning, middle, or end? Didn't that scene close an early chapter?) and choosing key words or phrases appropriate to the search (Which words in the question are keys? What key words are implied by the question?). When students think they have located the detail, they should stop to read the sentences around it to make sure they are correct. If they discover that they are frequently inaccurate when scanning, they should slow their pace for a while and check their choice of key words. Remind students to take notes when they scan.

You can give the class a timed practice in scanning during your vocabulary exercises. List on the board ten vocabulary words, out of alphabetical order, that are defined in the Glossary. Tell students to write down for each one the word that follows it in the Glossary. Explain that you will start the stopwatch when they begin scanning and after one minute will begin putting the time on the board in ten-second intervals. When each student has finished the last item, he or she can then write down the last time given on the board. Check the answers and response times in class, and suggest further practice at home to increase speed or improve accuracy.

References

Fry, Edward B. *Skimming and Scanning, Middle Level.* Providence, RI: Jamestown, 1982.

Nessel, Denise. "Reading Comprehension: Asking the Right Questions." *Phi Delta Kappan* 68 (1987): 442–444.

Poindexter, Candace A., a̶ nique for Teaching Students Text." *The Reading Teacher* 39 ᶜott. "A Technerences from ̶11.

Promoting the Growth of Students' Vocabulary

Many teachers have found that a concentrated effort on vocabulary during literature study results in great gains in students' active vocabularies. Often in such efforts you first must convince students of the value of a larger vocabulary. Besides continually sharing your own enthusiasm for words, you can easily demonstrate the necessity and power of language. Tell students to close their eyes for a few moments and to think thoughts for which there are no words. After a minute or so, the class will probably protest that it can't be done. This response is the point of the exercise: Words are essential to thought. Point out that the more words students know, the better able they will be to understand and communicate ideas.

In guiding students through vocabulary for the selections, you will probably find that a multifaceted approach is most effective—a combination of dictionary use, context study, and structural analysis.

Dictionary Use

Here are a few ideas for encouraging the dictionary habit.

• Have students turn to the Glossary during your general introduction to the anthology. Go over the pronunciation key to review common symbols for sounds, and point out the abbreviations for parts of speech. Remind students that many words have multiple meanings, and note that the Glossary defines words according to their use in the selections.

• Use a short, timed exercise to check students' basic dictionary skills. Provide dictionaries, and give the class five minutes to look up and write down the pronunciation and first definition of three words from a selection. Check responses for the third word, asking about problems in following guide words, alphabetization, or pronunciation symbols.

• Show students how to use dictionaries quickly and effectively when reading literature. Tell them to keep handy a supply of blank index cards. As they encounter unfamiliar words, they can jot down each one on a card, with the page number for reference, and later look up several words at once. Direct them to write the pronunciation under the word, say the word aloud, and, on the back of the card, write the part of speech and meaning that fit the context. Have students bring in their cards every week or two and compare their collections.

• Pay special attention to words with interesting histories. Help students discover that a word is borrowed from another language, for example, or that it derives from an old custom. Show students how to use special dictionaries of word and phrase origins.

• Review usage labels in the dictionary when the class studies Americanisms, jargon, colloquialisms, and so on.

• Be sure students understand that a dictionary's method of numbering definitions is significant. Some dictionaries begin with the oldest sense of a word, others with the most frequent usage. Have the class look up words such as *dashboard*, *temperance*, and *wardrobe* to see how the use of certain words has changed over time.

• Emphasize pronunciation in your dictionary drills to help students "sound out" new words.

Context Study

The following activities will help students learn *and use* new words through recognizing context clues, making connections between words, and creating new contexts through original writing. The first six items offer ways to reinforce students' use of context clues when they are reading or listening.

• Before class begins, write on the board a sentence about the day's literary topic that uses two or three new vocabulary words, with some clue to their meanings. Underline the vocabulary words. When students arrive, ask them to write a paraphrase of the sentence, without using the underlined

... ss their responses,
... se the exercise as a
... ussion of the selection.
... ion aloud, stop occasionally
words, while you call ... ulary word, and ask students for
asking what context ...
springboard to yo...
• If you are ...ning.
when you co...ulary words in your own comments to let
context clu...
• Use ...em in context.
studer... the vocabulary list for a selection is long, assign
• ...nt words to different students. Ask them to find for
...ch word a context clue, a synonym, and an antonym, to
be shared in a class discussion.

• Have students look for abstract vocabulary words in
contexts other than the text selection. For example, ask
them to locate and paraphrase famous quotations in which
the words appear.

• For quick reviews, write on the chalkboard the sentences from the selection that contain the vocabulary words,
but replace the words with blanks. Ask students to fill in the
blanks with the correct word from an alphabetized list, and
discuss how they made their choices.

The next two activities emphasize word relationships.

• Review synonyms or antonyms for vocabulary words by
devising short matching quizzes. You might have students
create them: Assign a small group to select ten words and
put together a scrambled list of synonyms (or antonyms).
Check the group's work, and have them write the two lists
on the chalkboard, one list numbered, the other lettered.
Ask the rest of the class to match the words.

• Review any group of related words with a simple
crossword puzzle using the words' definitions as clues. You
may create the puzzle yourself or have students volunteer to
do it. Give the puzzle a title that classifies the group of
words, such as "Vivid Adverbs" or "Words That Describe
[a character's name]." Some teachers also find such puzzles
effective as a review of literary terms: "The Elements of
Drama," "Sound Effects in Poetry," and so on.

The following activities require students to create new
contexts for the words they are studying; they put new
words to use through writing. Several suggestions also take
advantage of the strategy of centering word study on a
concept.

• Have students create their own direct context clues for
new words. Ask them to write sentences for vocabulary
words, giving a clue to meaning by definition, example,
restatement, comparison, or contrast.

• To explore connotative meaning, have students use five
vocabulary words in original sentences and then substitute a
synonym for each vocabulary word. How well does the
synonym work in the same context? Ask students what
difference in meaning or feeling is created.

• Choose two or three vocabulary words that have
distinctive multiple meanings, and ask students to write a
sentence using each meaning.

• If the vocabulary words for a selection number fewer
than ten, offer students the challenge of writing one sentence using as many of the words as possible. However
fanciful, the sentence must be intelligible.

• When the vocabulary list for a selection is long, group
the words by part of speech. Have students write a sentence
using one word from each group and compare their sentences.

• For a group of adjectives, ask students to create comparisons.

• Promote students' personal use of active verbs by having them write sentences in which they apply new verbs to a
school situation.

• When several vocabulary words for a selection relate to
a particular geographical or cultural setting, introduce the
words as a group. For example, *adobe*, *arroyo*, *mesa*,
mission (church), and *tumbleweed* are words of the West or
Southwest. Have students identify the common element
through definitions and etymologies and then write sentences or a paragraph using the words.

• If students are learning descriptive words that apply to a
character in a selection, ask them to write sentences applying the words to other characters they have studied.

• Assign different students, one or two at a time, to use
vocabulary words in writing three or four quiz questions
about a selection's plot, characters, or setting. At the
beginning of class, the students can call on classmates to
answer the questions, orally correcting the answers and
clarifying the meanings of the vocabulary words when
necessary.

• For a review of words from several selections, group
them according to an emotion or idea. Have students write
new sentences using each word.

• Encourage regular attention to new words by offering
bonus points for the appropriate use of vocabulary words in
the text writing assignments and in class discussions.

• On Fridays, have students vote on their favorite new
word from the week's vocabulary. Ask them to explain their
choices.

Structural Analysis

Students can often learn and remember new words by
breaking them into recognizable parts. Try these activities
for a morphemic approach focused on roots and affixes. A
selected list of common Greek and Latin word parts follows
the activities.

• Have students build a personal set of flashcards of roots
and affixes. Introduce a few roots, prefixes, and suffixes at
a time, having students write each one on an index card. On
the other side of the card, students should write the meaning

of the root or affix, along with an illustrative word that you provide (preferably a vocabulary word or literary term already assigned). Then direct students to be alert throughout the term to vocabulary words (as well as words from other sources) that contain these roots and affixes and to add the words to their cards. Remind them that some words, such as *infallible*, will be recorded on more than one card.

Every week or two, ask students to bring in their collections. Divide the class into small groups for peer quizzing with the cards. Spot-check the cards and quizzing to evaluate students' progress and to decide on review strategies. (After you have introduced several groups of word parts, you may want the students themselves to begin presenting new roots and affixes obtained from their assigned vocabulary or from other reading.)

• Present in one lesson prefixes that show position. Guide students in identifying and defining words with these prefixes. The examples might be vocabulary words from the selections, literary terms, or more familiar words encountered in the text.

• Encourage students to recognize prefixes that create a negative or opposite meaning. Ask students to complete a list of "not" definitions with words they have studied.

• To help students recognize the grammatical function of an unfamiliar word in context, show them how suffixes often—*not always*—signal a particular part of speech. Students can make a note on their suffix flashcards or list the groups in a vocabulary notebook, but remind them to watch for exceptions. In some words the ending looks like a suffix but actually is part of a root or base word.

• After you define a common Greek or Latin root in a new word, divide students into small groups, and, setting a time limit, have them list familiar words built on the same root. The group with the longest list could receive bonus points.

• Occasionally review small groups of prefix, suffix, and root definitions with oral and written quizzes. For variety in the quizzes, you could create crossword puzzles or conduct a group competition on the pattern of a spelldown.

There are hundreds of roots and affixes, and the following lists contain only a selection of those that students may learn through their vocabulary study in literature. As you introduce the study of word parts, point out that the spellings of roots and affixes sometimes vary, that affixes almost always alter the root's meaning in some way, and that the meanings of some Latin and Greek roots have undergone slight changes over time.

Roots

Greek

-bio-	life (*biography*)
-chron-	time (*chronological*)
-cris-, *-crit-*	separate, judge (*crisis, critical*)
-cycl-	circle (*Cyclops*)
-glos-, *-glot-*	tongue (*glossary, polyglot*)
-graph-	write, record (*biography, photograph*)
-log-, *-logy-*	speaking, study (*chronology, dialogue*)
-ops-, *-opt-*	eye (*Cyclops, optical*)
-phon-	sound (*phonetic*)
-stereo-	firm, solid (*stereotype*)

Latin

-aud-	hear (*audible*)
-cred-	believe (*incredulous*)
-dict-	tell, say (*prediction*)
-duc-, *-duct-*	lead, draw (*deduction, produce*)
-fac-, *-fic-*	make, do (*benefactor, fiction*)
-flect-	bend (*deflect, reflection*)
-ject-	throw (*projectile, reject*)
-leg-, *lect-*	read (*lecture, legend*)
-loqu-	speak (*eloquent, soliloquy*)
-mis-, *-mit-*	send (*commission, noncommittal*)
-mort-	die (*immortality*)
-quer-, *-quest-*, *-quir-*	seek, ask (*inquiry, quest*)
-sci-	know (*omniscient*)
-scrib-, *-script-*	write (*describe, manuscript*)
-spec-, *-spic-*, *-spect-*	look at, examine (*circumspect*)

-tens-, -tent-	hold (*contention, tension*)
-vers-, -vert-	turn (*adverse, invert, versatile*)
-vid-, -vis-	see (*videotape, visage, visual*)
-viv-	live (*vivacious, vivid*)

Prefixes

Greek

a-	not, without (*atheist, atypical*)
ant-	against (*antagonist*)
auto-	self (*autobiography*)
dia-	through, across, between (*dialogue*)
exo-	out of, outside (*exodus*)
mono-	one (*monologue*)
poly-	many (*polytheism*)
pro-	before, first (*protagonist*)
syn-	with, together (*synthesis*)

Latin

a-, ab-, abs-	away, from (*abominable, abscond, averse*)
ante-	before (*antecedent*)
bene-	well (*benediction, benefactor*)
circum-	around, on all sides (*circumstance*)
com-, con-	with, together (*complicity, connotation*)
contra-	against (*contrary*)
de-	from, down (*denotation, denouement*)
dis-	apart, away (*dispel, disrepute*)
e-, ex-	out (*evade, exorbitant*)
extra-	outside of, beyond (*extravagant*)
il-, im-, in-, ir-	not (*incredulous, irresolute*) *or* in, into, on (*impetus, inversion*)
inter-	between (*intermediary*)
non-	not (*nonentity*)
omni-	all, everywhere (*omniscient*)
per-	through (*perpetual*)
post-	after, behind (*postpone, postscript*)
pro-	forward (*projectile*)
re-	again, back (*redress, reference*)
soli-	alone, only (*soliloquy, solitude*)
sub-, sup-	under, beneath, below (*subversive*)
super-	above, over, outside (*superficial*)
trans-	across (*translucent*)

Suffixes

-able, -ible	able to (*formidable, infallible*)
-age, -ance, -ence, -ity, -ment, -ness, -ship, -tion	a state or condition (*atonement, calamity, carnage, gyration, indulgence, vigilance*)
-an, -ee, -eer, -er, -ian, -ist, -ite, -or	a person, one who (*barbarian, mountaineer, strategist, writer*)
-ate	to act or do (*evaluate, perpetuate*)
-er, -est	degree (*shadier, shadiest*)
-ful, -ous	full of (*fearful, ominous*)
-less	without (*aimless, ruthless*)

Varying Teaching Techniques

Using a variety of teaching techniques keeps students' interest high, fosters personal involvement with literature, and takes advantage of individual learning styles. With the following teaching suggestions, you can make the study of literature a thoroughly active, multifaceted experience for your class.

Collaborative Learning

To foster regular collaborative learning, you may want to assign students to groups (no more than five or six members) and to matched pairs early in the year, using a random-selection method such as counting-off. Then you will waste no time forming groups for each new activity. You may change the groups and pairs at some point, but do not change them too frequently. Students benefit from working with the same classmates for an extended period: They begin to appreciate different learning styles and abilities, and they develop a team spirit. The two group methods that follow have many applications in a literature course.

Expert Groups. In this technique, members of a small group become highly knowledgeable about one aspect of a topic or literary work and serve as experts for the other students. When you are reading *Macbeth*, for example, one group might become experts on the Globe Theater and another on Shakespeare's sources for the tragedy. The expert groups report to the class and stand for questions. The benefit of this strategy is twofold: Group members gain experience in intensive research, and all students gain more information about a topic or a work.

Jigsawing. Jigsawing, which uses two levels of groups, is another method by which students become each other's teachers. The method is particularly effective for covering lengthy or complex material when class time is limited. For example, suppose you want your class to paraphrase five paragraphs of difficult prose. Divide the students into five groups, assign one paragraph to each group, and set a time limit for the paraphrase. (Whenever possible, use any standing groups for this first jigsaw level.) When the students have finished, make a second-level group assignment: Within each group, have students count off (or designate themselves by letters, colors, etc.) and then move into their second groups—all 1's (A's, reds) together, 2's (B's, blues) together, and so on. Each student now becomes the "expert" for the paragraph paraphrased in his or her original group, presenting the information to members of the new group. Jigsawing also works well with lengthy vocabulary lists or an exercise containing many items. In those cases, divide the words or items equally among the first-level groups and then proceed as before to the second-level groups.

Into, Through, and Beyond Techniques

Many teachers think of three distinct stages in teaching a selection: preparing students for it, guiding them through it, and offering them bridges from it to other works, ideas, and activities. What follows is a summary of types of activities appropriate to each stage. (Detailed descriptions of concept formation, imaging, debating moral dilemmas, journal writing, sensory recall, and readers' theater follow the summary.)

To lead students *into* a work:

• Use filmstrips, films, or recordings to arouse students' interest.

• Invite lecturers to provide special background on a selection. The speakers may be knowledgeable about a particular work, author, or literary topic or may have experience that relates to a selection (someone who has visited or lived in Dublin, for example, could provide background for "Araby").

• Introduce the work with a variety of background information (history, the author's biography, technical explanations), using the text's introductions and the supplementary information in this manual.

• Distribute plot summaries, study guides, or character lists for difficult or lengthy works.

• Have students master vocabulary words before they begin to read, using a variety of strategies (see "Promoting the Growth of Students' Vocabulary").

• Encourage skimming as a prereading step, and guide students in posing questions for a close reading (see "Teaching Students to Vary Reading Rates").

• Use the techniques of concept formation, imaging, and journal quick-writes.

• Read portions of the selection orally.

To guide students *through* a work:

• Assign the questions following the text selections for discussion or writing. Assign the creative and critical writing exercises for individual or collaborative work.

• Pause during in-class readings to allow students to predict narrative outcomes.

• Assign groups of students to dramatize and perform brief scenes from a story or novel.

- Organize debates on issues and moral dilemmas raised by a work.
- Have students keep dialectical journals.
- Schedule readers' theater presentations.
- Lead imaging and sensory recall exercises.
- Assign reports and projects for class presentation, encouraging forms of expression other than writing (creating maps, illustrations, charts, timelines; performing; composing original music; etc.).

To lead students *beyond* a work:

- Encourage students to make connections between the work and other works in the same genre, as well as between works in different genres. Possible connections include subject, theme, major symbols, imagery, allusions, historical setting, and so on. Students may present their comparisons and contrasts in compositions, reports, and projects.
- Suggest further reading of works by the same author, of books and articles related to the selection's background, and of works in the same genre.
- Have a group of students write and produce an original video play inspired by some aspect of the selection (a moral dilemma, a character, a striking element such as horror).
- Have students create games based on literary selections.
- Have a group of students assume the personae of characters from different works and engage in a panel discussion on a specific topic. Instruct students to prepare carefully for their roles so that they can respond in character, correctly reflecting their different fictional settings.

Concept Formation

When students use concept formation to approach a new work, they practice both classifying and predicting. To use this technique, present students—without any preliminary explanation—with a list of words, objects, names, or ideas taken from or related to the selection. (You may restrict the list to one category of information or mix the categories.) Ask the students to group items that seem related and then to formulate predictions about the selection based on the items and their common elements. For example, from the vocabulary list for *The Rime of the Ancient Mariner*, students might isolate *drift*, *Albatross*, *shroud*, *tack*, *veer*, and *skiff-boat*, predicting—even without knowing the poem's title—that the sea will figure largely in the tale. Advanced students might go further, forming a concept about genre and predicting that the novel is a fable or an allegory.

Concept formation, in addition to sharpening critical thinking, involves students actively in a work even before they begin reading. An unexplained list can be an intriguing puzzle, and once students have made predictions from it,

they may read a selection with more eagerness and more purpose.

Imaging

Imaging taps students' imaginations, leading them into a literary work through sensory awareness. Acting as guide, you ask students to close their eyes and then "talk" them into a specific time, place, or mental state. Play mood-setting or period music if possible, and tell students to draw on their sensory memories to participate vicariously in the experience you evoke.

Imaging is effective with image-rich poetry as well as with narratives; you may use it to introduce a selection as well as to focus on individual passages and sections. For example, you may want to set the stage for *Beowulf* by guiding students in imagining the sights, sounds, and smells of the marshes and fens where the monsters have their lair. Imaging not only helps remove barriers of culture, time, and place but also shows students their own considerable power to invoke sensory experiences from words.

Moral Dilemmas

Moral dilemmas arising from conflicts within literary works are excellent ways to engage students' feelings and stimulate their critical thinking. You may use an actual situation from a work (the moral dilemma Eve faces in *Paradise Lost* when she weighs the serpent's words against God's injunction) or an extrapolation from it (a similar situation involving a person who is persuaded by logical reasoning to do something illegal). Whichever you choose, describe the situation in such a way that students are forced to take sides. (Some other provocative conflicts are those pitting individual conscience against law and those forcing a choice between loyalties to two friends or two family members.)

Have students articulate the opposing positions, write each as a statement on the board, and ask students to take sides by a show of hands. Divide students on each side into smaller groups for developing supporting arguments. Allow sufficient time, and then, taking one side at a time, have each group's spokesperson present one supporting argument. Go from group to group until supporting arguments are exhausted, and then allow a free exchange of rebuttals, guiding the discussion as necessary. Be sure each student comes to some formal closure about the moral dilemma, perhaps through a journal entry or a brief essay.

Journals

Journals are excellent tools for literature study: They encourage personal responses to literary works; allow freer, less formal writing; build a repository of writing ideas; and offer students a full year's record of their changing perspectives and thoughts. A loose-leaf notebook will allow students to make both private entries and assigned entries for your review. When you make journal assignments, specify those that must be turned in.

Two specialized uses of journals follow.

Dialectical Journals

Sometimes called dialogue journals, dialectical journals are double-entry records in which students take notes about a literary work and then add their own reflections about the notes. Each page is divided into two columns labeled "Note-taking" and "Note-making." Notes about the work may include facts, passages, quoted dialogue, significant plot developments, and so on. The students' recorded musings about these notes will be personal, but occasionally you may want to direct a response (for example, you could direct students to "take" notes about a poem's imagery and then to "make" notes about their emotional responses to the images).

A dialectical journal is valuable because students are forced to go beyond facts to reflection; they must think about what they read. Encourage students also to review all their entries for a selection, synthesize the thoughts, and write a summary, or distillation, of their personal response.

Quick-Writes

The aim of a quick-write journal entry is an immediate, spontaneous, unedited response to a stimulus. Possible stimuli are many: a passage from a selection, an idea you supply, music, guided imaging and sensory recall, and so on. Quick-writes can be used in all three stages of teaching a selection (into, through, and beyond).

Sensory Recall

Literature presents all readers with emotions and situations far removed from their own experience; sensory recall, a technique by which professionals prepare for acting roles, is one means of making these foreign experiences more understandable. An actress playing a character who, after extreme provocation, physically attacks someone may have no experience with such violence, for example. The director may ask her to remember being driven crazy by mosquitoes and to act out the resulting scene. Under the director's coaching, the actress begins to understand her character's response to the provocation and can then build a believable series of emotions for her role.

An adaptation of this theatrical approach can help students identify with unfamiliar characters and understand emotions otherwise out of their reach. As an introduction, students may enjoy watching a classmate with acting experience demonstrate the technique, but all students can participate in sensory recall through writing. First isolate an experience in a selection, build an appropriate parallel situation (or brainstorm situations with students), and then direct students to put themselves in the situation and to write their thoughts and feelings. You might use sensory recall, for example, to make accessible the bizarre events in "The Pit and the Pendulum," beginning with the narrator's awakening in the pitch-black dungeon. If you ask students to recall awakening in the middle of the night in a strange room, eliciting from them memories of the common feelings of disorientation and momentary panic, they will begin to feel more acutely the narrator's horror.

Initially, you will have to lead students in using sensory recall, but after practice, they will be able to create their own parallel situations and record their responses in their journals.

Readers' Theater

Readers' theater is simply a group oral reading of a selection, whether the work is a play, story, poem, or essay. Effective readers' theater is not impromptu, however. Students are assigned roles, or passages, and practice their reading outside of class. Readers' theater hones students' skills in oral interpretation and makes a work come alive for the whole class; it is a dramatic presentation with a minimum of production worries (you need only stools or chairs) and stage-fright problems (most students are less frightened of sitting and reading than of acting).

Students may read whole plays or single acts or scenes; they may create their own scripts from short stories, novels, and epics; they may present poems and essays by alternating the reading of stanzas and paragraphs. One way to accomplish the latter is to count off the stanzas or paragraphs according to the number of readers: The first reader reads all the stanzas or paragraphs numbered one, the second reads those numbered two, and so on. Remember also that, for scripts, one reader should be assigned the scene setting, necessary stage directions, and any prologue or explanatory narrative.

You may want to assign roles for certain dramatic readings, but at other times students may form their own groups and choose roles. If students in a particular small group want to read a script in which the number of roles exceeds the number of members, some students can read more than one role, indicating their character changes with simple props (hats, glasses, shawls, etc.) or with name signs.

Obtaining Audio-Visual Aids

Guides and Indexes

The following sourcebooks contain information about the wealth of educational audio-visual materials available.

AV Instruction: Technology, Media, and Methods. Ed. James W. Brown, Richard B. Lewis, and Fred F. Harcleroad. 6th ed. 1983. McGraw-Hill Book Co., 1221 Avenue of the Americas, New York, NY 10020.

Educational Film/Video Locator. 3rd ed. 2 vols. 1986. R. R. Bowker Co., 205 E. Forty-second St., New York, NY 10017. (This reference includes 194,000 titles held by members of the Consortium of University Film Centers.)

Educational Media and Technology Yearbook. Ed. Elwood E. Miller. 13th vol. 1987. Libraries Unlimited, Inc., P.O. Box 263, Littleton, CO 80160. (The yearbook is published in cooperation with the Association for Educational Communications and Technology.)

Educators Guide to Free Audio and Video Materials. Ed. James L. Berger. *Educators Guide to Free Films* and *Educators Guide to Free Filmstrips and Slides.* Ed. John C. Diffor and Elaine N. Diffor. Annual eds. Educators Progress Service, Inc., 214 Center St., Randolph, WI 53956.

NICEM Index Series. 1984, 1985 eds. in hardcover, monthly bulletins (separate multivolume sets for tapes, films, videotapes, slides, and transparencies). National Information Center for Educational Media, Access Innovations, Inc., P.O. Box 40130. Albuquerque, NM 87196. (The center works closely with the Library of Congress to update indexed titles.)

Suppliers

The following producers and distributors publish catalogs of their offerings.

Agency for Instructional Technology (formerly AITelevision), Box A, Bloomington, IN 47402.

AIMS Media, 6901 Woodley Ave., Van Nuys, CA 91406.

Allyn and Bacon, Inc., 470 Atlantic Ave., Boston, MA 02210.

Association Films, Inc., 866 Third Ave., New York, NY 10022.

Barr Films, P.O. Box 5667, Pasadena, CA 91107.

Blackhawk Films, Eastin-Phelan Corp., 1235 W. Fifth St., Davenport, IA 52808.

Bowmar Records, 622 Rodier Dr., Glendale, CA 91201.

Cassette Information Services, P.O. Box 9559, Glendale, CA 91206.

Center for Humanities, Inc., Communications Park, Box 1000, Mount Kisco, NY 10549.

Churchill Films, 662 N. Robertson Blvd., Los Angeles, CA 90069.

Classroom Film Distributors, Inc., 5610 Hollywood Blvd., Los Angeles, CA 90028.

CRM/McGraw-Hill Films, 110 Fifteenth St., Del Mar, CA 92014.

Encyclopaedia Britannica Educational Corp., 425 N. Michigan Ave., Chicago, IL 60611.

Epcot Educational Media (Walt Disney Co.), 500 S. Buena Vista St., Burbank, CA 91521.

Films for the Humanities, Inc., P.O. Box 2053, Princeton, NJ 08540.

Films, Inc. (also distributes Audio Brandon, Macmillan, and Texture Films), 1144 Wilmette Ave., Wilmette, IL 60091.

Folkways Records, 43 W. Sixty-first St., New York, NY 10023.

Great Plains Instructional TV Library, University of Nebraska, P.O. Box 80669, Lincoln, NE 68501.

Grover Film Productions, P.O. Box 12, Helotes, TX 78023.

Guidance Associates, Communications Park, Box 3000, Mount Kisco, NY 10549.

HBJ Video (Harcourt Brace Jovanovich, Inc.), 6825 Academic Dr., Orlando, FL 32821.

Holt, Rinehart, and Winston, School Division, 1627 Woodland Ave., Austin, TX 78741.

Indiana University Audio-Visual Center, Indiana University, Bloomington, IN 47405.

International Film Bureau, 332 S. Michigan Ave., Chicago, IL 60604.

Listening Library, Inc., 1 Park Ave., Old Greenwich, CT 06870.

Lucerne Films, Inc., 37 Ground Pine Rd., Morris Plains, NJ 07950.

National Audio-Visual Center, National Archives and Records Service, General Services Administration, Washington, DC 20409.

National Council of Teachers of English, 1111 Kenyon Rd., Urbana, IL 61801.

National Education Association, Audio-Visual Instruction, 1201 Sixteenth St. N.W., Washington, DC 20036.

National Film Board of Canada, 1251 Avenue of the Americas, New York, NY 10020.

National Public Radio, Educational Cassettes, 2025 M St. N.W., Washington, DC 20036.

National Video Clearinghouse, Inc., 100 Lafayette Dr., Syosset, NY 11791.

Phoenix/BFA Films and Video, Inc., 470 Park Ave. S., New York, NY 10016.

Public Television Library (Public Broadcasting System), 475 L'Enfant Plaza S.W., Washington, DC 20024.

Pyramid Film and Video, P.O. Box 1048, Santa Monica, CA 90406

Silver Burdett Co., 250 James St., Morristown, NJ 07960.

Simon and Schuster Communications (also distributes Centron, Coronet, LCA, and Perspective Films and MTI Teleprograms), 108 Wilmot Rd., Deerfield, IL 60015.

Smithsonian Recordings, P.O. Box 23345, Washington, DC 20026.

Society for Visual Education, Inc., 1345 Diversey Pkwy., Chicago, IL 60614.

Time-Life Films and Video, 100 Eisenhower Dr., Paramus, NJ 07652.

Vineyard Video Productions, Elias Lane, West Tisbury, MA 02575.

INDEX OF AUTHORS AND TITLES